STRATEGIC
SALES
MANAGEMENT

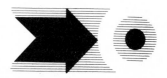

STRATEGIC
SALES
MANAGEMENT

G. David Hughes
Burlington Industries Professor of Business Administration,
University of North Carolina

Charles H. Singler
Sales Management Consultant,
former Vice President for Sales, Burroughs Wellcome Company

ADDISON-WESLEY PUBLISHING COMPANY
Reading, Massachusetts • Menlo Park, California
London • Amsterdam • Don Mills, Ontario • Sydney

Library of Congress Cataloging in Publication Data

Hughes, G. David (George David)
  Strategic sales management.

  Bibliography: p.
  Includes index.
  1. Sales management. I. Singler, Charles H.
II. Title.
HF5438.4.H83 1982   658.8′1   82-11513
ISBN 0-201-10260-9

ISBN 0-201-10260-9
ABCDEFGHIJ-HA-898765432

To Our Families

PREFACE

A more complete title for this textbook would be *Learning to Manage Strategically through Field Sales Management.* This title would reflect two points that are stressed in the text. First, all of the management functions and activities that are practiced by higher-level executives are practiced by a first-line field sales manager who may be just a few years out of college. Only the weightings given to each activity will differ. The latter fact was established by a survey of over 700 sales managers and marketing managers. Second, 25 percent of the chief executives in the *FORTUNE* 500 Companies have a background in sales management—more than any other functional area. This fact was established by Heidrick & Struggles, a leading executive placement firm.

It is unfortunate that contemporary sales management is not recognized as an excellent training experience for management at all levels, not just for managing the sales force. The out-of-date image of sales management is that a sales manager is simply a super salesperson who is a recruiter and a cheerleader. This image is robbing some students of excellent management experience as well as exciting and rewarding careers in sales management, sales training, and sales administration. The authors hope that this text will help to update this image.

This text covers the usual topics such as recruiting, training, motivating, evaluating, and compensating the sales force. It also covers additional sales management topics such as the following:

Behavioral modeling

Delegating

Developing personnel

Managing change and conflict

Coordinating

Coaching and counseling

Problem solving

Communication skills

Developing managers

Formulating policies and procedures

Profit-center management of accounts, territories, and districts

Microcomputer applications at all levels of sales management

The changing economic, social, and demographic environment of sales management

Recent laws and cases that affect the representative and sales manager.

This text uses a *career path* approach to examine the theories, research, and practice of sales management. Sales careers are examined at the territory level as seen by the representative, at the first-line field sales management level, and finally at the level of general sales management, which positions the personal selling function in the marketing mix. The traditional approach is to consider only the general sales management level, which does not provide the student with the skills to reach this level. The text demonstrates the challenge of first-line sales management as well as the management skills that can be developed at this level. This approach allows students to examine the potential of careers at all levels of sales management as well as careers in staff positions such as sales administration and sales training.

Because management is basically getting things done through people, this text emphasizes the development of *people skills* and the process of solving *people problems.* Cases provide opportunities to practice these skills. These cases were written by the authors for this text, using real situations from their experiences and field work done by graduate students. Additional cases from the Intercollegiate Case Clearing House are recommended in the Instructor's Manual.

Many persons have made important contributions to this book. First, we thank our families for their support and tolerance. Next we thank students who helped to sharpen our ideas. Then we must acknowledge contributions from colleagues at the University of North Carolina, reviewers from other universities, and persons from industry who kindly provided material or permitted cases to be written. At the University of North Carolina, Professor Carl Anderson provided insights regarding management activities and behavioral modeling. Professor William Bigoness provided materials on managing conflict. Professor Barry Roberts gave a critical review of legal discussions. Case researchers included Ms. Lynn Wilson, Ms. Terryn Douglas Owens, Mr. Bryan Joyner, and Mr. Edward Martin. All of these efforts are gratefully acknowledged.

We would like to thank the following persons for critical reviews of the manuscript at various stages in its development: Professors Richard P. Bagozzi, MIT; Joesph Bellizi, Colorado State University; Stanley Cort, Case Western Reserve University; William Cron, Southern Methodist University; Harrison Grathwohl, University of Washington; Eugene M. Johnson, University of Rhode Island; Wesley Johnston, Ohio State University; Adrian B. Ryans, Stanford University; Barton Weitz, University of Pennsylvania; and Ms. Barbara A. Pletcher, Executive Director, National Association for Professional Saleswomen. These reviewers may be surprised to see how many of their criticisms were accepted and incorporated into the text.

Persons in industry have been generous in providing materials. We would like to thank Ms. Margaret Anderson and Victor MacDonald, IBM Corporation; John H. Burns, Agway; William Jefferson, Datec; F. Stuart Keene, Petro Tech Institute, Inc.; Frank Mitchell, Cessna Aircraft Company; J. F. Munroe, Jr., Burroughs Wellcome Co.; Dr. Charles Smith, consultant in collaborative problem solving; J. Donald Staunton, National Starch and Chemical Corporation; Tom Hausman, Mead Corporation; Paul D. Wetenhall, Xerox Corporation; and Alan Ziegler, The Service Bureau Company. We thank also The Conference Board and the American Marketing Association for permission to reproduce many exhibits from their publications.

With such excellent assistance and cooperation, it has not been easy to introduce errors. No doubt there are many. We would be indebted to readers who call them to our attention.

Chapel Hill and   G.D.H.
Cary, North Carolina   C.H.S.·
August 1982

CONTENTS

Part III   FIELD SALES MANAGEMENT   170

I.

WHAT
IS SALES
MANAGEMENT?

1

THE
ROLE OF
SELLING

THE GROWING IMPORTANCE OF SALES REPRESENTATIVES

Selling plays an important role in a complex society by providing two-way communication links between supply and demand. This two-way communication becomes more important as products become more complex. Complex products, such as computers, must be adapted to the individual needs of customers. In fact, the importance of selling in the communication mix correlates positively with the complexity of products or services. Highly technical and industrial companies, such as computer or chemical companies, depend more heavily on personal selling than does a grocery products manufacturer, with products such as cereals, soaps, or soups. The latter companies will give greater emphasis to one-way communications methods, such as advertising and market research.

Greater competition, from domestic and foreign sources, can also increase the role of sales representatives in the marketing effort of a firm. The sales representative can respond immediately to a change in a competitor's offer. One-way communications may cause a delay of months to detect the change through market research, to revise the strategy, to change the advertising, and to get the cooperation and understanding of the channels of distribution, such as wholesalers and retailers.

CAREER OPPORTUNITIES IN SALES AND SALES MANAGEMENT

The variety and challenge in selling and sales management go unnoticed because many of the opportunities appear in industries that are not obvious to the casual observer. To illustrate the diversity of industries that depend on salespersons, we may refer to the classified advertising in just one issue of the *Wall Street Journal.*[1]

> LEASE SALES REP. A Minneapolis fleet management company seeks an experienced sales representative to contact major corporations in the Southeast. A business, finance or MBA degree in conjunction with a minimum of 2 years successful selling experience, preferably in the car leasing field, is desirable.
> FOOD SERVICE SALES. We are a nationally known manufacturer of bakers' supplies and food service specialties. If you have prior food service or bakers' supply sales experience we would like to talk to you.
> N.J. based US subsidiary of European Office Machine Manufacturer has exciting opportunity for a NATIONAL SALES MANAGER. The ideal candidate for this position should have previous exposure in the sales of word processing equipment or electronic typewriters and have experience hiring, leading and motivating sales persons.
> SALES MANAGER. We are seeking a Sales Manager with a proven track record to represent our Electric Utilities Division. This division provides turnkey systems and software services to both nuclear and fossil fuel power plants and is growing in excess of 50% per year.
> SALES MANAGER. Profit oriented heavy duty truck parts distributor covering N.C. & S.C. needs a seasoned professional to continue growth. The ideal candidate will have: MBA or BA degree in Business Administration or Marketing, 5–10 years combined direct sales & sales management experience with truck parts industry.
> DISTRICT SALES MANAGER. As a growing leader in the facing brick and cement block industry we are in search of an aggressive hands-on Sales Manager. The ideal candidate will have a progressive background which includes 3–4 years of outside sales supervisory experience in a construction related industry, knowledge of product display and promotions, excellent verbal and written communication skills and thorough familiarity with New York City and surrounding areas. Opportunities for personal growth. Will report to Regional Sale Manager.

These advertisements represent a very small sample of the diversity of industries that depend on personal selling to match their capabilities to the needs of the market.

Sales and sales management careers can lead to the chief executive officer position in major companies. A survey of the chief executive officers of the Fortune 500 companies is conducted regularly by the executive placement firm of Heidrick & Struggles. Its 1980 survey revealed that the functional backgrounds of these chief executives were as follows: engineering and research, 11.2 percent; finance, 18.5 percent; manufacturing and operations, 30 percent; and sales and marketing, 31 percent.[2] An earlier study by this company revealed that 74 percent of the chief *marketing* executives had careers in selling.[3] Thus at least 24 percent of the chief executive officers have had a background in sales management. This textbook will reflect why sales management is good training for becoming a chief executive. Sales management requires analytical and creative thinking. It requires a knowledge of planning, the law, and, most important, how to get things done through people.

Selling careers are not limited to private and profit organizations. Selling is used in the public sector. For example, states have development persons who sell companies on the benefits of locating plants in their states. Nonprofit organizations use sales representatives. For example, health organizations, such as Blue Cross-Blue Shield, use representatives to sell companies on using their services as part of an employee-benefit program. Universities use recruiters to sell the benefits of the university to potential students and athletes.

AN OUT-OF-DATE IMAGE

The image of personal selling and sales management has lagged behind reality.[4] The stereotype of a salesman, as recorded in American plays and novels, is that of a fast talker, slick dresser, high-pressure persuader, and one with loose morals while away from home. The play *Death of a Salesman* and the musical *The Music Man* help to form this stereotype for individuals who have no other knowledge of the role of a contemporary sales representative. Such an image is unfortunate because it turns many people away from careers in personal selling and sales management who would have found this a challenging, intellectually stimulating, and financially rewarding career.

Not everyone is suited to a career in selling and sales management. The goal of this text is to present personal selling and sales management as they are practiced in reality in the 1980s so that the reader may make a more informed decision regarding careers in these areas.

DISADVANTAGES OF SELLING CAREERS

We should note at the outset that selling has many disadvantages as a career. There is the problem of a poor public image. A person who is status conscious may find this the most important reason for rejecting selling as a career. Individuals who have a need for continuous positive reinforcement may find selling uncomfortable because they may regard a rejection as personal rather than a rejection of the product or the sales presentation.

This textbook focuses on a selling career known as "outside representative," in contrast to salespersons in a retail store or the inside person for a wholesaler. Outside sales representatives are subject to extensive travel and the loneliness of living on the road. Promotion to a larger territory or a higher level of sales management generally means relocation of one's family and establishing new friends. A sales representative will typically spend fifty hours or more a week, which would include evening and weekend work, completing reports, studying, and planning future activities. Because the representative generally works without much supervision, the selling career requires considerable self-discipline.

There is also considerable uncertainty, risk, and frustration in selling. A representative may work for years attempting to sell a new system, such as a computer, only to lose out to a competitor.

ADVANTAGES OF SELLING CAREERS

A disadvantage to one individual might be an advantage to another. For example, one individual might reject selling because of the lack of close supervision, while another would welcome this fact because it provides independence, an opportunity for initiative, and an opportunity for achievement. Similarly, while one person might want to stay in the community in which he or she was raised, another individual would welcome travel and relocation as a stimulating and challenging experience.

The contemporary sales representative is a problem solver and a consultant to the client. A person who engages in this kind of selling will find the work socially acceptable and psychologically rewarding.

There are few business careers in which a young person can have such complete control over his or her daily activities. As we will see shortly, many representatives run their territory like a business, thereby sharpening their skills for advancement.

Compensation and advancement are based on an individual's performance and productivity. An individual who likes activity outside of an office and who prefers making a variety of contacts may prefer personal selling to a career that is centered largely within an office.

If an out-of-date image has kept some people from a rewarding career in selling, our first order of business becomes one of presenting a more contemporary image of personal selling and sales management.

CONTEMPORARY SELLING

PERSONAL SELLING DEFINED

The new sales representative has been described in a variety of ways:

> The representative is the manager of a market area, a problem solver, an educator, an empathizer, and a strategy developer with profit responsibilities. . . .[5]

The new representative is a Micro-marketer for the territory. . . .[6]

Selling is a process that results in benefits to both parties—a win-win situation, as differentiated from a win-lose situation where an individual sells a product that is not needed. In the latter case, personal selling can be defined as a persuasive communication to satisfy a nonexistent need. . . .

Personal selling is an interpersonal process that exchanges information, goods, services, and money in which all parties of the exchange benefit. . . .

Personal selling is solving a client's problem or satisfying a client's needs with your products and services. . . . (This definition views the representative as a consultant.)

THE REPRESENTATIVE AS A CONSULTANT[7]

The professional sales representative has come a long way from the days of the fast-talking drummer who moved westward during the nineteenth century carrying all of his inventory in his wagon. Fast talking and no commitment to the buyer were characteristic of this type of selling. During the last 150 years, personal selling has passed through many stages to reach its present stage in which the representative is a consultant. Exhibit 1.1 summarizes the strategies that are appropriate to each of these stages. In examining this exhibit, we should recognize two important points. First, only the more sophisticated companies have reached the top level of personal selling in which the representative acts as a consultant to the clients and manages his or her territory as a business. Second, not all selling tasks require such a high level of sophisticated selling. The general sales manager must be certain to identify the level of personal selling that is necessary so that persons who are recruited are neither overqualified nor underqualified. We will consider briefly the strategies that are appropriate to each of the stages that are outlined in Exhibit 1.1.

Communication Strategies

At this lowest level of personal selling, the representative is an alternate medium for communicating information about the product or service offered by the company. In this case, the representative does little more than show the product, ask for the order, and leave. The only strategy appropriate for increasing sales at this point is walking more and talking more. There is little reason to use representatives as a communication medium when there are alternative mass communication media such as radio, television, newspapers, magazines, and direct mail.

**Exhibit 1.1   The Changing Role of the Sales Representative:
From a Communicator to a Business Manager**

Strategies for Selling   *Activities*

Business Management Strategies

- Manage accounts and territory as a Strategic Business Unit.
- Invest time and expenses in the most profitable opportunities.

Client Profit-
Planning
Strategies

- Sell to meet the client's total system and long-term needs. *Be a consultant.*
- Become part of the client's plan.
- Expand to other departments.
- Find new uses for your product.
- Services are an important part of the offer at this point.

Negotiation
Strategies

- The *customer* becomes a *client*.
- Perceive, classify, and serve the customer's needs.
- The product is adjusted to meet the customer's needs.

Persuasion
Strategies

- The representative understands the immediate and narrow needs of the *customer*.
- The representative tries to fit the customer into the existing product mix by skillfully overcoming objections.

Communication
Strategies

- The representative is a personal communicator, providing product and service information close to the point of the buying decision.

Developed from M. Hanan, J. Cribbin, and H. Keiser, *Consultative Selling* (New York: American Management Association, Inc., 1970).

Persuasion Strategies

The persuasion level requires the representative to go beyond merely the role of a communicator to the role of understanding at least the immediate and narrow needs of the *customer*. At this stage, the representative tries to fit the customer into the existing product or service mix by skillfully anticipating and overcoming objections. This stage of personal selling could be described as the "product concept" approach, not the contemporary "marketing concept" approach in which the customer's needs are considered first.

Negotiation Strategies

The marketing concept reminds us that the customer's needs should come first, and that the attributes of the products and services offered should be adjusted to meet these needs. Personal selling at the negotiation stage is in marked contrast to the two previous stages. During negotiation, the product is adjusted to meet the customer's needs rather than just attempting to skillfully overcome objectives, as is the practice in the persuasion stage of personal selling, or simply moving on to the next prospect, as would occur at the communication stage.

The critical skill at this stage of selling is analyzing and understanding the customer's needs and determining how the representative's products and services can meet these needs. At this point, the *customer* becomes a *client* and consultative selling begins.

Client Profit-Planning Strategies

Services are an important part of the representative's activities as we move from negotiation strategies to client profit-planning strategies. At this stage of personal selling, the representative seeks an understanding of a client's total profit-planning system—research, development, production, finance, management, and marketing. The representative must consider the long-term needs of the client, even foregoing a short-term sale if such is not in the best interest of the client. Consultative selling puts the representative on the client's team for the development of profit-planning strategies.

A representative must have empathy for a client. Thus we may ask, "What does an industrial buyer look for in a representative?" *Purchasing* magazine conducts an annual study to answer this question. The top ten qualities in rank order were: (1) willingness to go to bat for the buyer within the supplier firm, (2) thoroughness and follow-through, (3) knowledge of product line, (4) market knowledge and keeps buyer posted, (5) imagination in applying his or her product to the buyer's needs, (6) knowledge of the buyer's product line, (7) preparation for sales calls, (8) regularity of sales calls, (9) diplomacy in dealing with operating departments, and (10) technical education. Winners in *Purchasing* magazine's annual top industrial salespersons awards are individuals who have gone out of their way to meet clients' needs.[8]

Business Management Strategies

A sales representative has a loyalty both to the client and to his or her company. Carried to an extreme, consultative selling could be unprofitable. The professional representative, however, will manage his or her territory as a business. In Chapter 5, we will see how concepts from accounting and finance can be readily applied to a sales territory to produce income statements, return-on-investment calculations, and a portfolio of accounts.

THE REPRESENTATIVE AS A STRATEGIC MANAGER

To manage a territory as a business, it is necessary for the representative to have knowledge of the principles of accounting and finance. Similarly, a consultative representative who sells to the complete system of a client must understand production and marketing systems. Thus a thorough training in business administration is becoming a prerequisite for selling careers in many companies.

A representative may run his or her territory like a small business or a profit center. Some companies are beginning to require sales managers to state proposals in terms of return-on-assets managed. Many companies are using a system of national account management in which a manager is responsible for all sales to a few key accounts. Territory representatives, sales managers, and account managers are responsible for developing strategies and for bottom-line responsibility. How these activities are done by these individuals will be discussed in later chapters.

Exhibit 1.1 helps also to summarize the development of professional selling. It can also serve as a diagnostic tool when evaluating sales representatives. A representative who is operating at the level of persuasion strategies while the company is operating at a level of negotiation strategies is a representative who needs additional training.

TYPES OF REPRESENTATIVES

Sales & Marketing Management magazine identifies five types of salespeople in its annual survey.[9]

Account Representative

An account representative is a person who calls on established clients in industries such as foods, textiles, apparel, and wholesaling. This representative tends to be low-key with less pressure to develop new business than some other types of representatives. These representatives average from three to five calls per day and average $15,000 to $31,000 per year in compensation.

Detail Salesperson

A representative who concentrates on promotional activities and introducing new products, but does not directly solicit an order, is a detail representative. For example, pharmaceutical detail representatives call on doctors, hospitals, universities, and drugstores to encourage the use of their products. The sale actually takes place through a wholesaler or a pharmacist when the patient's prescription is filled. The detail representative averages eight to twelve calls per day and has an average compensation from $15,000 to $27,000.

Sales Engineer

A sales engineer must have a salesperson's expertise in identifying, analyzing, and solving problems in technical terms. Sales engineers are common in the chemical, machinery, and heavy-equipment industries. They average from three to six calls per day and have an average compensation ranging from $17,500 to $39,000.

Nontechnical Industrial-Products Salespersons

Many companies selling industrial products have found that a high degree of technical knowledge is not necessary. Some companies prefer representatives with a strong background in selling and business whom they can train in the technical aspects of their product. These companies have found that such a representative is more productive than the highly technically trained one. Nontechnical representatives are used by the office equipment and packaging materials industries. These representatives average from four to seven calls per day and receive a compensation that ranges from $16,100 to $37,000.

Service Salespersons

A representative who sells intangibles, such as insurance or advertising, has one of the more difficult jobs of selling because the benefits are intangible. These representatives average from five to nine calls per day and receive an annual compensation ranging from $16,500 to $35,700.

THE EXPANDED ROLES OF PERSONAL SELLING

The representative who practices profit-planning strategies assumes a new set of roles, such as a market analyst, a competitive analyst, and a financial analyst, for the client. These roles require additional skills that, in turn, will require a more highly trained representative. Many companies are hiring MBAs who already have the additional training for these expanded roles of the representative. A representative with a good business background would be able to make a presentation to a client that expressed benefits in terms such as return-on-investment. A knowledge of marketing analysis techniques and computers would help the representative to examine the potential in his or her territory and to assist clients in measuring the potentials in their markets.

The multiplicity of buying influences in a client firm has resulted in many companies using a team-selling approach in which the representative is a manager of a team of staff persons who provide technical support. IBM and the Bell System use such an approach. When this approach is used, the representative takes on the additional role of being a manager of a selling team. In this role, the representative assumes the tasks of isolating the influence structure in the customer firm, identifying the problems that these customers face in the development of their business, determining the criteria by which they will evaluate possible solutions to these problems, and organizing and managing the sales resources to develop an effective solution to these problems.[10] This team-selling approach provides the representative with the opportunity to practice management skills early in his or her career. From the company's point of view, this approach requires the identification of representatives who have these management skills or in whom they can be developed.

THE NEW COMPLEXITY OF PERSONAL SELLING

Changes in the personal selling function have not been limited to an expanding role for personal selling or the movement toward client profit-planning strategies or business-management strategies. There has also been a change in the environment of personal selling. Products and services have become more complex. Buyers and their criteria for buying have become more sophisticated. Purchasing managers use economic analysis and value analysis to build profit into the purchasing function. Domestic and foreign competition have increased greatly. Government regulations, such as pollution controls, complicate the sale of existing products and create market potentials for new products. Federal policies have given more importance to product benefits, such as energy savings and product safety. There has been a general erosion of prices and an increased demand for service. Multilevel buying decisions and team buying have complicated the buying process. Franchising and vertical integration have led to the centralized decision process where buying decisions are made at the home office, putting some buying influences outside the reach of the territory representative. In such cases, long-term relationships must be negotiated between the top executives of the seller and the buyer. Specialized selling teams have been developed to call on government accounts, schools, and export markets. National account managers, a new selling title, have been created to negotiate with the major accounts.[11]

This new complexity in the personal selling function has also altered the sales management function. More careful selection and training of sales managers is required. There is a need for a stronger role for sales management, and a corporate commitment to first-level sales management that is capable and full-time. The practice of having the first-line field sales manager also carry part of the territory will therefore decline in frequency.

THE NEW REPRESENTATIVE

By this point it is easy to see that the new representative is quite a different person from the old drummer who was the fast walker and talker. The selling function now requires greater training and provides greater opportunities to be creative. The personal selling function is taking on more importance in organizations such as banking, where it previously played a minor role.

GREATER TRAINING REQUIRED

Understanding the client's complete system needs and the use of business strategies when running the territory requires the new type of representative to have substantial business training. Exhibit 1.2 illustrates how some companies are actively seeking MBAs as representatives. Many MBAs are finding that consultative selling enables them to perform the consulting function that they seek with the additional responsibility of bottom-line profitability, which might provide them with better training for top management positions. Sales management provides an early opportunity to manage people.

OPPORTUNITIES TO BE CREATIVE

Opportunities to be creative in selling can be illustrated by an experience of a technical salesman with the Chemicals and Plastics Group at Union Carbide. (See Exhibit 1.3.) The customer wanted a safety bumper for one of its car models. Because this would be a multi-million dollar commitment for both parties, the first step was to arrange a meeting between the top executives of the two firms so that Union Carbide could demonstrate that it had the technical support and the capacity commitment that was required. At this point, the salesman's responsibilities began.

**Exhibit 1.2   A Recruiting Advertisement for an MBA Sales
Representative**

"It took me two years to get my MBA. And two more to realize I wasn't getting to use it.

"Getting my MBA took a lot of discipline and a lot of energy. And also a lot of time. I was glad when it was finally over. But after all that pushing, I felt let down. Something was missing. I had a friend who was in sales for SBC. And from the way he described it, it sounded like it was what I was looking for. Things like a constant challenge, real opportunity, not being chained to a desk, and the chance to go as far as your abilities will take you. I went to work for SBC. Sure, there was a risk in deciding to go into sales. But it was the best decision I ever made. I've never worked harder, played harder or felt better compensated. And when friends ask why I like sales, I tell them it's because I always know where I stand. I like the fact that the people I deal with are top executives in FORTUNE 1000 companies. I also like being with the leader in an industry that's growing over 20% a year . . . and that SBC promotes you to manage that growth. Most of all, I like the feeling that I'm in charge of my own life. That's why I end up asking my friends 'Why don't you go into sales?' "

SBC is looking for more people who aren't satisfied being anything less than the best they can be.

"We're looking for people who've made it, but still want more out of life.   ●   The kind of people who can't settle for coming in second. In anything. The kind of people who welcome challenge, thrive on hard work, seek recognition and the rewards that come with success. If you're that kind of person, we will guarantee you every opportunity here at SBC. You'll be given the best training in the industry. You'll get the support and backup you need. Your business talents will be developed to their maximum. Your abilities will be taxed to the limits. And I am confident that three years from now you'll say 'SBC was the best decision I ever made.' " *Robert Kleinert, President*

The opportunity is now. Your future is waiting. Send your resume to Bill Baker, Recruiting Manager, The Service Bureau Company, 500 West Putnam Avenue, Greenwich, Connecticut 06830.

THE SERVICE BUREAU COMPANY

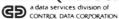 a data services division of
CONTROL DATA CORPORATION

An Affirmative Action Employer M/F
© 1977 The Service Bureau Company

Exhibit 1.3   Consultative Selling

UNION CARBIDE CHEMICALS AND PLASTICS

Could you solve this, company's problem?

One of our technical sales people did.

(continued)

Exhibit 1.3   Continued

Here's how one of our technical salesmen solved the problem:

His customer wanted a safety bumper for one of his car models. Because this project was a big one—involving a multi-million dollar commitment both for his customer and Union Carbide, the salesman's first step was to arrange for a meeting at our New York office with the customer and Chemicals and Plastics Marketing people. The purpose of this meeting was to agree on a joint effort, involving a commitment from Union Carbide to provide technical support, the capacity to make the large volume of chemicals required, and a clear definition of the economics of this unique system.

After the total organizational commitment was made, his work really started. While the customer was building prototype molds from concept drawings, we were supplying materials which were screened for properties and performance. Together we developed the bumper material and set material specifications to meet the requirements.

We also assisted in mold design, pour patterns and mold venting.

Meanwhile, the customer was installing the production line and the system for bulk storage of chemicals. Union Carbide material handling experts were called in to help work out bulk chemical handling techniques.

Many other important items had to be covered:
- Quality control methods

Courtesy of Union Carbide Corporation.

- Mode of delivery—trucks or tank cars
- Tank car unloading procedures and safety precautions
- Paint problems
- Stability in paint bake cycle
- Weathering and durability tests
- Volume and delivery schedules
- Negotiations for contract for the chemicals

Then—the contract was signed—the first bulk shipment was made—his customer's line was started up and debugged—the design level of production was reached—and there were smiles all around, especially on the face of the new car owner when he found that the cost of a "parking lot bump" was $0 instead of the usual $100-200.

Sound like a challenge that could turn you on?

This booklet has been designed to acquaint you with selling and sales management careers with the Chemicals and Plastics Group at Union Carbide. To do this, we've asked ourselves the questions we are most often asked by people considering joining us. As you read the answers, we hope you will focus particularly on certain aspects of our career opportunities that we feel are outstanding—the professionalism of the work, the career flexibility we offer, the importance of our career development process, and the chance all of our representatives have to solve important customer problems. If you like what you read—and you are truly interested in facing up to the demands of professional selling—we hope you will further explore a career with Union Carbide.

He worked with the customer on conceptual drawings, prototype molds, and the properties and the performance standards for the plastics. He assisted in technological matters such as mold design, pour patterns, and mold venting. The representative was involved in decisions about quality control methods, mode of product delivery, tank car unloading procedures and safety precautions, paint problems, stability in paint bake cycle, weathering and durability tests, volume and delivery schedules, and, finally, negotiations for the chemical contract. After the first bulk shipment was made, he worked with the customer in starting up and debugging the production line and bringing it up to a full level of production output. The result was a satisfied client and a satisfied customer of the client because the new car owner would not have a repair bill from a minor bump in a parking lot.[12]

SELLING SERVICES

Personal selling is an important function in many service organizations. The more familiar services include architectural services, insurance, stockbrokers, advertising, radio and television time, and newspaper and magazine space. Less familiar are selling services such as computer time and software (Exhibit 1.2), consulting services, banking services, and selling computers to the petroleum industry (Exhibit 1.4). Commercial bankers call on customers and help them solve their needs for capital. This role can be a mixture of consulting, selling, and financing. A commercial banker may be specialized in areas as diverse as construction, retailing, and international trade. Many banks seek individuals with an interest in finance and sales.

WHERE SELLING FITS INTO THE ORGANIZATION

The positioning of the personal selling function within the corporate organizational structure will vary greatly among companies and industries. There is one possible generalization. The personal selling function tends to dominate advertising in industrial firms, but it shares equal or lesser roles than advertising in the consumer fields, such as the grocery package industry.

SALES MANAGEMENT DEFINED

Definitions of sales management may vary greatly according to the industry and the firm in which the sales manager is operating. A very limited definition could be, "The personnel manager of sales representatives." This definition would be appropriate when the functions of the

Exhibit 1.4   Women Sell Computer Systems to the Petroleum Industries

Photo courtesy of International Business Machines, Inc. Ann Loidl, Denver, helped five oil, gas and mining companies apply the capabilities of new IBM computers, software and distributed processing techniques to produce significant productivity gains in geographically dispersed operations.

sales manager were limited to hiring, training, motivating, and rewarding salespeople.

In many companies, the sales managers include more than just these staffing functions; they include also the functions of planning, organizing, directing, and controlling—in short, all of the functions of management. In the latter cases, the sales manager becomes a micromarketing manager. Procter & Gamble defines sales management as people management, business analysis, and creative problem solving.

Sales managers may carry a variety of titles. The first-line sales management position may be called a field manager, a unit manager, or a district manager. The next level sales manager may be known as a division manager, a regional sales manager, or a zone sales manager.

Some companies, however, call the first line of sales management a zone manager. The titles "general sales manager," "national sales manager," and "director of sales" describe the next higher level of sales management. These latter titles would describe the top sales management position in those companies that do not have a vice-president of sales. From this position, an individual may proceed to division or corporate president.

CONSUMER PACKAGE GOODS

Exhibit 1.5 shows the positioning of personal selling in the Procter & Gamble Company. Here we see that sales management is on the same organizational level as advertising.

In this exhibit we see that there are four levels of sales management between the representative and the vice-president. Some companies use a position, such as a unit manager, as an early training ground to determine if a representative has management capabilities.

Exhibit 1.5   P&G Sales Structure

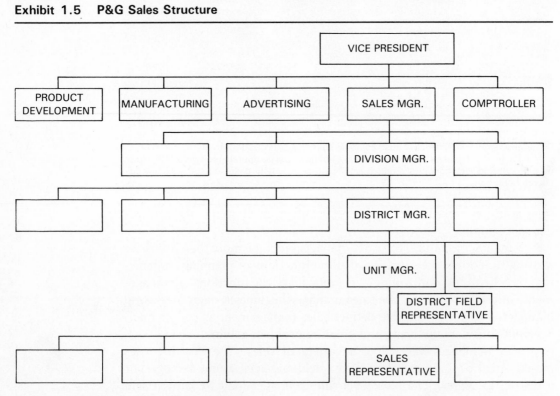

Courtesy of The Procter & Gamble Company.

Exhibit 1.6 Marketing and Sales Organization, Industrial Chemical Group, FMC Corporation

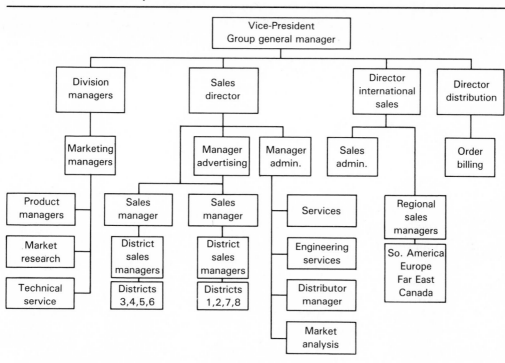

Courtesy of FMC Corporation Industrial Chemical Group.

INDUSTRIAL GOODS

Exhibit 1.6 shows the marketing and sales organization of the Industrial Chemical Group of the FMC Corporation. Here we note that the manager of advertising is under the sales director, in contrast to the P&G design where the advertising and sales managers were on equal levels. This organizational design reflects the fact that the technical selling function tends to dominate industrial marketing organizational designs.

SELLING OPPORTUNITIES BY INDUSTRY

If I decide on a selling career, which industry should I choose? To answer this question, one may consider the reply of the famous bank robber, Willy Suttin, when he was asked why he robbed banks. His reply was simply, "Because that's where the money is." A person who is serious about a sales management career will want to examine those industries where selling is an important part of the marketing function. One way of identifying these industries is to examine their sales force selling expenses as an percentage of company sales.

Sales & Marketing Management annually publishes the expenditures of industries on personal selling, expressed as a percentage of company sales. The top industries in 1980 were: office and educational supplies and equipment, 7.5 percent; printing and publishing, 6.9 percent; ethical pharmaceuticals, surgical supplies, and equipment, 5.6 percent; apparel, 5.2 percent; computers, 4.4 percent; and automotive parts and accessories, 3.0 percent.[13]

A person who is considering marketing as a career will want to compare the income of sales executives with the incomes from other marketing careers. Companies with sales of at least $750 million reported the following compensation packages (in thousands): top sales, $93; top marketing, $92; international marketing, $75; top advertising, $60; top public relations, $59; marketing research, $56; and sales promotion, $50.[14]

The number and variety of sales opportunities are extensive. To illustrate this point, Exhibit 1.7 shows the channel of distribution in three industries—real estate, snack foods, and apparel—that sell products that are familiar to the reader. It will be noted that outside selling functions are performed at a variety of points within these channels and represent great diversity in the knowledge required for successful selling.

Exhibit 1.7   The Selling Function in Selected Channels of Distribution

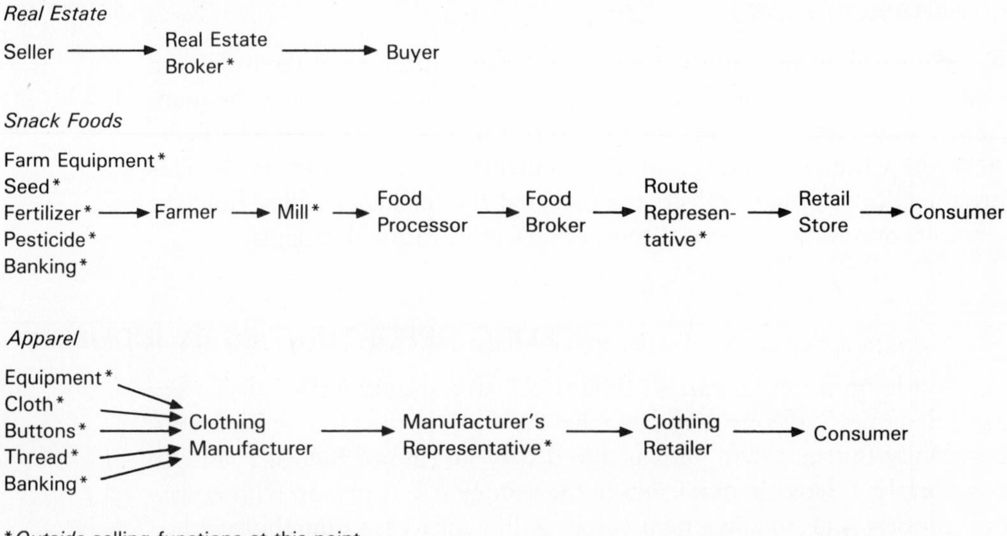

Real Estate

Seller ⟶ Real Estate Broker* ⟶ Buyer

Snack Foods

Farm Equipment*
Seed*
Fertilizer* ⟶ Farmer ⟶ Mill* ⟶ Food Processor ⟶ Food Broker ⟶ Route Representative* ⟶ Retail Store ⟶ Consumer
Pesticide*
Banking*

Apparel

Equipment*
Cloth*
Buttons* ⟶ Clothing Manufacturer ⟶ Manufacturer's Representative* ⟶ Clothing Retailer ⟶ Consumer
Thread*
Banking*

*Outside selling functions at this point.

SUMMARY

The personal selling function has come a long way from the old image of the slick-dressing, fast-talking salesman. Today's salesperson may perform the expanded roles of a consultant and a manager. Persons who still hold this out-of-date image of a sales representative may be overlooking a career opportunity that could be personally rewarding.

ASSIGNMENTS/DISCUSSION QUESTIONS

1. Analyze the want ads in the *Wall Street Journal* for positions in sales and sales management. Tabulate them according to industry, requirements, and compensation.

2. Contact the Placement Office of a university for the names of former students who have gone into sales. Write to these students and ask them for their evaluation of personal selling as a career. Their responses could be in written form, a tape that could be played in the classroom, or a conference call that would take place during the class hour.

3. Complete the following table for Xerox and Campbell Soup by estimating the percent of each of the communication tasks that is performed by the communication mix variables of advertising, personal selling, promotion, publicity, and market research. Be prepared to discuss your estimates during the class hour.

COMMUNICATION TASK	ADVERTISING		PERSONAL SELLING		PROMOTION		PUBLICITY		MARKET RESEARCH		TOTAL	
	C	X	C	X	C	X	C	X	C	X	C	X
Communicate the Product Benefits											100%	100%
Gather Feedback											100%	100%

C = Campbell's Soups
X = Xerox photocopy division

4. Prepare a list of potential employers (companies or organizations) in a field in which you are interested. Rate the companies as to their desirability and identify the criteria you used in your rating system.

5. Identify one specific type of job in which you are interested and list the job-related behavior required for the job.

6. Identify the criteria you would use in selecting a job in selling.

7. Conduct a survey among class members to rank the criteria in Question #6 in terms of their relative importance.

8. Compare the relative advantages and disadvantages of a career in selling with one other type of business-related activity you might consider.

CASE 1.1:
Acme Information Systems Company

After considerable needling by his brother Fred, who had graduated two years earlier, Jack Lodge thought seriously about what he was going to do next June after graduation from the state university. He had considered continuing his education to get an MBA, but like most of his classmates he felt he had had enough of school for a while, and, besides, he wasn't certain an MBA was what he wanted or was necessary for the field he thought he wanted to get into. He started at the university in liberal arts, but, as a result of part-time work during the summer and on holidays at Sears and the University Men's Shop, he switched to business administration. The interest he had developed through high school in math had led him into several computer courses, which he enjoyed. As a result he watched the bulletin board for placement interviews with companies that manufactured or distributed computers and other types of business equipment.

Jack's first several interviews didn't progress very satisfactorily. He approached each interview with a feeling of uncertainty and apprehension, until he encountered an older interviewer who stopped the interview midway to give Jack some advice. He suggested that Jack give some serious thought to what he wanted to do. If he didn't know, then he should talk with as many people as he could think of who were already employed in different kinds of jobs until he identified one or several that he thought might interest him, then discuss the pros and cons of those jobs with a number of individuals who held those jobs. After that, he should try to analyze his own strengths and weaknesses in the light of the comments those people made about the qualifications for their jobs. If he wasn't able to analyze himself, perhaps he could ask others to help him. Once he had a clearer picture of what he wanted to do and what he had to offer, he should make a list of the companies in this field, try to decide which company he wanted to go to work for, using whatever criteria he could obtain, and then make as strong and persistent an effort as possible—starting with the number one company on his list to be interviewed—and get a job with them. That way he would maximize his chances of getting what he wanted, minimize his time and efforts in the interviewing process, and at the same time impress his interviewers with his preparation.

Jack did just that. In the process, he decided that his interests and talents best equipped him for a career in selling some type of business equipment, and that the leaders in the field he was interested in were Info-Quipment Inc., Acme Information Systems Co., and Capitol Business Equipment Co. Inquiries at the college placement office enabled him to schedule interviews with the recruiters from Acme Information Systems and Capitol Business Equipment. A letter and resume sent to Info-Quipment brought a reply that they were not adding any sales personnel at this time, but they would keep his resume on file for six months. Jack readied himself as well as he could for the two interviews and surprised himself with the conviction with which he presented his qualifications. Both interviews seemed to go well and both interviewers indicated they had other applicants they were considering and would be getting back to him within a week. A few days later, he received a polite turn-down letter from Capitol Business Equipment, and a telephone call from Acme asking him to complete the application they were sending him and to make an appointment for another interview with the local Account Manager. After the second interview, Jack was invited to the branch office in Atlanta for a third interview with the Branch Manager. He was hired on the spot as a Sales Trainee beginning the first of the following month. He would be assigned a territory on the completion of his training, which would take four to five months. The Branch Manager, George Hampton, seemed pleased with Jack's qualifications and told him they had checked his references and previous employers, and that he had the qualifications to do well.

Jack was trained at the branch office, along with two other sales trainees, by Bob Webster, a Special Accounts Manager. Together, they spent a month in the office reviewing Acme's policies, procedures, the company organization, compensation and benefit plans, the fundamentals of selling and operating a territory, and the basic information about a limited number of Acme office products. Jack was particularly interested to learn about the five sales job classifications Acme used for its field sales staff, and the increasing salary ranges that went with promotions to the next level. As a sales trainee in the Office Products Division, Jack would start selling typewriters and copy machines to small businesses. On successful completion of his training, he would be promoted to Sales Representative and have several other categories of office products added to his catalogue. The next two levels were that of Account Manager who operated out of the General Products Division, which included the sale of small- and medium-sized computers to medium-sized companies; and the Special Accounts Manager who operated out of the Data Processing Division and sold medium- and large-sized computers to larger customers, and to those with multiple facilities where planning and coordination of the purchase of business information equipment was essential. The top level in sales below the managerial level was that of Consulting Account Manager. This individual was assigned to major and special accounts, such as university systems, manufacturers with multiple divisions and multiple sites, various governmental departments, etc., whose planning and purchasing required unusual coordination and follow through. In addition, the Consulting Account Manager was used for special assignments, training assistance at the Advanced Training Center, consulting in areas of special expertise, introducing new products, and for marketing research.

Jack was to start out selling typewriters and copy machines. While he initially had visions of selling expensive computer equipment, he soon learned that there was more to the simpler equipment than he realized. He hadn't been aware of the number of competitors, their advantages and disadvantages, prices, service, rental agreements, leasing agreements, and the size of the market. While his experience at the University Men's Shop and Sears was useful in giving him some insights into the selling process, he realized that now he was required to operate at a much more professional level. Through lectures and discussions, programmed learning courses, video tape, and tape/slide programs, Jack's knowledge increased steadily; so that when Bob Webster moved into role playing and video taping, Jack, along with the other sales trainees, began to feel more confident in handling and demonstrating the equipment. During the second month, Jack made field calls with Mr. Webster, two local Account Managers, and Customer Engineers on a number of small businesses, during which Jack was progressively included in the sales presentations. After his first solo call, he took some consolation in learning that fear of failure was not an uncommon concern of sales trainees, and that the customer was not rejecting him when he or she said "no," only the product. With Bob Webster's help, Jack soon learned to use turndowns to advantage in furthering his sales presentations and, ultimately, made his first sale. He also learned that building his knowledge and skills increased his confidence and gradually put the fear of failure in its proper perspective. With increasing experience his knowledge and confidence grew and he found himself looking forward with eager anticipation to the field training sessions. These were alternated with one-on-one coaching sessions during which the previous calls were reviewed, analyzed, restructured, and the next call planned. After three months' training at the branch and in surrounding territories with the local Account and Special Accounts Managers, Jack was invited to attend the advanced training school in St. Louis.

His three weeks at the Advanced Training Center were an experience he long remembered. He established lasting friendships with a significant number of the twenty sales trainees in the class and with the staff. In addition to an in-depth review of the products he was already selling, Jack's product mix was expanded to include portable, desk and telephone dictation equipment, graphics equipment to set type for audio-visual purposes, advertising and printing, and word-processing systems with storage, retrieval, and processing capabilities Jack didn't believe possible. But the aspect of training that Jack enjoyed and capitalized on most was the classes on salesmanship and the psychology of selling. His experience prior to the advanced training class made him realize that there was a lot more to selling than simply communicating facts about a product and asking for the order. As the class progressed, he began to understand the reasons behind the numerous classifications of sales personnel that Acme had devised, and how the skills of communications, persuasion, negotiation, client profit planning, and consultant selling became increasingly more important as the customer grew in size and business volume and Acme's products grew in complexity and price. He also began to appreciate the importance of knowing the customers' business, aims, objectives, and needs as thoroughly as possible if he were to provide the most suitable information processing products and systems.

On graduation, Jack was pleased to shed the title of sales trainee and become a professional Sales Representative of Acme's Office Products, and to enjoy the salary increase that went with his achievement. He was assigned and moved to Miami, Florida, where he reported to the Miami Branch Manager, Bill Harper. Mr. Harper made a point of telling Jack that the territory to which he was being assigned was a considerable challenge in that it was an above-average producing territory in a growing area, and that current sales were above the branch average in dollars and in sales versus quota.

Jack's territory comprised approximately 350 identified small business accounts and upward of 400 small business prospects located within 10 geographic sections of the greater Miami area. He learned that he was expected to call on as many as possible of the customers on his active call list during the first year to evaluate their potential, develop at least one prospect as a replacement for each active account, and make approximately eight calls per day. His itinerary would put him in two sections each month, with call-backs on some priority accounts in other sections more frequently as business opportunities were developed. Considering the effect of holidays, vacation, and one-day meetings at the branch every other Monday, Jack knew he would have to plan well to measure up to these standards. His first task was to get located and to learn his way around his territory. Mr. Harper was helpful in assigning Joe Mason, a Consulting Account Manager, to help him get started. For the first six months, Joe also worked with him on Jack's territory two days a month. This was in addition to the two days each month that Mr. Harper worked with him. This field training enabled Jack to have his questions answered quickly and to expand his knowledge and skills gradually about his own territory. In the process, he acquired a working knowledge of the importance of maintaining his call objectives and setting dollar quotas monthly, quarterly, and annually on each of the product lines he was selling.

After the first year in his territory, Jack reappraised the accounts on the basis of their potential use of Acme products. While his early efforts had been directed toward the sale, rental, or leasing of typewriters and copiers, he realized that the benefits of Acme's word-processing systems could significantly speed up the processing of information, improve the efficiency, and reduce the cost of operation of many of his customers. Just as he had to calculate the value of the economic life versus the physical life of the typewriters and copiers he was selling or leasing, and persuade the customers to recognize the financial benefits of trading in their old machines and depreciating the cost of new ones, now he had a different objective. He had to calculate for his customers the financial benefits of being able to act more quickly on the availability of speeded up information input, processing, and output—with fewer people—in less space and at lower cost. The ability he generated in doing that with his class of accounts over the next year earned Jack the admiration and respect of his peers, plus a significant bonus and growing recognition from Mr. Harper, the Branch Manager, and Mr. Longridge, the Marketing Manager of the Office Products Division. Jack was asked to discuss his methods at the Branch Managers' Conference, and to work with several sales trainees in adjoining branches. During the same period, Jack noticed the resignation or separation of several other Sales Representatives who had been members of his advanced training class. Max Merriman, his roommate in St. Louis, felt after two years that he "didn't want to be a salesman all his life," while several others evidently didn't enjoy the job or weren't willing to exert the necessary effort or self-discipline. To Jack, selling provided the opportunity to use his personality and verbal skills to interact with customers, persuade them to his point of view, and, in the process, satisfy their business needs with Acme information systems. He particularly enjoyed the freedom of being his own boss and managing his territory in the most productive way he knew.

A little more than two years after joining Acme, Jack's way of managing his territory and the sales results he produced earned him a promotion to Accounts Manager and a shift to the General Products Division within the Miami Branch. At first he was disappointed to learn that this entailed another series of training sessions at the Advanced Training Center. A review of the objectives during the first session of the course made Jack realize that he had been promoted to an area that required another dimension of knowledge about products and business needs with which he was only vaguely familiar, and a new set of selling skills that hadn't been required in selling office products. Selling small- and medium-sized computers, along with more complex word-processing systems, required a more extensive knowledge of bookkeeping (general ledgers, accounts receivable/payable, etc.) inventory control, payroll, customer data, production control, billing systems, sales analyses, territory customer classification, etc. The thrill of writing an order for a computer system and software programs worth $250,000 and above helped make up for the frustration he had felt during his first several months in his new role in not receiving the repeated ego rewards that went with frequent orders he had written for sales, leases, or rental agreements on typewriters and copiers. He appreciated the rapid feedback to a successful effort as a typewriter/copier salesman, and recognized the psychological growth and self-discipline he had to develop to fully enjoy the fruits of his promotion. It was a different world of operations that he was encountering to guide the efforts of an Acme team, including a sales engineer, product specialist, and Account Manager, either as a consultant or team leader, in identifying the customer's immediate and extended needs, designing the package, and then gaining the necessary multiple approvals to obtain the order. It required coordination skills, patience, and persistence. Jack's ability to grasp the customer's information processing needs, identify the bottleneck, and apply the vital one-on-one personal interacting skills, helped him feel a sense of achievement as they passed the checkpoints in the development of an order. It also helped him recognize his role as a member of an account planning team or account managing team. His toughest assignment and most impressive personal growth occurred as he went from one type of customer to another and learned their functions, language, and objectives, and the role of Acme Information Systems in such diverse fields as medicine, law, finance, manufacturing, insurance, communications, and banking.

Jack's promotion to Special Accounts Manager came a year and a half later. As pleased as he was to receive the recognition (and the salary increase!) for his efforts, he realized that his previous promotion had been the critical one in expanding his customer universe, his world of knowledge and skills, and his field of effort. The area of activity of the Special Accounts Manager for Acme was much the same as that of the Account Manager, only larger and with bigger and more complex computers and Acme Information Systems. The selling process was longer, required a larger team and more patience, and the payoff was bigger—as were the disappointments. The personal and selling skills were much the same, but at a higher level. The Special Accounts Manager usually was the team leader. Jack settled into his new responsibilities with confidence, but with a greater recognition of his interdependence on others.

CASE QUESTIONS

1. Who could Jack Lodge have talked with about the qualifications required for a job in the business equipment field?

2. Who could Jack Lodge have talked with about his strengths and weaknesses relative to the qualifications for a job in the business equipment field?

3. What talents or qualifications are best suited to a career in selling?

4. What are the advantages and disadvantages of being assigned as a salesperson in an above-average and below-average producing territory?

5. What is the importance of having territory sales above the average both in dollars and in sales versus quota?

6. How might turndowns be used to advantage to further a sales presentation?

7. What qualities could Jack Lodge have developed in his summer and holiday employment at the University Men's Shop and at Sears that could have been useful in his job with Acme? Define these qualities.

8. Identify the categories in Exhibit 1.1 of this chapter that correspond with the five Acme sales classifications and explain.

9. What behavioral characteristics or qualities that were identified and defined in Question #7 can be related to the four jobs Jack Lodge held with Acme Information Systems Co.?

REFERENCES

1. *Wall Street Journal* (November 10, 1981): 33–40.
2. Heidrick & Struggles, Inc., "Profiles of a Chief Executive Officer," 1980, p. 6.
3. Heidrick & Struggles, Inc., "Profile of a Chief Marketing Executive," 1976.
4. D. L. Thompson, "Stereotype of the Salesman," *Harvard Business Review* 50 (January–February 1972): 20–29.
5. Leslie M. Dawson, "Toward a New Concept of Sales Management," *Journal of Marketing* (April 1970): 33–38.

6. M. A. Jolson, ''Business Courses Must Change to Reflect 'New Salesperson' of 1980s,'' *Marketing News* (July 25, 1980): 20.

7. Mack Hanan, James Cribbin, and Herman Heiser, *Consultative Selling* (New York: American Management Association, Inc., 1970).

8. ''Buyers Choice,'' *Sales & Marketing Management* (August 20, 1979): 38–40.

9. Thayer C. Taylor, ''A Letup in the Rise of Sales Call Costs,'' *Sales & Marketing Management* (February 25, 1980): 24–30.

10. P. T. Fitzroy and G. D. Mandry, ''The Salesman-Manager,'' *Management Review* 64, no. 7 (July 1975): 51–53.

11. B. Charles Ames, ''Build Marketing Strength into Industrial Selling,'' *Harvard Business Review* 50 (January–February, 1972): 48–60; A. F. Doody and W. G. Nickels, ''Structuring Organizations for Strategic Selling,'' *MSU Business Topics* (Autumn 1972): 27–34; Benson P. Shapiro and Ronald S. Posner, ''Making the Major Sale'' *Harvard Business Review* (March–April 1975): 68–78; ''The New Supersalesman: Wired for Success,'' *Business Week* (January 6, 1973): 44–49.

12. Union Carbide recruiting brochure, 1979.

13. *Sales and Marketing Management* (February 25, 1980): 58.

14. John A. Fischer, ''The High Cost of Keeping Up,'' *Sales & Marketing Management* (November 17, 1980): 52–55. Based on a survey of 725 companies in 1980.

2

APPLYING
THE MANAGEMENT PROCESS
TO THE SALES FORCE

After decades of examining what managers do, most management scholars agree that there is an identifiable set of skills, functions, and activities that are performed by all managers, whether they are in production, finance, accounting, or sales.[1] This chapter will illustrate how these basic management skills, activities, and functions apply to sales management. This review will emphasize the point that even young sales managers have the opportunity to practice all phases of management. This opportunity explains why more chief executives come from sales management than any other functional field of business.

A definition of management seems in order at this point. Mackenzie defines management as "achieving objectives through others."[2] The manner in which objectives are established and achieved becomes the *management process*.

THE MANAGEMENT PROCESS[3]

The management process may be described at three different levels. At the lowest level, we find management activities. Clusters of similar activities form a management function. In order to perform these functions and activities, the manager must possess the basic management skills for analyzing the problem, making decisions, and communicating effectively.

The authors thank Carl R. Anderson, Associate Professor of Management, University of North Carolina, for helpful comments on this chapter.

MANAGEMENT SKILLS

At this point in our discussion we will simply define management skills. Later in the text there will be an opportunity to develop these skills through case analysis. These skills are necessary to perform each of the management activities.

Analyzing the Problem

The analysis of a sales problem or opportunity requires skills in gathering and analyzing the facts, identifying opportunities and problems, and determining the cause of a problem or opportunity. For example, a common sales management problem is the creation of territories to assure adequate coverage of a market. The sales manager will need to analyze the market potential, the workload, travel time, expenses, and the abilities of the sales representatives before developing alternative territory designs.

Making Decisions

To make a decision, a manager must first create alternative courses of action, such as territory designs, and then evaluate the gains and losses that are associated with each alternative. Then the most desirable course of action must be selected. Until this selection is made, we have no decision; we have only studies and analyses.[4]

The sales representative engages in decision making when he or she sets priorities, decides which products to promote, chooses which product features to emphasize, or selects a sales strategy to overcome competition. Field sales managers make decisions when they structure territories, solve account problems, and choose representatives for promotion. General sales managers make decisions when they choose a promotional strategy, select field sales managers for promotion, and determine the size and organizational structure of the sales force. Because all of these decisions are made in a state of uncertainty, the decision maker must assess the probabilities and outcomes that are associated with each decision. Thus the sales manager can use the concept of *expected value* when making a decision.

Communicating Effectively

Communication is the effective transfer of information from a sender to a receiver. The information is communicated effectively when the receiver gains understanding, not just its content, from the message. Communication is a critical skill for sales and sales management.

It is obvious that representatives must be effective communicators with prospects and buyers, but it is less obvious that they must be effective communicators with contact persons within their company. Effective communication with peers, superiors, credit personnel, the billing office, shipping clerks, engineers, production scheduling personnel, and research and development personnel will make the representative more effective in his or her assigned area of responsibility and more promotable to the next level of management. The vehicles by which representatives communicate include reports, itineraries, telephone calls, memos to managers and company departments regarding the success of promotions, customer complaints, and recommendations.

Field sales managers communicate upward with reports, itineraries, and memos. They communicate downward with staff bulletins, individual memoranda, training sessions, sales meetings, and personal counseling. They communicate in both directions when they evaluate representatives' past performance and report these evaluations to the representative and to the next level of sales management.

General sales managers monitor the communications at lower levels. They communicate to lower levels regarding new plans, policies, procedures, and overall company sales performance. They communicate upward with regard to goal accomplishment and recommendations for changes. Their ability to communicate well will help them achieve current goals and be promoted.

MANAGEMENT FUNCTIONS

Management is a continuous process that begins with the function of planning. It then moves sequentially to organizing, staffing, directing, controlling, and then moves back to planning. This continuous and sequential process is illustrated in Exhibit 2.1.

Strategic Planning

Strategic planning is *not* predicting and preparing for the future; it is marshalling of resources to make the future happen in your favor.[5] To make the future happen in your favor, you must control those events that are controllable and adapt to those events that are uncontrollable.

Wisdom and experience are required to distinguish between controllable and uncontrollable events.

Organizing

Organizing is the designing of a structure of roles to be performed by individuals so that there is an effective accomplishment of objectives. Departments are formed by grouping together persons who perform the similar roles. This grouping of role specialties expands the number of subordinates who can be managed, thereby making the organization more efficient and controllable. Line and staff relationships are established by the *kind* of authority that is allocated to subordinates. The degree of decentralization of authority is determined by *how much* authority will be allocated to subordinates. The physical location can also affect the degree of delegation. A representative who is far from the office may have more authority delegated.

Staffing

Staffing consists of choosing *qualifiable* persons for each position in the organization. We must recognize that it is not always possible to recruit persons who are qualified for a position, thus we must identify characteristics that make them qualifiable, after additional training. We will see later in the text that this distinction is important in conforming with federal regulations regarding equal employment opportunities.

Directing

Directing is the bringing about of purposeful actions by persons in order to achieve the desired objectives of the organization. *Directing* is a broader term than *leading* because the concept of directing includes delegating, motivating, coordinating, and managing change and conflict.

Controlling

Controlling ensures that the system progresses toward the objectives of the organization according to the plan. When a system is out of control, minor adjustments may bring it back. This out-of-control state of the system may also reveal that the objectives and the plan were not realistic. Thus it may be necessary to cycle back through the planning stage and repeat the whole sequence of functions.

Exhibit 2.1 The Management Process

Management Skills for All Activities:	1. Analyze Problems and Opportunities: Gather facts, define problems and opportunities, determine causes. 2. Make Decisions: Create alternatives, evaluate, and select the most appropriate course of action. 3. Communicate: Transfer information effectively.		

Sequential Functions:

Plan
• Make the future happen in your favor.

Organize
• Structure roles for effective accomplishment of objectives.

Staff
• Choose qualifiable persons for each position in the organization

Sequential Activities:

Forecast
• Estimate future events, environment, and results from present actions.

Set Objectives
• Determine desired end results.

Develop Strategies
• Decide how and when to achieve objectives.

Develop Policies
• Make standing decisions regarding strategic matters.

Develop Programs (Tactics)
• Break the objectives and strategies into manageable action steps.
• Schedule these action steps.

Set Procedures
• Standardize programs for efficiency and uniformity.

Budget
• Allocate resources (people, capital, and information) to programs.

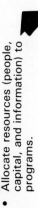

Establish Organizational Structure
• Identify and group work to be done and define liaison lines to facilitate coordination.

Create Position Descriptions
• Define scope, relationships, and responsibility.

Establish Position Qualifications
• Define qualifications for persons in each position.

Recruit/Select
• Locate, identify, and hire qualifiable persons.

Orient/Train
• Familiarize new persons with job environment and responsibilities.
• Make them proficient through instruction and practice.

Develop Personnel
• Counsel and coach to improve knowledge, skills, and attitude.

Sequential Functions:

Sequential Activities:

Direct
- Bring about purposeful action toward desired objectives.

Delegate
- Assign responsibility, authority, and accountability for results.

Motivate
- Create conditions on the job to persuade, inspire, and challenge individuals to take desired action.

Coordinate
- Relate efforts of individuals in most effective combination.

Manage Change/Manage Conflict
- Encourage independent thought and manage conflict.

Control
- Ensure progress toward objectives according to plan.

Establish Reporting System
- Determine needed critical data, how and when reported.

Develop Performance Standards
- Establish dimensions of satisfactory performance for critical duties.

Measure Performance
- Appraise deviation from standards and objectives.

Take Corrective Action
- Counsel to attain standards.

Reward
- Praise, remunerate, promote, discipline, or separate.

Return to Plan, revising objectives, strategies, and programs as necessary.

Adapted from R. Alec Mackenzie, "The Management Process in 3-D," *Harvard Business Review* (November–December 1969): 80–87; Louis A. Allen, *The Professional Manager's Guide*, 4th ed. (Louis A. Allen Associates, 1969); R. L. Ackoff, *A Concept of Corporate Planning* (New York: Wiley/Interscience, 1970); Harold Koontz and Cyril O'Donnell, *Management: A Systems and Contingency Analysis of Managerial Functions*, 6th ed. (New York: McGraw-Hill Book Co., 1976). © 1981 G. David Hughes, all rights reserved.

MANAGEMENT ACTIVITIES

As can be seen in Exhibit 2.1, each of the management functions may be further subdivided into a sequence of activities. A brief discussion of each of these activities will help us to see how they are incorporated into sales management. More detailed activities appear in the general sales managers' job description, Exhibit 16.1, Chapter 16. Later in this chapter we will see how these definitions may be translated into the excitement of consulting by using them to make a "sales management audit."

Planning Activities

Forecasting.   A forecast consists of estimating future events, estimating the future environment, and estimating the results that will take place from present actions given these future events and environment. Estimates of future technical events may include the research and development findings by us or our competitors. Economic and political environments will be an important part of this forecast. Once we understand these events and environment, we are in a better position to decide whether our present actions will bring about the desired results. Sales managers forecast sales, expenses, personnel needs, and training needs.

Setting Objectives.   When we determine the desired end results of an organization, we are setting its objectives. There may be a hierarchy of objectives where a lower objective is necessary in order to achieve a higher one. For example, to achieve a selling objective a representative may have objectives for the number of calls per day, the number of presentations made, and the number of new accounts established. Corporate objectives must be translated into sales force objectives and individual objectives.

An objective must be defined in measurable terms that state the *magnitude* of a result that is to be achieved and the *time period* for achievement. For example, "Increase sales 15 percent during the next six months," is a good statement of an objective because it is expressed in measurable terms (sales), the magnitude of the objective is specific, and the time period for achievement has been clearly identified.

Developing Strategies.   In its most basic form, strategy development is deciding how and when to achieve the objectives of the organization. *Stratagem*, in its ancient Greek form, means a trick for deceiving an enemy. Hence, strategies are what generals and admirals do. In an organizational context, *strategy* takes on a less belligerent meaning. It is simply the method that an organization would use to achieve its objectives, given a set of environmental constraints and organizational policies. Representatives and sales managers develop strategies for tapping opportunities and meeting competition.

Developing Policies. Policies are standing decisions regarding recurring strategic matters. Policies place limits on the kinds of strategies that are acceptable for achieving objectives. An understanding of a policy keeps the planner from developing a plan that would not be acceptable to top management. A policy is an automatic decision maker. It provides uniformity, fairness, control, efficiency, and simplified communication.

There are many sales management policies. Representatives will be bound by corporate policies regarding ethics, returned goods, dress codes, pricing, and trade-ins. The field sales manager will have corporate policies regarding recruiting, selecting, evaluating, promoting, and separating representatives. These policies must comply with federal policies regarding equal employment opportunities. The general sales manager will monitor these policies for compliance, as well as develop and suggest new policies.

Developing Programs. Programs break the objective and the strategy into manageable action steps that can be identified, delegated, and implemented, and the results measured. These action steps are also known as *tactics*, another term of Greek warfare meaning the science or art of maneuvering troops or ships in the presence of the enemy. A *schedule* is that part of a program that places a priority on the completion of action steps and specifies the time sequence in which these steps will be performed. Sales managers create selling programs that will direct representatives toward the sales objectives.

Setting Procedures. Procedures are standardized programs of actions regarding recurring tactical matters. Procedures are frequently the most efficient way for performing a task. They also provide uniformity for completing the task. The record of an order may require conforming with standard procedures. Selling procedures will include detailed descriptions for completing order forms, handling expenses or accident reports, and so on.

Budgeting. Budgeting is the allocation of resources to programs so that the programs may achieve the objectives of the organization. Resources include people, working capital, and information. Information about the market and competitors is becoming an increasingly important and costly resource in sales management. Representatives and sales managers must budget their time, expenses, and promotional materials.

Organizing Activities

Establishing Organizational Structure.   When roles have been identified and similar ones grouped together into departments, liason lines must be established to facilitate coordination. It is now possible to draw an organizational chart. This organizational chart should reflect the strategy of the organization. Unfortunately, strategies change and organizations frequently remain the same due to vested interests in old organizational structures. Strategies may fail because the old organizational structure may be incapable of implementing a new strategy.

The liason lines among roles within an organization are communication links that convey the kind and magnitude of authority that is appropriate for each role. These communication links report external threats and opportunities facing the organization, as well as the management activities. The communication links may become overloaded, thereby confusing role relationships and reducing the effectiveness of an organization.

Sales managers must decide whether to specialize the sales force by product or geography. They must decide how many field managers to use at each level of management. Exhibit 2.2 illustrates various sales force organizations.

Creating Position Descriptions.   The job description defines the scope, relationships, responsibilities, and authority assigned to a specific position within an organization. In sales management, the representatives' job description is the basic document for recruiting, training, evaluating, and rewarding the representative. Examples of job descriptions for representatives, district sales managers, and general sales managers will appear in Chapters 3, 7, and 16, respectively.

Establishing Position Qualifications.   The position qualifications represent the criteria by which persons will be selected and evaluated if hired. Defining the qualifications for persons in each position therefore becomes an important part of organizing. Representatives' qualifications include product knowledge, attitudes toward selling, selling skills, and habits in managing their territories.

Exhibit 2.2   Various Sales Management Organizational Structures

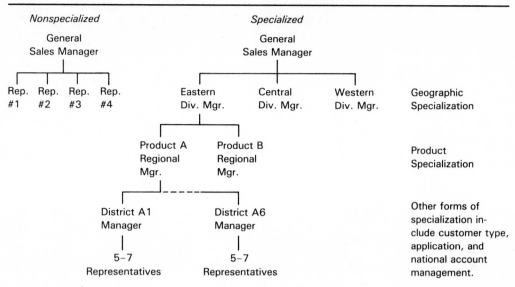

Staffing Activities

Recruiting/Selecting.   The initial stage of staffing includes the recruiting, screening, and final selection of qualifiable persons for each position in the organization. All of these steps consist of identifying those persons who have a high potential for performing the roles that are required by the job description.

Some companies have representatives participate in the process of recruiting and selecting by having them recommend prospects from social contacts, customers, and competitors, and by recruiting at schools and universities in their territories. The screening function may be performed in part by the representative if the company requires prospects to ride with a representative for a day. The representative then files a report on the potential of the prospect, which will become part of the final screening process.

The field sales manager must identify sources for recruiting, screen applicants and follow recruiting procedures, contact references, conduct a hiring interview, and make selections on job-related behavior characteristics.

The general sales manager monitors the field managers' recruiting and selecting activities to be certain that they comply with company and federal policies. The general sales manager must also select the field managers.

Selection includes not only selecting individuals into the organization, but also selecting those out of the organization who did not perform as required. Terms such as *separation, termination,* and *dehiring* are used to describe this process. Federal regulations regarding equal opportunities during hiring apply also to equal opportunities at the time of separation. Thus reasons for termination must be carefully documented to give a representative opportunities to correct deficiencies and to make certain that the company is not discriminating in its hiring, training, and promotional activities. It seems unfortunate that it has taken a federal regulation to bring about what seems to be a good management procedure, that is, more careful consideration of why people fail to perform well in a given job.

Orienting/Training.   Familiarizing the new representative with the company, the environment, and the territory becomes the responsibility of the field sales manager. A good orientation will prevent later misunderstandings, unhappiness on the job, and demotivation.

Training makes a qualifiable candidate proficient through instruction and practice. We will see later that there is great variance among the training programs for sale representatives due to differences in the characteristics of the products they sell and the selling tasks that are assigned to them.

Developing.   Representatives and managers are expected to improve their knowledge, skills, and attitudes by using self-development techniques and company programs.

Development for the representative requires gaining knowledge about products, processes, procedures, programs, and people for his or her company, its customers, and its competitors. The skills of analysis, decision making, and communication must be developed. Field sales managers provide training programs and informal on-the-job training.

Field managers also engage in their own personal development to make themselves promotable. Part of the latter activity is developing a replacement for himself or herself. The general sales manager provides field managers with opportunities for training and development, establishes career counseling, and monitors compliance with policies for development. Because selling and sales management require a high level of energy, some companies encourage health development and physical fitness programs.

A critical management activity is the counseling and coaching of subordinates so that they improve their knowledge, skills, and attitudes.

Directing Activities

Delegating. Delegating consists of assigning responsibility and authority to a subordinate and holding him or her accountable for the results.

The sales representative is largely on the receiving end of delegation. The field sales manager may delegate to the representative certain activities for the short term, such as training new representatives. The field sales manager has line responsibility delegated to him or her for the field sales staff. The general sales manager may be responsible for warehousing, service personnel, brokers, manufacturers' representatives, the selection of distributors, and the training of distributors' representatives.

Motivating. Motivating involves creating conditions on the job to persuade and inspire people to take the desired action that is necessary to achieve the objectives of the organization. The motivating process will include removing factors that are demotivating and creating environments to help the individual motivate himself or herself. Motivating representatives is the most important activity of the sales manager.

Coordinating. Coordination of efforts is required so that all individuals are pulling toward a common goal. The selling plan coordinates the advertising and personal selling efforts within the marketing mix. It also coordinates sales management activities such as staffing and training.

Managing Change/Managing Conflict. Change and conflict are inevitable in any dynamic, innovative organization. Some companies, such as IBM, build conflict into the planning process to assure that planners will be challenged to develop the best plan possible. An organization that encourages creative and independent thinking must expect conflict and must learn how to channel this conflict for the good of the organization. Organizational theorists have changed their position regarding conflict. Heretofore they thought in terms of conflict resolution. Now they discuss managing conflict. Thus an organization that does not have some conflict may be an organization that lacks innovation and dynamic growth.

Controlling Activities

Establishing Reporting Systems. Reporting systems ensure that the system is moving toward its objectives. To establish these systems it is necessary to determine what critical data are needed, and how and when they will be reported. We will see later in this text that the development of the computer and operations research techniques have greatly improved sales management reporting systems. The microcomputer will alter greatly sales reporting systems (Chapter 5).

Developing Performance Standards.   Performance standards identify the dimensions and the achievement along these dimensions that will exist when key duties are done well. For example, a sales representative who does not make ten calls per day may not be performing adequately, if such is the standard of the company. There will be similar standards for all levels of sales management. For example, the field sales manager may be required to recruit and train representatives so that no territory is without a representative for more than 5 percent of the year.

Measuring Performance.   The control system must include procedures for measuring results to ascertain the extent of deviations from the objectives and standards established for the organization. Control may be automatic when these results are supplied to the representative in readily usable form. Sales quotas provide self-performance measures for a representative.

Taking Corrective Action.   When the measures of results indicate that there are deviations from objectives and standards, it will be necessary to counsel personnel to help them attain standards and objectives. Replanning and repeating the management process will be necessary when the original plan was not realistic or unexpected environmental changes occurred. Sales management corrective action will include reassignment, demotion, and termination.

Rewarding.   Rewards for superior performance include social psychological rewards, such as praise, and financial rewards.

SALES MANAGEMENT FUNCTIONS AND ACTIVITIES

In Chapter 1 and Exhibit 1.2 we saw that many sales forces have two, three, or more levels of sales management. How are these management functions and activities assigned to the different levels of sales management? The authors conducted a survey of sales managers at three levels to answer this question. This survey included over 700 managers who were at three levels of sales management in twenty-five companies that represented five different industries. The results of this survey are summarized in Exhibits 2.3 and 2.4. (Additional findings will be reported in Exhibit 18.3, Chapter 18.) These findings provided the basis for organizing the discussions regarding the activities of field sales managers and general sales managers.

**Exhibit 2.3   The Percent Importance of Management Functions and Activities
to Own Job as Perceived by First-Line, Second-Line,
and General Sales/Marketing Managers**
(Respondents Allocated One Hundred Points among Twenty-Two Activities)

	IMPORTANCE TO OWN JOB			
FUNCTIONS/Activities	First-Line Managers %	Second-Line Managers %	General Sales/ Marketing Managers %	Probability of Nonsignificant Differences Across Management Levels
PLAN	17.6	24.7	36.5	
Forecast	2.2	3.5	7.1	.01*
Self Objectives	3.8	5.0	5.9	.01
Develop Strategies	3.4	5.1	5.6	.01
Develop Policies	1.6	2.7	4.0	.01
Develop Programs	3.5	4.6	6.5	.01
Set Procedures	1.8	2.1	4.2	.01
Budget	1.3	1.8	3.1	.01
ORGANIZE	4.2	5.2	7.9	
Establish Organ. Structure	1.9	2.3	3.5	.01
Create Position Description	1.1	1.3	2.3	.01
Estb. Position Qualifications	1.2	1.5	2.1	.01
STAFF	34.7	22.7	10.1	
Recruit/Select	8.7	6.0	1.9	.01
Orient/Train	9.2	5.4	3.6	.01
Develop Personnel	16.8	11.3	4.7	.01
DIRECT	21.1	23.0	21.4	
Delegate	4.3	5.9	5.3	.01
Motivate	9.6	8.5	7.9	.17
Coordinate	3.3	4.0	4.1	.07
Manage Change	3.8	4.7	4.0	.09
CONTROL	22.4	24.4	24.1	
Establish Report Systems	2.5	3.3	4.5	.01
Develop Standards	3.3	4.0	4.3	.02
Measure Performance	5.8	6.0	7.0	.32
Take Corrective Action	5.5	6.0	4.5	.16
Reward	5.4	5.2	3.8	.05
Totals (subject to rounding error)	100.0%	100.0%	100.0%	
Total No. of Managers	600	86	24	

*To be read as follows: There is one chance in one hundred that the difference in the perception of the importance of forecasting across these management levels is due to chance.

Respondents were asked to allocate one hundred points to reflect the importance of each activity in their job.

Exhibit 2.4   **The Percent Importance of Management Functions and Activities as Perceived by First-Line Field Sales Managers in Five Industries** (Respondents Allocated One Hundred Points among Twenty-Two Activities)

FUNCTIONS/Activities	All First-Line Managers	INDUSTRIES				
		Pharma-ceutical	Other Medical	Office Supplies/Equipment	Petroleum/Rubber	Clothing Manufr.
	%	%	%	%	%	%
PLAN	17.6	15.2	23.8	23.6	26.5	21.2
Forecast	2.2	1.7**	3.8	3.2**	4.7*	2.8**
Set Objectives	3.8	3.4**	4.2	5.2**	4.3	4.4**
Develop Strategies	3.4	3.1**	4.4	4.3*	4.1	4.0**
Develop Policies	1.6	1.3**	2.1	2.3	2.5	2.9**
Develop Programs	3.5	3.2**	3.9	4.5**	5.2	3.6**
Set Procedures	1.8	1.6**	2.5	2.4*	2.6	2.2**
Budget	1.3	1.0**	2.9**	1.8**	3.1**	1.3**
ORGANIZE	4.2	3.2	8.8	5.9	7.6	6.1
Establish Organ. Structure	1.9	1.5**	4.3**	2.5	3.6	2.4**
Create Position Description	1.1	0.8**	2.3	1.7*	2.0	1.8**
Estb. Position Qualifications	1.2	0.9**	2.2	1.6	2.0	1.9**
STAFF	34.7	37.2	23.4	32.8	17.6	27.2
Recruit/Select	8.7	8.9	5.7	10.2*	3.0	7.8
Orient/Train	9.2	9.4	5.8	10.7**	6.6	7.6
Develop Personnel	16.8	19.0**	11.9	12.0*	8.0	11.9**

DIRECT	21.0	21.3	21.9	18.8	23.4	22.3
Delegate	4.3	4.1*	5.2	3.7**	6.8	5.7*
Motivate	9.6	10.2**	8.7	8.2	7.4	8.6**
Coordinate	3.3	3.2*	3.6	3.4	4.2	4.4*
Manage Change	3.8	3.8	4.4	3.6	5.0	3.7
CONTROL	22.4	23.0	22.2	19.0	24.9	23.2
Establish Report Systems	2.5	2.2**	4.0	2.7	3.9	3.5**
Develop Standards	3.3	3.2	4.0	2.6**	5.4	4.1
Measure Performance	5.8	6.3**	4.6	4.1**	5.5	5.3**
Take Corrective Action	5.5	5.7*	5.0	4.9	5.3	5.2*
Reward	5.4	5.7	5.0	4.8	4.8	5.2*
Totals (subject to rounding error)	100.0%	100.0%	100.0%	100.0%	100.0%	100.0%
Total No. of Companies	25	16	3	3	2	1
Total No. of First-Line Managers	600	428	31	93	21	27

* = 0.05; ** = 0.01: Probability of the *industry* average activity percent differing from the percent of *all other* first-line managers.

Respondents were asked to allocate one hundred points to reflect the importance of each activity in their job.

COMPARING FUNCTIONS AND ACTIVITIES
ACROSS MANAGEMENT LEVELS

Exhibit 2.3 compares the management functions and activities at different levels of sales management. The findings for functions are consistent with what would be expected. As managers move to higher levels, they regard the functions of planning and organizing as more important and staffing as less important. The importance of directing and controlling are similar across all levels. This similarity suggests that a young sales manager gains good experience in these two functions for use later when he or she is promoted.

The seven planning activities illustrate how planning becomes more important as one moves up the administrative ladder. In each activity, the second-line manager weighted these activities as more important than did the first-line manager. Similarly, in each case, top management considered them more important than did the second-line managers. These patterns held true also for each of the organizing activities.

Responsibility for staffing is clearly the responsibility of first-line management. Thus a young sales manager who may be out of college only three years will be responsible for recruiting, selecting, orienting, training, and developing personnel. Such can be the challenge of sales management.

COMPARING FIRST-LINE FUNCTIONS AND
ACTIVITIES ACROSS INDUSTRIES

Exhibit 2.4 compares the perceived importance of functions and activities across five industries, with some interesting results. Each industry is compared with the perceptions of all respondents who are not in that industry.

The activities in the planning function indicate that first-line managers in the petroleum/rubber and office supplies/equipment industries regard planning activities as more important than average, and the first-line managers in pharmaceutical companies regard them as less important. These findings may be explained by the role of the representative in these industries. The pharmaceutical representative performs a communication-persuasion role, while the representatives in the other two industries perform a more consultative role.

Staffing functions tend to be more important in the pharmaceutical and office supplies/equipment companies and less important in the petroleum/rubber companies. Such dissimilarities may be explained by differences in turnover rates and growth rates among industries. These differences in importance of management activities among industries raise doubts about the wisdom of hiring sales managers from other industries. Furthermore, an additional analysis of the sixteen pharmaceutical companies revealed significant differences within one industry, thereby raising doubts about hiring managers from other companies within the industry. The pirated manager may not perceive the subtle differences in the importance of activities in the strategies of companies, which could create organizational conflicts.

SALES MANAGEMENT APPLICATION OF THESE CONCEPTS

JOB CLARIFICATION

The data in the survey were not collected for mere academic curiosity but to help sales managers and trainers. All cooperating companies were supplied with their averages and the 95-percent confidence intervals for their company and industry. They were supplied with instructions for interpreting the results and applying them to their organizations. Some companies made the results part of the training sessions for managers. Managers were asked to complete questionnaires that required them to record their perception of the importance of the various activities by allocating one hundred points among them. The survey results were then presented and differences were discussed. The approach can clarify errors in job perceptions that occur among persons at different levels of management.

SALES MANAGEMENT AUDIT

Consultants may use the management functions and activities as the basis for a sales management audit. Exhibit 2.5 illustrates how this may be accomplished. A sales manager does not need to wait for a consultant to perform this audit.

The pattern in Exhibit 2.5 suggests several management problems. The general manager in this case seems to be dealing with short-run problems such as developing programs, procedures, and budgets, but does not take care of the longer-range activities such as forecasting, setting objectives, and developing strategies and policies. Further probing

Exhibit 2.5   An Audit of a Sales Manager's Performance

FUNCTIONS/Activities	Not Done	Poorly Done	Outstanding					Weight	EVALUATION × Weight
									(3)
PLAN			(1)					(2)	(1) × (2)
Forecast	⓪	1	2	3	4	5	6	2.2	0.0
Set Objectives	0	①	2	3	4	5	6	3.8	3.8
Develop Strategies	0	1	2	③	4	5	6	3.4	10.2
Develop Policies	0	1	②	3	4	5	6	1.6	3.2
Develop Programs	0	1	2	3	④	5	6	3.5	14.0
Set Procedures	0	1	2	3	④	5	6	1.8	7.2
Budget	0	1	2	3	④	5	6	1.3	5.2
ORGANIZE									
Establish Organ. Struct.	0	1	2	③	4	5	6	1.9	5.7
Create Position Descrip.	0	①	2	3	4	5	6	1.1	1.1
Establish Position Qualif.	⓪	1	2	3	4	5	6	1.2	0.0
STAFF									
Recruit/Select	0	1	2	3	4	⑤	6	8.7	43.5
Orient/Train	0	1	2	③	4	5	6	9.2	27.6
Develop Personnel	0	1	②	3	4	5	6	16.8	33.6
DIRECT									
Delegate	0	1	②	3	4	5	6	4.3	8.6
Motivate	0	①	2	3	4	5	6	9.6	9.6
Coordinate	0	1	②	3	4	5	6	3.3	6.6
Manage Change	⓪	1	2	3	4	5	6	3.8	0.0
CONTROL									
Estb. Report Systems	0	①	2	3	4	5	6	2.5	2.5
Develop Standards	0	①	2	3	4	5	6	3.3	3.3
Measure Performance	0	1	2	③	4	5	6	5.8	17.4
Take Corrective Action	0	1	2	③	4	5	6	5.5	16.5
Reward	0	1	2	③	4	5	6	5.4	16.2
Totals								100.0	235.8

The weighted total in this case of 235.8 may be compared with an average of 350 or with the scores of other managers, and it may be used as a benchmark from which to set goals for improvement in the management of the sales force.

will be necessary to determine the cause of the problem, such as the following: this general manager does not think that these steps are important, does not have the time to do them, or does not know how to do them.

Some of the reasons for preoccupation with short-term planning are found in the other functions. The position descriptions are poorly done and there are no position qualifications. These deficiencies may increase the time that is required to recruit, select, orient, and train new representatives and evaluate existing ones, leaving little time for long-range planning. This hypothesis could be tested by having the manager indicate the percent of time that is spent on each activity and then comparing these percents with the percents of more successful managers.

The directing and controlling activities show similar weaknesses. Additional probing will be necessary to identify alternative means for correcting the situation. At one extreme, it may be necessary to redesign the entire sales management organization. At the other extreme, some management training may be all that is necessary. Between these two extremes are the alternatives of firing or demoting the general sales manager.

By adding a column of importance weights (column 2, Exhibit 2.5) and multiplying the evaluation scores by these weights, we reflect both the importance and performance of each management activity (column 3). The sum of these weighted evaluations may be compared with other managers and they may serve as a benchmark for establishing goals for improving a manager's performance.

SUMMARY

The goal of this chapter was to present a brief overview of the skills, functions, and activities of management, thereby providing the framework for the remainder of the book. The findings of the survey reported in this chapter revealed that all levels of sales management engage in all of the management activities, but there are differences in the weightings of importance among levels. The higher levels of sales management engage more heavily in planning and organizing, while the lower levels are more involved in staffing. The findings of this study reveal that even the most junior sales manager can begin to develop management skills.

These management functions and activities may appear to be simply an academic exercise, but they can be used to clarify the roles of managers and to audit sales managers at different levels. These audits require measures of perceived importance, time spent, and evaluations of how well the activities are performed.

ASSIGNMENTS/DISCUSSION QUESTIONS

1. Do a sales management audit for the Westmont case at the end of this text, using Exhibit 2.5.

2. Discuss which of the management skills and activities a sales representative will have an opportunity to practice.

3. Identify and explain the differences between management activities and skills a field sales manager may be involved in regularly or to a greater degree than a manager of any other type with which you are familiar.

4. Give the names of three companies in different industries that have a specialized sales management structure by product as shown in Exhibit 2.2.

5. If "line" authority or relationship in a group of two or more persons is the identity of the person who makes the final decision, and the relationship or role of the others in the group who advise and serve the individual who makes the decision is described as a "staff" relationship, identify the line and staff individuals in the following situations:
   a. The field sales manager and the sales administration manager in achieving the sales objectives within the district
   b. The field sales manager and the marketing services manager in conducting a field market survey within the district
   c. The field sales manager and the sales rep in setting territorial objectives
   d. The field sales manager and the sales rep in making sales calls together to achieve the territorial objectives.

6. If a properly stated objective is *specific* (defines a targeted area for action), *behavioral* (way of conducting one's self on the job), *individual* (identifies the involvement of a person), *measurable* (quantifiable and time oriented), and *realistic* (achievable), evaluate the completeness of the following objectives:
   a. To increase sales
   b. To double the sales of the three major products within the next six months

    c. To increase the number of calls on new accounts in each territory by 25 percent without reducing the number of calls on active accounts

    d. To maintain the sales in each territory of product X at or near quota for this fiscal year on the introduction of product Y.

7. What is the relationship between job qualifications and a job description?

8. Why do you think the three levels of managers shown in the survey in Exhibit 2.3 agree that recruiting and selecting are clearly the responsibility of the first-line management?

9. Why do you think the first-line managers in the survey in Exhibit 2.3 believe overwhelmingly that to "develop personnel" is their most important management activity?

10. Explain the relationship between the information in Exhibit 1.1 (Chapter 1) and the explanation of the findings in Exhibit 2.4 that the pharmaceutical sales rep performs a communications-persuasive role, while the representatives in office supplies/equipment industries perform a more consultative role.

11. If a survey of the first-line and second-line managers of a company were to show a statistically significant lower rating by the first-line managers of the relative importance of setting objectives, what possible explanations are there?

12. If a survey of the first-line and second-line managers of a company were to show a statistically significant higher rating by the first-line managers of the relative importance of developing personnel, what possible explanations are there?

CASE 2.1:
I-30 Truck Center

Sharon O'Kelly, six months a district sales manager for Marshall Motors Inc., a medium- and heavy-duty truck manufacturer, couldn't help laughing to herself as she drove to her call on the I-30 Truck Center, Marshall's Jamestown truck dealer. The characters who ran the dealership had always been a source of jokes among the Marshall personnel assigned to District 110. Unfortunately, the problems with this large dealer were no laughing matter. I-30 suffered from inadequate inventory and orders in process, no working prospect system, and falling market penetration percentages, which were not only serious problems, but continuous.

Sharon's stated job accountabilities were to meet a sales quota of 1,700 units, to maintain adequate dealer inventory and a three-times inventory turnover, to train dealer salespersons, to call on large customers of dealers, to promote company programs, and to enforce company sales policies. Since starting with Marshall Motors as a sales trainee, Sharon had sold trucks at a company-owned dealership for a year and had worked for the regional marketing staff for six months. As a district sales manager, she managed a "sales force" of eighteen dealers in a territory 300 miles wide and almost that long. Although she had the authority to terminate dealers and to recommend new ones, this was an alternative used very infrequently. Her overriding objective was to increase sales of Marshall Trucks through the franchised dealers. After a brief time in the district, Sharon realized that very little of her time and effort were spent selling trucks. Instead, she found she was most effective in improving the dealers' inventory and order systems, setting up prospect listings, sales planning, sales department organization, and overall sales efficiency.

Currently, industry sales were booming, and lead time at the factory was eight to ten months for most of the truck models. The district sales managers were being pressed by the company's regional management to get their dealers to reserve production time at the factory by submitting orders to meet their sales for the next twelve months. In response, Sharon developed sales projections and a simple order planning, tracking, and control system that several of her dealers had successfully adopted. Problems had arisen in implementing the plan at the I-30 Truck Center.

I-30 was founded by three brothers who had moved from the mountains in the western part of the state in the 1950s to start a dairy farm in the eastern Piedmont. Their success in farming led them to start an agricultural implements business, which, in turn, led them into truck sales, parts and service, and a contract with Marshall Motors Inc. in the early 1960s. The truck operation expanded into a small trucking company and a truck leasing business. As the area grew, the farmland they owned became increasingly valuable, so the brothers opened a real estate company and began some speculative building.

These many overlapping businesses were master-minded by the older brother, "H.V." By default, he was overseer of the financial affairs and general manager of every business except the dairy business. William, the second brother, ran the dairy farm, but occasionally stepped in to help with any other businesses where he thought he was needed. In theory, Max, the youngest, ran the truck dealership. A friendly, gregarious, likeable fellow, Max loved to sell.

Sharon's boss had described Max as ''a good ol' boy who just wants to be left alone to sell trucks.'' Max spent most of his time on the dealership floor or on the telephone with customers. He sold trucks to people all over the eastern United States. The salaried salesmen he hired acted mainly as Max's assistants, completing paperwork, delivering trucks, and covering the floor when Max was out.

On one of her early sales calls on the I-30 Truck Center, Sharon reviewed her customer inventory and order printout and realized that I-30 did not have enough units on hand or on order to begin to meet forecasted sales. After lengthy discussions with Max, in which he raised all the typical dealer objections—high cost of inventory, risk of ordering so far in advance, and the difficulty of stocking units to meet customer specifications—he agreed to order eight units with staggered production dates and to implement the order control system. Next month, under pressure from the regional sales manager, Sharon called the factory to see if the orders had been received. None had been submitted.

With fire in her eyes, Sharon made a special call on the I-30 Truck Center. When she asked Max why he hadn't ordered the units after agreeing to do so, he responded, ''Oh, H.V. wouldn't let me order them because he said we didn't need them, and the dealership couldn't stand the inventory interest expense.'' H.V. was out, but Sharon waited for his return. She met with him in his office, explained her sales and order system, and asked why the orders had not been submitted after Max had agreed to do so. H.V. answered, ''Max doesn't think we can sell those trucks, and, anyway, William went to a used truck broker in Columbus last week and loaded us up with enough used trucks to last at least a couple of months. Right now we have $750,000 in used units, $200,000 in new units, and our credit line is for $1,000,000. It will take six months, if we're lucky, to get out from under all this used junk. If we find a customer for a new piece we don't have in stock, we'll just have to buy it from another dealer since your lead times are so ridiculously long.''

''H.V., Max gave me a different story,'' Sharon responded. ''I need to know who makes the ordering and inventory decisions here. Let's get Max in here and decide what to order *today!*'' Max came in, and a little later William wandered through on his way to the noon milking. The discussion got heated, with each brother accusing the other of meddling in his business and making poor inventory decisions. Max walked out, using the excuse he had a customer to meet. William left to take care of the milking. H.V. closed his office door and said, ''Sharon, the dealership is supposed to be Max's, but he won't take the responsibility for running it; he doesn't even manage the sales department. We hired a general manager one time, but he quit because Max owns the business and is too pigheaded to take orders from anybody else. What do you think we should do?''

CASE QUESTIONS

1. How many business operations are the three brothers involved in?
2. What are the management problems at the I-30 Truck Center?
3. What are the specific sales management problems that Sharon O'Kelly and I-30 have?
4. In addition to the lack of leadership or sales organization, what other causes are responsible for their falling sales penetration?
5. Should Sharon seriously consider recommending that Marshall Motors terminate the dealership with I-30 Truck Center? Why?
6. How should Sharon answer H.V.?
7. How should Sharon answer H.V. if he presses her for some solution?
8. What recommendations should Sharon make to her regional sales manager?
9. What legal complications could arise from actions taken as a result of Question #8?
10. What are the five prerequisites for the survival of the I-30 Truck Center?
11. How would you rate the long-term chances of survival of the I-30 Truck Center? Why?

REFERENCES

1. Mintzberg, who does not agree that managers perform these functions and activities, seems to confuse skills, especially communications, with activities. He sees managers reacting to a continuous flow of information. His examples could be classified as poor time management, which is the activity of budgeting resources—a planning function. See Henry Mintzberg, ''The Manager's Job: Folklore and Fact,'' *Harvard Business Review* (July–August 1975): 49–61.
2. R. Alec Mackenzie, ''The Management Process in 3-D,'' *Harvard Business Review* (November–December 1969): 80–87.

3. Ibid.; Louis A. Allen, *The Professional Manager's Guide,* 4th ed. (Louis A. Allen Associates, 1969); R. L. Ackoff, *A Concept of Corporate Planning* (New York: Wiley/Interscience, 1970); Harold Koontz and Cyril O'Donnell, *Management: A Systems and Contingency Analysis of Managerial Functions,* 6th ed. (New York: McGraw-Hill Book Co., 1976).
4. Koontz and O'Donnell, *Management,* p. 196.
5. Ackoff, *Concept of Corporate Planning,* p. 6.

II.

MANAGING
THE TERRITORY

3

WHAT SALES
REPRESENTATIVES DO

Casual observers have a very limited view of the activities of a salesperson. They would probably never guess that face-to-face contact with a client or prospect represents only 20 percent of a salesperson's time. The other 80 percent of the time is spent in analysis, planning, and developing strategies and tactics. Exhibit 3.1 illustrates that these face-to-face activities are like the tip of an iceberg, with the largest part of the iceberg beneath the surface. The greatest opportunity for increasing the productivity of sales representatives is to make them more proficient in these "beneath-the-surface" activities.

A salesperson may be the final link between a company and its customers. Exhibit 3.2 illustrates the types of customers that are the responsibility of a Beecham sales trainee. This trainee must quickly learn four separate businesses—food, drug, variety, and mass merchandising.[1]

Coordinating all of these activities is known as *time and territory management*. The difference between success and failure in selling can frequently be traced to the salesperson's ability to manage his or her activities effectively. It is this early opportunity for management that makes personal selling such a good training ground for general managers. Exhibit 3.3, which summarizes a typical day in the life of a pharmaceutical representative, illustrates that self-management is needed.

An examination of Exhibits 3.1 and 3.3 will reveal that a representative performs many of the management activities that were described in the previous chapter.

Exhibit 3.1   Selling Activities Beneath the Surface

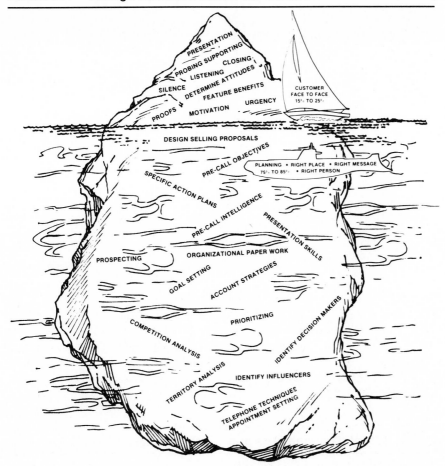

"Control Your 'Sales Berg,'" Professional Sales Marketing System, PTI, Houston, Texas. Used by permission of Petro Tech Institute, Inc. (5206 FM 1960 West, Suite 106, Houston, Texas 77069), a multi-dimensional human resource and training company specializing in sales, management, and technical training.

In this chapter, we describe the total activities of the representative. In the next chapter, the selling process is discussed.

EXAMPLES OF REPRESENTATIVES' ACTIVITIES

The authors analyzed twenty-five job descriptions for representatives in industries such as packaged grocery products, pharmaceuticals, publishing, oil, chemicals, plastics, telecommunications, tires, tobacco, insur-

Exhibit 3.2   Customer Responsibilities of a Beecham Representative

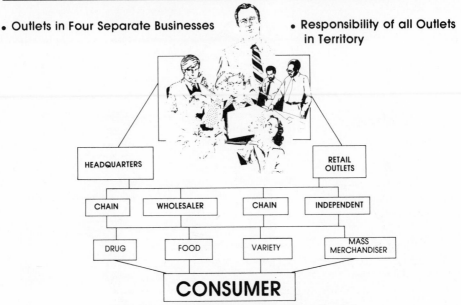

● **Outlets in Four Separate Businesses**   ● **Responsibility of all Outlets in Territory**

The Beecham Products Sales Representative is the vital
link between the Company and the Consumer........

YOU MANAGE YOUR OWN BUSINESS

Recruiting brochure of Beecham Products. Products include Calgon, ClingFree, Aqua-Fresh, Massengill, Sucrets, and Brylcreem.

Exhibit 3.3   A Day in the Life of a Pharmaceutical Representative

1. *Plans Calls for Next Day and Week*

The starting point in the daily schedule of a field sales representative is the official general schedule or WORKING ORDER, approved by the field sales manager, listing the sections, cities, or accounts within the geographic confines of the representative's territory. It is based on the grouping of cities or sections according to their geographic travel distances, and includes the schedule for sequencing the return trips (call-backs) on accounts and areas with high sales potential. Its length or duration is usually related to the duration of the selling plan or sales promotion cycle, i.e., monthly or quarterly. With the approval of the field sales manager, the WORKING ORDER is permanently revised as often as business conditions require.

From the WORKING ORDER the sales representative prepares a monthly FORWARD ITINERARY for the following six weeks (to allow overlap into the next month). Although the WORKING ORDER is to be followed religiously in preparing the FORWARD ITINERARY, scheduling variations are necessary because of convention attendance, sales meetings, vacations, holidays, and previously scheduled appointments.

(continued)

Exhibit 3.3 Continued

The FORWARD ITINERARY will include the dates the sections will be worked, and the addresses and phone numbers of hotels where the sales representative can be contacted. It is imperative that the FORWARD ITINERARY accurately reflect the representative's working schedule and location. The reasons are that the field sales manager uses the monthly FORWARD ITINERARY of his or her eight to twelve sales representatives in preparing his or her FORWARD ITINERARY and scheduling field trips with the representatives. The national sales manager and the sales administrative department use this document daily in contacting the representatives. Companies with field staffs numbering several hundred or higher find this document extremely important.

It is from the FORWARD ITINERARY that the sales representative makes plans for the following day and week. Considering previous appointments, previously acquired information about the best time to call, plans for new (cold) calls, and special requests for action (marketing surveys, recruiting calls, etc.), the representative will draw up a schedule for each day which includes a surplus of calls to allow for broken appointments, customers who are away or too busy, etc.

2. *Telephones for Appointments and Makes Travel Arrangements*

Call for or confirm appointments and make hotel and travel arrangements if out-of-town calls are scheduled.

3. *Establishes Call Objectives, Strategy, and Tactics*

Review sales records and/or files to identify individuals to be contacted, establish sales objectives, and review strategy and tactics for achieving the objectives.

4. *Packs Material*

Pack or replenish equipment, sales catalogues, and selling materials needed for scheduled calls.

5. *Makes Scheduled and Unscheduled Calls*

Make calls as scheduled and appointments for future calls. Follow up on leads, interruptions, emergencies, unscheduled distributor calls, complaints, special requests, etc.

6. *Records Information in Permanent Records*

Record pertinent information in permanent territory records or logs about personnel seen, summary of discussions, products ordered, follow-through required, etc.

7. *Writes Orders, Call Reports, and Correspondence*

Write orders, prepare daily call report, and necessary correspondence about unanswered questions or comments, marketing feedback, competitive activities, items or schedule requiring follow-up action by someone else, complaints, etc.

8. *Analyzes Calls and Establishes Objectives for Follow-Up Calls (Call-Backs)*

Analyze call. Were objectives achieved, advanced, developed, or in need of redefinition? Establish objectives and timing of next call (call-backs) on same accounts.

ance, and airplane manufacturers. This analysis revealed that all sales representatives are assigned a set of general responsibilities, which may be summarized as follows:

1. Sell the products or services to customers and prospective customers within the assigned territory in amounts equal to or in excess of assigned sales and profit quotas.
2. Service the accounts and prospects in accordance with company programs, policies, and procedures.
3. Maintain appropriate records and communicate with appropriate company personnel.
4. Maintain a current knowledge of company products, policies, procedures, programs, selling skills, marketing conditions, and competition.
5. Cooperate in the attainment of company and district sales objectives.
6. Plan personal activities so that time is used productively. Be responsible for the efficient use of company resources such as the automobile, expense monies, and samples.

These general responsibilities may be divided into the specific activities of selling, distribution, planning, decision making, communications (including market research, staffing, and self-development). A review of these job descriptions will illustrate the variety of selling activities.

SELLING

Consumer goods representatives and industrial products representatives may both engage in consultative selling, but the contents of their consultation will differ. The consumer goods representative gives merchandising advice, while the industrial representative consults on the manufacturing of a product. In Chapter 1 we saw how a representative for Union Carbide helped an automobile manufacturer design a new safety bumper.

Consumer Goods

"A creative merchandiser with imaginative ideas" is how Procter & Gamble describes its sales representative. The P&G representative will call on grocery chain owners or buyers to discuss new products, new deals, displays, and promotional support, and help to develop newspaper advertising, creative layouts, and promotional tie-ins.

Industrial Goods

The Uniroyal representative sells tires, tubes, batteries, and accessories for passenger, truck, farm, and industrial uses. Territories include tire dealers, materials handling concerns, and fleet accounts. This representative performs both a merchandising function and consultation on production activities. A call on a Uniroyal dealer requires that a representative have a fundamental knowledge of the selling plan, policies, billing, shipping, sales promotion, and adjustment policies of the company. But the representative must also have sufficient knowledge of the tire dealer's business to be able to recommend merchandising strategies, run successful dealer meetings, train dealer sales representatives, stimulate and motivate dealers' enthusiasm, and be able to do a financial analysis of the dealers' business so that recommendations may be made and appropriate action may be taken when necessary. The representative must also understand the company policies with regard to the antitrust regulations regarding the relationships between manufacturers and their independent dealers. The representative will work with the dealer analyzing the market so that the best product and promotional mix are used to maximize Uniroyal's sales. The representative will also instruct and assist in the installation of management controls and procedures regarding inventory and accounting systems. Therefore, the Uniroyal representative is more than a sales representative; he or she is a business consultant to the retailers. When calling on truck, farm, and industrial users, the representative needs to understand the cost structure of these businesses so that he or she can make appropriate and competitive recommendations for Uniroyal products.

Industrial sales representatives sell products that are not used directly by consumers, but may be components, such as motors for refrigerators or transistors for television sets. Industrial representatives also sell raw materials, such as petroleum or plastics, that are fabricated into industrial and consumer goods. The industrial representative must call on the persons who influence the decisions, such as the company president, the plant manager, the engineering department, the production department, the design department, and the purchasing manager. An industrial representative is truly a consultant because he or she must be very familiar with the production process of the customer. For example, a representative who sells bottles or cans for soft drinks must be certain that his or her packages will fit the machinery of the soft drink bottler. These representatives must learn the clients' long-range plans, help them write specifications for new products, demonstrate new products, find new uses for existing products, prepare bids, make proposals, participate in final negotiations, and give extensive service after the product is delivered to assure that it meets specifications and performs as promised.

The National Starch and Chemical Corporation requires its representatives to develop a knowledge of the industry and customer needs. They are to work closely with customers and prospects on new product ideas, calling on National Starch's technicians where additional assistance is needed. They are to develop and maintain contacts between National Starch and the customer's technical group.

After the products are delivered, the National Starch representative is required to follow through and investigate any problems or complaints. Additional activities of the National Starch representative include prospecting for new customers; increasing one's product and market knowledge through the study of technical bulletins, exposure to technical persons, trade publications, trade associations, and conferences; and maintaining an open mind toward new selling methods.

The business forms representative must have an extensive knowledge of the business and accounting systems that are used in a variety of industries. Business forms include products such as checks, invoices, work orders, inventory control sheets, ledgers, and other basic documents of business systems. The representative for a firm such as UARCO will manage the accounts in his or her territory so that they will use as many types of UARCO's forms as possible. These persons will sell standard forms and forms designed by them to meet customers' specific needs. Their activities include a knowledge of products, a knowledge of systems in various industries, account management, estimating and pricing nonstandard products, preparation of orders, maintaining relations with business machine representatives who will need these forms, and maintaining relationships with their own production facilities. Thus a business form salesperson, like a computer salesperson, does considerable consultative selling.

DISTRIBUTION

Representatives for consumer goods manufacturers and industrial goods manufacturers that use channels of distribution have the responsibility for maintaining the relationships with retailers, wholesalers, and distributors. For example, Monsanto salespersons are required to evaluate their dealers' sales results. Uniroyal representatives are required to evaluate present distributors and seek out new ones. They assist dealers with problems and merchandising, and counsel them in their planning for sales, profit, and expense control. They work with wholesalers and distributors to help them select new retailers.

The P&G representative works with the retailer checking inventory, shelf facing, and cooperative advertising to assure that the products are getting the maximum exposure. The American Greeting Card representative helps the retailer by ordering stock, fixtures, display accessories and merchandising aids, and by recommending a store layout and a product mix that are appropriate for the retailer's market. The representatives will then train store personnel in the display, sale, and reordering of American Greeting Cards.

PLANNING

In the previous chapter we saw that planning was a major management function and that it included the activities of forecasting, establishing objectives, developing strategies, developing programs, developing budgets, and creating or adhering to procedures and policies. An examination of sales representatives' job descriptions reveals that each of these activities is a central part of managing a territory.

The more sophisticated job descriptions describe how a representative should analyze the market and make projections for future trends that will alter or reflect the changing needs of customers. The National Starch and Chemical Company requires its representatives to identify the market potentials by end-use segments, to interpret trends and inform their district sales managers of any changes, and to maintain complete sales records for efficient performance, coverage, and continuity for representatives who may follow them in the territory. From this market analysis, they develop their territory strategies. The Bell Marketing System requires its representatives to understand customers' businesses and demonstrate how its products and services can help customers achieve their objectives. Job descriptions are now noting the fact that the representative will be supplied with computer printouts to analyze sales results, determine product penetration, and target untapped sales potentials.

Most job descriptions emphasize the need for the representative to establish a schedule for calling on accounts. Some descriptions require representatives to establish a definite itinerary with account names, dates, and objectives of the call. They are not to alter their itinerary without the approval of their district manager.

Sales representatives are frequently held accountable for the expense budgets assigned to their territory. The National Starch and Chemical representative is instructed to spend company money judiciously and to develop improved methods to lower selling costs. Some representatives are instructed to keep the cost of carrying an account to a minimum by keeping a customer's payments current.

Representatives are usually on the receiving end of procedures and policies. Burroughs Wellcome, a pharmaceutical company, states in its job description that its representatives must comply with all company procedures, programs, and policies, including those pertaining to statutory regulations governing equal employment opportunities, fair employment practices and safety requirements, and to ensure compliance with state and federal regulations. The Burroughs Wellcome representative is not limited solely to compliance, but is asked also to recommend changes in programs, policies, and procedures.

DECISION MAKING

The representative gets considerable opportunity to practice decision-making skills when managing a territory. Basic decisions are made by the P&G representatives when they decide how to organize their territories; the sequence, frequency, and timing of visits on accounts; and the merchandising recommendations that they will make to an account. The recruiting brochure for P&G states that a representative will manage the territory like a business with the support of other business experts in Product Development, Manufacturing, Advertising, Data Processing, etc.

COMMUNICATIONS

Communications are obviously the most important activity of a sales representative. These communications include not only the selling activities with the customers, but the communications with the sales management hierarchy along with contacts in production, shipping, accounting, credit management, etc. Written reports, records, and correspondence can be as important to the management of the territory as oral communications with customers and prospects. Burroughs Wellcome representatives collect and report field data to their district manager.

If the representative is to perform a marketing research activity, the job description must include this activity and the compensation scheme must be adjusted accordingly. For example, a representative who is paid a straight commission cannot be expected to be motivated to perform a market research activity.

Motivation for providing feedback must begin with proper sales training. Some companies, such as DuPont, require sales trainees to work in the market research department using the reports sent in by sales representatives, thereby emphasizing the point that the data are necessary and are actually used. Some companies use sales representatives' reports as an early warning device. Carpenter Technology Corporation, which sells stainless and alloy bars, has found that it gets a three-month lead on competitors by having representatives report changes in market conditions. Carpenter can trace savings of more than $5 million directly to market feedback from its sales representatives.[2]

Routine communications from the representative include reports of competition, expense reports, recommendations for changes in products and services, evaluations of new candidates for sales positions, and suggested changes in sales programs. Some companies require a broader type of communication, that of communicating to the public-at-large the role of their industry. The pharmaceutical and telephone industries encourage their representatives to make speeches at service clubs, to give television interviews, and to seek similar opportunities for communicating the role of their industries to the public.

STAFFING

The activities that are included in staffing are recruiting and selecting, training, and development. Because the representative is at the end of the line, he or she may have little or no involvement in staffing activities. Some representatives, however, become heavily involved in recruiting and selecting candidates for sales positions. Burroughs Wellcome, for example, includes in its representatives' job description the responsibility for calling on local colleges to recruit. Candidates for a sales position spend one day observing with each of two representatives to expose the candidate to the job activities and for initial screening. This information is weighed carefully by the district manager in deciding whether to hire a candidate. Some companies will give additional training and compensation to outstanding representatives and assign to them the additional activities of training young representatives. Top sales representatives are frequently brought into the home office as instructors for training courses. Thus a young representative may be at the end of the chain of command, but he or she may be involved in some staffing functions.

SELF-DEVELOPMENT

Self-development is an important activity for all sales representatives, and it receives extensive treatment in many job descriptions. The UARCO representative is expected to maintain his or her health and to develop a good mental attitude toward the job; to study during off-territory hours to learn products and attend sales courses and conferences; to develop a working knowledge of the company's policies and procedures; and to have a program of self-improvement to develop sales skills and performance.

The National Starch and Chemical Company representative is required to have a self-development program for knowledge, attitude, skills, and habit. These representatives must learn the company, the industry, the market, the language of the industry, the selling processes, and the selling goals. The development of proper attitudes includes the desire to learn, the development of confidence, dedication, the ability to motivate others, a selling personality, and a drive to achieve personal goals. They are expected to develop skills in prospecting, developing personal relations, analyzing information, making oral and written presentations, entertaining, preparing reports, following procedures, organizing their time and territories, anticipating changes in the marketplace and competition, and thinking creatively. They are expected to develop good habits in organizing their activities, studying, research, physical care and appearance, and automobile driving.

Pharmaceutical representatives may be required by the company to pass a proficiency examination on the ingredients of products, the recommended dosages, possible side effects, interactions with other drugs, and the specific illnesses for which a drug has been approved by the Food and Drug Administration. Companies may be held legally responsible if a drug product is misrepresented by a representative.

The representatives for Monsanto agricultural chemicals have an interesting dimension in their self-development requirements. They are required to evaluate their own achievements with regard to their goals, strengths, and weaknesses. They are then required to recommend the actions that they plan to undertake to correct their weaknesses. Many companies encourage their representatives to actively pursue their self-development toward career goals, and have educational reimbursement programs to help finance this self-development.

ORGANIZATIONAL RELATIONSHIPS

The line relationships of the sales representative may be limited to contacts with his or her district sales manager. Rarely does someone report directly to the representative. While the direct links are few, there are many dotted-line links between the representative and other functional areas of the company. The representative may be responsible for credit and collections. We have already seen that he or she may have market research responsibilities. The links with advertising and promotion may require feedback on the effectiveness of promotional efforts and the proper use of advertising, direct mail, and promotional pieces in selling. Representatives for industrial products are expected to consult and co-operate with their companies' technical staff personnel.

The direct and indirect reporting relationships for a sales representative are generally included in a job description. Addison-Wesley Publishing Company provides a representative with an abbreviated organizational chart showing his or her position within the company.

The sales representative is one of the few persons within a company who continuously interacts with the environment. This environment includes not only customers, competition, and the government; it also includes broad social and economic trends. The salesperson should sense and report these trends.

The representative is expected to establish working relationships with buying influences within the company, as well as persons of initial entry such as receptionists and secretaries. Organizational theorists have labeled this frontier relationship as a *boundary role*.[3] Organizational theorists and academic marketing researchers are beginning to examine the complexity of boundary roles and the types of individuals who can perform these roles successfully. These subtle organizational relationships cannot be defined fully in a job description. Most of them must be left to the selling personality of the representative.

JOB-RELATED BEHAVIORS

There is a trend away from giving detailed personal characteristics that are desired for the sales representative. Some job descriptions will list the attributes and behavioral patterns of representatives who have been successful in the job. These attributes typically include communication skills, high energy level, motivation, career ambition, sales ability, listening skills, tenacity, initiative, independence, planning and organizational abilities, problem analysis skills, judgment, and decisiveness. (See Chapter 9.) Because no one person has all of these attributes, tradeoffs must be made. Showing such a list to a candidate may discourage him or her from applying for the job, unless it is made clear that this list describes a perfect applicant who does not exist.

Great care must be used when writing the personal characteristics section of a sales representative's job description in order to comply with federal regulations regarding equal employment opportunities. For example, a requirement of five years previous selling experience may be discriminating against minorities if these minorities were not accepted in this type of selling five years ago. The company must be prepared to prove that specified knowledge, skills, and previous experiences are bonafide requirements for the job. It is more a matter of hiring candidates who are qualifiable than hiring those who are qualified.

The Northwestern Mutual Life Insurance Company states that it seeks individuals who are interested in their own personal development and have personal needs for an above-average income, a desire to have a self-image of a successful independent businessperson, a personal satisfaction from growth and knowledge, and the satisfaction of selling a product that has social value.

The Chevron Chemical representative is expected to have the ability to work independently and with others, be intelligent, be a problem solver, have planning and organizational skills, operate effectively under stress, be committed to the job objectives, have a cost and profit awareness, have written and oral communications abilities, and be decisive and self-assured. A careful identification of job-related behaviors is important not only for hiring, but for evaluating the performance of the representative. In too many cases, representatives are hired according to one set of criteria and evaluated according to an entirely different set. To prevent this management error, Burroughs Wellcome has combined its job description and evaluation forms into a single document. Thus when the applicant is hired, he or she knows what the criteria will be for evaluation and promotion.

THE JOB DESCRIPTION

The representative's job description indicates activities to be performed, the organizational environment in which a representative works, and those personal behavioral attributes that lead to success or failure in performing these activities in this organization. This job description positions the role of personal selling in the entire marketing mix. It makes clear which of the marketing activities are the responsibility of sales management, advertising, promotion, and market research. It is the most important tool for sales management.

To understand fully their role within the organization, representatives need to know their organizational environment and reporting relationships. Who is their boss and does anyone report to them? Are there staff relationships that provide technical expertise when necessary? What are the relationships between the representatives and functions such as credit and collections, logistics, product management, legal, and accounting?

Personal behavioral attributes should represent the minimum qualifications that are necessary for a representative to be trained for the job.

Hence, the search is for a qualifiable candidate, not necessarily one who is qualified and certainly not the ideal candidate. Tradeoffs will be necessary. The profile of the candidate should be realistic, thereby avoiding overqualified as well as underqualified candidates. A candidate with too much of a behavioral attribute for a job may be unmanageable. In selling, for example, he or she may lose interest, become too independent, too sensitive, or too tenacious to the point of being inflexible, all of which would make it impossible to manage this representative. The underqualified individual will have difficulty keeping up and become frustrated.

CONTENT

There are common elements in a job description, but there is no standard or ideal job description for a salesperson. The reason can be explained simply by the fact that the activities of the representative are determined by a company's sales strategy, which is determined by its marketing strategy. Because a company strives to have a unique marketing strategy, it follows that the job description will be unique for each company. *The representative's activities should determine the outline for a job description.* It is not simply a matter of using a sample outline to create a job description. When the strategies change, the description must change. The ultimate test of a job description is whether it can be used to manage the sales force effectively. This description is the basis for establishing performance standards and evaluation methods. These evaluations are the basis for pay, promotion, and other positive recognitions, as well as negative outcomes such as probation or termination.

Exhibit 3.4 summarizes elements that are frequently used in a job description. These items should be regarded as a minimum of items; they are not an outline of an ideal job description.

PROCEDURE FOR WRITING

The drafting of a representative's job description is the responsibility of the sales manager to whom that representative is immediately responsible. This manager should review the description regularly with the representatives. Minor adjustments for local conditions can be made by a district manager.

A sales organization that has changed its strategy or plans to increase in size will need to change sales representatives' job descriptions. The general sales manager will convene a workshop that includes a first-line sales manager and a sample of representatives. This workshop

Exhibit 3.4   Frequent Topics in Job Descriptions

Title: Sales representative, territory manager, or account manager.

Objectives: Achieve assigned quotas within the assigned territory and within the approved level of expenses.

Responsibilities: Activities that a representative is obligated to perform in filling the role of a sales representative.

Planning:
- Analyze market conditions and forecast future needs of customers and prospects.
- Establish objectives for individual calls and for the territory that are consistent with district, regional, and corporate objectives.
- Develop strategies for each account.
- Develop tactics for each call.
- Control expenses within approved budgets.
- Maintain company supplies and equipment in an orderly and usable state.

Organizing:
- Budget time and activities according to account potential.
- Develop and maintain an attitude of cooperation with and support for other representatives, the field sales manager, and other company personnel.
- Keep territory records current.

Selling:
- Interact effectively with customers to develop a personal awareness of their operations and needs and to provide maximum consulting service.
- Perform the steps in the selling process that are required by the selling plan. (See Chapter 4.)
- Provide service that is appropriate for account potential.

Personal Development:
- Develop skills in selling, planning, time and territory management, and communication.
- Develop knowledge about the company, the industry, and competitive products.
- Maintain a knowledge of current company policies, procedures, and programs.
- Analyze success and failures to learn from previous experiences.

Organizational Relationships:
- Reporting Relationships: Reports directly to the district sales manager. Communicates as necessary with persons in production, research and development, credit, and accounting.
- Authority: The authority for performing activities, such as pricing or specifying delivery dates, without seeking permission is specified in the company policies and procedures for representatives.
- Accountability: Representatives have an obligation to see that assigned activities are performed, and report the level of performance to the district sales manager and others through regular reports.
- Communication: Communicate regularly and punctually with the field sales manager and other company personnel regarding performance, orders, complaints, inquiries, market conditions, the effectiveness of selling programs, and competitive activities.

(continued)

Exhibit 3.4   Continued

Qualifications:
- Job-Related Behaviors:
  a. Good oral and written communication skills
  b. A good planner
  c. A self-motivator
  d. Tenacious
  e. A realistic ego drive
     (For additional items, see Exhibits 9.2 and 9.3 in Chapter 9.)

- Education: Some college education; a degree in business administration; a degree plus two years of selling; selling experience may be substituted for a completed degree.

would define the representatives' responsibilities and the levels of performance that are regarded as standard.

The workshop would produce a preliminary document that would be reviewed by other field managers and representatives. After many refinements, it would be forwarded to the general sales manager for his or her review and acceptance.

A company that has not written job descriptions may decide to use a specialist from the personnel department or an outside consultant to help in the task. In such cases, it will be necessary to begin with a complete analysis of the activities of the sales representatives.[4]

INFREQUENT ITEMS IN THE JOB DESCRIPTION

This review of representatives' job descriptions has revealed that products, pay, and territories are rarely found in the job descriptions of progressive companies. This is probably explained by the fact that the job description takes on the characteristics of a contract between the representative and the company, and that products, compensation, and territory assignments change. These topics will frequently be included in recruiting brochures or in letters that make a specific offer.

SUMMARY

This review of job descriptions from many companies provides an overview of the complex activities that are performed by sales representatives. It emphasizes a point made earlier that the representative is truly a manager of his or her territory. It also introduces a point that will be developed later in the book. A sales representative's job can be a good entry-level position into management because it provides direct experience in the knowledge and skills required within the selling process, as well as opportunities to develop so many management skills. These topics are covered in later chapters.

ASSIGNMENTS/DISCUSSION QUESTIONS

1. What is the purpose of a job description?

2. If you were hired for a job, what would you expect (or want) to be told relative to your job responsibilities?

3. Evaluate the following job description:

JOB DESCRIPTION

Title: Salesperson

Basic Responsibilities: To fulfill the role of the sales representative consistent with the purposes of the company and with the company image.

The field sales representative must:

Display technical and practical intelligence.

Reflect suitable personality characteristics, including
   a. self-discipline
   b. restraint
   c. proper degree of curiosity and assertiveness
   d. persuasiveness
   e. sociability
   f. ethical conduct
   g. creativity, imagination, and initiative
   h. reliability and dependability.

Be well-organized and punctual.

Have acceptable appearance, grooming, and dress.

Plan well.

Communicate effectively orally and in writing.

Have acceptable personal habits.

4. Evaluate the job descriptions for representatives of the National Starch and Chemical Corporation (Exhibit 3.5).

5. Rewrite the job description in Exhibit 3.5 and make it clearer by reducing long lists to subclassifications with appropriate headings.

6. Write a representative's job description for Westmont Business Forms, Inc., Chapter 23.

7. Make arrangements with a local company to write a job description for its representatives.

**Exhibit 3.5   National Starch and Chemical Corporation:
The Role of the Professional Salesman**

Definition: Basic function is to supply first-level customer contact and to promote the sale of specified products in an assigned territory so as to obtain maximum sales volume in accordance with company profit objectives.

A. *General Responsibilities*
Involve selling, customer service, sales planning, sales liaison, and time and expense control.

B. *Functional Relationships*

District Sales Manager
Explanation

1. *Market Research & Product Planning*
Total awareness of customers' operations should be developed along with trends and changes in the related industries; continuous feedback supply of appropriate information in clear, concise, complete form. This should include practical, accurate recommendations based on cumulative developed judgment.

2. *Marketing Administration*
Increased awareness of account credit, traffic, inventory, and customer service status to contribute to the control of the cost-profit relationship.

3. *Advertising and Promotion*
Ascertain advertising and promotion effectiveness in assigned accounts and feedback consistent with customer orientation information. Integrate ads, direct mail, and promotional efforts with selling efforts.

4. *Technical and Staff Personnel*
Consults and cooperates with appropriate personnel in a manner that will result in meeting sales objectives.

5. *To Line Manager*
Responsible to District Sales Manager for all assigned territorial responsibilities stated herein. Should develop an open communication for purposes of developing, mutually, job targets and standards of performance.

C. *Specific Responsibilities*
1. *Selling*
   a. Strengthens and develops personal and professional customer and prospect relations through personal contact, correspondence, and attendance at trade meetings.
   b. Counsels and advises customers regarding related business problems and as to new developments in application techniques relevant to their problems.
   c. Prospects his [or her] assigned territory on a continual basis to develop new desirable accounts so as to produce maximum sales volume (new business).

(continued)

Exhibit 3.5   Continued

    d. Maintains an open and progressive mind to new selling methods for increasing effectiveness of personal sales techniques.

    e. Increases knowledge of product and marketing through study of technical bulletins, taking maximum advantage of technical personnel exposures, and through trade publications and technical associations so as to better serve prospects and customers.

    f. Increases knowledge of customers' present and future business plans.

2. *Customer Service*
    a. Confers with customers on product and application problems and provides assistance through personal knowledge, or when necessary, requests assistance from appropriate company personnel.

    b. Works closely with present and potential customers in developing plans to meet customers' end use needs and, where necessary, requests assistance from appropriate personnel.

    c. Works closely with customers in developing new product ideas, and calls in appropriate company personnel to provide technical advice or conduct tests and experiments as necessary.

    d. Follows through on all orders from initiation to delivery.

    e. Investigates customers' complaints, prepares accurate reports, and follows through to satisfactory conclusion in accordance with established procedures.

    f. Develops and maintains current and adequate knowledge of mechanical application equipment and related materials involved in customers' production.

    g. Establishes and maintains contacts between company's and customers' technical groups.

3. *Sales Planning*
    a. Analyzes and evaluates territory for desirability of accounts and methods of approach, and plans selling efforts across complete product line so as to meet or exceed established targets.

    b. Maintains complete sales records for efficient performance, to provide continuity of coverage, and to facilitate periodic pattern analysis.

    c. Identifies market by end-use category, customers within end-use category compared with total market volume.

    d. Interprets customer trends so as to anticipate new volume and usage changes, keeping District Manager informed of any such changes.

(continued)

Exhibit 3.5 Continued

4. *Sales Liaison*
   a. Keeps supervisor informed of competitive activity, product development needs, and pricing practices.
   b. Cooperates with customer service office manager in a full exchange of information in a maximum effort to promote and maintain teamwork.
   c. Prepares required reports accurately and completely so as to effectively provide information as requested in accordance with established procedures.
   d. Prepares realistic forecasts of sales and shipments by customers and products as required by sales management for sales planning.

5. *Expense Control*
   a. Spends company money judiciously in carrying out sales activities so as to secure maximum volume of business and service to customers at a proper cost.
   b. Studies all phases of sales activities to develop and apply any improved methods or procedures that will result in lower selling costs.

Developed from a number of N.S.S.T.E. editorials (twelve years ago) for use with National Starch and Chemical Corporation Sales Managers. Reprinted with permission.

8. Contact a store selling greeting cards or an earth-moving or agricultural equipment dealer to obtain information about the different problems in successfully operating a business on the basis of capital, number of inventory turns, factors that stimulate demand, collections, etc.

9. What are the advantages to an applicant and the company of having an applicant for a position as a field sales representative make customer calls with a company representative for a one- to two-day period?

10. What are the benefits to a field sales representative and to the company of participating in nonselling activities such as recruiting, conducting marketing surveys, training, etc.?

11. Identify at least one company from the text of this chapter and explain the activity of the sales representative that corresponds with each of the categories in Exhibit 1.1 of Chapter 1.

12. Prepare a list of examples showing why inward communications from the sales reps to various departments in the company are valuable.

13. What is the value to a company of daily or weekly reports of client calls by sales reps?

14. What is the relationship between applicant qualifications and job-related behavior?

CASE 3.1:
Addison Construction Equipment Co.

When he entered the offices of the Addison Construction Equipment Co. on his first call as a manufacturer's representative for Hardman's, Harold Patrick thought he would enjoy calling on this dealership. The facility was a particularly clean, professional-looking one for the small coal-mining town in which it was located. Addison's sat on a hill, and the earthmoving and mining equipment it offered for sale made an impressive display on the clean graveled lot below. Inside, on the showroom floor, was a large indoor garden with all sorts of blooming plants and vines. A pretty gray cat scooted out from under the receptionist's desk as Harold entered.

Harold Patrick, age 25, had sold earthmoving equipment for three years before being offered a job as a sales representative for the Hardman Equipment Co., an internationally known manufacturer of earthmoving equipment. Although this was his first call on Addison's, his boss had told him that the dealership had been bought out the previous year by a former Hardman regional sales manager, Sherwood "Shirt" Howell. Harold knew that the buyout had left Mr. Howell in a tight cash position, but with several experienced employees, a new sales manager, and the additional salesman he had hired, Mr. Howell felt that the business would expand quickly.

Having reviewed Addison's sales and market penetration for the past several years, Harold hoped that during this first call on Mr. Howell he could establish a good relationship and get a general idea of the dealer's sales goals and inventory plans for the next year. Addison's was a medium-sized full-time dealer, probably eighth in dollar volume of Harold's twelve dealers. They had done well historically in heavy equipment, but had sold little of the medium-sized equipment being bought in their area.

Just as Harold was introducing himself to the receptionist, a burly man in his mid-forties with sunglasses and a bright yellow sports jacket came down the stairs onto the showroom floor. "Hi, I'm Shirt Howell. You must be a new rep. Glad to have you aboard. I hope we can be of some help to you." He paused to pick up the cat.

"How do you like the flower garden? A bit different from most heavy-equipment dealers, huh? Come on upstairs," he said as he turned and picked up Harold's card from the receptionist. "I used to work downstairs where I could keep my fingers on everything. Now, with Ernie Pelham as my sales manager, I just oversee him, my parts and service manager, and my office manager." In response to Harold's questions, Mr. Howell enthusiastically described his twenty years with Hardman's and his decision to buy the dealership in Mountain City, his hometown, and move back with his family. He was delighted with small-town life and the time he now had to spend with his wife and children in community activities. "In fact," he said, "I'm leaving at 4:00 today to referee a football game. You're welcome to come."

Soon, the conversation turned to the business. Mr. Howell admitted concern over the general economic slowdown. He thought that coal mining and his total sales were down somewhat, but he blamed it on the high interest rates and the cost of financing new equipment. He repeatedly referred Harold to a large color aerial photograph of opening day at the dealership a year ago when the lot was crowded with people and beautiful new equipment. "I manage this place like a big business," he claimed. "Each manager is independent; we have weekly meetings to coordinate the whole organization."

"Well, Mr. Howell," said Harold, "that's exactly what I wanted to talk about today. As you know, I'm relatively new to the earth-moving business with Hardman's, although I had three years experience selling the same kind of equipment with National immediately prior to joining Hardman's. From my experience, I realize that I need to get to know my dealers and the characteristics of their businesses as quickly as possible, if I'm to do my job properly and be of service to the dealers. One way to do that is to sit down with the dealer and his sales manager and write out an expected sales and inventory plan for the next year. If you don't already have one, I'd like to do that today."

"Great, I'll get Ernie up here right away," Mr. Howell replied as he paged his sales manager. He continued, "Ernie Pelham and I played football together at Mountain City High. He's a great guy and he's really working hard to learn this business. You could help him a lot. He sold greeting cards until I hired him three months ago."

When Ernie came in, Harold introduced himself and they chatted cordially for a while until Harold suggested they could both learn more about Addison's business by working up a sales and inventory plan. Harold began by asking the two men what they would like to inventory in each model and capacity rating. He was surprised at the large figures Mr. Howell gave him, but continued, "What do you expect to sell in the next year by model and capacity rating?" Again, the figures Shirt volunteered were clearly unrealistic, almost double the preceding year's sales. To reach those sales levels in a year forecasted to be a poor one for the industry, Addison would have to get a market share of 75 percent, which was most unreasonable. In addition, some of the models he said they planned to inventory were poor sellers in the medium-duty line. In fact, several of Harold's other dealers had adamantly refused to stock this line because the markets were declining and the turnover and profit margins were low.

To clarify things, Harold asked, "Who did you sell to last year? What did they buy and will they buy again?" Ernie, of course, didn't know, and Howell said he never called on customers. They suggested that Harold talk with Larry Tompkins, the older salesman who had been with Addison's since the previous owner's day, to get the names of the heavy-duty customers. Mr. Howell thought that Ernie would be able to develop the medium-sized equipment business. Harold then said, "Why don't we take a look at your past sales records and current orders, and then make some projections of your inventory needs, given the necessary factory lead times?" Neither Shirt nor Ernie "had those records handy." Harold had complete records by model of the actual sales and market penetration for the last three years in his briefcase. He knew, however, if he brought them out, both Mr. Howell's and Ernie's complete ignorance of their market and its trends, their customers, and the inventory turns required for a profitable sales operation would be obvious.

CASE QUESTIONS

1. What are the problems?

2. What is the prognosis for the Addison Construction Equipment Co. if they were to proceed with the purchase and sales forecast originally stated by Mr. Howell and Ernie Pelham? Explain.

3. What are the specific sales problems Harold has to deal with?

4. What are the primary problems facing Mr. Howell and Ernie Pelham?

5. Explain what actions could be taken to satisfy Ernie Pelham's needs.

6. How should Harold handle the immediate situation?

7. How would you recommend proceeding with Ernie to solve the problem? What should be Harold's objective and what tactics should he use to reach them?

REFERENCES

1. Beecham Products recruiting brochure, 1981.
2. T. M. Rohan, "Getting (and Using) Good Feedback from Salesmen," *Industrial Week* (January 19, 1976): 24–30.
3. J. S. Adams, "Interorganizational Processes and Organization Boundary Activities," *Research in Organizational Behavior,* vol. 2 (1980): 321–355.
4. C. Lambert, *Field Sales Management Performance Appraisal* (New York: Ronald Press, 1979).

SUGGESTED READING

McCormick, E. J., *Job Analysis: Methods and Applications* (New York: AMACOM, 1979.)

4

THE SELLING PROCESS

The selling process is a complex communication and learning experience for the representative and the prospect. The sales representative learns the needs of the prospect and the prospect learns whether or not the representative's product or service will meet these needs. The successful representative controls this communication process by going through various activities that are known as steps in the selling process. This process requires the basic management skills of analysis, decision making, and communication.

All selling processes contain the same basic steps, but the detail of each step and the time required to complete it will vary according to the products that are being sold. For example, a door-to-door sales representative may go through all the steps from prospecting to a close in a matter of ten or fifteen minutes. In contrast, the selling process for a million-dollar computer system may take several years. Each industry and each company will label these steps differently. The representative for Xerox photocopy machines uses five steps in the selling process—approach, survey, demonstration, proposal, and close. Representatives who sell word-processing equipment (a combination of a typewriter and a computer) may be calling on the same prospects, but the steps that they use in their selling process have different labels and sequences of events—application identification, demonstration, current methods study, systems analysis and proposal, and closing presentation. In this chapter we will examine the steps of a generalized selling process that are appropriate for all outside selling representatives. This process can be adapted easily to a specific company.

Each company will want to train its representatives in its own procedure, but the following section provides a summary of steps that are common to many company training programs. This highly distilled presentation in tabular and flow chart form provides a minicourse in personal selling. This condensation may also give the incorrect impression that selling is a mechanical, highly structured process. Such is not the case. The communication may be verbal and nonverbal, such as body language. Listening can be as important as talking for a sales representative. Asking questions can be a key skill in the selling process. Exhibits 4.1 and 4.2 provide a means for organizing the complex interpersonal behavior that occurs between a salesperson and a prospect. Some of the contributions to the selling process from the behavioral sciences are discussed later in this chapter and in Chapter 11, which discusses motivation.

STEPS IN THE SELLING PROCESS

The selling process that will be considered here consists of the following nine steps: (1) prospecting, (2) classifying leads, (3) developing a selling strategy, (4) making the approach, (5) presenting, (6) trial closing, (7) handling objections, (8) closing, and (9) handling details after the close, which includes a post-case analysis. These steps are commonly used by industrial representatives, pharmaceutical representatives calling on physicians and hospitals, grocery products representatives calling on supermarket chains, and other industries where the nature of the sale is relatively complex. Each of these steps will be discussed in detail and linked to Exhibits 4.1 and 4.2. These exhibits may be used by sales managers to train new representatives and to counsel present representatives. They may also be used by representatives to prepare their sales interviews and to evaluate their effort.

PROSPECTING

Prospecting (Step #1) is the identification of potential new customers. It consists of identifying individuals with unmet needs or needs that are not fully met by their present suppliers.

Prospecting is an important part of the selling process because of the dynamics of the marketplace. Present customers may move, go out of business, have changes in needs, or have their needs met by competition. Thus a successful representative will allocate some of his or her time to the process of generating quality prospects.

Exhibit 4.1 Representatives' Activities in the Selling Process

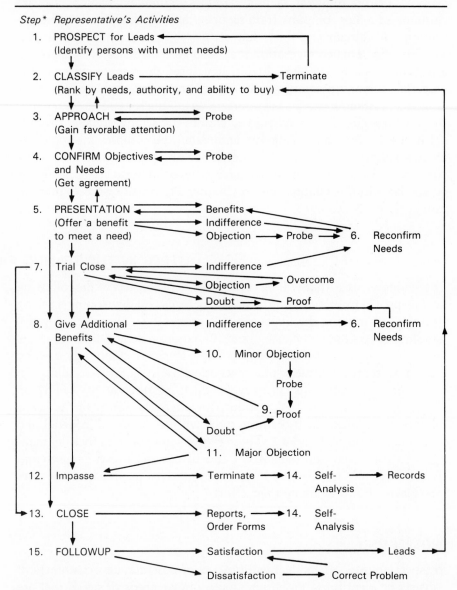

Step *Representative's Activities*

1. PROSPECT for Leads
   (Identify persons with unmet needs)

2. CLASSIFY Leads → Terminate
   (Rank by needs, authority, and ability to buy)

3. APPROACH ← Probe
   (Gain favorable attention)

4. CONFIRM Objectives ← Probe
   and Needs
   (Get agreement)

5. PRESENTATION ← Benefits
   (Offer a benefit → Indifference
   to meet a need) → Objection → Probe → 6. Reconfirm Needs

7. Trial Close → Indifference
   → Objection → Overcome
   → Doubt → Proof

8. Give Additional → Indifference → 6. Reconfirm Needs
   Benefits
   → 10. Minor Objection
        → Probe
   → 9. Proof
   Doubt
   → 11. Major Objection

12. Impasse → Terminate → 14. Self-Analysis → Records

13. CLOSE → Reports, → 14. Self-Analysis
    Order Forms

15. FOLLOWUP → Satisfaction → Leads
    → Dissatisfaction → Correct Problem

*These numbers refer also to steps in Exhibit 4.2.

Of the many procedures for identifying prospects with a high probability of buying, one of the most fruitful is referral from present satisfied customers. A similar approach is an applications approach where the successful sale for one application can identify other prospects with similar needs. For example, a word-processing salesperson with a successful installation in a law firm will seek out other lawyers for prospects. A new company coming to town may be reported in a newspaper announcement or by the issuing of a building permit for a new factory or store. Industrial sales representatives frequently use sources such as the *Thomas Register*, which lists companies according to the types of products they sell, thereby identifying needs for raw materials and component parts. Prospects' potential may be estimated from sources such as the "Survey of Industrial Buying Power," published annually by *Sales & Marketing Management*, and *County Business Patterns*, which is published by the U.S. Department of Commerce. These sources will be discussed in more detail in Chapter 17.

Territory records, suggestions from other sales representatives in other territories, and the company selling plan are all sources of stimulating ideas for generating prospects. The company selling plan will reflect the company's forecast for certain industries, its estimate of competitive activity, and the comparative advantages of its product. The plan will also reflect those products that are scheduled for major selling effort so they will receive promotional and advertising support, thereby making the representatives' prospecting job easier.

CLASSIFYING LEADS

Prospecting in selling is like prospecting in gold mining: the prospectors want to spend their time where the payoff is the greatest. Payoff is the combination of the percent chance of finding gold and the size of the nuggets found. In selling, the payoff, or expected value, is the probability of the prospect buying times the magnitude of the sale. The process of prospecting in selling has therefore become one of estimating probabilities of buying and sales potential. The representative will want to classify the prospect (Step #2) as early in the process as possible to prevent wasting time—the major resource in selling.

Low cost sources, such as library directories and asking other businesspersons in town, will give a rough estimate of the size of the business and the *magnitude of its needs* for the products. But a prospect must have more than a need to qualify as a potential customer. Prospects must have the *ability* and the *authority to buy*. The ability to buy is reflected in measures such as income and credit rating. The authority to buy is more difficult to define. Many representatives have been frustrated to learn at the end of a presentation that they were not dealing with the person who had the authority to buy, but who, in effect, had only the authority to turn down the proposal. Frequently the customer contact was simply gathering information for someone else, or was simply a member of a buying committee, meaning that the representa-

Exhibit 4.2 The Selling Process

SITUATION	REPRESENTATIVE'S ACTIVITY	PROSPECT'S RESPONSE	REPRESENTATIVE'S RESPONSE (STEP)
ASSESSING NEEDS			
1. Persons have unmet needs.	Prospect for leads using the company selling plan, secondary data, and territory records.	No response or a low-level response, such as an inquiry for more information after reading an advertisement.	Classify lead using secondary data and judgment (2).
2. The lead is classified as a prospect according to needs and ability to pay.	Identify a general need and match to a product benefit for the approach. Set call objective (e.g., sale, demonstration, survey, or proposal). Develop a selling strategy and contact prospect for an appointment.	Appointment granted. Prospect revealed information that changed the classification to unqualified.	Prepare for the approach (3). Develop another prospect (1).
3. The prospect remains qualified and can be contacted.	Use the planned approach.	Prospect gives attention and shows interest.	Continue to qualify. Move to presentation (5). If needs not fully understood, probe (4).
4. Needs must be identified or confirmed.	Confirm needs and objectives. Probe, using open or closed questions.	Prospect reveals needs in more depth.	Needs are ranked and presentation begins (5), or needs are not sufficient for a qualified prospect, then terminate the call (12).

MAKING THE PRESENTATION

5. General and specific needs identified and matched to product/service benefit.	Begin planned presentation with an important need and a matched product/service benefit.	Benefit accepted.	Present additional benefits (8).
		Indifference.	Reconfirm needs (6).
		Objection.	Handle minor (10) or major (11) objections.
		Reaction not classified.	Probe for more information (6).
6. Representative does not fully understand the needs, or they must be confirmed in the mind of the representative and the prospect.	Reconfirm needs. Probe with open or closed questions.	Needs confirmed.	Return to planned presentation (5, 8).
		Reaction classified.	Proceed to 7 through 12, according to classification.
		Needs not confirmed.	Use next most important need and continue (5, 8). If insufficient needs remain, terminate call (12).
7. Benefit accepted or objection handled successfully.	Use a trial close.	Trial close is accepted.	Close for call objective (2) if sufficient benefits have been accepted (13).
		Indifference.	Reconfirm need (6).
		Objection.	Handle minor (10) or major (11) objection.
		Doubts product or company has stated benefits.	Provide proof (9).
8. Insufficient benefits accepted to close.	Present additional benefits, using a trial close.	Trial close is accepted.	Close if sufficient benefits accepted (13), or present additional benefits (8).
		Indifference.	Reconfirm needs (6).
		Objection.	Handle minor (10) or major (11) objection.
		Doubts product or company has stated benefits.	Provide proof (9).

(continued)

Exhibit 4.2 Continued

SITUATION	REPRESENTATIVE'S ACTIVITY	PROSPECT'S RESPONSE	REPRESENTATIVE'S RESPONSE (STEP)
9. Prospect doubts that your product or company provides the benefit.	Offer proof.	Proof accepted.	Trial close (7), close (13), or provide additional benefits (8).
		Indifference or doubt remains.	Reconfirm need (6) and provide additional proof (9).
		Objections.	Handle minor (10) or major (11) objection.
10. Minor objection not based on fact.	Paraphrase the objection as a question, and answer the question with facts.	Objection overcome.	Continue presentation with a trial close (7), additional benefits (8), or a close (13).
		Objection not overcome.	Probe for more information (6) or reclassify as a major objection (11).
11. Major objection based on fact.	Paraphrase the objection as a question and offset it with other benefits relevant to prospect's needs.	Objection overcome.	Continue presentation with a trial close (7), additional benefits (8), or a close (13).
		Objection not overcome.	Probe for more information (6), use more offsetting benefits (11), or terminate the call (12).
CONCLUDING THE PRESENTATION			
12. Impasse reached.	Keep calm, thank the prospect for his or her time and attention, leave, and plan to call again.	Interview ended.	Record the call and do a self-analysis of the call (14).

13. Prospect agrees to sufficient benefits.	Close, using one of several closing strategies: 1. direct close 2. assumptive close 3. physical action 4. negative close 5. special offer 6. recommended action 7. summative close	Prospect agrees to the object of the call (2).	
		A sale, or	Write order and call report (14).
		A demonstration, survey, or presentation.	Make arrangements for next call and prepare (5).
		Close not successful.	Summarize needs and benefits and use a different close.

AFTER THE PRESENTATION

14. Interview terminated.	Complete territory records, noting needs, benefits, and objectives for next call. If a sale, complete order and other arrangements. Complete call report showing product/service weaknesses. Conduct a self-analysis of strengths and weaknesses in the selling process, noting where there is a need for more product knowledge and improved selling skills.	No response.	No response.
15. Followup	Check for delivery, installation, promised results, and satisfaction. Ask for additional leads.	Dissatisfaction Satisfied, provides leads.	Correct problem. Qualify leads (1).

tive had to go through the process of selling again. In small companies, it is frequently difficult to gain access to those individuals who make the buying decision because they are busy running the company. New representatives sometimes make the mistake of calling on prospects who are not *eligible to buy* from the company directly. For instance, a policy of selling only through wholesalers would eliminate retailers as prospects, unless the representative solicits orders to be processed by the wholesaler.

The representative would classify a lead as a prospect when the lead had a reasonable probability of buying, had sufficient needs to justify a profitable sale, had the financial resources to buy, and was consistent with company policy of eligibility.

DEVELOPING A SELLING STRATEGY

Need-Benefit Match

The representative uses the information from prospecting to develop a rough selling strategy (Step #2). Strategy development consists of identifying a general need of the prospect and matching a product benefit to that need. This need-benefit match will be used for the initial approach.

The representative will contact the prospect and use the generalized need that has been identified and the matched benefit as an inducement to gain favorable attention and an interview. This generalized need and matching benefit may also be used in the approach, which is the critical first thirty seconds in the sales interview.

Call Objective

The next step in the development of this initial strategy is to set the objective for the first sales interview. This objective is the action that the representative wants the prospect to take. Does he or she want to make a sale on the first call, or to get agreement for a demonstration, survey, or proposal? These objectives may change as the selling process develops. A representative who had planned to get permission for a survey may be pleasantly surprised to learn that the prospect is ready to buy on the first call.

Company Selling Plan

The company selling plan will help the representative to develop an effective selling strategy because it will give call objectives, opening benefits, additional benefits to stress, and suggested closes. Selling plans may vary throughout the year. For example, a pharmaceutical representative may have a plan that stresses a nasal decongestant during the flu season, and a product to treat swimmers' ear infections during the summer.

This process describes developing a selling strategy for a new prospect. The development of a selling strategy for a present customer is simplified by the fact that the representative can review territory records and past selling plans, and will have information about the customers' business objectives, competition, previous objections, and needs-benefit matches that were successful in the past.

Identifying the prospects' needs and meeting these needs with product or service benefits are central to the selling process. Therefore we must examine the different kinds of needs that a prospect experiences.

THREE TYPES OF NEEDS

A prospect will constantly be seeking ways to meet his or her professional needs, the needs of the organization, and personal needs.

Professional Needs

Professional needs, which may be defined as on-the-job needs, are created by the role that the individual plays within an organization. Problem solving consists of meeting a collection of needs. For instance, the manager of the automobile fleet for sales representatives has the problem of choosing among a wide variety of automobiles to meet the multiple needs of transportation, comfort, efficiency, economy, and corporate prestige. The sales representative who can best meet all these needs with the benefits of his or her automobile will solve the fleet manager's problem and make a sale.

Organizational Needs

The organizational needs of a prospect will be linked closely to the needs of the organization. The organizational needs may include growth; better utilization of resources, as reflected in financial ratios; more effective use of personnel, as reflected in productivity measures; and the enhancement of the company's prestige and credibility among its customers, suppliers, and the public at large.

A sophisticated representative will understand the professional and organizational needs of a prospect and include them in a statement of benefits. For example, a sales trainer in the grocery products industry instructs his or her representative to identify the criteria that are used for promoting a chain store buyer. Is the buyer evaluated according to profit, turnover, margin, or return-on-investment? A representative who can appeal to these criteria will create a win-win selling situation: the buyer looks good in his or her organization and the sales representative makes a sale.

Hierarchy of Personal Needs

Personal needs have been classified by many authors, but the most widely used classification is the one provided by Maslow, which is as follows: physiological, safety, belonging and love, esteem, and self-actualization.[1] The physiological needs would be an individual's need for food, shelter, and clothing. When these basic needs are met, the individual may move to the next need in the hierarchy—that of safety.

A prospect with a high need for safety would avoid risks and seek certainty or security. To meet these needs, the representative would want to match benefits such as the long and successful reputation of the company for delivery of a reliable product, the technical support that will be supplied, and the fact that the product has been used by many other companies known to the prospect. This same prospect may also want order in the selling proposal so that it has a definite structure and clear definitions of benefits.

Belonging and love needs may take several forms in the selling situation. An insecure prospect with high needs for belonging will want to have others in the buying decision, or to be assured other successful companies used the product or service. Conversely, a power-oriented prospect will want self-esteem. In the latter case, the representative will want to stress how the purchase of the equipment will enhance the organizational power and prestige of the prospect. For example, a larger computer system may require everyone in the organization to come to the prospect for information, thereby enhancing one's power and prestige in the company.

A prospect's esteem will be enhanced in the organization when he or she makes the right decision in buying a product or service. Prospects who feel that their esteem is at risk will frequently buy products from only the leading manufacturers, thereby minimizing later criticism. Representatives from other companies will have to supply many additional benefits to offset this perceived possible risk to esteem.

Self-actualization is a philosophical, internal experience that is usually achieved only by a few persons, and therefore cannot be central to many selling situations. For some individuals, it may be achieved with a sense of achievement for having affected change within the organization by making a wise purchase. For others, achievement may be simply a physical one—that of increased productivity.

The skillful representative will identify these complex need patterns early in the selling interview by probing with careful questions, listening carefully, and observing nonverbal communications, such as body language and the decor of the prospect's environment. An understanding of these need patterns will help the representative to tailor the presentation to include benefits that will meet these three types of needs.

BENEFITS DEFINED

By now it is probably apparent that people do not buy products or services; instead, they buy a bundle of benefits to meet their needs, thereby solving a problem. Physicians do not want a drug; they want their patients to get better. We do not buy an automobile; we buy transportation, comfort, and prestige, subject to the constraints of our budget. A manufacturer does not buy a numerical-controlled lathe; he or she buys higher productivity and lower set-up costs. Thus a benefit occurs when a product or service attribute satisfies a customer's need.

MAKING THE APPROACH

When the prospect remains classified as a prospect (Step #2), the representative turns to the approach (Step #3)—that crucial step in the selling process where the representative must gain the attention and interest of the prospect so that he or she may move into the presentation stage. The approach is the beginning of the two-way communication process that has been defined as, "finding a window and keeping it open."

Types of Approaches

A variety of approaches may be used. The strongest approach is the *benefit approach* that was previously described. The representative opens with a statement of general need, such as, "Would you like to increase productivity in your production line? Would you like to save money? Would you like to make money? Would you like some enjoyment in your life?" Having gained the attention of the prospect, the representative turns to the benefits of his or her offer that will meet these general needs. If the prospect shows interest, the representative may proceed with the presentation phase. If interest is insufficient, the representative will need to probe for a better understanding of the prospect's needs (Step #4).

The *referral approach* may be a strong approach if the reference person is highly regarded by the prospect. Less strong approaches are the *introductory approach*, where the representative introduces himself or herself and the company; and the *product approach*, where the representative hands the product to the customer to gain interest and attention. The product approach may be effective when the product is portable, when customer relationships are well established, when there is little time for a presentation, and when the customer needs to dominate the buying process. A representative selling high-fashion clothing to a department store buyer may use this approach by simply bringing the latest fashion item and placing it on the desk of the buyer.

Probing during the Approach

Tactical probing will occur at many points in the selling process. Shortly after the approach is completed, the representative will probe to learn additional needs of the buyer in order to earn the right to continue the interview. Probing at this stage amounts to the gathering of primary data that could not be collected prior to the interview. Later in the presentation when a prospect does not accept a stated benefit, the representative will use probing to confirm the prospect's needs and gain acceptance of the benefit.

Probing amounts to asking the right question at the right time. Open-ended questions, such as how, what, where, when, why, and who, yield the maximum amount of information. Closed-ended questions that can be answered with a yes or a no are used to clarify a point, reach agreement, or get a response from a nontalkative prospect. A chemical manufacturer's representative would be asking a closed question by asking, "Did your present suppliers meet delivery schedules during the petroleum shortage?" A representative for word-processing equipment could ask, "Does your secretarial staff spend a lot of time retyping a page to correct a minor error?"

Asking the right question at the right time is only half of successful probing. The other half of probing is hard, effective listening. One must listen for what the prospect does not say as well as what is said.

PRESENTING

Two-way communication between the representative and the prospect is the heart of the steps of the presentation (Steps 5 through 11).

Presenting Benefits

The salesperson presents benefits and the prospect responds by accepting the benefits, objecting, doubting that the product can produce the benefits, indifference, or no clear reaction. The representative must analyze these reactions and decide how to respond. If the prospect agrees with the opening benefit, the representative may proceed to a trial close (situation 7) or a presentation of additional benefits (situation 8). If the prospect is indifferent or if the response cannot be classified, the representative should probe for more information. To reconfirm a need, the seller should get agreement on a statement of the buyer's objectives and needs (situation 6). If there is doubt that the product has the benefits, proof should be offered (situation 9). Objections must be classified as minor or major ones (situations 10 and 11). It is important for the representative to wait for the prospect's reaction before proceeding to the next benefit.

Probing Needs Further

Probing (situation 6) may be necessary in order to classify the prospect's response or to confirm the need to which the benefit had been matched. This probing stage should be a natural part of the conversation. It requires careful listening.

Presentation Styles

Each company will want to develop its own style of presentations. A grocery products manufacturer instructs its representatives in the following steps: (1) summarize the situation, (2) state the idea, (3) describe how the idea works, (4) state the benefits, and (5) recommend action. To aid in the presentation, companies provide representatives with sales aids that include brochures and visual aids, such as charts, slides, and movies, to emphasize features that produce the benefits claimed for their products. Some companies prefer highly structured or "canned" presentations.[2] These presentations may be useful to simplify the training of new representatives who sell simple or standardized products.

Trial Closing

When several benefits have been accepted or objections handled successfully (situation 7), a trial close may be used to see if the prospect is ready to buy. A trial close consists of an early attempt to gain a commitment by the prospect on details of the order or a minor point such as the color, the delivery date, or the payment method that will be used. If the prospect is ready to make a decision on a minor point, then he or she is close to making the major decision of buying the product or service.

Handling Objections

Objections may take the form of *doubts, minor objections,* or *major objections.* A doubting prospect is asking for proof that a product or company has features that provide the stated benefits. The salesperson may provide this proof with a demonstration, samples, additional information, such as research results, or by quoting authorities in the field.

A minor objection (situation 10) is an objection that is based on incomplete facts. For example, "Your price is too high," may mean that the prospect has not been shown sufficient benefits, quality, and service that create a total value that more than justifies the price. To overcome this type of objection, the representative should paraphrase the objection as a question and answer it with facts.

A major objection (situation 11) is based on the fact that there is some disadvantage of the product when applied to the prospect's need. If the need is a minor one, in comparison to other needs that will be met by the product, the representative may offset this objection by summarizing the many other benefits of the product. If, however, the need is central to the prospect's problem, then it may be necessary to terminate the presentation at this point (situation 12). For example, "Your microcomputer is not portable," may be offset with features such as color graphics and extensive software.

Objections Provide Feedback

Objections provide the representative with feedback for those points where the prospect does not agree with either the definition of the needs or the stated benefits that will meet these needs. Objections will require backing up in the selling process to confirm needs, to provide features that produce agreed upon benefits, or to summarize benefits. It may also be necessary to reclassify the prospect. Are the needs, ability to buy, and authority to buy really there? An objection may be the prospect's way of asking for more reasons for buying. Perhaps the seller has not dealt with the buyer's personal or organizational needs, such as the risks associated with making a wrong buying decision.

The seller must listen carefully to minor objections because they may be major objections in disguise. A prospect may choose to hide the real objection. For example, a prospect may complain about the price of a new computer, when the real objection is that he or she is unwilling to invest the time and energy in learning a new computer system. Once the representative identifies this hidden objective, it is possible to deal with it directly by showing how the benefits more than offset the need to learn the new system. Procrastination can also be a hidden objection. The procrastinating prospect may be moved to a buying decision by pointing out the costs of foregoing the benefits.

Experienced salespersons welcome objections as an important part of feedback in the selling process. They will anticipate objections and prepare their responses as part of their selling strategy.

CONCLUDING THE PRESENTATION

Termination Short of the Objective

An impasse may be reached in the selling process (situation 12) when the prospect's needs do not justify a purchase, or when a major objection reveals that the product's benefits will not meet a central need of the prospect. At this point the salesperson needs to keep calm, thank the prospect for his or her time and attention, and leave the door open for another call in case there is a change in the needs of the prospect or a redesign of the product. The representative should analyze the reasons for the call being unsuccessful (situation 14).

Achievement of Objective

When the prospect has agreed to a sufficient number of benefits, the representative should close the presentation and seek the goal of the call. How many benefits are sufficient? There is no general answer to this question. The number will depend on the nature of the product and each selling situation. Trial closes will help the representative decide when to make the final close.

Types of Closes

Some representatives are afraid to *ask directly*, "Will you buy?" because they fear that they will be rejected and they have a strong need to be accepted by the prospect. Rather than use a direct closing strategy, this representative may want to use one of the other closing strategies that are available.

The *assumptive close* assumes that the sale is made and the representative proceeds to questions such as the spelling of names, the proper address, the quantity desired, the size, the color, etc. Handing the prospect a pen to sign the order or handing him or her the car keys represents a *physical action close*. A *negative close* occurs when the representative urges the need to buy now because the product is in short supply or a price increase would occur shortly. *Special concession closes* are used frequently in the grocery products industry: the representative may agree to give a special advertising or promotional allowance for buying now. If the close is not successful, the representative should summarize the needs and benefits and try a different close. In some cases these closes may boomerang because the prospect feels manipulated.

When the object of the call is a demonstration, survey, or presentation, the closing strategies will differ only slightly. An assumptive close may be on the details of where and when the demonstration should be held. If the call objective is a survey of needs, an assumptive close may be a request for the names of the persons who would be involved in such a survey and an introduction to these individuals.

AFTER THE PRESENTATION

Arrange for the Next Call

Several important selling activities are required after the interview is terminated. If the interview results in a sale, it will be necessary to complete the appropriate order forms. If the goal of the interview was a demonstration, it may be necessary to make arrangements for the equipment that will be demonstrated.

Administrative Tasks

The representative should complete the territory records for this account showing needs, benefits, and objections that occurred during this interview so that he or she will be well prepared for the next interview. Completion of the weekly call report may include an evaluation of the product when it was impossible to overcome objections. If other representatives share these problems, it may be necessary to redesign the product.

Post-Call Analysis

The representative will want to do a self-evaluation (Step 14) of the call, thereby identifying personal strengths and weaknesses in product knowledge and selling skills that need improvement. Many post-call analysis questions will need to be answered. Was the call successful? Why? What benefits triggered the sale? Are there other customers with similar needs who might respond to the same presentation? Was the presentation unsuccessful? Why? Why was the sale postponed? What proof or selling material will enable you to reclose the sale successfully? How long should you wait to call again?

This self-analysis could include measures of the successful managing of accounts, such as performance this year with last year using sales volume, market share, contribution, expenses, and perhaps return-on-investment as criteria.

Followup

Service after the sale is an important part of account and territory management. Sales followup (Step 15) assures that the order will not be cancelled, and it paves the way for future orders by building confidence in the customer that the representative will deliver as promised. It can also be a good source for new leads.

SYSTEMS SELLING—APPLIED ORGANIZATIONAL BEHAVIORAL SCIENCE

FOUR BASIC ORGANIZATIONAL STRUCTURES

Industrial selling requires a thorough understanding of the complexities of the buying organization. Hanan, Cribbin, and Donis suggest a *systems selling strategy.*[3] They note that a buying organization has four structures—the power structure, the group structure, the role structure, and the status structure.[4] Each of these structures has a life of its own, complete with behavioral codes, performance standards, vocabulary, objectives, and criteria for entry. The system seller must identify these structures and their leaders so that he or she may help them meet their personal and group objectives. Extensive checklists are available to assist in this identification.[5] Negotiation is the process by which a seller penetrates these four organizational structures.[6]

Negotiation is a vital component in the selling process when the product, associated services, delivery arrangements, and the price can be adapted to meet a prospect's needs. Many purchasing managers have been trained in how to negotiate, so industrial sales managers are finding it necessary to train their representatives in the art of negotiation.

What Is Negotiable?

Dow Corning created a two-day negotiation course for its representatives based on the principles developed by Chester L. Karrass.[7] The Dow Corning program uses a negotiation worksheet that includes items that may be subject to negotiation, such as characteristics of the product, special features, packaging, inventory, delivery, price, technical support, and safety factors. Each of these negotiable dimensions is then analyzed according to the customer's requirements, the value of that dimension to the customer, whether Dow Corning meets the requirements, which competitors meet the requirements, which items are not negotiable to Dow Corning and which are not negotiable for the customer, and, finally, the limits beyond which Dow Corning and the customer will not go on negotiable dimensions. Representatives are trained to know the limits of their authority, to be patient, and to concede slowly. Patient negotiating traits are more common in eastern cultures than in western ones.

Telephone Negotiations

The danger of negotiating on the telephone is noted because the initiative lies with the caller, and mistakes are frequently made under the pressure of a phone call. The negotiator needs to know the power structure of his or her organization and the power structure of the customer's organization. An appreciation of hidden personal values becomes an important component in negotiating. These subtleties cannot be achieved on the telephone.

Team Negotiations

Team negotiation has many advantages. In addition to providing greater expertise and moral support, it provides better listening, better planning, and a show of strength. Its principal disadvantage is a lack of unanimity among the team members, thereby making it difficult to make a counter-proposal.

Greater competition in the marketplace, more than any other single factor, will require that many industrial representatives be trained in the art of negotiation. But this training must be built on a sound, basic training in the selling process because negotiation requires an understanding of the prospect's needs and the product benefits that will meet these needs. The major difference between selling and negotiating is that in negotiating many product attributes are variable, while in selling they are fixed.

PARTNERING

According to Hanan, Cribbin, and Donis, systems selling requires turning a customer into a partner, not an adversary.[8] There is the need to develop common objectives, common strategies for achieving the objectives, common risks, and common defenses against outside threats. Systems selling is an extension of consultative selling that was discussed in Chapter 1. These authors stress the need to know the motives of prospect partners in the selling-buying partnership. They provide insights into the types of decision makers who make good or bad partners. The good partners include bureaucrats (rational, formal, and impersonal), zealots (impatient, outspoken, independent loners), executives (dominant, directive, but keep others at arm's length), integrators (egalitarian, excellent interpersonal skills, team builders), advocates (competent, politically skilled, need group support), developers (trust people, coach and counselor), gamesmen (fast-moving, impersonal, upwardly mobile), and paternalistic autocrats (benevolent, patronizing, not open to new ideas). The following decision-making styles do not make good partners: Machiavellians (self-oriented, shrewd, devious), missionaries (overly concerned with people and their opinions), exploitive autocrats (arrogant, self-insistent, demeaning), temporisers (procrastinating, compromising, vacillating, always complaining), climbers (striving, driving, nonloyal), conservers (status quo defender, resist change), and glad-handers (superficial, deceptively friendly, adept politicians, superior survival instincts, fluent, humorous, but may lack substance).[9]

BEHAVIORAL SCIENCES STUDIES
OF THE SELLING PROCESS

HISTORICAL PERSPECTIVES

Behavioral scientists have had a long interest in the selling process. In 1925, Edward K. Strong published an article in the *Journal of Applied Psychology* titled, "Theories in Selling."[10] This article discussed three models of the selling process. The first model was the well-known AIDA model that instructs the salesperson to gain Attention, stimulate Interest, create Desire, and move the prospect to Action. The second model was the stimulus-response model that is common to many communication and learning theories: the prospect will respond, given proper stimuli by the salesperson. The third model stressed the importance of identifying and creating wants in the mind of the prospect. In this model, the emphasis is placed on the representative's understanding the needs of the prospect. Strong made reference to an article published in 1898 by E. St. Emlo Louis who stressed the need to "attract attention, maintain interest, and create desire." Strong noted also that Sheldon added "secure satisfaction," in 1905. Of course, these models were based largely on the authors' personal observation without the benefit of rigorous experimental design and statistical analysis.

Studies of buying-selling behavior have followed developments in social psychology. The early studies considered changes in the prospect, as is reflected in the stimulus-response model or the AIDA model. With the development of personality research and multivariate statistical techniques, researchers' interests turned to the question of, "What characteristics of a representative can we identify to predict a successful and productive one?" The more recent studies examine the buyer-seller process as an interactive one. As we will see later, this type of research is extremely difficult.

FOCUS OF RESEARCH

To help us better understand behavioral science studies of the selling process, we will examine briefly some of the research dealing with changes in the prospect, characteristics of the salesperson, the buyer-seller interaction, models that attempt to integrate all of these concepts, and some of the difficulties in selling research. To keep this discussion within the limitations of this chapter, we will refer to the most frequently cited articles and to several recent excellent critiques of the hundreds of research articles on the selling and buying processes. The reader who is interested in exploring these topics in greater depth will want to refer to the citations in these summary articles.

Changes in the Prospect

In 1968, Gwinner summarized four theories of selling, noting the advantages and disadvantages of each. This summary emphasized the point that the sales strategists must consider different theories of selling for different products, customers, and representatives.[11]

The stimulus-response theory may be the appropriate strategy for low-priced products, simple selling situations where the product is uncomplicated, and when time is a factor so that only a short presentation may be made. The stimulus-response theory requires the representative to use a memorized or canned presentation. This strategy simplifies the selection and training of representatives, but it has the disadvantage of little two-way communication taking place between the salesperson and the prospect.

The AIDA theory assumes that the prospect goes through a series of mental states from attention, to interest, to desire, and, finally, to action. This strategy would be useful in industrial sales where the sale is complicated and repeat calls are necessary.

The AIDA model gives the new representative a structure for learning the selling process and encourages representatives to plan their sales calls in advance. There are two limitations of this model. First, it is difficult to identify these mental states as a particular "moment in time." Second, the selling process is dominated by the representative, with little consideration for feedback from the prospect.

A need-satisfaction theory shifts the attention of the selling process to the prospect because it assumes that purchases are made to satisfy needs. This selling strategy is used by representatives selling household goods, insurance, automobiles, and some industrial products. The salesperson attempts to avoid persuasion and concentrate on identifying the needs of prospects by encouraging them to do most of the talking. The disadvantage of this approach is that it requires a more highly trained representative who has an understanding of the psychology of communication, has empathy for the prospect, and who is willing to spend an appropriate amount of time with the prospect.

The problem-solution theory is a logical extension of the need-satisfaction theory because it helps the prospect to identify his or her needs. Furthermore, it helps prospects to identify and analyze alternative solutions to their problems—solutions that may not include the products and services of the seller. At this point the representative becomes a true consultant to the prospect, as was discussed in Chapter 1 and Exhibit 1.1. This strategy would be appropriate in highly technical sales or perhaps when selling to a buyer for a chain store, but it would be used rarely in direct sales to consumers. The disadvantage of this approach is that it requires a highly trained representative who is willing to make a long-term commitment to working with a prospect in the hopes of turning it into a long-term account.

Recent studies of changes in prospects' mental processes apply concepts from communication theory that assume a sales stimulus will induce a change in the prospect's beliefs and attitudes about needs and the products offered by the representative. A field experiment by Hughes revealed that the effectiveness of a call made by an adding machine salesperson could be measured in changes in beliefs and attitudes.[12] Capon, Holbrook, and Hulbert summarized fifteen selling-process studies that used the Source-Message-Response model, but made no generalizations regarding the contents of these studies. Their conclusions focused only on process by noting that the research showed a progression of sophistication.[13] Generalizations are difficult with these kinds of research because they use such a wide variety of techniques, products, buying environment, and sales stimuli. There seems to be little effort toward replication of previous research findings.

Characteristics of the Salesperson

The high cost of recruiting and training a representative led to the search for attributes of applicants that would predict high sales performance. Researchers used performance scores from personality tests, ability tests, and application form information. Weitz reviewed twenty-one studies that were reported after 1950, in which researchers attempted to predict sales performance using measures of personality and interest. He concluded that "the success in predicting sales performance has actually been quite limited."[14] He found inconsistent relationships between representatives' sales productivity and their age, knowledge, educational level, empathy for customers' needs, sociability, and forcefulness. It appears, therefore, that broad generalizations of what makes a representative productive are not possible, so that these criteria need to be established for each company.

In a separate study, Weitz and Wright concluded that the adaptive and technical abilities of salespersons may be a good predictor of sales performance because these abilities would allow them to adjust their message to the uniqueness of each selling situation.[15] These authors then propose a sales process model, with elements very similar to those in Exhibit 4.1.

Buyer-Seller Interaction

The next logical step in studying the buying process after focusing first on the buyer and then the salesperson, is to study the interaction of these two individuals during the sales process. In 1963, Evans examined the dyadic relationship between insurance salespeople and prospects, regarding the similarity of their attributes such as age, education, height, and politics. He concluded that there was an increased likelihood of a sale when the salesperson and the prospect had similar attributes.[16] This study stimulated other researchers to examine other buyer-seller interaction processes using advanced experimental and statistical techniques. Some of these later studies challenged the findings of Evans. Capon, Holbrook, and Hulbert reexamined the Evans data and found that the differences were not statistically significant.[17]

Weitz suggested that a rival hypothesis could explain Evans's findings. This is the hypothesis of *cognitive consistency*. Weitz points out that Evans's customers were contacted after they made the decision to purchase life insurance; thus, to avoid cognitive dissonance, they perceived the salesperson as being similar to themselves.[18] The cognitive consistency hypothesis seems to be supported by the experimental findings of Farley and Swinth who found that subjects who chose the product instead of money evaluated the product and the representative higher than did those who chose money.[19] Studies of the Evans type may also be criticized for failing to examine the dynamics of the buying-selling process. Essentially they make a comparison of two static measures of individuals.

Researchers have turned their attention to other variables in the interactive process. Woodside and Davenport examined the sales effect of the buyer and seller having similar interests and the effect of the relative expertise of the salesperson. The product was a head and capston cleaner kit for tape recorders. The experimental setting was a music store in Athens, Georgia. They concluded that prospects were more likely to buy if the representative expressed similar interest in tapes rather than dissimilar interest (55 percent vs. 33 percent), and if the content of the presentation was that of an expert in tape cleaning rather than a nonexpert (76 percent vs. 22 percent).[20] Spiro and Perreault concluded that selling situations tend to influence the styles that are used by representatives.[21] Speckman suggests that the concept of boundary role persons and boundary spanning activities apply to industrial salespersons because of the ways in which they link the selling and the buying organizations.[22]

Prior to developing his theory of the personal selling process, Capon concluded that:

> Scientific progress is made when hypotheses developed from soundly based theory are subject to empirical verification. Regrettably for the field of buyer-seller interaction the theoretical developments in this area have spurred virtually no empirical research and further, the twenty or so empirical studies extant either have no theoretical underpinnings whatsoever or are embedded in theoretical perspectives drawn from widely different fields, so that a coherent body of knowledge has not developed in the area.[23]

Weitz, reflecting on the fact that situational characteristics modify the buying-selling process, proposes a contingency theory of salesperson performance that would be based on the salesperson's behavior patterns, situational characteristics, and personal characteristics.[24] Salespersons' behaviors would include the extent of their information gathering, the extent of their adaptation to specific customers, their concern for customer satisfaction, the extent that they use manipulative or deceptive sales tactics, and whether they use expert or referent higher-based strategies. Characteristics of the situation would include the seller's anticipation of future interaction, characteristics of decision making (complexity, involvement, and size of order), the relative power of the customer and the salesperson, the level of conflict during interaction, and the characteristics of the customer, including the information possessed and the customer's personality. Salesperson characteristics would include knowledge about the products and customers, Machiavellianism, self-monitoring and adaptation during the selling process, and empathy for the customer's needs. It is interesting to compare this model proposed by Weitz with the model outlined in Exhibits 4.1 and 4.2 in this chapter, which are based on sales training procedures used in industry. The similarity between the proposed model and these training models suggests that a convergence is taking place between the practice and research of sales management.

Integrated Models of Industrial Buyer Behavior

The complexity of the industrial buying process has led many authors to develop models of the industrial buying process. Defined broadly, industrial selling includes all of those buying and selling encounters that do not involve the ultimate consumer, such as selling to manufacturers, assemblers, the government, and wholesalers and retailers. These selling situations are complex because of the nature of the products that are sold, the criteria that are used for purchasing, and the fact that the selling process may take place over a period of months or years.

One of the earliest studies of industrial buying was conducted by Robinson, Faris, and Wind, who developed a taxonomy of the industrial purchasing process.[25] They identified three buying situations—new tasks, modified rebuy, and straight rebuy. The steps in the buying process were identified as need identification and a general solution, characteristics and quantity of items needed, qualification of sources, proposals, evaluation, selection of supplier, selection of an order routine, and an evaluation of the entire process.

The Sheth model of industrial buyer behavior is a complex flow chart of the stimuli and responses that may take place in any industrial buying process. It is based on existing behavioral research that includes individual, intraorganizational, and interorganizational influences.[26] Webster and Wind present a general model for understanding organizational buying behavior by integrating interpersonal, intrapersonal, and interorganizational submodels, plus environmental factors, into a single framework, thereby attempting to identify the variables that should be considered in any study of the buying process.[27]

Wilson presents a decision process model of organizational buying behavior and attempts to synthesize other general models.[28] He notes that the dyadic interaction should be considered an exchange process. Busch, Bush, and Hair develop a theory of buyer behavior based on the literature of social power.[29] They emphasize that social power is an important concept in studying buyer-seller relations.

Bonoma, Zaltman, and Johnston reviewed over 200 studies of industrial and organizational buying behavior and concluded that there is little structure in the literature, it does not identify causal relationships in the buying process, research is based on some questionable assumptions, and there is a dearth of theoretical and empirical evidence for identifying variables that should be included in this research.[30] They emphasize the point that industrial buying behavior is a social process. They suggest also that the transaction should be the basic unit of analysis. These authors are of the opinion that much of the "leg work" in industrial buying behavior remains to be done and that there is a need for tedious, pick-and-shovel descriptive studies that would provide the taxonomies for variables to be included in studies of the industrial buying processes.

The Difficulties of Selling Research

Research on the industrial buying process is particularly difficult because it is a dynamic process involving the interaction of not only the buyer and seller but the members of the organizations of each. No one has created an experimental design to examine this complex process as it takes place over a period of time. We need unobtrusive instruments that will measure the process without interacting with it. A researcher riding with a salesperson raises doubts about altering the latter's behavior, a phenomenon known in behavioral research as the "Hawthorne" effect. The salesperson may increase or decrease his or her productivity because of the presence of the researcher. Some researchers have used a wireless microphone in retail selling to monitor the behavior of a specific salesperson, but this type of selling is a single-encounter sale, unlike the usual selling in industrial marketing. To control part of the interaction process, researchers have used a computer as either a buyer or the seller in a laboratory situation. Such computer-controlled behavioral experiments provide an opportunity to test hypotheses and build models, but these models still need to be validated in the field.[31]

SOME GENERALIZATIONS

This brief research review provides us with some generalizations regarding the buying-selling process. Researchers view it as an exchange process that uses social encounters and social power. They emphasize the need to understand customer wants and satisfaction. Recent researchers stress the importance of the selling situation, emphasizing that the sales representative is a mini-marketing strategist and tactician who must adapt to the uniqueness of each sale. Some researchers suggest that the transaction should be the basic unit of analysis. Selling research has moved from communication research, which appears at the bottom of Exhibit 1.1 (Chapter 1), to research that views the representative as a problem solver for the prospect—consultative selling—which appears at the top of Exhibit 1.1.

Recent researchers have made substantial contributions to buyer-seller process research by introducing new experimental and statistical techniques and by building on the findings of previous research. There are several areas, however, where this research may be criticized. For example, there is little direct replication of previous findings, which is so necessary to build empirical regularities and then, finally, theory. Research from related disciplines needs to be introduced. For example, the extensive literature on bargaining behavior may be appropriate to the study of buyer-seller interaction.[32] These researchers could be criticized also for not considering some of the writings of early marketing theorists. For instance, in 1957 the late Wroe Alderson discussed the evolution of market transactions, the exchange process, fully negotiated transactions, and routinized transactions, and he suggested the exchange transaction as the basic unit of marketing activity.[33]

It is comforting to see convergences between the practice of personal selling, the early theorists, and contemporary sophisticated research findings. This convergence provides some validity for the findings of future research in the area of buyer-seller interaction.

SUMMARY

This chapter summarizes the selling process as viewed by practitioners and researchers. The first part of the chapter summarizes the steps in the selling process that are common to many training programs and textbooks on personal selling. The steps in the selling process are presented graphically (Exhibit 4.1) and in tabular form (Exhibit 4.2) to facilitate the learning process. This material may be used by new representatives to learn how to sell, by experienced representatives to sharpen their skills, and by sales managers while counseling representatives.

A discussion of systems selling is viewed as an application of organizational behavioral science. The seller must recognize that each buying organization has four structures—the power structure, the group structure, a role structure, and a status structure. The representative must identify these structures and their leaders, and develop selling strategies accordingly. To penetrate these structures, the salesperson must be able to negotiate.

Behavioral science studies of the selling process have reflected the changes in thinking of the roles of a salesperson from being a communicator to that of a consultant. These studies have also reflected advances in experimental and statistical methodology. Recent criticisms of this research suggest that there is a convergence in thinking regarding the process of selling as viewed by practitioners and researchers.

ASSIGNMENTS/DISCUSSION QUESTIONS

1. What are the purposes of having a structured selling process?

2. Distinguish between product features and user benefits and give three examples of each.

3. What are the advantages and disadvantages of a "canned" selling process?

4. Give three examples of a "need-benefit match."

5. If a rifle manufacturer were to claim that the rifle is "perfectly balanced," list five benefits that this feature would provide the buyer or user.

CASE 4.1:
Analyzing the Selling Process:
Herman Miller, the Periodicals Representative

"Mr. Winkler, on my last call we were discussing periodicals that you send regularly to your field sales staff and you commented that your company might be looking for something new to restimulate the enthusiasm of representatives. Are you still in the market for such a product?"

"Yes, I suppose so." (Somewhat disinterested.)

"I didn't follow up your lead at that time because you had just contracted for our *Sales Managers Quarterly Bulletin* and I wanted you to see the benefits it provides your field Sales Managers before discussing a new publication we're in the process of releasing. In selecting a periodical for your field sales staff, what objectives do you have in mind? What do you want it to provide?"

"Well . . . we think it should give some tips on selling, some success stories, some material from a different point of view than the usual company material."

"I'm certainly glad to confirm that these are your objectives, Mr. Winkler, because our new *Suggestions for Successful Selling* publication will give you just what you're looking for. Here's a mock-up of our first issue scheduled for September. The Selling Tips are practical, field-tested contributions from members of Sales and Marketing executives whom we've contracted with. In addition, there's a regular column by a Marketing Professor from a School of Business Administration. And to provide some good background information, every other issue will include a commentary on current business trends. In combination, these articles should provide considerable information to your field staff, and make them appreciate the company's concern for keeping them. How does this sound to you?"

"Well . . . that sounds pretty good."

"Mr. Winkler, *Suggestions for Successful Selling* will be mailed monthly at a cost of $18 for twelve issues. There's a 10-percent discount for all original subscribers before July 1. Could I sign you up?"

"Well . . . let me think about it. We really haven't made up our minds about changing. We're still just looking."

"I can understand your hesitation. The subscription rate for your staff of 500 would be $9,000 less 10 percent, or $8,100. This could be made in quarterly payments. Would that arrangement be attractive to you?"

"Well, that's interesting, but I believe we'll wait. I've got another appointment in a few minutes. Thanks for coming by."

Use Exhibits 4.1 and 4.2 to determine what went wrong and why. If you were the sales manager observing this selling process what coaching would you give?

CASE 4.2:
Analyzing the Selling Process:
Selling a Purchasing Agent

"Mr. Franklin, your company has established a well-earned reputation for high-quality products that provide predictable and dependable results. As a result, your salespeople have had to continually prove the value of your products against cheaper competitive products by showing the benefits when compared with the higher price you charge. Wouldn't you agree with that analysis?"

"I sure would. I hear our Sales Manager discussing this with our salespeople all the time, and constantly hammering home the benefits our products bring to the user in comparison to cheaper competitors."

"That's my point, Mr. Franklin. Quality costs more but it pays off. We feel the same way about the products we've sold you. Admittedly they cost more than the line you are now considering, but the dependability of performance is certainly worth something in comparing our prices with our competition."

"Well, I understand that, Joe, but headquarters says I have to make some savings in my purchases and this is the largest expenditure we'll make this year. As you know, this recession has hit everybody and we have to make some cuts."

"OK, that's a fact I can't refute, but the service we've given you over the past three years has provided longer wear, fewer replacements, and less down time on your production line."

"I'm not so sure I can agree with you on that, Joe. How can you measure what didn't happen? That's only a lot of sales claims and you know it."

"Come on, Mr. Franklin, you know we've worked closely with your production people, and had our engineers in here on emergency calls at night and on weekends to help get some important orders out on schedule. Are you saying that that didn't save your company some penalties they would have had to pay if you hadn't met your contract dates?"

"No, I'm not saying that, Joe, and I don't want you twisting what I'm saying, but anyway, that's Production's problem. I'm in charge of Purchasing and I've been told to trim my purchases by 10 percent. Since you can't give me a lower price, I've decided to go with your competitor. Their specifications seem OK to me. If their products and service don't live up to their claims, we'll find out soon enough, and you'll have another crack at it the next time."

Use Exhibits 4.1 and 4.2 to determine what went wrong and why. If you were the sales manager observing this selling process what coaching would you give?

CASE 4.3:
The Selling Process

To help students practice analysis, decision making, and communication skills of selling, the class should be divided into teams with three persons in each team. Each person will play the role of the salesperson, the prospect, and the field sales manager who is observing and coaching.

The Selling Process, Part A
Linda (or Larry) Walter, The New Office Equipment Representative

In May 1980, Linda Walter was completing her second month as a new sales representative for the Edwards Office Equipment Company. Edwards grossed about $3.1 million per year, selling office furniture, adding machines, office supplies, typewriters, and small hand-held calculators. Most of their customers were small businesses and professionals such as lawyers and doctors. Some of their biggest customers were insurance agencies, real estate brokers, and banks.

Linda had become fascinated by the new hand-held calculator that had been designed for business use, was small enough to fit in a shirt pocket, and sold for less than $40. She had taken one of these machines home along with the instruction manual and played with it several evenings, much to her fascination. It seemed perfect for the businessperson because it would do all the functions that were needed for business analysis. It would perform the standard arithmetic functions of addition, subtraction, multiplication, and division, but it did much more than these basic functions. In one of its three calculating modes it could compute the cost, selling price, and margins that are calculated by retailers. The financial mode would calculate compound interest, annuities, amortization, bonds, and mortgage payments. With this calculator it would not be necessary for a loan officer or a real estate agent to carry a book that gives mortgage rates. A loan officer could quickly calculate different payments for varying interest rates and terms of a mortgage. Linda worked through the many examples in the instruction book that accompanied the calculator. She was amazed at how clearly the book explained financial calculations. It was practically a mini-financial course.

The third mode of the calculator was a statistical one. This mode permitted the calculation of the mean averages, standard deviation, linear regression, and trend-line analysis. Following the simple examples in the manual, a businessperson could easily analyze and project sales.

Reflecting on the various prospects in her territory, Linda decided that bank loan departments would be the place to begin to try to sell those units. She decided to start with the Metropolitan Bank and Trust Company, a medium-sized bank in her territory. This bank had four retail loan officers who arranged loans for the public to purchase large items such as homes, automobiles, and boats. Metropolitan had seven commercial loan officers who arranged loans for business expansions, inventories, purchase of new equipment, etc., for the business community. Mr. Charles Monet was the Vice President in charge of the Commercial Loan Department. The bank had recently purchased office furniture for a branch from Edwards.

The economic outlook for the summer was not good. The prime lending rate for favored customers had been 18 percent and inflation was approaching 20 percent. The money market funds had siphoned funds out of savings accounts, thereby reducing the funds that were available for loans. There were indications that there would be a recession during the summer. The economic issues were clouded by the politics of a presidential election year. The Metropolitan Bank had recently introduced a new promotional campaign to commercial accounts titled "Creative Banking," in which it claimed it took its customers' needs to heart.

Linda began to map out her strategy for selling some of these calculators to Monet.

The Buying Process, Part B
**Charles (Or Claudette) Monet, Vice President,
Metropolitan Bank and Trust Company**

Charles Monet, Vice President of the Commercial Loan Department, had been in banking for twelve years, but he had not seen anything like this year. The prime lending rate for favored business customers was 18 percent, the inflation rate was approaching 20 percent, and the sales of some loan customers, such as automobile dealers, had dropped 25 percent. This was really a period for creative banking and identifying new market opportunities. A major dimension of the present job was keeping old customers happy when there was no money to lend. Mr. Monet reasoned that if there was a recession the situation could reverse quickly—the demand for commercial loans could drop quickly and the supply of money for lending could increase.

"Creative Banking" had become the theme of Metropolitan's Commercial Department during these difficult times. Commercial loan officers became more involved in the daily businesses of old customers and new prospects. They helped them with their financial decisions and showed them ways to make their investments work harder by such techniques as faster turnovers, taking discounts on invoices, etc. Thus these loan officers were engaging in the consultative selling of the bank's services.

During a recent board meeting, Mr. Monet had explained the strategies of creative banking and consultative selling. Other bank officials explained some of their strategies for solving their problems. For example, there was a promotional drive to increase the dollar deposit so there would be money to lend. Some of the strategies included certificates of deposit for the larger customers and premiums for the smaller customer.

One morning shortly after the bank opened, Mr. Monet received a call from Linda Walter, a sales representative of the Edwards Office Equipment Company, asking for an opportunity to present some ideas of how a new calculator might be helpful in Mr. Monet's daily operations. The Metropolitan Bank had bought some office equipment from Edwards when the bank opened a new branch office, so Mr. Monet decided to grant this representative an interview.

CASE QUESTIONS

1. How should Linda go about making an appointment with Monet?

2. What must she do to prepare for this interview?

3. Assume you are Linda. How would you proceed when you walk into Monet's office?

4. If you were Charles Monet, what would be some of the problems that were on the top of your mind?

5. What benefits would you be looking for in a hand-held calculator?

6. How many of these calculators would you buy and how would you distribute them?

7. Could these calculators be a useful part of programs for creative banking and consultative selling?

REFERENCES

1. A. H. Maslow, *Motivation and Personality* (New York: Harper & Row, 1954).
2. Marvin A. Jolson, "The Underestimated Potential of the Canned Sales Presentation," *Journal of Marketing* (January 1975): 75–78.
3. Mack Hanan, James Cribbin, and Jack Donis, *Systems Selling Strategies* (New York: American Management Association, 1978).
4. Ibid., p. 50.
5. Ibid., pp. 59–64.
6. Ibid., p. 50.
7. C. L. Karrass, *Give and Take: The Complete Guide to Negotiating Strategies and Tactics* (New York: Crowell, 1974).
8. Hannan, Cribbin, and Donis, *Systems Selling,* Chapter 8.
9. Ibid., pp. 69–77.
10. Edward K. Strong, "Theories in Selling," *Journal of Applied Psychology* 9 (March 1925): 75–86.

11. R. F. Gwinner, "Base Theory in the Formulation of Sales Strategy," *MSU Business Topics* 16 (Autumn 1968): 37–44.

12. G. David Hughes, "A New Tool for Sales Managers," *Journal of Marketing Research* 1 (May 1964): 32–38.

13. Noel Capon, Morris B. Holbrook, and James M. Hulbert, "Selling Processes and Buyer Behavior: Theoretical Implications of Recent Research," in *Consumer and Industrial Buying Behavior,* ed. A. C. Woodside, J. N. Sheth, and P. D. Bennett (New York: North-Holland, 1977), pp. 323–332, 327.

14. B. A. Weitz, "A Critical Review of Personal Selling Research: The Need for Contingency Approaches," in *Critical Issues in Sales Management: State-of-the-Art and Future Research Needs,* ed. G. Albaum and G. A. Churchill, Jr. (Eugene, Oregon: Division of Research, College of Business Administration, University of Oregon, 1979), pp. 76–120, 83.

15. B. A. Weitz and Peter Wright, "The Salesperson as a Marketing Strategist: The Relationship between Field Sales Performance and Insight about One's Customers," (Cambridge, Mass.: Marketing Science Institute, Report No. 78–120, December, 1978), p. 4.

16. F. B. Evans, "Selling as a Dyadic Relationship—A New Approach," *American Behavioral Scientist* 6 (May 1963): 76–79.

17. Capon, Holbrook, and Morris, *Consumer and Industrial Buying,* p. 325.

18. Weitz, "A Critical Review of Personal Selling Research," p. 102.

19. J. U. Farley and R. L. Swinth, "Effects of Choice and Sales Message on Customer Salesman Interaction," *Journal of Applied Psychology* 52 (April 1967): 107–110.

20. Arch G. Woodside and William J. Davenport, "The Effect of Salesman Similarity and Expertise on Consumer Processing Behavior," *Journal of Marketing Research* 11 (May 1974): 198–202.

21. R. L. Spiro and W. D. Perreault, "Influence Strategy Mixes and Situational Determinants," *Journal of Business* 52 (July 1978): 435–455.

22. R. E. Speckman, "Organizational Boundary Behavior: A Conceptual Framework for Investigating the Industrial Salesperson," in *Sales Management: New Developments from Behavioral and Decision Model Research,* ed. R. P. Bagozzi (Cambridge, Mass.: Marketing Science Institute, 1978), pp. 133–144.

23. Noel Capon, "Towards a Theory of Personal Selling Process," in *Sales Management: New Developments from Behavioral and Decision Model Research,* ed. R. P. Baggozi (Cambridge, Mass.: Marketing Science Institute, 1978), pp. 243–262.

24. Weitz, "A Critical Review of Personal Selling Research," pp. 103–120.

25. P. J. Robinson, C. W. Faris, and Y. Wind, *Industrial Buying and Creative Marketing* (Boston: Allyn and Bacon, 1967).

26. J. M. Sheth, "A Model of Industrial Buyer Behavior," *Journal of Marketing* (October 1973): pp. 50–56.

27. F. E. Webster, Jr. and Y. Wind, "A General Model for Understanding Organizational Buying Behavior," *Journal of Marketing* 36 (April 1972): 12–19.

28. David T. Wilson, "Dyadic Interactions," in *Consumer and Industrial Buying Behavior,* ed. A. C. Woodside, J. N. Sheth, and P. D. Bennett (New York: North-Holland, 1977), pp. 355–365.

29. Paul Busch, R. F. Bush, and J. F. Hair, Jr., "Social Power Theory in Buyer Behavior," in *Consumer and Industrial Buying Behavior,* ed. A. C. Woodside, J. N. Sheth, and P. D. Bennett (New York: North-Holland, 1977), pp. 333–343.

30. T. V. Bonoma, G. Zaltman, and W. J. Johnston, *Industrial Buying Behavior* (Cambridge, Mass.: Marketing Science Institute, Report No. 77-117, 1977).

31. G. D. Hughes, and P. Naert, "A Computer-Controlled Experiment in Consumer Behavior," *Journal of Business* 43 (July 1970): 354–372; G. D. Hughes, P. Naert, and S. Tinic, "Analyzing Consumer Information Processing," *Proceedings,* American Marketing Association (August 1969): 235–240; G. D. Hughes and J. Guerrero, "Testing Cognitive Models Through Computer-Controlled Experiments," *Journal of Marketing Research* 8 (August 1971): 291–297.

32. D. L. Harnett, L. L. Cummings, and G. D. Hughes, "The Influence of Risk-Taking Propensity on Bargaining Behavior," *Behavioral Science* 13 (March 1968): 91–101; G. D. Hughes, J. B. Juhasz, and B. Contini, "The Influence of Personality on the Bargaining Process," *Journal of Business* 46 (October 1973): 593–604.

33. Wroe Alderson, *Marketing Behavior and Executive Action* (Homewood, Ill.: Richard D. Irwin, Inc., 1957), chapter 10.

SUGGESTED READINGS

Bagozzi, Richard P., "The Nature and Causes of Self-Esteem, Performance, and Satisfaction in the Sales Force: A Structural Equation Approach," *Journal of Business,* 53, no. 3 (1980): 315–331, pt. 1.

Bagozzi, Richard P., "Salesperson Performance and Satisfaction as a Function of Individual Difference, Interpersonal, and Situational Factors," *Journal of Marketing Research,* 15 (November 1978): 517–531.

Corey, E. Raymond, "The Organizational Context of Industrial Buying Behavior," Preliminary Research Report (Cambridge, Mass.: Marketing Science Institute, Report No. 78-106, August, 1978).

Falvey, Jack, "Basic System One," *Training and Development Journal* (November 1979).

Moriarty, R. T., and Galper, M., "Organizational Buying Behavior: A State-of-the-Art Review and Conceptualization," Preliminary Research Report (Cambridge, Mass.: Marketing Science Institute, Report No. 78-101, March, 1978).

Pasold, Peter W., "The Effectiveness of Various Modes of Sales Behavior in Different Markets," *Journal of Marketing Research* 12 (May 1975): 171–176.

The Research Institute of America, Inc., "Persuading a Group to Buy" (New York: The Research Institute of America, Inc., Special Analysis, 1981).

Shapiro, B. P., and Posner, R. S., "Making the Major Sale," *Harvard Business Review* 54 (March–April 1976): 68–78.

Weitz, Barton A., "Relationship between Salesperson Performance and Understanding of Customer Decision Making," *Journal of Marketing Research* 15 (November 1978): 501–516.

Young, A. M., "The Principles of Salesmanship." *The New Handbook of Sales Training,* ed. Robert F. Vizza (Englewood Cliffs, N.J.: Prentice-Hall, Inc., 1967), pp. 134–161.

5

MANAGING
THE TERRITORY
LIKE A BUSINESS

In this chapter we will see how the modern sales representative manages the territory like a business. Management concepts, such as the statement of goals and objectives, resource allocation, financial analysis, return-on-assets managed, and investment portfolios, can be applied to a sales territory in the same manner that they can be applied to the total business. We will see how the modern representative uses these concepts and, in the process, prepares himself or herself for management.

TERRITORY OBJECTIVES

To establish territory objectives, the representative must have a clear understanding of the company objectives, as well as his or her personal objectives. First, we must acknowledge that there is considerable confusion about the terms *goals* and *objectives.* In most companies these terms are used interchangeably. Where there is a distinction, *goal* will mean the broader, almost philosophical, results that an organization or an individual seeks. For example, the goal of an athletic program at a university may be to develop character. The goal of a pharmaceutical company may be to reduce suffering and pain in human beings. In contrast, *objectives* are more precise with regard to time, magnitude, and our ability to measure results. For example, the objective of the athletic program may be to win the football game this weekend. The objective of a pharmaceutical company may be to increase sales of a new product by 10 percent this year. These objectives are expressed in precise terms because they identify a time period for accomplishment and a magnitude. While some organizations find this distinction useful, it creates so much confusion that we will follow the trend of using objectives and goals interchangeably.

PERSONAL OBJECTIVES[1]

Development of territory goals and objectives must begin with an understanding of one's personal objectives. The representative must ask himself or herself a series of very personal and penetrating questions. What do I want out of life? What do I want to be five or ten years from now? What do I want out of my job? Will this job enable me to achieve these personal objectives in five years? What are my personal goals for this year, this month, and this week? Are they consistent with my long-term personal objectives? How will I know when I have achieved these objectives? Are these objectives realistic in the light of my personal strengths and weaknesses? Should I be seeking higher goals and objectives, given my personal resources? Having answered these questions, the representative may turn to a fuller understanding of the objectives of the company.

COMPANY OBJECTIVES

What are the objectives of the company? Is it an old company that is concerned primarily with survival, a mature company that focuses on profits, or a young company that is striving for growth? What are the organizational, product, and financial strengths and weaknesses of the company? Similarly, what are the strengths and weaknesses of my territory? Are the company objectives realistic for my territory, given these strengths and weaknesses? How will changes in competition, the economy, government regulations, and research and development affect these objectives and available resources?

Most of these questions will be answered for the representative in the action plan objectives that are part of the company's annual selling plan and the representative's assigned sales quota, or they can be a subject for discussion with the field sales manager.

ACTION PLAN OBJECTIVES

At this point the representative must ask the question, "How are these corporate objectives translated into the company's expectations of me?" Are the company objectives and my personal objectives consistent? Does the company expect me to travel more days per week than I care to be away from my family? Are the rewards consistent with my personal needs? If the corporate and personal objectives are inconsistent, the representative can never develop an effective territory action plan and may as well turn to other career opportunities.

In this chapter we will see that territory objectives may be expressed in financial terms such as sales, contribution to profit, and return-on-assets managed (ROAM). Nonfinancial selling activity objectives may be expressed in terms of the number of new prospects that are generated, the number of calls made per day, or improvement in the rate of closing prospects. The achievement of these objectives is subject to the limitation of available resources.

RESOURCE ALLOCATION

A representative will have available to him or her a variety of intangible and tangible resources. The intangible resources include the strengths of the organization, its goodwill, its prior reputation, and its technical support persons who can be used by the representative to aid in making a sale. Time—the most important intangible resource of the representative—is an unusual resource in that it becomes available constantly and evenly; it cannot be used in advance; it cannot be stored. The difference between a successful and an unsuccessful representative is in the effective use of time. The representative's time enters the company's income statement in terms of a salary, fringe benefits, and a commission or bonus. Because time is the representative's major resource, much of the discussion in this chapter will focus on time management.

To use time effectively, the representative must analyze the potential of accounts, establish an objective for each active account, design a selling strategy to achieve the objective, and estimate the time that will be required to implement that strategy. Having developed this plan, the next step is to schedule the activities for all accounts in the most efficient sequence possible.

The more tangible territory resources include travel expenses, entertainment expenses, promotional materials, and cooperative advertising. Each territory will also represent an investment in accounts receivable, inventory, automobiles, office and representatives' equipment, display racks, and demonstration products. These investments constitute the base for calculating the territory return-on-assets managed.

These resources are allocated by the representative to accounts and products. As we will see shortly, not all resources-account-product matches are profitable. When a resources-account-product match is not profitable, the representative must seek ways to make it profitable or reallocate resources to another combination.

ALLOCATING CALLS TO REGULAR CUSTOMERS

Planning the territory begins with analyzing the assigned geographic territory and ranking the accounts according to their potential. This ranking will include those accounts that are present customers, which we will call *clients,* and those that are not customers, which we will call *prospects.* A ranking of clients and prospects will identify quickly those cases where we should shift our resources from poor clients to good prospects.

We will examine first those cases where representatives make regular calls on clients. Examples of this type of selling include representatives for clothing manufacturers calling on department stores, hardware distributors calling on hardware stores, stationery supply representatives calling on office managers, and pharmaceutical representatives calling on physicians, drugstores, and hospitals.

THE ABC RULE OF ACCOUNT CLASSIFICATION

Many companies have examined the proportion of customers that provides the largest share of their sales or profits. The patterns are so strikingly similar across companies that they have become known as the "ABC Rule of Account Classification." This rule states that the first 15 percent of your clients will produce 65 percent of your sales, the next 20 percent yield 20 percent of the sales, and the last 65 percent will produce only 15 percent of the sales. These three types of accounts are known as A Accounts, B Accounts, and C Accounts. This account classification is illustrated in Exhibit 5.1. The importance of this classification to territory management has been examined by many authors.[2] In the example in Exhibit 5.1 we see that 130 of the accounts produced only 15 percent of the sales. We need to rethink the allocation of calls to these C accounts.

Exhibit 5.1   ABC Account Classification

CLASSI-FICATION	NO. OF ACCTS. (1)	% OF TOTAL ACCTS. (2)	SALES ($000) (3)	% OF TOTAL SALES (4)	IF EQUAL CALLS PER CUSTOMER:	
					TOTAL CALLS PER CLASSIF (5)	SALES ($) PER CALL (6) (3/5)
A	30	15%	$1,300	65%	150	$8,667
B	40	20	400	20	200	2,000
C	130	65	300	15	650	462
TOTALS	200	100%	$2,000	100%	1,000	$2,000

THE MARGINAL APPROACH TO CALL ALLOCATION

If it were possible to apply economic theory to territory management, each representative would call on an account until the marginal costs of calling on that account equaled the marginal profit of that last call. Unfortunately, cost accounting techniques do not permit this concept to apply to territory management; however, the principle is a sound one and the representative is expected to apply this principle judgmentally. The economic principle is a reminder that one should not move to the next lower-ranked account until the potential of the present account has been fully exploited. This economic concept would be violated when a representative called on all accounts an equal number of times.

THE ERROR OF EQUAL CALLS PER ACCOUNT

Columns 5 and 6 of Exhibit 5.1 illustrate the error of calling on all accounts an equal number of times instead of calling on them according to their potential. Column 5 shows that if each account receives five calls per year, the A accounts will receive a total of 150 calls; the B accounts will receive a total of 200 calls; and the C accounts will receive 650 calls. Dividing these total numbers of calls into the total sales for each classification (column 3), one arrives at the sales per call for each classification. Column 6 shows that a call on an A account will generate $8,667, while a call on a C account will generate only $462. Clearly the representative would want to reallocate calls from the C accounts to the A accounts in order to generate more sales for the limited number of calls that are available.

THE UPPER AND LOWER LIMITS OF REALLOCATION

Sales calls cannot be added to an A account indefinitely. At some point there are diminishing returns. The hypothetical example in Exhibit 5.2 illustrates that the second call will produce $35,000 in sales, while the seventh call yields only $2,000. There may be many reasons for this upper limit. Beyond a certain point the calls become social calls, and little selling takes place. Perhaps the customer has a limit on the share of business that will be given to any one supplier, to assure a constant supply during periods of shortages. Additional calls would therefore be wasted.

There is also a lower limit to call frequency. In many industries the supplier must make a minimum number of calls in order to overcome competition and to assure the buyer that the business is important to the supplier.

Exhibit 5.2   Diminishing Returns of Calls

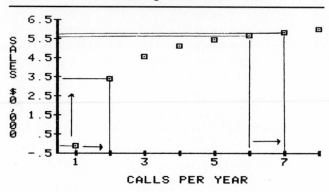

Note: These data are hypothetical. In practice the sales representatives would estimate the returns per call or they would be estimated using statistical techniques.

If the representative and his or her sales manager were to develop
this call-response curve for all of the accounts, they would be well on
the way to applying the marginal approach to allocating sales calls. A
microcomputer could make this task an easy one. The representative
could estimate sales at selected call frequencies. The computer would fit
a curve that could be used for allocating sales calls.

COMPUTER ALLOCATION MODELS

The allocation of calls to accounts using response curves such as the one
shown in Exhibit 5.2 would become very complicated as the number of
accounts increased and other realities of territory management were introduced. These realities include the fact that accounts buy different
mixes of products. There are differences in travel time among accounts.
The response functions differ according to various industry classification segments of accounts. The number of calls available may be expanded by the use of better time management. Operations researchers
have applied the power of the computer to the problem of call allocation.

Lodish developed a model called CALLPLAN that produces an account call frequency schedule that maximizes anticipated profit, given
limited time available to make calls. The input to the model is the representatives' estimate of the sales responses that would follow from various call frequencies, travel time, time per call, and account profitability.

An adjustment factor is used to represent the contribution of various product mixes or to establish priorities for account types. Fudge and Lodish tested CALLPLAN using twenty representatives for United Airlines.[3] The ten representatives who used the CALLPLAN model had 8.1 percent more sales at the end of the test period than the ten representatives in the control group who did not use the model. In a later model, Lodish[4] introduced the effect of the product mix on sales. This model will also estimate the optimal size of the sales force.

Zoltners, Sinha, and Chong note that the incremental analysis algorithm in CALLPLAN can significantly overallocate sales representatives' time. Incremental techniques can also be expensive with regard to computer time. These authors suggest an integer programming approach that uses response functions that are approximated by concave piecewise linear functions.[5] Zoltners and Sinha suggest a general integer programming model for sales resource allocation that incorporates multiple sales resources, multiple time periods and carry-over effects, nonseparability, and risks. While this more complex model would generally not be used by the sales representative, it would be appropriate to the broader task faced by the division or corporate sales manager who must allocate sales resources geographically, among products and between clients and prospects, to market segments and to channels of distribution.[6] This article also provides an excellent review of the literature on sales resource allocation modeling.

STRATEGIES TO INCREASE ACCOUNT POTENTIAL

To develop selling strategies, it is necessary to understand the components of account potential and how they may be modified in favor of the representative. First we need to estimate these components for each account and then develop selling strategies that will increase these components, thereby increasing the expected sales potential of each account.

The Components of Sales Potential

Exhibit 5.3 summarizes the components of the sales potential for each account, as well as the total territory. The analysis begins with the account's total requirements for the last period and the estimate of the growth for the next period. This growth rate estimate may come from a variety of sources, such as the client, industry studies, the representative's judgment, and the company's economics department. This growth rate may be linear or nonlinear. The rates in Exhibit 5.3 are linear. These

Exhibit 5.3   Sales Forecast

| | FOR   [1]PERIOD(S) | | | |
| | A C C O U N T S | | | |
	CENTRAL	WESTERN	NORTHERN	OTHER	TOTALS
TOTAL REQUIREMENTS LAST PER	[500]	[1250]	[713]	[6245]	8708
ESTIMATED GROWTH/PERIOD	[1.2]	[1.05]	[.95]	[1.00]	1.01
FORECASTED TOTAL REQUIRMT.	600	1312	677	6245	8835
OUR SALES LAST PERIOD	[200]	[125]	[214]	[1249]	1788
OUR SHARE POINTS LAST PERD.	40.00	10.00	30.01	20.00	20.24
FORECASTS					
SHARE POINTS	[47.50]	[20.00]	[30.00]	[20.00]	22.63
SALES ($000)	285	262	203	1249	2000
CALLS/PERIOD	[11]	[10]	[20]	[839]	880
SALES/CALL ($000)	25.91	26.25	10.16	1.49	2.27

Figures in brackets [ ] are entered by the planner. The computer enters all other data.

This table was printed on an Epson MX 100 printer using an Apple II Plus computer and VisiCalc, by Visi Corp.

calculations could be made by hand, but in this table (and in subsequent tables) they were made on an Apple II[tm] microcomputer using VisiCalc[tm], which is a planning software package.

Having projected the client's requirements for the next period, the representative will estimate his or her market share for the next period. This estimate will be based on the share for this period, which the computer can compute once the sales for the last period are entered. The share for the next period will be based on the representative's evaluation of competitive pressures, the company's selling plan for the next period, and his or her selling strategy. This strategy will determine the number of calls per client. The salespersons or the microcomputer will forecast the sales potential per account and per call. At this point the representative or the computer could classify accounts by total sales per account and sales per call. If the representative has a microcomputer, the ABC account classification could be done automatically.

The computerized model in Exhibit 5.3 could be used to project sales. By changing the number of periods at the top of the table, the computer will compute the total requirements, the company sales, and the sales per call. The computer will then transfer these projections to later models, shown here as Exhibits 5.5, 5.6, 5.9, 5.10, 5.11, 5.13, 5.15, and 5.16.

The representative can use the forecasting model to ask "what if" questions regarding key elements in the projection. For example, he or she may want to test various levels of market share for the Western Tool account to estimate the effect of a new strategy to convince this account that if it were to increase its purchases there could be financial advantages, such as a discount or a savings in freight costs. By changing the estimated share of Western's purchases, the representative can estimate the effect on sales, contribution, and return-on-assets managed.

Translating the Strategy into a Plan

The salesperson will want to translate the preceding strategy into account selling plans. An account card, such as those shown in Exhibit 5.4, will help in the development of an account selling plan. This card can be part of the territory records that the present and future representatives use for account development.

The data across the top of Exhibit 5.4 comes from Exhibit 5.3. In fact, if the salesperson has access to a microcomputer, the accounts could be ranked by the computer and the computer could print these account records.

How should the accounts be ranked? In Exhibit 5.4 they have been ranked by sales potential, with Central Manufacturing number one. If they were ranked according to potential per call, then Western Tool would be number one and Northern Engineering would be a distant third. We will see that these rankings will change again as we examine gross and net contributions per account. This switching of ranks emphasizes the importance of defining the objectives for the sales force. Should it be sales, contribution, sales per call, or contribution per call? The marginal approach noted earlier in this chapter suggests that the best objective is contribution per call.

When the account cards are arrayed in descending order of expected potential for the year, the representative may begin to develop a strategic plan for the territory. First he or she may want to know if the available number of calls will produce the expected potential that is required to meet the sales quota. To accomplish this, it is simply necessary to add the number of calls for each account until the total number of available calls is reached, say 1,000 calls per year. The next step is to add all of the expected potentials between the first account and this cut-off account to determine if the expected potential will give the sales quota that has been established for this territory. Later in this chapter we will see that it is

Exhibit 5.4   Account Records for Territory Management

Class	Acct. Name	Buying Req. Last Year ($000)	Growth Rate	Buying Req. This Year ($000)	Percent Share Last Year	Planned Share	Exp. Potential This Year ($000)	Rank	Calls This Year
A	Northern Engineering	$713	0.95	$677	30	30	$203	3	20
A	Western Tool	$1,250	1.05	$1,312	10	20	$262	2	10
A	Central Mfg.	$500	1.20	$600	40	47.5	$285	1	11

Address:

Their Products:

Their Competitors:

Buying Influences (Name, Title):
1.
2.
3.
4.

Benefits Emphasized Previously:

Our Products:

Our Competitors:

Our Strengths:

Our Weaknesses:

Strategies to Increase Share
→ Quantity Discount
→ Promotional Support
→ Lower Delivery Costs
→ More Technical Support
→ Custom Design
→ Product Benefits_____
→ Service Benefits_____
→ Price/Value Benefits____
→ Other_____

Strategies to Increase Buying Requirements
→ More Intensive Use of Product_____
→ Sales to Other Depts._____
→ New Uses for Products_____
→ New Products_____
→ Other_____

Factors That Influence Account's Growth Rate
→ Population Size and Age Distribution_____
→ Economic Factors 1._____
                   2._____
→ Competition_____
→ Govt._____
→ Other_____

possible to make additional refinements in this account record by noting figures such as net contribution and the return-on-assets managed of each account.

The lower section of each account card enables the representative to develop a *selling strategy*. The left-hand side of the card records information such as the address of the client, their products, their competitors, and the persons who have a buying influence in this purchase. It also provides space for summarizing benefits that were emphasized during a previous call, products that had been recommended, competitors with regard to these products, and a summary of strengths and weaknesses. The lower section of the card considers the factors that influence an account's growth rate and therefore their need for the organization's products. Factors such as population size and age distribution, economic factors, competition, and government regulations will give the representative insight into the dynamics of the account's business.

The right-hand section of this card provides space for developing a selling strategy for this account. Strategies to increase buying requirements include more intensive use of the company's products, sales to other departments, new uses for the products, and new products. Buyers may be encouraged to give the company a larger share of their business by using strategies such as quantity discounts, promotional support, lower delivery cost, more technical support, and custom design to meet their specifications. Representatives may improve the probability of the sale to a client with better statements of benefits regarding product, service, and value, as well as using effective promotional tools. After developing these strategies, the representative will want to reconsider the estimated calls that are required this year.

STRATEGIES TO INCREASE AVAILABLE SELLING TIME

After the representative has analyzed the expected potential of each account and the number of calls that are required, he or she will probably be motivated to find means for increasing the selling time that can be used to call on accounts. This section will consider some of the alternative strategies that can be used by a representative to make more selling time available.

Time Management

The activities of a representative are classified in Exhibit 5.5 into five time classifications—management, overhead, preparatory, productive, and personal. Management time includes those activities of planning, organizing, and evaluating previous selling efforts. Overhead time includes travel, waiting to be seen by a buyer, servicing, and administrative activities such as completing orders, filing reports, and investigating credit levels. (Some representatives use unproductive waiting time to do administrative chores or to plan for future calls.) Preparatory time

Exhibit 5.5   Daily Time Management and Plan

FOR   1 PERIOD(S)

ACTIVITY	PRESENT PERIOD MINUTES	PRESENT PERIOD PERCENT	NEXT PERIOD PLAN A PERCENT	NEXT PERIOD PLAN A MINUTES	NEXT PERIOD PLAN A %CHANGE	NEXT PERIOD PLAN B PERCENT	NEXT PERIOD PLAN B MINUTES	NEXT PERIOD PLAN B %CHANGE
AVERAGE DAY	[420]	100	100	[480]		100	420	
MANAGEMENT ACTIVITIES	[35]	8	8	40		8	35	
(PLAN,ORANIZE,EVALUATE)								
OVERHEAD:								
TRAVEL	[90]	21	21	103		[19]	80	
WAITING	[40]	10	10	46		[9]	38	
SERVICE	[15]	4	4	17		4	15	
ADMINIST	[20]	5	5	23		5	20	
PREPARATIION:								
LEARNING	[20]	5	5	23		5	20	
PROPOSAL	[45]	11	11	51		[9]	38	
PERSONAL TIME	[45]	11	11	51		[9]	38	
PRODUCTIVE TIME:								
PROSPECTING	[25]	6	6	29		6	25	
SELLING TIME(COMPUTED)	85	20	20	97		27	112	
AVERAGE CALL LENGTH	[25]			25			25	
COMPUTED CALLS/DAY	3.40			3.89			4.47	
SELLING DAYS	[220]			220			220	
TOTAL CALLS/YEAR	748			855			984	
SALES ($ 000)	2000			2000			2000	
NET TERR. CONTRIB.	218			218			218	
$SALES/CALL ($000)	2.67			2.67			2.67	
CONTRIB/ CALL($000)	0.29			0.29			0.29	
SALES PROJECTED				2285	14.29		2630	31.53
CONTRIBUTION PROJECTED				249	14.29		286	31.53
QUOTA ($000)				2400			2400	
PROJECTED PERCENT OF QUOTA				95			110	

Note: Minutes for present period are from a sample of call reports.
The planner changes the figures in columns A and B to test the effect of various objectives for more effective use of time.

would include the activities of learning about products, prospects, and industry changes. It also includes preparing to make presentations. Productive time includes selling and prospecting. Personal time would include lunch, personal errands, etc. When representatives conduct analyses of their activities, they will want to sample at least ten days selected from various parts of their territory. They will probably be surprised at the small percentage of time that is actually spent face-to-face with clients and prospects.

This activity analysis will help to identify why time is lost. Was it because of disorganization, diversion to unproductive activities, excessive involvement beyond levels that were necessary, paper work, a lack of motivation, or by not budgeting enough time to do the task properly the first time?

The right-hand columns in Exhibit 5.5 illustrate how a computer can help a salesperson become a better manager of time. Plan A tests the effects of increasing the workday by 60 minutes, from 420 to 480 minutes. Plan B tests the effect of reducing travel, waiting, proposal and personal time, and using this saved time to make additional calls. The computer estimates the increase in calls per day and per year, the projected sales, and the percent of quota. In the example Plan B, working smarter rather than longer is the better plan.

Costs per Call

By computing the costs per call, a representative moves closer to the economic theory of adding a dollar of effort to an account until it fails to produce a dollar of profit—the marginal concept. The procedure for computing the average cost per call is summarized in Exhibit 5.6 for a hypothetical young representative of an industrial products company.

In this exhibit we see that the compensation consists of salary, commissions or bonuses, and fringe benefits. Expenses include transportation, lodgings and meals, entertainment, telephone, samples, promotional literature, and miscellaneous items. The total selling expenses are $46,300. The maximum number of days for calling are 220. If the representative makes an average of 4 calls a day, this would mean that there were only 880 calls to be allocated for the entire year. Using these estimates, the representative can now compute the cost of an average day as $210.45 and the cost of an average call as $52.61.

The number of calls that can be made per day and the cost of a call will vary according to the industry, the concentration of accounts in a territory, and companies. *Sales & Marketing Management* magazine estimates that salespersons in a metropolitan territory make the following number of calls per day: account representative, 5; detail salesperson, 8; sales engineer, 5.5; industrial products salesperson, 7; and a service salesperson, 9. Representatives in rural territories make only about half of these numbers in a day. Returning to Exhibit 5.6, we see that our young representative is about average if the territory is a rural one, but if it is a metropolitan territory there is a definite need to increase the number of calls per day.

Exhibit 5.6   Computing the Cost of a Call for a Young Representative of an Industrial Products Company

COMPENSATION

Salary, commissions, bonuses	$26,000	
Fringe benefits (hospital, retirement, life insurance, social security)	3,900	29,900

EXPENSES

Transportation (20,000 miles × $0.35 per mile for ownership and operating costs)	7,000	
Lodging and meals	4,000	
Entertainment	2,500	
Telephone	1,200	
Samples, promotional literature	1,500	
Miscellaneous	200	16,400
Total Selling Expenses		$46,300

CALLS PER YEAR

Total selling days		
Total days	365	
Less weekends	110	
Days Available for Calling	255	
Less:		
Vacation 10		
Holidays 10		
Sickness 5		
Training 10	35	
Net Days for Calling	220	

AVERAGE CALLS PER DAY	4
TOTAL CALLS PER YEAR (4 × 220) =	880
COST OF AN AVERAGE DAY $46,300/220 = $210.45	
COST OF AN AVERAGE CALL $46,300/880 = $ 52.61	
EXPENSES PER CALL $16,400/880 = $ 18.64	

The average cost of a sales representative's call in a metropolitan territory has been estimated as follows: account representative, $32; detail salesperson, $17; sales engineer, $37; industrial products salesperson, $21; and service salesperson, $17. The McGraw-Hill survey of industrial representatives estimates that the call costs in 1977 were $96.79. Dartnell's survey concludes that consumer-goods industries, which have lower costs per call, experience a cost of $71.90 per call.[7]

If our young representative sells a product mix that averages a 20-percent margin, the break-even sales volume may be computed as follows:

Break-even volume per day = \$210.45/.20 = \$1,052, and
Break-even volume per call = \$52.61/.20 = \$263.

These calculations mean that the representative must sell \$1,052 per day and \$263 per call in order to cover his or her compensation and expenses.

Scheduling Calls

After the representative has developed a selling strategy for each account, it is necessary to schedule the calls on these accounts in the most efficient manner possible. Because scheduling is the allocation of time to activities over space, scheduling must deal with the fact that time is linear and space occurs in two dimensions.

Some representatives develop their routing patterns by plotting the expected potential of an account on a map along with the travel time between accounts. They then route themselves to clusters of accounts using the most efficient travel pattern possible. Some typical routing patterns include the four-leaf clover, the loop, and the figure eight. An experienced representative does this routing intuitively, but an inexperienced representative would be well advised to work out the routing on a map of the territory.

The Burroughs Wellcome Daily Planner. The call schedule is then translated into a daily planning sheet, such as the one used by Burroughs Wellcome Company, which appears in Exhibit 5.7. This sheet requires the representative to schedule two calls per half-hour time period, identify the classification of the customer, state the objectives for the call, identify the competition, and record preplanning remarks to be included in the selling strategy. The objective should be expressed in measurable terms so that the representative can record the degree of accomplishment.

The Xerox Daily Planner. When representatives call on regular customers, it is assumed that these selling calls are of equal length. Such is not the case when representatives are developing new accounts or, as in the case of the word-processing representative, the products are bought infrequently. New account selling requires a more precise daily plan,

Exhibit 5.7   Burroughs Wellcome Co.

TIME	CUSTOMER	TYPE	OBJECTIVES FOR CALL	COMPETITION	PRE-PLANNING REMARKS
8.30					
9:00					
9:30					
10:00					
10:30					
11:00					
11:30					
12:00					
12:30					
1:00					
1:30					
2:00					
2:30					
3:00					
3:30					
4:00					
4:30					
5:00					
5:30					

DATE_____

CITY_____

Burroughs Wellcome Co.

DAILY PLANNING SHEET U.S.A. 1494

Wellcome

*NOTE: List two calls per half-hour time period

Representative

Used by permission of Burroughs Wellcome Company.

such as the one shown in Exhibit 5.8, which is the Xerox daily planner. In this example, the representative for photocopying equipment must indicate whether the step in the sale call is the approach to survey, a demonstration, a proposal, or a close. He or she must also indicate a planned date for recalling on this account in order to move to the next step in the sale. We note also in this form that the type of call must be recorded. The type may range from a new business lease to the supplies order. Thus the Xerox representative engages in the two forms of selling that have been discussed here—calling on regular clients and prospecting for new ones.

When the representative has a selling plan and a call schedule, it is possible to evaluate an emergency to determine if the schedule should be interrupted in order to meet the emergency. Without a clear plan and schedule, a representative may give an emergency a higher priority than it deserves.

Exhibit 5.8 The Xerox Daily Planner

Type Call: **NBL** = **New Business Lease**
NBS = **New Business Sold**
QT = **Quantrum Trade**
STR = **Trial**
OTP = **Option To Purchase**
ST = **Sale Trade**
SUP = **Supplies**

Step of Sale: **A** – **Approach**
S – **Survey**
D – **Demo**
P – **Proposal**
C – **Close**

Day _____   Date ___/___/ **79**

Priority A. B. C	Establishment	U/N	Appt Time	Call Type	Step of Sale	Product Recom.	Results/Remarks/Next Action	Planned Recall Date

Messages/Notes	Must Things for Today	Done (✓)

Mileage _____   Expenses _____   Supplies { Daily Target _____
Sold Today _____

Permission granted by Xerox.

Paperwork Reduction

Sales representatives, by their very nature, do not like paperwork. Many companies will streamline forms, provide dictating machines, use computer cards for call reports, and develop any means possible to reduce the paperwork required of representatives. Xerox Corporation increased representatives' face-to-face selling time from 38 percent to 50 percent by improving the reporting routine. It hopes to increase this time to 55 percent with additional refinements in the system.[8]

Other Selling Methods

Representatives may increase their productivity by using selling methods that do not require them to make a personal call on an account. As the selling costs increase, the following techniques will become more popular.

Mail.   Mail is used by representatives in a variety of ways. It may be used for prospecting, setting up appointments, and introducing new products, thereby greatly saving a representative's time. Mail may also be used as a means for good will or image building. A prospect would be pleased to receive a letter thanking him or her for the interview.

Mail may not be glamorous, but it works, and it has some unique advantages. It can be very selective in targeting prospects. It is not as personal as a sales representative's call, but it is more personal than a magazine advertisement. It is easier to measure the productivity of personal letters than mass media campaigns. Mail can be a low-cost medium. Finally, mail that supports the representative can reduce the number of calls that are necessary and make more productive those calls that are made.[9]

Telephone.[10]   The telephone may also be used as a substitute for a personal call. A toll-free number and a catalogue may encourage customers to call in orders, thereby reducing the number of personal calls. Inside sales representatives may be assigned to an outside sales representative to supplement the calling patterns, especially for remote customers. Customer support representatives may be used in the home office to handle problems that would normally require a personal call.

Representatives' Assistants.   Assistants to senior sales representatives come in a variety of forms. Some companies use junior representatives as a training position. Grocery products companies hire housewives to stock the shelves and put up the promotional displays in their neighborhood chain stores. These assistants free the sales representative to concentrate on selling calls, and the housewives like the job because the flexible hours enable them to be home after school. Some industrial firms, such as printing companies, have customer support persons who handle the needs of clients while the representative is out in the field.

Exhibits. Exhibits are trade shows where vendors have booths to display equipment such as business machines, farm equipment, or boats. Exhibits are used extensively in industrial selling and in the fashion clothing industry. They are an efficient means for prospecting because the accounts come to the company.

Conventions. Conventions differ from exhibits in that an exhibit is the sole event, while a convention will have meetings, papers, seminars, and vendors' booths. For example, textbook publishers have displays at the professional association conventions of professors.

Distributors. Small distant accounts can easily become unprofitable when the cost of selling increases. Many companies turn the smaller accounts over to distributors who have representatives in the area. In such cases, the representative would be calling only on the distributors for these smaller accounts.

Improved Selling Skill

The representative may make more selling time available by improving selling skills. The representative who becomes more efficient in identifying qualified prospects wastes less time with losers. By improving closing rates, he or she can increase sales with the same number of prospects. The representative who increases the average order size makes each call more productive. Hence, personal improvement is an important element in increasing available selling time.

DEVELOPING NEW ACCOUNTS

The dynamics of the marketplace require the representative to prospect continuously for new clients. Old clients die, they move away, their needs change, and their needs may be met by competitors. Furthermore, an increase in quota may require adding new clients. In many cases, the representative must develop new accounts because of the very nature of the product. Durable products such as computers, earth-moving equipment, word-processing equipment, and new office buildings are purchased infrequently so that the representative cannot depend on frequent repeat purchases. In such cases prospecting becomes an important dimension of the selling job. The successful representative is the one who has an active list of good prospects and can qualify them quickly.

There are many sources for identifying prospects. Some of the frequently used ones are: the territory records, company records, trade associations, state directories of companies, local financial institutions, Chambers of Commerce, credit services, trade publications, business libraries, noncompetitive representatives, building permits, company employees, satisfied customers, and the personal observations of the representative. Because the prospect list may be quite extensive, the representative must decide how many prospects to interview in order to meet the territory objective.

STEPS TO CREATE A CLIENT

The sale of durable equipment requires the representative to go through every step in the selling process. It has been estimated that a representative for a word-processing company must spend 12 hours with each prospect as follows: prospect identification, 4; application identification, 1.5; demonstration, 1; current methods studied, 2; systems analysis and proposal, 1.5; and closing presentation, 2. The assistance of a specialist and sales support personnel would add approximately 25 more hours to the selling process.[11] If the representative had a closing rate of .16, or six prospects per customer, the time investment would be 72 hours per successful customer. If we assume that the representative can spend 8 hours a day on selling activities, we may estimate the completed sales per month as approximately 2.5 word-processing machines. If the closing rate could be improved to .25, or four prospects per successful closure, the representative could increase sales to 3.6 machines per month, a 50-percent increase.

A STRATEGY FOR PROSPECTING

The model in Exhibit 5.9 analyzes the present prospecting process and alternative new strategies for prospecting. The salesperson enters the number of accounts, prospects, accounts lost, prospects qualified, needs surveys, demonstrations, proposals, and closes from daily call reports. The computer provides the percent of success at each step. After studying these percents, the representative may evaluate alternative strategies for improving his or her selling process.

Exhibit 5.9 Prospecting Analysis

	PRESENT PERIOD		PLAN A		PLAN B	
	AMOUNT	PERCENT	PERCENT	AMOUNT	PERCENT	AMOUNT
NUMBER OF ACCTS. JAN. 1	[101]			95		95
ACCTS. LOST DURING YEAR	[10]			5		5
ADDITIONS BY PROSPECTING						
PROSPECT LIST	[400]			[600]		400
QUALIFIED	[80]					
%QUALIFIED		20	20	120	[30]	120
NEEDS SURVEY	[50]					
SURVEY/QUALIFIED %		63	63	75	63	75
DEMONSTRATIONS	[25]					
DEMO/SURVEY %		50	50	38	[65]	49
PROPOSALS	[19]					
PROPOSAL/DEMO %		76	76	29	[90]	44
CLOSES	[4]					
CLOSES/PROPOSAL %		21	21	6	[33]	14
NUMBER OF ACCOUNTS DEC. 31	95			96		104
PERCENT CHANGE		-6	1		10	
SALES /ACCOUNT	21.05			21.05		21.05
ACCOUNT CHANGE	-6			1		9
SALES FROM PROSP .($000)				21		200
SALES ($000)	2000			2021		2199
QUOTA ($000)	2100			2400		2400
PERCENT OF QUOTA	95			84		92

EFFECT OF PLANS ON REP.'S COMPENSATION:	BASE	RATE	($000)	BASE	RATE	($000)
SALARY($000)			10.00			10.00
COMMISSION:						
1% FOR $1000-1999	1000	1	10.00	1000	1	10.00
2% FOR $2000 OR +	21	2	0.42	199	2	3.98
$500/NEW PROSPECT	1	0	0.00	9	.5	4.74
TOTAL COMPENSATION($000)			20.42			28.72

COMMISSION RATES

BASE	%RATE	BASE	%RATE
-2000	0	-2000	0
0	1	0	2
999	1	999	2
2500	1	2000	2

NEW ACCTS	BONUS ($000)
-50	0
1	.5
50	.5

Note: Data for the present period come from call reports. Plan A analyzes the effect of generating more prospects. Plan B analyzes the effect of improving selling skills.

Two plans are considered in Exhibit 5.9. Plan A evaluates an increase in prospects from 400 to 600. It assumes that all the success percentages will remain the same. This plan provides a net increase of one prospect. Plan B assumes that the number of prospects will remain at 400, but the salesperson will improve his or her selling skills for qualifying, needs surveys, demonstrations, and closes. Plan B will generate nine new customers.

The lower portion of this model translates the outcomes of these plans into the representative's total compensation. Plan A would generate an income of $20,420, while Plan B would produce $28,720. The compensation plan includes a salary, a 1-percent commission on sales between $1 and $2 million, a 2-percent commission on sales over $2 million, and a bonus for each new customer. This automatic translation of a prospecting plan into compensation should help motivate representatives. A sales manager could also use this model to test the effect of proposed changes in the compensation plan on each representative.

CUSTOMER-PRODUCT MIX ANALYSES

Unless a company sells only one product, or all products in the mix make the same contribution to profit, the profitability of a customer will be determined by the mix of products that it buys. A representative will greatly improve the profitability of the territory by improving the customer-product mix.

DIFFERENCES IN PRODUCT MARGINS AND LOGISTICS COSTS

The margins on products may vary greatly. A new product may have a large margin, but as competition enters, the margin may be reduced to meet price competition. Conversely, learning curves that occur during the production process may reduce costs and increase the margin of a product. Promotional allowances may reduce margins.

The logistics costs that are associated with inventory and transportation functions will vary greatly according to the characteristics of the product. For example, a very valuable product will have a heavy insurance cost, a higher pilferage rate, and higher shipping costs. A large bulky product may be subject to heavy damage and greater storage costs. Perishable products, such as frozen foods, incur such additional costs as cold storage. Some companies will include these costs in the general heading of freight and inventory costs, but a better analysis will result if it is possible to allocate these costs directly to products.

CUSTOMER-PRODUCT MIX CONTRIBUTION

Exhibit 5.10 illustrates how an analysis of the customer-product mix can change the ranking of a customer. The planner enters the margins that are associated with each product and the proportion of each product that is purchased by each customer. The computer carries forward sales forecasts and computes the dollar contribution that each customer product combination makes to the company. The total customer-product contribution and contribution per account are provided by the computer. In this example we see that Northern Engineering makes the largest contribution because it buys those products with the largest margins, but it has the lowest contribution per call. This finding suggests that the representative develop a strategy for lowering the calls to this account and reallocating them to another account, such as Central Manufacturing, which has the fastest growth rate.

The representative or a sales manager may use this model to test the effect of strategies that would alter the mix of products that an account purchased. For instance, a special promotional effort may induce Central Manufacturing to buy more clutches and drums. This shift in mix would greatly improve the contribution of this account, even if it bought the same total dollar volume.

Exhibit 5.10   Contribution from Account-Product Mix

FOR   1 PERIOD(2)

		CENTRAL MANUFACTUR		WESTERN TOOL		NORTHERN ENGINER.		OTHER ACCOUNTS		TOTALS	
SALES FORCST($000)			285		262		203		1249		2000
PRODUCT	PRODUCT MARGIN	PRODUCT MIX	CONTRIB ($000)	PRODUCT MIX	CONTRIB ($000)	PRODUCT MIX	CONTRIB ($000)	PRODUCT MIX	CONTRIB ($000)	PRODUCT MIX	CONTRIB ($000)
AXLES	[.1]	[.5]	14.25	[.3]	7.87	[.1]	2.03	[.3]	37.47	0.31	61.63
BARS	[.2]	[.3]	17.10	[.3]	15.75	[.1]	4.06	[.3]	74.94	0.28	111.85
CLUTCHES	[.3]	[.1]	8.55	[.3]	23.62	[.5]	30.48	[.2]	74.94	0.23	137.60
DRUMS	[.4]	[.1]	11.40	[.1]	10.50	[.3]	24.38	[.2]	99.92	0.18	146.20
TOTAL CONTRIBUT		1.00	51.30	1.00	57.75	1.00	60.96	1.00	287.27	1.00	457.28
CONTB.%OF SALES			18.00		22.00		30.00		23.00		22.87
CALLS/PERIOD			11		10		20		839		880
CONTB/CALL($000)			4.66		5.77		3.05		0.34		0.52

Data in brackets [ ] would be entered by the planner.

ACCOUNT COSTS, SELLING COSTS, AND NET CONTRIBUTION

To compute the net contribution of each customer, we must determine those marketing costs and selling costs that are caused by the unique characteristics of each customer. For example, the speed with which a customer pays its bills will determine its accounts receivable costs. Schiff and Schiff[12] identified the following account costs that can be related directly to the buying behavior of a client: freight, technical services, advertising and promotion, accounts receivable costs, and inventory costs.

FREIGHT

When the seller pays the freight, these costs will vary according to a customer's distance and order size. Naturally, the more distant customer will have a greater freight cost. The customer who buys in small quantities will also have high freight costs for several reasons. Shipping rates for smaller lots are generally higher. The fixed costs in preparing a bill-of-lading, insurance documents, and related shipping documents are fixed, regardless of the order. The customer who buys in small quantities will generate greater quantities of this paper work for the seller. The representative should include in his or her strategy reasons why the buyer should purchase in larger quantities.

TECHNICAL SERVICES

A representative who sells technical products such as electronic equipment, office equipment, computers, chemicals, and production machinery will frequently have technical service representatives who can be called upon to assist in a sale. A client with a small technical staff of its own will place greater demand on its suppliers for its services. A representative who is weak in product knowledge may call upon these support services more than necessary. By comparing the costs for services across territories, this weakness in representatives can be identified quickly. Excessive demands by customers may be identified by comparing the cost of these services across customers within a territory.

The cost of technical services may be analyzed further by examining the types of services used and the frequency of use. The types of services would include expensive design specialists, engineers, or installation persons. A customer who uses the design specialist will clearly incur more costs to the seller than the one who uses the lower priced installation staff. The customer who demands services frequently will obviously incur greater costs for the seller.

ADVERTISING AND PROMOTION

Advertising and promotion expenses that can be traced directly to a customer include cooperative advertising allowances, special promotional expenditures, and any other expenditure that is authorized by the sales representative for a particular customer. These expenses would not include general corporate advertising, which cannot be traced to a customer or an account.

ACCOUNTS RECEIVABLE COSTS

A customer who receives merchandise without paying cash is essentially receiving a loan from the seller for the period of time between the sale and payment. When a customer purchases $120,000 per year and normally pays thirty days after shipment, the seller is essentially granting the buyer a loan equal to $10,000 per year (30 days/360 days $\times$ $120,000 = $10,000). The annual cost for carrying this account would be determined by each seller's cost of capital. If this seller had a cost of capital of 15 percent, the annual account receivable cost for this customer would equal $1,500 ($10,000 $\times$ 0.15 = $1,500).

INVENTORY COSTS

Inventory costs include the investment in the finished goods, the cost of warehousing, handling costs, insurance, and special treatment that may be required, such as refrigeration.

Relating inventory costs to specific customers may be difficult because of the subjective factor of customer satisfaction. The company may have a policy of 95 percent satisfaction, which means to them the shipment of 95 percent of the items on an order within a specified time period, such as forty-eight hours. An important customer who buys specific items and wants them shipped immediately may result in the company carrying a larger inventory of these items. In such a case, it would be necessary to estimate the size of inventory that is required to make this customer 100 percent satisfied.

A customer who orders in large quantities and on short notice could also increase the amount of inventory that is carried on his or her behalf. We saw earlier that large orders could reduce the freight costs, but we see here that in some cases there may be an offsetting increase in the inventory costs. The inventory costs per customer would be computed by multiplying the estimate of the inventory that was carried for the benefit of that customer times a percentage that represented the cost of capital associated with these finished goods and the expenses previously noted.

THE MODEL FOR NET CONTRIBUTION

A salesperson may compute the contribution per account by entering the costs per account as a percent of sales in the computer model in Exhibit 5.11. The computer then calculates the costs per account and subtracts these costs from the account-product contribution that was carried forward from Exhibit 5.10. At this point the representative or sales manager can ask "what if" questions regarding changes in the percent of costs. What if we increased our discount for an earlier payment of accounts receivable? This model will compute the benefits for comparison with the cost of increasing the discount to aid in making a decision.

The salesperson may compute the total cost of personal selling per account by using either an average cost of a call or the specific account

---

Exhibit 5.11   Account Costs and Net Contribution

	CENTRAL MANUFCT.		WESTRN.	FOR TOOL	NORTH.	1 PERIOD(S) ENGINER.	OTHER ACCOUNTS		T O T A L S	
	%SALES	$(000)	%SALES	$(000)	%SALES	$(000)	%SALES	$(000)	%SALES	$(000)
SALES FCST. ($000)	100.00	285	100.00	262	100.00	203	100.00	1249	100.00	2000
ACCT-PROD CONTRIB.	18.00	51.30	22.00	57.75	30.00	60.96	23.00	287.27	22.87	457
ACCOUNT COSTS										
FREIGHT(DIRECT)	[1.00]	2.85	[3.00]	7.87	[6.00]	12.19	[3.00]	37.47	3.02	60
INVENT.(IMPUTED)	[3.00]	8.55	[4.00]	10.50	[2.00]	4.06	[1.30]	16.24	1.97	39
ACT REC(IMPUTED)	[3.00]	8.55	[2.00]	5.25	[4.00]	8.13	[3.00]	37.47	2.97	59
TEC SVC(DIRECT)	[1.00]	2.85	[0.00]	0.00	[1.00]	2.03	[1.00]	12.49	0.87	17
ADV/PRO(DIRECT)	[0.00]	0.00	[0.00]	0.00	[2.00]	4.06	[1.00]	12.49	0.83	17
TOTAL ACCOUNT COST	8.00	22.80	9.00	23.62	15.00	30.48	9.30	116.16	9.65	193
PERSONAL SELLING										
COST/CALL($000)		[.053]		[.053]		[.053]		[.053]		
CALLS/ACCOUNT		11		10		20		839		880
SALES COST/ACCT.	0.20	.583	0.20	.53	0.52	1.06	3.56	44.47	2.33	47
TOTAL MKTG. COSTS	8.20	23.38	9.20	24.15	15.52	31.54	12.86	160.62	11.99	240
NET CONTRIBUTION	9.80	27.92	12.80	33.59	14.48	29.42	10.14	126.65	10.88	218
% OF TOTAL CONTRB.	12.83		15.44		13.52		58.21		100.00	
% OF TOTAL CALLS	1.25		1.14		2.27		95.34		100.00	
NET CONTB/CALL$000		2.54		3.36		1.47		0.15		0.25

Figures in brackets [ ] are entered by the planner. The computer provides all other data.

costs per call. The latter costs help to identify those accounts that have unusually high selling and entertainment costs.

The number of calls per account is carried forward automatically from Exhibit 5.3, but the representative can override this automatic feature to test the effect of changes in the number of calls per account.

The statistics at the bottom of this exhibit emphasize again the need to define clearly sales force objectives. Western makes the largest dollar net contribution. Northern makes the largest net contribution as a percent of sales, but it has the lowest net contribution per call.

The comparison of the percent of total contribution with the percent of total calls reveals that we are spending 95 percent of the calls on accounts that yield only 58 percent of the contribution. A reallocation of calling effort seems in order.

TERRITORY FINANCIAL ANALYSIS

Many of the financial analysis techniques that are used to evaluate a business may be used to evaluate a sales territory. In this section we will see how the concepts of return-on-assets managed, investment portfolios, income statements, and productivity measures are applied to a sales territory.

TERRITORY RETURN-ON-ASSETS MANAGED (ROAM)[13]

We have already seen that the investments in a territory constitute largely the accounts receivable and inventories that are associated with specific customers. Two customers, A and B, may have the same sales volume and net contribution, but they may produce different return-on-assets managed because their buying habits require different investments, accounts receivable, and inventories. The following simple example will illustrate this point.

	COMPANY A	COMPANY B
Sales (000)	$400	$400
Net Contribution	$ 40	$ 40
Territory Investment	$100	$200
Return-on-Investment (Contribution/Investment)	.40	.20

The assets required by Company A are used more productively than those required by Company B.

While the return-on-assets managed may be computed directly as follows:

ROI = Net Contribution/Investment,

this ratio conceals the sales level and the important concept of asset turnover, which is a measure of how hard the assets are being used. The expanded equation is as follows:

$$ROI = \frac{\text{Territory Net Contribution}}{\text{Territory Sales}} \times \frac{\text{Territory Sales}}{\text{Territory Assets}}$$

$$= \text{Contribution Rate as a Percent of Sales} \times \text{Asset Turnover Rate}$$

Exhibit 5.12   Computing the Territory Return-on-Assets Managed

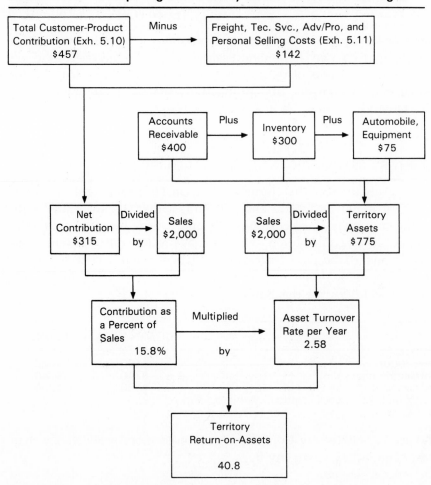

This concept is presented in graphic form in Exhibit 5.12, which is generally credited to the E. I. duPont Co. because of its use as a management planning tool for duPont's divisions. Exhibit 5.12 computes the return-on-assets for our young industrial representative, using the expense and contribution data from Exhibit 5.11.

Exhibit 5.13 summarizes the return-on-assets managed calculations for each account. It will be noted that the costs of carrying inventory and accounts receivable are added back to the net contribution so that we do not double the count, given the fact that these costs are based on assets invested in inventory and accounts receivable.

If we evaluate accounts according to return-on-assets managed, then Northern is the best account and Central is the worst. Once again, we see how accounts shift in their ranking as we use different criteria. Some companies are now evaluating their sales forces according to ROAM. In such cases the compensation scheme should be related to ROAM so that rewards and evaluations are based on the same criteria.

Exhibit 5.13   Return-on-Assets Managed

FOR   1 PERIOD(S)

	CENTRAL	WESTERN	NORTHRN.	OTHER	TOTAL
SALES FORECASTED	285	262	203	1249	2000
ASSETS MANGD($000)					
ACCTS. (DIRECT)	[57.3]	[35.3]	[54]	253.4	[400]
INVENT. (DIRECT)	[57.3]	[70]	[27.3]	145.4	[300]
DEM EQT(% CALLS)	0.73	0.66	1.32	55.30	[58]
OFF EQT(% CALLS)	0.13	0.11	0.23	9.53	[10]
AUTO (% CALLS)	0.09	0.08	0.23	6.67	[7]
TOT.ASSETS ($000)	115.54	106.15	83.07	470.31	775
% ASSETS/ACCOUNT	14.91	13.70	10.72	60.68	100.00
ASSET TURNOVER (SALES/ASSETS)	2.47	2.47	2.45	2.66	2.58
NET CONTRIB. %	9.80	12.80	14.48	10.14	10.88
ADD INT INVENT.	3.00	4.00	2.00	1.30	1.97
INT ACCT REC	3.00	2.00	4.00	3.00	2.97
TOTAL CONTRIB.	15.80	18.80	20.48	14.44	15.82
RETURN ON ASSETS	38.96	46.49	50.09	38.35	40.82

Data in brackets [   ] are supplied by the planner. The computer enters all other data.

ACCOUNT INVESTMENT PORTFOLIO

Strategic planners have found the concept of an investment portfolio useful when evaluating products or business units. These portfolios are usually expressed as a two-dimensional matrix. There are no standard variables that are used along these two dimensions. The Boston Consulting Group use the dimensions of market growth and relative market share. The consulting firm of McKinsey and Company and the General Electric Company use the dimensions of business strengths and industry attractiveness. The consulting firm of Arthur D. Little uses the dimensions of competitive position and stage of industry maturity. Planners at Shell International use the dimensions of the company's competitive capabilities and the outlook for sector profitability. For this example we will use two financial dimensions—growth rate and return-on-assets managed. Both of these dimensions appear in Exhibit 5.14. All of the key data in this example are summarized in Exhibit 5.15.

By expressing the account in terms of an investment portfolio, we gain better strategic insight than would be possible with a simple ABC classification. Here we have four classifications—winners, comers, goers, and losers. Central Manufacturing and Western Tool are both classified as winners because they have a favorable growth rate and a high return-on-assets managed. Northern Engineering, on the other hand, is a goer because it has a growth rate less than 1.00, which indicates that its need for our product will decline each year. We should retain this account, however, because it still has a very favorable return-on-assets managed. Account Z is a clear loser because it has a declining growth rate and a very low return-on-assets managed. The representa-

Exhibit 5.14   Portfolio of Accounts

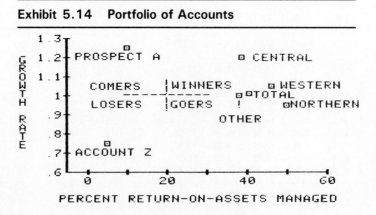

Exhibit 5.15   Account Summary ($000)

FOR   [1]PERIOD(S)

ACCOUNTS	REQUIRMTS	GROWTH RATE	FORECAST REQUIRE.	SHARE PRESENT	SHARE FORECST	FORECASTED SALES	FORECASTED NET CONT	CALLS	SLS/CALL	CONT/CAL	ROAM
CENTRAL	500	1.20	600	40.00	47.50	285	28	11	25.91	2.54	38.96
WESTERN	1250	1.05	1312	10.00	20.00	262	34	10	26.25	3.36	46.49
NORTHERN	713	0.95	677	30.01	30.00	203	29	20	10.16	1.47	50.09
OTHER	6245	1.00	6245	20.00	20.00	1249	127	839	1.49	0.15	38.35
TOTAL	8708	1.01	8835	20.24	22.63	2000	218	880	2.27	0.25	40.82

FOR   [2]PERIOD(S)

ACCOUNTS	REQUIRMTS	GROWTH RATE	FORECAST REQUIRE.	SHARE PRESENT	SHARE FORECST	FORECASTED SALES	FORECASTED NET CONT	CALLS	SLS/CALL	CONT/CAL	ROAM
CENTRAL	500	1.20	720	40.00	47.50	342	34	11	31.09	3.06	46.86
WESTERN	1250	1.05	1378	10.00	20.00	276	35	10	27.56	3.53	48.83
NORTHERN	713	0.95	643	30.01	30.00	193	28	20	9.65	1.39	47.52
OTHER	6245	1.00	6245	20.00	20.00	1249	127	839	1.49	0.15	38.35
TOTAL	8708	1.03	8987	19.90	22.92	2060	223	880	2.34	0.25	42.04

FOR   [3]PERIOD(S)

ACCOUNTS	REQUIRMTS	GROWTH RATE	FORECAST REQUIRE.	SHARE PRESENT	SHARE FORECST	FORECASTED SALES	FORECASTED NET CONT	CALLS	SLS/CALL	CONT/CAL	ROAM
CENTRAL	500	1.20	864	40.00	47.50	410	40	11	37.31	3.68	56.33
WESTERN	1250	1.05	1447	10.00	20.00	289	37	10	28.94	3.71	51.30
NORTHERN	713	0.95	611	30.01	30.00	183	26	20	9.17	1.32	45.08
OTHER	6245	1.00	6245	20.00	20.00	1249	127	839	1.49	0.15	38.35
TOTAL	8708	1.05	9167	19.50	23.26	2132	231	880	2.42	0.26	43.53

The planner enters only the number of periods to be forecasted. The computer supplies all other data.

tive may want to drop this account and use those available calls to develop prospect A. This prospect has a very high growth potential, but presently would yield a low return-on-assets managed. The representative will want to explore ways for increasing ROAM.

TERRITORY INCOME STATEMENT AND PLAN

If the salesperson is using a microcomputer for territory analysis, it will now have sufficient data to produce automatically the income statement shown in Exhibit 5.16. The two right-hand columns are for territory planning. The representative may change estimates of sales, account-product contribution, and costs to determine the effects on the territory statistics.

A sales manager can use the model in Exhibit 5.16 to manage a district or a region by adding columns for each territory or district. Differences in percentages across columns identify areas for administrative action.

Exhibit 5.16   Territory Income Statement and Plan

FOR	1 PERIOD(S) PRESENT PERIOD		NEXT PERIOD PLAN	
	$000	%	$000	%
SALES	2000	100	[2500]	100
ACCT-PRODUCT CONTB. EXH. 2	457	22.87	572	22.87
ACCT. COSTS EXH. 3				
FREIGHT	60	3.02	[65]	2.60
INVENTORY	39	1.97	[30]	1.20
ACCTS.RECEIVABLE	59	2.97	[75]	3.00
TECH. SERVICES	17	0.87	17	0.69
ADV. & PROM.	17	0.83	[35]	1.40
TOTAL CUSTOMER COSTS	193	9.65	222	8.89
PERSONAL SELLING COSTS				
COMPENSATION	29.90	1.50	[33.00]	1.32
TRANSPORTATION	7.00	0.35	[5.00]	0.20
LODGING & MEALS	4.00	0.20	4.00	0.16
TELEPHONE	1.20	0.06	[1.70]	0.07
ENTERTAINMENT	2.50	0.13	[1.00]	0.04
SAMPLES & LITERATURE	1.50	0.08	1.50	0.06
MISC.	0.30	0.02	0.30	0.01
TOTAL PERS. SELLING CST	46.40	2.32	46.50	1.86
NET TERRITORY CONTRIB($000)	217.82	10.89	302.81	12.11
RETURN ON ASSETS MANAGED:				
TERRITORY ASSETS ($000)	775		775	
ASSET TURNOVER(SALES/ASSTS)	2.58		3.23	
ADD: INTEREST INV.		1.97		1.20
INTEREST A/R		2.97		3.00
TOTAL CONTRIBUTION PERCENT		15.83		16.31
RETURN ON ASSETS MANAGED		40.85		52.62

Note: The planner enters only those budget items that are likely to change during planned period.

At this point in the example it is obvious that a microcomputer can help a representative manage the territory like a profit center using data from daily call reports and financial data that could be supplied from the accounting department.

The microcomputer could be used by the representative to rank accounts according to potential, to maintain prospect lists, to create calling schedules, to write standard letters, and to complete expense and order forms—all of the tasks that most representatives hate. It could also be used to keep vital records for telephone marketing and it could even be programmed to dial the prospect's number.

A district sales manager could use the microcomputer to create territories based on potential and ZIP code numbers. Columns for each representative in Exhibit 5.9, Prospecting Analysis, would identify areas where training is needed.

SUMMARY

This chapter has examined how strategic planning concepts may be used by the representative to develop a selling plan for a territory. The plan must begin with an understanding of the individual's personal goals and objectives, the corporate goals and objectives, and the corporate objectives for the individual and the territory. The representative must then examine the expected potential of all accounts—present clients as well as prospective ones. The next step in the plan is to develop a selling strategy to make each account a profitable one. When an appropriate strategy has been developed for each account, the representative must then consider the allocation of scarce resources, the most important of which is his or her time. Personal time management becomes an important skill in order for a representative to manage a territory productively. The manner in which this time is allocated will differ according to whether the representative is calling on regular customers or developing new ones.

Financial concepts such as income statements, return-on-assets managed, productivity measures and investment portfolios may be used to analyze present situations, develop strategies, evaluate previous strategies, and plan for the future. Many companies have computerized these concepts so that the representative receives frequent reports that enable early detection and correction of problems. The microcomputer and low-cost software will make major contributions to increasing the productivity of salespersons.

This chapter emphasized a point that was made in earlier chapters: Today's sales representative is truly running his or her own small business. The young salesperson has ample opportunity to practice the knowledge that has been gained through a business education. The salesperson performs many of the roles of a consultant and a product manager, but with the important difference that there is bottom-line accountability. A representative who manages the territory well will be identified for a rapid promotion.

ASSIGNMENTS/DISCUSSION QUESTIONS

1. What are five business concepts that a representative may use to run a territory like a business?

2. Using the model in Exhibit 5.5, compute how many minutes longer per day the representative would have to work to make Plan A equal the productivity of Plan B.

3. Develop a selling strategy to improve the account-product mix for Central Manufacturing.

4. Discuss how a microcomputer may be used to manage a territory.

5. Assume that a training program resulted in the representative in Exhibit 5.10 changing the product mix of Central Manufacturing as follows: Axles .3, Bars .2, Clutches .3, and Drums .2. What would be the effect of this shift on the contribution of this account and the contribution per account call? Would this product mix shift affect the representative's compensation? (See Exhibit 5.9 for the compensation scheme.)

REFERENCES

1. Many of the ideas in this section are courtesy of Mr. John H. Burns, Sales Training Manager, Agway, Inc., Syracuse, N.Y.

2. For example, Porter Henry, "The Important Few — The Unimportant Many," *1980, Portfolio of Sales & Marketing Plans* (New York: Sales & Marketing Management, 1980), pp. 34–37.

3. W. K. Fudge and L. M. Lodish, "Evaluation of the Effectiveness of a Model Based Salesman's Planning System by Field Experimentation," *Interfaces* (November 1977): 97–106.

4. Leonard M. Lodish, "A User-Oriented Model for Sales Force Size, Product, and Market Allocation Decisions," *Journal of Marketing* 44 (Summer 1980): 70–78.

5. A. A. Zoltners, P. Sinha, and P. S. C. Chong, "An Optimal Algorithm for Sales Representative Time Management," *Management Science* 25, no. 12 (December 1979): 1197–1207.

6. A. A. Zoltners and P. Sinha, "Integer Programming Models for Sales Resource Allocation," *Management Science* 26 (March 1980): 242–260.

7. T. C. Taylor, "S&MM's Eighth Annual Survey of Selling Costs," *Sales & Marketing Management* (February 25, 1980): 26–28.

8. Thomas M. Rohan, ''New Twists Help out Sales Costs,'' *Industry Week* 190, no. 5 (Sept 6, 1976): 37–42.
9. John D. Yeck, ''Reducing the Cost of Sales through Marketing Support Mail,'' *Industrial Marketing Management* 6, no. 2 (1977): 95–97.
10. For an extensive discussion, see Murray Roman, *Telephone Marketing* (New York: McGraw-Hill, 1976).
11. ''Selling Time: A Curb on Market Growth?'' *Sales and Marketing Management* (September 13, 1976): 54.
12. J. S. Schiff and M. Schiff, *Strategic Management of the Sales Territory* (New York: Sales and Marketing Executives International, 1980).
13. Michael Schiff, ''The Sales Territory as a Fixed Asset,'' *Journal of Marketing* 25 (October 1960): 51–53; Michael Schiff, ''ROI: A New Criterion for Salesmen,'' *Marketing Insights* (April 29, 1968): 14–15; J. S. Schiff and Michael Schiff, ''New Sales Management Tool: ROAM,'' *Harvard Business Review* 45 (July–August 1967): 59–66.
14. Schiff and Schiff, *Strategic Management,* p. III–32.

SUGGESTED READINGS

Hall, W. P., ''Improving Sales Force Productivity,'' *Business Horizons* (August 1975): 32–42.
Smackey, B. W., ''A Profit Emphasis for Improving Sales Force Productivity,'' *Industrial Marketing Management* 6, no. 2 (1977): 135–140.
Smith, Charles W., ''Gearing Salesmen's Efforts to Corporate Profit Objectives,'' *Harvard Business Review* (July–August 1975): 8ff.

6

THE LEGAL DIMENSIONS OF PERSONAL SELLING AND SALES MANAGEMENT*

The legal and regulatory environment requires each representative to have sufficient knowledge of marketing laws and regulations to know when he or she should consult the legal department of the company. This chapter will be limited to a discussion of those regulations that apply directly to field selling and sales management. Discussion of the legal considerations when recruiting, evaluating, and terminating representatives will appear in later chapters. More extensive discussions of public policy toward business may be found in the suggested readings at the end of this chapter.

THE U.S. PHILOSOPHY TOWARD THE REGULATION OF MARKETING ACTIVITIES

PROTECT CITIZENS

For thousands of years, governments have had rules to protect their citizens from careless craftsmen and dishonest merchants. Over 4,000 years ago the Code of Hammurabi required a careless craftsman to make repairs at his own expense. The need for standard weights and measures is noted in the Bible and the Magna Carta. As the Industrial Revolution brought more complex products, methods for protecting society became more complex. Public policy in the United States has been designed to preserve competition, protect the consumer, and conserve national resources and the environment. The sales representative will be concerned largely with policies for preserving competition.

*The authors thank Barry S. Roberts, Associate Professor of Legal Studies, School of Business Administration, University of North Carolina, for his helpful comments.

ECONOMIC PLURALISM

Antitrust legislation to preserve competition is an economic analogue of the pluralistic political model. The political model places the power in the individual voter, the smallest political unit. The economic model attempts to place the power in the marketplace, so that no one firm can dominate the market structure and therefore the price. The goal of antitrust regulations is to have the price mechanism allocate scarce resources through the marketplace. One of the important tests of whether competition is taking place is the price flexibility that occurs in the marketplace. Thus, as we will see below, activities that unreasonably prevent price flexibility are generally regarded as a violation of antitrust legislation.

Responsibility for enforcing antitrust laws is becoming more of an individual responsibility. Court cases of the 1970s expanded the responsibilities for antitrust compliance to the lower echelons of the firm. A national sales director was charged with price fixing. A person who violates the Sherman Antitrust Act (1890) may be fined $100,000, is subject to a three-year jail term, and his or her firm could be fined $1 million.

REPRESENTATIVES' LEGAL RESPONSIBILITIES

A representative as an agent has many legal responsibilities to the company, such as protecting company secrets and not making unauthorized contractual arrangements on behalf of the company. The representative must be careful when discussing the developments of new products so as not to leak competitive information. Letters must be written carefully and checked by the legal department to be certain that what the representative thought was an informal proposal did not become a binding contract. The representative must adhere to approved claims for products and services. This chapter will attempt to alert the representative to some of the subtleties of price fixing, price discrimination, controlling distribution, and unfair selling practices.

COLLUSIONS TO FIX PRICES

THE LAW

The Sherman Act of 1890 is the basic law in the United States that outlaws monopolies and collaboration. Section 1, as interpreted by the courts, makes it illegal to enter into a contract, combination, or conspiracy that unreasonably restrains trade. Section 2 makes it illegal to monopolize, attempt to monopolize, or combine or conspire to monopolize trade. The courts have interpreted price fixing as illegal *per se* under Section 1 of the Sherman Act. A *per se* violation means that it is not necessary to prove that the activity restrained trade or created a monopoly. The *per se* rule is a reaction to the high costs of economic analysis and extended court trials.

Any activity that reduces the flexibility of price and therefore its ability to allocate resources is assumed to be not in the public interest. To help illustrate price fixing concepts, we will examine several of the classic cases.

COLLUSION CASES

A landmark price-fixing case involved rigging bids for heavy electrical equipment. Decades of collusion were ended in 1960 when the major manufacturers of transformers, switch gear, and generators were found guilty of rigging bids and increasing prices by as much as 20 percent.

> The defendant had allocated contracts, selecting the low bidder by drawing names out of a hat, by rotating them in alphabetical order, and by making allotments according to a formula based upon the phases of the moon. The low bidder had then informed others regarding his bid, and they had adjusted their bids accordingly. The conspirators had met under assumed names in luxury hotels in various cities, and motels and mountain-top retreats, in cabins in the Canadian woods, and at a Milwaukee bar known as 'Dirty Helen's.'[1]

Twenty-nine companies, including General Electric and Westinghouse, pleaded guilty or offered no defense. Seven officers spent brief prison terms. Philadelphia Electric Company collected $28.8 million, in a treble damages suit. (Treble damage suits allow the damaged party to recover three times the amount of the damage.) The companies then settled out of court with total payments estimated at $405 million.[2]

Another classic case occurred between 1960–1974 and is known as The Folding Box case. In this case twenty-three major manufacturers of paperboard boxes that are used for foods, drugs, household supplies, and textiles, held 70 percent of the market. The case included Container Corporation, Federal Paperboard Company, American Can Company, International Paper Company, Weyerhauser Company, and fifty officials. The price-fixing procedure included price-information sharing, rotation of winning bids, and uniform price increases to customers shared by several companies. The Antitrust Division of the Justice Department sought an average eighteen-month jail term and an average fine of $50,000, but the judge hearing the case rendered an average sentence of ten days, and a fine averaging $5,000.[3]

Antitrust pressure has carried over into professionals, such as lawyers, doctors, stockbrokers, druggists, architects, engineers, and others, who had practiced either not announcing their prices or following a fee schedule that was suggested by their association. The classic case occurred in June 1975, when the Supreme Court decided in favor of Goldfarb, who found that none of the thirty-seven lawyers whom he had contacted would budge from a fixed fee to check the deed for his house. As a result of this and subsequent cases, lawyers, druggists, and optometrists are advertising their fees for services.

Charges of price fixing are not limited to large companies. The Federal Trade Commission (FTC) found the American Art Clay Company, Binney & Smith Inc., and Milton Bradley Company had engaged in a price fixing conspiracy when selling art supplies to public school systems. The $1.2 million refund will be allocated by State Attorneys General according to the number of students in each state in grades kindergarten through 12.[4]

CONDITIONS THAT CREATE COLLUSION

A summary of price-fixing cases identifies those conditions that lead to collusion. The concept of the product life cycle reminds us that price competition becomes severe as products become mature and there is little product differentiation among sellers. High fixed costs increase the break-even level of a firm, and put pressure on the selling function to maintain high levels of sales, which, in turn, is an inducement to fix prices with competitors. Similar cost structures among manufacturers help to support a collusion because a low-cost or high-cost rival will be tempted to break the pricing agreement. Manufacturers of folding boxes seemed to have met these three conditions. Barriers to entry, such as licensing requirements, large investments in production equipment, or a lack of access to raw materials, may lead to collusive pricing because new firms cannot enter easily. The fewer the sellers in a market, the easier it is to implement collusion because a price cutter can be found and penalized quickly.

PRICE DISCRIMINATION

A seller need not engage in collusion with other sellers to reduce competition. A seller may build a monopolistic position or direct resources away from their most efficient use by individual efforts through price discrimination.

THE LAW

Section 2a of the Clayton Act (1914), as amended by the Robinson-Patman Act (1936), makes it illegal to discriminate among purchasers of goods of like grade and quality where the effect of price discrimination may substantially lessen competition or create a monopoly, unless the discrimination reflects a difference in costs or an attempt to meet the price of a competitor. The content of the Robinson-Patman Act is explained by the economic environment of the times: The country was emerging from a great depression, a period of unemployment that could be worsened by the elimination of small, locally owned grocery stores. The aim of the Act was to eliminate unfair buying advantages that the chain stores had over smaller competitors, which could be translated into predatory price cuts to drive these small competitors out of business, and then restore prices when the chain stores became monopolists.

Chain stores used a variety of techniques to induce their suppliers to give them a better price. In addition to seeking direct differential discounts, they would set up a phantom brokerage firm and require a brokerage allowance, they would require special cooperative advertising allowances, they would get quantity discounts that would be available to only a few buyers, and they would induce a lower price by claiming that a competitive seller had offered such a price. We will also see that predatory pricing has not been limited to chain stores.

DEFENSES

Price discrimination occurs when one party is put at a disadvantage that results in a lessening of competition. A weak competitor may claim price discrimination when in fact the alleged price discriminator was lowering prices to reflect lower cost, quantity discounts, functional discounts, the clearance of perishable or obsolete goods, or in a good faith meeting of competition. Thus the law provides for these defenses against a charge of price discrimination.

Costs

Price differentials are permitted where there is only due allowance for differences in the cost of manufacture, sale, or delivery resulting from differing methods or quantities in which commodities are sold or delivered. This defense is not as popular as it was previously because of the difficulty of establishing cost for a specific product when a company sells a large number of products and the allocation of joint production and marketing costs is difficult, if not impossible.

Quantity Discounts

Quantity discounts are permitted as long as they reflect a true cost saving in the manufacture, sale, or delivery of the product. The Federal Trade Commission has placed upper limits on the quantities that must be purchased to get a discount. In 1952, it established one carload as the upper limit for rubber tires to limit the price advantage that Sears Roebuck enjoyed over smaller distributors. The Commission found many instances in which quantity discounts were available to only a few buyers, thereby creating price discrimination. Such a discount would not be discriminatory if the buyers had different end uses for the product or if it could be proved that there was no harm to competition.

Functional Discounts

A functional discount is a means for paying a member of a channel of distribution for performing certain functions, such as storing, financing, advertising, or shipping. A functional discount could be a suitable defense, but problems are created when this discount is passed along the channel of distribution and a subsequent competitor finds herself or himself at a price disadvantage. In the case of Standard Oil (Indiana), the Federal Trade Commission found that discounts to jobbers were being passed along through the channel to their retailers, with the result that severe competition occurred between these retailers and Standard's own retail customers. While this functional discount may have reduced competition, Standard Oil was able to demonstrate that it was using another defense—the good faith meeting of competition.[5] The Supreme Court decided in favor of Standard Oil.

While functional discounts raise questions of cost allocation and meeting competition, the Act is clear on the matter of brokerage discounts. It is illegal for a seller to pay any broker's fee or to allow a discount in lieu of a broker's fee to a buyer. This provision was to stop large firms such as A&P from setting up phantom brokerage firms simply to get a larger discount.

Functional discounts may become discriminatory if they are not given proportionally to all buyers. For example, if a chain store is given an advertising allowance equal to five cents per case for a cooperative newspaper advertisement, the little family-owned corner grocery store must be given the same allowance to enable it to distribute handbills to its customers.

Perishable or Obsolete Goods

A seller of a perishable good, such as vegetables, a fashionable product, such as clothing, or a technologically obsolete product, such as a computer with a limited core memory, may give a discount to move the product quickly. Such a discount is not price discrimination.

Meeting Competition

The Robinson-Patman Act makes provision for charging a lower price to a customer in good faith to meet an equally low price of a competitor. In this case, price discrimination is not illegal, even if competition was reduced as a result.[6] The burden of proving good faith falls upon the seller, which introduces two problems. First, was there a genuine offer by a competitor or was this just a negotiation tactic? Second, how does one determine a competitive price without appearing to engage in price fixing? These questions will be addressed in the next two sections.

BUYER LIABILITY

The Robinson-Patman Amendment (1936) to Section 2 of the Clayton Act (1914) makes it unlawful to knowingly induce or receive a price that is discriminating. This provision protects the sales representative from being drawn into an illegal act by a hard-bargaining buyer. It also protects the seller from competing with a nonexistent competitor or *meeting* an offer that was not bonafide. It is difficult, however, to distinguish between discrimination and competition. In reversing a lower court decision, the Supreme Court (1979) decided that A&P had not knowingly induced a better offer from Borden, Inc., because Borden had simply made the offer in an attempt to meet competition.[7] The complexity of this case suggests that a representative should seek legal advice early in price negotiations that are made to meet competitive offers.

EXCHANGING PRICE INFORMATION

A seller who is attempting to meet a competitor's price in good faith must establish exactly what that price is. The Robinson-Patman Act permits us to meet the price, even though it may limit competition, but we may not go below the competitor's price. Hence, accurate knowledge of the competitor's price is necessary for both bargaining purposes and legal purposes. Can a seller call a competitor directly to confirm a price or ask for a price list? The Supreme Court (1978) decided that direct contact with a competitor regarding price is a violation of Section 1 of the Sherman Act.[8]

There are at least two legal ways for a representative to meet a competitive offer in good faith without engaging in an activity that could be interpreted as price fixing. One approach is to have the prospective buyer supply a copy of the competitor's offer or price list. These documents should be marked clearly by the buyer and the representative as having come from the buyer, not the competitor. If a competitor's written quotation is not available, a seller may decide to include a statement on the invoice to the effect that the seller's price is given on reliance of the buyer's representation of the competitor's offer and that the buyer will cooperate in any later investigation regarding charges of price discrimination.

Many companies instruct their representatives to refuse to discuss prices with competitors. Some companies even advise that their representatives should be dramatic, and even knock over a chair to emphasize the fact that they will not discuss prices. These instructions are to help the competitor to recall correctly the fact that this company will not discuss prices should the competitor ever be called on the witness stand in a grand jury investigation of price fixing.

PREDATORY PRICING

The Robinson-Patman Act is frequently criticized for limiting effective competition by limiting price cutting. A seller is afraid to use price as a competitive tool for fear of being charged with price discrimination. This concern is real because a variety of industries have been represented in predatory pricing cases. Standard Oil Company selectively cut prices to force small competitors into more favorable merger terms.[9] Anheuser-Busch cut prices in St. Louis in 1953 to try to improve its fourth-place market position. It was exonerated because it had responded to sales losses, its prices were not below its cost, its competitors still made profits, and its share slipped back when price cuts ended.

The courts decided in favor of a small bakery, Utah Pie, when it found that Continental Baking, Pet Milk, and Carnation engaged in predatory price cutting by selling below their average total cost and below Utah's prices. The court's inference of predatory pricing was supported further by evidence of industrial spying. It is interesting to note that two-thirds of the predatory pricing cases occurred in the food-products industry.[10]

CONTROLLING DISTRIBUTION

THE LAW

The price mechanism is not the only way for creating a monopoly. There can be many contractual arrangements that limit the vertical freedom of a buyer. Competition may be reduced by restricting a buyer's alternative sources of supply or the conditions under which the buyer may resell the product of the seller. These arrangements may reduce competition directly, or they may reduce it indirectly through vertical price fixing, which is illegal under the Sherman Act, Section 1.

Section 3 of the Clayton Act (1914) prevents tying contracts and exclusive dealership arrangements when they may substantially lessen competition. Other forms of controlling distribution, such as mergers, joint ventures, and interlocking directorships, would generally not be the concern of the representative or the sales manager, so they will not be discussed in this text.

VERTICAL PRICE FIXING

Vertical price fixing, like horizontal price fixing, is illegal, but it was legal between 1937 and 1975, under the "Fair Trade Laws." Vertical pricing allows a manufacturer to require a retailer to sell at a fixed price. The Fair Trade Laws were created after the depression of the 1930s to protect small retailers from discount stores. The growth of the discount stores challenged these laws, but it was not until 1975 that the Consumer Goods Pricing Act repealed the Miller-Tydings Act (1937) and the McGuire Act (1952), which had made vertical price fixing legal.

TYING ARRANGEMENTS

There can be several forms of tying arrangements. A tying arrangement occurs when the buyer is required to buy Product B in order to get the desired product, Product A. This condition exists when the seller has a comparative advantage for Product A because it is a new product that is selling well or has a patent advantage. In order to move a slower moving product such as B, the seller links this inferior product to Product A. When the seller forces the buyer to purchase a whole line of products, the arrangement is known as "full-line forcing." Tying arrangements may violate the Clayton Act or the Sherman Act because other sellers are foreclosed from competing for this buyer's business.

Tying contracts may also be a subtle way of price discrimination. A seller could bundle a group of products and sell them at a total price that was discriminating, claiming a savings in the cost of distribution. If the discounts cannot be justified on the basis of a cost saving, the bundled price may be a discriminatory one.

There have been some classic cases in tying arrangements that will help illustrate the application of these laws. IBM (1936) could no longer require users of its equipment to purchase all tabulating cards from IBM. The American Can Company (1949) was found in violation of Section 3 of the Clayton Act because it required food-processing leasees of its can-closing machinery to buy all of their cans from American Can on a five-year contract. To encourage this purchase, the machines were leased at a low rental. International Salt Company (1947) can no longer require users of its patented salt-processing machines to use only its salt in these machines. The block selling of movies for local theaters was found to be an illegal tying arrangement (Paramount, 1948); block sales tied poor movies to hit movies. After 1956, Eastman Kodak could no longer tie film processing to the purchase of film, so that buyers could choose freely among several processors. A tying arrangement that merely extracts a profit, without reducing competition, may not be illegal. Angry fans sued six football teams for requiring season ticket buyers to buy preseason tickets, but the teams were acquitted. The court concluded that this action did not reduce competition in preseason games. There is also the possibility that the amounts were too small to affect materially leisure-market activities. Furthermore, the antitrust legislation has tended to be lenient toward sporting activities.[11]

EXCLUSIVE DISTRIBUTION

The job description for a sales representative frequently includes establishing new dealerships to handle the company's products. The question of exclusive dealing will generally enter these negotiations. In some instances, the seller will want to require the dealer to handle his or her products exclusively, while the dealer may want to handle competing lines. Conversely, there will be occasions when a manufacturer wants to have several dealers in a territory, but a new dealer refuses to sign-on unless given an exclusive coverage of the territory. Exclusive dealing can be very complex and has become the subject of many court cases. A review of some of these cases will help the young representative or sales manager to recognize the complexities of the issue and seek legal counsel early.

Cases in Exclusive Dealing

The trend in the court decisions on exclusive dealing is that *contractual* requirements by a seller to exclude others from competing or supplying a buyer do have anticompetitive effects and are illegal. Whether *persuasive* methods are illegal is less clear, as has been seen in some cases of franchising. The key test in exclusive dealing cases is the market share of the seller, but the courts have not established the percent of market share that constitutes anticompetitive behavior.

Standard Fashion Company (1922) was prohibited from exclusive dealership arrangements in the sale of its dress patterns because it controlled 40 percent in the marketplace and it excluded the competitors from the best stores in each city. Carter Carburetor was stopped in 1940 from giving special discounts to dealers who bought exclusively from it.

Cases in Exclusive Territories

Exclusive territorial arrangements have been particularly troublesome for the court. The Topco incident is an important case in this field. Topco was a cooperative of independently owned local grocery chains that was formed in 1940 to compete with the larger chains. By 1967, its sales of $2.3 billion placed it fourth after A&P, Safeway, and Kroger. Topco members agreed not to sell Topco-brand products outside of their assigned territories. The Supreme Court (1972) held that this agreement was a *per se* violation of Section 1 of the Sherman Act because it was a horizontal territorial limitation on competition.

One of the most precedent-shattering decisions of the Supreme Court was its reversal of its position regarding exclusive dealing. The Court (1967) had found Arnold Schwinn & Company in violation of Section 1 of the Sherman Act, *per se*, because of its vertical restrictions on bicycle distributors and retailers. Distributors had been limited to dealing with franchised dealers and these retail dealers had been limited to selling only to consumers. The Court held that when a seller relinquishes the risk, domain, and title of a product, the seller can no longer establish conditions governing its sale.[12] The Court reversed its position in the GTE Sylvania (1977) case.

To improve its 2-percent market share, in 1962 Sylvania decided to change its channel strategy from one of saturation to the use of selective distribution, thinking that a few loyal franchised dealers would promote its television sets more aggressively. Dealers were franchised for a specific location and agreed not to move merchandise to other locations. Sylvania remained competitive by not giving an exclusive dealership for an area and by authorizing at least two dealers in major markets. The strategy seemed to be successful because its market share increased to 5 percent. Continental TV, one of Sylvania's largest dealers, violated the agreement not to move merchandise to an unfranchised location, so Sylvania terminated its contract. Continental sued Sylvania, citing the *per se* rule in the Schwinn case. The District Court favored Continental, but the Circuit Court of Appeals reversed the decision, stating that the trial judge was too liberal in his application of the *per se* rule in the Schwinn decision. The Supreme Court (1977) affirmed the decision of the Court of Appeals. Thus, "location clauses which allow a franchisor to select the location from which its franchisees may sell and to exercise sole discretion both in increasing or decreasing the number of dealers and in requiring its product to be sold only from its franchised location was held to constitute a reasonable marketing device."[13] The Court found no distinction between the customer restriction in Schwinn and the location restriction in Sylvania. The Sylvania decision would seem to make it possible for franchisors to use location clauses in their contractual arrangements with franchisees. Such clauses should be used with care, however, because they may still be an unreasonable restraint of trade. Some observers think that the Sylvania case would have been decided differently if the market share had been 12 or more percent.[14]

Cases in Franchising

While the franchising arrangements regarding territories may have been clarified by the Sylvania case, franchise arrangements regarding sources of supply for fast-food franchisees are not clear. Chicken Delight, Inc., required its franchisees to buy its chickens and supplies from it because it thought that these essential items made its food distinctive. The Appeals Court (1972) concluded that this arrangement restrained trade because Chicken Delight was distinct in the market, even though it had only a small market share. In the Chock Full O' Nuts (1973) case, the FTC affirmed that the franchisor of chains cannot make a franchisee buy from itself or designated suppliers, but it can try to persuade the franchisees that these products are necessary to ensure quality.[15] The point at which persuasion becomes coercion will be difficult for the courts and franchisors to decide.

In concluding the discussion of exclusive distribution, we should note that there are advantages for both the seller and the buyer. The seller may enjoy lower selling and promotional and production expenses because goods flow automatically and more predictively to the buyer than would be true in an open-market situation. The exclusive franchising arrangement is superior to the manufacturer's integrating forward, because franchising reduces the seller's need for a large capital investment.[16] Furthermore, as was seen in the Sylvania case, exclusive dealership may stimulate the buyer to promote the brand more aggressively.

Advantages to the buyer include making the supply more certain, which is important during times of shortages. Deliveries may be automatic, thereby reducing buying and paperwork expenses. Investments in inventories of products, spare parts, and training service personnel are reduced when the number of brands is limited.[17]

RECIPROCITY

"If you buy from me, then I will buy from you" constitutes reciprocity, which may be anticompetitive. In extreme cases, reciprocity becomes coercion. General Motors was indicted by a federal grand jury on charges of using its vast economic power to monopolize the manufacture and sale of railroad locomotives, a violation of Section 2 of the Sherman Act.[18] GM routed rail shipments of its products to favor those railroads that purchased GM locomotives, and withheld rail shipments from those railroads that purchased from competitors. The government charged that this reciprocity helped to create General Motors' 84-percent marketshare of the railroad locomotive business.

The Federal Trade Commission issued three cease and desist orders under Section 5 of the FTC Act, charging that reciprocity was unfair competition. These three cases involved food processors who forced suppliers to use railroad facilities or equipment in which the processors had an interest.[19]

The sales representative must be very alert not to enter inadvertently into reciprocity. He or she should not attempt to intimidate a buyer by threatening to withdraw the company's purchases from that buyer. Simply supplying one's purchasing department with the sales figures for particular customers will be interpreted as an attempt to engage in reciprocity. Conversely, if a customer indicates that it wishes to become a supplier of the representative's company, the representative should refer it to the purchasing department with the understanding that it must bid for the business on the basis of its own merits, without reference to its status as a customer.

UNFAIR PRACTICES

THE LAW

Many unfair trade practices are regarded as illegal under the Federal Trade Commission Act (1914), Section 5, as amended by the Wheeler-Lea Act (1938). Section 5 has been used vigorously by the FTC against deceptive advertisers, but it also is used to stop deceptive selling. Door-to-door sales representatives have engaged in many unfair and pressure selling tactics. Some representatives claimed they were doing a market survey, not selling books. Salespeople for heating contractors claimed they were doing fire inspections. Representatives for courses in computer programming claimed they were career counselors. In 1974, the FTC introduced a "cooling off" rule that required the door-to-door salespersons to give customers who placed orders of $25 or more a form stating that they could cancel their purchase within three days. Industry claims that this form is no longer necessary because most door-to-door companies now give a 100-percent money-back guarantee and because only a few hundred of the one billion forms have ever been used to cancel purchases. Industry claims it would be easier to train a representative to say, "We have an unlimited money-back guarantee," than to explain the 228-word form with its legalistic references.[20]

The Magnuson-Moss Warranty Federal Trade Commission Improvement Act (1975) attempted to make consumer product warranties more easily understood and enforceable. Some marketers concluded that this act added to the complexity of warranties and chose instead to remove the warranty from their products. In such cases, the consumer will have to rely on the Uniform Commercial Code for remedies.[21]

The sales representative, in his or her enthusiasm for the product, may unintentionally promise more than the product can deliver or imply a warranty that the company does not wish to support. Representatives should make guarantees with great care and within the bounds of the corporate policy.

BRIBERY

Influencing a buyer's employee to decide in favor of the seller can constitute bribery, a violation of Section 5 of the Federal Trade Commission Act. In 1960, the FTC successfully prohibited payments by record manufacturers and distributors to disc jockeys to push the sale of certain records. The court concluded, however, that push money (PM) given by a manufacturer to a retailer's sales force to encourage the sale of the manufacturer's product was not illegal. The reasoning was that competition among the manufacturers had ceased so that this manufacturer could not be attacked for engaging in unfair competition.[22] The Federal Alcoholic Administration Act takes a stricter view of push monies and prevents a distiller from giving any incentive to a barmaid or barkeeper. The Foreign Corrupt Practices Act (1977) makes it a criminal offense to pay a foreign official for help in selling to a foreign government.

SUMMARY

The legal dimensions of personal selling are involved primarily in preserving competition so that the marketplace will be the means for allocating resources according to the demands of the public. The purpose of this chapter has been to alert sales representatives and sales managers to those laws and court decisions regarding price fixing, price discrimination, controlling distribution, and unfair practices that may, in the eyes of the courts, result in a reduction of competition. After learning these laws and court cases, the representative will be better prepared to know when to turn to the legal department for advice. The general rule, of course, is, "If in doubt, seek advice."

ASSIGNMENTS/DISCUSSION QUESTIONS

1. Review the "Legal Developments in Marketing" in recent issues of the *Journal of Marketing* for recent cases of interest to sales management. Discuss these cases in class.

2. Develop a table of relevant law and cases to train sales representatives in the following industries:
   a. Folding boxes
   b. Grocery packaged goods
   c. Door-to-door books.

REFERENCES

1. S. Shepherd and C. Wilcox, *Public Policies Toward Business,* 6th ed. (Homewood, Ill.: Richard D. Irwin, Inc., 1979), p. 203.
2. Ibid., p. 204.
3. Ibid., pp. 204–205.
4. *FTC News Summary,* vol. 39–80 (July 4, 1980): 2.
5. M. C. Howard, *Legal Aspects of Marketing* (New York: McGraw-Hill Book Co., 1964), p. 66; I. M. Stelzer, *Selected Antitrust Cases,* 6th ed. (Homewood, Ill.: Richard D. Irwin, Inc., 1976), pp. 262–266.
6. Howard, *Legal Aspects of Marketing,* p. 56.
7. 99 S. Ct 925 (1979).
8. U.S. v. United States Gypsum Co., et al., 98 S. Ct 2864 (1978).
9. Shepard and Wilcox, 236.
10. Ibid., pp. 237–238.
11. Ibid., p. 247.
12. R. O. Werner, "The 'New' Supreme Court and the Marketing Environment, 1975–1977," *Journal of Marketing* (April 1978): 60.
13. Ibid.
14. Shepherd and Wilcox, 251.
15. Ibid., p. 253.

16. Howard, *Legal Aspects of Marketing,* p. 96.
17. Ibid.
18. Ibid., p. 93.
19. Ibid.
20. B. Schorr, "Salesmen Ask FTC to Relax Refund Rule," *Wall Street Journal* (August 14, 1980): 21.
21. B. S. Roberts, "The Magnuson-Moss Federal Warranty Act and Failure of its Essential Purpose, Uniform Commercial Code 2-719(2)," *The Business Lawyer* 33, no. 3 (April 1978): 1845–1858.
22. Howard, *Legal Aspects of Marketing,* p. 136.

SUGGESTED READINGS

Areeda, Phillip, *Antitrust Analysis,* 2nd ed. (Boston: Little, Brown and Co., 1974).

Briggs, J. A., "For Whom Does the Bell Toll?" *Forbes* (June 25, 1979): 33–35.

Gellhorn, Ernest, *Antitrust Law and Economics* (St. Paul, Minn.: West Publishing Co., 1976).

Howard, M., *Legal Aspects of Marketing* (New York: McGraw-Hill Book Co., 1964).

Hughes, G. David, *Marketing Management: A Planning Approach* (Reading, Mass.: Addison-Wesley, 1978), Chapter 10.

Hughes, G. David, "Antitrust Caveats for the Marketing Planner," *Harvard Business Review* (March–April 1978): 42–46ff.

Posner, Richard, *Antitrust Law* (Chicago: University of Chicago Press, 1976).

Shepherd, William, and Wilcox, Clair, *Public Policies Toward Business,* 6th ed. (Homewood, Ill.: Richard D. Irwin, Inc., 1979), Part II.

Smith, R. A., "The Incredible Electrical Conspiracy," *Fortune* (April and May 1961).

Sonnenfeld, J., and Lawrence, P. R., "Why Do Companies Succumb to Price Fixing?" *Harvard Business Review* 56 (July–August 1978): 145–157.

Stelzer, Irwin M., *Selected Antitrust Cases,* 5th ed. (Homewood, Ill.: Richard D. Irwin, Inc., 1967).

Welch, J. J., *Marketing Law* (Tulsa: Petroleum Publishing Co., 1980).

III.

FIELD
SALES
MANAGEMENT

7

OVERVIEW OF FIELD SALES MANAGEMENT

THE IMPORTANCE OF FIRST-LINE SALES MANAGEMENT

The first line of management in the sales force is the field sales manager, who is generally called a district sales manager or unit manager. Davis noted that there is considerable evidence that field sales managers are the forgotten persons in selling and managing.[1] Their counterparts in production are the foremen. The field sales manager will share many of the problems of the new foreman who, like the new sales manager, may have been promoted because he or she was successful at selling and there was a sudden need for a manager.

Successful selling depends on good first-line sales management. Davis cites a study that found that a sales representative had almost twice the chance of succeeding under a good supervisor as under a poor one.[2] The study found also that a weaker representative with a strong manager had the same chance of success as a strong representative with a poor manager. Ryans and Weinberg found that sales decreased as the span of control increased, adding additional evidence to the importance of the first-line field sales manager.[3]

CRITICAL DIFFERENCES BETWEEN SELLING AND MANAGING

Many district sales managers fail to make the distinction between selling and managing. In a study of 150 field managers, Davis found that their strongest skills were in the mechanics of the job and in human relations with customers and superiors, but they were weakest in analysis, plan-

170

ning, and human relations with subordinates.[4] He concluded that many local managers are super sales representatives instead of administrators. They do, instead of delegating, and they react, instead of planning.

ACTIVITIES

The primary responsibility of the sales representative is to develop accounts, while the sales manager is expected to develop people. In Exhibit 2.3 (Chapter 2) we saw that the most important activity of the first-line and second-line field sales managers was the development of people. Some companies promote and reward district sales managers according to how rapidly they bring people along in the business.

The working relationships of the sales manager are those of getting work done through others, while the representative can be a loner. The representative is a player, while the manager is a coach. The manager must remember that he or she is now a part of management. The diversity of responsibility between being a representative and being a manager is quite extensive, as is shown in Exhibit 7.1. A more detailed list of daily activities for a field sales manager may be found in Exhibit 7.2.

The failure of representatives to become good managers may be explained by the results of one study that found that more than one-half of the sales managers interviewed never saw a good description for their job; 78 percent were dissatisfied with their training or never received any management training; and only one out of forty-four companies had any kind of sales management training program.[5] The district sales manager seems to be a forgotten member of management in some companies.

Exhibit 7.1   Critical Differences Between Selling and Managing

ACTIVITY	REPRESENTATIVE	SALES MANAGER
Primary responsibility	Develop accounts	Develop people
Working relationships	Loner	Through others
Role	Player	Coach
Part of management?	No	Yes. Must sell the company plan to representatives.
Diversity of responsibility	Make calls, sell, and service	Develop people, recruit, select, train, motivate, compensate, run branch office, see key accounts, correspond, work with departments such as advertising, engineering, and credit.

Adapted from Ronald Brown, *From Selling to Managing* (New York: American Management Association, 1968), pp. 2–5.

Exhibit 7.2   Activities of a Field Sales Manager

Working with Representatives
- Assisting representatives with routine or difficult customers in a variety of calls, sales projects; trouble shooting.
- Coaching and motivating representatives.
- Calling on distributors with representative.
- Evaluating, appraising, counseling representative.
- Analyzing territory, market area, competitive activities, and the effectiveness of selling program and materials.
- Disciplining activities and rewarding.
- Resolving concerns and grievances.

Recruiting
- Contacting primary sources of applicants (colleges, employment agencies, government agencies, newspaper and magazine advertisements).
- Checking references and previous employers.
- Contacting minority, female, handicapped, and protected age group applicant sources.
- Conducting information sessions with spouses.
- Interviewing or reinterviewing applicants individually or in groups.
- Corresponding with applicants regarding required information, hiring, or turndown.
- Selecting applicants to be hired.

Training and Development
- Conducting training sessions individually or in groups.
- Conducting sales meetings.
- Coaching, delegating.
- Supplemental education.

Appraising, Counseling, Coaching, Correcting
- Annual and semi-annual performance reviews.
- Salary and bonus recommendations.
- Writing trip reports after working with the representative.
- Taking appropriate disciplinary actions.

Administrating
- Preparing forecasts for sales objectives, personnel needs, expense budgets, working materials, and office space.
- Communicating market information to appropriate corporate departments.
- Writing district bulletins.
- Writing general correspondence.
- Making compensation recommendations.
- Complying with administrative procedures.
- Making routine reports.
- Analyzing the statistical data regarding performance of representatives, the district, and the nation.
- Providing feedback about people, programs, procedures, and policies.
- Making expense analyses.
- Complying with the company's policies, procedures, and programs and relevant statutory regulations.

Self-Managing
- Achieving personal and professional objectives.
- Maintaining technical and management knowledge and skills.
- Maintaining favorable climate within the working unit.

PERSONAL DIFFERENCES

It is frequently difficult to identify those attributes that will single out a representative as a prime candidate for sales management. In a study of 135 salespeople and 35 managers who engaged in the technical selling of steel and plastic strapping, Bagozzi concluded that the overall profiles of salespeople and sales managers were relatively homogeneous.[6] He measured variables such as job satisfaction, motivation, self-esteem, other-directiveness, inner-directiveness, fatalism, verbal intelligence, role ambiguity, and job-related tension. The only significant differences were that sales managers had greater job satisfaction, were better able to cope with ambiguity and tension on the job, and had a stronger sense of controlling their fate.

The perception of the qualifications for district sales management positions will vary according to the perceiver's position in the administrative hierarchy. Spencer found a 0.87 correlation between the perceptions of the sales representatives and the district (first-line) managers regarding the qualifications that were necessary for first-line sales management.[7] Both groups ranked leadership, organizing ability, knowledge, and the ability to get along with people in their top five attributes of district sales managers. In contrast, division (second-line) managers ranked their criteria for district sales managers in the following order: sales performance, integrity, intellectual ability, and initiative and enthusiasm. There was only a 0.49 correlation between the attributes listed by the district managers and those listed by the division managers. While the Spencer study was an exploratory study that focused on a packaged-food manufacturer, it does suggest that many companies need to clarify the role and the attributes desired in their first-line sales managers. We will return to this point in Chapter 18, which discusses organizing the sales force.

ACTIVITIES OF FIELD SALES MANAGERS

Berkowitz notes that if a field sales manager is to perform the boundary role between management and the representative, then there must be some agreement by all parties on the importance of specific duties, the time to be allocated to duties, and the criteria that are used for rewarding field sales managers.[8] He found significant differences between the perceptions of sales representatives, regional managers, and the field manager. These results are particularly surprising because the study was conducted in one company, a large industrial chemical manufacturer, that had job descriptions and training manuals for the field sales managers. While these results may not be generalized to other companies, they do indicate the need for role clarification.

Berkowitz found that representatives ranked the field sales manager higher in importance on the duty of developing salespersons, personal selling activities, and inventory control. They ranked managers lower in importance on the activities of recruiting and training new salespersons, evaluating representatives' performance, and conducting district meetings. The comparison of the regional managers and field managers revealed that the regional managers thought that inventory control and evaluating representatives' performance was more important than was the perception of the field sales manager. The comparison of perceptions regarding how a manager spends his or her time revealed that regional managers thought that field managers spent more time on training new salespeople, in the field with experienced salespeople, and on inventory control, and less time on personal selling, office activities, and communication activities than were reported by the field sales manager.

There was also a lack of clarity on criteria for evaluation. Comparisons of perceptions of how field sales managers are evaluated revealed that representatives thought that they were evaluated according to personality, the meeting of quotas, the number of new accounts, and personal sales volume. There was also a misperception between field and regional sales managers regarding the use of personal sales volume as a performance criterion. Because these perceptions occurred in a company with a job description and a training manual for field sales managers, it is safe to assume that even more disruptive perceptions are present in companies that do not have a job description or a manual.

Most of the studies reported in the literature examined the perceived activities of district sales managers within one company. The study reported by the present authors in Chapter 2 (Exhibit 2.3) was a survey of twenty-five companies representing a variety of industries. This study compared the importance of management activities as viewed by the district managers themselves and their superiors. It found that only three of the twenty-two management activities differed in the perceptions of first-line, second-line, and general sales/marketing managers (Chapter 18, Exhibit 18.3). Differences among industries and companies will be discussed in Chapter 18.

FIELD SALES MANAGER JOB DESCRIPTIONS AND EVALUATIONS

The first-line sales manager has not been the forgotten person in all companies. Many companies have excellent job descriptions and evaluation schemes for this management position. To illustrate this point we will examine the job descriptions and evaluation forms for Cessna Aircraft Company and Burroughs Wellcome, a pharmaceutical firm. The roles of these field sales managers are quite different.

CESSNA AIRCRAFT COMPANY DISTRICT SALES MANAGER

The Cessna District Sales Manager's Job Description (Exhibit 7.3) illustrates that some first-line sales managers do not manage sales representatives. Instead, these managers accomplish their sales objectives by working with dealers. Many of the functions are similar. For example, the Cessna manager trains sales representatives, but they are the dealers'

Exhibit 7.3   Cessna Aircraft Company: Commercial Aircraft Marketing Division Management Position Guide

---

I. *Position Title:*   Manager, District Sales (Single Engine)
                               (Multi Engine)

II. *Organizational Relationship:*
    Line: Reports to Manager, Zone or Manager, Zone Sales
    Staff: Coordinate with Zone personnel to attain Zone objectives.

III. *Primary Function:*
To manage a domestic district for assigned product line in accordance with stated policies to accomplish approved sales objectives.

IV. *Specific Duties and Responsibilities:*

1. Implement various marketing programs at the dealer level to help achieve unit and dollar sales goals.
2. Train and assist dealer personnel for the purpose of increasing retail sales. Work with dealer personnel to implement new model introductions.
3. Provide instruction in aircraft demonstration techniques to dealers and assist in preparing and scheduling customer demonstrations as requested.
4. Coordinate problems encountered regarding aircraft sales and the management of product inventory, demonstrations, displays, advertising sales promotions, and merchandising.
5. Maintain and improve relations with dealers, customers, government officials, and organizations in the district.
6. Coordinate and cooperate with Zone support personnel on service, parts, flight training, and dealer procurement matters.
7. Oversee and monitor the performance of existing dealers. Locate, evaluate, and recommend appointment of new dealers and termination of dealers.
8. Maintain and monitor the status of Zone programs, dealer prospects, and aircraft prospects, and make reports as appropriate. Advise Supervisor on the effectiveness of materials and programs furnished, and on additional materials and programs desired.
9. Maintain flight proficiency and knowledge of aircraft, associated equipment, and sales features.
10. Prepare sales forecasts and order projections for assigned district.
11. Maintain contact with competitive dealers to gather knowledge of competitive products.
12. Attend and participate in aviation shows, conventions, and other meetings as assigned.
13. Advise Supervisor of product improvement suggestions and aircraft operational discrepancies encountered.

(continued)

Exhibit 7.3   Continued

Sample Worksheet

KEY RESPONSIBILITIES AND TASKS	AUTHORITY LEVEL	(STANDARD) SATISFACTORY PERFORMANCE EXISTS WHEN:
(1)		
(2)		
(3)		

Level of Authority

Level 1—Complete Authority: exists when the subordinate is expected to take necessary action to carry out a key responsibility *without consulting or reporting to the manager.*

Level 2—Considerable Authority: exists when the subordinate is expected to take necessary action but *must report the action to the manager.*

Level 3—Limited Authority: exists when the subordinate is expected *to present recommendations and action taken only upon manager's approval.*

Courtesy of Cessna Aircraft Company.

personnel. Marketing programs are implemented through the dealers rather than through company salespersons. The title of "District Sales Manager" is used also by heavy duty truck manufacturers who market through distributors. The recruiting function in these cases might include assisting a dealer in recruiting salespersons as well as recruiting dealers to handle the product.

The Cessna Aircraft Company job description for a district sales manager, Exhibit 7.3, identifies the organizational relationship, primary function, and specific duties and responsibilities. An interesting feature of this job description is the worksheet that is used to identify key responsibilities and tasks for this position. The authority level and the standard of satisfactory performance are specified for each responsibility and task, thereby reducing job ambiguity.

**Exhibit 7.4   Burroughs Wellcome Company
DSM Position Description and Performance Appraisal
U.S.A. 579**

DSM_____Date_____

Key Objectives: To plan, organize, lead, and control the activities and personnel of the District to achieve the planned level of sales within the approved level of expenses. To promote the prestige of the Company and the pharmaceutical industry. To provide stable employment with opportunity for the District Sales Staff.

Rate the DSM's performance in each of the major areas listed below entering the appropriate initials in the box in each category. ("O" Outstanding, "AA" Above Average, "S" Satisfactory, "M" Marginal, "US" Unsatisfactory, and "UA" Unacceptable) and add appropriate explanatory comments in the Remarks area.

Remarks

C.O. 1 To prepare projections for expenditures, equipment, services, and personnel requirements for the District Sales Staff.

C.O. 2 To collect Field marketing data and current marketing information, and to recommend programs and procedures to the Regional Sales Manager and appropriate departments.

C.O. 3 To develop and implement a district recruiting program to ensure the continuing availability of sales personnel.

C.O. 4 To maintain adequate District Sales Staff.

C.O. 5 To train and develop District Sales Staff to ensure capable management succession.

C.O. 6 To train and motivate the personnel within the District Sales Staff to work together and with other Field personnel and departments of the Company in order to:
  A. Achieve the sales objectives.
  B. Control expenses to maximize profits.
  C. Promote the prestige of the Company and the pharmaceutical industry.
  D. Provide stable employment with opportunity for District personnel.

C.O. 7 To maintain performance criteria and evaluate, review, and report performance of all members of the District Sales Staff regularly.

(continued)

Exhibit 7.4 Continued

C.O. 8 To apply within the District Sales Staff all standard Company procedures and policies including those pertaining to relevant statutory regulations governing labor relations, equal employment opportunities, fair employment practices and safety, and to ensure that such compliance is within the State and Federal regulations.

C.O. 9 To recommend to the RSM such programs, policies, and procedures as would improve the Company's performance, and inform the RSM immediately to recommended changes for approval as soon as possible when conditions arise which indicate an approved plan, program, policy, or procedure is unlikely to be achieved or implemented.

C.O. 10 To keep District Sales staff informed of Company objectives and programs.

C.O. 11 To resolve and/or communicate the achievements, needs, concerns, and grievances of the District Sales Staff to the RSM and appropriate departments.

C.O. 12 To adequately compensate the District Sales Staff within Company guidelines.

C.O. 13 To maintain an adequate level of Technical and Management knowledge.

C.O. 14 To achieve the District Sales Objectives.

C.O. 15 To create and maintain a favorable climate within the District.

Used by permission of Burroughs Wellcome Company.

BURROUGHS WELLCOME COMPANY DISTRICT SALES MANAGER

The Burroughs Wellcome Company is a pharmaceutical company with a field staff of over 500 sales representatives who call on physicians, hospitals, pharmacists, and medical centers. The Burroughs Wellcome position description for district sales managers (Exhibit 7.4) is unique in that it also includes performance appraisal. Thus the activities of the position and the criteria for evaluation are identical and are made clear to the new manager from the outset. A careful reading of this position description will illustrate that some district sales managers perform all of the activities that are basic to top management, as noted in Chapter 2, Exhibit 2.1.

EVALUATION

The performance appraisal form for Cessna Aircraft Company, Exhibit 7.5, is divided into four sections. The first section examines results attained from managing resources (finances, facilities, equipment, supplies, materials, and products), from managing information (information obtained, analyzed, communicated, and the resulting judgments and decisions), from managing people (supervision, motivation, control, selection, assignment, delegation, overcoming objections, human relations, subordinating development, and compliance with personnel policies and government regulations), and from self-management (self-discipline, planned usage of time, setting examples, and keeping commitments). It is interesting to note that this evaluation identifies information as a resource in itself.

The second section of this evaluation form by Cessna examines *how* these results were obtained. In this section the manager is evaluated according to basic management skills and functions, including: self-motivation and drive; leadership and motivation of others; planning and development; organizing, delegating, and followup; communicating and presenting; creativity; and judgment and decisions. The third and fourth categories in this form are open-ended questions regarding special problems and significant changes during the past year.

Burroughs Wellcome Company quantifies its evaluation of district sales managers with the aid of the DSM Activities Appraisal Summary that appears in Exhibit 7.6. Here we see all of the activities that appeared in Exhibit 7.4, summarized and weighted under the major headings of technical, operational, personal, and sales objectives. Summaries such as this one should reduce greatly the ambiguity between the expectations of the district managers and those of their superiors.

Weights, such as those shown in Exhibit 7.6, might be derived statistically, using multiple regression. An overall performance measure, such as sales, could be regressed on the individual performance evaluations such as forecasting, recruiting, etc. The coefficients in this regression model would be the estimated importance weights for each of the performance criteria.

Exhibit 7.5   Cessna Aircraft Company Performance Appraisal

Cessna
AIRCRAFT COMPANY
PERFORMANCE APPRAISAL

Employee Name_____
(FIRST, INITIAL, LAST)

Full Title_____

Employee No._____ Dept. No._____ Division_____

Monthly Salary ☐   Weekly Salary ☐

I.   **RESULTS ATTAINED** - In this section SUMMARIZE and EVALUATE the RESULTS ATTAINED by this employee in each of the areas below. Compare results to established standards of performance. Be sure to consider all established goals, targets, and objectives.

1. RESULTS FROM MANAGING RESOURCES:
Using finances, facilities, equipment, supplies, materials, products.
COMMENTS:

☐ Outstanding

☐ Above Average

☐ Satisfactory

☐ Needs Help

2. RESULTS FROM MANAGING INFORMATION:
Information obtained, analyzed, communicated, and judgment and decisions based on it.
COMMENTS:

☐ Outstanding

☐ Above Average

☐ Satisfactory

☐ Needs Help

3. RESULTS FROM MANAGING PEOPLE:
Supervision, motivation, and control of others. Selection, assignment, delegation, overcoming objections, human relations, subordinate development, compliance with personnel policies and government regulations.
COMMENTS:

☐ Outstanding

☐ Above Average

☐ Satisfactory

☐ Needs Help

Attach additional sheets when necessary.

(continued)

Exhibit 7.5   Continued

4. **RESULTS FROM MANAGING SELF:**
    Self-discipline, planned usage of time, good example, commitments kept.
    COMMENTS:

    ☐ Outstanding

    ☐ Above Average

    ☐ Satisfactory

    ☐ Needs Help

5. **OVER-ALL RESULTS:**
    Over-all results during the last year.
    CLARIFYING COMMENTS:

    ☐ Outstanding

    ☐ Above Average

    ☐ Satisfactory

    ☐ Needs Help

II. **RESULTS ANALYSIS:** In this section analyze HOW this employee obtained the types and levels of results appraised above. In your COMMENTS, pinpoint WHY you rated this individual as you did.

1. **SELF-MOTIVATION AND DRIVE:**
    Enthusiastic, self-starter, aggressive, persistent, a doer.
    COMMENTS:

    ☐ Outstanding

    ☐ Above Average

    ☐ Satisfactory

    ☐ Needs Help

2. **LEADERSHIP & MOTIVATING OTHERS:**
    Guides constructively, sets example, stimulates, is respected, and has self-confidence, aids development of subordinates.
    COMMENTS:

    ☐ Outstanding

    ☐ Above Average

    ☐ Satisfactory

    ☐ Needs Help

(continued)

Exhibit 7.5   Continued

Employee Name_____

3. PLANNING & DEVELOPING:
Looks ahead, logical, sets goals and priorities, innovative, methodical.
COMMENTS:

☐ Outstanding

☐ Above Average

☐ Satisfactory

☐ Needs Help

4. ORGANIZING, DELEGATING, AND FOLLOW-UP:
Utilizes capabilities of people and resources, administers and controls.
COMMENTS:

☐ Outstanding

☐ Above Average

☐ Satisfactory

☐ Needs Help

5. COMMUNICATING & PRESENTING:
Speaking, reading, listening, gets the point across, sells ideas, generates action.
COMMENTS:

☐ Outstanding

☐ Above Average

☐ Satisfactory

☐ Needs Help

6. CREATIVITY:
Inventive, unusual and unique ideas. Creates own breakthroughs. Independent
thinker, Problem solver.
COMMENTS:

☐ Outstanding

☐ Above Average

☐ Satisfactory

☐ Needs Help

(continued)

Exhibit 7.5   Continued

7. JUDGMENT & DECISIONS:
 Realistic, common sense, gets facts, considers alternatives, timely, decisive.
 COMMENTS:

                   ☐ Outstanding

                   ☐ Above Average

                   ☐ Satisfactory

                   ☐ Needs Help

III. Have the employee's RESULTS been affected by any special problem or situation during the last year? If so, specify.

IV. Has this employee's performance CHANGED SIGNIFICANTLY during the past year?

Appraised by_____Title_____ Date_____

   Signature_____

Appraiser's Supervisor_____Title_____ Date_____

   Signature_____

Supplementary Comments by Appraiser's Supervisor

Attach additional sheets when necessary.

Courtesy of Cessna Aircraft Company.

Exhibit 7.6   Burroughs Wellcome Company: DSM Activities Appraisal Summary

DSM ACTIVITIES APPRAISAL SUMMARY   U.S.A. 598

DSM _____ Submitted by _____ Date _____

Appraise DSM's performance by assigning the appropriate number in the box provided, using the following key: "5" Outstanding, "4" Above Average, "3" Satisfactory, "2" Marginal, "1" Unsatisfactory, "0" Unacceptable. For performance considered between evaluation categories use the decimal 3.5, 3.4, 3.3 etc. Copies: White (GSM), Yellow (RSM), Gold (DSM).

TECHNICAL

☐ Manpower
    Annual
    Forecast
    Changes

☐ Recruiting
    Col/Min Srcs.
    Applic, Flow
    Processing

☐ Dist. Staff
    Lost Days
    Hires/AAPs
    On Staff

☐ Training
    Sales Mtg.
    Rep. Trips
    Use PK/SS/Tools
    Tips/Planner
    PSS
    DDD

☐ Personnel Dev.
    Promotable
    Develop Tr.
    Counseling

☐ Compensation
    Annl. Sal. Rev.
    Inter. Sal. Rev.
    Bonus
    Benefits

☐ Perfor. Appraisal
    Annual
    Trip Reports
    Achievements
    Deficiencies
    Sp. Obj. Warrn/Prob.

____ Avg. Points Col. 1

OPERATIONAL

☐ Marketing Feedback
    Marketing Data
    Recommendations
    "Info Please'

☐ Communications
    Reps
    RSM
    Company

☐ Co./Indust. Image
    Wholesaler
    Speakers Bur.
    Rx Groups

☐ Expense Control
    Audits
    Equipment
    Specimens

☐ Co. Policies
    Supr. Manuals
    AAP Support
    Reps Compliance
    Recommendations

____ Avg. Points Col. 2

PERSONAL

☐ Self
    Set objectives
    Example
    Positive Attitude
    Accept. Crit.
    Evaluate Facts
    Take Action
    Realism
    Tolerance
    Self dicipline
    Deadline Control
    Mgt. Knowledge
    Tr. Ability

____ Avg. Points Col. 3

SALES OBJECTIVES

☐ Motivation
    Team Work
    Challenge
    competence
    Encourage
    excellence
    Leadership

☐ Achieve Sales Obj.
    DDD
    QP
    OTC
    Other

____ Avg. Points Col. 4

CALCULATIONS

	Col. Pts.	Factor	T. Points
1.	_____	x 3	= _____
2.	_____	x 1	= _____
3.	_____	x 4	= _____
4.	_____	x 2	= _____

GRAND TOTAL _____

AVERAGE (÷10) _____

Briefly discuss Strengths:

Briefly discuss areas needing improvement:
(Explain less than Sat. Perf. [less than 3.0] .)

Used by permission of Burroughs Wellcome Company.

TIME MANAGEMENT

Time is an unusual resource because it is linear, meaning that it comes in even units, it cannot be stored for future use, and it cannot be borrowed from others. The new district sales manager will find time management a critical skill for the successful completion of expanded responsibilities. Many textbooks, corporation programs, and short courses are available on the subject of time management. This section will be limited to specific suggestions that have been made for newly-appointed sales managers.

TECHNIQUES FOR MANAGING TIME

A *schedule* is the basic time-management technique. A schedule breaks a sales program into manageable steps, places a priority on the completion of each step, and specifies the time sequence in which these steps will be performed (Chapter 2).

Brown suggests that the new district sales manager should create two schedules: one for actions to be taken monthly and a second for tasks to be performed less often than monthly.[9] Exhibit 7.7 illustrates a schedule for monthly activities, and Exhibit 7.8 illustrates a schedule for activities throughout the year.

Exhibit 7.7 assumes that each activity can be completed in a single day. When this is not the case, the x's may be replaced by bars spreading across the days needed to complete the activity. This control technique is known in production as a GANTT chart. This table assumes also that each activity is independent of the others. Complex tasks require the completion of one activity before another can begin. These tasks might require a more complex scheduling technique such as PERT (Program Evaluation Review Technique) or CPM (Critical Path Method). District sales managers should be encouraged to begin with simple scheduling techniques before moving to the more complex ones.

By having a definite schedule, the young manager is better able to distinguish between important activities and urgent ones. Urgent events come in all sizes, and are not of equal importance. Without a schedule, a manager may fall into the trap of completing minor urgent tasks without having time to complete the important tasks. The manager who has not carefully planned activities may resort quickly to crisis management, which is responding to events rather than making them happen in your favor—the basis of planning.

Exhibit 7.7   Field Sales Manager's Monthly Action Schedule

	1	2	3	4	5	S	S	8	9	10	11	12
Work with Representatives[1]												
Sam Brown	x	x										
Nancy Smith			x	x								
John Black								x	x			
Frank Peterson										x	x	
Henry Green												
Special Calls												
Recruiting, interviewing reference checking	(as required)											
Personal accounts												
Annual calls on distributors' management												
Desk Work[2]												
Trip reports (work with reps.)					x							x
Correspondence		x			x					x		x
District bulletins (1–2/mo.)				x								
Development program (reps.)												
Personal expense accounting												
Forward itinerary												
Review own activities against plan												
Review sales data vs. quota		x		x					x		x	
Review expenses vs. budget		x		x					x		x	
Review reps' activities reports		x		x					x		x	
Review progress vs. objectives		x		x					x		x	
Miscellaneous[3]												
Dist. Sales Mtg. preparation											x	
Conventions, exhibits	(as required)											
Prepare performance reviews												
Disciplinary actions	(as required)											

[1]Work with half of representative staff every two months.
[2]May require considerably more time than scheduled.
[3]Miscellaneous activities occur irregularly, but are time-consuming.

Some authors suggest that there is an 80–20 rule of time management. This rule states that a manager places 80 percent of his or her time on those activities that represent only 20 percent of the importance of management. A clear schedule of activities and dates for completion should lead to a better allocation of time.

S	S	15	16	17	18	19	S	S	22	23	24	25	26	S	S	29	30	31
		x	x															
				x														
					x				x							x		
						x												
				x		x					x		x			x		x
						x							x					
																		x
																		x
																		x
																		x
			x															x
			x															x
			x															x
			x															x
																	x	
										x								

For example, some companies supply their district sales managers with high-quality dictating machines that can transmit over telephone lines at high speed to the home office word-processing center, thereby reducing the field manager's paper work. Other companies supply their managers with portable microfiche readers that can plug into their auto-

Exhibit 7.8 Annual Activities Checklist/Schedule

Activity	JAN	FEB	MAR	APR	MAY	JUN	JUL	AUG	SEP	OCT	NOV	DEC
Annual Sales Forecast	x											
Annual Expense Budget	x											
District Objectives	x		(and as required)									
Marketing Planning Conf.	x						x					
Personnel Requirements	x											
Promotables Recommendation		x										
District Sales Meetings (quarterly or bimonthly)	x			x			x			x		
District Sales Managers Conferences			x			x			x			x
Appraisal & Counseling (Reps)						x						x
Appraisal & Counseling (by Boss)						x						x
Quarterly Progress Reviews			x			x			x			x
Training Activities			(as required)									
Review/Revise Job Descriptions												x
Compensation Recommendations					x							
Vacation											x	
Holidays												

Note: Annual activities are scheduled usually one month in advance of start of fiscal year.

mobile cigarette lighters so that they may read extensive computer print-outs of territory analysis without the burden of the large computer output.

Some district managers are beginning to buy their own microcomputers for word processing and analysis of territory data. In the future we may expect companies to supply district managers with microcomputers for these applications, as well as for use in training programs for representatives.

Twedt found that a time-and-duty study of managers could be helpful in identifying the activities of high-performing managers.[10] His study of one company revealed that managers who made high progress toward company sales goals spent more time on inventory control and personnel administration. Conversely, the poorer managers spent more time on advertising and promotion. Studies such as this one could be helpful in preparing a job description for field sales managers.

SUMMARY

This overview of field sales management reveals that it is difficult to make generalizations about the sophistication of the first-line sales manager. In some companies he or she may be the forgotten person, without a job description and without clear criteria for measuring performance. The resulting ambiguity will reduce the effectiveness of the field sales force and increase its turnover, adding great expense to the selling function.

ASSIGNMENTS/DISCUSSION QUESTIONS

1. Evaluate the Cessna job description for a District Sales Manager (Exhibit 7.3). Compare it with the activities of a sales manager (Exhibit 7.2) and explain any differences.

2. Evaluate the Burroughs Wellcome District Sales Manager position description (Exhibit 7.4). What changes do you recommend?

3. Why do you think that first-line field sales managers are neglected in some companies?

4. What are the job-related activities of a field sales manager who tends to be a super sales representative instead of a manager?

5. What are some reasons that a field sales manager might neglect developing his or her representatives? What are the benefits from developing the sales representatives?

6. Arrange to be interviewed by a campus recruiter and identify and comment on the role of the field sales manager in interacting with the sales reps in the following procedures of that company:
   a. Training program
   b. Performance review system
   c. Compensation plan
   d. Career development
   e. Customer calls.

7. Compare the relative importance of the characteristics of salespeople and sales managers reported by Bagozzi in the section on Personal Differences, by listing them 1–2–3, etc.

8. To what would you attribute a significant difference of opinion between the perceptions of sales reps, field sales managers, and general sales managers about the importance of specific duties of the field sales manager?

9. What is the primary difference in management activities between managing a group of reps employed directly by the field sales manager's company and working with reps employed by a distributor?

10. Explain the relationship between a position (job) description, performance review, compensation, and promotion (advancement) system.

11. By assigning values to total 100 percent, weight the four categories in Section I of the Cessna Aircraft Company Performance Appraisal, Exhibit 7.5.

12. What are the factors that could interfere with the manager adhering to the monthly schedule as shown in Exhibit 7.7?

CASE 7.1:
The Inter-Con Pharmaceutical Co.

As he reread the annual report he had prepared for Steve Collins, his regional sales manager, and fleetingly relived the highlights of his first year in supervision, Brian Dexter shook his head in wonderment and muttered to himself, "Boy, what a year!"

He'd never forget the terrific surge of pride he felt when Jane Smithfield, his former district sales manager, met him last June and asked him whether he'd like to call Steve Collins to let him know whether or not he wanted to accept a promotion to district sales manager for the Dallas area. As he remembered, he couldn't get to the telephone quickly enough, and it was only after Steve asked him how Brian's wife, Patty, had taken the news that he realized he had forgotten to ask her. He corrected that oversight immediately and found that, as expected, Patty was as delighted as he was, both with his promotions and their move to Dallas, even though neither one of them had been there before. Brian did remember, however, to express his appreciation to Jane for all the help she had given him in helping him qualify for the promotion.

Now aged twenty-seven, Brian had joined Inter-Con Pharmaceuticals as a sales rep immediately following graduation from Arizona State. While he'd been mildly interested in science in high school, and had taken one course in chemistry and another in biology at State, he was more interested in communications. When Inter-Con recruited at the college in his junior year and again in the spring of his last year, Brian decided he might combine his interests in science and communications as a sales representative. He was interviewed, hired, and assigned to a traveling territory out of Salt Lake City in Jane Smithfield's district. Brian's willingness, personality, and communications skills, plus Jane's encouragement and guidance, aided him in quickly achieving a better-than-average level of productivity and helped him win a transfer to a territory in metropolitan Denver. The new territory offered him additional experiences in working with drug and food chain headquarters, large hospitals, and drug wholesalers. Brian recalled these experiences with considerable pleasure as he reviewed the events of the past year. Jane worked regularly with him, and delegated to him some of the training of new reps, which he found challenging and particularly rewarding when the trainee did well. His selling skills flourished in the new customer universe, as did his income and the recognition of his achievements by Jane and the regional sales manager. A year later, he was selected to attend the company's leadership training program, which was a milestone in his progress.

Even before his first trip to Dallas, Brian was asked by Dick Holloway, the general sales manager, to spend a couple of days at the corporate headquarters in Philadelphia with him and various department heads in marketing, legal, and personnel. They were all very complimentary about his past performance and how much he deserved his promotion, but each of them in a different way seemed to repeat the same message: "Managing people is different from selling products." How well the events of the past year were to bear that out. The thrust of Mr. Holloway's message was a little different. He wanted Brian to realize that he had full confidence in his ability, that Brian had earned his promotion, and that although Brian was a sales rep one day and a district sales manager the next day, the company recognized the change wouldn't occur overnight and it would provide him with further training. In the meantime, he counseled Brian that the Dallas district was productive, operating efficiently, and staffed with well-trained sales reps, and that he was not expecting Brian to be a "new broom" and make radical changes. He also emphasized that (1) Brian should give the sales reps in Dallas time to know him and him them; (2) he would be surprised and disappointed to discover that all the reps didn't operate with the same efficiency he did, nor use the same methods he used when he was a rep; (3) he shouldn't try to correct too many deficiencies at one time; (4) telling someone to do something doesn't necessarily get it done; (5) everyone doesn't remember hearing something the same way; and (6) it's better to have three sales reps working with you than ten working for you.

A year later, Brian realized that at the time he and Mr. Holloway talked, he didn't understand or appreciate the full meaning of that advice. The legal department wanted him to be aware of his increased responsibilities as a manager in speaking and acting for the company, and their availability when issues were not clear. The various departments in sales, marketing, and personnel emphasized the importance of his new role and his support in administering the company's promotional programs and gaining the compliance of his sales reps. Increasingly, he realized the duality of his role as a member of management and of the field sales staff. The sales management training programs he attended during the succeeding months reinforced these points and helped prepare him for the types of problems he was to encounter.

His introduction to the nine sales reps in the Dallas district went smoothly. His predecessor, Jim Franklin, who was retiring after twenty-six years with Inter-Con, fully reviewed with him all of the sales statistics for the district and the personnel records of the reps, and gave him the benefit of his thoughts for the future and what Brian's immediate concerns should be. Brian had inherited a district that was operating on target both for sales and expenses, and appeared to have no major personnel problems other than one territory that had been open for three weeks. Jim even had resumes on two promising applicants who needed processing.

So, in setting up his first itinerary, Brian telephoned both applicants and scheduled interviews for the following week, along with the working trips of two days each with two of his reps. The interviews seemed to go well, but they took up the better part of a full day. On his first day at his desk the following week, Brian called the references and previous employers of both applicants, scheduled a second interview several days later with Jed Turner, the most promising applicant, and, in accordance with the company's interviewing procedure, set up an information session with Jed and his wife for the following evening. Since this was Brian's first session of this type, he was pleased that it went well and was happy when it ended. Mrs. Turner had numerous questions about transferring, the amount of travel, and the amount of paperwork her husband would have to do at night. Brian was glad he was able to address her concerns. The telephone conversations with the applicants' references and previous employers had been an interesting experience and tended to confirm what the applicants had said, except in two instances. A previous employer and one reference were guardedly enthusiastic about the applicant. When Brian pressed the issue, the reference refused to say more, while the previous employer provided specifics which confirmed an earlier impression Brian had noted at the initial interview. Comments about the other applicant, Jed Turner, all emphasized the great personality he had and what a terrific job they thought he'd do in sales. Following the second interview with Jed Turner and the spouse information session, Brian completed the company's applicant appraisal reports on both applicants and decided that Jed was the better of the two. He telephoned his RSM, Steve Collins, to set up a final interview for Jed, forwarded Steve his applicant appraisal reports, and wrote the other applicant a polite turndown letter.

The day following Jed's interview, Steve Collins called to say that while he had some misgivings, he had hired Jed to begin his training in a class at the regional office the first of the month. Brian's reaction was a sigh of relief because of all the time he had put into the screening, and the hope that he wouldn't have to do that too often. The reports he completed on his first field trips with the sales reps with whom he'd worked had been his first and took longer to prepare than he anticipated. Coupled with the correspondence and appraisal reports on the applicants, Brian realized that written communications were going to be a bigger part of the job than he had realized, and that he'd have to learn how to communicate in writing faster and more effectively if he were to have the necessary time for his other responsibilities.

Brian's relationships with his sales reps seemed to go well during the early months, with the exception of Frank Heston, an above-average producer, aged 50, with twelve years experience, and the senior man in the district. Frank had been described by Jim Franklin, the retiring DSM, as a friendly, outgoing individual with a good sense of humor and a highly individualistic style of selling. As Brian worked with Frank, he was able to confirm in Frank's interaction with his customers the general description Jim had given him. However, in his personal interaction with Brian, Frank was curt, relatively subdued, and at other times almost hostile. For the next several working trips, Brian tried to ignore Frank's conduct and concentrated on the calls they were making and the objectives they were trying to achieve. At a recent sales meeting, Frank seemed to take delight in being argumentative and disruptive until Brian jokingly asked him if he would like to take over the meeting. After that, Frank settled down but made almost no contributions to the discussions for the rest of the meeting.

The situation came to a head immediately following the last physician call, during which Frank introduced Brian without indicating who he was or his purpose for being there. The physician's reaction was, "Oh, a new rep, eh?" and to Frank, "Are you being promoted?" This forced Frank, somewhat embarrassed, to indicate that Brian was his new district sales manager. As they left the office, it was clear that Frank was furious, as he muttered in a sarcastic manner, "Are you getting promoted?" Brian decided it was time to take action, whereupon he said emphatically, "Frank, I don't know what the hell is eating you, but I think it's time we got it out in the open. You've been on the muscle from the day I arrived. You're sarcastic, uncooperative, and downright unfriendly. If you and I are going to continue to work together, this has got to change! I don't know what I've done that's upset you, but whatever it is or whatever I've said, it certainly wasn't intentional and I'm sorry. You're too good a man to go around perpetually angry. What's bothering you?"

Frank's reaction was an angry, somewhat subdued and embarrassed, "Aw, I guess it's not your fault or anything you did. The fault is Jim Franklin's or Dick Holloway's or I don't know who. I've been here twelve years, and I'm the best sales rep in the district. Jim even told me so. And then you got promoted! Boy, that's gratitude for you."

Now that the problem was out in the open, Brian realized how long Frank had been carrying his anger locked up inside himself, and felt sorry for him. With that, he said, "Frank, I've sure been blind. Let's knock off, and sit down somewhere to talk this out." Three hours later they shook hands and parted on a much better understanding. Their relationship improved steadily, and now, as Brian reflected on the district's productivity for the past year, he realized that Frank's support had contributed measurably to their success.

Thinking about the successful year reminded him of Linda Ferrell, the trainee who was doing such a terrific job. She was the one who took Jed Turner's place. When he thought of Jed Turner, his brow furrowed and he winced a little thinking about the mistake he'd made. Jed was the first rep he'd recruited. He'd completed the basic training class, but just barely. The report from the sales training manager was anything but encouraging. Jed had difficulty acquiring the necessary product knowledge and his scientific communication skills were marginal. The qualities that saved him from being dropped from the training class were his desire, his willingness to work, and the fact that he was such a great guy—everybody loved him! Notwithstanding Jed's shortcomings, Brian was convinced he could turn Jed around. He worked with him every opportunity he had, quizzed him, coached him, and drilled him in an effort to improve his knowledge and skills so Jed would be able to capitalize on his sincerity and personality.

As the months wore on, Brian became increasingly aware that while Jed's customers liked him, he couldn't sell and his sales showed it. It was a tough decision Brian had to make to let Jed go, and an even tougher decision to implement, but Brian realized it really was in everyone's best interests. As he looked back on all the time and effort he had put into Jed's ultimate failure, Brian realized that it was at the expense of the time and effort he should have spent with his more productive reps. He also realized with some chagrin that in spite of the overwhelming evidence, he had carried Jed much longer than he probably should have, and was thankful that Steve Collins did not remind him of it. Sometimes, however, events have a bright side. As much as Brian regretted the amount of time it took to recruit Jed's replacement, he felt he lucked out with Linda Ferrell. She seemed to do everything right. In the four months since she'd been on the territory, sales had taken a noticeable increase and her enthusiasm was infecting the other reps in the district. Brian hoped her progress and productivity would continue on that trend.

Linda's performance, however, didn't eliminate the log jam that recruiting her had created in Brian's other activities. Her interviews, reference checking, early orientation and training, plus the extra time he had spent over the previous months trying to help Jed succeed, extended the intervals since he last worked in the field with his above-average sales reps, to the extent that several were beginning to make humorously sarcastic comments about being "orphans." Brian tried to explain that they were practically self-sufficient, while others needed his help more urgently. While they were willing to listen, Brian could see they weren't buying the excuse.

To further compound the problem, he received notice that the semi-annual appraisal and counseling interviews were to begin within thirty days. This would be the second time he would be holding these performance reviews, but it would be his first time alone since his RSM, Steve Collins, had helped him when they were last scheduled, which was shortly after his promotion. As Brian began to review the trip reports and correspondence in each rep's file, along with the pertinent sales performance data, he realized the accuracy of the beefing by the above-average producers. Their files were relatively thin, compared to those of reps with whom he had been spending the bulk of his time. If it hadn't been for the in-depth nature of the sales data, Brian would have been at a serious loss to justify his appraisal of their performance and productivity.

The process of accumulating the data and information, evaluating it, scheduling the interviews, sending copies of the appraisal form on which the reps could evaluate their own performance, and then conducting the interviews, was a time that, as Brian reflected on it, he really earned his salary. Throughout the year on field trips, at sales meetings, in correspondence, during telephone conversations, on reports of all kinds, and on reams of statistical print-outs, Brian had accumulated bits of information about the performance of each of his reps. It was at this time that it was his responsibility "to bite the bullet" and assess the value of this accumulated information, determine its meaning, and then communicate that value judgment to the individual. When the reps and Brian had different evaluations, which was not uncommon, the differences were resolved and then it became a matter of their jointly agreeing on a plan of action or set of objectives on the best way to close the gap between the actual and desired performance. As difficult as it was to achieve the agreement at times, and harder still to implement the agreed-upon plan, Brian felt that it was at this point that he was making a significant contribution to the success of the company and the growth and development of the individual. He also realized that he needed to mobilize his efforts and organize his time better throughout the year and to prepare for these sessions, for in the process he was evaluating his own performance in being able to help his staff achieve its objectives.

The second appraisal and counseling session of the year had had its peaks and valleys. It had been a pleasure to provide Stan Wychek, Henry Hartman, one of his two black reps, and Dave Chapman with the recognition their performances merited, and to help them define the goals they would next achieve. In the case of Bill Kensington, it was another matter. Bill had been in the training class at the time Brian was hired. He had done reasonably well, but nothing compared with the potential he appeared to have. Lately, Bill seemed to have lost interest, and, while his performance did not merit any drastic action, the trend was certainly in the wrong direction. When Brian challenged Bill's own evaluation of his performance and let Bill read what Brian had written, Bill sheepishly commented that he "wondered whether you'd let it pass." When Brian pressed him for an explanation of his performance in view of his better-than-average potential, Bill quickly replied, "I didn't know you cared that much."

Brian acknowledged the fact that he'd spent much of his time in the field working with inexperienced reps and in helping Jed Turner, but he also stated that he felt that Bill had sufficient experience and intelligence to exert the necessary self-discipline to do what was required without a lot of personal attention from him. At this point, Brian said, "Bill, I think it's time you made a decision whether or not you want to continue in this job. You have the capabilities to be an above-average performer, and nothing better could happen to you, me, and the company. On the other hand, the performance trend you're presently on can't end in anything but a disaster for all of us. Oh, you could continue getting by, but sooner or later a day of reckoning will come and the decision will be made for you. Why not face the issue now? If you decide you want to do a better job, I'll help you in every way possible, but you'll have to want to work at it. If you don't want to, then I think you're wasting your time and talents, which you could invest better elsewhere probably. So, why prolong it? Therefore, what I want you to do is to go home, think about what I said, talk it over with your wife, and then let me know what you decide. It's your decision to make at this time. How about if we get together next Wednesday morning, and at that time we'll plan how to implement your decision.''

The problem Brian faced with Fred Winkler was almost the opposite. Fred was a young, single rep with three years' experience in a fairly heavy traveling territory in the Texas panhandle. He had just about every good quality anyone could want in a salesman, except maturity and self-control. He was smart, eager, highly motivated, very productive, and extremely ambitious. His favorite question of Brian was, ''What else do I have to do to get promoted?'' and he posed that question on every field trip and frequently at sales meetings. In addition, Brian could count on Fred calling him at least three nights a week and dropping by his home on weekends now and then. In a way, Brian wished he had more reps who were as productive and as eagerly cooperative, but he also wished Fred would develop more patience and self-discipline. While Brian certainly didn't want to do anything to dampen Fred's enthusiasm, he was running out of ways to help Fred grow up.

As he thought about the different challenges he had with Fred Winkler, Bill Kensington, Linda Ferrell, Frank Heston, Stan Wychek, Henry Hartman, and Dave Chapman, and the administrative log-jam he'd created as a result of his recruiting activities, he realized he had to formalize a set of objectives for the coming year to discuss with Steve Collins, during his own appraisal and counseling session two weeks away. Although the year had been a successful one and they had met their overall sales objectives, their performance on a couple of major products could have been better, and he'd have to get the reps together to figure out some kind of action plan to correct that situation. And then there were the territory revisions to be done to take advantage of the growth potential in the Ft. Worth area. Not the least important or urgent matter he needed to address was to evaluate his own performance during the past year and to set some personal objectives.

As Brian let these thoughts filter through his mind, he realized that his activities anticipated, supported, corrected, or reinforced the activities of his sales reps. Yes, his job included innumerable administrative forms of documentation, planning activities, and reward systems in the form of marketing plan recommendations, changes in territory content or design, sales, expense and personnel forecasts, specific objectives, salary reviews, career recommendations, selling plan evaluations, surveys of various types, etc. In the main, however, his problems and opportunities were people problems and people opportunities, and their interaction and interdependence were what made his job challenging and fun.

CASE QUESTIONS

1. What could be some of the negative effects of the "new broom" efforts of a new district sales manager?

2. Why do new field sales managers initiate changes prematurely?

3. What is the purpose of checking references and previous employers?

4. Why would a reference or previous employer give anyone a bad reference?

5. What is the purpose of the spouse information session?

6. How might Brian Dexter have prevented or minimized the impact of the Frank Heston problem?

7. How else might Brian Dexter have handled the crisis with Frank Heston?

8. What would you say to Frank when you sat down with him and "talked it out," in an effort to resolve the problem?

9. How would Brian terminate Jed Turner? What would he say?

10. Discuss the pros and cons of Brian spending his time working in the field with less experienced or less productive sales reps versus above-average producers.

11. Identify the individuals whom the case indicates were probably affected by the imbalance of Brian's time in the field with Jed, and discuss the effects.

12. How can Brian help Fred Winkler develop more patience without becoming dispirited?

13. Identify a list of objectives Brian can set for his reps and for himself during the next year.

REFERENCES

1. Robert T. Davis, *Performance and Development of Field Sales Managers* (Boston: Division of Research, Graduate School of Business Administration, Harvard University, 1957).
2. Robert T. Davis, "Sales Management in the Field," *Harvard Business Review* 36 (January–February 1958): 91–98.
3. A. B. Ryans and C. B. Weinberg, "Territory Sales Response," *Journal of Marketing Research* 16 (November 1979): 453–465.
4. Davis, "Sales Management," p. 95.
5. Research by the American Management Association quoted in C. G. Stevens and D. P. Keane, *Marketing News* (May 30, 1980): 1, 20.
6. Richard P. Bagozzi, "Salespeople and Their Managers: An Exploratory Study of Some Similarities and Differences," *Sloan Management Review* (Winter 1980): 15–26.
7. Hollister Spencer, "Salesmen and Sales Managers Look at the District Manager," *California Management Review* 15 (Fall 1972): 98–105.
8. Eric N. Berkowitz, "Organizational Perceptions of Sales Managers," *Industrial Marketing Management* 7, no. 1 (1978): 37–42.
9. Ronald Brown, *From Selling to Managing* (New York: American Management Association, 1968), pp. 96–97.
10. D. W. Twedt, "What Time Allocation Is Most Productive for Sales Managers?" *Journal of Marketing* 30 (July 1966): 63–64.

SUGGESTED READINGS

Dodge, H. R., *Field Sales Management* (Dallas: Business Publications, 1973).

Hanan, M. et al., *Take-Charge Sales Management: Successful First Year Strategies for the Newly Appointed Sales Manager* (New York: AMACOM, 1976).

Henry, Porter, "Manage Your Sales Force as a System," *Harvard Business Review* 53 (March–April 1975): 85–95.

Loen, Raymond O., "Sales Managers Must Manage," *Harvard Business Review* 42 (May–June 1964): 107–114.

MacDonald, Morgan B., *The First Line Sales Supervisor* (New York: The Conference Board, 1968).

Steinmetz, L. L., and Todd, H. R., Jr., *First-line Management: Approaching Supervision Effectively* (Dallas: Business Publications, 1975).

"Time and Territory Management," Sales Builders Division, *Sales & Marketing Management,* 1976.

8

PLANNING AND DEVELOPING STRATEGY BY FIELD SALES MANAGERS

The new field sales manager will have experienced some planning and strategy development as a representative. Planning calls, managing the territory like a profit center, deciding which product and service benefits to sell to a client, and developing selling approaches and closes introduced the representative to the concepts of planning and strategy development, and provided an opportunity to practice them in a limited environment. The representative was on the receiving end of the selling strategy as it was developed by top management and adapted by a field sales manager to his or her territory.

A new field sales manager is provided with an expanded opportunity to develop planning and strategy skills. First, the selling strategy must be adapted to individual territories. Second, territory resources, such as representatives' time, expense accounts, samples, promotional materials, and, perhaps, local office expenses, must be planned and allocated in the most optimal means possible. And finally, a field sales manager is required to evaluate company sales strategies and make recommendations for change. The new field sales manager suddenly realizes that planning is now for a longer term than the planning that is practiced by a representative. The new field sales manager will need training to develop these skills.

THE FIELD SALES MANAGER'S ROLE IN PLANNING

Planning lacks the excitement and immediate fulfillment of achievement that is present in a representative's activities of making presentations, meeting objectives, and closing a sale. Planning requires many desk-oriented activities in which the new manager has little expertise, and, perhaps, less interest. The manager would rather be spending time sharing his or her expertise by engaging in such activities as training, counseling, and coaching, which provide almost immediate feedback. The new field sales manager will therefore need training, coaching, and counseling during the early development of his or her planning skills. This period may be disillusioning for the new manager who thought a manager was simply a super salesperson.

By reading across the rows of Exhibit 8.1, we see that planning becomes a more important function as one moves up the sales management hierarchy. General sales managers regard planning more than twice as important for their jobs as do first-line managers (36.5 vs. 17.6).

If we distinguish between activities that create change (planning and organizing) and implementing changes that have been specified by higher managers (staffing, directing, and controlling), we see in Exhibit 8.1 that the implementation functions decline as one gains higher management responsibilities (from 78.2 to 55.6). Thus first-line managers must learn to implement the plans of others before they acquire sufficient experience to develop their own plans.

The fact that first-line managers spend most of their efforts implementing plans is fortunate because the implementation activities of staffing, directing, and controlling give them immediate feedback, while planning and organizing give delayed feedback.

Exhibit 8.1 Management Functions at Three Levels
(Importance Weights)

	SALES MANAGEMENT LEVELS		
FUNCTIONS	First Line	Second Line	General
Create Change:			
Plan	17.6	24.7	36.5
Organize	4.2	5.2	7.9
Total Plan and Organize	21.8	29.9	44.4
Implement:			
Staff	34.7	22.7	10.1
Direct	21.1	23.0	21.4
Control	22.4	24.4	24.1
Total Implementation	78.2	70.1	55.6
Total Importance	100.0	100.0	100.0

Adapted from Exhibit 2.3, Chapter 2.

FORECASTING

A forecast is an estimate of future events, their effect on the selling environment at that time, and a prediction of the outcomes of alternative strategies in this environment. Forecasting is not predicting and preparing for the future, but an attempt to understand and influence the future in favor of the forecaster. This chapter will focus on the forecasting activities of the first-line sales manager. The forecasting responsibilities of the field sales manager tend to be for a one-year time horizon and include the following subjects: market conditions, staffing needs, compensation and expense needs, and management activities. This time horizon is longer than that of the representative who typically plans for a day, a week, or a few months. Hence, the new manager must stretch his or her horizons.

MARKET CONDITIONS

In many companies the representative participates in the sales forecast by estimating the sales to key market segments or accounts for the coming year. This "bottom-up" forecasting approach is then reconciled with the "top-down" forecast that is generated by corporate economists using macroeconomic data. Representatives' forecasts are frequently larger than those of management because of the basic optimism of sales representatives, their lack of information about company plans, and their lack of knowledge of broad economic forces and their effects on customers. Sales force participation in forecasting generates a greater commitment on the part of representatives for quotas that are based on these jointly derived forecasts.[1] The field sales manager must reconcile these forecasts without dampening the representatives' enthusiasm. The manager will need to find hard evidence to support the representatives' claim.

Sales managers are required to forecast sales by key market segments that may be defined geographically, by product, by industry of end user, or by key accounts. They are required also to estimate the growth of the market by customer class, market shares, and the sales of key competitors. First-line field sales managers are required also to assess the effect of the economy, local economic conditions, and local competition on the sale of major products in their sales districts. These managers will provide feedback on a corporate forecast's reliability and validity. The psychological tug-of-war the field sales manager encounters in sales forecasting is that of being optimistic to the representative and being realistic in what can be achieved, because the manager will be committed to whatever he or she forecasts above the "top-down" forecast.

STAFFING NEEDS

To estimate the need for sales representatives in the coming years, the field sales manager must consider the growth or decline in the customer universe, the change in the number of competitive salespersons, the effect of the company selling plan, the capacity of the sales staff as it will be affected by loss of personnel because of resignations, terminations, promotions, transfers, rotations, and retirements, and the time to train replacements to an equally productive level. The manager must consider also the effect of new products, new competitors, new markets, and the company's Affirmative Action Program (AAP). This Program sets requirements for applicant flow, hiring, and other fair employment practices that will determine the size and composition of the sales force relative to the agreed upon AAP hiring goal.

Some companies hire only to fill existing vacancies, which may require several days or months in order to locate qualified applicants, interview them, check references, hire, and then train them. Other companies avoid this delay and an open territory by hiring a "floating" representative in anticipation of a vacancy occurring. The latter procedure increases the number of representatives on the staff, thereby increasing the expenses for salaries and fringe benefits. Because the "floater's" ultimate assignment is unknown, there will be additional relocation costs when the final assignment is made. The manager must balance these costs against the losses from an open territory.

COMPENSATION AND EXPENSE NEEDS

Once these staffing needs have been identified, the manager will need to forecast the need for the training of new hires, the development of existing staff, and the development of future managers. The field sales manager will also need to forecast the need for equipment, supplies, office space, and related expenses to achieve the sales objectives within the approved budget.

In forecasting the budget for compensation, the sales manager must anticipate applicant qualifications, changes in job descriptions because of new products or technology, and competition. It may be necessary to pay more for the more qualified applicant. It may also be necessary to increase the compensation package for present representatives to prevent competitors from pirating the best representatives.

Expenses that must be forecasted include automobile and other forms of travel, lodging, meals, entertainment, equipment, activity fees, telephone, postage, selling materials (such as samples and literature), sales meetings, and training expenses. Travel and lodging expenses have been especially sensitive to inflation. Some companies are supplementing expensive personal sales calls with less expensive methods, such as mail and telephone selling.

FORECASTING SALES MANAGEMENT ACTIVITIES

After the field sales manager has forecasted the needs of the sales district, he or she must forecast personal management activities such as recruiting, hiring, training, trips with representatives, evaluation, counseling, and coaching. The manager must estimate the time requirements for each of these activities for each representative. In allocating scarce management time, the sales manager must allocate his or her effort to those activities that will yield the greatest productivity of the sales force. The manager will also need to forecast changes in staff support, such as secretaries, systems engineers, and repair personnel. He or she will also need to consider the logistical problems associated with producing and distributing sales literature and promotional materials such as samples, display materials, and selling aids (audio tapes, records, and slides). Some of these materials may require twelve months to produce.

SETTING OBJECTIVES

Setting objectives consists of determining the desired end results to be achieved by the sales district. A sales organization may have a hierarchy of annual objectives. For example, the company may have as its objective increasing its profit by 25 percent before taxes. This company goal may be translated into a sales management goal as, "Increase sales of the three most profitable items by 15 percent and reduce expenses by 5 percent." This sales management objective may be translated into a representative's objective such as, "Increase the sales of products A, B, and C by 15 percent; make one more call per day; and route calls more efficiently."

MANAGEMENT BY OBJECTIVES

The field sales manager will probably be implementing a corporate MBO (Management By Objectives) program. MBO programs integrate the company's need for achieving sales growth and profit with the representatives' needs for income, recognition, and development. An effective MBO program channels the energies of each representative within the district toward mutually established and agreed upon goals. The representative and the sales manager gain an understanding of the work to be done, the costs and the deadlines to be met, and how the results will be measured. MBO programs give greater control within the sales organization, but they also permit greater freedom for self-expression once the objectives have been established. MBO systems are flexible because objectives are renegotiated on a regular basis, thereby permitting modifications to reflect changes in the environment and in strategies.

There are many benefits to MBO programs. A manager and a representative define responsibilities in terms of results, not work, thereby giving the representative the freedom to work out his or her own strategies and tactics. Performance standards, controls, evaluation, and feedback are made easier by MBO programs because objectives must be measured in terms that are observable and measurable. In order for an objective to be measurable, it must be stated in terms of magnitude and time for completion. Thus, "Increase sales of product A by 10 percent within the next six months." is a well-stated objective because it identifies a magnitude to be achieved and a time frame within which the objective must be attained. This time frame helps to establish priorities and encourages the allocation of time to those accounts with the greatest potential.

Well defined objectives must also meet other criteria. They must be achievable, i.e., not too difficult but not too easy to accomplish. They must be specific to a particular area of performance, rather than overall performance. The objectives must be traceable to the efforts of an individual rather than a group. The measurability should include a time schedule that will put the components of an objective in a time frame, and, where possible, express the costs of reaching an objective in terms of a budget.

The output of the manager-representative interchange is a document that reflects the results the representative is committed to achieve. These results may be long- and short-term ones. The MBO process can save management time because it encourages self-commitment, self-analysis, and self-supervision by the representative.

The process for implementing an MBO program frequently begins with the president of the company, who defines his or her objectives and passes them along to the next level of management. The process cascades through various levels of management until it finally reaches the sales representatives. Each individual in the MBO process should be encouraged to take some risks and stretch his or her abilities. Each individual should be motivated to prepare for greater responsibility. This process should develop a cohesive relationship between a superior and a subordinate.

What should be included in MBO?—any objective that contributes to the end result of helping the representative to meet the sales quota.

REPRESENTATIVES' OBJECTIVES

Exhibit 8.2 illustrates objectives of a representative for a soap manufacturer. These objectives are in four activity classifications—sales closing, product distribution, self-development, and territory management. The time frame for accomplishment has been established as December 31, 1982. The objectives for three of the four activities have been expressed in precise quantitative terms—the orders-to-call ratio, percent distribution, and days in a territory. Each of these objectives may be evaluated by data sources that are currently in existence—invoices, daily reports, account analysis, and expense reports. The self-development objective is more difficult because it involves skill improvement, which is difficult to measure. Perhaps the training department has tests for measuring skills in overcoming objections. Generally, such measures are based on the subjective observations of field managers during coaching sessions and field trips.

The activities for which objectives are set by representatives include sales by product and by accounts, share of the market in comparison with potential, increases in the market, correction of an imbalance of product mix sold, improvements in compliance with administrative procedures, and improvements in knowledge or skills.

The MBO process can greatly aid the field sales manager by transforming qualifiable skills objectives into quantifiable objectives that can be monitored more effectively. The skills that a representative uses include the judgment exercised in selecting accounts for a call, in selecting

Exhibit 8.2   Objectives for a Soap Representative for December 31, 1982

ACTIVITY	OBJECTIVE	DATA SOURCE FOR EVALUATION
Sales Closing	Increase orders-to-call ratio from 63% to 72% in accounts to which we ship direct.	Invoices and Daily Call Reports.
Product Distribution	Achieve distribution of new Family Size Detergent in 70% of key accounts, with no loss of distribution for other sizes.	Quarterly Analysis of Key Accounts.
Self-Development	Improve skills in overcoming objections, with no reduction in calls.	Training Department test and field manager's observations.
Territory Management	Revise my route plan so that I spend three more days in the western part of my territory where potential is untapped.	Call Report, Expense Report.

the product benefit that will be stressed during the call, and the amount of effort to be expended for each account-product-benefit match. The sales manager must monitor, evaluate, coach, and counsel each representative in these skills. While it is difficult to express selling skills as measurable performance standards that are acceptable to the representative and manager, some measurable or observable standards are necessary for the objective supervision of and the communication with the representative.

FIELD MANAGERS' OBJECTIVES

The first-line field sales manager, who may be known by a variety of titles, such as the district sales manager or division manager, will also have a set of objectives. These objectives may be stated in terms of improving the total district performance or improving the performance in certain product groups. Many of this manager's objectives will be focused toward the development of personnel. Thus there may be objectives for developing team spirit, improving or replacing the poorest representatives, getting a good representative promoted, and making MBO programs work. There will also be administrative objectives, such as taking appropriate action on delinquent reports or maintaining optimum inventory levels. Exhibit 8.3 illustrates a sales manager's action plan for maintaining optimum inventory levels by reducing stock-out conditions without increasing inventory carrying costs.

MBO procedures are not limited to managers who are selling tangible products. Commercial banks have lending officers who are really bank sales representatives. These lending officers have managers who perform functions that are first-line sales management functions. These managers analyze current industry characteristics, competitive factors, and the bank's current industry position. They develop industry objectives and set a division plan for commitments, loans, balances, fees, and profitability. They will work with individual calling officers in setting personal goals and objectives for specific accounts. They then monitor the performance of lending officers according to mutually agreed upon objectives.

NATIONAL ACCOUNT MANAGERS

Companies with a program of national account managers might have objectives for key account managers that are broader than the objectives that are assigned to representatives. Exhibit 8.4 summarizes some key account objectives.

Exhibit 8.3   A Sales Manager's Action Plan

Key Activity: Maintaining Optimum Inventory Levels
Objective: To reduce stock-out conditions from 10% to 3%
with no increase in inventory carrying costs.

Action Plan Steps	Completion Date
1. Identify stock-out items during the previous six months.	10/15
2. Classify frequency of out-of-stock by stock number and customer type.	10/16
3. Analyze usage pattern and profitability of customer types.	11/01
4. Examine customer purchasing procedures and analyze our purchasing/manufacturing procedures.	11/14
5. Discuss and review findings with persons who impact inventory levels.	11/17
6. Define the problem and create alternative solutions.	11/22
7. Evaluate the alternatives and recommend one.	12/01
8. Gain management approval, agreement, and support at each level.	12/07
9. Implement recommended changes.	12/31
10. Evaluate the recommendation by determining stock-out conditions.	03/31
11. Review, monitor, and modify the system as needed.	

Adapted from a presentation to the National Society of Sales Training Executives by R. V. Lippincott, Director, Training and Management Development, Sterling Drug Incorporated, December 6, 1976.

Quarterly account objectives for a manufacturer of packaged groceries will include sales volume, the number of in-store displays, and promotional objectives, such as the amount of cooperative advertising. An important activity of the account manager is the coordination of the activities of key personnel within the account to implement display and advertising programs and to troubleshoot out-of-stock situations. The account manager must work closely with the client's buyer, merchandising manager, advertising manager, data processing manager, and store supervisors. This manager will have objectives for these activities.

The key account manager will be evaluated also according to his or her ability to get things done through the district sales managers and representatives of his or her company. Objectives will include the writing of information bulletins and making presentations at sales meetings.

Business reviews and management presentations will be judged according to their timeliness, the presence of all key customer and company personnel, the use of market research data, and the clarity of the verbal and written presentation. Sales presentations to clients will be

Exhibit 8.4   Objectives for a Key Account Manager

PERFORMANCE EVALUATION—QUARTERLY REVIEW

DEFINITIONS OF CATEGORIES:

Outstanding: Performance at a consistently high level. Objectives accomplished. Effective in all respects. Little room for improvement.

Above average: Objectives almost always met. High level of effectiveness in most respects.

Satisfactory: Objectives usually met. Effective in most respects. Definite strong points offset weaknesses.

Marginal: Some objectives being accomplished. Performance not effective. Needs to improve before satisfactory performance will be obtained.

MARGINAL	SATISFACTORY	ABOVE AVERAGE	OUTSTANDING (Max.)
1–3	4–6	7–9	10

POINTS

☐ *ESTABLISHMENT AND ACCOMPLISHMENT OF QUARTERLY ACCOUNT OBJECTIVES* . . . Review quarterly objectives established for each assigned account and evaluate the overall level of attainment of those objectives relating to *volume* objectives, *listing* objectives, *display* objectives, and *promotional* objectives. (Attach a separate commentary outlining objectives and accomplishments by account.)

☐ *EFFECTIVENESS OF COORDINATING ACCOUNT ACTIVITIES* . . . Consider the coordination established in the account between account personnel such as the buyer, the merchandising manager, the advertising manager, the data processing manager, and store supervisors. This could relate to implementing a new display program, advertising program, or other type of promotional programs, or troubleshooting out-of-stocks.

☐ *EFFECTIVENESS OF COORDINATING FIELD FORCE ACTIVITIES* . . . Consider ability to get things done through others. Include the drafting of information bulletins, ability to work with district managers and territory representatives to get merchandising, display, and promotional programs implemented.

☐ *BUSINESS REVIEW AND MANAGEMENT PRESENTATIONS* . . . Consider the timeliness of reviews and presentations. Are all key customer personnel in attendance as well as company personnel? Consider content of each presentation. Are sales statistics, Nielsen data, SAMI data, and other source materials properly organized to fit the objectives of the presentation? Consider the verbal presentation and written materials with regard to clarity.

☐ *SALES PRESENTATIONS* . . . Review the use of personal selling skills, profit charts, and other sales tools, and the organization of materials. Consider the creativity and imagination of developing promotional programs for each assigned account.

☐ *CUSTOMER CONTACT* . . . Is frequency of contact in accordance with the established plan for headquarter calls, store supervisors, and retail surveillance calls?

☐ *ADMINISTRATIVE WORK* . . . Consider neatness, accuracy and timely submitting of reports, maintaining of records, etc.

☐ *OVERALL ATTITUDE* . . . Consider the key account manager's willingness to take on additional assignments and special projects. Consider whether the key account manager performs at levels consistent with individual potential.

☐ TOTAL POINTS

David S. Hopkins, ''Marketing Performance Evaluation,'' *The Conference Board Information Bulletin* 53 (February 1979): 9. Reprinted with permission.

judged by objectives such as personal selling skills, profit charts, and the creativity for developing promotional programs for each assigned account.

Objectives will be established for the number of calls on headquarters, store supervisors, and retail stores. Key account managers will be evaluated according to the neatness, accuracy, and timely submission of reports, as well as their maintenance of account records. Finally, the key account manager will be evaluated according to objectives, such as his or her overall attitude toward taking on additional assignments and the performance of duties at levels that are consistent with individual potential.

LEVELS OF OBJECTIVES

Objectives may be defined at various levels within an organization. Allen uses the terms "key objectives, critical objectives, and specific objectives" to distinguish between those objectives that are central to the organization and those objectives that are required for the day-to-day operation of an organization.[2] "Key objectives" are the primary result that the enterprise is organized to accomplish. The key objective for a sales department is to sell the company's products and services at a profit. This departmental objective is translated into a key objective for district sales managers, such as the following objective: "Attain sales quotas within assigned territories and budgets."

To attain key objectives, it is necessary to perform critical activities. These critical activities will have "critical objectives." For example, a district sales manager's critical objectives would include the successful performance of forecasting and budgeting for district personnel needs for the next fiscal year.

"Specific objectives" are those objectives that are designed to overcome performance deficiencies in attaining critical objectives. For the field sales manager, specific objectives could be specified for working with each representative to improve closing skills. Specific objectives may be set also for positive activities, such as creating a new promotional program for a client.

PROBLEMS WITH MBO

MBO systems, like all planning systems, can become an end in themselves so that too much time is spent planning and too little time implementing. While MBO procedures have been enthusiastically presented by their supporters, some researchers have concluded that there has been little empirical support for the effectiveness of these procedures.[3] It is frequently difficult to evaluate their effect on morale or productivity because MBO programs were only one of several management changes that were implemented.

If the representatives managed their territories like a business, complete with income and productivity statements (Chapter 5), the groundwork will have been established for Management by Objectives. By comparing these income and productivity statements for all representatives in the district, the sales manager can quickly identify those representatives who have weaknesses, and then negotiate objectives with them to improve their performance on those activities that will improve their productivity.

DEVELOPING STRATEGIES

Strategies may be defined briefly as deciding how and when to achieve objectives. The field sales manager begins with the company selling plan and then adapts the plan and its objectives to his or her district by developing objectives and strategies that are appropriate for each representative and local conditions. Local conditions may include a regional brand that is selling at a lower price, a high unemployment level, or an out-of-stock condition for very popular products. The manager must work with the representatives to develop benefit statements that will overcome these deficiencies in the short run and make recommendations to senior management to correct them in the long run.

The sales manager will need to identify ways that his or her representatives can build on the company's strengths, avoid competing against the primary strengths of competitors, satisfy customers, and make the most efficient use of existing channels of distribution. The manager must review the strategies of the representatives as reflected in their activity plans. This review will assure that the representatives' strategies are consistent with the corporate selling plan.

A field sales manager may be required to implement a new sales strategy, or he or she may recommend one, such as the following strategies that were developed by several companies to increase the productivity of their selling effort:

1. A chemical company combined the sales forces of two divisions;
2. Selective directing the sales force to specific accounts increased sales productivity for a foundry;

3. A major appliance manufacturer improved productivity by organizing the sales force according to tasks or selling objectives instead of by geography;

4. A large machinery company decided quarterly whether each territory should be serviced directly or through distributors;

5. Manufacturers' representatives were used to supplement the sales force during peak seasons;

6. The servicing of low volume accounts or territories with mail, catalogs, and telephone selling was used by many companies; and,

7. More local advertising in newspapers and radio was used by some companies to supplement personal selling effort.[4]

A field sales manager will recommend creating smaller territories and adding representatives if the potential cannot be handled by the present sales force. Conversely, when markets are declining, a manager may recommend combining territories and reducing the number of representatives in a district.

MANAGING FOR FAST GROWTH

Hanan provides several growth laws and strategies that a sales manager will want to consider when he or she is developing strategies. The six laws are as follows:

1. The only real growth is profit growth. All other forms of growth—company size, product volume, share of market—enlarge costs rather than net worth.

2. Policy is the allocation of assets to maximize profit growth.

3. People must be managed as growth assets.

4. Branded products and services are difficult to create and even more difficult to market. This makes them extremely difficult to be knocked off by competition.

5. The role of marketing is to create perceptions of unique added value in the minds of a market.

6. The most important sensitivity in managing a growth business is customer sensitivity.[5]

Hanan also provides strategies for fast-growth leadership and management.

Fast-Growth Leadership Strategies:

1. Make policy and delegate decisions to others. Hire implementers. Do not become one yourself.

2. Manage people, not functions. Success depends on people.

3. Be a builder of customer businesses, not just a seller to them. Help them to make a profit by doing business with you. Remember that *customers are the sources of growth funds.*

Fast-Growth Management Strategies:

1. Put profit objectives first—not volume. Treat the business like a money machine. Bring more money down to the bottom line. To do this one must maximize margins of growth, minimize the costs of growth, concentrate on the product-market matches with the best growth-rates, and institutionalize the return-on-investment approach for calculating growth.

2. Position your products as brands—not commodities. Premium profits come from premium pricing, not commodity pricing.

3. Use marketing for leverage—not product technology. Except in rare instances, product technologies will condemn a business to slow growth or no growth. Product technologies make products better, but marketing technologies benefit customers better.

4. Dominate your category preemptively, not as a competitor. Monopoly profits are premium profits and the source of fast growth.[6]

ORGANIZATIONAL STRATEGIES

The organizational design plays an important role in successful strategy making. Miller and Friesen analyzed eighty-one cases on business organizations as published in *Fortune* and the Harvard Case Clearing House to identify successful and unsuccessful methods for coping with hostile environments.[7] The competitive response styles of the firm, its organization, and its strategies are summarized in Exhibit 8.5. The lessons in this table should help a strategist to develop strategies within existing organizations and to avoid some fatal organizational designs and strategies.

Strategy formation is extremely important within an organization. It is also very difficult. Mintzberg notes that, "There is perhaps no process in organizations that is more demanding of human cognition than strategy formation. Every strategy-maker faces an impossible overload of information (much of it soft); as a result he can have no optimal

Exhibit 8.5   **Organizational Designs and Strategies for Dealing with Environments that are Dynamic, Heterogeneous, and Hostile**

COMPETITIVE RESPONSE STYLES	ORGANIZATIONAL DESIGNS	STRATEGIES
SUCCESSFUL STYLES		
The adaptive firm under moderate challenge	Vigilant-Traditional (delegates, strong leader, intelligence systems)	Adaptive-Positive (expertise, proactive, adaptive)
The adaptive firm in a very challenging environment	Organic-Cerebral (delegates-centralized, intelligence systems, technocratic)	Assertive-Analytical (product-market innovation, proactive, adaptive, analytical)
The dominant firm	Hierarchical (initial strategy, strong leader, adequate resources)	Extrapolation (expertise, integrated innovative, and adaptive)
The giant under fire	Decentralized (delegates-centralized, intelligence systems, technocratic)	Incremental-Analytical (analysis, expertise, conscious strategy, caution)
The entrepreneurial conglomerate	Charismatic (centralized, delegates, intelligence systems)	Manipulation-Expansion (analytical, risk taker, proactive)
The innovators	Encephalized (centralized, initial strategy)	Innovation within Niche (product-market innovator, proactive, expertise, conscious of strategy)
UNSUCCESSFUL STYLES		
The impulsive firm	Top Centered-Differentiated (centralized, low intelligence systems, lack of controls, differentiated)	Overextension (risk taker, proactive, analytical)
The stagnant bureaucracy	Rigid-Bureaucratic (centralized, low intelligence systems, poor communications, internal conflict)	Ultra Conservatism (low risk taker, low in innovation, adaptiveness, and proactiveness, and high in traditions)
The headless giant	Leaderless-Diversified (no leadership, responsibility divisionalized, low intelligence systems, low controls and communication)	Muddling Through (high in traditions, low in integration, innovation, multiplexity, and proactiveness)
The aftermath	Makeshift (past trouble, centralized and low resources)	Grafting + Groping (moderate risk taker and low integration of decision with other areas)

Adapted from Danny Miller and P. H. Friesen, "Archetypes of Strategy Formulation," *Management Science* 24 (May 1978): 929, 932.

process to follow."[8] The magnitude of the task is apparent when one considers that the environments that must be considered include the government, the workers, the market, the suppliers, the owners, and the public, all of which may provide opportunities and threats.[9] At best, the strategist can only scan these environments for threats and opportunities.

TOOLS FOR MAKING STRATEGIES

Mintzberg and Shakun note that management science has contributed enormously to analytical processes at the operating levels of organizations since the 1920s and middle management since the 1940s, but strategy formulation requires descriptive studies in order to generate prescriptive techniques.[10]

While no models exist that will guarantee optimal strategies, some descriptive techniques have been developed for analyzing cost patterns that determine pricing strategies,[11] portfolios of products,[12] competitive environments,[13] and management styles.[14] The field sales manager is not likely to be involved with these techniques. The general sales manager, however, should be familiar with them because they will probably be used by a marketing manager during the development of marketing strategies.

IMPLEMENTING POLICIES

The first-line sales manager, who rarely produces but sometimes influences policy, must understand and implement those policies that come down from above. Because of the physical distance that separates the field sales manager and the representative, and the distance of both from the headquarters, incorrect policy interpretations sometimes occur, particularly in the time press of a selling situation. As a result, the manager frequently is involved in arbitrating or settling requests that grew out of a policy conflict. The manager will also make recommendations for changes in policy and, in emergencies, find ways for operating outside policies.

Policies may be defined as standing decisions regarding recurring strategic matters. Policies are boundaries on acceptable alternatives for achieving objectives. Policies have many advantages in administering a complex organization. They are automatic decision makers that free managers to attend to nonrecurring tasks. They provide uniformity across the company, so that all representatives are treated equally. Policies also simplify the control of representatives and simplify the communication networks.

Managers and representatives will be subject to a variety of corporate policies such as dress codes, adherence to good ethics, a return-goods policy, pricing and trade-in policies, antitrust policies, and adherence to affirmative action programs when hiring, promoting, compensating, or separating.

DEVELOPING PROGRAMS

WHAT ARE SALES PROGRAMS?

A program is a series of action steps that are designed to achieve an objective. When they are arranged in an order of priority with times for completion, they are known as a *schedule.* In military terms, these action steps are known as *tactics.* Exhibit 8.3 presents a sales manager's action plan for maintaining optimum inventory levels. It includes a schedule because each step is assigned a completion date.

Managers will become involved with programs at many different levels. They will recommend national programs to their representatives. They need to know about competitive programs and estimate their effect on company sales. They need to work with representatives to develop programs to achieve each of their key objectives. And finally, managers need to develop programs so that they can achieve their management objectives and objectives for their self-development.

When implementing the national selling program, the manager's principal role is to make certain that the program is understood, supported, introduced, and implemented with vigor. He or she must make certain that tools are available and used for implementing the program, that pitfalls are spotted and corrected early, that enthusiasm is generated and sustained, that coaching is provided where needed, and that programs are evaluated and feedback provided to headquarters along with recommended changes.

ESTABLISHING PRIORITIES

Priorities are necessary because representatives and managers have multiple objectives that have activities that compete for the scarcest of resources—time. By establishing priorities, it is possible to distinguish between important activities and emergency ones. Emergencies may not necessarily be important, but when they are, the establishment of priorities provides the basis for returning to normal activities.

Representatives establish priorities when they allocate the length of time and frequency of their calls according to the potential for each account. They also create daily and long-term itineraries to carry out the programs and meet their specified objectives. Prioritizing activities is an important part of time and territory management (Chapter 5).

A field sales manager will have an itinerary for making trips with representatives, meeting important customers, training, market planning, appraising, counseling, coaching, staffing, and self-development. An important management task is making certain that representatives comply with their scheduled itineraries, product promotion schedules, appointments, and regularly scheduled call-backs on major accounts.

Priorities must be reevaluated constantly as environmental changes occur. The manager must distinguish between those actions that are "must do" versus those that are "could do." The short-term "could do" activities have a way of crowding out the long-term "must-do" ones. Samples of a manager's activity schedule appeared in Chapter 7.

SETTING PROCEDURES

WHAT ARE PROCEDURES?

Procedures may be defined as standardized programs that foster management efficiency and uniformity. A representative's procedures manual will include items such as: expense reports, automobile-operating procedures, standardized field selling manual, special account manual, working conventions procedures, sick and accident plan, order-writing procedures, classification of prospects, call-reporting procedures, sampling procedures, complaint handling, relocation and moving procedures, and recruiting procedures. A manual with such procedures eliminates the need for managers to make decisions in these areas, thereby making managers more efficient and freeing them to develop programs for nonrecurring events. Procedures, like policies, provide control, fairness throughout the sales force, and simplified communication.

Field managers must be certain that representatives understand procedures, their nonnegotiability, and the futility of fighting them. Representatives' noncompliance with procedures is a major problem for managers, especially in nonselling activities such as gathering market research data and processing memos, orders, returns, credits, and correspondence.

PROCEDURES FOR MANAGERS

Many companies have procedure manuals for field managers. The new manager will find that these manuals will help him or her anticipate problems and know how to handle them when they arise. Field managers' manuals will cover such topics as product promotions, recruiting procedures, warning and probation procedures, separation routines, spouse information sessions, territory redesign, salary review, bonus procedures, performance review, and procedures for promoting representatives.

Policies, procedures, and programs must be written clearly because of the distance between the persons who wrote them and those who must implement them. There is little opportunity to ask for interpretation.

BUDGETING

Budgeting is the translation of a program of action into the resources that are necessary to implement it. The budget is the link between the planning and controlling functions. At the planning stage, the budget is an estimate of the resources (people, capital, and information) that are necessary to implement the program. These resource estimates may lead the planner to develop a new program if the existing one will not meet profit goals or if the program cost exceeds the budget. Once the program and the associated budget are adopted, the budget then becomes a control device for measuring results in financial terms and taking appropriate corrective action.

The sales manager must become familiar with concepts such as controllable and uncontrollable expenses, account codes, sales and expense quotas, break-even analysis, marketing cost analysis, and promotional costs (conventions, seminars, etc.), as well as representatives' resources that include time, expenses, equipment, and promotional materials. A budget is an important management tool, so a new manager must learn how to use this tool effectively. The availability of microcomputers with standard programs can greatly simplify the young manager's budgeting process. These computers can also make it possible to do "what if" planning and determine the effect on the budget.

ORGANIZING

The organizing function consists of structuring roles of individuals for the effective accomplishment of the objectives of the organization and the individuals. Of the five management functions—planning, organizing, staffing, directing, and controlling—first-line sales managers reported that organizing was the least important of their responsibilities (Exhibit 2.3, Chapter 2). These managers do have input into some organizational activities such as participating in the job description for representatives and themselves, and establishing position qualifications, territory alignment, and promotion recommendations.

The primary organizational activity of the field sales manager is re-organizing. The field sales manager will generally be promoted into an existing district, but changes in the market and the needs of the company will require the addition or deletion of territories and districts. As a result, the field sales manager's ongoing organizational responsibility is to remain flexible to the conditions that create a need for organizational change and make appropriate recommendations for new organizational designs of the sales force.

SUMMARY

The new field sales manager will have an opportunity to develop further those planning and strategy skills that he or she learned as a representative. The domain and time horizon of the field manager is considerably greater than that of the representative. This expansion of skills in planning and strategy formation provides good training for promotion to higher levels of management.

At first the new sales manager may miss the excitement of selling and the more immediate response from his or her efforts. While the new manager is involved in planning, most of his or her efforts will be spent in implementing the plans of others through functions such as staffing, directing, and controlling.

Forecasting can be an important activity for sales managers who must forecast market conditions, competition, staffing needs, compensation, and expenses. The time horizon of the young manager moves from a few weeks or months to a year. The manager must also forecast what management activities need to be accomplished during the year.

Field sales managers must translate the selling objectives in the company selling plan into objectives for the district and each territory. The objective must be a balance between being achievable and challenging. The manager and the representative will work together to establish personal objectives so that the representative is committed to them. This process may be part of a company MBO (Management By Objectives) program.

National account managers may have a separate set of objectives that reflect their total responsibility for the account. These objectives will reflect the need to work effectively with people at all levels in the client firm and in the account manager's firm.

Objectives become more precise and involve a shorter time horizon as one moves down the organization. *Key objectives* are translated into *critical objectives*, which are further refined into *specific objectives*.

Field sales managers implement strategies that have been developed at higher levels, they provide feedback about these strategies, and they make strategy recommendations in both directions—to representatives and to superiors. In preparation for promotion, the young manager will want to begin to think in terms of growth strategies.

The first-line sales manager rarely produces policy, but sometimes influences policy making through recommendations. This manager will be called upon to interpret policies and settle conflicts that they may create.

Sales programs and procedures must be translated into local environments. They must also be evaluated. First-line managers are given early opportunities to develop skills in evaluating and, to some extent, developing programs and procedures.

ASSIGNMENTS/DISCUSSION QUESTIONS

1. Develop a management-by-objectives program for the sales organization in the Westmont case at the end of this text.

2. Which of the criteria for an objective are present in the following objectives?

   _____ To do better.

   _____ To turn in reports on time.

   _____ To triple sales on product X within the next quarter.

   _____ To triple sales on your territory within the next fiscal year while maintaining complete coverage of your territory.

   _____ To maintain a 10-percent increase in sales on products X and Y in your territory during the next fiscal year while improving the coverage of all major customers to meet the minimum call standard.

   _____ To submit your daily call reports by the first of the following week without fail for the next six months.

3. Write an objective for your first job after graduation. Include all necessary criteria.

4. Write a sample procedure to be used by the representatives in the case of sickness or accidents.

5. Contrast the planning steps by a sales representative and the district sales manager in splitting the representative's territory into two territories.

6. How can a field sales manager convince a representative that his or her sales forecast is overly optimistic?

7. Since the cost of a "floater" is considerable, what are the disadvantages of leaving a territory vacant until a suitable applicant can be found?

8. Using any industry, what change in the product mix for that industry could require hiring applicants with different qualifications?

9. What is the relationship between the general sales manager's dollar sales objective and that of the district sales manager, and what would it be based on?

10. Create two alternative solutions to Action Step #6 in the program outlined in Exhibit 8.3.

CASE 8.1:
Leland Publications, Inc.

Mike Branden, the Southeastern District Supervisor for Leland Publications, Inc., wasn't certain he agreed with the company's policy that allowed transfers of sales representatives, but in this case he felt he had more to gain than to lose when his Regional Manager, Paul Hancock, had approved the transfer of Ken Adams to fill the open territory in Atlanta. Mike wasn't convinced that the advantages of getting an experienced sales representative whom he didn't know was better than hiring an applicant of his own selection. His current experiences with Ken Adams confirmed his judgment.

The company's thinking was that if there were sales representatives unhappy in their present assignments, or for other reasons wanted to live elsewhere, their extra motivation for having been allowed to transfer would reflect their personal happiness or that of their family, and make the representative more productive. This logic resulted in Leland's transfer policy that allowed experienced sales representatives with more than two years' experience to transfer to any open territory at their own expense, providing they received at their last performance review a rating of at least "satisfactory," and their present sales supervisor approved the request.

Ken Adams, a seasoned representative with six years' experience in a territory headquartering in Charleston, West Virginia, and a sales record of above-average productivity, had requested the transfer because his wife, Nancy, had been raised in Birmingham, Alabama, and wanted to get back to the south. Ken, who had graduated from the University of West Virginia, had been happy to have been assigned initially to Charleston, his hometown. Although he traveled extensively into adjacent parts of Ohio, Kentucky, and Virginia, he liked the area and felt at home with the people.

Yes, it had taken Ken and his family a while to find a home in an Atlanta suburb, and the difference in the cost of living between Charleston and Atlanta was a bit of a shock to them, but they seemed to have adjusted well, and the reduced time on the road for

Ken pleased Nancy and the kids. Allowing for the differences in Charleston and Atlanta, and the time for Ken to learn his way around, Mike expected Ken to be performing at least at an acceptable level eight months after his move. In fact, Mike had expected Ken to become one of his top people because he had been given what he wanted. The problem was that it hadn't worked out that way.

The call averages in Mike's district averaged slightly under fourteen calls per day, with the company performance standard set at ten. Ken Adams's had consistently run at eight initially, and for two of the last three months had moved to nine. When Mike told Ken about the district average, and that nine was unsatisfactory, Ken was surprised. He intimated that this was an acceptable level in his previous district. Since Mike was not familiar with Ken's previous district or its manager, he felt reluctant to make any comparisons. But, to make matters worse, Ken's dollar sales were only in the "marginally satisfactory" range for the district.

Mike's preliminary analysis was that Ken was not getting the sales return he should from the metropolitan sections of his territory where the potential was considerably greater. By contrast, he was doing better in Columbus, Macon, and Augusta, which have smaller sales potentials. A brief review of Ken's call pattern indicated to Mike that Ken was not allocating the proper amount of time to the metropolitan Atlanta sections. Three months previous, Mike and Ken reviewed the daily and weekly planning guide used by the other sales representatives, after which Ken's call average picked up for a while. Unfortunately, a corresponding increase in sales was not forthcoming, and last month Ken's call average was down to its previous level. Mike also suspected that Ken was not using the specific call objectives kind of planning used by the others. During his last review with Paul Hancock, Mike was asked what he planned to do about it.

CASE QUESTIONS

1. What is the problem?

2. What are the possible causes of the problem?

3. Is the evaluation of Ken's dollar sales productivity as "marginally satisfactory" a valid criticism of his performance? Why?

4. What are the possible reasons for Ken's low call average?

5. How could Mike Branden confirm whether Ken Adams's problem is poor planning?

6. If Ken's problem is poor call planning, how could Mike attempt to correct the problem?

7. What is the possible reason Ken was "doing better in Columbus, Macon, and Augusta," which had smaller potentials?

8. Could a call average of nine have been acceptable in Ken's previous territory? Why?

9. What are the advantages and disadvantages of a transfer policy as used by Leland Publishing, Inc.?

10. Discuss the reasons for each of the conditions in the transfer policy.

REFERENCES

1. T. R. Wotruba and M. L. Thurlow, *Journal of Marketing* 40, no. 2 (April 1976): 11–16; B. G. Ammons, "Greater Commitment by Letting Salespeople Help Set the Quotas," *Sales and Marketing Management* (April 7, 1980): 88–93.

2. L. A. Allen, *The Professional Manager's Guide,* 4th ed. (Palo Alto, Calif.: Louis A. Allen Associates, 1969).

3. C. M. Futrell, J. E. Swan, and C. W. Lamb, "Benefits and Problems in a Salesforce MBO System," *Industrial Marketing Management* 6, no. 4 (1977): 265–272; J. N. Kondrasuk, "Studies in MBO Effectiveness," *Academy of Management Review* 6, no. 3 (1981): 419–430.

4. "Senior Executives Tell How They Increased Marketing Productivity," *Marketing News* (August 7, 1981): 1–2.

5. Mack Hanan, *Fast-Growth Management* (New York: Amacom, 1979), p. 1.

6. Ibid., pp. 33–127.

7. Danny Miller and P. H. Friesen, "Archetypes of Strategy Formulation," *Management Science* 24 (May 1978): 921–933.

8. H. Mintzberg, "Patterns in Strategy Formation," *Management Science* 24 (May 1978): 948.

9. Y. Aharon, Z. Maimon, and E. Segev, "Performance and Autonomy in Organizations: Determining Dominant Environment Components," *Management Science* 24 (May 1978): 949–959.

10. H. Mintzberg and M. F. Shakun, "Introduction to a Grouping on Strategy Formulation," *Management Science* 24 (February 1978): 920.

11. For a discussion and citations, see D. N. Thompson, "Pricing and the Experience Curve Effect," in *Macromarketing: A Canadian Perspective,* ed. D. N. Thompson, P. Simmie, L. Heslop, and S. J. Shapiro (Chicago: American Marketing Association, 1980), pp. 100–123.

12. For a discussion of techniques, see G. S. Day, "Analytical Approaches to Strategic Market Planning," in *Review of Marketing 1981,* ed. B. M. Enis and K. J. Roering (Chicago: American Marketing Association, 1981).

13. M. E. Porter, *Competitive Strategy* (New York: Free Press, 1980).

14. R. R. Blake and J. S. Mouton, *The Managerial Grid* (Houston: Gulf Publishing Co., 1964). For a discussion of the origins of this grid, see T. F. Stroh, *Managing the Sales Function* (New York: McGraw-Hill, 1978), pp. 400–408.

SUGGESTED READINGS

Factors Related to Salesman Turnover, Report No. 1972-11 (New York: The Conference Board, 1972).

Jackson, D. W., Jr., and Aldag, R. J., "Managing the Sales Force by Objectives," *MSU Business Topics* (Spring 1974): 53–59.

Katzenbach, J. R., and Champion, R. R., "Linking Top-Level Planning to Salesman Performance," *Business Horizons* (Fall 1966): 91–100.

Morrisey, G. I., *Management by Objectives and Results* (Reading, Mass.: Addison-Wesley, 1970).

Sims, J. Taylor, "Industrial Sales Management: A Case for MBO," *Industrial Marketing Management* 6, no. 1 (1977): 43–46.

Steinmetz, L. L., and Todd, H. R., Jr., *First-Line Management* (Dallas: Business Publications, Inc., 1975).

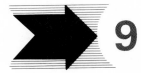

9

RECRUITING
AND SELECTION

A survey of 600 field sales managers revealed that recruiting and selection was their fourth most important activity, following the activities of developing, motivating, and training personnel (Chapter 2, Exhibit 2.3). These four activities are interrelated. A company that does poorly in developing, motivating, and training personnel will have a high turnover and therefore find it necessary to spend more time recruiting and selecting. Similarly, a company that does poorly in recruiting and selection will increase its problems in training, motivating, and developing.

Recruiting and selection are important because the success of every other sales management activity depends on the success of recruiting and selecting salespersons in order to maintain the quality and quantity of the sales force. The field sales manager must strike a balance between two conflicting goals—continuing the search for the perfect candidate and the cost of an open territory. The cost of the open territory is more obvious than the cost of long-term administrative problems from hiring the wrong candidate. Hence, there are probably more errors in hiring the wrong candidate.

PLANNING SALES FORCE REQUIREMENTS

The recruiting and selection process begins with an understanding of the factors that determine the quantity and quality of the sales force and the methods for determining the sales force size.

FACTORS DETERMINING QUANTITY AND QUALITY

The Job Description

The activities to be performed by the sales representative appear in the job description. The behavior required to perform these activities determines the qualifications of persons needed. These behaviors will appear in the job description. The job description will also show links with supporting staff members, such as systems engineers, product managers, installation clerks, service persons, and customers' relations persons. The existence of such supporting staff members simplifies the selling process and therefore simplifies recruiting. The level of supervision will also determine the qualifications of the sales force. A less qualified representative may be hired if there is close supervision. Recruiting and selecting quality salespersons is made more difficult by the fact that few field sales managers have received specific training for these activities.

Personnel Forecasts

The sales forecast (Chapter 17) is the basic document for determining the quantity of representatives to be recruited. Here, we identify changes in demand and competition that will affect the size and location of the sales force. For example, some companies are reducing the size of their staff in the northeastern part of the United States and increasing their sales force in the sunbelt areas, thereby reflecting population and industrial shifts. These forecasts will also estimate competitors' share of the market and their share of the sales force, thereby enabling us to estimate if we are falling behind in our share of selling effort.

We must also estimate the turnover of the sales force, which will require separate estimates of promotions, retirements, and voluntary or involuntary separations. With these turnovers in mind, the sales manager must recruit in advance of needs. Some managers have a policy of recruiting to replace the poorest performer on the staff. The length of a training program will determine how far in advance a forecast must be made. A long training program requires an early identification of sales force staffing requirements.

The forecast must also include predictions of new product introductions by our firm and our competitors. These introductions can affect greatly the quality and quantity of salespersons required, as well as lengthen training programs.

Sales force organizational strategies must also be anticipated. For example, a company that splits its sales force into an industrial and a consumer sales force will have different processes for recruiting salespersons and managers. The candidates for the consumer products will need to have skills in mass merchandising. The candidate for the industrial products will need to be applications oriented.

The Selling Plan

The selling plan reflects the objectives of the company, its marketing strategies, the role of personal selling in these strategies, and, finally, the selling strategies of the sales force. This document gives the field sales manager a means for assigning the tasks to be performed with the staff available to perform them. This selling plan and the manager's forecast for his or her district will reveal any gaps that must filled through recruiting.

METHODS FOR DETERMINING SALES FORCE SIZE

Incremental Method

In Chapter 5, "Managing the Territory Like a Profit Center," we saw that a sales representative could take the fixed resource of a limited number of sales calls and apply it to those accounts that will make the greatest expected contribution to profits. In economists' terms, this is the *marginal* or *incremental approach* toward allocating the sales effort.

Time management (Chapter 5) is an important component of the incremental method for determining sales force size. The sales manager will want to examine the proportion of representatives' time being spent on selling, traveling, and nonselling activities. Better time management may make it unnecessary to hire an additional representative. After examining the territory records, such as those shown in Chapter 5, the sales manager may decide that the expected potential profit contribution by penetrating present customers further and developing prospects justifies adding salespersons. The sales manager may use a microcomputer, as illustrated in Chapter 5, to test the critical assumptions in the analysis leading to this conclusion. He or she may challenge assumptions regarding growth rates and expected market shares to see if additional representatives can be justified. The key element in the incremental method is the subjective estimate of the effect on sales of making additional calls. As we saw in Chapter 5, there are upper and lower thresholds for determining the sales calls to be made per account.

Equal Load

The equal-load method is less desirable than the incremental method because of its tendency to overgeneralize the number of calls that are necessary per account. With this method, it is necessary only to estimate the total number of calls that are required per district and divide this total by the number of calls that can be made by a representative during the year. For example, if the average representative makes 1,000 calls per year and the number of calls required for the territory is 7,000, then the district must have seven representatives (7,000/1,000). This approach would be most appropriate for selling tasks that were routine, of the order-taking variety. Thus a route salesperson calling on grocery stores performs predictable activities so that accurate estimates can be made of the average calls per representative and the total district calls needed. Such estimates could not be made when consultative selling is involved (Chapter 1).

Computer Models

The sales manager's decision process for determining the size of the sales force becomes more complex as he or she examines the question of allocating sales effort geographically, among products requiring different efforts, between clients and prospects, across different market segments and the effect of diminishing returns from additional sales calls. Some of the recent computer allocation models that were discussed in Chapter 5 could be used by sales managers to estimate the number of representatives needed for a territory, given the complexity of allocation decisions. These models depend heavily on representatives' estimates for such variables as sales responses that would follow from various call frequencies, travel time, time per call, account profitability, and various product mixes that would be purchased. In many cases, users of such models have found that the greatest benefit came from requiring representatives to analyze their accounts in such detail that they could make these estimates. The dominant theme in Chapter 5, "Managing the Territory Like a Profit Center," is that representatives should be making these estimates routinely and that microcomputers make it easy for the representatives and managers to analyze the data.

RECRUITING

SOURCES OF CANDIDATES

Who recruits? The answer to this question will vary among companies. Some companies make recruiting part of a sales representative's job description because the company representatives are located throughout the country where interested applicants are located. Recruiting is almost always part of the job description for a district sales manager, if only to screen applicants identified by others. Sales recruiting may be handled also by a team from headquarters and, to a lesser degree, by the recruiting staff from the personnel department. These teams may travel to regular recruiting sites or areas where territories are vacant.

Sources of applicants for sales positions are numerous. The initiative may come from the applicant who writes to the company or contacts one of its employees. Additional sources include social contacts; college placement offices for students and alumni; private, state, and federal employment agencies; customers; competitors; company personnel in other departments (service, production, or office staff); noncompeting companies; persons calling on the company; clubs; high schools; newspapers; trade associations; and university faculty. Representatives may call on some of these sources as part of their routine job activities.

Over the years, companies will identify those sources that provide the most productive applicants. Companies may use a college as a prescreening device when they find the students in previous years have been very successful in selling careers. Successful graduates employed by a company usually provide a reliable source for other student applicants.

LEGAL CONSIDERATIONS

Some companies that have federal contracts must have written Affirmative Action Compliance Programs that comply with the *Federal Contract Compliance Manual.* Presidential Executive Orders might exempt companies with fewer than one hundred employees and contracts less than $50,000. These Executive Orders tend to be political and change with elections.

The *Compliance Manual* is designed to assure minorities equal treatment with regard to recruiting, selecting, training, compensation, and promotion. Sales managers must have active programs for recruiting minorities and other protected groups (women, veterans, handicapped, and protected age groups) from minority colleges; female colleges; minority referrals from college placement officers or alumni placement officers; state employment agencies; private employment agencies; private agencies specializing in minorities, females, handicapped; protected age groups; and organizations that represent minorities (e.g., the Urban League, the Urban Coalition, and NAACP).

One of the factors in recruiting that must be carefully monitored in the process of selection is the applicant flow of potentially affected classes of applicants (black, Hispanic, Asian/Pacific, American Indian, and female). The federal regulations state that, "A selection rate for any race, sex, or ethnic group which is less than four-fifths (or eighty percent) of the rate for the group with the highest rate will generally be regarded by the federal enforcement agencies as evidence of adverse impact, while a greater than four-fifths rate will generally not be regarded by federal enforcement agencies as evidence of adverse impact."[1] If a selection process causes adverse impact, the process must be modified to eliminate the adverse impact or the employer must validate that this process is justified by business necessity or that a less onerous procedure is not available. Examples of adverse impacts might be educational requirements or experience.

To determine if there is an adverse impact, the recruiter must compute the "impact ratio" for each race, sex, or ethnic group. Assume, for example, that forty persons are hired from one hundred white applicants, fifteen are hired out of fifty black applicants, and five are hired out of twenty-five Hispanic applicants. The relevant percentages and ratios are summarized in Exhibit 9.1. The white acceptance rate is 40 percent (40/100), the black acceptance rate is 30 percent (15/50), and the Hispanic acceptance rate is 20 percent (5/25). Because the 40-percent white acceptance rate is the largest number, it becomes the base for computing the impact ratio of other applicant categories. The impact ratio for blacks then is .75 (.3/.4), and the Hispanic acceptance rate is .5 (.2/.4). The recruiting and selection process in this case would be deemed to have a negative impact on blacks and Hispanics because both ratios are beneath the guideline of 0.80. Additional legal considerations will be discussed in the next section, which examines the selection process.

Exhibit 9.1   Computing Impact Ratios for Affirmative Action Programs

RACE	NUMBER OF APPLICANTS	NUMBER OF HIRES	PERCENT OF APPLICANTS	IMPACT RATE
	(1)	(2)	(3) $((2/1) \times 100)$	(4) $((3)/(40) \times 100)$
White	100	40	40%	
Black	50	15	30%	$(30/40) \times 100 = 75\%$
Hispanic	25	5	20%	$(20/40) \times 100 = 50\%$

An Affirmative Action Program that results in selection levels less than 80 percent is a clear violation, but those programs that meet this 80-percent test are not necessarily free of biases in their hiring. For example, screening devices such as tests might still bias against minorities but not in sufficient numbers to be detected by the four-fifths rule. In such a case, an individual could bring suit. Furthermore, the four-fifths rule does not assure that the test is valid, i.e., that there is a verified relationship between the items in the test and the types of behavior that are required to be a sales representative. The EEOC rulings accept standard psychological procedures for the validation of this relationship.

THE SELECTION PROCESS

The selection process requires a careful consideration of all important dimensions for hiring and, where possible, standardization of these dimensions. The selection procedure should minimize overemphasizing one dimension and personal biases, such as the tendency to hire a person in one's own image. The selection process should minimize the tendency to jump to a decision simply to fill the territory. Because the selection process is expensive in terms of managers' time for interviewing, interview guides should be designed to minimize duplication of coverage of topics by several interviewers, unless such duplication is planned. The selection process includes criteria for selection, selection procedures, selection tools, and legal dimensions.

Selection can be a major undertaking. One pharmaceutical company screened 2,200 applicants before hiring 85 representatives.

CRITERIA FOR SELECTION

Personality

Personalities represent personal styles for dealing with one's environment. Thus we may think of an individual as sociable, forceful, or having empathy for others. There have been numerous studies using personality variables as predictors of sales productivity, with very mixed results.[2] D. Mayer, H. M. Greenberg, and J. Greenberg have found that empathy and ego are predictors of sales success.[3] Empathy is the ability to sense the reactions of another person. Ego-drive is the inner need to persuade another individual as a means for gaining one's own gratification.[4] It is easy to see how these two personality traits could combine to produce a forceful sales presentation.

Demographics

Demographic variables include age, sex, marital status, education, race, and prior work experience. For years, sales managers have used these variables as screening devices when hiring sales representatives. Greenberg and Greenberg report that in their studies of 350,000 individuals for selling positions since 1961, demographics were not good predictors of sales success.[5] They concluded instead that the "personality dynamics" of empathy and ego-drive distinguished between successful and unsuccessful sales representatives, and that there were no important differences in these personality dynamics with regard to age, sex, race, education, or experience. Not all researchers would agree with these findings. Busch and Bush compared thirty-nine salesmen and thirty-nine saleswomen according to their job satisfaction, values, role clarity, performance, and propensity to leave.[6] Subjects were matched according to time on the job and work experience, but the women tended to be slightly younger. These researchers found no differences between job satisfaction, job values, and performance, but they did find that women were lower in role clarity and had a higher propensity to leave.

Many companies have more than ten years' experience with the hiring of women and minority representatives. Some companies report extensive analyses of their experiences in an effort to hire and retain these representatives. Singler has studied the problems of 125 women as pharmaceutical representatives.[7] In 1977, he surveyed the women representatives and their district sales managers in order to examine both sides of the problem. Both surveys revealed that the number one problem was relocation and travel. The dimensions of this problem include loneliness and isolation caused by relocation, the lack of opportunities to make friends, the absence of a business-role model, problems of independent living (e.g., handling finances and housing arrangements), and a concern for safety while living at home and on the road. These findings suggest that the recruiting process must include better descriptions of the job and improved methods for screening out unsuitable candidates.

The field sales managers and the women representatives identified credibility as a major problem. This problem emerged as a lack of acceptance of the female representative by customers, peers, and the business community in general. Customers would continue to quiz these representatives in depth to test their competence.

Field sales managers also reported that emotionalism was a problem that revealed itself as more emotional peaks and valleys, more sensitivity to criticism, and a greater need for positive reinforcement. Sales managers reported that some women had less of an understanding of business, the profit concept, paperwork, and planning.

In 1981, Singler surveyed the reasons for separating (resignation or termination) 183 women field sales representatives during a thirteen-year period. The reasons given by the district sales manager, and confirmed by the regional sales manager at the time of separation, were as follows:

Personal Relationships

Husband transferred or objected to travel	9%
Marriage, boyfriend moved, increased social life	16%
Pregnancy	2%

Aptitude for the Job

Lack of comprehension or communication skills	10%
Lack of assertiveness or adaptability	14%
Loneliness or lack of maturity	16%

Attitude Toward the Job

Not working, lack of interest	18%

The difficulties faced by women in the sales force may be summarized as problems in relocation, travel, loneliness, independent living, credibility, acceptance, and understanding of the business processes.

These findings suggest that companies must improve their recruiting processes so that the selling tasks are described more accurately. Some companies make riding with a representative part of the screening process, so that the recruit sees the job first-hand. Many recruits will screen themselves out at this point. Recruiters will need to develop a greater sensitivity for identifying past behavioral traits that will predict an ability to overcome these difficult problems. Furthermore, companies are requiring sales managers to give special attention to new women representatives during the orientation phase to help them overcome these problems.

Job-Related Behavioral Traits

The limitations of personality and demographic variables became a legal matter when the Equal Employment Opportunity Commission required that companies have an Affirmative Action Program for hiring minorities, women, and other protected groups. These programs must validate all measurement techniques that are used for screening applicants. As we have seen, very few personality and demographic variables predict selling performance. For these reasons, many sales managers are returning to measuring job-related behavioral traits on the assumption that past behavior is the best predictor of future behavior on the job.

Relevant job-related behavioral traits that appear frequently in interview guides and are used by sales recruiters appear in Exhibit 9.2. Reading through the list, it is easy to see how some of these apply to selling activities. The representative must have a high level of physical and mental energy, be ambitious, have analytical abilities, seek challenges, and be not easily depressed. A person who is seeking a sales position will want to review this list prior to an interview.

The sales manager who is probing for these behavioral traits will find Exhibit 9.3, "Sources of Information for Behavioral Traits," useful. This table identifies previous behavior patterns that will help identify behavioral traits, sources of information for identifying these traits, and suggested interview questions.

THE SELECTION PROCEDURE

The selection procedure is a series of steps designed to reduce the applicant pool to those persons who have the highest probability of successfully fulfilling those activities appearing in the job description.

Exhibit 9.2   Behavioral Traits Used for Selecting Sales Representatives

Analytical abilities, problem analysis	Decisiveness
Adaptability	History of successfully overcoming
Ambitiousness	obstacles
Average or above-average intelligence	Aggressiveness
Communication skills, oral and written	Individualistic
Breadth	People and results oriented
Average creative ability	Realistic ego drive
Energy level high, physical and mental	Objective view of abilities and
Deals with failure realistically	potentials for achievement
Competitive	Healthy maturity level
Self-motivated	Self-confident
Stress tolerance	Requires less outside enforcement
Sensitivity	Decisions not affected by emotions
Tenacity	Not easily depressed
Planning and organizing abilities	Seeks challenge
Resilience	High degree of perceived self-worth
Learning abilities	Trusts others only to a realistic degree
Integrity	Not really affected by peer or societal
Sales ability	pressures
Judgment	

Sources consist of various screening documents for sales recruiting.

Exhibit 9.3 Sources of Information for Behavioral Traits

BEHAVIORAL TRAITS	PREVIOUS BEHAVIOR	SOURCES OF INFORMATION
ADAPTABILITY	Geographic mobility; career or company mobility; variety of organization memberships.	Resume; "How did you feel about the shift from a small (school, town, company, etc.) to a large one? (Or vice versa.) What kinds of problems did you face after your last move (of any kind)? How would your family adjust to a move?"
ANALYTICAL ABILITIES	College courses requiring analysis (e.g., case courses); previous job requiring analysis and problem solving.	Resume; references; "Describe how you have analyzed a recent problem and solved it. Do you see problems before others do? Do people think that you are logical in your thinking processes?"
BREADTH	Hobbies, clubs, civic organizations, vacations, concerts, plays, lectures, reading habits.	Resume; "What interesting books have you read in the last year? Concerts? Plays? Movies? What magazines did you read during the last month? How do you spend your spare time? Where have you spent your vacations recently?"
COMMUNICATION SKILLS		
Oral	Course selection; membership roles in clubs, organizations; speeches, public-speaking courses.	Resume; "How do you prepare for running a meeting? What are your tough communication problems? What presentations have you made? How effective do you think you were?"
Written	Articles published; writing courses; creative writing such as poetry or short stories; jobs requiring reports or memos.	Resume; "What reports have you written in the last year? How were they received? How do you go about writing a report? Do you make major contributions to team reports?"

(continued)

Exhibit 9.3 Continued

BEHAVIORAL TRAITS	PREVIOUS BEHAVIOR	SOURCES OF INFORMATION
CREATIVITY	Art, writing, photography; creative alternatives to problems.	Resume; "Describe some recent problem where you came up with an alternative that solved the problem. What is the most creative or imaginative thing that you have done in the last few months? What conditions stimulate your imagination? Which ones deter your imagination? Do you prefer new or old solutions to problems? Describe how you did something different from your predecessor when you took over a job. Do you have a tendency to prefer a new solution even if the old one works?"
ENERGY LEVEL	Previous employment; extra-curricular activities, community activities.	Resume; "How do you use your leisure time? What sports have you participated in during the last month?"
LEARNING ABILITY	Scholastic record.	School transcript; references; "What subjects came easily? What were the hard ones?"
MOTIVATION	Previous accomplishments; evidence of goal setting; number and focus of career changes.	Resume; references; "What goals have you set for yourself in the last two years? For the next two years? Describe your accomplishments and life style five years from now. Describe your last big accomplishment. Why did you choose selling as a career? What previous careers have you considered? Describe a situation in which you are most comfortable. What self-development do you plan for the next year? What position do you want after your initial selling position? What do you want to be in ten years?"

PERSUASIVENESS	Previous leadership or selling roles, course selection, hobbies, previous employment.	Resume; references; "Describe the most recent time when you persuaded someone to accept your approach to a problem. If you have sold, describe the most satisfying sale. Have you had courses in selling, debate, or negotiation?"
PLANNING ABILITIES	Past accomplishments requiring planning and good use of time; college extra-curricular activities. Educational plan.	Resume; references; "How do you establish personal priorities? How do you organize your day? Your week? What procedure do you use to keep track of future activities that need your action? What are your goals for the next six months? Next year? Do you encourage others to plan? Do you delegate effectively? How do you keep informed on items you delegate?"
SENSITIVITY	Openness; willingness to listen; hobbies; previous employment.	References; "Describe the last few times that someone came to you with a personal problem. How did you handle him or her? Are you doing anything to become a better listener?"
STRESS TOLERANCE	Previous jobs; physical activities; college experiences, recreational role.	Resume; references; "Under what conditions are you most productive? Creative? When do you feel under pressure? How do you handle it? How do you handle interpersonal conflicts? How do you relieve tensions?"
TENACITY	Number of career changes; accomplishments with a distant payoff.	Resume; references; "Why did you change your college major? Describe a major obstacle that you overcame during the last year. How long should you persist on a sale before giving up? How do you feel when someone rejects your ideas?"

Steps in the Selection Process

Exhibit 9.4, "Steps in the Selection Process," describes the steps that are used by field sales managers of Burroughs Wellcome Company, a pharmaceutical manufacturer, in recruiting sales representatives. The first contact with a candidate is frequently at a slide presentation, showing the typical day of a pharmaceutical representative. After a preliminary interview with a candidate, the sales manager will complete his or her screening interview notes. At this point, the manager decides whether to continue the process or send a turndown letter to the applicant. The second screening stage occurs when the applicant sends a completed application and college transcripts. The application is screened by the district sales manager who then interviews the candidate and either sends a turndown letter or arranges for the candidate to spend two days in the field with representatives for a first-hand view of the job.

If the decision remains to continue the screening process, the field sales manager will obtain a Motor Vehicle Report from the state in which the applicant is licensed, conduct a Spouse Information Session with the applicant and spouse (if applicable), and contact the applicant's references and previous employers. On the approval of the field sales manager, the candidate will be interviewed by the regional sales manager at the regional office. If hired, the necessary documents will be completed and arrangements will be made to have the applicant receive a physical examination.

Each step in the selection process must be documented very carefully. Exhibits 9.5, 9.6, and 9.7 provide examples of an application blank, a screening interview form, and an interview planning grid. Exhibit 9.8 provides a summary form of the appraisals by the district sales manager and the regional sales manager.

Screening Tests

The use of tests and other selection procedures for screening applicants must conform to a uniform set of principles that have been established by the Equal Employment Opportunity Commission, the Civil Service Commission, the Department of Labor, and the Department of Justice. These guidelines are built upon court decisions, previous agency guidelines, the experience of agencies, and standards of the psychological profession.[8]

These guidelines apply to all tests and procedures for hiring, promotion, demotion, union membership, referral, retention, and licensing. Any selection procedure that has an adverse impact on the hiring, promotion, or other employment decision on members of any race, sex, or

Exhibit 9.4 Steps in the Selection Process

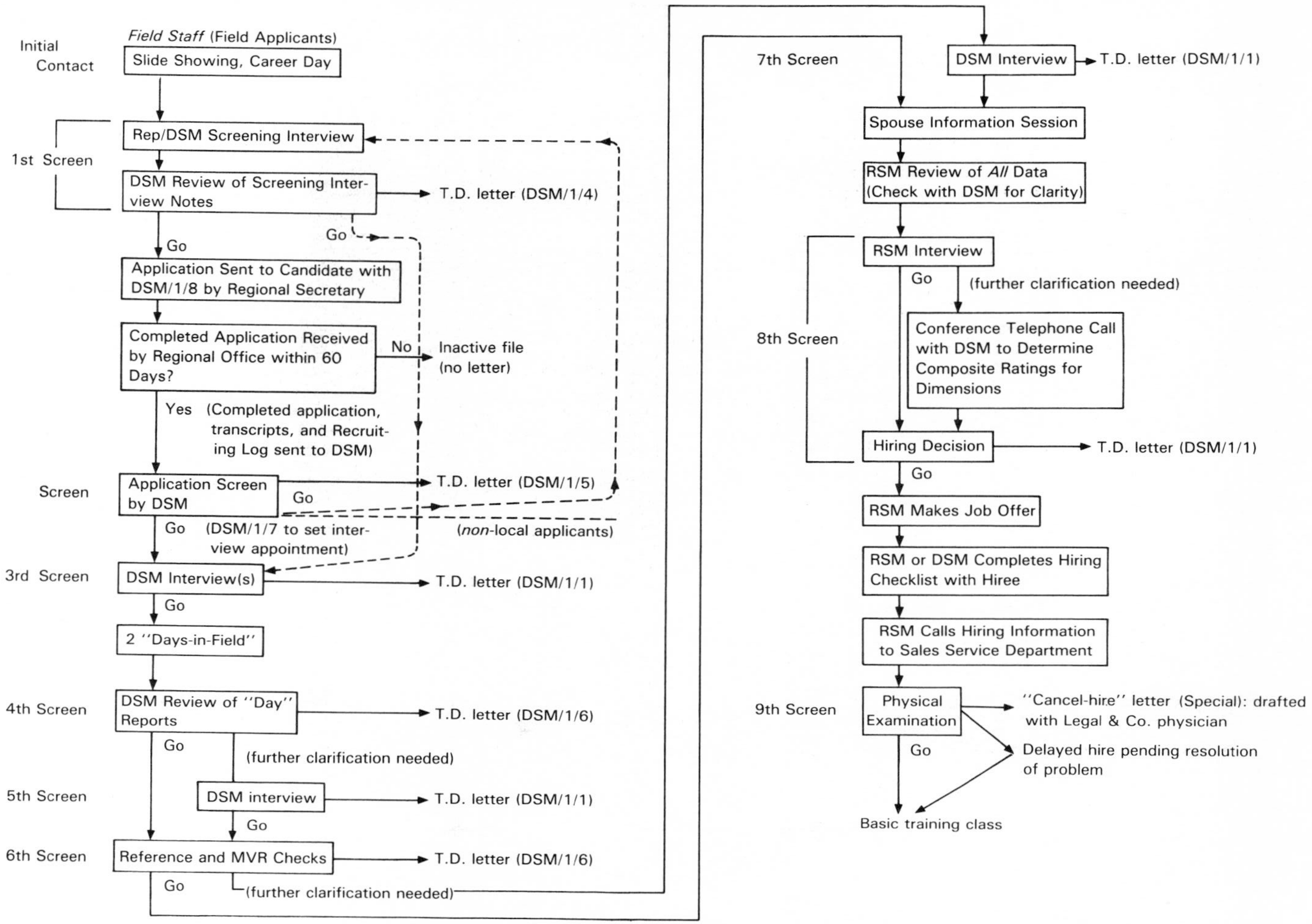

Note: DSM means district sales manager, T.D. letter is turndown letter, and MVR is motor vehicle report.

Used by permission of Burroughs Wellcome Company.

ethnic group is discriminatory unless the procedures have been validated for identifying traits that are necessary for the job.

To assure that sales management personnel policies do not have adverse impacts on these protected groups, the sales manager must apply the "four-fifths rule" to all personnel decisions from recruiting through promoting or firing. This rule, as previously described, when applied to the selection decision, states that the selection rate for minorities must not be less than four-fifths, or 80 percent, of the majority group selection rate.

Procedures and criteria for validating tests for selection should conform to the professional standards of educational and psychological testing associations.[9] Selection procedures should be administered and scored under standardized conditions. A nonvalidated approach may be used if it reduces adverse impact and is job related.

Statistical Approaches to Selection

After job-related criteria have been established and measuring instruments have been validated, a variety of multivariate statistical procedures may be used for screening candidates. Perreault, French, and Harris suggest using discriminant analysis.[10] Cooper and Johnston suggest the use of an additive conjoint model.[11]

Selection Outcomes

The obvious selection outcomes are rejection of the applicant or hiring for immediate employment. Less obvious are outcomes such as advance hiring. In such cases, sales managers process all of the paper and promise to hire a representative as soon as there is an open territory. Some companies have found this a very beneficial procedure for their needs and those of the applicant. It reduces uncertainty for the applicant and it reduces the number of days of open territory for the company.

Recruiting Documentation

There are many good reasons for keeping extensive records regarding the selection and rejection of sales applicants. The most obvious reason is the need to document a decision in case the company faces a suit regarding adverse impact on a minority group or a complaint by the applicant. But there can also be positive reasons for documenting recruiting procedures. A company will want to identify those sources of

Exhibit 9.5   The Application Blank

NAME: _____

FILE NUMBER: _____

SOURCE: _____

Representative's Application

OUR EMPLOYEE RELATIONS POLICY

The Company's employment policy has been and will continue to be to insure equal opportunity for all persons employed by it or seeking employment with it, without discrimination as to race, color, religion, age, sex, national origin, handicap, or status as a disabled or Vietnam era veteran.

The Company is committed to a program of affirmative action to further the utilization of members of minority groups, women, qualified handicapped, qualified disabled and Vietnam era veterans at all levels and in all segments of its work force.

BURROUGHS WELLCOME CO.
3030 Cornwallis Road
Research Triangle Park, N.C. 27709

(continued)

Exhibit 9.5   Continued

This form has been especially designed to help you. If you are employed by us, it will be our intention to assist you in making progress. The more we know about your interests, abilities and aspirations, the better we can train, supervise and encourage you. Please answer all questions carefully. You can be assured that all information will be treated as a personal matter, and will be kept confidential.

PERSONAL HISTORY

Name in full _____ Date _____
                    (last)   (first)   (middle)

Home address _____   Area Code and
                    (street and number)   (city, state and zip code)   Phone No. _____

Upon employment, can you provide us with proof of citizenship or appropriate work visa? _____

Social Security Number _____

PHYSICAL HISTORY

Employment is contingent upon passing a physical examination at the Company's expense. Do you have any physical conditions which may limit your ability to perform the job of Sales Representative? For example uncorrectable speech? _____

Hearing? _____ Sight? _____ If yes, give details, _____

_____

_____

How much time have you lost through illness in the past three years? _____

For what reason(s)? _____

_____

_____

(continued)

Exhibit 9.5 Continued

MISCELLANEOUS

Do you have a valid driver's license? _____ Driver's License No. _____ What state? _____

List any moving traffic violations recorded in the last 3 years. _____

_____

Describe briefly any automobile accidents you have had in the past three years. _____

_____

Is spouse employed by a competitive pharmaceutical company? _____

Have you been convicted of a crime* excluding misdemeanors within the last 7 years? YES_____ NO _____ If yes, please explain: _____

_____

Have you ever been terminated or disciplined because of drug abuse? YES _____ NO _____ If yes, explain: _____

_____

*(Conviction of crimes is not necessarily a bar to employment, but is one factor considered by the Company in hiring.) Factors such as age and time of the offense, seriousness and nature of the violation and rehabilitation will be taken into account.

TERRITORY PREFERENCES, TRAVEL

Are you willing to accept a sales territory in any part of the U.S.? _____ If no, state geographic areas in which you will accept

employment:_____

Are there any states or areas of the U.S.A. in which you would not like to work? _____

Reasons for geographic limitations: _____

_____

Are you willing to travel in your job? _____ Maximum number of nights you are willing and able to be away from home per

month. _____

EDUCATION

IMPORTANT: TRANSCRIPTS OF ALL EDUCATIONAL COURSES MUST BE INCLUDED WITH THIS APPLICATION. APPLICATIONS ARE CONSIDERED INCOMPLETE WITHOUT THESE TRANSCRIPTS.

Type of School	Name and Address of School	Major Course	Dates Attended	Did You Graduate	Degree
College			From To		
Graduate School			From To		
Business College			From To		
Other			From To		
			From To		

Name of academic advisor, university & dept. _____

Name of professor in major, other than academic advisor, university & dept. _____

List any scholastic awards or scholarships _____

(continued)

Exhibit 9.5   Continued

EMPLOYMENT HISTORY: Give employment record as completely as possible, including employment during college period starting with your present or last employer. For any unemployed or self-employed periods, show dates and locations.

Dates	Name, address (street, town, state & zip code), and telephone & area code number of employer	Salary	1. Position,
From		Starting	
To		Ending	
From		Starting	
To		Ending	
From		Starting	
To		Ending	
From		Starting	
To		Ending	
From		Starting	
To		Ending	

On what date will you be available? _____

May we contact your present employer as a reference? YES _____ NO _____

BUSINESS REFERENCES (Previous employers or other business contacts.)

Name and Address (street, town, state and zip code)	Area Code & Telephone Number	Business or Profession	How Long Known?
1. _____	Home_____		
_____	Bus._____	_____	_____
2. _____	Home_____		
_____	Bus._____	_____	_____
3. _____	Home_____		
_____	Bus._____	_____	_____
4. _____	Home_____		
_____	Bus._____	_____	_____

PERSONAL REFERENCES *(Use professional or business persons, not former employer or relatives.)*

Name and Address (street, town, state and zip code)	Area Code & Telephone Number	Business or Profession	How Long Known?
1. _____	Home_____		
_____	Bus._____	_____	_____
2. _____	Home_____		
_____	Bus._____	_____	_____
3. _____	Home_____		
_____	Bus._____	_____	_____
4. _____	Home_____		
_____	Bus._____	_____	_____

Exhibit 9.5 Continued

2. Name and title or position of immediate supervisor,   3. Number supervised by you,   4. Nature of duties,   5. Reason for leaving.

Referred By: Write-in/Phone-in/or Walk-in _____ , Private Employment Agency _____ , College Placement Office _____ ,

State Employment Agency _____ , Referred by Outside Person _____ , Community Agencies _____ ,

Burroughs Wellcome Employee _____ , Other _____

Have you previously applied to B.W. Co. for a position? _____ If so, when? _____

Have you ever been employed by B.W. Co.? YES _____ , NO _____ . If yes, when and what position? _____

In what special activities, trade or professional organizations do you actively participate that you feel are related to the position of Sales Representative (past and present other than those indicating your race, color, religion, sex, age or national origin).

Offices Held: _____

(continued)

Exhibit 9.5   Continued

MILITARY SERVICE RECORD
in the Armed Forces of the United States or in a State Militia

If you did serve in the Armed Forces: Date you entered Service _____ Branch of Service _____

Date discharged or separated _____

Duties performed _____

_____

Rate or rank when discharged or separated _____

Special training courses taken during period of service: _____

_____

Are you an Obligated Reservist? _____ If so, for how long? _____

Do you take an active part in: Reserve ☐   or National Guard Training? ☐   (check one)

If so, indicate name and location of unit _____

Do you participate in annual
2 weeks' training duty? _____ Do you regularly attend drills? _____Weekly? _____ Monthly?_____

(continued)

Exhibit 9.5 Continued

What do you consider your strongest qualification in selling? ______________________

____

____

Which of your assets (background, education, territory knowledge, etc.) do you feel would be most valuable in any association you might make with us? ______________________

____

____

State briefly why you think you would make a successful B.W. Co. medical representative:

APPLICANT'S CERTIFICATION:

THE FACTS SET FORTH IN THIS APPLICATION ARE TRUE AND COMPLETE, AND I AUTHORIZE BURROUGHS WELLCOME CO. TO MAKE SUCH INVESTIGATIONS AND VERIFICATIONS OF DATA AS IT DEEMS APPROPRIATE, INCLUDING THE OBTAINING OF WRITTEN REFERENCE CHECKS. I UNDERSTAND THAT ANY MISREPRESENTATIONS WILL BE SUFFICIENT CAUSE FOR DISMISSAL OR VOIDING OF APPLICATION.

______________________ ______________________

DATE SIGNATURE OF APPLICANT

U.S.A. 183 R 10/78

Used by permission of Burroughs Wellcome Company.

Exhibit 9.6 The Screening Interview Form

SCREENING INTERVIEW U.S.A. 1811 Rev. 6/81

Interviewee _____
Address _____
_____
Phone_____
Interviewer_____
Date _____ Terr. # _____
Source _____

(The following is a suggested format. Feel free to paraphrase it in your own words. However, please adhere to the text of the interview questions as closely as possible!)

Hello, I'm _____ , _____
(Your Name)   (Title)

from Burroughs Wellcome Co.

I'm glad you could spare the time to talk with me.

The purpose of our discussion is for us to get to know as much as possible about each other. That is the only way you and we can make an intelligent decision about a possible career in pharmaceutical sales.

Please understand that this is merely a screening interview; *no* hiring offer will be made here. That comes at a later stage of the application process.

The sales representative job itself is very complex, as indicated in our "A Time to Decide" slide program and on our *Information Sheet.* Have you seen them yet?

Yes_____ (Continue)   No_____ (Have applicant read Information Sheet first)

Do you have any questions about what you read or saw?

Do you have any questions about what you read?

(Don't spend more than a minute answering questions now! Tell applicant you will answer questions at the end of the interview, if time permits.)

Okay. Now I'd like to ask a series of questions and I'll take notes of your answers so I won't miss any of the important information you give me.

When I finish, you may ask as many questions as time permits.

DSMs: The Screening Interview questions are intended to elicit behavioral data relative to the following dimensions. Use the spaces in the margin for recording your numerical rating of each dimension.

_____ Motivation for Sales
(Questions 1, 2 & 7)

_____ Resilience
(Question 3)

_____ Sales Ability
(Questions 4 & 5)

_____ Planning and Organization
(Question 6)

_____ Oral Communication Skill
(Question 8)

(Ratings Scale: 5-Outstanding; 4-More than effective;
3-Effective; 2-Less than effective; 1-Poor)

DSM Action:

Application requested _____
(date)

Turn-down letter sent _____
(date)

Interviewee decided not to pursue job further for the following reasons: (List reasons below, then forward entire file to Sales Recruiting Coordinator).

_____
_____
_____

(continued)

Exhibit 9.6   Continued

1. Why did you choose this particular major (or job)?

2. What have you done in college (or on jobs) to prepare yourself for a pharmaceutical sales position?

3. What were your biggest disappointments in life? How did you pick yourself up again after each?

4. Describe any situations in which you tried very hard to change a teacher's (or boss') mind about something, but you were *not* successful. Why weren't you successful?

5. Describe any situations in which you *were* successful in changing a teacher's (or boss') mind. Why were you successful?

(continued)

Exhibit 9.6   Continued

6. Please outline your major study and extra-curricular (or occupational and non-occupational) activities of the past week. Just start with last week and tell me how you spent the many time segments of each day.

7. Exactly how are you conducting your present job search?

Note: do not write below this line!

(continued)

Exhibit 9.6   Continued

Now, you've been excellent answering my questions; so it's only fair that I answer your questions about Burroughs Wellcome Co. and the sales representative job.

(Answer as many questions as time permits.)

It's been a pleasure meeting you. At any given time, we have several candidates, so you will receive a letter from our District or Regional office within two weeks concerning the next step in the selection process.

Reps: AFTER INTERVIEWEE LEAVES THE ROOM, answer question #8 and complete the EEOC section below.

8. (Evaluate candidate's ability to communicate ideas and to listen effectively during the interview).

Reps: Detach and send EEOC Data to Regional Office and Screening Interview Form to DSM.

Interviewee _____

Interviewer _____ Terr. # _____

EEOC Data:

- ☐ White   ☐ Male
- ☐ Black   ☐ Female
- ☐ Hispanic
- ☐ Asian
- ☐ American Indian
- ☐ Unknown

Used by permission of Burroughs Wellcome Company.

Exhibit 9.7 Interview Planning Grid

INTERVIEW PLANNING GRID

USA 1810   Applicant   Date

Instructions:

1. Use this Grid as the cover page of your interview notes.

2. DSMs - (a) If applicant is turned down prior to being offered an RSM interview, the Ratings column of the Grid must be filled out with ratings of observed dimensions; or (b) if applicant is offered an RSM interview, ratings of observed dimensions must be written on the Dimension Appraisal Form instead.

3. Forward entire file to RSM.

Ratings Scale: 5 - Outstanding; 4 - More Than Effective; 3 - Effective; 2 - Less Than Effective; 1 - Poor; 0 - No Opportunity to Observe; W - Weak Data; H - Too High

Critical Dimensions	Portions of Interview									Future	Other	Ratings
Sales Ability												
Oral Communication Skill												
Integrity												
Motivation For Sales												
Resilience												
Planning and Organization												
Energy												
Practical Learning												
Initiative												
Tenacity												
Judgement												
Work Standards												
Problem Analysis												
Oral Fact Finding												
Adaptability												
Decisiveness												

Exhibit 9.8   Applicant Summary Form

REPRESENTATIVE SELECTION SYSTEM
DIMENSION APPRAISAL FORM U.S.A. 1807

_____

Applicant

INSTRUCTIONS:

DSMs/FSs — Review the entire applicant's file, then rate each dimension in the "DSM" column. From all reports in the file, transcribe the behavioral data that substantiates your rating of each dimension. Forward this form and the entire file to the RSM.

RSMs — 1. Review your interview notes, then rate each dimension in the "RSM" column. From your interview notes only, transcribe behavioral data that substantiates your rating of each observed dimension.

2. Next, fill in the "Composite" ratings. If your ratings in the "RSM" column differ significantly from the "DSM" ratings, you should conduct a data integration session with the DSM to determine the composite ratings.

Ratings Scale: 5—Outstanding; 4—More than effective; 3—Effective; 2—Less than effective; 1—Poor.

Dimensions: Ratings:

	DSM	RSM	COMPOSITE

Sales Ability —
Utilizing appropriate interpersonal styles and methods of communication to gain agreement or acceptance of an idea, plan, activity, or product from clientele such as physicians, pharmacists in drugstores and hospitals, P.A.'s in institutions and others.

Oral Communication Skill —
Effective expression in individual or group situations, when pre-planned or when impromptu (includes gestures and non-verbal communications).

Integrity —
Maintaining social, ethical and organizational norms in job-related activities.

Motivation for Sales —
The extent to which sales activities and responsibilities available in the job overlap with experiences, duties and responsibilities which help product personal satisfaction.

Resilience —
Maintaining effectiveness in spite of disappointment and/or objection.

Planning and Organization —
Establishing a course of action to accomplish a specific goal; planning appropriate allocation of resources including samples, time and literature.

Energy —
Maintaining a high activity level for an extended period of time while sustaining an effective performance level.

Practical Learning —
Assimilating and applying job-related information, taking into consideration rate and complexity.

(continued)

Exhibit 9.8   Continued

	DSM	RSM	COMPOSITE

Initiative —
Active attempts to influence events to achieve goals; self-starting rather than passive acceptance. Taking action to achieve goals beyond those called for; originating action going beyond the norm.

Tenacity —
Staying with a position or plan of action until the desired objective is achieved or is no longer reasonably attainable.

Judgment —
Developing alternative courses of action and making decisions which are based on logical assumptions and which reflect factual information.

Work Standards —
Setting high goals and standards of performance for self, including work activity. Dissatisfied with average performance.

Problem Analysis —
Identifying problems, securing relevant information, relating data from different sources and identifying possible causes of problems.

Oral Fact Finding —
Obtaining and using information from oral communications.

Adaptability —
Maintaining effectiveness in varying environments (including physical and interpersonal), varying tasks and varying responsibilities.

Decisiveness —
Readiness to make decisions, render judgments and take action or commit oneself.

DSM/FS _____ /Date _____   RSM _____ /Date _____

Used by permission of Burroughs Wellcome Company.

candidates and selection procedures that generate candidates who have the highest probability of success on the job. Careful documentation will build a history of data that can be analyzed through multivariate statistical techniques.

LEGAL DIMENSIONS OF SELECTION

Today companies must have an Affirmative Action Compliance Program (AACP) in order to implement Title VII of the Civil Rights Act of 1964. The Equal Employment Opportunity Commission (EEOC) was created to administer Title VII and has direct access to the courts.

A sales manager's affirmative action compliance program should include a guide on preemployment inquiries so that recruitment does not discriminate. This guide should indicate what questions regarding sex, marital status, physical data, etc., may be asked without violating federal regulations. The guide must identify criteria that are "bona fide occupational qualifications (BFOQ)." Age and sex may be BFOQs when hiring a fashion model, but may be illegal when hiring a sales representative. Exhibit 9.9 provides an interview guide of the types of inquiries that are discriminatory and those that are acceptable. Such lists can never be complete because they are continuously affected by court decisions. Therefore a company should prepare such a list by consulting current publications of the Equal Employment Opportunity Commission.

EVALUATING THE RECRUITING AND SELECTION PROCESS

Recruiting and selecting, like other sales management activities, must be evaluated continuously. Two procedures for such an evaluation are measuring turnover rates and productivity levels. Operations researchers have also suggested evaluation models that evaluate these processes in terms of return-on-investment.

TURNOVER RATES

Turnover rates may be computed as follows:

Number of Representatives Who Left / Average Sales Force Size (1)

For example, if there were 22 representatives who left or were terminated, and if the beginning sales force for the year was 200 representatives and the closing sales force was 240, the average sales force size would be 220 and the turnover rate would be 0.10. The computations are as follows:

$$22/\ ((200 + 240)\ /\ 2) = 22/220 = 0.10 \tag{2}$$

Exhibit 9.9 An Interview Guide for Affirmative Action Compliance Programs

SUBJECT	DISCRIMINATORY INQUIRIES	ACCEPTABLE INQUIRIES
Name	The original name of an applicant whose name has been changed. Maiden name or father's surname.	Whether the applicant has worked or been educated using a different name, if necessary to verify qualifications.
Sex		Notice appearance.
Birthplace or Residence	Make comments or notes unless sex is a BFOQ. Birthplace of applicant or parents. Requirements that applicant submit a birth certificate.	
Creed or Religion	Religious affiliation, holidays observed, name of spiritual leader.	Whether special arrangements need to be made for working on Saturdays or Sundays (e.g., convention duty).
Race or Color	Applicant's race, color of skin, eyes, or hair. Photographs are not permitted.	
Marital Status	Are you married, single, divorced, or engaged? Who lives with you?	These questions may be asked after hiring for insurance purposes.
Children	How many children do you have? Who cares for them? Do you plan to have children?	Number and ages of children after hiring, for insurance purposes.
Age	How old are you? (Or simply estimating age.)	After hiring, "Are you over 18?" and age for insurance purposes.
Physical Data	Height or weight (which will have an adverse impact on Spanish-surnamed or Asian-Americans)	Explain manual labor, lifting, or other requirements of the job. Show how the job is performed. Require a physical examination.
Criminal Record	Have you ever been arrested, convicted, or spent time in jail? (Minorities are arrested more frequently.)	Number and kinds of convictions if they are related to the job. For example, a theft conviction for an applicant applying for a job as a bank teller, or a drug conviction by an applicant applying for job as a pharmaceutical representative.

Category		
Military Experience	Experience in armed forces other than U.S. Dates, conditions, or type of discharge. Reserve or draft status. Whereabouts during war years. (Minorities have had a larger proportion of unfavorable discharges.)	Are you a veteran? Any job-related experience?
Housing	Do you own or rent your home? Do you live in an apartment? Do you live with your parents? (These are "economic status" questions that do not reflect favorably on minorities. Similar questions deal with length of residence, car ownership, past garnishment of wages, and personal bankruptcy.)	If you have no phone, how can we reach you?
Citizenship	Any inquiry into whether the applicant is now or intends to become a U.S. citizen. (The law protects lawfully immigrated aliens.)	Are you in the country on a visa that would not permit you to work here?
Education	Education may not be asked if it is not job related, because minorities tend to have less education.	
Organization	Any clubs, social fraternities, sororities, societies, lodges, or organizations to which the applicant belongs.	Membership in union, trade, or professional organizations.
Language	Applicant's mother tongue, language learned at home, how the applicant acquired knowledge of a foreign language.	Language spoken and written if job related.
National Origin	Applicant's lineage, national origin, or that of parents or spouse.	
Relatives	Name and/or address of any relative of applicant.	Name and address of person to be notified in case of an emergency

Sources: Adapted from "How to keep bias out of job interviews," *Business Week*, May 26, 1975, p. 77; collected corporate screening documents based on EEOC regulations.

There are many different costs associated with turnover. There is the cost of lost business. There are termination costs, such as severance pay and storage of idle equipment. There are hiring costs, which include agency fees, advertising expenses, interviewing time for all persons involved, travel costs for the applicants and interviewers, relocation expenses, and screening expenses such as medical and psychological examinations. There will be additional training costs at training centers and by field trainers, training materials, and travel associated with training. Additional supervision will be required by field sales managers. A rough estimate of all of these figures will give a total monthly impact per representative who left the company. Multiplying this expense times the number of terminations will give the total expense of representative turnover. Dobbs thinks that 30 to 50 percent of the conditions that lead to turnover can be controlled by the sales manager.[12] He lists as the controllable factors the representative's inability to perform the job, not being well suited to the job, not motivated, and ill-defined criteria for success. Dobbs cites the following factors as difficult to control: changes in the company's competitive position, insufficient opportunity for promotion, compensation systems, ineffective supervision, and raiding by competitors. Thus the high cost of turnover cannot be completely the blame of poor recruiting and selection procedures. But in many instances an examination of the total cost of turnover will suggest that spending more on recruiting and selection would be a good investment.

PRODUCTIVITY LEVELS

Two different forms of productivity measures may be used to evaluate the recruiting and selection process. First, we may measure the steps in the recruiting process, such as the number of visits to college campuses, the number of applications processed, or the number of minorities interviewed. We may also measure the effectiveness of the recruiting selection process by measuring its failure—the number of days that territories were open. Some companies evaluate sales managers on the percent of days that territories were open.

EVALUATION MODELS

Finding the applicant with the highest probability of succeeding as a sales representative represents a series of tradeoffs among the cost of an open territory, the turnover costs, the costs of recruiting and selecting, and the costs of managing a poor candidate. Darmon suggests a sequential decision theory model to help decide how many candidates should be sought before selecting one representative.[13] He notes that choosing an average candidate instead of a competent one introduces an opportunity loss, consisting of the difference in profit flows between an average and a competent representative. The decision tradeoff is between the additional recruiting costs and the higher level of sales productivity. He applied his approach to a Canadian pharmaceutical company and concluded that if it increased its recruiting budget thirteen times its present budget, it would realize an increase in discounted profit flow of 6.8 percent.

SUMMARY

Subsequent sales management tasks are made easier by a good system for recruiting and selecting candidates. This system begins with planning the sales force requirements with regard to the quantity and quality of representatives that will be needed. The job description, the selling plan, and the sales forecasts will help the sales manager to determine the sales force requirements. In recruiting candidates, the sales manager must make certain that sources used will not adversely impact minority persons. The selection process begins with criteria for selection that are job related. The selection process represents a tradeoff between the immediate need to fill a territory and finding the ideal candidate. The Civil Rights Act of 1964 adds many new dimensions to the process of recruiting and selecting. Interviewers must phrase their questions carefully and keep complete records.

Evaluation of the recruiting and selection process may use measures such as turnover rates, productivity levels, and financial concepts such as present value of discounted profit flows. Productivity levels include such measures as the number of days the territories were open and statistics on recruiting activities such as the number of persons interviewed.

ASSIGNMENTS/DISCUSSION QUESTIONS

1. Students should exchange resumes prior to a class session and prepare questions for interviewing each other. During the class session, students will be called upon to serve as the interviewer and the candidate. The class will be required to evaluate the process. The instructor will assign various cases in this text as the company doing the recruiting.

By selecting different companies, students will see the following critical questions emerge: How much technical knowledge is required? Is the product a standard off-the-shelf one, or must it be modified to meet customer needs? How much training will the applicant require?

Some interviewers like to ask personality questions, such as the following: What activities do you find exciting and which ones are monotonous? Describe your lifestyle five years from now. What has been your most outstanding disappointment in life? What do people criticize about you?

2. What are the objectives of the selection interview?

3. What is the value to the interviewer of a written application?

4. What are selection criteria and what is their importance?

5. Where are selection criteria derived from?

6. Which subject should be covered first in the selection interview—the information about the job or about the applicant? Why?

7. What are the relative advantages of turning the applicant down in person and in writing?

8. What rewards or benefits can be expected from recruiting and selecting qualified applicants?

9. What costs can be expected from poor personnel selection?

10. What is the purpose of checking references, previous employers, resume information, professors, etc.?

CASE 9.1:
The Case of Sally Simpson

Sally Simpson was hired by National Business Forms, Inc., in June, three weeks after graduating from St. David's College with a B.A. in history. St. David's is a liberal arts college with an enrollment of approximately 4,000 undergraduates, located in Schenectady, New York, thirty-five miles from Amsterdam, where Sally's family has lived for two generations. Sally is the youngest of six children. While at St. David's, Sally was a member of the drama club, a cheerleader, a member of the honor society, and graduated *cum laude*. She spent her junior year in France in a language program and worked each of the past three summers at a prep school in New England.

National Business Forms, headquartered in Baltimore, was expanding its sales force in the mid-west, and in recruiting at St.

David's had hired three graduates with whom Sally had shared classes. The initial screening interview was conducted by a recruiting team from National's personnel department, with the final interview by the personnel manager in Baltimore. Along with two other applicants recruited from Kansas City and Chicago, Sally was assigned to Scott Johnson's district and given a territory radiating out of St. Louis into parts of Illinois and Missouri, which required her to be away from her St. Louis home base a total of fifteen working days out of a nine-week cycle. National Business Forms relocated about two-thirds of all new representatives they hired. They paid for a trip to St. Louis for Sally to locate an apartment and all of the expenses of Sally's move. They provided a car, base salary, bonus, and reasonable expenses.

Sally's District Sales Manager, Scott Johnson, headquartered in Chicago, supervised eleven sales representatives in Illinois, Indiana, Missouri (four in St. Louis), Wisconsin, and Iowa, including two other women representatives in Chicago and Milwaukee.

Sally got off to a good start in the training class in Baltimore, and worked with two representatives in their territories for two weeks before returning to St. Louis, where John Faircloth, the senior representative in St. Louis, helped her get started. For the four months following her field training, Sally had been very busy making a full trip around her territory, including the three weeks of travel, setting up her records, preparing the required reports, and expanding her knowledge of the industry and the company's products via the correspondence courses sent to her by the sales training department.

During this interval, Scott Johnson had spent two days with her in field training activities during each of the past four months, as he did with all of his trainees. In his last trip report on Sally, he had expressed his approval of her sustained effort and the progress she was making. He complimented her on her positive attitude, the way customers responded to her personality and friendly approach, the improvement he had noted in her knowledge and skills on each of the past three trips, and her general understanding of the job.

Sally had mentioned several times the heavy volume of the work and the fact that the job was tougher and took more of her personal time than she had expected, but that she thought she was gradually getting on top of the job. She complained somewhat that the training assignments, study time, reports, and travel had so limited her free time that she hadn't had the opportunity to make any friends.

Scott did his best to put her immediate concerns in perspective and to make Sally realize that, while field sales was tough at first, as she became more knowledgeable she would be able to accomplish the required reporting and planning more quickly. He also assured her that as she worked her territory repeatedly she would establish friendships with many of her customers' employees. He tried to make her realize that the period of training required more concentration and effort on everyone's part to enable her to achieve the required level of competence, and that her progress to date was ahead of that of the average trainee.

Sally was pleased to receive his evaluation and reassurances, and reaffirmed her determination to qualify for the next advanced training class. As a result, Scott was surprised and disappointed on his return from working with the Cedar Rapids representative to receive a telephone call from Sally saying she had just returned from an out-of-town swing and was so discouraged that she was resigning and wanted to be checked out as quickly as possible. When pressed for an explanation, Sally said she had tried her best but she felt that she just wasn't suited for the work. Scott reluctantly accepted her decision and planned to fly to St. Louis on Monday.

CASE QUESTIONS

1. What major job-related behavioral characteristics are required for the job of a field sales representative?

2. How would these behavioral characteristics differ from those required for an in-plant salesperson?

3. Would any different behavioral characteristics be required for a sales representative with a territory where a significant amount of traveling (up to 50 percent) is required?

4. What qualifications does Sally Simpson have that match the behavioral characteristics for the job for which she was hired?

5. For what business reasons might an interviewer hire an applicant whose qualifications did not reasonably match the required job-related behavioral characteristics?

6. Who should conduct the final hiring interview: (a) a member of the personnel department, (b) the field sales manager to whom the applicant will report, (c) any field sales manager? List the advantages and disadvantages of each.

7. Should Sally Simpson have been hired? Was this a mistake in interviewing and hiring or orientation and training?

REFERENCES

1. ''Testing and Selecting Employees' Guidelines,'' *Employment Practice Guide,* vol. II (Chicago: Commerce Clearing House, Inc., 1978), pp. 2223–2224.
2. See Chapter 4 for discussions and citations. A tabular summary may be found in G.A. Churchill, Jr., N. M. Ford, and O. C. Walker, Jr., *Sales Force Management: Planning, Implementation and Control* (Homewood, Ill: Richard D. Irwin, Inc., 1981), pp. 280–281.
3. D. Mayer and H. M. Greenberg, ''What Makes a Good Salesman?'' *Harvard Business Review* 42 (July–August 1964): 119–125; J. Greenberg and H. M. Greenberg, ''Predicting Sales Success—Myths and Reality,'' *Personnel Journal* 55, no. 12 (December 1976): 621–627.
4. Greenberg and Greenberg, ''Predicting Sales Success,'' pp. 621–622.
5. Ibid.
6. Paul Busch and R. F. Bush, ''Women Contrasted to Men in the Industrial Salesforce. . . ,'' *Journal of Marketing Research* 15 (August 1978): 438–448.
7. C. H. Singler, ''Suggested Solutions to Potential Problems with Women as Field Sales Representatives,'' Editorial for the National Society of Sales Training Executives (NSSTE), September 1, 1977; C. H. Singler, ''A Thirteen-Year Study of the Reasons for Separation of Women as Field Sales Representatives,'' NSSTE Editorial, July 1, 1981.
8. ''Testing and Selecting Employees' Guidelines,'' pp. 2221–2225.
9. Ibid., pp. 2223–2224.
10. William D. Perreault, Jr., Warren A. French, and Clyde E. Harris, Jr., ''Use of Discriminant Analysis to Improve the Salesman Selection Process,'' *Journal of Business* 50 (January 1977): 50–62.
11. Martha Cooper and W. J. Johnston, ''Analyzing the Sales Force Selection Process,'' College of Administrative Science, The Ohio State University, Working Paper Number 80-33, May, 1980.
12. J. H. Dobbs, ''Sales Force Turnover Can Make You—Or Break You,'' *Sales & Marketing Management* (May 14, 1979): 53–58.
13. R. Y. Darmon, ''Sales Force Management: Optimizing the Recruiting Process,'' *Sloan Management Review* (Fall 1978): 47–59.

SUGGESTED READINGS

The Conference Board, *Salesmen's Turnover in Early Employment* (New York: The Conference Board, 1972).

Ewing, D. W., ''The Right to Be Let Alone,'' *Across the Board* (October 1977): 62–70.

Kanter, R. M., and Stein, B. A., ''Birth of a Saleswoman,'' *Across the Board* (June 1979): 14–24.

Kanuk, Leslie, ''Women in Industrial Selling,'' *Journal of Marketing* 42 (January 1978): 87–91.

Lamont, L. M., and Lundstrom, W. J., ''Identifying Successful Industrial Salesmen by Personality and Personal Characteristics,'' *Journal of Marketing Research* 14 (November 1977): 517–529.

Modern Sales Management: Checklists, Forms, Procedures (Boston: Warren, Gorham & Lamont, Inc., 1981).

Newton, D. A., "Get the Most Out of Your Sales Force," *Harvard Business Review* 47 (September–October 1969): 130–143.

Robertson, D. H., and Hackett, D. W., "Saleswomen: Perceptions, Problems and Prospects," *Journal of Marketing* 41 (July 1977): 66–71.

Seigel, Jerome, *Personnel Testing Under EEO* (New York: Amacom, 1980).

Swan, J. E.; Futrell, C. M.; and Todd, J. T., "Same Job—Different Views: Women and Men in Industrial Sales," *Journal of Marketing* 42 (January 1978): 92–98.

10

ORIENTING, TRAINING, AND DEVELOPING REPRESENTATIVES

A young sales trainer may be given the same advice that a newspaper editor gave a young cub reporter who was told to find the story by answering the questions who, what, when, where, why, and how. The sales trainer needs to answer these questions, but in a slightly different order. Why is sales training necessary? Who should be trained? What should be the content of the training program? When should the training be given? How should the training be done? Who should the trainers be? Where should the training take place? And how should the training programs be evaluated?

The field sales manager plays an important role in orienting and training representatives. These managers must orient and train new and experienced representatives in selling and they must also identify representatives who are candidates for management positions and help prepare them for these new roles. Thus the sales manager is helping to develop the future management capabilities of the company. The importance of such development has been expressed by the Chinese philosopher Kuan Teu who, in 300 B.C., said, "If you are going to plan for a year, plant corn; if you are going to plan for a decade, plant trees; if you are going to plan for a lifetime, train and develop people."

The relationship between training and other sales management functions may be seen in Exhibit 10.1. The job description guides the recruiting and selection effort, which, in turn, produces applicants with varying qualifications and therefore varying training needs. Some companies prefer to recruit applicants with no previous sales experience and who have similar backgrounds so that they may use a standardized

Exhibit 10.1   The Relationship Between Training and Other Sales Management Functions

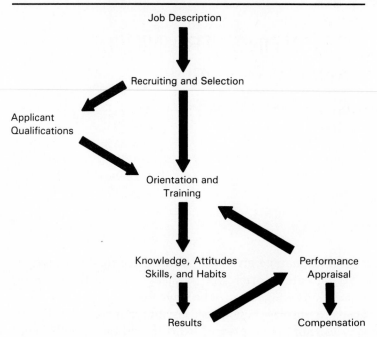

orientation and training program. The applicant's qualifications and the company's orientation and training program produce knowledge, attitudes, skills, and habits that will lead to results. Performance appraisals are used to evaluate these results and identify the need for more training. This appraisal will also determine the compensation levels.

WHY TRAIN?

The training goals will vary according to the experience of the sales representative. The goals for new representatives may be to create positive attitudes, to orient them toward the company, company products, territory, and community, and to help them satisfy their personal needs. The training goals from the company viewpoint may be to lower the cost of new recruits by speeding their personal development. The company will also have goals for expanding the sales force or providing a flow of qualified persons to meet future needs.

Training for experienced representatives may have goals of improving morale, motivation, or customer relations. Training may be needed for new products, new markets, new competition, new technology, and new marketing strategies—changes that have occurred at an accelerated rate. There may be special training programs for older representatives with declining performance who have been resisting changes in the selling environment, or whose skills have not kept pace with the changing environment. Increases in productivity may be sought by improving skills in territory management, time utilization, negotiation skills, closing and other elements of the selling process, consultative selling, and knowledge of the entire marketing process. Better training may also have as its goal reducing necessary supervision and reducing the turnover of the sales force. Some companies will have goals of improving territory reports, forecasts, and record-keeping in general. And finally, representatives with a potential for management may be given training in management.

ASSESSMENT OF TRAINING NEEDS

Mager reminds us that training is only one of many alternatives that can be used to help an individual overcome a deficiency in human performance.[1] Other alternatives for improving performance include motivation programs (Chapter 11), compensation schemes (Chapter 22), better feedback to the individual (Chapter 13), and reassessment of the goals as described in the job description.

Exhibit 10.2 is Mager's flow diagram of questions that may be asked to find solutions to performance deficiencies. First, if the discrepancy is not important, it should be ignored. If it is important, the next question is, "Is the performance deficiency due to a skill deficiency?" If the sales representative has the skills but is not performing, perhaps there is a need to remove the punishment dimensions of the task, arrange for better motivation and compensation, or remove obstacles that prevent performance. If the representative does not have sufficient skills, then the next question is, "Did he or she ever have these skills?" If the answer is no, then formal training must be arranged. If the answer is yes, the next question is, "How often are these skills used?" If they are not used frequently, it may be necessary to arrange for practice. If they are used frequently, then it is a matter of providing better feedback. There is always the final question, "Does the individual have the potential for performing the job?" If the answer is no, then the manager must face reality and

Exhibit 10.2   Finding Solutions to Performance Deficiencies

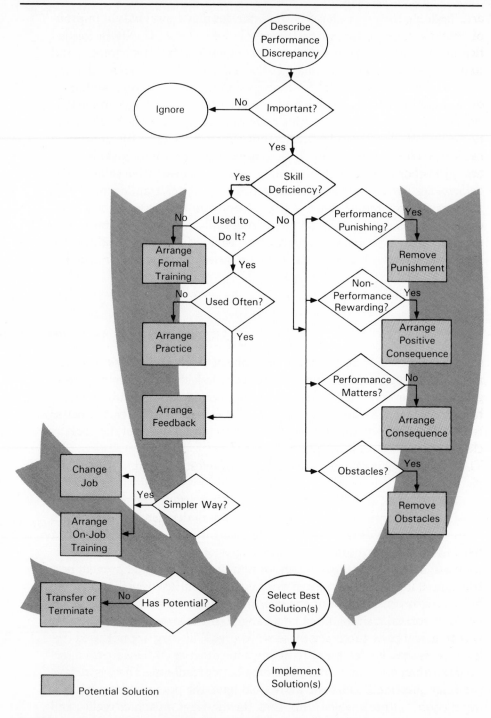

R. F. Mager, *Analyzing Performance Problems* (Belmont, Calif.: Pitman Learning, Inc., 1970).

arrange for a transfer or termination. Having considered the alternatives of training, motivation, compensation, better feedback, and goal specification, the manager must then select the best alternative and proceed toward implementation.

A variety of techniques may be used for identifying performance deficiencies that could be corrected through training. Performance deficiencies may appear through productivity measures, such as sales levels, turnover, absenteeism, new account prospecting, presentations, closing rates, sales lost to competitors, and territory costs. The job description and performance evaluation reviews will be the basis for identifying the deficiencies in these productivity rates.[2]

Survey techniques may be used also to identify deficiencies. Some companies survey representatives, field managers, and general sales managers, asking them to identify their own strengths and weaknesses, and those areas where they would like to develop their own knowledge and skills. Small-group discussions with the representatives are used to identify problem areas and possible solutions. Customer surveys are used to identify what customers want in a representative and the deficiencies in company and competitive representatives.[3]

When training needs have been identified and agreed upon, the person in charge of training should establish priorities for training with management and then proceed to develop a training program. This program should concentrate on an individual's strengths, not try to make him or her over into a new person. It should be made clear that training is a routine part of the job. Organizing for training should include a clear outline of objectives, the results of which can be measured clearly. Time spans, methods, and materials should all be identified during this planning stage.

WHO SHOULD BE TRAINED?

Because training is a continuous process, the question, "Who should be trained?" can be answered very simply: everyone. The content of the training, however, will depend on the position of the representative in his or her career life cycle.[4] Training for the new representative must be heavy in orientation and selling skills. The experienced representative will need training in marketing, new products, and management. Problem representatives will need training that is specific to their particular needs. The older representative will need encouragement to learn new products and methods. The sales manager will also want to tap the knowledge of these older representatives by using them as field sales trainers.

WHAT SHOULD BE THE CONTENT OF THE TRAINING PROGRAM?

The content of training programs may be divided into three parts—orientation, selling activities, and follow through.

ORIENTATION

The orientation program requires an understanding of the needs of the new employee. The new college graduate entering a sales career, for example, faces uncertainty, anxiety, and discomfort as he or she leaves the familiar surroundings of the college campus. The orientation program should be designed to reduce these uncertainties and reassure the candidate that the right career decision was made. Complete orientation programs will include materials about the industry, the company, the role of personal selling in the marketing mix, the channels of distribution, the territory, the community, and the informal social structure of which the applicant will be a part.

Company orientation will include its history, its products, corporate policies, and procedures for accomplishing routine tasks. The new applicant's position in the organization will be identified with organizational charts that clearly define reporting relationships. The role of personal selling in the marketing mix will also be described in the discussion of company policies. At this point the new representative will learn whether the representative in this company is a communicator or a consultant (Chapter 1, Exhibit 1.1).

Orientation into the territory will include details such as trading areas, streets, travel routes, parking facilities, and territory records that will include customer and prospect names, past strategies, and buying patterns. Much of this type of training will take place on the job.

Community orientation will include social and athletic structures available, churches, banking, and housing details such as telephone, gas, and electricity. Field sales managers who take this phase of orientation seriously will help the new trainee overcome many initial anxieties. As noted in the previous chapter, new women representatives tend to need more support during this phase of orientation.

The informal company social structure can help the new candidate bridge the gap between the college life and the corporate life. This structure will provide opportunities for meeting people individually as well as at social gatherings and recreational activities. A company that has high turnover among young representatives will want to examine carefully its orientation program.

SELLING ACTIVITIES

The content of training programs in selling may be divided into four categories—knowledge, attitudes, skills, and habits. While this sequence provides a useful acronym—KASH—some trainers feel that attitudes are most important, habits are second in importance, followed by skills and knowledge.[5] A successful salesperson must have a positive mental attitude. He or she must be sold on the product and company in order to sell these to others. Personal pride in the company, its products, its industry, and in the career of a salesperson will create confidence and enthusiasm for everything the representative does. The new applicant needs to understand the importance of personal selling to the company and to the industry, and that without this function all other functions in the company would come to a halt.

Training in developing good habits will include self-discipline, effective time utilization, adequate planning, proper travel routing, and good record-keeping. In short, this is managing the territory like a business (Chapter 5).

Skill development training will be required in all phases of the selling process from prospecting through needs identification, probing presentation, meeting objections, and closing, all of which have been discussed in detail in Chapter 4. Representatives may also need training in effective listening.

The representative must have extensive knowledge, not only about his or her company and products, but also about industry trends, competitors' activities, and economic conditions that will influence customers' buying decisions. In industrial selling, the representative must understand the production process of prospects in order to make proper product applications. He or she will also need to know technical details of the product, pricing, production scheduling, warehousing and shipping details, servicing, and corporate credit policies. All of these subject areas may be included in initial and continuing training programs.

The concept of account management requires new forms of training. The representative now must develop skills in estimating account potential, developing selling strategies, negotiating, demonstrating to buying teams, persevering, and handling turndowns.

FOLLOW THROUGH

Follow through is receiving increased attention among sales trainers. Representatives are trained in analysis of prospects' problems, decision making, and communication, all of which are part of problem-solving skills. A failure to make the sale requires analysis of the steps of problem solving to determine where the representative needs skill development. These problem-solving skills should be examined also when the sale is made so that the representative knows his or her strengths, as well as reasons for failure.

Sales follow through, by working out the logistics of delivery, installation, payment, and customer satisfaction, can make subsequent sales to a customer easier.

WHEN SHOULD THE TRAINING BE GIVEN?

The timing of the training will depend on many circumstances, for example, the stage in the representative's career, the complexity of the material being sold, and special occasions such as new products, new markets, new strategies, new promotional campaigns, and new competition. Special occasions would include problems that were identified during the analysis of training needs for the entire sales force and during the performance appraisal of specific representatives. Training philosophies will differ among companies within the same industry. Some companies prefer to give some training at a centralized location prior to sending a new representative into the field, while other companies prefer on-the-job training and therefore send representatives into the field immediately to work with experienced representatives. Some companies will have a combination of initial training after hiring, on-the-job training, and then returning to the home office for advanced training.

Several examples will illustrate the diversity of corporate sales training programs. Procter & Gamble begins sales representatives' training with a twenty-week structured on-the-job training program. The recruit works with the Unit Manager, which is the first level of field sales management at Procter & Gamble. The Unit Manager explains each step in the sales call, demonstrates it, and then lets the recruit try it. Then the trainee makes sales calls with the trainer who observes and makes suggestions for improvements. The new representative next attends a training program at corporate headquarters in Cincinnati where small, problem-solving discussion groups are used to study the business in depth and to learn advanced selling techniques. On-the-job training will continue with regular sales meetings, organized reading programs, district bulletins, company and trade publications, and interactions with other sales representatives. When the young representative has demonstrated the maturity and ability to handle additional responsibilities, he or she will be promoted to District Field Representative, which presents the opportunity to work with District Managers and Unit Managers calling on major accounts, recruiting, training, and other marketing operations at the district level. The next step is to attend the Sales Management Training School in Cincinnati. Successful completion of this phase will earn the representative a promotion to Unit Manager, the first level of field sales force management.[6]

The timing of the IBM training program and its contents are summarized in Exhibit 10.3. Completion of this training can take more than one year. The program begins with training in computers and their applications. About six months into the training program, the trainee and the company must decide whether the best career path is being a sales representative or a systems engineer (SE).

The Conoco Chemicals Division of Continental Oil Company has a detailed training program for marketing trainees that begins in its Houston office with an explanation of employee benefits and the signing of an invention agreement. The trainee then sees a slide show of the first one hundred years of the company, receives cash advances, and is given instructions regarding expense account procedures and progress reports. He or she then spends fifteen to thirty minutes each interviewing persons in functional areas such as marketing, manufacturing, planning, and product development. The trainee is then sent to his or her first field training assignment where one-half day each will be spent with regional managers. The trainee then observes a Technical Sales Representative on a regular sales call. At the completion of this call, the trainee must complete an observer's checklist of what took place in the selling process. This checklist sensitizes the trainee to the important steps in the chemical sales process. The individual then proceeds to eight weeks of product and technical training, and then attends plant training modules that include tours of production facilities, laboratory operations, and administrative operations. Topics include plant safety, transportation activities, and plant engineering. The trainee now returns to the Houston headquarters for instruction in the Sales Manual, regional office administration, sales forecasting, contract logs, customer files, and progress reporting. At this point, the trainee is instructed in supply and distribution systems, customer service, and credit activities. These steps take about eight months.

Sales training at Conoco is accomplished with in-house courses given by company personnel or consultants, outside courses, and individual training by sales managers and technical sales representatives. The company has used the American Management Association training program on Time and Territory Management.[7]

Exhibit 10.3   Roadmap for a New Curriculum (March 1, 1982)

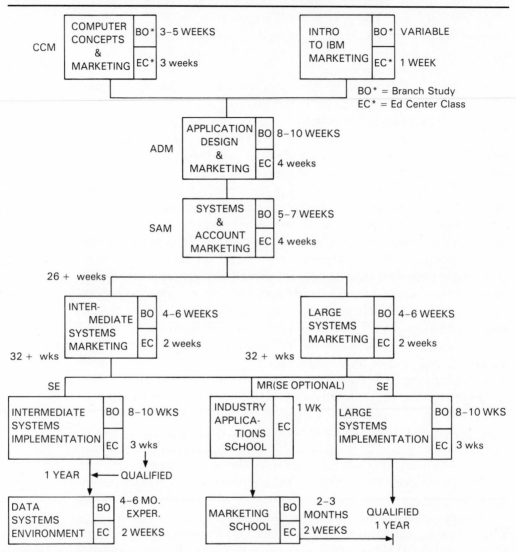

SE = Systems Engineer
MR = Marketing Representative

Reprinted with permission of IBM.

HOW SHOULD THE TRAINING BE DONE?

Sales training, like any training process, carries responsibilities for the teacher and the learner. These responsibilities may be summarized as follows: relevance, benefits, experience, feedback, classroom application, self-evaluation, and on-the-job application. These responsibilities and the teaching process as viewed by the teacher and the learner are summarized in Exhibit 10.4.

TRAINING METHODS

Training methods may be classified by the degree of involvement permitted the trainee. The lecture method has the minimum involvement and should be used in sales training only to convey factual information, such as the history of the company, its products, policies, and procedures. Demonstrations provide some visual involvement by trainees and maximum involvement when they are permitted to practice demonstrating. Conference and small-group discussion methods permit a high level of involvement. With these methods, the trainees may introduce their personal experiences and try out ideas on other members of the group. Small-group discussions of case material represent one of the best means by which trainees can develop and sharpen their problem-solving skills. Role playing is perhaps the most frequently used method for developing selling skills. (The instructor or another trainee plays the role of the buyer while another trainee plays the role of the sales representative.) Such experiences can be frightening, but they make the real-world experience seem less difficult.

Exhibit 10.4   Adult Teaching and Learning Responsibilities and Processes

RESPONSIBILITY	TEACHING PROCESS	LEARNING PROCESS
1. Relevance	1. Define why it is necessary to learn the subject.	1. Recognize the need to learn.
2. Benefits	2. Specify gains to learners.	2. Perceive the training goals as my goals.
3. Experience	3. Offer learning through participation.	3. Learn the subject matter in a way that makes use of my experience and allows me to participate.
4. Feedback	4. Test the learner's understanding.	4. Test my understanding of the material.
5. Classroom Application	5. Allow learners to use their new knowledge to produce some result.	5. Practice using the new knowledge.
6. Self-Evaluation	6. Help the learner to evaluate himself or herself without fear.	6. Evaluate my practice in a supportive climate.
7. On-the-Job Application	7. Provide supportive climate on the job.	7. Apply my learning on the job.

Some training methods can be both individual and personal. For example, there are tutorial methods, which are frequently known as "curbstone conferences," where the field sales manager gives immediate advice after having observed the representative in action. Correspondence courses are another form of individual, high-involvement learning methods.

The good training programs recognize the strengths and weaknesses of each of these techniques by using a combination of them to train future sales representatives. Many trainers use the old selling dictum of, "Tell them, show them, let them do it, and review it." Confucius said, "I hear and I forget. I see and I remember. I do and I understand." Sales trainers will want to follow the advice of Confucius by involving trainees in the learning process.

COACHING

Coaching is an important activity for sales managers. It is unusual because it contains elements of training and control. Hence, it will be discussed in this chapter and in Chapter 13, which discusses control. It will be presented also in Chapter 19, where a new method of training, behavioral modeling, is used to train field sales managers in coaching.

The training dimensions of coaching sustain, develop, and improve skills to an agreed-upon level of performance through the use of discussion, observation, demonstration, transfer, and practice. The coaching process may be divided into five steps:

1. *Discuss and agree on the skill to be developed and the level of proficiency to be achieved.*   There is no motivation for learning unless there is agreement on the importance of developing the skill and on the necessary level of proficiency to achieve agreed-upon goals. Because there may be many ways to develop the skills, it may be necessary to negotiate the best methods for each representative, thereby recognizing each person's needs. Some coaches stress the need to learn one technique well before adapting it to individual differences.

2. *Observe the performer in action on the job.*   The observation phase should focus on having the performer do a self-evaluation. What was the objective? What was achieved? What do you think that you did well? What needs improvement? How could this improvement be achieved? These and similar questions encourage a self-evaluation by the representative. Most people learn better through self-discovery than by being told. The self-evaluation approach has the additional advantage of continuing after the coach has left.

3. *Demonstrate the desired method of performance in a nonthreatening manner.* Greater learning will take place when the representative is involved in this demonstration. This involvement may include feedback from the representative on the level of skill performance exhibited in the demonstration. It is important to maintain a nonthreatening environment during this step.

4. *Transfer the skill to the job.* There will be no improvement in performance unless classroom skills are transferred to the job. The coach must again observe the representative in the field and ask self-evaluation questions. It may be necessary to repeat steps #3 and #4 until the desired level of proficiency is achieved.

5. *Practice to develop confidence, proficiency, and habit.* Classroom skills frequently are lost on the job because insufficient time for practice did not result in sufficient levels of confidence, competency, and habit.

During the early training of a representative, coaching will take place in the classroom and in role-play situations. In Chapter 13 we will see that field sales managers will use "curbstone coaching."

TRAINING MATERIALS

Training materials reflect a wide range of technologies from such basics as books and blackboards to the electronics of recordings, television, and computers. Programmed learning represents one teaching procedure that has used a range of techniques. Perhaps the earliest form of programmed learning, and one that is still frequently used, is to train sales representatives in a "canned" presentation. This type of programmed learning is appropriate in industries in which there is a high turnover among representatives and the product is relatively uncomplicated.[8] Workbooks provide another means for programmed learning. Computer-assisted learning programs permit branched learning experiences where correct decisions are reinforced and incorrect choices result in additional information. Such computer applications can greatly reduce the cost of training by reducing the cost of traveling.

Learner controlled instruction (LCI) is an individualized training approach. LCI begins with a needs assessment. The trainer or sales manager and the representative then agree on those areas that need additional training. The trainer provides the representative with materials or identifies resource persons and turns him or her loose to proceed at his or her own speed. The trainer and the representative will make a contract as to what is to be learned and the time period for learning it. Such approaches work well with highly motivated individuals.

Business games have been created to help representatives learn about business in general and marketing in particular, to develop sales strategies, and to develop a skill for routing their time through the territory. These games may be hand-scored or may use a computer.

The electronic age has had its impact on sales training. Video tape recording enables the trainee to make a self-evaluation of a sales presentation. New product information and strategies can be described on tape and sent to representatives who may listen to them at home or while driving to call on customers. Microcomputers may be used by sales managers in performance appraisals by comparing the productivity ratios of representatives in different territories. The development of newer techniques should not blind us to the fact that basic sales training materials, such as outlines, bulletins, letters, and flip-charts, are very effective and frequently used.

WHO IS THE TRAINER?

Who is the sales trainer? Broadly speaking, anyone and everyone can be a sales trainer for a sales representative. It could be persons outside the company who are not generally in training roles, such as a smart buyer or a sharp competitor who has just taught a sales representative a lesson that he or she will never forget. It could be a football coach or a politician who is particularly inspiring. But generally when we think of sales trainers we are focusing on formal sales training programs that use company or outside personnel in structured training programs. Company personnel are not limited to those in marketing, as we saw earlier in the Conoco example. Persons in engineering, production, research and development, and finance all play important roles in training salespersons.

Marketing persons who are involved in sales training include trainers and managers at headquarters, field personnel such as the field sales manager, and special representatives who have been trained to assist in instructing new representatives.

Deciding who will conduct the training results in a series of tradeoff decisions. Line personnel at headquarters have extensive experience and introduce substantial authority into the training process, but they lack time and may lack teaching ability. There is also the cost of moving trainees to the headquarters location. Staff trainers, at headquarters or field locations, are trained in teaching methodology and are aware of the latest in teaching aids, but they lack the authority that goes with line control over trainees, and their department adds a fixed cost to the selling function.

Field sales managers know the personal needs of the representative, as well as unique features of the territory, but, unfortunately, few field sales managers have received any instruction in training. Outstanding representatives are sometimes given special instruction in training and additional compensation to assist in training recruits.

Outside training personnel may be used by companies that have small sales forces and low turnover rates, thereby not requiring a fixed investment in training departments. These outside personnel include sales training consultants; trade associations; sales clubs; continuing education programs through local colleges, the American Management Association, or the Sales and Marketing Executives Club; correspondence courses; and rented materials such as movies. The quality and appropriateness of these training sources vary greatly. Many of the outside training sources will be excellent for training skills, such as the Professional Selling Skills II as produced by Xerox Learning Systems. A company that uses such programs must find other means for providing its representatives with knowledge of the company's products and industry. Some industry-specific training may be provided by consultants who specialize in an industry or by trade associations that provide sales training for their members.

WHERE SHOULD THE TRAINING TAKE PLACE?

Sales training is a continuing process. Every time a manager checks a salesperson's report, sends a note, discusses business on the phone, passes along something to read, criticizes or compliments, then the manager is training. Training, therefore, is not limited to classroom experiences.

Formal training programs may be held at the home office, a training center, university facilities, a conference center, or a motel. Centralized locations have the advantages of better facilities, equipment, and materials, and they provide an esprit de corps when representatives from many regions are brought together. These centralized locations can be expensive in terms of time, money, and administrative problems, but may be less costly than repeating the training individually in numerous locations.

Decentralized locations include a local motel, the branch office, traveling clinics, or with field managers who train using material supplied by the headquarters, training by other representatives, coaching by the sales manager, and correspondence courses. Decentralized procedures are less expensive in terms of representatives' time and travel expenses. Local programs also tend to receive more support from the local manager. Decentralized programs have disadvantages, however, in that there may not be time or capacity for training at the local level.

The length and location of sales training tend to vary according to broad industry groupings. Industrial product companies do most of their training at field offices, but they also use the home office, regional offices, plant locations, and central training facilities. Consumer products firms also favor the field office, but they use the home office, the regional office, and occasionally a central training facility. Service industries (including insurance, financial, utilities, transportation, etc.) use the home office, field office, regional office, and sometimes a central training facility. The median training period for industrial firms is twenty-six weeks, while it is nineteen weeks for consumer products, and twelve weeks in service industries. Training costs, including salaries during training, were approximately $20,000 in industrial product firms and $13,000 in consumer goods and service industries.[9] It is interesting to note that while the service industry is the most rapidly growing sector of the economy in the United States, it spends the least amount of time and money on training its sales personnel.

HOW CAN THE TRAINING PROGRAM BE EVALUATED?

How to evaluate the training program has long been a problem for sales trainers. If clear and measurable goals were established prior to training, then this step becomes simpler, but not easy. If the goal of sales training is to improve statistics such as the size of the sale, increased profit, lower expenses, sales forecasting accuracy, a higher closing rate, or sales of a more balanced product mix, then the success of the training effort should be measured in these terms. Before-and-after measures of these variables need to be made in a control and experimental group, where the experimental group receives the training and the control group does not.

If the training goal is to increase representatives' knowledge about product benefits, applications, or competitors, then the effectiveness of training may be measured by giving representatives objective tests covering these topics.[10] Most sales training, however, focuses on behavioral variables dealing with attitudes, skills, and habits that are extremely difficult to measure. Training in sales skills would fall in this category.

McGraw-Hill Publishing Company developed techniques for measuring the effectiveness of its sales training program.[11] It adapted the Xerox Professional Selling Skills program materials. These materials include programmed instruction, enactments of sales situations as recorded on audio tapes, and role playing. Several techniques were used to evaluate the program. Participants were asked first to evaluate the program upon completion and then again thirty days later.

McGraw-Hill used a more objective test of training effectiveness by having the trainees role play a sales presentation to their managers before and after training. These tapes were later content-analyzed for key dimensions in the sales training, such as initial benefits statement, probing, supporting statements, handling objections and offering proof, and closing. These tests showed marked improvement on sixteen of the twenty points that were covered in training, a clear indication of the effectiveness of the training program.

Another experimental procedure that was used by McGraw-Hill was a before-and-after survey of prospects. This survey revealed that while training stimulated representatives to do more probing, this probing raised objections in the minds of the prospects—objections that representatives were not equipped to handle. Thus there was a need for more training in handling objections. This survey revealed, however, that trained representatives performed better in closing. And finally, some significant portion of the growth in sales three years after the training program was attributed to the program.

Perhaps the difficulty in evaluating training programs is the philosophical difference in the accounting procedures for expenditures on equipment and expenditures on humans. Expenditures on equipment are generally treated as an investment, while expenditures on humans are expensed. Accountants would probably change this philosophy if sales trainers could demonstrate more clearly the fact that expenditures on sales training have effects that last many years.

WHY TRAINING PROGRAMS FAIL

Training programs, like all human endeavors, are subject to failures. Parry has provided the following eleven reasons why sales training programs succeed or fail:

1. Top management gave only lip service to the training effort.
2. Training drove a wedge between the trainee and his or her sales manager because the manager objected to time taken out of the territory.
3. Lazy and unstimulating participants destroyed the enthusiasm of the program.

4. There was one-way communication because too much information had been scheduled for the session or the instructor had an ego-need to share knowledge.

5. The material was not relevant to the needs of the participants and their companies.

6. The topics were safe, theoretical ones that did not deal with real problems.

7. There was little link between the classroom and performance on the job.

8. The program was evaluated only on its popularity, not its effectiveness.

9. The training session was not part of an overall training program; instead, it was bits and pieces of popular methods.

10. The instructor had little knowledge of the participants and their needs.

11. The instructor lacked credibility because he or she did not know the organizational dimensions of the participants or did not know the subject matter that was being taught.[12]

DEVELOPING PERSONNEL

A survey of sales managers (Chapter 2, Exhibit 2.3) revealed that the most important activity of first- and second-line managers is developing personnel. *Developing personnel* may be defined as helping a subordinate develop goals, knowledge, skills, habits, and energies beyond those that are necessary to perform the present job. This process is sometimes known as developing a "life plan."

In the next chapter, which discusses motivation, we will see that a major demotivator is a dead-end job. A job situation may become unbearable when an individual senses that a job is not only a dead-end, but no one cares and there is no effort made to correct the situation.

It is in the best interest of a company to develop as fully as possible the capabilities of its employees in order to maximize its return-on-investments in recruiting, hiring, and training. Many companies develop compensation plans, benefit programs, and promotion policies that stress promotion from within. Benefit programs may include programs of continuing education and reimbursement of the costs of advanced studies. Some companies evaluate supervisors on their ability to develop subordinates. Thus career counseling can be an important part of a sales manager's job, but few managers receive formal training in this activity.

CAREER COUNSELING

The first-line field sales manager's primary task in developing sales representatives is to help them gain a realistic understanding of the process for "getting ahead." Many representatives express a strong desire to get ahead without realizing that the first step is be successful in their present assignment. Hence, the first step is for the manager and the representative to work on the knowledge, attitudes, habits, and skills that are necessary to succeed as a representative. At this point, the manager turns to helping the representative develop plans for the next step in his or her career.

In order for a career planning system to work, the company must reward a manager for personnel development. Without such rewards, the manager has a natural incentive to "hang on" to a good representative.

LIFE PLANNING

Several steps have been identified by some sales managers to help a representative develop a life plan after he or she expresses a desire to get ahead. These steps are:

1. Have the individual rank-order several jobs that he or she finds most attractive.

2. Beginning with the top-ranked job, help the representative identify the knowledge, attitudes, habits, and skills that are necessary to qualify for that job.

3. The representative should then list his or her assets and liabilities in terms of this job.

4. The job qualifications are then matched against the representative's qualifications to determine what is necessary to become qualified.

5. The manager must then help the individual determine how he or she will be able to acquire the needed qualifications, by when, and at what costs.

6. The manager identifies what the company can provide to help the individual qualify.

7. The manager and the representative must develop a realistic program of self-development, with resources, checkpoints, and realistic outcomes.

8. Perhaps the most sobering step is the assessment of the chances of the individual's getting the job of his or her first choice after becoming qualified. Perhaps such opportunities rarely occur.

9. If all indications are positive, the representative begins to implement the career planning program. If steps 7 or 8 lead to the conclusions that the first-choice job is not feasible, then the manager and the representative move to the second-choice job and cycle through the analysis again. The process is continued until a feasible plan is developed.

SUMMARY

Orientation and training provide qualifiable applicants with the knowledge, attitudes, skills, and habits that are necessary to produce sales results. The performance appraisal conducted by the sales manager evaluates these results and, with the concurrence of the representative, determines what additional training is necessary.

To develop a training program, the sales manager or training specialist must answer a series of questions. Why train? The answer to this question will identify the training goals and express them in terms that are measurable, thereby facilitating the evaluation of the training program. A training needs assessment may be necessary to identify these training goals. Who should be trained? Because training is a continuous process, the answer is simple—all representatives must be trained. But the type of training that they receive will differ according to their position in their career path development. What should be the content of the training program? The new representative will need to have orientation into the company, the role of personal selling in the marketing mix, the territory, the community, and the social structure of the company. All representatives will need training in selling activities, new markets, new products, new competition, new market strategies, and territory management. Training in following through is also becoming an important part of the sales training. When should the training be given? The point at which training is given will vary among industries and companies. Some companies prefer to give training before sending the representative into the field, while other companies prefer initial on-the-job training. Training programs will be offered also on special occasions, such as the introduction of new products and when problems are identified during performance appraisals of representatives. How should the training be done? Most training programs combine lectures, demonstrations, group discussions, role playing, and tutorials to create the maximum learning experience. Training materials range from elementary devices, such as blackboards, to electronic equipment, such as video tape recorders and computers. Who is the trainer? Trainers may be staff personnel from a training department, line sales managers, or outside consultants and associations. Where should the training take place? The training planner must balance the advantages and disadvantages of centralized and decentralized locations. How can training programs be evaluated? The answer to this question is simplified somewhat by a clear statement of training goals, but some goals are easier to measure than others. For example, if the goal was to communicate knowledge about products and markets, trainees may be given a simple objective test to evaluate the training effectiveness. If, however, the training was to develop behavioral changes, such as selling skills, it may be necessary to develop elaborate before-and-after measures to evaluate the training program. Programs may be evaluated also by changes in statistics, such as sales and profits, closing rates, and reduced expenses.

Developing representatives is the most important single activity performed by field sales managers. The development begins by qualifying them first as representatives and then helping them to develop a realistic life plan for their career.

ASSIGNMENTS/DISCUSSION QUESTIONS

1. Complete a sales training worksheet, such as Exhibit 10.5, for the Procter & Gamble, IBM, and Conoco training programs as described in this chapter. Explain why these programs differ.

Exhibit 10.5   Sales Training Worksheet

IMPLEMENTATION DECISIONS

Content (What?)	Why?	Who Trained?	When?	Where?	How Done?	Who Trains?	Where?	How Evaluated?
Knowledge								
. .								
. .								
. .								
Attitudes								
. .								
. .								
. .								
Skills								
. .								
. .								
. .								
Habits								
. .								
. .								
. .								

2. Develop a training program using the training worksheet approach for one of the cases in this textbook as assigned by the instructor.

3. What should the content of a training program be based on?

4. If orientation is a training process of acquainting the trainee with the existing situation or environment, to whom and to what should a trainee be oriented, in addition to those items listed in the text?

5. Briefly define sales training.

6. In periods of depressed economic conditions and reduced budget expenditures, should training be increased or decreased and why?

7. At what point does the training process begin?

8. At what point does the training process end?

9. Compare the advantages and disadvantages of training inexperienced versus experienced sales representatives.

10. Who is fundamentally responsible for the training of a field sales representative? Explain.

11. What are the benefits to the individual of an effective company program of personnel development?

12. Compare the training responsibilities of the organization and the individual participants.

CASE 10.1:
Sally Simpson, Revisited
Reread the Sally Simpson Case in Chapter 9.

CASE QUESTIONS

1. What is the problem from the standpoint of orienting and training?

2. What advance indications were there of the development of the problem?

3. Could the problem have been prevented? If so, how? If not, why not?

4. Should Scott try to dissuade Sally?

CASE 10.2:
Shelby Building Supplies Company

Shelby Building Supplies Company was a typical, successful member of the industrial community in the Southwest. Established in Los Angeles in 1960 by Jim Shelby, the company took advantage of the explosive growth in southern California before expanding its distribution to northern California, Oregon, and Washington, and ultimately to eleven western states. With sales representatives and warehouses in the major metropolitan and growth areas, Shelby Building Supplies provided numerous opportunities during its growth for career advancement for its employees by following a policy of promotion from within. All of its division sales managers and most of its warehouse managers came from the ranks of the sales representatives. Although Jim Shelby's two sons, John and Sam, expected to inherit the major share of the business, it was common knowledge that long-time employees, particularly among the senior managers, were given the opportunity to buy into the company. In a recent announcement to all employees, Mr. Shelby told of expansion plans and the opportunity to participate in a profit-sharing plan that would be offered when these plans were implemented next April at the beginning of the new fiscal year.

Four years ago, after graduation from Sacramento State College, Tim Brush started with Shelby Building Supplies Co. as a salesman in Sacramento. Tim developed into an aggressive, hardworking salesman, ambitious, imaginative, and with a friendly ability to get along with customers and peers. Tim worked northern California and western Nevada in addition to the Sacramento and San Joaquin Valley areas. This required him to be on the road better than 50 percent of the time, which didn't please his wife, Mary, whom he had married soon after graduation. However, Tim convinced Mary that this assignment enabled him to prove his abilities in a variety of working conditions, and his predictions were borne out in an excellent sales record that attracted the attention of Doug Webster, the Vice President of Sales. Two years ago, Tim was offered a transfer to Oakland, which he promptly accepted. Although Tim had no added responsibilities, Oakland was a boom market for building supplies. It offered the opportunity for greater income and his travel was cut by 75 percent, which pleased Mary greatly. The transfer proved advantageous for Tim, and he continued his above-average performance. The metropolitan Oakland area provided him with a new set of insights into the sales of Shelby Building Supplies and the added income from his increased sales enabled Tim and Mary to buy their first home. However, as pleased as Tim was with his prosperity, he wanted more responsibility. Specifically, Tim wanted a promotion to Division Sales Manager.

Although Tim knew this would get him back on the travel circuit, Mary had reluctantly agreed. In addition, he discussed it with Don Goodman, his Division Sales Manager. In fact, he talked with Don about it during his annual counseling session immediately following his transfer, which was just about the time the company instituted a career planning program. Tim believed that the only way to get ahead was to keep bringing up the subject, and on each working trip with Don, Tim would figure out some way to press the issue as to when he could expect to be promoted.

Don Goodman recognized Tim's talents and considered him to be one of the most productive sales reps in his division. Don also recognized Tim's impatience and desire to be promoted, which sometimes clouded his judgment. When Tim first voiced his interest in additional responsibilities, Don asked him what he was doing to prepare himself for these added responsibilities. He reminded Tim of the company's educational program that provided 75 percent reimbursement of tuition for job-related courses taken during time off. Also offered was a variety of packaged programs, some of which were in programmed learning and other correspondence forms. Don also suggested that Tim would benefit from further training in verbal and written skills. It wasn't that Tim couldn't express himself effectively, for he had demonstrated his ability for the past four years as a salesman. Tim's grammar and vocabulary were a bit unpolished and Don was concerned about Tim's ability to express himself properly at division sales meetings, managers' conferences, and before large groups at building supplies meetings and conventions, which was part of the responsibility of a division manager, but not of a sales representative.

In addition, Don had some reservations about Tim's commitment to handling all the paperwork that came across a division manager's desk. Tim's attention to paperwork was not up to the level of his other skills as a salesman and Don wasn't sure how Tim would react when the volume of correspondence increased, as Don knew it would as a division manager. Tim wasn't necessarily tardy, but he was rarely first in sending his reports and he almost never submitted more than what was required. In contrast to the initiative displayed in the field in search of new sales opportunities, Tim's unsolicited written feedback was almost nonexistent. Don had kidded him about it, commenting that he couldn't understand how anyone with Tim's sales record and nose for business never had any information to share about the marketplace or the competition. Tim's response was that he was too busy selling to take time to write. Don's analysis was that Tim was less confident expressing himself in writing and avoided doing so whenever possible.

To Tim's credit, he took Don's advice and enrolled in an advanced public speaking course at the University Extension Division. This wasn't exactly what Don had in mind, but it was a start. Tim's initial reaction to the class was somewhat hesitant, but he soon learned to enjoy the challenge, and, after completing the course, he joined the local Toastmasters Club. At the end of a ten-day field trip that Don made with several sales reps culminating with two days with Tim on Thursday and Friday, they discussed Tim's continuing lack of interest in paperwork while professing a strong ambition to be promoted. To make a point, Don asked Tim to be at Don's office in San Francisco promptly at 9:00 A.M. the following Monday. He wanted Tim to see the volume of mail that had accumulated during his absence and to impress upon him the absolute need to be able to handle that volume of correspondence if he wanted to become a division sales manager. Tim knew that Don had no way of knowing what correspondence was waiting for him on his return, and Tim was impressed with the quantity and variety of mail and the amount of work that would go into replying. Tim's reaction was that this was something he would have to learn to do if the job demanded it. From that point on, Tim's reporting and correspondence began to show some improvement.

Following the last division sales managers' conference in Los Angeles at the Shelby headquarters, Don discussed with Doug Webster Tim's performance and interest in moving up. Their conversation had been lengthy; every phase of Tim's performance and qualifications had been reviewed. The feeling of Doug Webster seemed to be that while Tim's sales ability was well recognized, his administrative skills and ability to manage people were unknowns. It was for these reasons that Don decided against making a formal recommendation that Tim be promoted to Division Sales Manager. He knew that if he pushed Doug Webster, Don would get a definite "NO," and he didn't want to have Mr. Webster go on record as having turned Tim down.

It was with a clear memory of that conversation that Don met with Tim on their next working trip. Don had completed the review of the quarterly sales by-product when Tim asked to change the subject. When Don inquired about what he had on his mind, Tim replied: "Don, I've been with the company for a little over four years as a sales representative. Judging by what you've said about my performance and my own estimation, I think I've done a better than average job. I've had a variety of sales experiences, both rural and metropolitan, and I think I'm ready for a promotion. I'd like to stay with Shelby and make a career out of it. It's a great company, they've treated me well, the new expansion plans sound exciting and I can see myself in a top management spot someday down the road. The problem is that I've been offered a job with a big increase by a competitor. While I would still be a salesman for a while, they promised to make me a division sales manager. I'd like to stay with Shelby, but the competitive offer is very attractive, particularly the promise of becoming a division manager. Can you make the same promise if I stay with the company?''

Don thought for a long time, to the point that Tim became a little uncomfortable. Finally, Don responded: ''Tim, let me make it perfectly clear. You've done a great job as a sales representative, one of the best in the division, and I want you to know that. I know you are ambitious and want to be a division sales manager so badly you can almost taste it. Moreover, you are convinced you are qualified right now! Let me ask you a theoretical, but a very real, question. If you were a division sales manager right now and one of your sales representatives were to ask you, 'Will you promise me that I will become a division sales manager?', how would you answer him?''

CASE QUESTIONS

1. How would you answer Don Goodman's question?

2. How do you think Tim Brush will answer Don Goodman's question?

3. Why do you think Don Goodman phrased the question the way he did?

4. How can you assure an employee who may be qualified and who asks the same question Tim Brush asked?

5. How would you evaluate Tim Brush's qualifications for division sales manager?

6. What qualifications are required for the job of a division sales manager?

7. What management development has Don Goodman provided Tim Brush?

8. If Tim Brush decides to stay, how could Don Goodman help Tim develop the needs identified by Doug Webster?

9. Should Don Goodman ask questions about the competitive offer? If so, what question could he ask?

REFERENCES

1. R. F. Mager, *Analyzing Performance Problems or 'You Really Oughta Wanna'* (Belmont, Calif.: Fearon Pitman Publishers, Inc., 1970).
2. T. A. DeCotis, and R. A. Morano, "Applying Job Analysis to Training," *Training and Development Journal* (July 1977): 20–24.
3. For additional discussions of training assessment procedures see Melvin Lamster, "Assessing Training Needs of New Salespersons," *The Management of Sales Training,* ed. Jared F. Harrison (Reading, Mass.: Addison-Wesley Publishing Company, 1977), pp. 23–33; Gerald E. Michael, "Methods of Identifying Sales Training Needs," *The New Handbook of Sales Training,* ed. Robert F. Vizza (Englewood Cliffs, N.J.: Prentice-Hill, Inc., 1967), pp. 112–126; Charles H. Singler, "Assessing Specific Training Needs," *The Management of Sales Training,* ed. J. F. Harrison (Reading, Mass.: Addison-Wesley Publishing Company, 1977), pp. 47–63.
4. M. A. Jolson, "The Salesmen's Career Cycle," *Journal of Marketing* 38 (July 1974): 39–46; J. D. Koser, "Career Paths: A Tool for Motivating Field Salesmen," in *New Directions in Marketing,* ed. F. E. Webster (Chicago: American Marketing Assoc., 1965), pp. 151–159; A. E. Pearson, "Sales Power through Planned Careers," *Harvard Business Review* 44 (January–February 1966): 105–116.
5. T. D. Fallon, "Sales Training Program Content," *The New Handbook of Sales Training,* Robert F. Vizza (Englewood Cliffs, N.J.: Prentice-Hill, Inc., 1967): pp. 127–133.
6. Procter & Gamble sales recruiting brochure, 1979.
7. Materials provided by the Training Department of Conoco Chemicals Division.
8. M. A. Jolson, "The Underestimated Potential of the Canned Sales Presentation," *Journal of Marketing* 39 (January 1975): 75–78; J. D. need, "Comments on 'The Underestimated Potential of the Canned Sales Presentation,' " *Journal of Marketing* 40 (January 1976): 76–78.
9. "Sales Meetings and Sales Training," *Sales & Marketing Management* (February 23, 1981): 66.
10. James F. Evered, "Assessment and Measurement of Training Effectiveness," *The Management of Sales Training,* ed. J. F. Harrison (Reading, Mass.: Addison-Wesley Publishing Company, 1977), pp. 233–244.
11. B. A. Johnson and J. Pierce, "Research Brings Proof of Value, Future Direction to Sales Training," *Training and Development Journal* 28 (November 1974): 25–32.
12. Scott Parry, "11 Reasons Why Sales Training Programs Succeed or Fail," a presentation given at the meetings of the National Society of Sales Training Executives, December 9–12, 1979, New Orleans.

SUGGESTED READINGS

Argyris, Chris, *Integrating the Individual into the Organization* (New York: John Wiley & Sons, Inc., 1964).

Connell, H. Stanley, III, "What to Do When the Selling Slump Hits," *Training and Development Journal* 31, no. 11 (November 1977): 14–17.

Falvey, J. J., "Myths of sales training," *Sales & Marketing Management* (April 3, 1978): 40–43.

Hahne, C. E., "How to Measure Results of Sales Training," *Training and Development Journal* 31, no. 11 (November 1977): 3–7.

Hall, W. P., "Improving Sales Force Productivity," *Business Horizons* 18, no. 4 (August 1975): 32–42.

Harris, C. E., Jr., "Training the Sales Neophyte." *Training and Development Journal* 29 (February 1975): 46–51.

Harrison, J. F., "On-the-Job Sales Training by Objectives," *Training and Development Journal* 28 (November 1974): 22–24.

J. F. Harrison, ed., *The Sales Manager as a Trainer* (Reading, Mass.: Addison-Wesley Publishing Company, 1977).

Hopkins, D. S., *Training the Sales Force: A Progress Report* (New York: The Conference Board, 1978, Report No. 737).

Mandia, R. J., "Sales Training: As Simple as P-A-C," *Training and Development Journal* 28 (November 1974): 15–20.

"Market Impact Team—The Coca Cola Co.," *Training and Development Journal* 31 (November 1977): 28–33.

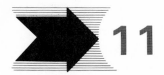

11

DIRECTING BY MOTIVATING REPRESENTATIVES AND FIELD SALES MANAGERS

The major role of field sales managers is directing and leading the efforts of sales representatives to achieve the forecasted sales results. (See Exhibit 2.3, Chapter 2.) These managers must recognize that the territory and company success depends in a very large part on their ability to motivate representatives to use the knowledge and skills that they acquired through orientation and training.

THE ENVIRONMENT FOR MOTIVATION

Motivation differs from the other activities of sales management (Chapter 2) because of its indirect nature of application. The action-oriented field sales manager must realize that it is not possible to command a representative to be motivated. It is possible, however, to create environments that encourage representatives to motivate themselves. Because all motivation is self-motivation, the first step in a motivation program is to create an environment in which self-motivation is possible. This process must begin with the removal of demotivators, which may be defined as those conditions that discourage the positive efforts of representatives. Thus the successful sales manager must generate an early awareness of the causes of demotivation and their effects on productivity.

JOB DEMOTIVATORS

One of the authors of this text has run many national seminars on motivation for sales managers. These hundreds of sales managers have identified demotivators that may be placed into the following classifications:

293

uncertain job requirements, misapplied qualifications, inadequate development, poor working environment, and poor reward systems.

Uncertain Job Requirements

Unclear Job Responsibilities. People may not know what they are supposed to do, the limits of their responsibilities, their interrelationships with others who have related responsibilities, and where they fit into the organization. "I didn't know I was supposed to do that, too." "That's not my responsibility." Such statements reflect a poor job description, inadequate orientation, poor training, or all three of these activities that should clarify job responsibilities.

Uncertain Performance Standards. "How well am I supposed to do the job?" "How do I know when I'm doing the job the way you want it done?" "Yes, I know you'll tell me, but I'd like to know, too, so I can evaluate my own performance." "The other supervisor said he wanted it done a different way." These replies by a representative reflect a system of inadequate performance standards. A clear definition of job responsibilities does not remove uncertainty unless the representative knows the level of performance that is expected.

Misapplied Qualifications

Wrong Job. An individual may be unsuited psychologically, temperamentally, or even physically for a career in personal selling. A manager who recognizes that a representative is in the wrong job might be doing the representative a favor by terminating an unsatisfactory relationship and suggesting other career opportunities that might be more suitable.

Under- or Overqualified. Underqualified persons frequently become discouraged or frustrated because of their inability to acquire the needed knowledge and skills within a requisite time, to perform within the job standards, or to compete successfully with their associates. In contrast, the overqualified individual frequently becomes bored or bitter because of the lack of opportunity to use his or her talents.

Dead-end Job. Related to the overqualified case is the individual who perceives the present job as a dead-end with no opportunity to develop personally and be promoted to higher responsibilities and recognition within the organization.

Inadequate Personal Development

Inadequate Training. To those individuals with the potential for development and a willingness to learn, the lack of proper training is frustrating and discouraging. This discouragement is particularly pertinent to new entrants into the field of selling.

Poor Supervision. To the average or above-average performer, supervision that is thought to be unfair or incompetent is highly demotivating.

Poor Communications. "Is anybody listening?" A new sales representative will, at times, feel frustrated and lonely in the sales territory. A manager who is a good listener can help prevent small problems from becoming major demotivators.

Poor Working Environment

Unsatisfactory Environment. The environment in which some jobs are performed may be depressing or unacceptable to some people, particularly for extended employment. Thus a comfortable and well equipped automobile may be important for a representative who spends many hours on the road. Creative individuals tend to be more sensitive to their environment and therefore find an unsatisfactory environment more demotivating. An individual with a metropolitan background may become demotivated if assigned to a rural territory that requires travel, and vice versa.

Unsatisfactory Peer Relationships. Relationships with one's peers can be an important part of the working environment. This demotivator is one of the less important ones for field salespersons because they do not interact with their peers frequently. Nevertheless, it is disturbing and demotivating to some individuals who may require a close working relationship with others.

Poor Reward Systems

Unfair Compensation. Unfair or inadequate compensation is viewed as lack of appreciation for efforts expended or results produced. It is important to note that unfair compensation can be a strong demotivator, but it is only one of many demotivators, not the only one. It is only one of many forms of recognition. An increase in pay, therefore, will have only a temporary effect if other demotivators are not corrected. Unfair compensation is a particularly strong demotivator in selling where productivity may be difficult to measure accurately.

No Recognition. "It isn't the hard work that gets me, it's the lack of recognition." Recognition can be a stronger reward than compensation for employees who have a strong need for social recognition. The acknowledgment of a representative at a sales meeting for having made an important sale or the winning of an incentive, such as a television set, may provide a stronger reward than the commission associated with the sale.

MANAGING THROUGH MOTIVATION

If management is defined as the process of getting work completed through people, then motivation is the process of creating job circumstances that will inspire, persuade, encourage, or challenge individuals to manage themselves. Managing through motivation is no easy task because it requires a change in management philosophy from one of being in direct control to indirect control by creating job circumstances in which individuals will direct themselves. Thus management is achieving results through people who are motivated individually.

Defining motivation as an individual process differs with more popular definitions that characterize motivation as a process of inspiring or persuading employees to want to work. While the importance of the leader's charismatic influence cannot be discounted altogether, behavioral scientists have shown that motivation is an individual process of meeting one's own needs. The manager who wants to motivate his or her representatives must therefore understand their individual needs.

A LOGICAL APPROACH TO INDIVIDUALIZED MOTIVATION

WHY DO PEOPLE BUY?

If we ask, "Why do people buy?" most people would respond, "To satisfy their needs." When faced with the realization of having made a mistaken purchase, we recognize that we improperly analyzed our need and say, "I didn't need that." We could also say that the saleperson failed to properly identify our needs and sold us the wrong product. We may resent such a purchase and may never deal with this salesperson again.

Most sales representatives and sales managers have been trained to identify the needs of buyers and sell the benefits of their products that will meet these needs. Managers frequently fail to see the analogy between buyers and representatives who have needs to be met on the job.

WHY DO PEOPLE WORK?

If we ask, "Why do people work?" the most common answer will be, "To acquire the means to satisfy their needs off the job." We earn money to buy goods and services that we need and want. While this answer recognizes the role of money as our exchange medium, it fails to identify the important role of job motivation in our industrial society.

Would the individual who works for money to satisfy needs off the job continue to work if he or she inherited a large sum of money? There are innumerable instances of persons who work hard, enjoy what they are doing, and receive no compensation. This leads to the conclusion that most needs are job-related needs that can be satisfied on the job. It is important to emphasize that the individual is working to satisfy his or her needs, not the needs of the employer. Just as a mistaken purchase that fails to satisfy the buyer's needs results in buyer dissatisfaction, a job that does not meet the employee's needs on and off the job leads to demotivation that appears in loss in productivity, unrealized use of potentials, requests for transfer, resignations, terminations, or worst of all, retirement on the job.

HOW SHOULD MANAGERS MANAGE?

If people buy to satisfy their needs, if people work to satisfy their needs on and off the job, and if management is the process of getting results through people, then how should managers manage? Clearly, their management style should be to help employees meet their needs.

There is a selling dictum that states, "If you would sell what John Brown buys, you must see John Brown's needs through John Brown's eyes." A management version of this saying could be, "If you would motivate how much John Brown tries, you must see John Brown's needs through John Brown's eyes." Douglas MacGregor noted that we can improve our ability to control only if we recognize that control consists of selective adaptation to human nature, rather than attempting to make human nature conform to our wishes.[1]

THEORIES OF JOB MOTIVATION

NEEDS HIERARCHY

In 1943, Abraham Maslow published his now classic article, "A Preface to Motivational Theory."[2] He theorized that motivation is an internal drive that stimulates an individual to action in order to satisfy personal needs. Maslow's need hierarchy provides the basis for a self-motivation

Exhibit 11.1   Maslow's Hierarchy of Needs

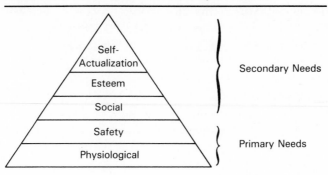

theory. The five basic need categories, which are summarized in Exhibit 11.1, include the following classifications: physiological, safety, social, esteem, and self-actualization. A need may be defined as a requirement that will enable a person to adjust optimally to his or her environment.

Physiological needs reflect the need to survive, so they include the need for air, water, food, shelter, rest, etc. When these needs are met, the next important category is safety needs, which include physical and emotional security that is necessary for survival. Industry attempts to satisfy these needs through various forms of job security, retirement benefits, and health and accident benefits. When these primary physiological and safety needs are met, social needs emerge as the next most important category. Social needs include being loved, the desire to belong, and to be accepted or cared for. A representative who wants to be liked by customers may have difficulty asking for the order for fear of being rejected. A field sales manager who wants to be liked by his or her representatives will unreasonably support his staff against the company. Esteem includes the dual needs for self-esteem and the esteem of others. Self-esteem is reflected in self-confidence, efforts to be in control, a sense of independence, and in being "your own person." The need for the esteem of others leads to high achievement, prestige, recognition, and status. In selling, satisfying these needs results in competitive achievements, recognition, promotion, and overall high levels of performance. Self-actualization needs are frequently identified as self-realization and self-fulfillment. These are the needs to realize an individual's full potential, not for esteem or social acceptance, but rather for the purpose of meeting one's life objectives or contributing to the good of society.

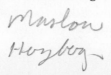

JOB SATISFACTION

In the 1950s, Frederick Herzberg conducted a series of studies about motivation in industry and the importance of work and working conditions. His research team measured the attitudes that workers had regarding specific work tasks and job surroundings. Specific content elements of the job that provided satisfaction were called motivators. He used the term *hygiene factors* to describe the context of the job that was dissatisfying or demotivating. He concluded that satisfying the hygienic factors is a prerequisite for effective motivation. Thus the demotivators must be removed before motivation can begin.[3] Exhibit 11.2 illustrates how demotivators are a barrier to motivation.

Herzberg concluded that one does not motivate people to succeed but instead provides people with an opportunity to succeed and they will be motivated. The key to motivation, therefore, is the work that one is given to do, the responsibility for doing the work, the feeling of achievement for doing the work well, the recognition that is received, and the advancement that derives from this accomplishment. In this context, job enrichment is the opportunity for an employee to grow psychologically through challenging work. Work enlargement is only the process of making the job structurally bigger.[4]

Exhibit 11.2   Hygiene Factors and Motivators

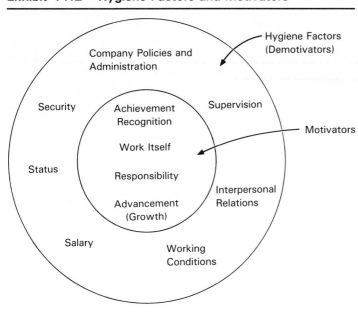

THE OPEN MANAGEMENT SYSTEM

In 1975, V. W. Kafka and J. H. Schaefer published a book titled *Open Management,*[5] in which they state three motivational principles for managers. These principles are: (1) see a situation from the other person's point of view, (2) identify and build on an individual's strengths rather than concentrating on how to improve weaknesses, and (3) understand and satisfy the individual's human needs.

The Other Person's Point of View

Because our point of view is the result of our total experiences, and because no two individuals have the same experiences, no two individuals can have the same point of view on all matters. The best that can be achieved is areas of understanding or agreement. If a manager wishes to see the situation from an employee's point of view, then he or she must express a sincere desire to be understanding, to be willing to listen, to be a good observer of nonverbal communications, to communicate well, to generate similar interests if necessary, and to achieve clearly defined, mutually agreed upon common goals.

Build on Strengths

Our contemporary value structure emphasizes the well-rounded individual, so that most of our training and reward systems emphasize the correction of weaknesses rather than building on individuals' strength. Emphasizing a person's weaknesses is demotivating, while emphasizing his or her strengths is a motivator. The management challenge, therefore, is to achieve superior performance by identifying persons' special talents and arranging circumstances that will allow them to use these talents to achieve mutually agreed upon goals. Activities that are enjoyed most are usually done best. Thus developing areas of strength should produce a happier and more productive individual by satisfying his or her needs.

Individual Needs

The Open Management System focuses on five basic human needs—the need for economic security, the need for recognition or prestige, the need to dominate or control, the need for emotional security or personal self-worth, and the need to belong. These needs are very similar to those that have been identified by Maslow and Herzberg.

Applying Open Management Principles

The Open Management System is directed more toward implementation than are the theories of Maslow and Herzberg. This system begins with the individual's point of view by understanding his or her self-image, human symbols, strengths, and individual needs. These basic concepts are summarized in Exhibit 11.3, as a circle of reference.

Self-Image. Individuals' self-images are a reflection of how they see themselves and how they want others to see them. These images are composites of the many roles the individual plays—adult, parent, spouse, employee, community member, church member, organization

Exhibit 11.3   Circle of Reference

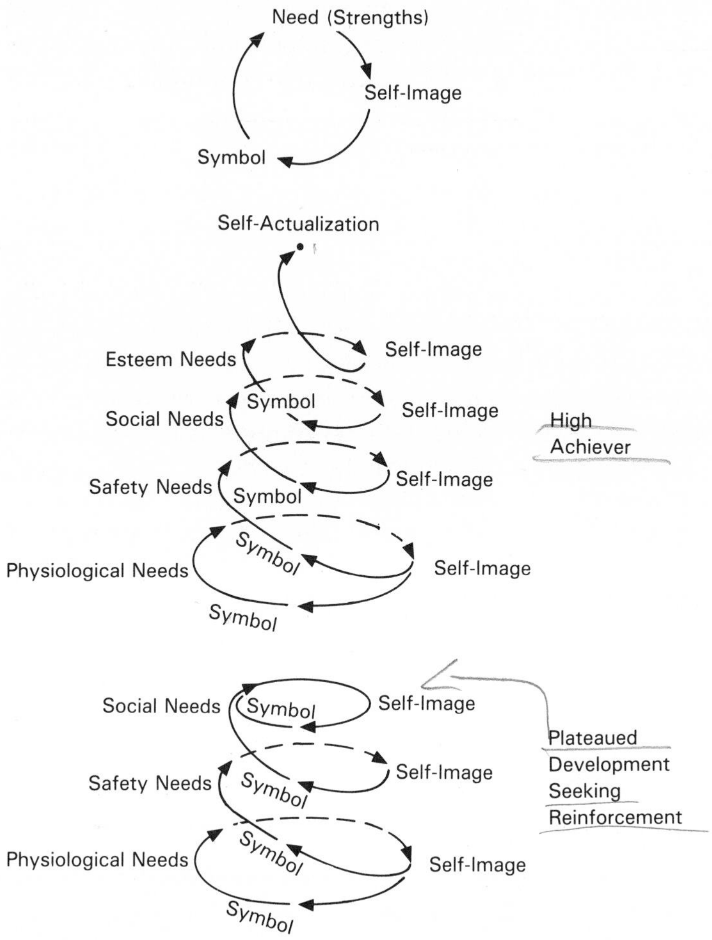

member, etc. It is important to understand how the individual sees himself or herself because he or she will be receptive to anything that reinforces a self-image and resist anything that threatens this image. To work effectively with an individual, we need to understand and reinforce the self-image by satisfying the related needs, building on strengths and not emphasizing weaknesses.

Symbols.   Human symbols are a way of telling others what is important to us. Our symbols include physical possessions like automobiles and houses; topics of personal interest, such as ideas and philosophies; and activities, such as sports, vacations, schools, and *occupations.* By observing these human symbols, the manager can identify persons' self-images and begin to identify their needs. The manager must look for a pattern of symbols that identifies an individual's needs and the importance of these needs to the individual. The manager must avoid making judgments regarding the values of these symbols and needs, thereby projecting his or her value system on the value system of the representative. Such judgments lose the perspective of the representative.

Needs.   A manager who uses symbols to identify needs must consider several important points regarding the relationships between symbols and needs. First, one symbol may reflect different needs to different individuals. Second, it is the needs that must be satisfied, not the symbols. Therefore a representative who wins a contest is satisfying a need for recognition, not the need for a color television set. Third, it is the use of a person's strengths on the job that satisfies the individual's needs. And finally, the circle of reference is really in three dimensions so that it is in the form of a cone, as appears in the middle section of Exhibit 11.3. As one set of needs is satisfied, a higher order of needs is sought, a concept that is reflected in Maslow's hierarchy of needs. The manager, therefore, must understand the representatives' present needs and anticipate their future ones. Thus, the Open Management System of motivation requires considerable empathy on the part of the manager. The lower section of Exhibit 11.3 reflects the fact that some individuals are satisfied with reaching a plateau, thereby foregoing the higher need satisfaction, but seeking continuous reinforcement at the plateau needs level.

WHY IS MOTIVATION THEORY RARELY APPLIED?

While Maslow's motivational theory was first published in 1943, this and subsequent theories have found little systematic application in industry. This lack of application is explained largely by the fact that the systems for motivating individuals run counter to society's and industry's preference for dealing with groups by setting up systems, methods, and procedures that apply equally to all members of the group. Organized society finds it easier and cheaper to deal with groups than with individuals. Furthermore, governments and unions mandate that everyone be treated equally. The aforementioned theories of motivation, however, suggest strongly that group motivation schemes will be only marginally effective.

To motivate individuals to the maximum of their abilities, it is necessary to identify their individual needs. This identification is difficult, time consuming, and could appear to be prying into the private affairs of individuals. Programs for individual motivation may also run into legal opposition from industry, institutions, government, and unions—all of which support standardized job categories and job descriptions, but for different reasons. Industry and institutions seek efficient assignment, evaluation, and compensation; governments want standardization for regulatory purposes and equal treatment; unions favor standardization because it facilitates organizing and controlling. It appears, therefore, that the gains in efficiency derived from standardized job descriptions and reward systems are offset by less than optimal individual productivity. Anyone who is concerned with the effects of motivation on productivity must consider the tradeoffs between organizational efficiency and increased individual productivity.

A second reason for not implementing individual motivation systems is that they require eliminating demotivators, which is a costly and time-consuming process. Some managers would prefer the short-range incentive systems that give immediate results, but they must be supplemented with other incentives as the short-run effect wears off.

ELIMINATING JOB DEMOTIVATORS

Herzberg stated that satisfying hygienic factors is a prerequisite for effective motivation. Failing to satisfy hygienic factors is like flipping the light switch where the wiring is defective. No matter how frequently one turns on the switch, the bulb will never produce light. Similarly, no amount of job enrichment will produce a motivated employee if the compensation is unfair or inadequate. It is essential to clean up the negative job environment before initiating positive motivational efforts. While this may appear to be a formidable task, current management practices provide the means to eliminate most demotivators. Practices that are relevant to sales management will be discussed in this section.

IDENTIFY THE JOB CLEARLY

Unclear job responsibilities and conflicting job standards are important—perhaps the most important—job demotivators. Recent studies of job satisfaction among sales representatives have revealed that dissatisfaction is caused by role ambiguity and conflict.[6] A job description that clearly defines the responsibilities of the representatives and their position in the organization will remove this demotivator. The organizational linkage becomes increasingly important as the organization grows. Field sales personnel who are separated from the home office for extended periods need to be reminded of their important function in the company.

HIRE QUALIFIED OR QUALIFIABLE CANDIDATES

Properly designed hiring standards based on qualifications that will produce the required job behavior will go far toward minimizing the hiring of overqualified or underqualified applicants. In certain types of selling, qualified applicants may not be available. Then it becomes necessary to identify and hire qualifiable applicants. This type of hiring requires identification of job-related *behavioral* qualifications that predict a high probability of success after proper orientation and training. These job-related behavioral qualifications are essential to the reduction of turnover of newly hired underqualified individuals and minimizing the hiring of persons for the wrong job. (See Chapter 9.)

ORIENT AND TRAIN CANDIDATES

Programs will be necessary to orient and train entry-level sales personnel so that they can develop the required knowledge and skills to become productive. Some flexibility will be necessary in these programs to reflect the varying needs of the applicants. The recent college graduate, the experienced salesperson who is changing companies or industries, and the experienced individual who is changing career paths all have different training needs.

Refresher training programs are necessary for the present sales force because of rapid changes in products, competition, market conditions, and channels of distribution. Training is needed also for individuals who have been promoted to additional responsibilities, such as field sales managers. These individuals must be trained in problem identification, analysis, decison making, motivational theory, and new forms of communication.

PROVIDE PROPER SUPERVISION

Poor supervision is clearly one of the most serious demotivators, resulting in immediate as well as long-term loss of sales, underdevelopment of salepersons with potential, unresolved personnel problems which become magnified, and turnover through resignation of salespersons with management potential. Proper supervision is critically tied to a strong sales management training and retraining program that produces managers who are evaluated on their supervisory skills, as well as the sales results produced by their district. Good supervision requires agreed upon job definitions and standards for the representatives and the field sales managers. If performance cannot be measured, it cannot be controlled. If it cannot be controlled, it cannot be managed.

REWARD EQUITABLY

While compensation and benefit programs do not necessarily motivate, or at best motivate for a short duration, perceived inadequate or unfair compensation is a strong demotivator. Constant reviews of compensation schemes are necessary to be as fair as possible to all representatives, given the variability of territories, market conditions, and competitive salespersons. A company will want to compare its compensation plan with those of competitive companies using data provided by research firms that exist solely for this purpose.

DEVELOP PERSONNEL

The lack of advancement opportunities and opportunities for personal growth are serious demotivators. Many companies fail to recognize that these demotivators are costing them those individuals on whom the company would depend most in the future to fill its management positions. Evaluation programs should identify early those sales personnel with management potential. Many companies provide advanced training for these persons or company-financed educational programs that are held outside the company. The apparent expense of such a management training program should be more than offset by the short-term benefit of motivating sales personnel and the long-term benefit of providing a pool of management personnel for future growth.

Some critics argue that a career development program is only effective if there are sufficient positions to which salespersons may be promoted. IBM disproves this argument. It has probably provided more top executives for competitive data-processing companies than any other organization, and yet it still remains at the top of its industry. IBM has a dual benefit from such a career development program. It has the opportunity to select from an elite core of managers. Equally important, IBM has the use of the services of a very large pool of managers while they are in their highly motivated developmental stage.

MONITOR CONTINUOUSLY

Eliminating job demotivators is a continuous process. Changes in market conditions, corporate marketing strategies, domestic and foreign competition, and federal regulations will require a continuous reexamination of job descriptions, evaluation systems, and training programs. Age distributions, economic conditions, and college students' images of sales careers will alter the supply of candidates available for hiring. These dynamics require a continuous reexamination of representatives' environment in order to identify and reduce demotivators.

MOTIVATING INDIVIDUALS

When the demotivators have been eliminated from the job environment, positive motivational efforts may take effect. Now the manager can turn to the question, "How can individuals be motivated?" This question has strategic and tactical dimensions. The strategic dimensions have been answered in the preceding discussion. Individuals must be motivated individually rather than collectively if they are to achieve their maximum potential. A commitment to individual motivation is mandatory if a serious attempt is made to motivate sales personnel. To implement this individual motivation strategy, managers must weight differently the tactical components of leadership style, technical resources, and individualized supervision.

LEADERSHIP STYLES

Few sales managers would claim to have the charismatic leadership style of John Kennedy, Vince Lombardi, or Martin Luther King, but these managers will have qualities such as warmth, integrity, fairness, realism, and decisiveness that will generate trust and respect, thereby making sales representatives want to work for the manager. Such leadership styles generate a positive atmosphere that produces team work and identification with the group's objectives. Managers will possess these qualities in varying degrees and should learn how to use them well.

TECHNICAL RESOURCES

Salespersons develop a sense of pride in being part of a modern progressive organization. They like to feel that their company has developed the best products, strategies, selling programs, and promotional support materials to help them sell effectively. We may refer to these technical competitive advantages as technical resources. The presentation of a new strategy, selling program, or support material to the sales force at a sales meeting can provide considerable motivation.

INDIVIDUAL SUPERVISION

The single most effective positive motivator that the field sales manager has is the ability to apply personalized supervision. This supervision will include individual need identification, job restructuring for motivation opportunities, and need-satisfying supervision. Individualized supervision recognizes that management is the process of getting the job done through people; that motivation is the process of creating job circumstances that will inspire, persuade, encourage, or challenge individuals to manage themselves; job-motivated individuals work to satisfy their needs on the job; and managers should manage not in the style that satisfies their needs but in the style that satisfies the needs of their employees.

Individual Need Identification

It is clear from the preceding discussion that the important needs are those of the employee, not the manager. But how should the manager identify the employee's individual needs? Methods could range from casual observation, through a case-study method, to highly structured record keeping. One company uses the case method in an unusual way to identify representatives' needs, symbols, self-images, and strengths. In this company, a sales manager and a representative jointly write a case about the representative that includes the following kinds of information: personal history, activities, interests, and hobbies; job histories; job performance; career goals; strengths and deficiencies; and behavioral characteristics (e.g., aggressive, takes charge, quiet, a loner, etc.). These cases are used to help the manager understand the representatives' motivations and are used in training programs for managers.

Job Restructuring for Motivational Opportunities

After identifying the representative's individual needs, the manager must confirm that the job does in fact possess the means for this representative to be motivated on the job. If it does not, the manager faces the options of terminating the representative, transferring him or her to a job that will be more satisfying for this individual's needs, or restructuring the job to provide individual need-satisfying opportunities. Restructuring requires job enrichment that will provide opportunities for psychological growth.

To restructure the job, the manager must know clearly the present requirement of a representative and requirements that may be expected in the future. The individual's needs must be related to these job requirements to determine if the job can be transformed into a motivating opportunity. The manager must then create need-satisfying opportunities for representatives. For example, a representative with a need for self-esteem may be asked to organize a presentation for the next sales meeting.

Need-Satisfying Supervision

Individualized supervision requires the continuous application of need-satisfying supervision. This supervision is the process of working with a sales representative to set his or her objectives and evaluating his or her performance in achieving these objectives.

IMPLEMENTING MOTIVATION THEORIES

Much of the discussion on motivation may seem theoretical and abstract, but these concepts are used daily by successful field sales managers and general sales managers. There are important distinctions, however, in how these motivation concepts are applied at different levels of sales management. In general, the field sales manager is working with a group of representatives whose motivational needs are in varying stages of identification, development, and satisfaction. In contrast, the general manager is directly responsible for field sales managers who have achieved success, have greater maturity, and whose motivational needs probably have been identified. These differences result in significantly different on-the-job applications of the motivational principles and in different motivational problems.

IMPLEMENTATION BY THE FIELD SALES MANAGER

The motivational problem of a field sales manager may be classified according to three representative categories—new or young representatives, experienced representatives, and older representatives—each with different motivational problems.

To Motivate New Representatives

New or young representatives who are in their first selling job tend to be a bundle of uncertainty regarding the company policies, their own abilities, specific responsibilities, performance standards, and the field sales manager's leadership style. This uncertainty provides the field sales manager with an excellent motivational opportunity to help the new representative identify with the company and thereby build trust, loyalty, and self-confidence. To establish this motivational foundation, the sales manager may proceed as follows:

1. Establish clearly identified goals using a job description, performance standards, performance appraisal forms, the compensation plan, and identification of promotional tracks.
2. Satisfy early needs through orientation about the company history, benefit programs, sales training in products, skills, planning, programs, policies, and procedures.
3. Minimize the effect of trauma by arranging early failures during training.
4. Identify early strengths, human needs, and areas of special training needs.
5. Orient the representative in the territory (including housing, banks, etc.), and introduce him or her to associates.
6. Arrange and guide the representative through early opportunities for achieving success.

To Motivate Experienced Representatives

The experienced representative group can be divided further into those who are successful and those who are having difficulties. In the case of the successful representatives, the field sales manager has the ideal situation for providing them with continuing opportunities to use their strengths, to be successful, and to satisfy their needs for achievement, control, self-worth, etc. This case provides an opportunity to apply Herzberg's "You don't motivate people to succeed; instead, you provide people with opportunities to succeed, and they will be motivated."

Methods for meeting representatives' needs are summarized in Exhibit 11.4, Field Sales Managers' Actions for Meeting Representatives' Needs. For example, the representative who has a strong need for recognition and prestige may be assigned a special session at a district sales meeting. The representative who needs to dominate a situation needs to be reminded that personal selling permits running one's territory as a profit center. Reviewing the fringe benefits will aid the representative who has a strong need for economic security. A strong need to belong can be met by keeping close contact with representatives and making sure that they are included in all business and recreational activities. By recognizing a representative's strengths and achievements, a manager can help meet this representative's need for emotional security.

When an experienced representative is having difficulty, the field sales manager has the opportunity to convince the representative that a

---

**Exhibit 11.4   Field Sales Managers' Actions
for Meeting Representatives' Needs**

Need for Recognition and Prestige

. . . the need to satisfy the desire for approval of actions

1. Acknowledge achievements in district bulletins, personal memos, at district sales meetings, in front of spouse, in person.
2. Assign responsibility for session at district sales meeting and work with him or her on it to help him or her succeed.
3. Assign attendance at convention, or responsibility as "Representative in Charge" at convention.
4. Arrange for him or her to be recognized as the district authority on a product (or procedure or skill) about which he or she is very knowledgeable, and assign him or her to help others in areas of his or her strengths.
5. Assign him or her to help screen promising applicants.
6. Help him or her qualify for promotion.
7. Assign him or her responsibility to head or coordinate a selling team.

Need to Dominate or Control

. . . the need to control a situation from one's own point of view

1. Assign responsibility for workshop leader or market surveys.
2. Solicit his or her suggestions for better territory management of time and effort, district needs, and goals.
3. Teach him or her better planning to achieve better territory and customer control.
4. Find ways to demonstrate the concept that representatives are managers of their own territories.
5. Reassign to more challenging territory.

(continued)

Exhibit 11.4   Continued

Need for Economic Security

. . . the need a person has to be free from economic want

1. Spell out performance standards to qualify for annual salary review and incentive bonus, and the importance of "extra sales."
2. Review the fringe benefits, such as life and health insurance, pension plan, automobile selection, and the employees' education fund.
3. Work closely with him or her to identify time saving and efficiency resulting from good working habits and territory management by objectives.
4. Help the representative plan his or her personal activities to maximize benefits from optional fringe benefits.
5. Emphasize the policy of salary and incentive bonus based on performance and productivity instead of seniority, and advise him or her of his or her relative standing in the group.

Need to Belong

. . . the need to feel like an accepted member of the group

1. Maintain closer contact by mail, telephone, or in person to build confidence and provide reassurance.
2. Reassure him or her as a person, with birthday card, employment anniversary, etc. Inquire about and know his or her family, community activities, church, or other organizations. Praise his or her efforts to the group.
3. Emphasize to him or her the interdependence of all activities within the company, the district and region; encourage his or her feedback.
4. Be sure he or she is included in all district activities, business or recreational, and arrange to have him or her invited by peers.
5. Encourage close working relationship with representatives in bordering territories.
6. Encourage him or her to join outside community or business-related groups.

Need for Personal or Emotional Security

. . . the need to satisfy his or her feeling of self-worthiness

1. At appraisal and counseling interview, review progress and achievements.
2. Assign him or her a series of reasonable projects and maintain close contact either personally or through trainer to emphasize their importance, and help him or her attain the objective so that he or she becomes accustomed to success.
3. Recognize his or her personal as well as business achievements, hobbies, customer rapport, and other areas of interest, and let him or her know you care.
4. Solicit his or her opinions and suggestions on promotion, marketing surveys, special assignments.
5. Emphasize strengths whenever possible.

deficiency exists and to help this representative identify the reasons for the failure to meet mutually agreed upon performance standards. The manager and representative may then develop together a program and schedule for improving performance. The manager can then work with the representative to achieve these goals and enjoy the consequences derived from improving selling skills.

To Motivate the Older Representatives

The motivational problems with older representatives can be traced to causes such as the following:

1. Declining performance resulting from a lack of interest, effort, self-discipline, a failure to keep current on new job requirements, or deteriorating selling skills;
2. Self-doubts because of growing seniority and the increasing number of younger associates who are moving ahead quickly;
3. Declining health or family problems;
4. Missed opportunities for promotion, real or imagined;
5. Unequal time with the field sales manager because of the manager's need to spend time with new representatives.

The motivational problems with older representatives provide the field sales manager with a real test of his or her motivational abilities. It will be necessary to put the deficiencies in their proper perspective relative to this representative's contribution to the total selling effort. The manager will need to get agreement on the variations between standards and performance. It will be necessary to correct the time discrepancies between the efforts with younger and older representatives. The manager could use the older representative to solve this problem by having him or her as a trainer for younger representatives.

In almost all motivational problems, whether they are with new, experienced, or older representatives, the field sales manager has the means for converting these problems into motivational opportunities that will inspire, encourage, persuade, or challenge the representatives to manage themselves productively.

IMPLEMENTATION BY THE GENERAL SALES MANAGER

Because most field sales managers are former sales representatives and have received their current status through previous successes, they tend to be highly motivated individuals. The task of the general sales manager is to keep them motivated.

To Motivate Field Sales Managers

During the transition from a sales representative to management, the new field sales manager suffers a letdown that requires support and encouragement. The reason is that the field sales manager recognizes that it is more difficult to satisfy his or her personal needs through the representatives' efforts than through direct efforts as a representative. The general sales manager must identify and provide circumstances in which the motivational needs of the field sales manager can be satisfied. Exhibit 11.5 identifies ways that the general sales manager can meet the basic needs of the field sales manager. Many similarities between this exhibit and Exhibit 11.4 illustrate the fact that motivation techniques are generalizable.

**Exhibit 11.5 General Sales Managers' Actions
for Meeting Field Sales Managers' (FSM) Needs**

Need for Economic Security

Date

_____ 1. Spell out the importance of the extra sales to qualify for annual salary review and incentive bonus.

_____ 2. Work closely with field sales managers (FSM) to identify time saving and efficiency resulting from good work habits and district management by objectives.

_____ 3. Help FSM plan his or her personal activities to maximize benefits from the optional fringe benefits.

_____ 4. Provide recognition among peers for his or her competence in economic areas such as expense control.

_____ 5. Stress stability of the industry and economic long-term security of FSM's job.

_____ 6. Reinforce his or her life style by complimenting him or her on economic achievement. Example: personal and family purchases, investments, etc.

Need for Recognition and Prestige

Date

_____ 1. Acknowledge achievements in regional bulletin, personal memo, memos to office, recognize his or her success at field sales managers' (FSM) conferences and other peer groups and in front of spouse and customers.

_____ 2. Assign responsibility for session at FSM conference.

_____ 3. Recognize and use the FSM as the authority on certain procedures, programs, or skills. Use participative management as much as possible.

_____ 4. Have him or her write editorial or regional bulletin on a subject of his or her expertise.

_____ 5. Assign him or her to conduct a basic training class.

_____ 6. Maintain close communications contact.

(continued)

Exhibit 11.5 Continued

Need for Personal Self-Worth

Date

_____ 1. At appraisal and counseling interview, review progress to show his or her achievements and help him or her set realistic objectives.

_____ 2. Recognize his or her achievements to him or her privately and the value of these achievements to the company, his or her peers, customers, and family.

_____ 3. Assign him or her a series of achievable projects and maintain close contact to help him or her attain the objectives.

_____ 4. Review his or her role within the region, the company, and industry to make him or her feel its importance, how needed he or she is, and what his or her contribution is to the total success.

_____ 5. Recognize his or her personal as well as business achievements, hobbies, customer rapport, and other areas and interests, and let him or her know you care.

Need to Dominate or Control

Date

_____ 1. Assign the responsibility for session at FSM conference, workshop leader, or arrangements for FSM conference, including suggestions for topics to be covered at meeting.

_____ 2. Allow and encourage individual variations in district management within accepted standards.

_____ 3. Help him or her to become regional authority on a procedure or skill, and assign him or her to help other district managers in areas of his or her strength.

_____ 4. Seek his or her counsel and use participative management as much as possible in those areas where control is a factor.

_____ 5. Develop district programs for all districts in the region that he or she has successfully used in his or her own district.

_____ 6. Let him or her help train new Field Supervisors by suggesting that the new Supervisor spend time with him or her to learn how he or she does the job of FSM.

Need to Belong

Date

_____ 1. Involve FSM in group activities such as workshops and/or panels.

_____ 2. Compliment him or her personally in front of a group, in front of spouse, or in a regional bulletin with an example of his or her participation to the regional achievements.

_____ 3. Encourage and help him or her personally, or suggest outside courses to develop his or her abilities to achieve an acceptable level within the group.

_____ 4. Ask older FSM to keep in touch with new FSM.

_____ 5. Maintain close contact by mail, telephone, or in person to build his or her confidence and to provide reassurance.

_____ 6. Keep him or her well informed of regional or company activities and of his or her value to the team effort.

To Motivate Field Sales Managers to Motivate Others

The general sales manager's motivational responsibilities also include monitoring the sales manager's activities in motivating representatives. The general sales manager will help the field sales manager in identifying the symbols, strengths, and human needs of the representatives. The general sales manager will also assist in providing representatives with motivational opportunities on a continuing basis, periodically reassessing the job of the representative to identify new need-satisfying opportunities, and check for the results from these motivational activities.

To Motivate Representatives

Recognizing that motivating the representatives is a direct management responsibility of the field sales manager, the general sales manager has a personal responsibility *indirectly* to inspire, encourage, persuade, and challenge all employees. This is particularly applicable to the general sales manager whose personal efforts can reinforce those of the field sales manager in building pride, loyalty, and confidence on the part of the representatives toward the company's management, its objectives, and its success.

FINANCIAL MOTIVATORS

Financial motivators, such as bonuses, contests, and recognition banquets are an important part of the motivation systems in many companies. In some companies the only motivational schemes are financial ones. Financial schemes can be effective over the long term only when the basic human dimensions of motivation have been cared for. A financial incentive that is used without consideration for other needs of the representative tend to have short-term effects. After a while, representatives tend to ask, "What have you done for me lately?"

RECENT DEVELOPMENTS FROM THE BEHAVIORAL SCIENCES

In Chapter 4, "The Selling Process," we saw that behavioral scientists have taken an interest in attempting to understand the behavior of buyers and sellers. They have also taken an interest in the study of salesperson performance as determined by individual and organizational differences. The organizational factors will be examined in Chapter 18, which will discuss sales organizational designs. The present discussion will be limited to research on individual factors that relate to motivating the salesperson to perform productively.

PERSONAL DIFFERENCES

Churchill, Ford, and Walker have conducted extensive research on the individual differences that may lead to sales representative performance.[7] They apply the findings from psychological research on job performance by considering the following variables: motivation, aptitude, skill level, role perception, and personal, organizational, and environmental variables. To explain the psychological process of motivation, Churchill, Ford, and Walker have chosen the expectancies model. This model attempts to explain the amount of effort that a salesperson wishes to expend on each selling activity. These authors define expectancy as the representative's estimate of the probability that effort expended on a specific activity will improve performance. For example, "If I increase my calls on potential new accounts by 10 percent (effort), then there is a 50 percent chance that my volume of new account sales will increase by 10 percent during the next six months (performance level)."[8] The total force or motivation to perform this activity is the sum of the expectancies associated with these activities times the valance of performance outcome. Valances are the salesperson's perceptions of the desirability of receiving increased amounts of the rewards he or she might attain as a result of improved performance.[9]

Churchill, Ford, and Walker tested this model by surveying 227 salespersons in two industrial companies. They examined the relationships between age, job tenure, marital status, family size, and educational level and the valance for each of the following needs: pay, job security, recognition, promotion, liking and respect, sense of accomplishment, and personal growth.[10] The findings indicated that in these companies financial rewards were most highly valued by older salespeople with long job tenure and by those married individuals with large families. Promotion and opportunities for accomplishment and growth were more valued by younger, less experienced salespersons who were single or had small families, and those with relatively high levels of formal education.

Attempts to measure motivation among sales representatives and other workers frequently yield nonsignificant results. This lack of significance may be due to characteristics of motivation and survey research methodology. As noted earlier in this chapter, motivation is a very personal characteristic with individuals giving different weights to different needs. Survey research, on the other hand, averages data in search of common traits. It is quite possible that these survey techniques in their averaging process bury patterns of individual motivation. We probably need to change our research methods when measuring motivation.

Luthans suggests that humanistic approaches, such as Maslow's and MacGregor's, and the most recent cognitive models such as Vroom's expectancy theory and Adams' equity theory, fall short in their ability to predict and control human behavior.[11] He suggests that behavioral psychological theories, in particular reinforcement and operant learning theories such as those of Thorndike and Skinner, can make important contributions to human behavior in organizations. A procedure is suggested that has the following steps: identifying the behaviors, measuring the behaviors, conducting a functional analysis to identify the antecedent queues that precede behavior and the contingent consequences that follow it, developing an intervention strategy, and evaluating for a performance improvement. It is useful to note that suggestions for intervention include activities such as attention and recognition, points that are included in Exhibits 11.4 and 11.5.

This brief summary of the theories of motivation as they relate to representatives suggests that what is needed is a theory that integrates all of these concepts. The motivational procedures that are recommended in the earlier parts of this chapter combine the humanistic and behavioral theories. The cognitive theories have not received wide application.

ROLE CONFLICT AND AMBIGUITY

Recent research is showing that a clear definition of what is expected of the representative is an important motivating factor. Statements such as, "That's not my job," or "I didn't know I was supposed to do that," are clear indications of role conflict and ambiguity. Donnelly and Ivancevich concluded that greater role clarity may play an important part in a representative's job performance.[12] Doyle and Shapiro concluded that the nature of the sales task has more to do with motivation than personality, compensation, or the quality of management.[13] They studied the sales systems of four companies—two with clearly defined sales tasks and two without. They found that salespeople worked longer hours on the job when the tasks were clearly defined and when they saw a positive relationship between their efforts and the results.

The presence of role ambiguity and conflict can probably be traced to the lack of an adequate job description, the lack of performance standards, vague recruiting standards, and poor training. Thus these important steps in sales management must be reviewed continuously to make certain that the representatives' roles are clearly understood by them.

DIRECTION OF CAUSALITY IN JOB SATISFACTION

There have been numerous attempts to measure job satisfaction of representatives. Churchill, Ford, and Walker developed a satisfaction scale that included items regarding the job, peer relationships, supervision, company policies, compensation, promotion, and customer types.[14] Researchers and practitioners, however, frequently question the direction of causality between job satisfaction and productivity. Practitioners argue strongly that a highly productive representative will be highly satisfied and that the management task is to make them productive, not to make them satisfied. Recent research by Bagozzi supports this position. He concluded, "Apparently salespeople are motivated by the anticipated satisfaction that comes with performance more than they are by the performance itself."[15] Bagozzi concluded that self-esteem is the key determinant of motivation. He recommends that, "Management should enhance self-esteem by regularly providing positive reinforcement in the form of personal recognition and monetary rewards, as well as socially visible acknowledgements of good performance."[16] In another study, Bagozzi has reported that role ambiguity seems to have its greatest adverse effect on self-esteem because this ambiguity weakens the representatives' self-regard and their self-competence on the job. He concluded further that role ambiguity and motivation appear to have about equal but opposite effects on performance, so that the optimum sales management action would be to reduce this ambiguity and increase motivation simultaneously.[17]

MOTIVATION IN A CHANGING CULTURE

Because motivation programs are built on individual needs and values, they must reflect changes in these values and needs as they occur in a changing culture. Yankelovich, an authority on national values, concludes that the productivity problem with the American work force is the growing mismatch between incentives and motivation.[18] Motivations have changed but incentives have not. He notes further that one of the problems is the fact that many top managers are trained to deal with the tangibles in business—finance, engineering, or production—so that they are uncomfortable in dealing with the intangibles of human behavior. He points out that these technology and capital investment decisions were once the key factors in productivity, but the human dimension is becoming relatively more important.

Rapid changes in cultural values can produce generation gaps. Dunn provides an interesting case about a sales manager of one generation who is unhappy about the lifestyle and values of one of his outstanding representatives.[19] This case raises serious questions about motivating representatives to produce or to conform to procedures.

SUMMARY

Motivation is based on the concept that all behavior is motivated behavior and each of us, without exception, plays, works, and does all the things that we do to meet personal needs. Resourceful sales managers will realize that the best that can be done is to arrange job circumstances so that these needs can be met on the job.

To develop the proper environment for motivating, a sales manager must first identify job demotivators—uncertain job requirements, misapplied qualifications, inadequate personal development, poor working environment, and poor reward systems. A logical approach for individualized motivation begins with an understanding of why people work. To gain insights into behavior on the job we may begin with the question, "Why do people buy?" This logical process leads us to the conclusion that sales managers should manage in a way that enables each representative to meet his or her needs on the job.

The development of a program of motivation begins with eliminating job demotivators. To eliminate job demotivators, a manager needs to identify the job clearly, hire qualifiable candidates, train these candidates, provide proper supervision, reward equitably, and develop personnel and monitor them continuously. To motivate individuals, the manager must develop appropriate leadership styles, use all available resources, and supervise representatives individually. This individual supervision requires the need to identify each individual's needs, restructure the job for motivational opportunities, and then use a management style of individualized need-satisfying supervision. The field sales manager must deal with motivating new representatives, experienced representatives, and older representatives who may have retired on the job. The general sales manager must motivate the field sales managers directly and representatives indirectly.

Financial motivators have been relegated to a minor role in this discussion because they have only short-term effects if the proper environment for motivating has not been created. The representative quickly forgets having won a contest if the total job environment is unsatisfactory.

Theories of motivation have included approaches that may be described as humanistic, cognitive, and behavioral psychology. The humanistic and behavioral approaches have been used in sales management more than the cognitive models, which are still in a state of development.

The complexity of motivating a sales force is increased by the fact that younger representatives' personal values may differ widely from those of managers. The manager must work hard at understanding the needs of the representative through his or her eyes, not the eyes of the manager.

ASSIGNMENTS/DISCUSSION QUESTIONS

1. Discuss the components of "good supervision."

2. Discuss the relationship between symbols, strengths, human needs, self-image, and point of view, as stated in the Open Management System. Give an example of how this theory might apply.

3. What is the relationship between motivators and demotivators?

4. Discuss the application of a career development program to motivational theory.

5. Discuss the motivational needs of a young sales representative in the "On-the-Job Application" section of this chapter.

6. Discuss the motivational needs of the older representative identified in the "On-the-Job Application" section of this chapter.

7. Discuss a program a field sales manager could implement with an older representative whose performance deteriorated because the representative did not keep pace with technological changes in the product line.

CASE 11.1:
Tri-Star Chemical Company

Tri-Star Chemical Company has enjoyed excellent growth over the past four years, doubling its sales of $48 million and exceeding the chemical industry growth trend by 37 percent. This growth has resulted primarily from their expansion in the Texas, Oklahoma, and Louisiana markets where Tri-Star increased its sales coverage from six to eighteen sales reps, with six having been added in the last twelve months.

Randy Johnson, the current Regional Sales Manager in this area, is fifty-two years old, having started as a salesman with Tri-Star twenty-seven years ago, covering half the state of Texas and part of Oklahoma. Randy's philosophy is that hard work produces results, and when people produce results you pay them accordingly. Recently, Tri-Star hired a new personnel manager, Jim Solomon, who has added some voluntary management training, including a course on the application of the theories of behavioral sciences on the job. While two of the four other Regional Sales Managers have enrolled in the program and sent several of their DSMs, Randy has not. Instead, he commented, "These kinds of programs may have their place but if you pay your people what they're worth you won't have any major problems. Money is what sales reps work for. That's their security."

Tom Hartman, who retired a year ago as District Sales Manager in Texas, trained both Randy Johnson and Gary Holmes, a salesman who is five years Randy's senior and who started with Randy. Tom had grown up with Tri-Star and was a major influence in its growth in Texas, where he had hired and trained a number of sales reps who had transferred to other areas. Some had been promoted to DSM, and two like Randy Johnson had been promoted to Regional Sales Manager as the company grew and the RSM level of management was added. Even though Tom hired and trained Randy and eventually worked for him, there was no resentment between them. In fact, Tom was Randy's biggest booster, even though his management style was considerably different. As Tom always said, "Randy is interested in results, and that's what the company hired him for. The strategies of how you get salespeople to produce the results is the responsibility of the District Sales Manager." While Tom as a salesman had personally covered most of the district his sales reps had, and knew most of the top management of the customers they sold to, his approach to management was to let his reps make the sale and be the heroes and he'd applaud their achievements, and provide technical support when it was needed and moral support when they failed. Tom was proud of his team and they worked together very productively, usually being at or near the top when the sales results were analyzed.

As the district expanded in personnel and ultimately was split, Tom recruited most of the new salespeople, including Judy Sampson three years ago, their first female sales rep. In the chemical sales field, where sales reps dealt with sales engineers and production managers in the plants and in the oil fields, there weren't many female applicants, and hiring Judy raised some eyebrows among the other representatives. Tom had to defend his actions to several other DSMs. Randy, however, never commented. Because Judy was a slow starter due to her lack of background in chemical sales, Tom had assigned two experienced sales reps to work with her in addition to the time he worked with her each month. Judy was twenty-six years old, divorced two years earlier, and had a three-year-old daughter at the time she was hired. Initially she had some difficulties making arrangements for her daughter when she worked out of town, but eventually she solved the problem with the regular help of an older neighbor woman as a temporary live-in babysitter. At present she is about an average rep.

When Tom Hartman retired a year ago, Skip Petersen was promoted to DSM from an adjoining region. Skip had been with Tri-Star six years, had moved laterally into two different territories, each more important than the last. He had built a reputation for being an innovative, hard working salesman who outsold the competition and attracted attention for the results he got. He invariably placed in the top five of every sales contest and enjoyed the publicity his successes rated in the regional and national sales bulletins. He's a natural athlete and very active in participative sports. Skip is an achiever. When Tom came up for retirement and Randy Johnson had the opportunity to select Skip from two other candidates, Randy identified Skip as the kind of manager he wanted.

In the year since his promotion, Skip has become increasingly concerned and impatient. Initially he tried to get to know his new district, the customers, their potential, the decision makers, who the major competition was in the area and how they were doing, and where the best sales opportunities existed for increased sales. Skip spent many evenings and weekends reviewing the records, analyzing the data, and making plans for the kinds of programs he wanted to introduce. In fact, he spent so much time his wife began to make some comments about whether his promotion was worth the price she and their young son were having to pay.

The problem Skip was encountering was hard for him to define. Sales had continued to grow at about the same rate as before he took over, but not in proportion to the sales opportunities that he saw. Although his nine sales reps were friendly enough, they weren't adopting his suggestions for improving their prospecting, planning, and selling skills the way he had suggested and expected. And then there were the problems with Judy Sampson and Gary Holmes, which he wasn't certain how to handle.

Judy was doing OK in her sales performance, even though he was sure that with more effort she could do better, but that wasn't the problem. Judy called him at home about one thing or another just about every other night. He realized she couldn't reach him during the day when he was out working with one of the other reps and she was on her own territory. The difficulty was the frequency of her calls, and the subject matter. If it wasn't some problem with one of her accounts, it was about some sale she had made that she wanted to hash over. And if that weren't enough, she'd tell him about some of the things her daughter Sally was doing. The fact was that Skip's wife was becoming increasingly annoyed. She even went so far as to ask sarcastically what was going on between them. At that point, Skip became angry and ended up in a minor row with his wife. Skip remembered that Tom Hartman had said something about Judy's calls. Skip couldn't remember what it was, but he sure didn't appreciate Tom allowing Judy to continue that practice.

The problem with Gary Holmes is quite different; in fact, it is almost the opposite of Judy's problem. Gary has been with Tri-Star a long time. In comparison to Skip, he's an old-timer even if he's in his mid-fifties. In addition, he and Randy Johnson, the Regional Sales Manager, were reps together and are still good friends. Gary is the independent type and rarely contacts Skip. He's one of the most productive reps in the District, and has his own way of selling, which doesn't match the methods Skip would like to see used in the District particularly by the new reps. Since Gary is one of the most productive reps, Skip would like to have him help in the training of the new reps, but he doesn't want them trained in the unorthodox way that Gary sells. Skip has talked with Gary on the last two field trips he made with him about the methods he uses, but without success. In fact, Gary seemed to resent Skip's comments about his methods, and kept referring to the results he was getting. The situation has become acute as a result of a telephone call Skip received from Randy Johnson. It seems that Gary told Randy that he wished Randy would "get Skip off my back. I don't need some young kid telling me how to sell. I've been getting top-notch results since before he was born." Randy told Skip he didn't want personnel problems to get in the way of productivity and he wanted the problem with Gary resolved promptly.

Assign each of the characters in this case to a student or group of students, and determine the answers to the following:

CASE QUESTIONS

1. Specify the predominating leadership style or needs of each of the persons in the case by identifying the pattern of actions (symbols) as they relate to the theories of Mazlow, Herzberg, Open Management, and/or others.

2. Identify and explain the major problems with each individual.

3. How could the problem(s) be resolved? How could Skip Petersen motivate Judy Sampson and Gary Holmes?

REFERENCES

1. Douglas MacGregor, *The Human Side of Enterprise* (New York: McGraw-Hill Book Co., 1960), p. 30.
2. A. H. Maslow, *Motivation and Personality* (New York: Harper & Row, 1954).
3. F. Herzberg, B. Mausner, and B. Snyderman, *The Motivation of Work,* 2nd ed. (New York: John Wiley, 1959). The two factor theory—that job satisfiers and dissatisfiers are separate dimensions—has been challenged by many researchers, e.g., R. J. House and L. A. Wigdor, "Herzberg's Dual-Factor Theory of Job Satisfaction and Motivation: A Review of the Evidence and a Criticism," *Personnel Psychology* 20 (Winter 1967): 369–89; M. G. Evans, "Herzberg's Two-Factor Theory of Motivation," *Personnel Journal* (January 1970): 32–35; N. King, "Clarification and Evaluation of the Two-Factor Theory of Job Satisfaction," *Psychological Bulletin* 74, no. 1 (1970): 18–31.
4. Frederick Herzberg, "One More Time: How Do You Motivate Employees?" *Harvard Business Review* (January–Febuary 1968): 53–62.
5. Vincent W. Kafka and John H. Schaefer, *Open Management* 2nd ed. (San Francisco, Calif.: Alchemy Books, 1979).
6. G. A. Churchill, Jr., N. M Ford, and O. C. Walker, Jr., *Sales Force Management* (Homewood, Ill.: Richard D. Irwin, 1981), pp. 231–241.
7. For a summary of this reseach, see Ibid.
8. Ibid., p. 379.
9. Ibid., p. 381; O. C. Walker, Jr., G. A. Churchill, Jr., and N. M. Ford, "Motivation and Performance in Industrial Selling: Present Knowledge and Needed Research," *Journal of Marketing Research* 14 (May 1977): 156–168.
10. G. A. Churchill, Jr., N. M. Ford, and O. C. Walker, Jr., "Personal Characteristics of Salespeople and the Attractiveness of Alternative Rewards," *Journal of Business Research* 7 (1979): 25–49.
11. Fred Luthans, "How PF/PR Pays Off for Human Resources Managers," *Training HRD* (December 1976): 17–19, 36.
12. J. H. Donnelly and J. M. Ivancevich, "Role Clarity and the Salesman," *Journal of Marketing* 35 (January 1975): 71–74. See also D. N. Behrman, W. J. Bigoness, and W. D. Perreault, "Sources of Job Related Ambiguity and their Consequences upon Salespersons' Job Satisfaction and Performance, *Management Science* 27 (November 1981): 1246–1260.
13. S. X. Doyle and B. P. Shapiro, "What Counts Most in Motivating Your Sales Force?" *Harvard Business Review* (May–June 1980): 133–140.
14. G. A. Churchill, N. M. Ford, and O. C. Walker, "Measuring the Job Satisfaction of Industrial Salesmen," *Journal of Marketing Research* 11 (August 1974): 254–260.
15. R. P. Bagozzi, "Performance and Satisfaction in an Industrial Sales Force: An Examination of their Antecedents and Simultaneity," *Journal of Marketing* 44 (Spring 1980): 70.
16. Ibid., p. 71.
17. R. P. Bagozzi, "The Nature and Causes of Self-Esteem, Performance, and Satisfaction in the Sales Force: A Structural Equation Approach," *Journal of Business* 53 (1980): 315–331.
18. Daniel Yankelovich, "Yankelovich on Today's Workers," *Industry Week* (August 6, 1979): 67–72.
19. A. H. Dunn, "Case of the Suspect Salesman," *Harvard Business Review* (November–December 1979): 38–52.

=== **SUGGESTED READINGS**

"Getting Ahead with Incentives," Special Section, *Sales & Marketing Management* (April 6, 1981): 59–96.

Scanlon, Sally, "Want Better Incentive Results? It's Simple," *Sales & Marketing Management* (September 19, 1977): 44–47.

Weeks, David A., *Incentive Plans for Salesmen* (New York: The Conference Board, 1970).

12

DIRECTING BY DELEGATING, COORDINATING, AND MANAGING CHANGE AND CONFLICT

Many new sales managers find the management function of directing the most difficult of the new tasks that they must perform. As a successful sales representative, one needs to direct only his or her activities. In contrast, the field sales manager must achieve the desired objectives of the organization by working through others. In the previous chapter, which discussed motivation, we saw that the manager cannot motivate other individuals, but only create the proper environment whereby individuals may motivate themselves. Motivation, it will be recalled, requires a thorough understanding of an individual's needs. Three additional directing activities are examined in this chapter—delegating, coordinating, and managing change and conflict. These activities, like motivating, require an understanding of an individual's needs.

DELEGATING

Delegating consists of assigning responsibility and authority to a subordinate and holding him or her accountable for the results. For example, a field sales manager may delegate to a representative certain activities for the short term, such as recruiting and training a new representative. To delegate effectively, the manager must clearly define the responsibilities, authorities, and accountabilities that are being delegated. Responsibility is an obligation to perform, which requires that the representative understand and accept the nature of the responsibility. Authority, the power to decide or act, must be clearly defined so that the representative knows his or her limits of authority. Account-ability, the obligation to produce results (i.e., beyond responsibility), requires mutual agreement between the manager and representative on how these results will be observed and measured.

PURPOSE OF DELEGATION

Delegation expands the capacity of an organization by freeing a manager from work that can be done equally as well by someone else, thereby freeing him or her for tasks that only a manager can do. Such managerial tasks include salary reviews, performance reviews, personnel development, and recommendations for promotion.

Delegation also performs an important role in developing subordinates. It provides job-enriching opportunities. It gives a subordinate insight into the problems of being a manager, which should make the subordinate more manageable. Delegation also expands the number of persons in the sales force who are qualified to perform expanded roles.

PROCESS OF DELEGATION

A process of delegation is necessary in order for the manager and the representative to achieve a shared understanding and acceptance of what is delegated. The process of delegation may be divided into the following six steps:

1. Define in writing what is to be delegated, the limits of authority, and the degree of accountability.
2. Make standards of performance clear, measurable, and achievable. These standards should identify goals that are expressed in terms of quality, quantity, cost, and time for performance.
3. Create an environment that encourages subordinates to be motivated to accept the responsibility, to exercise authority, and to fulfill the accountability requirements.
4. Build in checkpoints at reasonable intervals.
5. Support and check progress and final accountability.
6. Recall the delegation if necessary.

Failure to perform one of these steps when delegating may jeopardize the success of the delegation process.

LIMITATIONS OF DELEGATION

Because the manager is ultimately accountable, all authority cannot be delegated, or the manager would lose control. If all authority were delegated, the manager would be abdicating his or her accountability.

In addition to this organizational limitation of delegation, there are personal limitations. In order to delegate, a manager must have confidence in his or her ability to rescue a project if the subordinate fails. The manager must also have confidence in the representative's ability to perform the activity. Delegation may be limited by personal shortcomings of a manager. The manager may fear being replaced by a subordinate, or fear a loss of security or identity. There may be a reluctance to share recognition or credit. And finally, there may be a reluctance to admit that others can do the job as well or even better.

COORDINATING

Coordination of representatives' efforts is required so that all individuals pull toward the common corporate objective. Coordination begins, therefore, with the representatives' clearly understanding the corporate objectives, the sales objectives, and their individual objectives. If, for example, representatives are not certain whether their objectives are sales volume, profit, market share, or customer service, each representative may be allocating his or her effort in a different direction, making coordination impossible. The corporate selling plan provides the basis for the field sales manager's coordinating representatives by specifying the selling objectives and the relationships between personal selling efforts, advertising, and promotion. This plan also helps the field sales manager coordinate staffing and training activities because it gives an indication of the number of trained representatives that will be necessary during the coming year.

A clear communication of the objectives of the selling effort is only the beginning of the coordination process. The new field sales manager may face five to ten ambitious individuals, each of whom has quite different personal objectives and different selling strategies.

UNDERSTANDING RESOURCES

The basic task facing a sales manager is the allocation of limited resources to market potential so as to maximize the sales objectives. The coordination of this allocation requires an understanding of the nature of these resources.

The single most important resource is the time of the representative. The manager must understand the strengths and weaknesses of representatives, their needs, and what is required to motivate them. One representative may have greater success with larger accounts than with smaller ones, while the reverse pattern may exist for another representative. Understanding such strengths, a manager will design territories accordingly.

Travel expenses, entertainment funds, demonstration equipment, samples, and promotional literature are all limited resources that must be allocated to market potential in the most productive manner possible.

All of these allocation decisions must be consistent with corporate policies and procedures to assure uniformity across sales districts and regions.

COORDINATING RESOURCE ALLOCATION WITHIN THE DISTRICT

Coordinating the allocation of resources within the district requires the sales manager to strike a balance between the individual needs and strengths of representatives and the tasks that need to be done. The representative who likes responsibility, is a problem solver, takes risks, and understands organizational behavior may be the ideal representative to assign major, national accounts. Conversely, the representative who needs continuous feedback and avoids risks should be assigned to smaller accounts that generate small but frequent sales. The representative with a high need for achievement may be assigned high-visibility tasks, such as presenting a new product at a sales meeting or representing the industry's position on a local television program. (Some researchers have found that need for achievement distinguishes between high and low sales productivity.[1])

When assigning representatives to territories, the sales manager will want to consider many individual differences. The person with a high need for independence should be assigned a suburban or rural territory. A representative who needs close support should be assigned an urban territory near the sales manager. Similarly, different personalities and backgrounds may be required to call on headquarters, chains, distributors, wholesalers, government accounts, cold calls, and accounts requiring frequent call-backs. When a sales district is specialized according to different product types or end uses, the sales manager has an opportunity to match representatives' preferences for selling different product mixes. A representative who enjoys consultative selling may prefer to sell raw materials and component parts because these products require working closely with the manufacturing process of customers. Other representatives may prefer to sell finished products, so they would be assigned to retail accounts. A pharmaceutical manufacturer may have many opportunities for matching products to representatives. Product mixes include those sold only by prescription versus those sold over-the-counter (OTC) in drug stores, products for humans versus products for animals, products for large animals versus those for pets, agricultural products such as pesticides, and chemicals for laboratory diagnosis.

Precise matching of representatives' talents with the selling tasks required in the territory will greatly increase the clarity of the task, thereby increasing the productivity of the representative.[2] This matching is an ideal. (Keep in mind that it will never be possible to make *perfect* matches between representatives and territory needs.)

TEAM BUILDING

By building synergy into the sales force, a manager may make the district productivity greater than the sum of its parts. To create synergy, the manager will use combinations of circumstances and individuals to compound their effectiveness and productivity.

Contests are frequently used to stimulate competitiveness, to meet achievement needs, and to provide recognition. Team spirit can be generated by competing with adjacent districts, thereby developing a district identity. New representatives may be teamed against older representatives. City representatives may compete with representatives in other cities, or against the rural representatives in the same district. A district may compete with other districts for national competition or for individual honors, such as the President's Club that is used by some insurance companies.

Team building can also be generated by noncompetitive means, such as sales representatives' cooperating on a project or a call on an important customer. A representative who has become a specialist in an application or product may assist other representatives in making calls on accounts that are prospects for these applications and products.

In summary, coordinating, like delegating and motivating, requires an understanding of the individual needs of representatives. In addition, it requires an understanding of the limited resources available, the selling tasks that are required in the territory, and the company policies and procedures that will constrain the way resources are allocated.

MANAGING CHANGE

Because all change is seen as a separation from the familiar, it becomes a threat or risk to the personal security of the individual. As a result, the representative who is newly hired, trained, transferred, or even promoted needs additional support or assurance during the process. Changes in territories, compensation, and evaluation systems threaten personal securities and lead to conflicts.

Motivating, delegating, and coordinating sales representatives is done in an environment of constant change, due to the dynamics of the marketplace. The distinction between a manager and a true leader may turn on how he or she handles change. A manager may resist or, at most, cope with change, while a true leader will welcome the dynamics of change, benefit from it, and create it.

Representatives and field sales managers are at the leading edge of change. Changes in demand, new technology, competition, and government regulations will have substantial and immediate impacts on these individuals. Furthermore, they are part of the change process when they are encouraged to be innovators in developing new sales strategies, finding new product applications, and making recommendations for changes in sales promotion.

THE FIELD MANAGER CREATES CHANGE

The field sales manager creates change in a variety of ways. First, and perhaps foremost, is being open-minded regarding change, thereby encouraging creativity and innovation in others. There are also many opportunities for creativity and innovation in field sales management. The manager may search for more productive ways for structuring territories. He or she may develop new means for presentations, probing, overcoming objections, and closing. Managers may make recommendations for new products as suggested by customers, competitors, or representatives. The manager is also in a good position to make recommendations regarding packaging, advertising, promotion, pricing, and distribution methods so as to give the representatives a competitive advantage. New training methods may be developed and tested at the district level. Suggestions may be made for changing objectives, performance standards, developing evaluation methods, and developing reporting systems. The field sales manager may identify new sources for recruiting sales personnel and methods for training them. The field sales manager plays an important role in responding positively to regulations regarding women, minorities, handicapped, and protected age groups in the sales force. Special efforts will be necessary by these managers to orient these groups into the sales force.

HOW CAN CHANGE BE MANAGED?

Managing the Creative Process

To manage the creative process, one must begin with an open mind, and resist thoughts such as, "That's the way we've always done it." The manager must also resist the NIH (not invented here) trap. Having created the right frame of mind, the manager must then identify the innovators and creative thinkers on the staff. A climate must be created that supports ideas that are outside the normal corporate policies and procedures. Performing such a supporting role may be difficult for a sales manager because it puts him or her in the middle. On the one hand, the manager is to support the organization, which generally means the status quo. On the other hand, he or she is to encourage innovation, which is a rejection of the status quo and perhaps the organization.

Change may occur in the sales force from internal or external forces. Innovation and creativity represent internal sources of change. External sources at the field sales management level include changes in corporate policies and procedures, new technology, competition, and government regulations. With these many sources of change, the sales manager must have a program for managing change among the representatives. This program may include selling yourself on change, viewing change through the eyes of others, anticipating fears, understanding response levels, and choosing appropriate actions.[3]

Selling Yourself on Change

To implement a change, the manager must be sold on it. There will be no problem if the manager is the innovator, but if the change is one of company policy, the manager must sell himself or herself before attempting to sell it to the representatives.

The process of self-selling should begin when a change is contemplated. At this point, the manager should use every legitimate means for contributing to the decision and to weigh fairly the arguments in favor of change. Once the change has been established, the manager must be certain that he or she understands the facts, the reasons for the change, his or her reasons for resistance, means for overcoming this resistance, and the need to support the change.

Viewing Change through the Eyes of Others

Managing change, like the selling process and motivating, requires viewing the process through the other person's eyes. Failing to communicate the reason for change will probably create a misperception and therefore resistance to change. For example, a redesign of a call report to make better use of market data from the sales force was misperceived as saddling the representatives with more paperwork, thereby cutting down on available selling time. A new service group to handle technical equipment was misperceived as management's not trusting the sales staff. Thus, "To be sure a new idea flies, we must view change through John Brown's eyes."

Anticipating Fears

Representatives may be fearful of change if they view it as a threat to those systems that meet their needs. These are the same needs that were discussed in Chapter 11, which discussed motivation:

1. Security: Will the change cut my earnings? Am I being replaced?
2. Self-esteem: Will this change reduce my self-image?
3. Status: Does this change make me look less important?
4. Work load: Will I have to work harder? Must I change my work routine? Will this change add stress to the job? Are the rewards consistent with the additional effort?
5. Social: Will this change require me to make new contacts within the company, the community, and customers?

Change must be sold to each representative in the same way that representatives sell products and services to customers. The sales manager must consider each representative's needs, and translate the change into costs and benefits associated with these needs. Selling techniques, such as probing for objections, proof statements, handling objections, and closing, may all be used by the sales manager when selling change.

Understanding Response Levels

Responses to change may be either acceptance or resistance. Acceptance may be further divided into compliance, identification, and internalization. Resistance may be divided into active hostility, passive hostility, and neutrality.

Compliance occurs when an individual accepts change, not because he or she agrees with it, but to avoid unpleasant outcomes by disagreeing. For example, a representative may not agree with a decision to split territories, but he or she complies because failure to comply may place the job in jeopardy.

Identification occurs when a representative accepts a change because the change was accepted by a representative who is admired. For example, a young representative may accept a territory cut because a senior representative stated, "Now we'll have time to do some real consultative selling." *Internalization* occurs when the representative realizes that the change is consistent with his or her personal values. For example, the territory split may now require representatives to work more with plant engineers than to call on industrial wholesalers. The change may be seen as making it possible for the representatives to concentrate in the areas that they enjoy most.

Active hostility may take the form of outspoken bitterness and refusal to cooperate with a representative who will take over some present accounts. This hostility reduces productivity. *Passive hostility* occurs when a representative complains at the time of the change, continues to complain when given an opportunity, but maintains sales productivity. The *neutral* response is when the representative neither accepts nor rejects a change. This representative is probably withholding a decision for the present time and may change into one of the other levels of response in the future.

Choosing Appropriate Actions

The two most appropriate actions are those that should come naturally to the field sales manager—providing information and persuasion. Much of the resistance to change can be eliminated or avoided in the first place by effectively communicating the reason for the change, its benefits, and its costs. Persuasion may be necessary to reassure the representative that the change results in a net benefit to his or her need structure. If honest and active participation is sought for implementing the change, many resisters will become accepters. Resorting to authority and compelling representatives to accept the change will probably have a negative effect on the sales force productivity and motivation.

MANAGING CONFLICT

A manager should anticipate conflict because it is unlikely that delegation, coordination, and change will be implemented to everyone's satisfaction. Furthermore, some behavioral scientists conclude that, "A group that does not experience conflict is probably not very creative, active, or strong."[4] Some companies build conflict into the planning process to assure that planners will be challenged to develop the best plan possible. Therefore a sales manager who does not experience some conflict in his or her district is probably not encouraging creative and innovative thinking.

Likert and Likert define conflict as "active striving for one's own preferred outcome which, if attained, precludes the attainment by others of their own preferred outcome, thereby producing hostility."[5] "A conflict is viewed as resolved when all opposing parties are satisfied with the outcome."[6] The complexity of the systems for resolving conflict reflects the level of complexity of the social systems that generated the conflict. Thus the resolution must reflect the personal needs that created the conflict.

WHEN DO CONFLICTS OCCUR IN SALES MANAGEMENT?

Sales management conflicts, like most conflicts, are related to change and limited resources. The introduction of new procedures or policies, such as compensation, reporting, or vacations, has the potential for generating conflict. New personnel or changes in the status of present personnel, such as promotions, terminations, and resignations, may result in the reassignment of responsibilities—a potential source of conflict. Conflict may not be overt. It may be reflected in subtle changes in attitude, cooperation, support, or effort.

CONFLICT WITH WHOM?

A representative may be in conflict with headquarters personnel, the field sales manager, other representatives, and customers. Conflicts with headquarters personnel may revolve around policies, procedures, pricing, distribution facilities, shipping, returned goods policies, compensation, and misinterpretation of telephone agreements. Conflicts with one's field sales manager may revolve around imagined or misunderstood unequal treatment. Conflicts may also occur among representatives when one representative works harder, is more productive, is clearly moving ahead, or appears to be receiving favored treatment. Customer conflict may occur when a representative thinks that a customer is unreasonable or when a customer complains about a representative who is "not providing proper service."

RESOLVING CONFLICT

The first step in resolving a conflict is to understand its cause. Was it a lack of communications or a misunderstanding of communications? Did the representative have unreasonable or unsupported expectations? Was there a lack of sensitivity or courage on the part of the manager? To answer these questions, the manager must listen carefully, not take sides, be understanding, and collect the basic facts.

The ideal conflict resolution process would begin by having the conflicting parties jointly work their way through the problem-solving process by jointly defining their goals, identifying alternatives, evaluating the costs and benefits of each alternative, and then making a decision. Critical decisions may need to be reviewed with the next higher level of management. The solution and program of implementation should be discussed with the individual in conflict. The conflict and the solution should be reported for the file.

Styles for resolving conflict will be influenced by each person's concern for his or her relationship with the group, versus his or her concern for personal goals. Researchers have identified several behavioral styles for resolving conflicts. The "tough battler" seeks his or her own goals and is willing to sacrifice the goals of others. The "friendly helper" gives in to the goals of others, thereby placing a greater value on the group relationship than on personal goals. The "problem solver" seeks to find an outcome that meets his or her goals and the goals of others.[7]

Likert and Likert suggest that conflict may be managed most effectively by substituting a win-win alternative for a win-lose approach that will leave at least one party in a state of conflict. These authors present the profiles of four organizational types, labeled System 1 through System 4, and point out that System 4 organizations are better able to resolve conflicts. System 4 organizations have the following characteristics: (1) They have leadership styles in which managers have complete confidence in subordinates, encourage dialogue, and seek innovation. (2) Motivation is based on group-set goals. (3) Communication is down, up, and sideways. (4) Interaction is extensive and cooperative. (5) Decisions are well integrated throughout the organization with full involvement of subordinates. (6) Goals are established through group action. (7) Control is widely shared and control data are for self-guidance and problem solving.[8] The System 4 organizational design seems to be close to the "Open System" design that was presented in Chapter 11, which discussed motivation techniques.

ORGANIZATIONAL THEORIES OF CONFLICT

For several decades, organizational theorists have been exploring the origins of conflict. They have noted that conflict may occur when there is a difference in participants' perceptions of facts, objectives, means for achieving objectives, competition for resources, and competition for rewards. Theorists have noted also that hierarchical structures will produce competition and conflict. They have challenged the Anglo-American concept that competition is good.[9]

THE EFFECTS OF COMPETITION

Kraus argues that competition and conflict are intertwined. After reviewing the literature on competition, he concluded that,

> . . . there is overwhelming evidence that competitive structures and processes are not appropriate for life in organizations. They have consequences that outweigh their benefits. They are not good for individuals and they are not good for the organization. Yet they persist. Why? Because of the nature of socialization processes and because of the nature of the major component of organizational life—hierarchy.[10]

In reviewing the literature, Kraus notes that studies show that the school systems are the major supporters of the competitive model, and that American children are more competitive than children from other countries. Anglo-American competitive school systems produced students with more anxiety, less self-assurance, and a self-needs orientation. Adults in competitive industrial organizations are more anxious than in cooperative ones. Seven-year-old children in competitive environments were more destructive, boastful, and demonstrated deprecatory behavior, while children in collaborative environments were more sharing, helping, and had more friendly conversation.[11] He notes further that,

> There is a vast body of research that supports the proposition that cooperative goal structures encourage positive interpersonal relationships characterized by mutual liking, positive attitudes toward each other, mutual concern, friendliness, attentiveness, feelings of obligation to other students, and the desire to win the respect of other students.[12]

Competition is better than collaboration, however, when the task is drill and the goal is quantity of work. Furthermore, hierarchical structures will increase speed and accuracy, but they will decrease morale and flexibility.[13] As the tasks become more interdependent, the need for collaborative organizational designs becomes more necessary. Higher technology leads to increased specialization, which requires more interdependence. This interdependence requires more collaborative organizational designs to accomplish problem solving. The fact that hierarchical structures are best for simple activities, and collaborative designs are best for complex activities, suggests that hierarchical structures were appropriate during the industrial revolution, but that we have outgrown this design and must find new designs for the post-industrial revolution.

HIERARCHICAL STRUCTURES

A hierarchical structure is a system of superior and subordinate roles. Several authors have concluded that this structure will produce conflict. Thompson notes that this conflict arises from an inconsistency between the roles of specialists and line administrators in a hierarchy. It is difficult to acknowledge or legitimize these differences in this structure because such recognition is counter to the monocratic nature of a hierarchy.[14] In a hierarchy, only one claim, value, or course of action is permitted. "A pluralistic institution, on the other hand, accepts the legitimacy of conflict, the legitimacy of conflicting claims or proposals for action, and for that reason must provide procedures for effective compromises."[15] Hierarchies are therefore individual problem-solving organizations.

Thompson observes that "problem solving by a group should be superior to individual problem solving, providing the group is not formally structured into roles of superior and subordinates."[16] The group provides a constant evaluation of one's thinking, relative strengths, weaknesses, and affective attachments to one's own ideas. The group provides more viewpoints, specialized inputs, and more alternatives. Furthermore, group judgment is more likely to influence others than is an individual's judgment.

Thompson notes further that the use of group processes within a hierarchical structure is subject to basic weaknesses.

> Though attempts are often made to hide the hierarchical structure in the formal group-decision process and to pretend that it is not there, the hierarchy is *in fact* present and all group participants know it. Consequently, because of hierarchical control over personal goals, everything said and done in the group situation must be evaluated not only from the standpoint of its relation to the organization's goals but also from its relation to personal goals. In bureaucracy, ideas do not stand on their merits alone. It is not only an opinion or an idea that wins, but also a man. The situation is inherently competitive rather than co-operative; and, as Kurt Lewin pointed out, competition attacks group solidarity and consequently the ability of the group to employ specialization in pursuit of the group goal.[17]

Hierarchical designs increase the productive capacity of a group, but they also increase conflict because the distribution of powers, capacities, rights, and official value systems inhibit one's ability to achieve personal goals within the organization. And, as we saw in the discussion of motivation (Chapter 11), persons who do not have their needs met on the job will put their energies into activities off the job.

If one accepts the conclusion that job "satisfaction depends upon the degree of skill involved, the variety of activities, the degree of autonomy, the consistency of the job with the individual's self image, and the predictability of work relationships,"[18] then it is easy to see how a hierarchical structure that emphasizes a superior's right to assign activities and to supervise them will create dissatisfaction. The subordinate loses some sense of equality, dignity, independence, and a self-image.[19]

As one moves up the hierarchy, specialization declines, which leads to a decline in the ability to create operational performance standards, which then leads to a decline in job satisfaction from performing a job well. The satisfaction then comes from the exercise of authority and issuing rewards such as power, money, and prestige. Subordinates then develop bureaupathic practices such as hypocrisy, false personalization, excessive formalism, overstrict compliance with rules and regulations, and close supervision.[20] Kraus concluded that, "Organizations thus foster mindless individuals who are adept at the party line but who have lost their own individuality along the way. They have lost touch with their own value system, their feelings, and have diminished the boundaries between themselves as entities and the larger organization of which they are a part."[21]

PROCEDURES FOR DEALING WITH CONFLICT

Conflict is not bad in itself. It can be part of a learning process.[22] Robbins argues that conflict is necessary for change and that change is necessary for an organization to adapt and survive in a dynamic environment.[23] Conflict is bad when it is caused by forces within the organization that could be eliminated with a better organizational design. Kraus has argued that hierarchy is the major structural variable that reinforces competition and that individuals would be committed to more important goals if the competitive process were not so firmly entrenched.[24] In this section, we will examine how hierarchical organizations deal with conflict by repressing or resolving it and then how collaborative organizations preclude conflict.

Repressing Conflict

Repression is probably the worst way to deal with conflict. Nothing is solved. The morale of the organization deteriorates, and the conflict emerges elsewhere in different forms. Individuals will meet their needs off the job so that the organization will not receive their best efforts.

Miles has identified five commonly used methods for repressing conflict in an organization.[25] These methods are as follows:

1. Take no action. This approach will probably escalate conflict.

2. Practice administrative orbiting, which consists of keeping appeals for change "under consideration," during which time protagonists lose interest or go elsewhere, documents get lost, or key decision makers take vacations.

3. Use due-process nonaction, which is similar to orbiting, but it uses a formalized, extensive procedure for redressing grievances. This process is slow, costly, and risky. It is risky because it will probably escalate conflict.

4. Maintain secrecy regarding the features of operation that may elicit complaint. Secrecy enables preemptive moves that cannot be countered by opponents because they cannot be anticipated.

5. Law and order may be invoked by suppressing conflict with force.

Resolving Conflict

A variety of strategies exist for resolving intergroup conflicts. Neilsen arrays seven strategies along a continuum from behavioral solutions to attitudinal change solutions.[26] These strategies are as follows:

Behavioral Solutions

1. Separate the groups physically, reducing conflict by reducing the opportunity to interact.

2. Allow interaction on issues where superordinate goals prevail and decision-making rules have been agreed to beforehand.

3. Keep groups separated but use as integrators individuals who are seen by both groups as justifying high status for the job, possessing personal attributes consistent with both groups' ideals, and having the expertise necessary for understanding each group's problems.

4. Hold direct negotiations between representatives from each group on all conflictful issues, in the presence of individuals who are seen as neutral to the conflict and who have personal attributes and expertise valued by both groups.

5. Hold direct negotiations between representatives from each group without third-party consultants present.

6. Exchange some group personnel for varying periods of time, so that contrasting perceptions and the rationales for them are clarified through day-to-day interaction and increased familiarity with the other group's activities, and then attempt direct negotiations after returning members have reported to their groups.

Attitudinal Change Solution

7. Require intense interaction between the conflicting groups under conditions where each group's failure to cooperate is more costly to itself than continuing to fight, regardless of how the other group behaves.

Collaborative Designs

Kraus concludes that the behavioral science literature specifies three strategies for resolving conflict: win-lose, negotiation, and problem-solving. He notes further that the literature suggests that the conflict should be analyzed and the appropriate conflict strategy applied. He concludes that competition is such a pervasive force in organizations that the most logical strategy is win-lose strategy or perhaps a negotiated settlement.[27] Conflict, according to Kraus, is a learning process only to the extent that one must learn how to use the competitive process to cope with the organization. To exist within the organization, the individual must learn to play the organizational game.[28]

The human relations movement, as reflected in the Hawthorne studies, attempted to deal with power and control, but, according to Kraus, it failed because it did not deal with competition and hierarchy.[29] He concluded that the only suitable way to deal with competition is to move from hierarchical organizational designs to collaborative designs.

Collaboration Defined. "Collaboration is a cooperative venture based on shared power and authority. It is nonhierarchical in nature. It assumes power based on a knowledge or expertise as opposed to power based on role or role function. It utilizes Theory Y assumptions about people."[30] The collaborative process is based on the concept of pluralism, which recognizes that many solutions are acceptable and that there is no one "right solution."

Collaborative Value Systems. Kraus has identified clusters of values that are characteristic of collaborative organizations.[31] Some of these values are as follows:

1. Trust, openness, honesty, and personal growth.

2. Self-actualization, which is necessary for an individual's psychological survival. This means being excited about who one is, what one is, and what one can still become. Feeling good about others begins with feeling good about oneself.

3. Capacity for joy and affective functioning. The ability and desire to experience pure delight. The excitement of accomplishment. The joy of interdependence rather than the pride of independence.

4. Responsibility and dependability. These values are commitments to others as a part of oneself. These values quietly state that, "You can count on me and I can count on you." While individuals are committed to each other, they remain responsible to themselves.

5. Cooperation is the process of muting the boundaries to better mesh them for a larger objective. (Cooperation is a less drastic state than compromise.)

6. Psychic energy is generated by open-endedness.

7. Synergy is the seeking of the next higher level of interaction in analysis or process.

8. Homonomy is the belief in the larger or collective community. It recognizes that the boundaries of the individual and the system are intertwined and permeable.

Kraus concludes that, ". . . the role of the organization must become more consistent with who people are. If people are to change organizations, then they must be willing to look at who they are and who they wish to become."[32]

Characteristics of Collaborative Organizations.   Throughout Kraus's analysis, he identifies many characteristics of collaborative organizations, such as the following: focus less on roles and more on functions, Theory Y assumptions, shared power and responsibility, individual control over immediate work environment, no differences in authority (i.e., no hierarchy), permeable boundaries, interdependence, dispersed rewards (there is enough to go around), clear operational criteria, jointly defined objectives, rewards for skills and knowledge (rather than for making a superior look good), friendliness, and effective communication.[33] While these characteristics may seem highly idealistic, it should be noted that many of these concepts are discussed in operational terms in this textbook and are being applied by some sales managers.

Two Examples. Kraus provides several examples of cases where structural changes in organizations resulted in more collaboration. Two examples that are appropriate for this textbook occurred in an insurance company.

For years there had been a struggle between the underwriting department and the agency department. The agency department had the objective of increasing sales volume, while the underwriting department was responsible for producing an underwriting profit. The agency department would try to please the agents, while the underwriting department was concerned only with selecting that business that would produce a profit. There were conflicts on agency appointments, commission rates, refusing renewals, and payment of losses. Jealousy and political maneuvering abounded as the vice presidents of these divisions competed for the president's favor. The conflicts were eliminated when both departments were put under one leader and jobs were redefined so that everyone shared the same goal—profitable growth.

In the same insurance company, the administration department had many conflicts with other departments as it executed its responsibilities for policy processing, premium collection, and clerical services in the field offices. These administrators were perceived as the persons who said "no" because they were in charge of budgets. The forty-year struggle was eliminated by a structural change. These administrative functions were transferred to the new agency-underwriting department along with appropriate personnel. Being on the same team, common leadership, and common objectives transformed strife into cooperation.[34]

Difficulty in Implementing Collaborative Concepts. The task of transforming a competitive, hierarchical organization into a collaborative organization is overwhelming, given the vested interests of those in the hierarchical organizations who do not want to yield power and the related rewards. This task may appear both challenging and overwhelming. The rewards are great, including the survival of some organizations that need to adapt to the dynamics of their environment or die.

Kraus notes that the Corporate Responsibility Planning Service identified ten changes in employee-employer relationships that will occur as a result of changes in cultural values. These changes are consistent with the shift from hierarchical to collaborative organization, and they are consistent with many of the newer sales management practices that are discussed in this text. For these reasons, they are summarized as follows:

Shift 1:   Job Fit
Employers will have to make a much greater effort to ensure the optimum match of employees and job.

Shift 2:   Personal Development
Recognizing a generally greater value placed by employees on personal growth and expansion, employers will have to provide comprehensive, ongoing management and organizational development activities, not all of which will be limited to job-related skills.

Shift 3:   Nonfinancial Compensation
While direct financial compensation will probably never be completely supplanted, there will be less emphasis placed on it, especially as personal income taxes rise.

Shift 4:   Decreasing Importance of Academic Credentials
While the overall value of academic attainment will remain high, the degree to which employees are required to have academic credentials to qualify for positions will be reduced.

Shift 5:   Employee Involvement in Decision Making
Employees at all levels will have a greater role in decision making and overall governance.

Shift 6:   Employee Counseling
Prominent among the shifts away from the traditional approach to human resource management, is the trend toward greater corporate involvement with the personal lives of employees and their problems.

Shift 7:   Input to Job Transfers and Assignments
Increasingly, employees will have the right to refuse transfers and job assignments without negatively affecting their career standing.

Shift 8:   Blurred Job Distinctions
As the national workforce becomes increasingly service oriented (education, government, insurance, leisure, banking, retail, etc.), the distinction between white and blue collar, and professional and nonprofessional, will blur.

Shift 9:   Employee Rights
The Constitution's Bill of Rights, the protection of which citizens enjoy, will become a source of protection for employees.

Shift 10:   Employee Ownership
Employee ownership of corporations through pension funds and stock ownership will increase.[35]

SUMMARY

Directing sales representatives through the activities of delegating, co-ordinating, and managing change begins with an understanding of the representative's individual needs. Delegating assigns responsibility and limited authority to a subordinate for the completion of an activity, and holds the subordinate accountable for results. Coordinating assures that all representatives are pulling toward a common goal. The dynamics of the marketplace provide the sales manager the opportunity to practice managing change. To manage change, the sales manager must be open-minded regarding creativity and innovation. Conflict may result in a sales organization because of failures in delegating, coordinating, and managing change. Conflict is also the by-product of a creative and innovative organization. Thus a sales district with no conflict is a sales district that probably lacks the outward stimulation of creative thinking.

Organizational theorists have concluded that conflict may be inherent in hierarchical structures that reinforce competitive behavior that is encouraged by American culture, especially the school systems. A wide range of strategies are used in hierarchical organizations to repress and to resolve conflict. Kraus argues that these strategies do not provide a complete solution to conflict. He proposes using collaborative structures instead of hierarchical ones. A sales manager who works with a representative in developing objectives and counseling is using a collaborative organizational design.

ASSIGNMENTS/DISCUSSION QUESTIONS

1. How would you introduce the following changes?
   a. An increase in a commission rate that is accompanied by the requirement that a representative pay his or her own expenses.
   b. A reduction in territory size.
   c. A report form that requires more competitive information.
   d. The reorganization of the sales force from geographic territories to territories by end-use specialization.
   e. The transfer of an account from a territory to a national account manager.
2. Discuss the circumstances under which a manager (a) may allow a representative to fail at a delegated task, and (b) would not allow failure but would rescue the situation.

3. Select a product and list the departments of a company whose efforts are required to coordinate successfully the field sales staff during the introduction of a new product.

4. Discuss how each of the five basic needs of the representatives (defined in Open Management System in Chapter 11) can be satisfied by the successful team-building efforts of a field sales manager within a district.

5. If change is defined as "a shift from the familiar," identify the business experiences a sales representative may encounter that represent a change, and which require the support of the field sales manager.

6. What personal experiences may a sales representative experience that will impact adversely on job performance and require the support of the sales manager?

7. Why is change resisted?

8. What is the role of the sales manager during the process of change?

CASE 12.1:
A-1 Electronics Company

A-1 Electronics Company sales have mushroomed along with the industry from $12 million to $122 million in five years. While their distribution policy includes selling their products direct to major users, they also sell through selected distributors. The Western Sales Region comprises the eleven western states with Frank Sommers, the Regional Manager, headquartered in San Francisco. He now supervises the activities of seven representatives living in Seattle, Denver, Los Angeles, San Francisco, and Salt Lake City, having adding the last three—including a second in Los Angeles—in the past year. Frank personally calls on a limited number of major accounts in the Silicon Valley area south of San Francisco, having given up the major part of his territory to the new representative in San Francisco. The addition of the new territories reduced the amount of travel for almost everyone in the region; at the same time, it intensified the coverage.

For Frank Sommers, the additions expanded his management activities, for which he had limited background and very little training. He joined A-1 Electronics as a salesman in Los Angeles seven years ago, at which time the company had two representatives covering the entire region, plus the regional sales manager who worked a full territory. The company recently hired a sales training manager who is concentrating his efforts initially on the training of sales representatives.

Frank was a hard worker and expected a similar dedication from his people. He liked selling and spent much time in the field, somewhat to the detriment of his management responsibilities. When needled a bit on the subject by his boss, the V-P of Sales, Frank pointed to the sales figures for his region that, eight months into the fiscal year, were running at 132 percent of forecast. However, Frank was aware of some of his shortcomings and knew he had to begin doing something about them and soon, but he wasn't sure where to start. The problem was that whenever he wanted to set some time aside to approach the problem, some sales crisis demanded his attention, or it was time to work with the representative, or call on his headquarters accounts. And riding herd on the new sales representatives took more time than he expected because he "wanted to be sure they developed good working habits."

Then there was the problem he was having with Sue Harding and Chuck Taylor, who worked territories out of Denver and Seattle. As Frank described it: "Both of them are excellent producers with increases way ahead of the region, but they give me my biggest problem: I never hear from them. I can't be running off to those places because I have my own major accounts to cover and these new reps to keep an eye on, but you'd think they'd get in touch with me, at least periodically. They phone or write only in an emergency, when they have some kind of critical problem, or in answer to my requests. While I don't like this situation, it's not all bad because I don't want my people calling me or writing for instructions about every problem they encounter. I don't have time for that, and I'd have to spend all my time in the office. I prefer my people to be independent and self-reliant. However, these two have gone to extremes. I realize that's the way they grew up in the field. Out there, all alone, when we didn't have the staff we've got today, they had to solve their own problems. But times have changed, and anyway, they've gone to extremes. I've toyed with the idea of ordering them to send me reports, but that doesn't strike me as the right way, and anyway I'd have to reply to them. I'm really not sure how to proceed."

CASE QUESTIONS

1. What is the problem?
2. Is the apparent problem symptomatic of a more important problem(s)? If so, what are they?
3. What types of communications problems are evidenced?

4. Whose responsibility is it to maintain active communications—the representative's or the manager's?

5. What is the underlying cause of the communications problem?

6. Specifically, which management functions and activities does Frank Sommers need to improve?

7. How could Frank Sommers coordinate the efforts of Sue Harding and Chuck Taylor with the other sales reps in the region?

REFERENCES

1. S. X. Doyle and B. P. Shapiro, "What Counts Most in Motivating Your Sales Force?" *Harvard Business Review* (May–June 1980): 136.
2. Ibid.
3. This discussion follows that of "Managing Change—Without Pain," *RIA Marketing Alert: Special Analysis* (January 7, 1981).
4. E. Guthrie and W. S. Miller, *Making Change* (Minneapolis, Minn.: Interpersonal Communication Programs, Inc., 1978), p. 147.
5. R. Likert and J. G. Likert, *New Ways of Managing Conflict* (New York: McGraw-Hill, 1976), p. 7.
6. Ibid., p. 8.
7. A. C. Filley, *Interpersonal Conflict Resolution* (Glenview, Ill.: Scott, Foresman and Co., 1975), p. 53.
8. Likert and Likert, *New Ways of Managing Conflict,* pp. 91–93.
9. W. A. Kraus, *Collaboration in Organizations: Alternatives to Hierarchy* (New York: Human Sciences Press, 1980), p. 42.
10. Ibid., p. 99.
11. Ibid., pp. 95–97.
12. Ibid., p. 96.
13. Ibid., pp. 98–100.
14. V. A. Thompson, *Modern Organization* (New York: Alfred A. Knopf, 1961), pp. 109–110.
15. Ibid., p. 79.
16. Ibid., p. 88.
17. Ibid., p. 89.
18. Ibid., p. 93.
19. Ibid.
20. Ibid., pp. 93–94.
21. Kraus, *Collaboration in Organizations,* p. 161.
22. Ibid., p. 43.
23. S. P. Robbins, *Managing Organizational Conflict: A Nontraditional Approach* (Englewood Cliffs, N.J.: Prentice-Hall, Inc., 1974), p. 112.
24. Kraus, *Collaboration in Organizations,* pp. 42, 87.
25. R. H. Miles, *Macro Organizational Behavior* (Santa Monica, Calif.: Goodyear Publishing Co., Inc., 1980), p. 125.
26. E. H. Neilsen, "Understanding and Managing Intergroup Conflict," (Boston, MA: Intercollegiate Case Clearing House, 9-471-059, 1972), p. 6.
27. Kraus, *Collaboration in Organizations,* p. 43.
28. Ibid., p. 44.
29. Ibid., p. 41.

30. Ibid., p. 19.
31. Ibid., pp. 120–126.
32. Ibid., p. 127.
33. Ibid., pp. 163–190.
34. Ibid., pp. 216–218.
35. Stakeholder Issues & Strategies, *Ten Shifts in the Employee/Employer Relationship* (Philadelphia: Human Resources Network, 1976); quoted in W. A. Kraus, *Collaboration in Organizations: Alternatives to Hierarchy* (New York: Human Sciences Press, 1980), pp. 245–246.

SUGGESTED READINGS

Filley, A. C., *Interpersonal Conflict Resolution* (Glenview, Ill.: Scott, Foresman and Co., 1975).

Pondy, L. R., "Organizational Conflict: Concepts and Models," *Administrative Science Quarterly* 12, no. 2 (September 1967): 296–320.

13

CONTROLLING THROUGH APPRAISING, COACHING, COUNSELING, AND CORRECTING

INTRODUCTION

CRUCIAL DEFINITIONS

Controlling ensures progress toward the objectives of the organization according to its plan. Controlling requires the comparison of the performance of individuals with mutually agreed upon standards to accomplish specific goals. This comparison of individual performance against performance standards is known as *appraising*. Negative deviations from standards will require coaching, counseling, and correcting the behavior of sales representatives. Positive deviations from performance standards will trigger reward mechanisms, such as a memo of congratulations, a salary increase, or a promotion. Appraising also provides an opportunity for the development and growth of the representative.

Coaching consists of those managerial activities for developing the skills of a representative. These skills are generally those found in the selling process. The coaching sequence that is used by a sales manager is the same as that sequence used by any athletic coach—observe them, show them, let them try it, and provide feedback.

Counseling consists of working with the representatives to develop an agreed upon plan for the improvement or maintenance of current levels of performance. It is important to note that counseling is the giving of advice after mutual deliberation. It is not a one-way communication where the sales manager is playing God. There must be mutual agreement between the representative and the manager regarding the goals, the measurement of performance, and the development of rewards that are consistent with the individual's need for money, promotion, recognition, assurance, positive reinforcement, job enrichment, and vertical loading. Such mutual deliberations have been a part of the counseling programs of many sales managers, but they will become more common as companies adopt newer management styles that are emerging under various names such as open management, quality circles, and "Z" management styles.[1] Thus the representative has an active role in establishing the level of performance that is required, scheduling activities, establishing budgets, and identifying penalties for noncompliance with the plan.

Correcting may be automatic and instantaneous if the representative and the manager have spent sufficient time in getting consensus. A well-designed control system will allow the representative to make self-appraisals that will lead to self-corrections. Call reports, expense accounts, quotas, computerized sales analyses, and commission compensation plans all provide the representative with a means for personal self-evaluation and correction. These automatic supervisors also save the time of field sales managers.

The combined activities of appraising, counseling, and rewarding are frequently referred to in the literature and in business as the *performance appraisal* or *performance review*. A performance review is usually held annually or semi-annually and is a formal procedure. Another type of field sales performance review, which is less formal and used by many companies, is the trip report or field report. This is carried out by a field sales manager with the representative, usually after each working visit with the representative, which might be every two or three months. The review usually covers the business activities conducted during the visit, progress toward specific sales objectives, deficiency improvement, and/or growth objectives.

The review will cover some major area of the sales representative's responsibilities, as defined in the job description. On subsequent working trips, the sales manager will try ultimately to cover all major areas of the job description, as well as all major areas of the sales representative's territory. The evaluation will be based on performance standards, which are statements describing a specific degree of measurability of critical results that signify effective completion of a task.

The most informal and most frequent coaching or counseling session is the "curbstone conference," which may be held on the sidewalk, over coffee, or in the car. It is held for varying periods of time, perhaps several times each day following a sales call or suitable break, to discuss some aspect of the call that needs review. During the conversation, the sales manager could say something like this: "Joe, I noticed on the last several calls that each time you mentioned the price of our product, the customer objected to the amount of money he'd have to invest, etc. Let's talk about that. Why would that have triggered that reaction when you didn't get the same reaction this morning? Do you remember phrasing it differently then? Let's role-play that sequence for a minute before we make the next call you have scheduled."

OBJECTIVES OF CONTROL SYSTEMS

The objectives of a control system include the objectives of training—improving knowledge, attitudes, skills, and habits—because controlling is a form of training. Controlling, however, has the additional dimensions of rewarding positive behavior, correcting negative behavior, and maintaining improved performance. Because training is built upon a job description, hiring, and selection procedures, we may say also that appraising, counseling, coaching, and correcting are extensions of these earlier steps in sales management. Controlling also provides an opportunity to put motivation concepts into action. Hence, the ease or difficulty with which the sales force can be controlled depends on all of the earlier steps in sales management.

DIFFICULTIES IN APPRAISING

One of the difficulties of evaluating the performance of a sales representative is the fact that sales performance is determined by many variables that are not under his or her control. Ryans and Weinberg note that these variables include the environment, the company strategy and tactics, competition, territory characteristics, sales force policies and procedures, the field sales manager, and individual customer factors.[2] The relationships among these external forces appear as a flow diagram in Exhibit 13.1. Cravens, Woodruff, and Stamper suggest a model for the performance of a representative in a specific territory.[3] These authors consider variables such as market potential, territory workload, company effort in a territory, company penetration and reputation, and sales person characteristics such as past experience, training, and effort. This model is summarized in Exhibit 13.2. These authors used multiple regression to test the model for a specific company to illustrate that such analytical techniques could be used for evaluating a representative's performance.

Exhibit 13.1   A General Model of Sales Force Performance

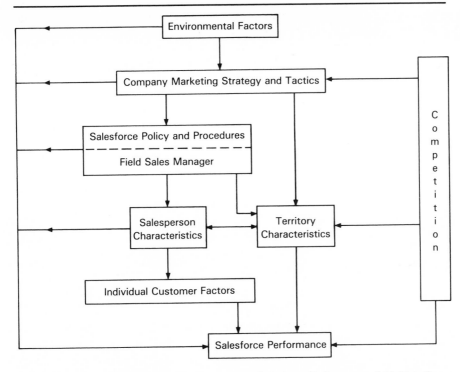

A. B. Ryans and C. B. Weinberg, "Determinants of Salesforce Performance: A Multiple Company Study," in *Sales Management: New Developments from Behavioral and Decision Model Research,* ed. R. P. Bagozzi (Cambridge, Mass.: Marketing Science Institute, 1979), p. 95.

A second major problem in appraising performance is the measurement of the representative's performance. Many performance measures are subjective because they measure behavior, not sales results. To measure this behavior, it must be observable. These subjective measures can become a basis for controversy between the sales manager and the representative, so that extensive negotiation and consensus are necessary on how crucial forms of behavior will be observed and evaluated.

Objective and subjective measures may be interrelated. For example, cancelled orders, lost accounts, slow pay, low reorders, and complaints may be measured objectively, but they may reflect a subjective behavioral trait—the representative tends to oversell accounts.

Exhibit 13.2   Conceptual Model of Determinants of Sales Territory Performance

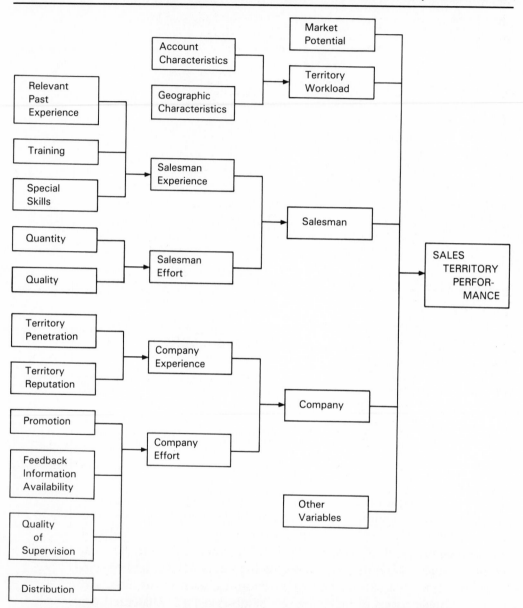

D. W. Cravens, R. B. Woodruff, and J. C. Stamper, "An Analytical Approach for Evaluating Sales Territory Performance," *Journal of Marketing* 36 (January 1972): 32. Published by the American Marketing Association.

In summary, appraising systems must focus on those determinants of sales performance that can be controlled by the representative. When the manager and representative have agreed on these variables, they must agree next on how they will be observed and measured.

ASKING THE BASIC QUESTIONS

The development of a control system, like the development of a training program, consists of answering a series of questions. Why is control necessary? How should this control be accomplished? When should it take place? What is the goal of counseling or coaching? How long should counseling or coaching take? How many levels of management participate? Where does it take place? What are the instruments for evaluation? And, ideally, who develops the instruments and standards? Each of these questions may be answered at varying levels of formality. Exhibit 13.3 summarizes possible answers to these questions at different levels of formality. For example, informal procedures may be used to solve immediate problems, while formal procedures are used to solve long-term problems and to present new objectives, strategies, or sales plans. These sessions may take place in the field, in the regional office, or in the home office, and they may last anywhere from five minutes to six hours. A counseling session may have as its goal correcting an immediate problem or setting objectives for the coming year. The final objective of a counseling session is a set of agreed upon steps to improve performance.

APPRAISAL

ESTABLISHING PERFORMANCE STANDARDS

Ideally, the development of performance standards will be negotiated between the representative and the first-line field sales manager, with the approval of the second-line field sales manager. The general sales manager will usually exert minimal control over these performance standards for the representative. The general sales manager, however, will work with the field sales managers in developing their performance standards. In many cases, each successive lower level of control will adapt a superior's performance standard to its own situation.

The performance standards are an extension of the job description, so if the job description is inadequate, it will not be possible to develop

Exhibit 13.3 Evaluation, Counseling, and Coaching Basic Questions

QUESTIONS	DEGREE OF FORMALITY		
Questions	**Informal**	**Semi-Formal**	**Formal**
Why is control necessary?	To confirm progress toward objective.	To adjust plans or revise objectives.	To solve long-term problems, tap opportunities, and present new objectives, strategies, or plans.
Why is counseling necessary?	To solve immediate problems.	To clarify the sales objectives and selling plan; develop skills.	To solve long-term problems and to present new objectives, strategies, or plans. During the Annual Performance Appraisal.
How should this control be accomplished?	Daily or periodic contact.	"Curbside" coaching and counseling.	
When should it take place?	After a substantial deviation from a standard. Correct an immediate problem.	After a short trend away from a standard. Improve performance in the immediate future.	After repeated trends away from a standard. Set objectives and improve next year's performance.
What is the goal of the counseling or coaching?	Five to fifteen minutes.	Fifteen to sixty minutes.	One to six hours.
How long should counseling or coaching take?			
How many levels of management participate?	First-line sales management.	First and second levels of management.	All levels of sales management.
Where does it take place?	In the field.	In the regional office.	Regional office or home office.
What are the instruments for evaluation?	Personal observation.	Performance standards and observations.	Performance standards.
Ideally, *who* develops instruments and standards?	Field Sales Manager uses company instruments and standards.	Field Sales Managers use company instruments and standards, but make recommendations for change.	General sales management with input from representatives and all levels of management develops instruments and standards.

clear performance standards. These standards must be based also on hiring criteria. Failure to link performance standards to job descriptions and hiring criteria is not only poor management, it may also be illegal under federal regulations regarding equal employment opportunities. In the case of the Albermarle Paper Company versus Moody, the U.S. Supreme Court concluded that "There is no way of knowing precisely what criteria of job performance the supervisors were considering; whether each of the supervisors was considering the same criteria—or whether indeed any of the supervisors actually applied a focused and stable body of criteria of any kind."[4] In ruling against the Union Carbide Corporation, the Fifth Circuit Court of Appeals concluded that the company failed to demonstrate that its evaluation procedures were substantially related to the particular job for which the individual was being evaluated, and that a high level of subjectivity resulted in promotional decisions that were based on conscious or unconscious prejudice.[5] Thus the Equal Employment Opportunity Commission focused first on hiring and selection procedures and has now moved to evaluation and promotion procedures.

The development of performance standards for representatives will generally be done with the assistance of the company's personnel department, and, perhaps, outside consultants, so that we need not go into further detail at this point. It is desirable, however, to see examples of the objective and subjective measures that have been developed by companies for their appraisal systems.

OBJECTIVE MEASURES

Data Generated by Representatives

The sales representative generates considerable information that can be used for controlling. Itineraries, orders, call reports, and expense reports all provide a basis for evaluation. The objectivity of these reports, however, can be questioned. The incentive for falsifying reports can be strong if too much weight is placed on data generated by the representative. Furthermore, only about 50 percent of companies use representatives' call reports in any way.[6] Believing that reports are unnecessary paper work, many representatives fail to submit them or do a superficial job.

Computer developments have simplified call reporting and improved techniques for analyzing sales representatives' activities. Exhibit 13.4 shows the Burroughs Wellcome Company computerized card that

Exhibit 13.4   The Burroughs Wellcome Computerized Call Card

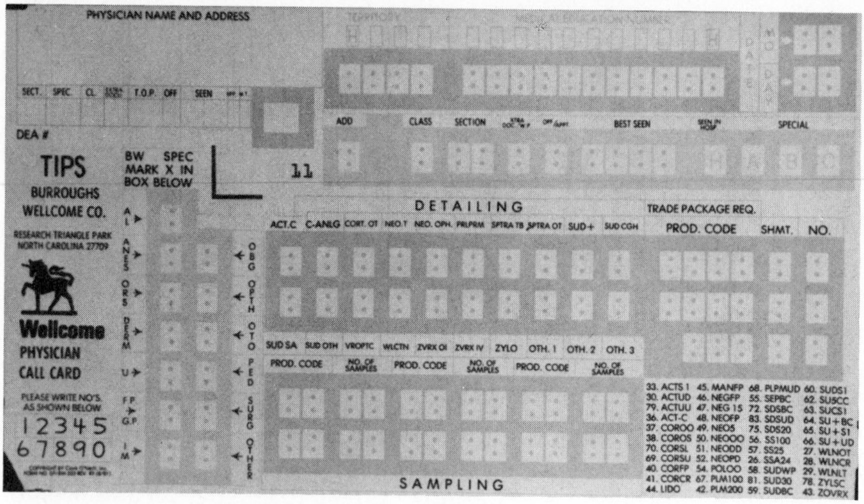

Used by permission of Burroughs Wellcome Company.

is prepared for each call the representative makes on a physician. Analysis of these call records and reports enables the company to determine if the representatives are following the sales plan.

Income and Productivity Statements

In Chapter 5 we saw how the representative may run his or her territory using territory income statements and productivity statements. These statements may be used also as a self-controlling device where the representative establishes detailed objectives for the coming year. Exhibit 13.5 illustrates this point by showing a representative's prospecting data for last period, the present period, and the objectives for the coming period.

The district manager may control the entire territory with a comparative statement in which there is a column for each representative. A comparative income statement appears as Exhibit 13.6. Such a statement can be an excellent tool for counseling sessions because it highlights the strengths and weaknesses of each representative in comparison with others in the district. The addition of a column for corporate averages would permit the evaluation of a representative against a national average.

Exhibit 13.5 Representative's Personal Plan

	LAST PERIOD		PRESENT PERIOD			NEXT PERIOD	
	AMOUNT	PERCENT	PERCENT	AMOUNT		PERCENT	AMOUNT
NUMBER OF ACCTS. JAN. 1	101			95			107
ACCTS. LOST DURING YEAR	10			5			7
ADDITIONS BY PROSPECTING							
PROSPECT LIST	400			500			400
QUALIFIED	80						
%QUALIFIED		20	[35]	175		35	140
NEEDS SURVEY	50						
SURVEY/QUALIFIED %		63	63	109		63	88
DEMONSTRATIONS	25						
DEMO/SURVEY %		50	[68]	74		[75]	66
PROPOSALS	19						
PROPOSAL/DEMO %		76	76	57		[85]	56
CLOSES	4						
CLOSES/PROPOSAL %		21	[30]	17		[35]	20
NUMBER OF ACCOUNTS DEC. 31	95			107			120
PERCENT CHANGE		-6	13			12	
SALES /ACCOUNT	21.05			[22.50]			22.50
ACCOUNT CHANGE	-6			12			13
SALES FROM PROSP .($000)				269			282
SALES ($000)	2000			2407			2689
QUOTA ($000)	2100			2400			2500
PERCENT OF QUOTA	95			100			108

EFFECT OF PLANS ON REP.'S COMPENSATION:	BASE	RATE	($000)	BASE	RATE	($000)
SALARY($000)			10.00			10.00
COMMISSION:						
1% FOR $1000-1999	1000	1	10.00	1000	1	10.00
2% FOR $2000 OR +	407	2	8.13	689	2	13.79
$100/NEW ACCOUNT	12	.1	1.20	13	.1	1.25
TOTAL COMPENSATION($000)			29.33			35.04

COMMISSION RATES

BASE	%RATE	BASE	%RATE
-2000	0	-2000	0
0	1	0	2
999	1	999	2
2500	1	2000	2

NEW ACCTS BONUS ($000)

-50	0
1	.1
50	.1

Note: [ ] = those areas where representative has improved or plans to improve.

Exhibit 13.6   District Comparative Income Statement for 1982

	E. MARTIN		J. TAYLOR		W. JONES	
	$000	%	$000	%	$000	%
SALES	2200	100	2500	100	2000	100
ACCT-PRODUCT CONTB.	479	21.77	613	24.52	457	22.87
ACCT. COSTS						
FREIGHT	63	2.86	65	2.60	60	3.02
INVENTORY	44	2.00	30	1.20	39	1.97
ACCTS.RECEIVABLE	64	2.91	75	3.00	59	2.97
TECH. SERVICES	18	0.82	18	0.72	17	0.87
ADV. & PROM.	21	0.95	35	1.40	17	0.83
TOTAL CUSTOMER COSTS	210	9.55	223	8.92	193	9.65
PERSONAL SELLING COSTS						
COMPENSATION	31.50	1.43	33.00	1.32	29.90	1.50
TRANSPORTATION	6.00	0.27	5.00	0.20	7.00	0.35
LODGING & MEALS	3.50	0.16	3.50	0.14	4.00	0.20
TELEPHONE	1.35	0.06	1.70	0.07	1.20	0.06
ENTERTAINMENT	3.00	0.14	1.00	0.04	2.50	0.13
SAMPLES & LITERATURE	2.00	0.09	2.00	0.08	1.50	0.08
MISC.	0.50	0.02	0.50	0.02	0.30	0.02
TOTAL PERS. SELLING CST	47.85	2.18	46.70	1.87	46.40	2.32
NET TERRITORY CONTRIB($000)	221.15	10.05	343.30	13.73	217.82	10.89
RETURN ON ASSETS MANAGED:						
TERRITORY ASSETS ($000)	800		890		775	
ASSET TURNOVER(SALES/ASSTS)	2.75		2.81		2.58	
ADD: INTEREST INV.		2.00		1.20		1.97
INTEREST A/R		2.91		3.00		2.97
TOTAL CONTRIBUTION PERCENT		14.96		17.93		15.83
RETURN ON ASSETS MANAGED		41.14		50.37		40.85
(% CONTRIB. X TURNOVER)						

Home Office Computer Reports

Many companies provide representatives with computerized statistical summaries of their performance. Exhibit 13.7 illustrates product sales by territory, the nation, the targeted product mix, and whether the territory and national sales were over or under the target product percentage. Exhibit 13.8 summarizes the travel expenses for a specific employee first on a monthly basis and then year-to-date. The needs of each company will vary; therefore these forms are simply illustrative and cannot be regarded as standard.

A lumber company supplied each representative with a printout of monthly sales and profit margins for the entire sales force. This common knowledge stimulated representatives not only to increase their sales, but to sell profitable items.

Exhibit 13.7 Territory Sales Report Tredwell-Shoe Company
Product Profile Report by Territory as of 11/30/79

	TERRITORY SALES AMOUNT	YTD SALES %	NATIONAL SALES AMOUNT	YTD SALES %	PRODUCT TARGET %	OVER/UNDER TARGET % TERR	NATIONAL
John B. Knight							
Women's Shoes	$145,983	43.6	$9,514,027	44.3	39.1	4.5	5.2
Men's Shoes	60,521	18.1	3,601,649	16.8	16.7	1.4	.1
Nurses' Shoes	683	.2	664,615	3.1	3.2	3.0 −	.1 −
Sporting Shoes	63,319	18.9	3,180,608	14.8	20.3	1.4 −	5.5 −
Children's Shoes	51,674	15.4	3,729,668	17.4	16.3	.9 −	1.1
All Other	12,595	3.8	783,825	3.7	4.4	.6 −	.7 −
Total	334,777		21,474,396				

Exhibit 13.8 Travel Expense Report Tredwell-Shoe Company

	CURRENT MONTHS					YEAR TO DATE				
	Miles Days	Amount	Per Mile Days	Region High	Low	Miles Days	Amount	Per Mile Days	Region High	Low
John B. Knight										
Travel	1,675	381	.22	493	77	4,379	1,430	.32	2,055	297
Living	5	222	44.40	402	44	16	773	48.32	1,908	241
Public Transportation										
Entertainment		39		449	3		70		1,202	3
Miscellaneous		74					239			
Totals		714					2,512			
Annual Budget							1,200			
Under/Over							4,688			
%.Y.T.D. Expense To Budget						35%				

In addition to the objective measures that appear in these forms, some companies have additional measures, such as the number of customer complaints, the implementation of promotional programs, sales forecasting accuracy, the number of competitive investigations, and the number of sales candidates who were recruited.

SUBJECTIVE MEASURES

Objective measures tend to be the outcome of representatives' behavior on the job. To evaluate the representative fully, it is necessary to observe and measure those behaviors that reflect skills in selling, problem solving, decision making, and communicating. Developing appraisal forms is an important step in sales management that is shared with persons from the personnel department and external consultants.

Developing Appraisal Forms

Appraisal forms must have three important characteristics. First, they must be relevant to the job being evaluated. Second, they must be valid; that is, they must truly measure the characteristic they purport to measure. Third, they must be reliable; that is, they must give consistent results over time and among raters. Appraisal techniques that are used frequently are the essay, graphic rating scales, critical incident appraisal, management-by-objectives, work-standards approach, ranking methods, and assessment centers.[7] Each of these techniques has its strengths and weaknesses, so many evaluation schemes use a combination of them. Several of the techniques that are frequently used in sales management will be illustrated briefly.

Essay Appraisals

The essay appraisal requires the manager to describe the main assignments of the representative and the results of his or her effort during the period covered by the evaluation. This description should cover strengths, weaknesses, and a program for improvement. While the essay method is highly personalized, it is difficult to compare and combine the evaluations of separate reviewers. An example of how an essay should and should not be written appears in Exhibit 13.9.

Verbal and Numerical Scales (BARS)

Some scaling techniques use a combination of verbal cues and numerical scales that will provide more uniformity across raters. When the verbal cues describe desirable or undesirable behavior, they are known also as Behaviorally Anchored Rating Scales (BARS).[8] The development of verbal cues with numerical ratings has a long history in psychology and is known as *psychometrics*. The pioneering work in scaling verbal cues was done by L. L. Thurstone.[9] The procedure consists first of generating a large number of statements that describe various forms of behavior, in this case that of sales representatives. These statements are then grouped into homogeneous categories using knowledgeable judges, such as sales managers, and statistical techniques, such as factor analysis. The resulting scales may then be tested on a sample of representatives and sub-

---

Exhibit 13.9   Essay Appraisal

Assignment/Results
(Describe the main assignment of this representative and the results of his or her efforts during the evaluation period.)

Jill's major objectives this year were to gain 80 percent distribution in her fifteen major accounts, increase sales volume 7 percent, and develop her skills in overcoming objections. She increased her sales volume by 8 percent, so she met that goal, but she got product distribution through only nine major accounts for a 60-percent distribution rate. Her ability to overcome objections is still weak. This weakness contributes to the failure to sell major accounts.

Jill is enthusiastic about selling, but is slow to see the need for completing reports and requests for market information. She is eager to accept new responsibilities that are related to selling. For example, she volunteered to develop a sales presentation for a new product and to make a presentation at a district sales meeting. Her presentation was well received.

How *NOT* to Write an Essay Appraisal

Jill is an eager representative who is liked and respected by her peers and customers. She fits well into a variety of social situations, which will help her to sell the large accounts. She is quick-witted, learns rapidly, and listens carefully to advice. She is almost a workaholic and thrives on responsibility.

---

jected to further statistical tests for validation and reliability. The sales managers would generally have the assistance of staff persons and external consultants during the development of such scaling instruments. The scaling instrument that appears in Exhibit 13.10 uses verbal cues, numbers, and provides space for open-ended comments.

Relating Appraisals to Job Descriptions

The activities of the Equal Employment Opportunity Commission have drawn attention to the fact that many companies use one set of criteria to recruit and select candidates and a different set for performance appraisal. To prevent this inconsistency, Burroughs Wellcome, a pharmaceutical company, developed a form that combines the representative's position description, performance standards, and performance appraisal. This form appears as Exhibit 13.11. This combined form enables the applicant to see what is expected and how he or she will be evaluated if hired. This appraisal form uses verbal cues, numerical evaluations, and open-ended responses. It also makes provision for the representative, the district sales manager, and the regional sales manager to sign that they have read the evaluation. A second form is used to evaluate measurable sales results.

Exhibit 13.10 Verbal and Numerical Scales for Evaluating Representatives

Check the number on the scale that describes this representative's performance for each dimension. Comment or give examples to explain your ratings. Write "Did not observe" where this statement applies.

*Performance Dimensions**

Sales Ability—ability to utilize appropriate interpersonal styles and methods to gain agreement or acceptance from customer.

1. No selling style. Just presents facts.
2. Uses same style with all customers, rarely listens or reacts to customer comments, and fails to ask for agreement.
3. Varies style and methods, but is reluctant to ask for agreement or acceptance from customers of ideas or proposal.
4. Reasonably effective in utilizing appropriate interpersonal and closing skills, but is unable to deal with certain customer types.
5. Utilizes interpersonal skills very effectively through intelligence and perseverence to gain customer agreement.
6. Combines natural sociability, intelligence, and persistence in exceptionally effective manner to gain customer agreement.

Comment:_____

Oral Communication Skills—ability to effectively express ideas in individual or group situations, preplanned or impromptu.

1. Oral presentations disorganized and inaccurate, replete with bad grammar.
2. Knowledgeable, but easily distracted, nervous, and becomes flustered.
3. Speaks reasonably well; uncomfortable with high-level professionals or groups.
4. Effectively communicates with individuals or groups in impromptu selling situations, but less effective with preplanned group presentations or complex interactions.
5. Very effective in variety of professional settings and groups, but style lacks warmth and sociability.
6. Tailors presentations to circumstances, interacts very well with audience, and uses personality to communicate effectively.

Comment:_____

Motivation for Sales—the extent to which sales responsibilities and activities produce job-related personal satisfaction.

1. Rarely evidences interest in job activities, seems bored, very little reaction to successful or unsuccessful sales calls, conversation directed to leisure or hobbies.
2. Welcomes opportunities to communicate technically, but avoids closing or gaining customer agreement or acceptance; likes people.
3. Gains agreement and closes on small orders, but lacks confidence on larger orders.
4. Challenged by opportunity to persuade others to accept ideas or to provide information; reacts positively to success, but overly depressed by failures; takes failures personally.
5. Expresses sense of achievement in persuading or convincing others, enjoys recognition, not dejected by failures.
6. Eagerly seeks out challenging opportunities to persuade and convince others; enjoys the selling process and is very effective.

Comment: _____

(continued)

Exhibit 13.10 Continued

Resilience—ability to maintain effectiveness despite objections, disappointments, or variety of selling situations.
1. Lacks self-confidence in most selling situations.
2. Usually dejected by disappointments or turn-downs; accepts customer's point of view without rebuttal.
3. While not depressed by turn-downs, seems unable to respond with different arguments when faced with differing viewpoint.
4. In normal situations, enjoys customer interaction and opportunity to use different behavioral styles in varying situations; somewhat argumentative.
5. Has above-average ability to rebound from objectives, understand them, and respond with different arguments.
6. Has exceptional ability to respond agreeably with additional information in a wide variety of selling situations.
Comment:_____

Energy—ability to maintain high activity level for extended period of time while sustaining an effective performance level.
1. Starts late or quits early; call activities and effectiveness diminishes late in day and week.
2. Quality of performance diminishes, although satisfactory activity level maintained throughout day.
3. While satisfactory overall, activity and performance level fluctuates.
4. Paces self at moderate level throughout day.
5. Maintains a consistently above-average level of activity and performance.
6. Has exceptional energy level that is manifest in activity level for extended period while sustaining an effective performance level.
Comment:_____

Practical Learning—ability to assimilate and apply job-related information in the job environment.
1. Limited ability to acquire technical job-related information.
2. Reasonably able to assimilate job-related information, but inadequate understanding and ability to apply it on the job.
3. Has job-related technical knowledge and skills, but has difficulty applying them under stressful selling situations.
4. Has satisfactory technical knowledge and ability to apply this knowledge on the job.
5. Has above-average knowledge and applies it diligently on the job.
6. Has exceptional knowledge and skills, and applies them on the job in an outstanding manner in all situations.
Comment:_____

Self-Discipline—ability to work independent of close supervision to achieve objectives.
1. Fails to do what is required unless closely supervised.
2. Requires frequent supervisory prodding or encouragement.
3. Usually works efficiently without frequent supervisory attention if assignments progress without change, interruption, or obstacles.
4. Works persistently with little or no supervision even in the face of interruption or obstacles.

(continued)

Exhibit 13.10 Continued

5. High degree of initiative and independent activity even with complex projects.
6. Exceptional ability to initiate activities to achieve goals; self-starting rather than passive acceptance.

Comment:_____

Problem Solving—ability to identify causes and practical solutions, and to follow through to their resolution.

1. Usually blames competition or company; defensive; suggests impractical solutions or maintains problem is beyond control.
2. Foggy, hesitant, or reluctant reasoning; vacillates; avoids confrontation or negotiated settlements.
3. Able to identify and solve simple problems; has difficulty with complex issues; willing and cooperative if supervisory solutions are provided.
4. Identifies causes well, but has difficulty in creating alternative solutions.
5. Dependable in reasoning out causes and solutions, and persistently follows through to resolution.
6. Quickly and imaginatively analyzes problems and creates solutions, and frequently reports resolved problems to supervisor.

Comment:_____

Initiative—self-starting ability rather than passive acceptance; originates actions to influence events to achieve goals.

1. Waits to be told what to do; lacks imagination.
2. Wants to initiate action, but reluctant to take responsibility; will contact supervisor for instructions; has difficulty changing.
3. Tends to originate actions impulsively without obtaining all the facts or considering the consequences.
4. Originates actions or activities of lesser importance.
5. Dependably responds to unplanned occurrences without supervision; welcomes change and adapts quickly.
6. Anticipates or creates change to achieve goals.

Comment:_____

Tenacity—perseverence or persistence in staying with an action plan until objective is achieved or is no longer attainable.

1. Accepts disagreement or resistance without rebuttal or second efforts.
2. Refuses to accept opposing viewpoint or disagreement except after lengthy discussion; lacks judgment.
3. Persists until objective is achieved, but does so in an offending or annoying manner.
4. Usually can be counted on to stick with action plan.
5. Uses good judgment in being graciously and persuasively persistent.
6. Has ability to use a variety of behavioral styles and arguments to stay with action plan to achieve objective.

Comment:_____

Judgment—ability to make decisions based on logical assumptions and factual information.

1. Jumps to conclusion on basis of emotions or limited facts.
2. Reluctant to analyze facts before making a decision.

(continued)

Exhibit 13.10 Continued

3. Analyzes facts, but does not sort them logically.
4. Analyzes facts clearly and logically, but does not translate them into alternate courses of action.
5. Above-average ability to develop alternative courses of action.
6. Can be counted on to logically identify the long-term consequences of alternatives and to enthusiastically support those adopted.

Comment:_____

Adaptability/Flexibility—ability to maintain effectiveness in varying physical and interpersonal environments including varying tasks and varying responsibilities.

1. Unable to produce effectively in changing environment or with a changing customer mix.
2. Effective with limited number of tasks in stable environment, but refuses other assignments.
3. Performs effectively with identified tasks and responsibilities in stable environment, but requires significant training and counseling when changes occur.
4. Adapts easily and maintains effectiveness in changing environment, with changing tasks or responsibilities.
5. Welcomes changes and maintains effectiveness in changing environment, with changing tasks or responsibilities.
6. Highly adaptable and requires frequent changes to maintain interest and job effectiveness.

Comment:_____

Decisiveness—ability to readily make decisions, render judgments, take action, or commit oneself and accept accountability.

1. Reluctant to accept and commit to a single alternative; vacillates.
2. Avoids suggesting or supporting unpopular or controversial alternatives; passes the buck.
3. Avoids suggesting or supporting alternatives of major consequences; defers to others.
4. Willing to render judgment, make suggestions, and commit to agreed upon alternative.
5. Welcomes opportunity to suggest or support alternatives, and take a firm stand.
6. Seeks out opportunities to control the decision-making process, accepts accountability even in difficult situations.

Comment:_____

Integrity—ability to maintain social, ethical, and organizational norms in job-related activities.

1. Documented violation of expense or time reports.
2. Some tendency to hedge on expenses, reporting, time on territory, or travel.
3. Gives effort proportionate to income and minimum performance standards, rarely more.
4. Cooperatively supports company policies, procedures, and programs, as well as personal time and effort.
5. Suggests ways to improve policies related to corporate integrity.
6. Maintains highest social, ethical, and organizational norms.

Comment:_____

(continued)

Exhibit 13.10   Continued

Work Standards—ability to set own high goals and standards of performance for work activities.
1. Does little or nothing to correct unsatisfactory performance level.
2. Aspires to higher goals, but effort inconsistent; outside activities claim time and energy.
3. Seems satisfied with average performance; no action plan or effort to improve.
4. Aspires to above-average performance goals and is working consistently according to plan.
5. Achieving top 10 percent of group which is the objective; not necessarily interested in promotion.
6. Outstanding performance is consistent with constantly challenging self to improve; has active career plan that is on target.
Comment:_____

Planning and Organization—ability to establish a course of action to accomplish goal; appropriating resources.
1. Does not plan ahead; waits until last minute and frequently misses deadline.
2. Does not establish priorities or adhere to plan.
3. Plans well, but responds too frequently to less essential "emergencies."
4. Plans well for normal circumstances.
5. Establishes realistic goals and sets contingency plans and schedules.
6. Establishes realistic immediate and long-range goals with contingency plans and schedules.
Comment:_____

*Note: These phrases should be scaled by a psychometric method on populations that are similar to those that are being evaluated. For a discussion, see J. C. Nunnally, *Psychometric Theory,* 2nd ed. (New York: McGraw Hill, 1978), pp. 77–80.

Weighting Activity Appraisals

Exhibit 13.12 illustrates how appraisal summary forms may be used to reflect the fact that some forms of the representative's behavior are more important than others. In this exhibit, technical dimensions are given a weighting of two, operational activities receive a weight of one, personal activities, such as attitudes, receive a weight of three, and sales activities receive a weight of four. These weighted evaluations are totaled and averaged in the lower left-hand corner of this exhibit for an overall evaluation. These weights may be subjectively determined or estimated by using multiple regression. In the latter case, a measure of performance, such as sales, would be regressed on the average points. The regression coefficients would be the weights.

Exhibit 13.11   Representative Position Description and Performance Appraisal

REPRESENTATIVE POSITION DESCRIPTION AND PERFORMANCE APPRAISAL U.S.A. 700 (R. 3/80)

Representative _____ Date _____ Submitted by _____ Date _____

Sec. _____

KEY OBJECTIVES: To plan, organize, lead and control the activities of the Territory to achieve the planned level of sales within the approved level of expenses. To promote the prestige of the Company and the pharmaceutical industry.

Appraise Representative's performance using the following *numerical* rating scale in the appropriate boxes: Outstanding (4.5-5.5), Above Average (3.5-4.49), Effective (2.5-3.49), Marginal (1.5-2.49), Unsatisfactory (0.5-1.49), Unacceptable (0.0-0.5), and add appropriate explanatory comments in the Remarks area. A plus (+) has no numerical value. A minus (−) is to be assigned a numerical value of up to 2.0.

CO1   To recommend territorial changes, expenditures, equipment and services.

PS1   Submit to DSM as needed:

+/−   ☐   a. Recommendations for territorial changes, with substantiating data.

b. Recommendations with substantiating data for attendance at meetings, seminars, exhibits, conventions as well as supplementary equipment, services and programs.

CO2   To collect field marketing data and current marketing information and to recommend programs and procedures to the DSM and appropriate departments.

PS2-1   ☐   Collect and submit field marketing data according to the outline supplied when requested.

PS2-1   ☐   Continue to submit worthwhile feedback, including competitive activity, as necessary and submit informative "Information Please".

CO3   To participate activity in the District recruiting program to ensure the continuing availability of sales personnel.

PS3-1   ☐   Make one call per period on assigned college, utilizing materials.

PS3-2   ☐   Make one call per period on assigned minority source.

PS3-3   ☐   Make every good faith effort to actively support the Company's

+/−

a. employment policy not to discriminate by reason of race, color, religion, sex, national origin, age, handicap or status as a disabled or Vietnam-era veteran, and

b. Affirmative Action Programs for members of minority groups, women, qualified handicapped and qualified disabled and Vietnam-era veterans.

PS3-4   ☐   Screen at least one desirable qualified candidate per year.

PS3-5   ☐   Accurately complete Screening Interview USA 1811 and "Day In Field" reports, submitting to DSM immediately.

REMARKS

(continued)

Exhibit 13.11 Continued

CO4   To achieve maintain and use acceptable levels of product knowledge, organizing, planning and sales skills to attain sales objectives.

    PS4-1   Know the following aspects of major Company products:

☐   a. Depth —
      —Ingredients
      —Dosages
      —Indications
      —Price, packing sizes and storage require-
        ments, including minor products
      —Symptoms or diseases for which they are
        used
      —Educational programs
      —PPE Program
      —Balance/full disclosure
      —Side effects
      —Contraindications, precautions, warnings
      —Common drug interactions

☐   b. Competition — Major competition

    PS4-2   Demonstrate effective professional selling techniques.

☐   a. Assessing needs
      —Utilize Tips program including daily
        written plan
      —Follow selling plan

☐   b. Planning presentation —
      —Set call objectives utilizing PAD data

☐   c. Opening Benefit —
      —Refer to general customer need
      —Introduce appropriate benefits of B.W. Co.
        products

☐   d. Probing —
      —Identify or confirm need or problem
      —Determine customer reaction

☐   e. Reinforcing Benefit —
      —Agree with customer remark
      —Introduce appropriate benefit of B.W. Co.
        product

☐   f. Benefit —
      —Describe what your product can do that
        the customer wants done

☐   g. Proving —
      —Utilizing literature
      —Utilizing reprints

☐   h. Handling Objectives —
      —Minor
      —Major

☐   i. Closing —
      —Ask for business

☐   j. Recording data for next call —
      —Enter in TIPS work plan book:
        —objective for next call
        —benefits to stress
        —objections to handle

☐   k. Specimens —
      —Utilizes samples to maximize sales
        potential

☐   l. Expressive Skills —
      —Speaks clearly
      —Presents material logically
      ··—Listens

    PS4-3   Demonstrate effective sales dynamics to maximize selling opportunities

☐   a. Effort/initiative/determination

☐   b. Sales sense

☐   c. Customer evaluation

REMARKS

(continued)

Exhibit 13.11 Continued

PS4-4   Time management

☐ a. Effective use of available time

☐ b. Proper balance of calls

CO5   To make the necessary calls to achieve the sales objectives.

PS5-1   Allowing for territorial differences, Representatives will maintain a minimum acceptable average of:

☐ a. 6.0 MDs/day

☐ b. 60% Class "A" seen/period

☐ c. 30% Callbacks on "A"s/period

☐ d. 3.0 Details/call

☐ e. 2.5 Retail calls per day.

☐ f. 3 key Rxing DDS's per week.

☐ g. Total calls minimum 10/day.

PS5-2   Contact the following hospital personnel/departments if available or where appropriate:

☐ a. Physicians
    1. Chief of Staff
    2. Director of Medical Education
    3. Department Chairmen
    4. Clinical Staffs and ER
    5. Committee members (P&T/Formulary, etc.)
    6. Residents/Interns/Students
    7. Oral Surgeons
    8. P.A.'s
    Nurses
    1. Directors/Assistant Directors
    2. In-service education nurses
    3. Department supervisors
    4. Specialty nurses (ICU, CCU, OR, ER, Infection Control, CRNA, etc.)
    5. Team nurses (IV, Catheter)
    6. Nurse Practitioners
    7. Corpsman
    Administration
    1. Administrator/Assistant/Secretaries
    2. Purchasing personnel/Procurement Officer
    3. Director of House Staff Affairs
    4. Medical Library

☐ b. Pharmacy
    1. Director
    2. Staff/Residents/Interns
    3. Clinic pharmacists
    4. Clinical Pharmacists/Pharm. D.'s
    5. Drug Information Center

☐ c. Clinics — Demonstrate knowledge of and work around clinic and ER schedules

+/− ☐ d. Laboratory
    1. Pathologists
    2. Technologists/Technicians

PS5-3   Complete hospital projects and/or sales objectives as agreed upon with DSM by:

☐ a. Projects —
    1. Prospecting for new sources of business
    2. Establishing new products
    3. Maintaining existing sales of products
    4. Expanding use of products
    5. Making routine calls on major departments for information gathering and maintaining rapport with key personnel.
    6. Coordinating key personnel contacts with other field personnel

☐ b. Sales — This year vs last year

REMARKS

(continued)

Exhibit 13.11 Continued

+/− [ ] PS5-4   Conduct at least one hospital exhibit each year. where profitable and worthwhile, or as many as agreed upon with DSM, for each hospital where permitted, and submit informative reports of hospital exhibit on weekly Activity Report.

PS5-5   Call on retail accounts to achieve and maintain sales objectives by:

[ ] a. Promoting Company image, products, promotions and services to the following key personnel:
1. Owner/Manager
2. Chief Pharmacist/Staff Pharmacists
3. Purchasing Agent/Buyer
4. Clerks

[ ] b. 1. Dispense B.W. Co.
—Encourage use of B.W. Co. products instead of generics

[ ] 2. Detail Pharmacists/Clerks

[ ] 3. Merchandising
—Increase product stock levels
—Increase OTC product position/facings

+/− [ ] 4. Returns
—Handle return goods

[ ] 5. Sales
—Create/generate turnover orders
—50% T.O.'s ratio to calls

[ ] 6. Rx Info
—Solicit Rx info on own and competitive products

PS5-6 [ ] a. Maintain good rapport with assigned wholesaler to ensure:
1. Adequate stock
2. Cooperation with
(a) Bids
(b) Contracts
(c) QPAs
(d) Special promotions
(e) Deals
(f) Stocking/Distribution of new products
3. Participation at sales meetings
4. Understanding of our Return Goods Policy
5. Compliance with our Charge Back Policy
6. Compliance with Promotional Service Agreement
b. Call on assigned wholesaler at least once per month and contact the following appropriate personnel as necessary:
1. House/Branch/Operations Manager
2. Sales Manager
3. Inventory Control Manager
4. Field staff personnel
5. Telephone personnel
6. Buyer
7. Credit Manager
8. Other executive personnel
c. Maintain a diary on the assigned wholesaler
d. Inform field personnel and appropriate departments of wholesaler activities
+/− [ ] e. All Reps who do not have an assigned wholesaler should maintain good rapport with any wholesaler personnel to ensure cooperation with Company projects and policies and have an understanding of procedures (i.e. policy/terms) of local wholesalers.

PS5-7 [ ] a. Contact, as necessary, the following personnel of assigned medical, pharmacy, dental and nursing schools or any other paramedical institutions to promote the Company's image and sales:
1. Dean/Assistant/Secretaries
2. Dean of Student Affairs
3. Professors/Instructors
4. Students

[ ] b. Check the current curriculum of these assigned schools and/or institutions and coordinate the use of Company educational programs and materials, eg, learning programs, blue brochures, educational projects, etc.

(continued)

Exhibit 13.11 Continued

PS5-8 Seek, identify and call on, as necessary, all Special Calls with high sales potential, including industrial accounts, podiatrists, Nursing homes, health and beauty aids and medical supply houses, etc.

    a. Promote Company image
    b. Sell Company products
    c. Explain promotions and services

CO6 To control expenses in order to maximize profits.

PS6-1 a. Properly use, care for and store sales materials such as:
    1. Trade packs
    2. Literature
    3. Samples
    4. Company records (TIPS, etc.)
    b. Efficiently utilize and care for consigned equipment such as:
    1. Automobile
    2. Typewriter
    3. Detail bag
    4. Exhibit units
    5. Audiovisual equipment and programs
    c. Realistically control territorial expenditures such as:
    1. Telephone expenses
    2. Postage
    3. Business entertainment
    4. Lodging and food
    5. Tolls and parking
    6. Automobile expenses

CO7 To communicate and cooperate with other field personnel and departments of the Company.

PS7-1

    a. Actively participate at meetings with constructive comments.

    b. Communicate and cooperate with fellow Reps to maximize sales.

CO8 To promote the prestige of the Company and the pharmaceutical industry.

PS8-1 Actively support Company-sponsored public relations programs, e.g., Pharmacy School, P.R. Program, Pharmacy Education Program, Clinical Pharmacology Awards, B.W. Speakers Program, etc.

CO9 To comply with all standard Company procedures, programs and policies, including those pertaining to relevant statutory regulations governing equal employment opportunities, fair employment practices and safety, and to ensure that such compliance is within state and federal regulations.

PS9-1 Punctually and accurately complete all required reports including:

    a. Day/Weekly
        —Daily and weekly reports
        —TIPS documents

    b. Itinerary
        —Monthly forward itinerary
        —Expense accounts
        —Automobile expense report

    c. Correspondence
        —Replies to correspondence

    d. Others
        —Automobile accident report
        —Adverse reaction report
        —Complaint report
        —Information Please
        —Other required reports

PS9-2 Comply with Company policies as set forth in or related to:

    a. Procedures Manual
    b. TIPS Manual
    c. Automobile Manual
    d. State and federal regulations
    e. Other Company directives

(continued)

Exhibit 13.11   Continued

CO10   To compliment existing programs, policies and procedures, and to recommend changes that would improve the Company's performance to the DSM and/or
appropriate departments.

REMARKS

PS10-1   a. Provide positive feedback to maintain and/or
expand existing programs, policies and procedures.

b. Immediately recommend to DSM constructive
changes or discontinuation of programs,
policies or procedures when conditions arise
which would indicate that they are unlikely
to be achieved or implemented.

CO11   To communicate the Representative progress, concerns
and achievements to the DSM and other appropriate
departments.

PS11   Communicate in writing to DSM and/or other
appropriate departments his/her progress, needs,
concerns, desires and achievements.

CO12   Set and achieve specific objectives.

PS12-1   Set one personal and two territorial specific
objectives.

CO13   To achieve the territorial sales objectives.

PS13-1   Cooperate and participate with DSM in establishing and achieving:

a. DDD territorial sales objectives such as:
1. Overall Performance Index
2. Balance of Product Performance Index
3. Product Sales vs. Goals
4. TCR Market Share
5. Other

b. QPA sales objectives

c. OTC sales objectives

CO14   To demonstrate a positive attitude.

PS14-1   Project professionalism within the job responsibilities by exhibiting personal and job-related behavior such as:

a. Job interest

b. Initiative

c. Industriousness

d. Acceptance and utilization of constructive
criticism

e. Punctuality

f. Self-discipline

g. Assertiveness

h. Self-motivation

i. Self-improvement

j. Realism

k. Maturity

l. Persistence

m. Tact

(continued)

Exhibit 13.11   Continued

PS14-1 (continued)   **REMARKS**

☐   n. Cooperation

☐   o. Positive attitude in negative situations

☐   p. Positive attitude with customers

☐   q. Enthusiasm

PS14-2   Prepare for and actively participate in the annual
☐   Counseling Session with DSM.

(continued)

Exhibit 13.11 Continued

*** *** *** *** *** *** ***

Date of last discussion with Representative
of promotability and/or future goals. _____

(Date)

Specific areas of interest to Representative.

Objectives and plans consistent with Representatives developmental goals.

Signatures Rep. _____

DSM _____

RSM _____

Revised March 1980

Used by permission of Burroughs Wellcome Company.

Exhibit 13.12 Representatives' Activities Appraisal Summary

CONFIDENTIAL

REPRESENTATIVES ACTIVITIES APPRAISAL SUMMARY U.S.A. 585 Rev. 3/80

Representative _____ **Submitted by** _____ **Date** _____

INSTRUCTIONS: Send to RSM for approval, copying and distribution. Copies to VP Sales — RSM — DSM — Rep

Appraise Representative's performance using the following *numerical* rating scale for each category and subcategory: Outstanding (4.5-5.5); Above Average (3.5-4.49), Effective (2.5-3.49), Marginal (1.5-2.49), Unsatisfactory (0.5-1.49), Unacceptable (0.0-0.49). Numbers in parentheses refer to Performance Standards on U.S.A. 700.

TECHNICAL

Product Knowledge
- _____ Depth (4-1a)
- _____ Compet. (4-1b)

Selling Skills
- _____ Opening Benefit (4-2c)
- _____ Probing (4-2d)
- _____ Reinforcing Benefit (4-2e)
- _____ Benefit (4-2f)
- _____ Proving (4-2g)
- _____ Handling Objections (4-2h)
- _____ Closing (4-2i)
- _____ Expressive Skills (4-2L)

Planning
- _____ Assessing Needs (4-2a)
- _____ Planning Presentation (4-2b)
- _____ Recording Data (4-2j)
- _____ Specimens (4-2k)

_____ Avg. Pts Col 1

OPERATIONAL

Recruiting
- _____ College (3-1)
- _____ Minority (3-2)
- _____ AAP (3-3)
- _____ Day in Field (3-5)
- _____ Results (3-4)

Reporting
- _____ Day/Weekly (9-1a)
- _____ Itinerary (9-1b)
- _____ Corresp. (9-1c)
- _____ Other (9-1d)

Feedback
- _____ "Info. Pls."/ Competitive (2-2)
- _____ Marketing Data (2-1)
- _____ Terr. Info. (1a,b)
- _____ Promo. Ideas (10-1)
- _____ Open Door (11-1)

_____ Avg. Pts. Col. 2

PERSONAL

Attitude
- _____ To Supv. (14-1d,e,n,o)
- _____ To Co. Pol (8-1,9-2)
- _____ Expense Control (6-1)
- _____ To Peers (7-1a & b)
- _____ To Cust. (14-1m,p)
- _____ To Pers. Perf. (14-1a,b, c,f,g,h,i,j,k,l,q)
- _____ Counseling Session (14-2)

Sales Dynamics
- _____ Effort/Init./Deter. (4-3a)
- _____ Sales Sense (4-3b)
- _____ Cust. Eval. (4-3c)

Specific Objective
- _____ Terr/Personal (12-1)

_____ Avg. Pts. Col. 3

SALES

Time Mgt.
- _____ Total Calls (5-1g)
- _____ Utilizes Time (4-4a)
- _____ Balance of Calls (4-4b)

Terr. Sales Obj.
- _____ DDD (13-1a)
- _____ QP's (13-1b)
- _____ OTC (13-1c)

Physician Coverage
- _____ MD Calls (5-1a)
- _____ 60% A (5-1b)
- _____ 30% CB's (5-1c)
- _____ 3.0 Details (5-1d)

Hosp. Coverage
- _____ Pers. Depts (5-2a)
- _____ Pharmacy (5-2b)
- _____ Clinics (5-2c)
- _____ Projects (5-3a)
- _____ Exhibits/Films (5-4)
- _____ Sales (5-3b)

Retail Coverage
- _____ Call Std. (5-1e)
- _____ Dispense BW (5-5b1)
- _____ Promote Image (5-5a)
- _____ Detail Phar/Clks. (5-5b2)
- _____ Mdsing (5-5b3)
- _____ Returns (5-5b4)
- _____ Rx Info. (5-5b6)
- _____ Sales (5-5b5)

Med/Phar/DDS/RN School Perf.
- _____ Stud/Teach & Ad. Pers. (5-7a)
- _____ Ed. Prog./Proj. (5-7b)

Special Calls
- _____ Wholesalers (5-6)
- _____ Labs (5-2d)
- _____ Industrial/Others (5-8)
- _____ DDS (5-1f)
- _____ Wholesaler Rapport (5-6e)

_____ Avg. Pts. Col. 4

Briefly discuss Strengths:

Briefly discuss areas needing improvement:
(Explain less than Effective Perf. [less than 2.5].)

CALCULATIONS

Col. Pts.	Factor	T. Point
1. _____ x	2	= _____
2. _____ x	1	= _____
3. _____ x	3	= _____
4. _____ x	4	= _____

GRAND TOTAL _____

AVERAGE (÷ 10) _____

Used by permission of Burroughs Wellcome Company.

Comparing Representatives with Each Other

Rating scales attempt to evaluate a representative according to some absolute standard. Another approach is to compare the performance of representatives against each other. Exhibit 13.13 illustrates a paired-comparison method. Here, each representative in the column is compared with each representative in the row to the left. In this illustration, Jones is better than Baker, Kerr, Thomas, and Wilson. The sum of the X's received by each representative produces a ranking of representatives. In this case, the ranking is Jones, Baker, Kerr, Thomas, and Wilson.

While Exhibit 13.13 provides an overall comparison of representatives, Exhibit 13.14 provides a comparison along specific criteria. These criteria give the sales manager direction for coaching, counseling, and correcting representatives' behavior. For example, while Jones is the top representative, he could use improvement in planning, reporting, and territory management. Because all representatives have scored low in reporting, the sales manager may want to have a special session on this topic. Wilson is strong in selling skills but weak in everything else. The manager must decide if Wilson should be terminated or a grand effort made to improve all of these major deficiencies.

Some companies require sales managers to prepare tables such as Exhibits 13.13 and 13.14 prior to making individual assessments. These simultaneous assessments have the advantage of reducing biases toward one person. They have the additional advantage of being completed at one point in time so that evaluations are not subject to changes in moods of the evaluator when ratings take several days.

Exhibit 13.13   Paired Comparisons of Representatives' Overall Performance

REPRESENTATIVE	THE BETTER REPRESENTATIVE OF THE PAIR*				
	Baker	Jones	Kerr	Thomas	Wilson
Baker		x			
Jones					
Kerr	x	x			
Thomas	x	x	x		
Wilson	x	x	x	x	
Totals	3	4	2	1	

*An X in the cell means that the representative in the column is superior to the one in the row. Thus Jones is better than Baker.

Exhibit 13.14   A Comparison of Representatives Across Criteria
(Scaled 1 to 5, with 5 the most favorable)

REPRESENTATIVES

Evaluation Criteria	Baker	Jones	Kerr	Thomas	Wilson
Product Knowledge	4	5	4	3	2
Planning	4	4	3	2	1
Reporting	3	3	3	2	1
Attitudes	4	5	4	3	2
Selling Skills	4	5	3	3	4
Territory Management	3	4	3	2	2
Totals	22	26	20	15	12

Appraisal Feedback

If the performance appraisal is to modify the behavior of the representative, then he or she must receive feedback from this appraisal. Poor feedback systems may aggravate an already negative situation.

Writing performance appraisals on subordinates is a perennial problem for most field sales managers for a variety of reasons. There is a psychological reluctance to put disparaging comments about performance in writing if the individual will receive a copy of the report. Yet, failure to note unfavorable performance will result in a continuation of that performance.

One counseling method that avoids the psychological problem for the field sales manager is called "positive-reinforcement." Instead of emphasizing the deficiency, it stresses methods for achieving the objectives. For example, if a representative has achieved only 75 percent of a sales goal, the sales manager would compliment him or her on achieving 75 percent of the sales and ask what methods were used and if these methods could be used to achieve the remaining 25 percent.

There are also the problems of sales managers' dislike for paper work and their preference for talking rather than writing. These conditions lead to performance reports that tend to evaluate everyone as average or above. They may be stilted and cryptic to the point of being useless in redirecting representatives' behavior. Yet, the application of good participative management practices and management communications dictate that *every* employee deserves a clear and accurate appraisal of performance. Furthermore, federal regulations require written evidence to prove a good-faith effort in compensation, upgrading or promoting, transferring, demotivating, or separating employees.

Singler describes a unique solution to these feedback appraisal problems.[10] First, he provided each field manager with a high-quality cassette recorder to dictate the reports, which appeals to managers' preference for talking over writing. The high-quality tapes made it possible to transmit the tapes over telephone lines at high speeds to the company's word-processing center for typing.

The second dimension of this innovation was to write the report to the representative being evaluated, with copies to the regional sales manager—the reverse of the usual procedure. With this innovation, the sales manager is speaking directly to the representative in the second person rather than reporting to the regional manager and referring to the representative in the third person. A few examples of sales managers' reports after spending a day with a representative will illustrate why both representatives and managers prefer reports in the second person (Exhibit 13.15).

The representatives and all levels of sales management think that dictating reports in the second person represents a substantial improvement in performance evaluation after the manager has spent a day with a representative. There is also the additional advantage of timeliness. Managers are more likely to complete their reports immediately after visiting with a representative when the reports can be dictated instead of written or typed by the manager.

Appraisal Pitfalls

There are many pitfalls in the subjective evaluation of representatives' performance. A brief discussion of these pitfalls will help the sales manager avoid them.

The manager must avoid letting personal feelings destroy the objectivity of the rating process. The evaluation should be limited to the representative's proficiency on the job, not personal behavior outside the job or his or her personal life. There is a danger of recency effects and dramatic incidents that may loom large in the mind of the rater, resulting in a favorable or unfavorable evaluation that does not reflect the representative's total performance. A halo effect may occur when a manager judges a representative as "good" on one activity and then continues this favorable evaluation for all activities. Similarly, a negative evaluation may carry over into all other activities. Because managers work closely with representatives, there is a tendency to be lenient and rate no one below a scale value of "average."

Exhibit 13.15   Writing Evaluations in the Second Person

Representative Trip Report #3   (Third Person)

Selling Skills
"Mary needs to be more aggressive in asking for the business. I had to put in my two cents' worth on several calls to get a commitment from the physicians to use the product."
Planning
"She will have to get more specific on her individual call objectives. She will have to zero in on the main reason for the call. We discussed this at length and set up some objectives for the next several calls, and her second day was more meaningful in this respect."

(Second Person)

Selling Skills
"I graded your selling skills on this trip, Mary, as 'Needing Improvement.' As I mentioned, you seem to close, but not strongly enough. As an example, you said on several occasions, 'I'd appreciate your keeping our product in mind.' I think, Mary, that you would be more successful in getting him to use our product on his next several patients if you ask him directly, 'Will you use it or try it on your next three or six patients, Doctor?' I think you will agree that this is asking for the business and getting a commitment at the same time. In the area of using selling tools, I think you'll agree that on that physician in Athens who was a member of the AAFP, you should have planned this call a bit better in advance. The CEU credit he will receive certainly pays off in good will and future support. Let's work on this, OK?"
Planning
"I realize you don't get into this area very frequently, but I was glad to see you using their appointment system. This should improve your time utilization. I also noticed you're getting more information from your stores and hospitals about new physicians in this area. These should be your future calls."

Representative Trip Report #4   (Third Person)

Product Knowledge
"He has the product knowledge to handle most details, but I had to fill him in on several instances when he didn't have all the information he should have. Knowledge of literature and other sales aids is OK."
Selling Skills
"Joe comes on strong when asking for the business and gets the pharmacist to commit himself on each product. He doesn't waste time getting to the close. Makes good comparisons of our products to competition and knows the right time to get to the crux of the matter in signing the order."

(Second Person)

Product Knowledge
"Joe, I think your product knowledge on this trip was effective and that you used good sales points, current literature, and other sales aids. While we didn't get into a lot of in-depth details, I felt that what you did present was adequate. However, as I pointed out on several occasions, your level of PK is not up to the same high level of expertise you show so very well in your selling skills. Improvement on several products should also pay off in increased sales."
Selling Skills
"It was good to see your continuing use of Personal Selling Skills. As an example, you continuously closed, and closed very strong. I don't believe there is anyone else in the District who asks for the business as convincingly as you do! Keep it up."

Scale misinterpretation can also be a problem. Managers should have adequate training manuals and receive training in evaluation. One approach to solving this problem is to give managers several standard scenarios of representatives' behavior and have them evaluate these representatives. These standard scenarios can then be used to coach managers in the process of evaluation.

One of the most difficult contemporary problems in evaluation is the effect of federal regulations on evaluations. There is a reluctance to evaluate accurately a deficient performance, not out of friendliness for the representative, but out of a fear of an inability to defend the rating if the representative contests it in court. The inability to defend salary, promotion, and separation decisions reflects a lack of measurable and observable standards that are agreed upon by the representative and supported by on-going counseling and documentation of performance.

Exhibit 13.16 provides guidelines for a performance appraisal review.

COACHING

THE COACHING PROCESS

Coaching consists of observing skill performance, demonstrating means for improving these skills, providing an opportunity to practice the skills, and giving feedback. Any sales manager who has taken a lesson in tennis or golf will recognize these steps in coaching. First, the pro says, "Hit a few for me." Then he or she will say a few kind things about the swing and then demonstrate means for improvement. This step will be followed by some practice and feedback. The manager will want to keep this process in mind as he or she prepares for a coaching session with a representative.

In preparing for a coaching session, the manager will want to review the past performance of the representative. Are there problems in implementing the selling plan? Is the problem with the representative or the plan? Perhaps the selling plan needs revision.

The coaching session should begin with a clear statement of the reasons for the session and the groundrules that will take place. The manager must explain that he or she will observe the representative in the selling situation, but not participate in the sale. The manager will then observe an actual selling situation, evaluating the message content, communication effectiveness, and interpersonal skills. Following this observation, there should be a mutual evaluation of the performance. First, the representative should be asked, "What was the objective of

Exhibit 13.16   Guidelines for Performance Appraisal Review

1. Review available reports of representative:
   - previous performance appraisals
   - recent working trips
   - critical incidents
   - important correspondence
   - sales statistics
   - activities data
   - specific objectives

   and review strengths and weaknesses of representative and working relationship between manager and representative.

2. Complete a preliminary overall performance rating only of all representatives in District, rating all representatives simultaneously on each item on the review form, rather than each representative consecutively on the entire form.

3. Obtain advance approval from the next higher field or national sales manager of the overall performance rating for all representatives in the district, before completing the preliminary performance appraisal form with full comments on each individual representative.

4. Advise representative in writing approximately two weeks in advance of the date and place for the review. Send representative a copy of the performance appraisal form to be used, and ask the representative to complete fully and be prepared to discuss.

5. At time and place of review, put representative at ease, arrange for comfortable setting as nearly neutral as possible, private, and allow ample time for the review with no interruptions.

6. Compare the representative's self-evaluation with your evaluation. Listen, discuss fully, and resolve differences, getting agreement or acceptance.

7. Agree on realistic objectives, programs, and schedules to correct the deficiencies, build on strengths, and establish innovative projects. If this step requires additional time and preparation, schedule an early follow-up meeting. Specify the roles of both parties in achieving new objectives. Discuss relative consequences of failure and success.

8. Prepare an agreed upon version of the performance appraisal form signed by both parties to be forwarded to the next higher field or national sales manager for approval and signature, with copies containing all three signatures to be distributed to all parties including the personnel department, consistent with company policy.

9. Follow through on objectives and programs as scheduled.

this call? What was your plan for accomplishing this objective? What do you think happened? Why?" The manager must be careful during this probing not to put down the representative. The manager will want to give positive feedback before noting deficiencies. At this point, the manager and representative should compare views of what happened, resolve disagreements, and then have the representative suggest a way that the objective could have been reached.

The next step in the coaching process is for the manager and representative to develop a short list of agreed upon improvement areas, create an improvement plan, and establish a priority for implementing this list. Many companies develop a form whereby this list becomes a self-improvement plan or a learning contract that is signed by the representative and the manager.

The coaching process is more than developing immediate skills. It has the longer-term goal of training the representative in self-discovery that will lead to self-evaluation and improvement without the need for close supervision.

TRAINING COACHES

Many companies report that their sales managers do not actively engage in coaching. Managers report that this is not a rewarding experience for the representative or the manager. Coaching can be a threatening situation because personal selling skills and interpersonal skills are on the line. There can also be problems when young managers find it necessary to coach older representatives. These situations probably reflect the fact that most managers view coaching as a negative process and fail to recognize it as an opportunity for providing positive and motivating feedback. Some managers, however, are skilled coaches who enjoy the process because it provides them with the opportunity to demonstrate the selling skills that helped to earn them their promotion.

Few companies train sales managers in coaching. Some companies provide a form for use during the coaching process. This form requires the sales manager to record the object of the call, statements of needs, benefits and proofs, the handling of objections, and post-call review. Companies that have trained managers in coaching have found that role playing can be very productive. Some companies have even used representatives in the manager's role as a coach to provide another viewpoint of the coaching process. To provide uniformity in coaching, one company has created the role of a field coach who assists managers in the coaching process. Efforts to improve the coaching process can greatly improve the selling skills of the sales force. (See Chapter 19 for an application of behavioral modeling for training sales managers in coaching.)

COUNSELING

THE COUNSELING PROCESS

Coaching deals with skills, while counseling deals with values. The clarification of company, management, and the representative's values is the beginning of the development of positive attitudes that will help the representative feel good about himself or herself, the company, the industry, and careers in selling. Thus counseling is not a lecture or a transferring of knowledge. It should not have as its goal the dispensing of advice or "straightening out" a representative. Instead, it is a process for mutual analysis and understanding that leads to the following outcomes: self-discovery and self-understanding by the representative, a commitment to mutually agreed upon goals, and a plan of action to improve performance and achieve these goals. Counseling sessions, therefore, should guide representatives to understand better their problems and their potentials.

TRAINING COUNSELORS

Counseling is another area where few companies provide sales managers with training. But the lack of training is not the only reason why many sales managers do not engage in counseling. Counseling is very time consuming and the increased demand on sales managers' time leaves little opportunity for it.

Counseling is time consuming because it requires the establishment of mutual trust, which cannot be done quickly. It also involves another time-consuming process—probing for the real problem, not the symptom.

Counseling takes time also because it must recognize the uniqueness of each individual and have separate objectives for each counseling session. It will be necessary to review the strengths and accomplishments of each representative, thereby providing guidance without criticism. Ideally, the representative will provide much of the self-evaluation and say the words that need to be said. The sales manager will want to identify the best place for the counseling session. It will vary with individuals. Should it be in the car, the manager's office, or some neutral territory?

The sales manager will seek consensus during the counseling session regarding the definition of the problem, the improvement plan, and the rewards and punishments associated with success and failure in these areas. Consensus will greatly simplify implementation. The manager needs to recognize the distinction between acceptance and agreement. Acceptance means that consensus has not taken place and the manager has had to resort to organizational power to bring about change.

Counseling sessions can be difficult for some managers because they must listen. Many sales managers are better at talking than listening. Training in counseling should therefore include sessions in effective listening.

CORRECTING

If consensus has been reached during coaching and counseling, and if all motivation is self-motivation (Chapter 11), then representatives will work to correct their own behavior. But such ideal conditions do not always exist. Managers will find it necessary to establish facts, impose solutions, and create plans of actions when self-discovery does not occur with the representative. Such corrective action, however, should be regarded as a temporary procedure until the representative can be trained in problem analysis and decision making. A representative who requires continuous corrective action should probably be transferred or terminated.

To move the representative along the road of self-correction, the manager will want to review the appraisal, the coaching, and the areas of agreement in the counseling sessions. This review should establish that there is a problem and what caused the problem. Then there needs to be a review of the activities necessary to correct the problem and when these activities will be performed. And finally, the manager and representative must come to a clear understanding of the consequences associated with various outcomes of performance, such as warnings, probation, and termination. (See Exhibit 13.17.) The consequences may also include positive rewards that are consistent with the needs of the representative, such as promotion, financial rewards, and social recognition.

This final stage in the controlling function completes the cycle of the management process and returns the field sales manager to phase one—planning where he or she may concentrate on developing better strategic plans and cycling through the management process again (Exhibit 2.1, Chapter 2).

Exhibit 13.17   Correcting Representatives' Behavior

Reprinted by permission. © 1981 NEA, Inc.

SUMMARY

The sales manager controls the sales force through a system of appraisals, counseling, coaching, and correcting behavior. This process builds on previous steps in the sales management process of recruiting, selecting, training, and motivating representatives.

Appraisal systems begin with the establishment of performance standards, which reflect the requirements as enumerated in the salesperson's job description. Performance is appraised using objective and subjective measures. Objective measures include statistics on activities, such as numbers of calls and numbers of demonstrations, as well as on outcomes, such as sales volume. Data for evaluating the representative's performance are generated by the representative, field sales management persons, and the home office.

Many of the representatives' measures of performance are based on observations of behavior in selling situations. A wide variety of measuring instruments has been developed by statistical psychologists. Each technique has its own strengths and weaknesses, so that most representatives' appraisal forms are combinations of essays and verbal and numerical scales.

Coaching is the individual continuation of training in selling skills. Unfortunately, few sales managers have received adequate training in coaching. Similarly, few managers have received training in counseling. Counseling is a time-consuming management activity because it requires the development of mutual respect and understanding in order to clarify values and goals. Ideally, counseling will lead to a process of self-discovery and self-development for the representative that will minimize the future need for counseling by the sales manager.

Because counseling and coaching are time-consuming activities, they frequently fail to get adequate attention by sales managers. Companies that have trained their managers in these skills find that they make an important contribution to sales productivity.

ASSIGNMENTS/DISCUSSION QUESTIONS

1. Define a performance standard and give an example for a field sales representative.
2. What is the overall purpose of the function of controlling?
3. While the representative's performance is influenced by many variables not under his or her control, what will enable the representative to accept these variables?

4. What conclusions would you draw from data that indicate an experienced representative is making the required number of calls but whose productivity is significantly below average?

5. Explain the differences between the two essay type appraisals in Exhibit 13.9.

6. Compare the advantages and disadvantages of Exhibits 13.13 and 13.14.

7. What is the purpose of a performance appraisal?

8. What are the benefits to the company and to the sales representative of an effective performance appraisal system?

9. What is the purpose of Step 3 in Exhibit 13.16?

10. Discuss the role of the manager during the performance appraisal interview in identifying and defining performance deficiencies.

11. What can the field manager do if "the extent the sales rep is able and willing to recognize his or her deficiencies is less than acceptable to the manager"?

12. Why do managers view coaching negatively?

13. What is the relationship between the position description, specific objectives (MBO), and sales results? Which should be used as the basis for the annual formal performance review?

CASE 13.1:
Skokie Tool Company

Jim Kelly, age 34, was a five-year veteran of Skokie Tool Company, headquartered in Cleveland, Ohio. He had worked for the previous eight years with Cleveland Pump Company in the same city where he had a great reputation with his customers. He left Cleveland Pump because they "were too conservative and had an archaic bureaucratic management system." While none of his customers was very specific, they did confirm that Jim was "a great guy, well liked, and well remembered." Cleveland Pump had a policy that they observed strictly about not giving out any information about previous employees. Prior to joining Cleveland Pump, Jim had spent a year with the Cleveland Browns as a fullback until injuring his knee, following a great college career at the University of Pittsburg.

Personally, Jim was an affable Irishman with a ready wit, "a way with customers," an ability to get to see important decision makers, some tendency to cut corners in ordering procedures and pricing, a continuing dislike for reports, a big entertainer, and "a born salesman." The personnel records indicated that he had been put on warning the previous year by his district manager for his repeated violation of the company's expense and pricing policies.

In an industry where inventory control was important because of the high cost of finished goods, there were only minor seasonal variations in sales, with peaks in the summer months. Jim's territory had larger than average swings. For example, with an annual quota of $6,500,000 last year, his sales for the winter quarter were $1,800,000, for the spring quarter were $1,300,000, for the summer quarter were $1,200,000, and for the fall quarter were $2,005,000. In the previous four years, sales in Jim's territory had totaled 102 percent, 84 percent, 96 percent, and 92 percent of quota.

This was the situation that Susan McCullough had found when she took over as the district sales manager (DSM) a year ago. At the end of that fiscal year, Susan had received a complaint from the comptroller about the excess inventory that they were carrying as a result of the inventory on hand during the summer months, which had been produced against the forecast negotiated between Jim and the previous DSM. This complaint was followed by a letter from the production manager and the shipping manager who complained that because of the lengthy production time they couldn't adjust their production rapidly enough to respond to the high sales in Jim's territory in the fall quarter. The result was shipping delays and customer complaints that had gone directly to the president because Jim had promised delivery early in the fall.

This year Jim's sales were at 96 percent of quota as of April 1, and 83 percent at July 1. In a telephone conversation, Jim had told Susan, "Don't worry, I'll make it up by the end of the year."

At the end of last year, Susan had asked Jim to evaluate his performance using the company's standard four-page Representatives' Performance Appraisal Report, which she wanted to compare with her evaluation during their annual performance review. Susan had felt the need to conduct her first annual appraisal with Jim on a thoroughly business-like basis because, frankly, she felt ill at ease in the role. Jim tended to overwhelm her and she had the feeling that in his friendly, boisterous manner he was really laughing at her and certainly not taking her seriously.

As a result, when Jim met her she wasn't prepared for the very sketchy comments he had scrawled over the Comments section of the first page: "I was hired to sell and I'm doing a very good job of it. My customers like me, and my sales are ahead of last year for every year I've worked for Skokie Tool."

When Susan challenged him on the quality and content of his report, he laughingly said, "Aw, come on, Susan, you know these reports are for new kids. You and I don't have to play these kinds of games, and nobody pays any attention to them anyway. We ought to be spending this time with customers creating sales instead of rehashing the past, which doesn't serve any useful purpose." Susan flushed and pointed out that he was being very selective in the facts he remembered because he had never made the sales forecast except the year he joined the company, even though he had been ahead of last year's sales each year. Jim laughed hard and countered, "Boy, you sure have a hard heart for such a pretty girl, and anyway I can't be held responsible for those unreasonable quotas established by the front office. Those guys don't know what it's like out in the cruel competitive world. My customers are giving me all their business on our type of products. If we'd bring out some new products once in a while, I'd be able to do better." Susan had a hard time maintaining her self-control for the balance of the interview, but she did manage to tell Jim she wasn't satisfied with his sales performance, his attitude, his advance planning reports which she rarely received, or his sales call summary reports which were frequently late or incomplete, and that she would confirm it in writing. This didn't seem to phase Jim who replied, "Susan, don't take your job so seriously. Can't we be friends?" which infuriated her all the more.

When Susan discussed her dissatisfaction with Jim Kelly's performance and attitude with John Freeman, the national sales manager to whom she reported, he told her that she'd have to figure out a way to solve the problem herself. He also mentioned that it was his understanding that Jim was well liked by his customers.

Susan decided to list in the annual report the specific deficiencies she had noted and asked Jim to reply in writing what he planned to do about them. When Susan worked with Jim in March, by which time she had not received his reply, he said that what she was asking of him was a difficult thing for him to do, that the previous DSM had not been as unreasonable in his demands, and that he was working on a set of plans that he hoped would satisfy her but that "they weren't finished as yet."

When Jim's plans did not arrive by the end of June, Susan scheduled herself to work with him the second week in July, only to learn that his forward itinerary indicated he was working out of town about 200 miles away, so she scheduled herself to work with Harry Wilkins, the other representative headquartered in Cleveland. As a result, Susan was shocked to see Jim's car parked in front of his home as she drove by at 10:00 AM enroute to the location where she had agreed to meet Harry. On the spur of the moment, she circled the block and parked about a half block from Jim's house where she was able to keep his car in full view. At 1:00 PM her vigil was rewarded when Jim came out in casual attire, a picnic basket in hand, with his wife and two children, got in his car and drove off.

For a moment Susan was afraid that Jim had spotted her.

After considerable thought, Susan continued on to work with Harry Wilkins. On returning home after her working trip with Harry, Susan decided to wait for Jim's sales call summary report for that week before doing anything. As luck would have it, Jim's report came in on time with full activities reported for the week that he was supposedly out of town.

CASE QUESTIONS

1. What was Jim Kelly's quarterly seasonal quota last year and what percentage was his sales ahead or behind for each individual quarter?

2. What is the immediate problem?

3. What are the long-term problems?

4. What additional unresolved problems have occurred since Susan became Jim's district sales manager?

5. What combination of clues provided some early warning signals?

6. What should Susan do?

7. If there is no company policy on falsification of reports, what should Susan do?

8. On what basis would Susan recommend termination (firing) of Jim Kelly if there is no specific policy on falsification of reporting?

9. If, for whatever reason, Susan were to decide or be told that she could not terminate Jim Kelly, how should she handle their subsequent working relationship?

10. If we assume that Jim Kelly had not falsified his reports, but instead had written Susan a letter, which she had not received, saying he was taking several days vacation and had sent in daily call summary reports for the vacation days marked "Vacation," what plan could Susan devise to correct their working relationship and Jim's productivity?

CASE 13.2:
Oklahoma Hardware Company

The Oklahoma Hardware Company manufactures and distributes a complete line of hand tools to retail hardware, discount, and general stores throughout the country. Recently, they expanded their line to include power hand equipment. As the company grew, they expanded their field sales force to its present structure of sixty-two representatives reporting to seven area sales managers who, in turn, report to Fred Stanfield, the General Sales Manager.

In addition to the regular individual bimonthly sales conferences conducted by the area sales managers for their representatives at the branch offices, Fred Stanfield held three annual Area Sales Managers Conferences. These were intended to maintain good communications between various department heads and the area sales managers, to provide the area managers with an opportunity to exchange experiences about market conditions and promotional programs, and to provide supplemental sales management training. One session that had been a part of each meeting for the past two years, and had become a favorite with the area managers, was the discussion of current personnel problems. Each manager presented a case about one of his or her sales representatives, explained the problem in detail, then fielded the questions of the other area sales managers, who acted as a panel of experts, and listened to their suggestions on how to solve the problem. As actual names were used and the sales reps were known by many of the other area managers, these sessions were not exercises in theory. Although the area manager presenting the case was not compelled to follow the suggestions made by the others, Fred Stanfield regularly recorded their suggestions, sent copies to everyone who attended, and, in follow-up working sessions with the manager, individually inquired about the action that had been taken in the cases that had been presented. On occasion, the managers would voluntarily present as their contribution to the conference a follow-up explanation of the effectiveness or lack of effectiveness of the action plan the panel had suggested.

As we listen in on the problem-solving session at the ongoing conference, Bruce Tomlin, the Southeast Area Sales Manager, explains: "I believe we have a fairly smooth-running district in the Southeast, which, as you fellows know, is leading the country in sales against forecast," (which provokes catcalls and boos from the other managers). "Most of my eleven reps are young and have from two to five years of experience. They're young, aggressive, and, until recently, I thought we had a very good team spirit. One of my reps is beginning to cause a problem and it's causing me increasing concern.

"The guy I'm referring to is our rep in Atlanta, Tommy Atkins, whom many of you know. He's been with the company about thirteen years and is the veteran on the staff, even though he's only thirty-eight years old. He's always been opinionated and somewhat of a loudmouth, but he had a pretty good sense of humor. Overall, he's an average, reliable performer, but nothing exceptional considering his experience. His territory is running at 102 percent of forecast, with sales for a rolling twelve months at about $700,000. This 102 percent of forecast used to be better than it is of late. With the area territory average at 108 percent and $825,000, he's not maintaining his relative position. His territory potential is about average for the area. Considering his years of experience, I feel he probably could do better, but somehow he seems to lack imagination.

"Recently, Tommy has become much more serious and tries to use his seniority, rather than the logic of his arguments, to exert influence over the others about programs, promotional opportunities and problems, etc. In addition, he's become negative about company policies, the way we do things, our promotional direction, his pay, and the job. At sales meetings, he spouts off, is negative, and challenges almost everything. He keeps coming up with 'we used that before and it won't work,' 'we're behind the times,' 'the competition does this better,' etc. Everything that fails to run smoothly or the way he wants it to irritates him. Lately, he's been riding Jeff Mailing, one of our new reps who works out of Jacksonville, and there is growing antagonism between them. Some of the other reps are rising to Jeff's defense and I can see a split in the ranks developing unless I do something promptly.

"This is not a situation that developed overnight. Tommy's always been a bit of a hard-head. Initially, I tried placating him and offering what I thought were reasonable explanations to the complaints he voiced, but—as you guys know—there aren't always solutions or immediate answers to some of the tactical problems that occur. For instance, he wanted an immediate drop in price to meet the price on National's new product line, then he criticized our deal structure when compared with the Peerless line. When we opened the new territory in Memphis, he complained all the way up to Fred Stanfield when I took Birmingham away from him, even though he had more active accounts in his remaining territory than he could cover comfortably and we covered him on his sales bonus.

"At our last appraisal and counseling session in January, I took a firm stand with him, told him what I saw and how I thought he was coming over to the other reps, as well as to me, and gave him examples of the instances when I thought he was out-of-line. As you might guess, he was very defensive, said I was playing favorites with the young reps, that I didn't realize how tough the competition was getting to be, and that the company wasn't keeping abreast of the changing marketplace. It got kind of hectic for a while, but I finally calmed him down. He never did accept the fact or admit that his attitude was causing the problem. We discussed his sales figures and territory penetration and he's convinced that he's more effective than his figures show. He finds it difficult to accept our classification of 'average' for year-end figures between 95 percent and 105 percent of forecast. Even though his sales fell in that range, he believes strongly that his overall performance is 'above average.' We left it that he'd think about what I had said about his attitude and that he would try to make his sales figures reflect the kind of performance he felt he was giving.

"His sales performance hasn't changed in the past six months and, in the light of his latest series of tirades and set-tos with Jeff Mailing, he's beginning to cause almost more trouble that he's worth. He certainly takes up more than his rightful share of my thinking time and my concern. He is productive and I would rather not terminate him, but I *am* concerned about the effect he's having on the other reps. I can't say that I'm looking forward to his semi-annual appraisal and counseling session next month. How do you guys see it?"

CASE QUESTIONS

1. What is the problem?

2. What are the possible causes?

3. How should Bruce Tomlin *prepare* for his appraisal and counseling session with Tommy Atkins?

4. How should Bruce Tomlin *conduct* the counseling session?

REFERENCES

1. C. G. Burck, "Working Smarter," *Fortune* (June 15, 1981): 68–73.
2. A. B. Ryans and C. B. Weinberg, "Determinants of Salesforce Performance: A Multiple Company Study," in *Sales Management: New Developments from Behavioral and Decision Model Research,* ed. R. P. Bagozzi (Cambridge, Mass.: Marketing Science Institute, 1979), p. 95.
3. D. W. Cravens, R. B. Woodruff, and J. C. Stamper, "An Analytical Approach for Evaluating Sales Territory Performance," *Journal of Marketing* 36 (January 1972): 32.
4. Albermarle Paper Co. v. Moody 422 U.S. 405 (1975).
5. Robinson v. Union Carbide Corporation 380 F. Supp. 731 (5th Cir. 1974).

6. "Missed Opportunity," *Sales & Marketing Management* (December 10, 1979): 23.

7. Winston Oberg, "Make Performance Appraisal Relevant," *Harvard Business Review* (January–February 1972): 61–67.

8. W. B. Locander and W. A. Staples, "Evaluating and Motivating Salesmen with the BARS Method," *Industrial Marketing Management* 7 (1978): 43–48; A. B. Cocanougher and J. M. Ivancevich, " 'Bars' Performance Rating for Sales Force Personnel," *Journal of Marketing* (July 1978): 87–95.

9. J. P. Guilford, *Psychometric Methods,* 2nd ed. (New York: McGraw Hill, 1964); J. C. Nunnally, *Psychometric Theory* (New York: McGraw Hill, 1978).

10. C. H. Singler, "What Sony and the Second Person Did to Our Performance Appraisals," Editorial Contribution to the National Society of Sales Training Executives, September, 1979.

SUGGESTED READINGS

Cravens, David W., and Woodruff, Robert B., "An Approach for Determining Criteria of Sales Performance," *Journal of Applied Psychology* 57 (1973): 242–247.

Grossman, J. J., and Frank, J., "Guidelines for Annual Evaluation," Dartnell Corporation, 1974, reprinted in J. M. Comer, ed., *Sales Management: Roles and Methods* (Santa Monica, Calif.: Goodyear Publishing Co., 1977), pp. 287–299.

Henry, Porter, "Managing Your Sales Force as a System," *Harvard Business Review* (March–April 1975): 85–95.

Herendeen, J. F., "MBO Applied to the Sales Territory," in J. F. Harrison (ed.), *The Sales Manager as a Trainer,* ed. J. F. Harrison (Reading, Mass.: Addison-Wesley Publishing Co., 1977), pp. 159–175.

Kafka, V. W., "Curbstone Counseling," *The Sales Manager as a Trainer,* ed. Jared F. Harrison (Reading, Mass.: Addison-Wesley Publishing Company, 1977), pp. 67–71.

14

PROBLEM-SOLVING SKILLS

INTRODUCTION

The major responsibility of the first-line field sales manager is that of problem solving. Sales management problems come in a variety of sizes, and, like all management problems, each one is unique. Thus the field sales manager cannot apply an automatic solution to a problem, but must treat each one individually through analysis and the creation of alternative solutions. This chapter suggests some procedures that will help a field sales manager identify and solve problems in an efficient manner.

The following are a few examples of the kinds of problems that require a sales manager's urgent attention:

1. A new competitive product, an unusually effective competitive salesperson, or a sudden price change will seriously affect the market, the morale of the representatives, and their chances of reaching their quotas.

2. A shortage of ingredients or packaging materials, a strike at the plant, a transportation strike, a flood, or a snowstorm may produce temporary shortages of company products.

3. A combination of promotions, retirements, resignations, or competitive pirating may deplete the sales staff and trigger a period of intense recruiting and training along with low productivity.

4. Individual productivity problems for specific representatives may be the result of personal problems, poor applicant screening, or demotivators that need to be eliminated.

5. Differences of opinions about policies, procedures, programs, strategies, and tactics will seriously affect compliance by representatives.

The solutions to these problems are complicated by the dynamics of the marketplace, the great variance in the skills of representatives, and the limited control that a manager has over the critical variables that determine sales results in his or her district.

This is the world of the first-line field sales manager whose responsibility it is to bring to fruition the combined efforts of the company's research, development, production, finance, and marketing through the efforts of the field sales staff. To reach corporate objectives, the field sales manager must be able to analyze problems, create alternative solutions, choose the best of these alternatives, and then implement it through an effective program of communication. The manager must be prepared to apply these skills to all of the management activities that have been identified as appropriate to first-line field sales managers.

Decision makers may be reactive or proactive. A reactive decision maker waits for a problem to happen and then *takes* the best decision that is available. A proactive decision maker anticipates problems and *creates* solutions that will make the future most favorable for his or her company. The reactive manager is a fatalist, while the proactive one is a strategist.

WHY PROBLEMS OCCUR

While the number of problems that occur seem almost limitless, they can be classified into a reasonably small number of types. This enables us to understand more clearly how to solve them. The sales manager's problems and appropriate action may be classified as follows:

PROBLEMS OCCUR BECAUSE INDIVIDUALS:	APPROPRIATE ACTION:
1. Don't know WHAT to do	Knowledge Training
2. Don't know HOW to do it	Skill Training
3. Don't know WHY they're supposed to do it	Communications
4. Aren't COMFORTABLE doing it	Coaching
5. Don't AGREE with what they're supposed to do	Counseling
6. Don't CARE about it	Motivation
7. Can't CONTROL what they're supposed to do	Communications
8. Other individuals don't know WHAT, WHY, HOW, etc.	All of the above
9. Have PERSONAL reasons	Counseling

The process of problem solving at any level of management includes generally accepted steps for analyzing the problem and for decision making. These steps will be illustrated first in the context of a personnel problem faced by a field sales manager, and then in a strategy decision faced by a general sales manager. The latter decision will illustrate some basic concepts in quantitative decision making.

STEPS IN ANALYZING THE PROBLEM

An analysis of the problem begins with a definition of the problem and identification of its causes. The contribution of each cause to the problem and the degree of control (or adaptability) of each of these causes must be determined in order to select a course of action.

DEFINE THE PROBLEM

A sales management problem is a deviation from a performance standard that is based on the job description and the selling plan. The problem definition should identify the principal actors who are involved in the problem, their objectives, needs, and values. The problem solver should try to understand how each of these principal actors defines the problem. Did they participate in the job description and performance standards development? Are these standards up to date? Are these individuals in the wrong job? The definition of the problem should be a joint, negotiated effort among all of the principal actors.

During the problem definition, the manager will need to describe the deficiency in terms of the performance standards that have been established and the importance of the activity to the selling program. The manager will then listen for causes, retaining neutrality and objectivity, ask for solutions, support those solutions that are viable, and be ready to suggest solutions.

To illustrate the analysis process, we will examine a problem that is common for sales managers—a representative who does not file daily reports. In this case, the representative filed the reports, but not at the end of each day. Instead, they were filed in batches two or three times per month. The reports were the basis for a direct mail program, as well as for controlling the representatives.

IDENTIFY THE CAUSES

Failure to submit reports as required is a symptom, not a cause. Problem solving requires a list of causes that may explain this behavior. These causes, sometimes known as subproblems, are part of the scientific process that identifies hypotheses and then tests these hypotheses through experimentation. The analyst must therefore follow basic scientific rules by listing all of the reasonable explanations and making certain that they are exclusive of each other.

Exhibit 14.1 suggests the following five possible causes for this representative's failing to file daily reports when required: (1) no space to work at home, (2) spouse objects to evening work, (3) the representative doesn't think that reports are important, (4) the representative does not know how to fill out the reports, and (5) the representative has an insufficient stock of forms.

DETERMINE THE CONTRIBUTION OF EACH CAUSE TO THE PROBLEM

Causes do not contribute equally to the problem. In the present case, the manager and the representative will need to determine how much each of the five causes contributes to the problem of not completing the reports. In this instance, the objections of the spouse to evening work was weighted as the most important cause. The second most important cause was the fact that the representative was not convinced that reports needed to be turned in daily. The third most important factor was that the representative had no space at home to do paperwork.

Exhibit 14.1   Ranking the Causes of a Problem
Problem Definition: The representative does not turn in daily call reports when required.

CAUSES (EXHAUSTIVE AND EXCLUSIVE)	PERCENT CONTRIBUTION TO PROBLEM	PERCENT CONTROL* (OR ADAPTATION)	ACTION INDEX	ACTION RANK
	(1)	(2)	(3) (1)x(2)	(4)
1. No space to work at home	20%	75%	1500%	2
2. Spouse objects to evening work	40%	40%	1600%	1
3. Doesn't think that it is important	30%	10%	300%	4
4. Does not know how to fill them out	5%	10%	50%	5
5. Insufficient forms in stock	5%	90%	450%	3
	100%			

Note: Column (1) must add to 100%. Column (2) does not add to 100% because the control of each cause is independent of other causes.

*Percent control by the representative in this case because the manager is helping the representative solve his/her problem.

DETERMINE THE CONTROL OVER EACH CAUSE

Managers must frequently accept the fact that they have little control over some of the most important causes of a problem. Column 2 in Exhibit 14.1 provides a means for quantifying this percent of control (or the ability to adapt to a situation). In this case, the control is exercised by the representative. It is important to note that the manager helps a representative to solve his or her problem by working through the problem-solving process. In this manner, the representative will be in a position to solve his or her own problem when next faced with one. If, in contrast, the manager had attempted to solve the problem, then the manager would be continuously faced with solving representatives' problems for them.

The representative's perception of the percent of control over each of the five causes appears in column 2.

PRIORITIZE THE CAUSES

Managers will want to focus on the most important causes of a problem. The causes in Exhibit 14.1 may be prioritized by multiplying the percent contributions and the percent of control in columns 1 and 2 to form an action index, column 3. For easy reference, this index may then be rank ordered in column 4. In this example, the most important causes were the objections of the spouse to evening work and a lack of space at home for completing paperwork. The manager and the representative may now turn to the decision making steps of problem solving.

STEPS IN DECISION MAKING

When the most important causes of the problem have been ranked, the manager may return to those steps that could eliminate causes and thereby solve the problem. Because this is a personnel problem, the manager and the representative will work on these steps jointly.

ESTABLISH DECISION-MAKING CRITERIA

A clear statement of the criteria for making a decision places boundaries around feasible alternatives; therefore these criteria are the initial step in decision making. These criteria, in turn, will be determined by corporate policies, procedures, performance standards, and the selling plan. These criteria, like all objectives, must be stated in quantitative terms that clearly identify the event and the time frame for completion. In the present example, the event is the completion of daily call reports and the time frame is the submission of these reports daily so they may be used in a direct mail campaign and for controlling the sales force. In other cases, the decision-making criterion may be a specified sales level, expense level, profit contribution, or rate of product distribution. Personnel problems, such as the present one, must consider the individual needs of the representative, such as maintaining harmony in the family. Translating such human dimensions into objective criteria is not always feasible, but these human needs must be considered when choosing among alternative solutions to a problem. The personal dimensions of this case make it even more important for the manager and the representative to agree on the decision criteria that are appropriate.

CREATE ALTERNATIVE PROGRAMS

The most creative step in management is the identification of alternative programs to eliminate the causes that result in problems. Ackoff has stated that the most essential properties of good management are competence, communicativeness, concern, courage, and creativity, and that the greatest of these is creativity. "Without creativity a manager may do a good job, but he cannot do an outstanding one. At best he can preside over the progressive evolution of the organization he manages; he cannot lead it to a quantum jump—a radical leap forward."[1] In the present case, the manager and the representative must explore, discuss, and test alternative solutions for the elimination of the two major causes of the problem.

Possible solutions to the spouse's objections to evening work are as follows:

1. Determine if other spouses are objecting to this evening work and modify the reporting system, using techniques such as punch cards or microcomputers to simplify the task.

2. Provide the representative with evidence of the importance of gaining promotional support from the direct mail programs generated by daily reports.

3. Point out that bad reporting habits are an early warning that frequently leads to termination of a representative.

4. Enlist the support of the spouse through an understanding of the importance of getting good evaluations, emphasizing how a successful representative can meet the needs of the family.

Possible alternatives to the lack of space include the following:

1. Enlist the support of the spouse in identifying a temporary time and space in the home for completing the paperwork. Make the spouse part of the solution.
2. Discuss with the representative the possibility that his or her family has outgrown its present accommodations.
3. Supply the representative with a desk at the company's expense.
4. Encourage the representative to buy a desk and install it in the bedroom.

All parties to the decision will want to explore, discuss, and test alternative solutions before making a decision. It may be advisable to discuss alternatives with other field managers or other representatives. It may also be desirable to try out one alternative solution for a limited period of time before making a final decision.

MAKE A DECISION

To choose among the alternatives, the decision maker must have an assessment of the costs and benefits associated with each alternative. These costs and benefits must be expressed in terms of the decision-making criteria that had been established. Because of the human nature of personnel problems, it is rarely possible to express the outcomes in numerical costs and benefits. The manager and the representative must subjectively evaluate the outcomes of each alternative and choose the most appropriate one. Later in this chapter we will see how decision theory and tree diagrams may be used to make a decision when outcomes can be quantified.

The manager and the representative must agree on the decision, what steps will be taken by whom, the standards, the schedule for accomplishment, the reevaluation date, and the consequences for performance or nonperformance. All of this should be in writing and signed by the manager, the representative, and other key parties.

IMPLEMENT THE DECISION

Implementing a decision requires a variety of steps, such as buying equipment and materials, hiring and training personnel, developing new products, time sequencing the events that are necessary to implement the program, and selling the program to all stake holders and superiors.

The present example may require a statement of activities that the representative agrees to perform in order to correct the problem of late reports. If the solution is the purchase of a new desk, the manager may suggest some furniture stores. If the long-range solution is larger living accommodations, the manager may introduce the representative to several real estate brokers.

The implementation step requires a negotiated agreement on the program, schedules, and standards for implementing the best alternative. Some negotiated agreements may also require the approval of the district and general sales managers. The agreed upon program and schedule must include measurable behavioral standards that demonstrate when the problem is solved. The manager and the representative must recognize the consequences of the success or failure of a program. Consequences such as termination, demotion, or probation must be understood now, rather than after the program fails.

Difficulty in implementing the decision may reflect failure to get agreement on each step in the problem-solving process. Failure to get agreement that a problem exists will assure failure in implementing a decision.

FOLLOW THROUGH

The final success of a program turns on the continuous monitoring of the results so that appropriate action may be taken if the problem continues and rewards given if it is solved. The manager will also want to ask questions such as, "How can this problem be avoided in the future? Can policies and procedures solve it automatically?"

QUANTITATIVE DECISION ANALYSIS

Quantitative decision analysis may be used by a sales manager when it is possible to quantify the costs and benefits associated with each alternative. To illustrate the application of quantitative techniques to sales management, we will examine the problem of a sales manager who was faced with the problem of a sales force that was reaching only $20 million in a market with a potential of $22 million. An analysis of the problem revealed that the most important cause was that the present sales force did not have sufficient capacity to prospect for new customers and maintain the eight-week calling cycle for present customers, as required by the selling plan. The sales manager wished to evaluate the costs and benefits of the following three alternatives: (1) add five new representatives, (2) use manufacturers' representatives, and (3) increase the calling cycle from eight to nine weeks and supplement the drop in calls per account with either direct mail or telephone sales.

DECISION TREES

The sales manager specified that the decision-making criterion would be highest net expected value, which is the expected value associated with the alternative minus its costs. To help organize all of this information, the sales manager developed the *decision tree* that appears in Exhibit 14.2. Each branch on this decision tree will be discussed briefly to illustrate how decision trees help to organize objective and subjective information when solving sales management problems.

The first step in the decision tree analysis is to draw branches that represent all of the alternatives that have been identified by the decision maker. In this example, there were three main alternatives—adding new representatives, using manufacturers' representatives, and increasing the calling cycle. If manufacturers' representatives were used, there were the additional alternatives of what commission rates to use and which accounts would be assigned to these representatives. The company rejected the alternative of giving manufacturers' representatives named accounts because this would conflict with its national account program. Instead, it considered only the alternatives of using manufacturers' representatives for accounts that generated less than $500 in sales per year, or the assignment of all rural accounts to these outside representatives. If it was decided to increase the calling cycle, it would be necessary to increase other promotional efforts. The sales manager decided to consider two alternative promotional efforts—direct mail and telephone sales. When the tree diagram has been drawn to reflect all of the alternatives, the next step is to evaluate each alternative in terms of the decision-making criteria that were established earlier. To simplify the example, the analysis is limited to one year, but it could be extended by discounting future benefits and costs to a present value.

Benefits associated with each alternative are expressed in terms of expected value. The sales manager estimates the expected value by estimating the potential of various fractions of the market and the probability of attaining these fractions. The expected value for adding five new representatives is $800,000. It was estimated that the compensation, fringe benefits, expenses, training costs, and administrative costs associated with each new representative was $80,000. Thus the total cost of this alternative would be $400,000. The net expected value of this alternative would be $400,000, which appears in the far left-hand end of this branch of the decision tree.

Exhibit 14.2   A Tree Diagram to Aid in a Decision-Making Process

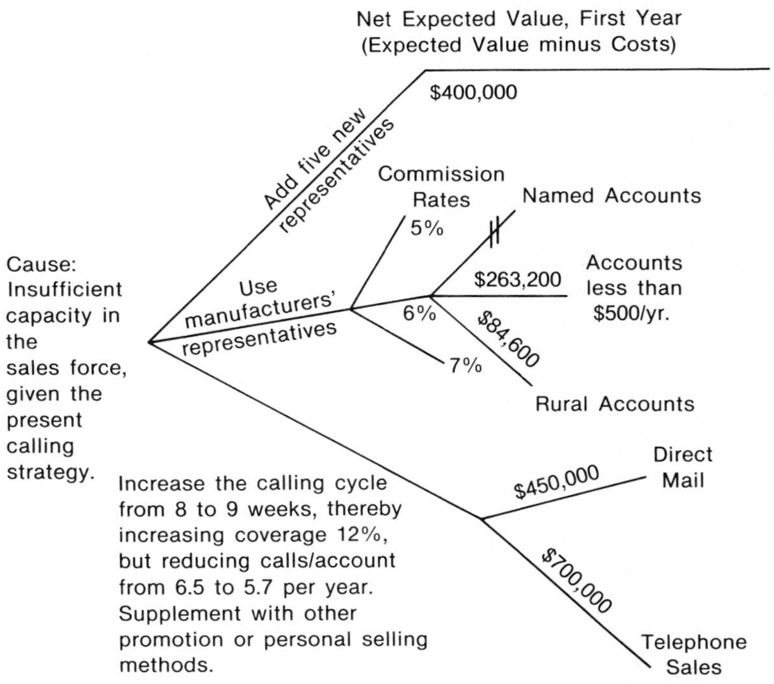

	Estimated Costs	Benefits — Market Potential	Expected Value
Net Expected Value, First Year (Expected Value minus Costs)	$400,000		
Add five new representatives	(Compensation, expenses, benefits, training, and admin. costs = $80,000/rep.) $400,000	$2.0 M	$800,000
Use manufacturers' representatives — Commission Rates			
Named Accounts: 5% / 6% / 7% ($263,200 / $84,600)	6% × $280,000 = $16,800	$1.4 M	$280,000
Accounts less than $500/yr.	6% × $ 90,000 = $5,400	$0.6	$ 90,000
Rural Accounts — Direct Mail ($450,000)	$150,000	Lost Sales $20.0	−$400,000
		New Sales $ 2.0	$1.0 M
		Net gain $600,000	
Telephone Sales ($700,000)	$200,000	Lost Sales $20.0	−$200,000
		New Sales $ 2.0	$1.1 M
		Net gain $900,000	

Cause: Insufficient capacity in the sales force, given the present calling strategy.

Increase the calling cycle from 8 to 9 weeks, thereby increasing coverage 12%, but reducing calls/account from 6.5 to 5.7 per year. Supplement with other promotion or personal selling methods.

If manufacturers' representatives were given the smallest accounts, they would have a market potential of $1.4 million. It was estimated that if they were paid a commission of 6 percent, the expected value would be $280,000. By paying them a fixed commission, the selling costs are easily computed to be $16,800. The net expected value of this alternative is $263,200. The analysis could be replicated at different commission rates using different probability estimates to determine which commission rate would yield the highest net expected value.

If the manufacturers' representatives were assigned rural accounts, their market potential was estimated to be $0.6 million, and the expected value was estimated to be $90,000. The net expected value associated with this alternative was $84,600.

The third alternative considered was increasing the call cycle from eight to nine weeks, thereby increasing the coverage by 12 percent, but dropping the calls per account from 6.5 to 5.7 calls per account per year. It was decided that either direct mail or telephone sales should be used to supplement the efforts of the salesperson. In evaluating these alternatives, we must acknowledge that there are negative outcomes as well as positive ones. The reallocation of selling effort from present customers to new customers may result in sales lost to competitors because direct mail and telephone sales are not perfect substitutes for personal selling effort. For example, in the case of direct mail, the expected loss to competitors from less intense market coverage was $400,000. This expected loss would be more than offset by the $1 million expected gain from new business.

A telephone sales supplemental effort was estimated to have a higher expected value than direct mail programs because telephone sales techniques had a lower probability of losing present business and a higher probability of gaining new business. The net expected value for the direct mail alternative appears in Exhibit 14.2 as $450,000, while the telephone sales alternative is $700,000. Given the decision criterion to select that alternative that generates the highest net expected value, the sales manager should choose the alternative of increasing the calling cycle from eight to nine weeks for present customers, using the sales calls that this makes available on new customers, and supplementing the effort of representatives with telephone sales.

SENSITIVITY TESTING ASSUMPTIONS

The sales manager will want to challenge many of the assumptions that appear in Exhibit 14.2. Estimates of market potential, probabilities, and costs may be changed and new net expected values computed to determine how sensitive each alternative is to these assumptions.

The manager may decide that some assumptions are critical and that subjective estimates must be replaced with more objective data that are derived through market research and cost analysis techniques. Additional decision-making techniques, such as Bayesian analysis, may be used by the manager to help decide how much should be paid for information that would refine these subjective estimates.[2]

Quantitative decision-making techniques can help the manager to organize the data and visualize the alternatives, but it does not deal with the creative dimensions of generating the alternatives or the human dimensions of implementing a decision. In many cases, the generation of alternatives and the implementation of a decision are the most critical steps in problem solving.

SUMMARY

Much of what a sales manager does can be classified as solving problems and tapping opportunities. (Opportunities may be considered as a special case of problems.) The process for problem solving may be divided into two processes—analyzing the problem and making the decision.

A problem is detected when there is a deviation from some performance standard. It is a symptom of underlying causes that must be identified and weighted according to their contribution to the problem and according to the control that the manager has over each particular cause. After determining the contribution and control of each cause, the manager may prioritize the causes and proceed to develop solutions.

The decision-making process begins with establishing criteria for choosing among alternative programs for eliminating the cause of a problem, generating these alternatives, analyzing the costs and benefits associated with each alternative, and then choosing one that best fits the decision-making criteria. The decision then must be implemented by developing detailed programs of action that may include activities such as purchasing equipment and training personnel. Implementation will also include communicating the decision to all relevant parties and selling them on implementing it. This communication and selling effort will be greatly simplified if these individuals have participated in the problem-solving process.

Follow through will include steps for measuring and monitoring the results. The manager will want to explore policies and procedures that will avoid these problems in the future or, if they occur, solve them automatically.

Quantitative decision-analysis techniques help a sales manager to organize subjective and objective data and to visualize the alternatives.

It must be recognized, however, that these techniques do not encompass the creative process that generates alternatives or the human process that implements a decision.

ASSIGNMENTS/DISCUSSION QUESTIONS

1. What is a problem?
2. Why do problems occur, and how can problems be classified?
3. Role play with a classmate the case of the representative who did not file reports daily. Switch roles so that each person has an opportunity to play the role of the representative and the sales manager. Evaluate each of the alternatives suggested in the text and suggest new ones. How would you resolve the problem?
4. Do a sensitivity analysis in Exhibit 14.2 varying the assumptions regarding the outcome probabilities and the costs associated with each alternative. What market research would you like to see conducted?
5. Give an example of a proactive and a reactive sales manager and how each would handle the problem.
6. Given the problem of a fifty-five-year-old representative whose productivity has decreased and who is 20 percent behind forecast while other representatives in his area are 15 percent above forecast, list five possible causes.
7. When should the sales manager become involved in a representative's personal problems?

CASE 14.1:
Superior Publishing Company

When Harry Bunting, the Northeast District Sales Manager for Superior Publishing Co., learned that Nancy Cunningham was pregnant but planned to continue working her field sales territory as long as possible, Harry had the feeling that his supervisory responsibilities were going to become considerably more complex.

Harry had been reviewing the current sales figures for the territories in his district and was troubled by the continuing flat-dollar trends. The Northeast District was running at 94 percent of forecast with only four months remaining in the fiscal year. This compared with sales of 101 percent of forecast for the Eastern Region, and 99.7 percent nationally. Six of the ten territories in Harry's district were at or very close to their quotas. Of the remaining four, Nancy

Cunningham's territory was the one most significantly behind, at 76 percent of quota. Mr. Shepherd, Harry's Regional Manager, had recently questioned him about Nancy's performance, and had remarked about the fact that the Northeast District was the only one in the Region behind quota. This would affect the share of the year-end bonus that Harry and his representatives would receive. He reminded Harry that he had asked previously for a program or plan of action to turn Nancy's performance around.

Nancy had been difficult for Harry to supervise ever since she was hired four years ago. She was a delightful individual, friendly, very well spoken, vivacious, and energetic. As a result, she was very well liked by her accounts. However, in spite of her ability to make friends easily, Nancy failed to make quota in any of the four years she was employed, with her year-end sales at 96 percent, 94 percent, 89 percent, and currently 76 percent. Although Harry had personally participated in Nancy's field training and had selected the other representatives to round out her training schedule, he had not been totally satisfied with her early progress. While his own observations and the reports from the trainers indicated her satisfactory performance during the training period, Nancy's use of methods and tactics outlined in the Selling Plan and of the selling tools provided by the company was too inconsistent and too awkward to suit Harry. He had the feeling that she followed the Plan only when he worked with her. His analysis was that she relied too heavily on her personality to do her selling for her.

In considering what he might do to help Nancy improve her performance, Harry's major concern was to be fair and to avoid the label of being prejudiced. (Nancy was the first female representative in Harry's district and, at the time she was hired, Harry's wife Virginia voiced her concern about Harry's working with Nancy on out-of-town trips.) While he recognized that one's selling style was individualistic and that Nancy's personality was an asset, Harry believed that her unconventional methods, for whatever reason, were behind her less-than-satisfactory productivity. Unfortunately, Nancy's personality and degree in business administration from UCLA, together with Harry's manner, did not make it easy for her to accept Harry's appraisal and counseling.

Nancy's response to Harry's efforts was an alternating defense of her individuality, with repeated references to the acknowledged warm relationships she had with her customers, and a friendly tolerance of his suggestions, all of which Harry found difficult to deal with. With little improvement, the status quo was maintained until less than a year ago when Nancy married. Her husband, a successful lawyer, supported Nancy's ambition to develop her own career. Unfortunately, Nancy's performance was anything but enhanced by her marriage. In addition to a continued slow decline in sales, Nancy's correspondence and reporting fell behind on more than one occasion, and she failed to make at least two scheduled out-of-town trips in compliance with her itinerary. When pressed for an explanation, Nancy admitted that her marriage was probably responsible, but insisted that it was a temporary lapse and that she would work out a better system to prevent any recurrence.

When Nancy telephoned Harry last weekend to announce her pregnancy, she told him that she was due to deliver in approximately six months, that she planned to work as long as possible, and that she planned to return to work after the birth of her child. To put it mildly, Harry was upset. Although he did not communicate his concern to her at that time, Harry calculated that Nancy would probably stop working six to eight weeks before her delivery date, would take another six to eight weeks personal leave of absence (without pay), and then she might decide that she didn't want to return to work. This would mean that her territory would be open for as long as four months—on top of the last eight months of declining sales—a set of circumstances he was certain his regional sales manager, Mr. Shepherd, would consider intolerable. Summarizing the situation in a lengthy memorandum to Mr. Shepherd, Harry reviewed the alternatives and made a number of recommendations for his approval.

CASE QUESTIONS

1. If we assume that the three other territories in the Northeast District that are behind forecast (in addition to Nancy Cunningham's) are equally so, what are their current sales as a percent of forecast or quota?

2. How might Nancy's "too heavy reliance on her personality" have interfered with her productivity?

3. Identify the following:
   a. Define the problem(s).
   b. Identify the causes.
   c. Determine the contribution of each cause to the problem.
   d. Determine the control over each cause.
   e. Prioritize the causes.
   f. Establish decision-making criteria.
   g. Create alternative programs.
   h. Make a decision.
   i. Implement the decision.
   j. Follow through.

REFERENCES

1. R. L. Ackoff, *The Art of Problem Solving* (New York: John Wiley & Sons, 1978), p. 1.
2. For more complete discussions of decision theory, including methods for handling different outcomes, see Howard Raiffa, *Decision Analysis* (Reading, Mass.: Addison-Wesley Publishing Company, 1968; B. M. Enis and C. S. Broome, *Marketing Decisions: A Bayesian Approach* (Scranton, Penn.: International Textbook Company, 1971); E. G. Hurst, ''Analysis for Management Decisions,'' *Wharton Quarterly* (Winter 1969): 2–7.

SUGGESTED READINGS

Blodgett, T. N., ''The Problem in Defining the Problem,'' *Training and Development Journal* 31, no. 11 (November 1977): 18–20.

Buzan, Tony, *Use Both Sides of Your Brain* (New York: E. P. Dutton, 1976).

Radford, K. J., *Modern Managerial Decision Making* (Reston, Va.: Reston Publishing Company, 1980).

Wickelgren, W. E., *How to Solve Problems: Elements of a Theory of Problem Solving* (San Francisco: W. H. Freeman, 1974).

 **15**

COMMUNICATION SKILLS

CHARACTERISTICS OF COMMUNICATION

COMMUNICATIONS DEFINED

Communication skills, like problem-solving and decision-making skills, are required to accomplish all sales management activities. The field sales manager must achieve all management objectives through communications of one type or another with representatives, senior sales managers, office administrators, personnel, production, shipping, and finance departments. Communications are so central to any organization that Boulding has defined an organization as a collection of roles connected by communications.[1]

Communication is a process by which meanings are exchanged through a common set of symbols, for the purpose of change. *Meanings* reflect those values, experiences, and judgments that are common to both parties. A lack of common values, experiences, and judgments probably makes communications impossible. *Exchange* highlights the fact that both parties must participate in communicating. It is a two-directional and interactive process that requires work to receive information as well as to send it. In the case of verbal communications, this means working hard at listening effectively. A *common system of symbols* that carries the same meaning to both parties is required in order to communicate. These symbols may be words, sounds, gestures, pictures, diagrams, or numbers. The new field sales manager must quickly learn the importance of exchanging information. This process includes effective listening and observing, as well as talking. Some new managers are effective listeners as representatives, but poor listeners as managers.

REASONS FOR COMMUNICATING

The reasons for communication follow closely from its definition. The reasons are to exchange information to bring about a change in awareness, understanding, and attitudes; to gain acceptance or agreement; and, finally, to bring a change in behavior. It should be noted that acceptance and agreement are different mental states. A representative may accept information but not agree with it. If there is no agreement, the probability of a change in behavior is greatly reduced. Acceptance is more of a fatalist approach, while compliance is dependent on punishment.

Each of these changes is a step in the communication process that has been studied by psychologists for decades. Of course, it is possible to change behavior without changing awareness, understanding, and gaining acceptance. When an individual's behavior is not consistent with his or her mental state, we have a situation of cognitive dissonance. Such a state may occur in sales management by short-term motivating techniques, such as compensation schemes or incentive schemes that temporarily increase sales, but do not meet the representative's psychological needs. Once the effect of the incentive has worn off, the representative is inclined to ask, "But what have you done for me lately?" Long-term motivation (Chapter 11) requires effective communication about basic needs.

There can be many purposes for a manager's initiating communications. The purpose may be to create loyalty, develop skills, motivate, or convey information about a product, the company, and its objectives.

The major difficulty that the field manager encounters is gaining understanding, agreement, and follow through. This difficulty occurs because the representative and the manager will have different values, different levels of interest, and different priorities with regard to the tasks at hand. The manager may gain short-run acceptance of the contents of a message, but not agreement with it. Failing to recognize that agreement was not attained, the manager will have difficulty moving toward a change in behavior.

A manager has many opportunities for communicating with a representative, including daily, weekly, and monthly reports and itineraries, and feedback from the representative regarding the success of promotions, customer comments or complaints, order follow up, and recommendations. Basically, managers communicate to fulfill their needs and to help others fulfill theirs.

THE PROCESS OF COMMUNICATING

The sender encodes a message through the use of appropriate symbols that convey the message to the receiver who, in turn, decodes the message, encodes a response, and conveys the response to the sender. The communication task for the field sales manager is frequently one of translating the symbols of general sales management into symbols that are more familiar to the representative. Thus the field sales manager must first determine those symbols that communicate most effectively to the representatives.

COMMUNICATION BARRIERS AND GATEWAYS

The receiver's experience, value system, and judgment (needs, wants, fears, beliefs, opinions, self-image, and intelligence) may be so different from those of the sender that symbols have different meanings and no communication takes place. The receiver must have an incentive for decoding the message. In short, "What's in it for me?"

In addition to the personal differences between senders and receivers being barriers to communication, there are environmental barriers. There may be distractions, such as a telephone call, that destroy the receiver's attention and cause him or her to miss the message. The manager must be careful to set an environment that is conducive to communication.

Perhaps the most important gateway to communications is for the sales manager to convey the message that the representative's needs are respected and understood. Reflecting on the discussion of motivation (Chapter 11), the manager must communicate in terms of the needs of the representative, not the manager.

COMMUNICATION SYMBOLS

Effective communication requires an ability to use the full range of communication symbols, including oral words and sounds, body language, written words, pictures, and numbers. The new sales manager generally feels comfortable in oral communication, but may feel inadequate using the other symbols. The most glaring deficiency among new managers is their low level of skills in written communications, such as memos, bulletins, letters, and proposals. This deficiency must be overcome promptly, not only for internal, corporate reasons, but also because so many of the field sales management documents are legal documents.

VERBAL SYMBOLS

The field sales manager will be involved in numerous forms of verbal communications. One-on-one verbal communication with representatives in solving problems, counseling, coaching, praising, and motivating represents the largest volume of verbal communications for the manager. But the manager must also make verbal presentations to buying groups, at sales meetings, at training sessions, and for parts of national sales meetings. Some managers have difficulty communicating upward to higher management.

The manager will also be called upon to represent the company at local civic clubs, television interviews, trade associations, and industry groups. The purpose for each of these oral communication experiences will differ and may include eliciting information, inspiring, persuading to take appropriate action, and challenging. Each purpose will draw upon different language skills, different forms of advance preparation, public-speaking abilities, and conference leadership skills.

BODY LANGUAGE

Some information is communicated more effectively with nonverbal means. For example, feelings and attitudes are expressed with words 7 percent of the time, 38 percent of the time with the tone of the voice, and 55 percent with body language such as gestures.[3] A good representative will recognize body language from a buyer. An interested buyer will lean forward, pick up the sales literature, maintain eye contact, and generally indicate to the representative that he or she is interested in the product or service being offered. Similarly, the representative sends body-language signals to the manager when he or she is not accepting the manager's message. A manager who is not sold on the industry, the company, the job, the program, or the message may be communicating these negative thoughts with body language while attempting to give a verbal message to the representative that is quite different. In this case, the body-language message probably more than offsets the verbal one. Gschwandtner reports that representatives who were trained in nonverbal communications increased their sales on an average of 41 percent.[4] Managers could also increase their effectiveness by learning nonverbal techniques. The representative may be saying, "I accept," verbally, but saying, "I don't agree," with body language.

WRITTEN WORDS

A sales manager was once overheard to say, "What do I do with a representative who is ready to be promoted to district sales manager but can't write a memo or a letter? If the verbal skills were poor we would send him to Dale Carnegie courses. We just cannot promote him while his written skills are so poor."

Most sales personnel dislike paperwork, but sales management activities require substantial written communications. The sales manager must communicate downward to representatives, upward to higher levels of sales management and general management, and outward to customers. The written communications include correspondence with customers, distributors, and wholesalers; bulletins and letters of encouragement to representatives; memos to general sales managers, legal, personnel, shipping, and accounting departments; job applicants and references for applicants; formal warnings and probations to representatives; annual performance appraisals; critical deviations from performance standards; and sales managers' reports after spending a day with the representatives. The field sales manager will also need to file reports on product promotions, marketing surveys, the performance of selling plans, competitive activities, and unusual economic activities in the district. He or she will want to recommend programs to meet local market and competitive needs. Thus the new field sales manager must develop written skills quickly to carry out the job responsibilities and expedite handling the workload.

Some companies are supplying field managers with dictating equipment because salespersons prefer to talk rather than write. These managers dictate all reports, memos, evaluations, and other correspondence. They then transmit them at high speeds to the home-office word-processing center for transcription. Companies are also supplying representatives with microcomputers that are capable of word processing. These types of investment should increase the productivity of the sales managers. They require mastering new forms of communication.

NUMBERS, GRAPHS, PICTURES, AND CHARTS

Pictures and charts will be used frequently by managers who train new and experienced representatives. The manager will frequently be supplied with these training materials. In other cases, he or she will develop them to meet local needs.

Numbers and graphs, like written communications, suddenly become an important part in the life of a representative who has been promoted to sales manager. Computerized district reports and graphic summaries of district performance require their own skills. The manager must learn how to analyze and interpret information in numerical and graphic form. As we saw in Chapters 5 and 7, microcomputers are playing an increasing role in the management of territories and districts. Some district managers are buying their own computers to maintain records. Some companies are supplying representatives and managers with computing equipment that will tie into the company computer for placing orders, checking on inventories, and electronic memos. We may expect more of this investment in capital equipment for the sales force in the near future.

New marketing survey data and inventory movement data, such as is available in the grocery products and pharmaceutical fields, can provide details of company and competitive sales to units as small as zip codes. Representatives' call reports are also computerized by many companies. Managers must analyze this selling effort and sales response by zip codes, territories, and districts in order to appraise performance and to reallocate selling effort more effectively. Some managers will need special training to help them develop the skills for communicating with these numbers.

COMMUNICATION NETWORKS

It is well for the field manager to recognize that there are several communication networks beyond those shown in job descriptions and organizational charts. Informal networks among representatives are usually made up of several representatives in a district with an informal leader. There may be similar networks linked to office personnel. Of course, the sales manager is excluded from these networks, but it is important to recognize their existence and to anticipate their early knowledge of most information and announcements. For this reason, formal announcements of product, price, and personnel changes should be made as early as possible.

ONE-ON-ONE COMMUNICATIONS

One-on-one communications probably represent 75 percent of the communications of the first-line sales manager. This type of communication requires empathy and people skills. Improving these skills would improve other activities of the sales manager, such as coaching and counseling. Two important dimensions of this type of communication are the negotiated agreement and documenting such communications.

NEGOTIATED AGREEMENTS

One very special type of one-on-one communications is the process of a negotiated agreement, which was discussed in the previous chapter as one step in the problem-solving process. This form of communication should have the following guiding principles: maintain the employee's self-esteem, listen and respond empathetically, ask the employee to solve his or her own problem, and take some form of specific action.

While the steps in this process will vary according to the type of problem, the following steps are common to many negotiated agreements in a one-on-one communication situation.

1. Describe the specific deficiency in terms of job-related behavior. Is it a performance problem or a work-habit problem?

2. Explain the agreed upon performance standard that is not being met and its importance to the company, the district, and the employee.

3. Ask the representative for his or her explanations for the deficiency. Listen carefully with sincerity, neutrality, and understanding. This mental and emotional state on the part of the manager is very important.

4. Ask the representative for solutions, supporting viable solutions that are recommended, and be prepared to suggest alternatives if none are forthcoming.

5. Agree on a course of action in writing that includes the following elements: what steps will be taken, what standards will be used to measure compliance, a timetable for these steps, and acceptance of the consequences for success or failure. This final step eliminates a misunderstanding of what was agreed upon and prepares both the manager and the employee for action.

DOCUMENTING COMMUNICATIONS

Federal and state regulations regarding equal employment opportunities place special requirements on sales managers for documenting communications regarding recruiting, hiring, evaluating, compensating, promoting, and terminating. This specialized form of communication requires accuracy, objectivity, and completeness. These documents become particularly important when the representative is handicapped, a female, a veteran, or a member of a minority group, a protected age group, or a religious group. The following are sensitive areas that require careful written documentation by the field sales manager:

1. Affirmative action recruiting efforts, including turndowns of offers made by the company.

2. Acceptances or turndowns of offers of promotion.

3. The agenda and date when company equal employment opportunity policies are discussed at sales meetings.

4. Performance appraisals of employees, giving specific examples of good and deficient performance on the job.

5. Disciplinary incidents, giving full information on who, what, when, where, and the action that was taken. The employee should be provided with a copy.

6. Warnings and probations, providing the employee with a copy.

7. Compliments and commendations, providing the employees with a copy.

8. Career counseling sessions and subsequent followup sessions, showing what activities were to be performed by the representative, what courses of action were selected, and which ones were completed.

9. Complaints about company biases or discrimination against employees, signed by the employee and witnesses, with copies for the employee and the personnel department.

10. The candidate should be evaluated immediately after a hiring interview, noting specifics about possible job behavior in comparison with job requirements.

11. Exit interviews, with summaries of the reasons for leaving.

12. Terminations, with details of previous disciplinary actions, efforts to salvage the representative, training, and counseling. Company personnel policies must be followed carefully, especially for representatives in the protected groups.

All documentation should be objective and limited to job-related behavior, excluding opinions or editorializing. This documentation should be for all employees, not just those in protected groups or problem employees. This documentation should be completed within twenty-four hours to record full details because complaints or law suits may not surface until many years later, at which time details will have been forgotten.

GROUP COMMUNICATIONS

The sales manager must also be an effective communicator with groups because he or she must frequently run sales meetings and conferences.

SALES MEETINGS

A new sales manager may become involved quickly in a variety of sales meetings. There is the weekly or monthly sales meeting for representatives that is designed to develop enthusiasm, provide recognition, train, and communicate information about products, programs, and company policies. There will be scheduled training meetings for new recruits and retraining for present representatives. The sales manager may be responsible also for designing and running sales meetings for distributors, dealers, and retail salespersons. National sales meetings will also involve presentations by sales managers from various levels of the organization. These meetings may introduce new products and programs, generate enthusiasm, recognize accomplishments, and provide incentives for the high achievers. Sales meetings are also a mechanism for a dialogue with the representatives. Top-management personnel can get feedback on selling programs, sales trends, employee attitudes, and information about competitors.

Companies that run frequent regional and national meetings will have an in-house director of conferences. This position is so frequent among insurance companies that there is even an association called Insurance Conference Planners. Other organizations of meeting planners include Meeting Planners International and Society of Company Meeting Planners.[5]

Planning is a major undertaking that begins with a clear definition of the reasons for the meeting. If the meeting represents a reward for accomplishments, then the site location should be in a resort such as Hawaii, Mexico City, or Miami. If, on the other hand, the purpose of the meeting is simply a training or retraining session, diversions will be minimized by holding it in a regional motel.

Site selection should begin two years in advance. Some companies will select a conference center or hotel where they will be the only or the largest convention in the hotel to assure that they get careful attention. While the site is frequently selected two years in advance, the hotel will generally not confirm room rates until one year in advance.

The planner will want to prepare a detailed budget of hotel costs, gratuities, meals, coffee breaks, cocktail parties, speakers' costs, transportation costs, and meeting room costs. *Sales & Marketing Management* magazine provides a directory of average costs for cities, conference centers, and cruise ships. These estimates can help the meeting planner choose among the wide variety of alternative meeting sites. This directory also provides information about union requirements for setting up exhibits and the availability of audio/visual equipment.

The meeting planner is not finished when the conference ends. Evaluation from participants and executives provides important feedback for planning the next meeting. Professional planners also share their experiences with other planners so that there is an informal communication network that aids in avoiding disasters.

Companies that do not have frequent or large meetings may not have a professional meeting planner. Hotels, conference centers, airlines, and consultants help meet their needs.

CONFERENCES

Conferences are small groups of individuals who are gathered together to communicate, to find answers to questions, and to create solutions for problems. Thus the problem-solving techniques described in the previous chapter are central to planning and implementing a conference. A sales manager will frequently be a conference leader on topics such as product problems, intense competition, incentive programs, compensation schemes, and sales strategies and tactics.

A conference leader must develop the skills for encouraging everyone to participate. This means practicing self-restraint. He or she must resist the desire to lecture in areas of personal expertise. The conference leader must develop questioning skills that open the discussion, stimulate interest, provoke thinking, accumulate data, distribute the discussion among participants, develop a subject, redirect the discussion, arrive at conclusions, and limit or end the discussion.

The conference leader must prepare for the conference. This preparation includes defining the problem, notifying conferees, and having the meeting room ready. The conference leader must ask himself or herself whether this meeting is really necessary. Is it an ego trip for the leader? Is the meeting called simply to present a decision that has been made by the leader? Such reasons will be detected quickly by conferees so that little communication will take place and future conferences will be avoided. Some conference leaders use an independent observer to keep the conference discussion moving objectively and to provide feedback to the conference leader and participants for better future meetings.

EXECUTIVE COMMUNICATION SKILLS

As a sales manager moves up the administrative hierarchy, skills must be developed to deal with a broader range of audiences outside the company. Some companies will provide future executives with training in subjects such as statistical, financial, and technical presentation skills. A sales manager may participate in the company's or its industry's speakers' bureau, which provides an opportunity for the individual to influence important community and national decisions. Senior executives are trained in pressure and confrontation communications that may be necessary for stockholders' meetings, media interviews, Congressional hearings, television talk shows, news programs, and appearances before hostile audiences. Hence, the young sales manager who has learned communication skills before groups has an excellent background for future top administrative roles.

SUMMARY

Communication creates change by the transfer of information through a shared set of symbols. The changes that take place include changes in awareness, understanding, attitudes, acceptance of agreement, and behavior. The sales manager seeks changes in behavior that will help the sales force to achieve its corporate objective. A newly-appointed sales manager will have excellent skills in dealing with verbal symbols and perhaps body language, but may need training in writing and communicating with numbers, graphs, and charts.

The most common form of communication for the first-line sales manager is one-on-one communication with representatives. This type of communication requires skills in negotiated agreements and careful documentation. This documentation is especially important because of federal and state regulations regarding equal employment opportunities.

As the young sales manager moves up the administrative hierarchy, it will be necessary to develop skills for communicating with groups. These skills include planning and implementing sales meetings and conferences. The development of these group communication skills can be helpful when the sales manager reaches the top levels in an organization that requires communicating with outside audiences, such as stockholders, Congressional hearings, the media, and hostile groups.

ASSIGNMENTS/DISCUSSION QUESTIONS

1. What are the reasons the same performance problem will recur repeatedly with the same representative?

2. What should a sales manager do if the representative poses a solution to a problem that the sales manager is reasonably certain will fail, and if the representative is unwilling to accept the manager's solution?

3. What could happen if the sales manager insists on the representative implementing the manager's plan to solve the problem?

4. What should a sales manager do if he or she cannot gain acceptance or agreement on the identification of a problem?

5. Use good graphics to present the data in the Westmont Case, Chapter 23.

6. Write a press release for a company of your choice:
   a. announcing a new plant opening
   b. responding to an FTC charge of price fixing or deceptive advertising
   c. responding to a Senate inquiry of overseas bribery.

CASE 15.1:
Standard Business Machines

Ron Williams joined the field sales staff of the Standard Business Machines Company eight years ago. His original territory was a section of downtown Chicago. After a slow start, Ron developed into a persistent, cooperative, and productive hard worker. His sales ability was recognized when Sam Steward retired in Milwaukee and Ron was asked to take a lateral transfer at company expense to this highly productive territory which Jennifer Engle, the district sales manager, felt matched Ron's temperament and capabilities. Eight months ago, Jennifer Engle was promoted to regional sales manager in Denver and was replaced by Pete Harrison, who had eleven years with Standard Business Machines and had been a special accounts representative in New York City prior to his promotion.

Last week, Mary Powers, a sales representative in Madison, Wisconsin, for the past five years, was promoted to district sales manager in Kansas City on the recommendation of Pete Harrison. Ron Williams received the announcement of Mary's promotion in his company mail on Monday evening. Tuesday morning Ron called Pete Harrison at his Chicago office and asked to see him about a problem that was bothering him. When Pete asked for particulars, Ron said he'd rather discuss it in person, whereupon Pete replied, "Fine, if you can make it down here from Milwaukee by 1:00 P.M., I'll keep the afternoon open."

When Ron walked into Pete's office at 1:00, Pete sensed that Ron was really upset because his usual smile had been replaced with a grim, set look. In fact, Ron's appearance prompted Pete to say in a jovial way, "It's good to see you, Ron. What's on your mind and where's your usual smile?" At which point Ron blurted out, "I don't see it as a laughing matter to have some gal who had half my seniority, and can't match my experience or performance, be promoted to DSM ahead of me, particularly when I was promised the next promotion. I could understand your being promoted because of your seniority, but this seems like reverse discrimination to me."

CASE QUESTIONS

1. List the apparent problems with which Pete Harrison has to deal.

2. How should Pete proceed in attempting to resolve each of the problems in Question #1?

3. What caused the problems?

4. How should Pete determine the facts about the "promised promotion"?

5. If we assume that Pete was unable to find any evidence to substantiate Ron's claim, what points should Pete cover in his next conversation with Ron?

6. After the matter has been resolved, what should Pete do? Why?

CASE 15.2:
Sterling Electric Products

Bill Dunham graduated last June from the state university with a B.A. in business administration, and had one part-time job before being hired by Sterling Electric Products as a sales representative. His performance during training was about average for his class. He's very friendly, generally cooperative, somewhat inexperienced, and progressing well, in general. He likes the job, and believes he's doing well. He's had a few paperwork problems, but he feels that they're no big deal. His sales are on target and it looks as if he'll make forecast.

Steve Hollings, his district sales manager, has worked closely with Bill, feeling that probably Bill would require some early guidance and extra attention. Steve has been generally pleased with Bill's progress. He's easy to work with, seems to like selling, and his sales are just about on target. However, Bill is having a problem in the area of reporting. Bill sends his reports on time to the computer company that processes them for Sterling, but about half of the customer computer cards are returned for correction or completion. In addition, the warehouse order department has had to telephone Bill at least once each week about product numbers that were transposed, incorrect prices entered, or incomplete shipping addresses. The incomplete or incorrect reports result in duplicate processing costs and delay the consolidation of current marketing and call data. The incorrect order forms delay the processing of the customers' orders. Because of this, Steve has decided to talk to Bill about this matter before letting his bad habit become deep-seated.

Using the Negotiating Agreement Outline and Objectives, three students will assume the roles of Bill Dunham, Steve Hollings, and an observer in a ten-minute role-play of this case.

CASE QUESTIONS

1. Identify the communications problems in this case.

2. Were the problems solved adequately in the role-play session?

3. Did the district sales manager use the Negotiating Agreement Outline and achieve the Negotiating Agreement Objectives?

CASE 15.3:
The National Hospital Supply Company

Jim Lee's gut feeling was that somehow he had a problem where none had existed previously, and he had the guilty feeling that, unintentionally, he had created the problem. Not that there wasn't ample evidence—at least as he saw it—that some changes ought to be made, but the reps were not responding as he had planned. And then there was the grumbling.

Jim Lee graduated from Ft. Sumpter College with a B.A. in History. He wasn't particularly interested in the subject, but by the time he became aware of that fact, he discovered that he would have had to spend another year in college to graduate with a business degree and his finances wouldn't permit that. In addition, he felt he'd spent enough time in college, at least for a while. His growing interest in business led him to apply to the National Hospital Supply Co., Inc., as a salesman when their recruiting team put in an appearance at Ft. Sumpter College in the spring of his junior year. Jim realized he knew nothing about selling medical or hospital equipment, but a fraternity friend had joined National Hospital Supply the previous year and was doing well, and Jim felt he liked the challenge of interacting with people.

The first year was a rough one for Jim and he found himself back in school, or at least in a training school. National Hospital Supply gave all new sales representatives a combination of six months' training in the classroom, in the field, and through home study courses. Jim's lack of technical knowledge was a hindrance, but he found that many others had no better background; perseverence saw him through. The company's training provided the required information and Jim learned how to use it. As Jim's experience grew, so did his productivity, confidence, and obvious enjoyment of the job and the recognition it brought him. Within four years, he was the top representative in the district and had gained a reputation for "getting things done." Whenever a special marketing project came down from headquarters, Jim's District Sales Manager delegated it to him. Jim also handled some of the training of new representatives. This latter assignment took him off his territory on occasion for extended periods. In at least one instance, it knocked him out of winning one of the special sales drives, which didn't please him; however, when his

Manager told him that his name had been added to the list of promotables for the region, Jim realized that the extra effort had paid off.

A year later, Jim Lee got his chance. He was appointed District Sales Manager in San Francisco to replace Tom Kelly, a fifteen-year veteran who was promoted to the headquarters division. The San Francisco district had qualified for the President's Cup in three out of the last five years, a record envied throughout the ranks of the DSMs. Tom Kelly had built his group of representatives into an enthusiastic team that worked well together and was considered to be innovative, hard-working, and resourceful. Most of the representatives had been on the staff for over five years, with only two of the ten having less than two years' experience. Tom was considered by his reps to be a "great guy." He was enthusiastic, highly supportive of their achievements, very encouraging, and helpful when they encountered problems. During sales meetings, he was "one of the fellows." The annual picnics and Christmas parties that he and his wife, Rita, hosted brought all the families together, including the kids. As a result, his farewell party was a festive occasion and the representatives had mixed feelings about his good fortune.

Jim Lee had worked in the district adjoining San Francisco, and over the years had interacted with some of the sales representatives in his new district on special projects, at conventions, or at joint sales meetings. He had observed some practices with which he didn't agree and had heard them complain about the way some things were handled. As a result, when Jim took over as DSM six months ago, he set about promptly to put some of his ideas into effect and, at the same time, solve some of the problems that he had heard about. But somehow, things were not working out as planned. He had a growing feeling that the changes in procedures and programs that he had initiated were not being followed, including those that reflected the problems he had heard about. To top it off, he had heard confidentially from a competitive district sales manager, who was a friend of his, that some of Jim's representatives were beginning to grumble to their peers, and one of the younger representatives had let it be known that he might be interested in changing jobs.

Somewhat bewildered by the current state of affairs and with his feelings alternating among annoyance, frustration, and apprehension, Jim sought the counsel of his Regional Sales Manager, Harvey Cotton. Mr. Cotton listened to Jim's explanation and then asked him what he thought caused the problem and how he planned to resolve it. To his credit, Jim admitted that somehow, in his eagerness to make a contribution, he may have caused the problem. Although Mr. Cotton had left word with his secretary to hold all incoming calls, his telephone rang. It was the President of National Hospital Supply who wanted to talk with him immediately. With apologies, Mr. Cotton asked Jim to spend the intervening time trying to identify his problems, what caused them, and how he thought he should set about solving them, and he would be back to discuss these questions with him as quickly as possible.

CASE QUESTIONS

1. What management problem(s) is represented in this case?

2. What caused the problem(s) identified in Question #1?

3. How might the sales representatives have interpreted the "changes in programs and procedures" that Jim Lee initiated?

4. How would you interpret the representatives' comments about the complaints they voiced to Jim when he was a fellow representative and their lack of compliance with the solutions to the same problems he initiated as a DSM?

5. What solutions should Jim Lee suggest to Mr. Cotton?

6. On what factors would the success of this meeting depend?

7. Depending on how you read his management style or human needs (Chapter 11), do you think Jim will follow through with the solutions that you believe that he should implement?

8. With reference to his future management activities, how should Jim Lee operate within his style and with the changes he thinks should be made?

REFERENCES

1. K. E. Boulding, *The Image* (Ann Arbor, Mich.: University of Michigan Press, 1956), Chapter 2.
2. Carl R. Rogers and F. J. Roethlisberger, "Barriers and Gateways to Communication," *Harvard Business Review* (July–August 1972): 46–52.
3. Gerhard Gschwandtner, "Non-Verbal Selling Power," *Training and Development Journal* (November 1980).
4. Ibid.
5. Peter Shure, "Meetings Are Their Business," *Advertising Age* (April 1979): S–14.

IV.

GENERAL
SALES
MANAGEMENT

16

AN OVERVIEW OF GENERAL SALES MANAGEMENT

The general sales manager performs the same management functions and activities as the field sales managers, but with different emphasis. Planning and organizing activities are twice as important to the general line sales manager, while staffing is only one-third as important (Exhibit 2.3, Chapter 2). General managers and first-line field sales managers gave similar weightings to the functions of directing and controlling. The discussion in this chapter will not repeat the discussion of those management activities that are shared with first-line managers. Instead, the chapter will focus on two general management activities that are critical and unique to the general sales manager—positioning personal selling in the communication mix and developing selling strategies. But first we will examine a job description for a general sales manager.

JOB DESCRIPTION

Exhibit 16.1 provides a detailed job description for a general sales manager. A comparison of this job description with that of a first-line field sales manager (Chapter 7) will illustrate the differences in how activities are performed at these two extreme levels of sales management. General sales managers' involvement in many of these management activities is limited to the monitoring of field managers' compliance with strategies, policies, selling programs, and procedures. Activities such as training and developing personnel, evaluating, counseling, and coaching are performed by a general sales manager, but the recipients of these efforts are the field sales managers, not the representatives.

Exhibit 16.1 General Sales Manager Job Description

OBJECTIVE

To plan, organize, lead, and control the activities and personnel of the sales staff to achieve the planned level of sales within the approved levels of expenses.

MANAGEMENT SKILLS

Analyzing information to identify opportunities, problems, and their causes.
Decision making by identifying alternative courses of action, estimating the costs and benefits associated with each alternative, and selecting the best alternative.
Communicating effectively downward through the sales organization and upward to top management.

FUNCTIONS/Activities

Plan

Forecast

- Sales, expenses, competition, environmental, technological, and regulatory changes
- Personnel needs
- Space and equipment needs
- Promotion and staff support needs
- Training needs
- Management succession needs
- Nonselling responsibilities, such as committees

Set Objectives

- Translate corporate objectives into sales objectives
- Establish goals for market penetration, changes in personnel, programs, procedures, and training
- Establish priorities for various dimensions of the job
- Make objectives behavioral, individual, specific, measurable, achievable, and time oriented
- Establish personal goals

Develop Strategies

- Create sales force strategies
- Participate in developing strategies for products, services, advertising, promotion, price, and channels
- Evaluate the effectiveness of selling strategies

Develop Policies

- *Monitor* policies (company and statutory) for compliance in the sales force
- Evaluate present policies
- Develop or suggest new policies as circumstances change or in anticipation of changes in the environment, competition, or regulation
- Interact with the company compliance officer and government inspector

Develop Programs

- Select the best mix of selling activities to achieve the sales goals
- Make strategic decisions regarding the deployment of resources
- Evaluate existing programs
- Develop new selling programs and promotions

(continued)

Exhibit 16.1   Continued

Set Procedures
- *Monitor* compliance with procedures
- Evaluate present procedures
- Develop new procedures

Budget
- Deploy resources to achieve financial goals, such as sales levels, expense ratios, and return-on-assets managed
- *Monitor* field sales managers' efforts in controlling representatives' expenses
- *Monitor* field sales managers' expenses
- Anticipate expense trends and suggest alternatives
- Create annual estimates of needs for compensation, expenses, promotional materials, equipment, automobiles, office space, and public relations

Organize

Establish Organizational Structure
- Determine the size and structure (e. g., product or geographic specialization) of the sales force
- Consider alternative personal selling methods, such as brokers, manufacturers' representatives, direct mail, and telephone selling

Create Position Descriptions
- Evaluate current position descriptions in the light of changes in marketing strategies, the environment, and competition
- Work with field sales managers, representatives, and the personnel department to revise position descriptions
- Evaluate and revise own position description

Establish Position Qualifications
- Evaluate current qualifications for representatives and field managers in the light of present flow of applications, federal regulations regarding equal employment opportunities, marketing strategies, competition, turnover, and performance levels
- Revise position qualifications as necessary

Staff

Recruit and Select
- Develop programs for recruiting and selecting to maintain an adequate sales staff, given objectives and strategies
- Evaluate turnover, pirating, and terminations to determine future needs and deficiencies in policies, programs, and procedures
- Evaluate competitive recruiting schemes
- Comply with Affirmative Action Plans (AAPs) to assure applicant flow from protected groups and minorities
- Evaluate recruiting sources
- Cultivate minority applicant sources
- Comply with federal and state regulations regarding interviewing
- Anticipate future skills that are required

Orient and Train
- Develop programs for orienting new representatives and relocated representatives into the company, territory, and community

(continued)

Exhibit 16.1 Continued

- Develop training programs for new and present representatives to improve their knowledge, attitudes, skills, and habits
- Be aware of the changing values, qualifications, and needs of the applicants
- Be aware of the changing expertise required because of new products, strategies, competition, and regulations
- Keep informed of new training methods and equipment
- Update company training programs
- Provide management training for field sales managers

Develop Personnel

- Be aware of the effect of turnover and training on sales productivity and market share
- Develop team spirit
- Recognize the "dead wood" and "walking wounded" and take appropriate action
- Anticipate future needs
- Identify changing behavioral requirements and technical requirements
- Identify potential promotables
- Provide growth, educational, and training opportunities
- *Monitor* developmental activities of field sales managers
- Provide rotation for experience
- Approve transfers and reassignments consistent with future needs, growth, and promotability
- Create a pool of qualified managers
- Develop your replacement

Direct

Delegate (assign responsibility and accountability for:)

- Training sales staff and distributors' representatives
- Recruiting, selecting, and hiring representatives
- Evaluating, counseling, and coaching representatives
- Customer service
- Distributor selection

Motivate

- Provide charismatic (emotional) and intellectual leadership
- Develop pride, self-esteem, loyalty, willingness to work
- *Monitor* the results of field managers' motivation efforts
- Provide opportunities for field managers to meet their individual needs

Coordinate

- Coordinate the activities of field sales managers
- Coordinate the activities of representatives through field sales managers
- Encourage time management
- Manage the technical work of the sales force

Manage Change

- Create flexibility in the systems and organizations so change is possible
- Encourage innovation and criticism by others
- Create early warning systems that will monitor the environment, competition, technology, and regulation for opportunities and problems
- React appropriately to emergencies and recover quickly
- Inform top management immediately when conditions indicate that an approved plan will not be achieved

(continued)

Exhibit 16.1   Continued

Control

Establish Reporting Systems
- Collect and present field marketing data in actionable form
- Provide field managers, appropriate departments, and higher management with appropriate information in an actionable form
- Develop information systems to evaluate policies, procedures, and programs
- Be aware of new technology in information development
- Be aware of new information sources that will signal changes in the environment, competition, technology, and regulation
- Understand the limitations of information systems and market research
- Detect early any unsatisfactory trends and deviations from plans

Develop Standards
- Establish performance standards for representatives and field sales managers
- Challenge job descriptions and performance standards on a regular basis
- Assure that standards comply with federal and state regulations for equal opportunities for compensation and promotion
- Assure that standards are observable, measurable, and mutually agreed upon

Measure Performance
- Develop measuring instruments that are valid, reliable, and acceptable under federal regulations for equal opportunities in employment
- Appraise field managers regularly, accurately, and fairly
- *Monitor* the appraisals of representatives as conducted by field managers
- Evaluate changes in performance since last evaluation and the resulting consequences from success or failure in performance
- Evaluate field sales managers' performance in management skills and activity performance

Take Corrective Action
- Take prompt, corrective action when unsatisfactory trends in behavior are noted
- Counsel and coach field sales managers in management skills
- *Monitor* the counseling and coaching of field sales managers
- Identify problems and alternative solutions, including training
- Take negative actions involving reassignment, demotion, or separation

Reward
- Reward favorable behavior in accordance with individual needs
- Keep compensation schemes competitive with industry
- Anticipate necessary changes in the compensation levels and methods
- Assure that compensation is consistent with performance
- Identify disparate impact of compensation schemes on protected groups and minorities
- Review regularly compensation schemes for field managers and representatives

Similarly, the management skills of analyzing, decision making, and communicating are common to all levels of sales management, but the content broadens as an individual moves up the management hierarchy.

General sales managers, like all managers, must have skills in analyzing, but the general sales manager must analyze long-term trends in the environment, economy, and technology to determine possible effects on sales of products, compensation, and changing applicants' requirements. These long-range influences may also change personnel practices. The effects of government regulations must also be considered when making recommendations for an appropriate corporate response to proposed changes in government regulations.

Much of a general sales manager's decision making will focus on problems that are not covered by existing programs, policies, and procedures. Many of the problems will be personal ones that require sensitivity without intrusiveness. Conflicts that must be resolved may come from personal problems; changes in programs, policies, and procedures; complaints (customers, government, and peers); income; and career objectives (planned versus achievement, progress versus lack of progress). In many instances, these conflicts must be negotiated because they cannot be resolved fully to everyone's satisfaction. The general sales manager must anticipate conflicts and have programs for dealing with them. These conflict management programs must maintain morale and not destroy the motivation of creative persons. Central to many conflict management programs is the translation of a win-lose outcome to a win-win outcome.

Communication skills take on a new importance for a general sales manager. He or she must maintain visibility at all levels within the sales organization by attending regional and district sales meetings occasionally, attending conventions, and communicating effectively through memos and other media. The manager will monitor the communications of lower-level managers to see if they are communicating effectively. A manager must take great care when reducing personal matters to a memo, remembering that the "sunshine laws" permit an individual to see his or her personnel file.

The general sales manager will have heavy communication responsibilities with other marketing and nonmarketing departments. Much of this communication will take place in formal and informal committee assignments. Similarly, the general sales manager will represent his company at industry association meetings, community organizations, and on regulatory hearings that affect his or her company.

POSITIONING PERSONAL SELLING IN THE COMMUNICATION MIX

The general sales manager must understand the corporate and marketing strategies in order to develop personal selling mix strategies and then implement them. Exhibit 16.2 shows how sales management is positioned in the corporate strategy flow. The corporate strategy begins with an analysis of its market and environment. This analysis identifies market segments with opportunities and problems. These opportunities and problems must be evaluated in the light of organizational capacities—managerial, financial, research and development, production, and marketing. After the market analysis and the evaluation of capacities, the corporate planners evaluate and select market segments that are consistent with the stated objectives of the company. Marketing mix strategies are then developed to tap these opportunities and problems. A communication strategy is then developed that assigns responsibilities to advertising, sales promotion, personal selling, and marketing

Exhibit 16.2   Positioning Sales Management in the Corporate Strategy

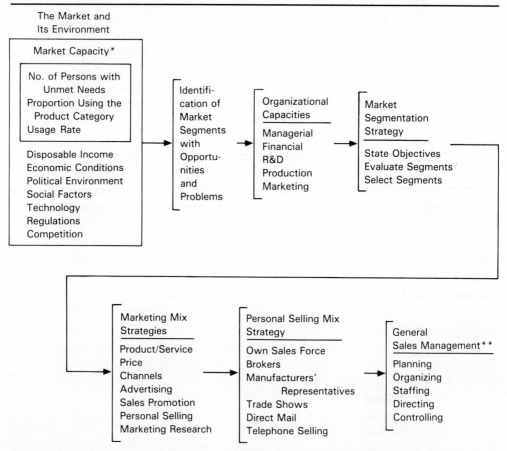

*See Chapter 17.
**See Exhibit 16.1 for details.

research. When the roles of personal selling are clearly defined, the general sales manager may then concentrate on developing an optimal personal selling mix that could include a company sales force, brokers, manufacturers' representatives, trade shows, direct mail, and telephone selling. Each of these personal selling alternatives requires different levels of general sales management involvement. The most extensive management requirements occur when a company has its own sales force. Thus most of the discussion in this text deals with the situation of a company sales force, with the understanding that these functions and activities apply to other personal selling strategies to a lesser degree.

COMMUNICATION TASKS

The communication tasks to be performed by the sales force will be determined by product characteristics, customer needs for information, and competition. During the discussion of consultative selling, we saw that personal selling strategies ranged from communication strategies, through persuasion and negotiation strategies, to consultative strategies (Exhibit 1.1, Chapter 1).

Column 1 in Exhibit 16.3 illustrates the fact that the communication tasks necessary to market a product differ across product categories. This simplified example compares the communication tasks required for a consumer product with those required for an industrial product that uses a direct sales force. A consumer product, such as a packaged grocery product, may require less emphasis in identifying customer needs than an industrial product that is custom designed. Similarly, market feedback may be less important for the industrial product than for the consumer product. Assuming that these two products have the communication tasks that are shown in column 1, we may turn to the question of developing a strategy for allocating these communication tasks among the communicators in advertising, personal selling, market research, and the channels of distribution.

ALLOCATION OF COMMUNICATION TASKS

In columns 2 through 5 in Exhibit 16.3 we see that, in the case of the consumer product, market research is assigned 100 percent of the responsibility for identifying customers' needs. Addressing product benefits is largely the task of advertising (50 percent), with contributions from personal selling (30 percent) and the channels of distribution (20 percent). Market feedback is provided by personal selling (20 percent), but is largely the responsibility of marketing research (80 percent). In contrast,

Exhibit 16.3 Positioning Personal Selling in the Communication Mix

COMMUNICATION TASKS (A PARTIAL LIST)	% OF TOTAL COMMUNICATION TASK	PERCENT TO BE DONE BY:				NET COMMUNICATION TASK BY:			
		Advertising	Personal Selling	Market Research	Channels	Advertising	Personal Selling	Market Research	Channels
	(1)	(2)	(3)	(4)	(5)	(1 × 2)	(1 × 3)	(1 × 4)	(1 × 5)
CONSUMER PRODUCT									
Identify needs	30%			100%				30%	
Stress benefits	50%	50%	30%		20%	25%	15%		10%
Market feedback	20%		20	80			4	16	
	100%								
INDUSTRIAL PRODUCT (DIRECT SALES FORCE)									
Identify needs	40%		70	30			28	12	
Stress benefits	50%	10	90			5	45		
Market feedback	10%		50	50			5	5	
	100%								

the industrial product communication tasks are dominated by personal selling for needs identification (70 percent) and stressing benefits (90 percent). The responsibility for market feedback is shared by personal selling and market research.

By multiplying the percent of the communication task in column 1 and the allocation of these tasks to advertising, personal selling, market research, and the channels (columns 2 through 5), we may derive the net communication tasks assigned to each of these communication activities, as appears in columns 6 through 9.

THE GENERAL SALES MANAGER AS A MARKETING STRATEGIST

The general sales manager will play an active role in developing strategies for marketing and sales management. He or she will probably be on a corporate marketing and policy committee, along with the managers of advertising, sales promotion, and marketing research. This committee, which is normally chaired by the vice president for marketing, develops the long-range policies and strategies for the corporation and reviews the annual plans for products. The sales manager also has primary responsibility for developing the personal selling strategy. In the latter role, the sales manager must be sensitive to changes in the marketplace, changes in the roles of the sales representatives, and changes in regulations that would affect selling strategies.

Some of the best managed companies have made strategic planning and management a single process. This combination has been achieved through three mechanisms:

1. A planning framework that cuts across organizational boundaries and facilitates strategic decision making about customer groups and resources
2. A planning process that stimulates entrepreneurial thinking
3. A corporate values system that reinforces managers' commitment to the company's strategy.[1]

To develop a personal selling strategy, a general sales manager must have answers to questions such as the following: What business are we in? What are the trends in this business? What is our competitive position? Answers to these questions will form a product-market portfolio matrix that will help the manager to develop his or her strategy. He or she will then develop a personal selling mix and programs for implementing these strategies.

A sales manager must guard against planning becoming an end in itself. To reduce the cost and save the time of management and staff persons, some companies have lengthened the planning cycle for some products from one year to three or more years. Businesses that result from the matching of a mature product to a stable market permit this lengthening of the planning cycle. Of course, the business will be monitored against its strategic goals every quarter, but an extensive strategic review will not be done every year.[2]

WHAT BUSINESS ARE WE IN?

A business is the matching of a market and a product. A single product like an automobile represents a different business when it is sold to consumers, the federal government, police departments, or to companies for fleet use by sales representatives. Each of these businesses is sometimes known as a "Strategic Business Unit" (SBU) in the terminology of strategic planners. Product-market matrices, such as those shown in Exhibits 16.4 through 16.6, help the strategic planner to organize vital information about strategic business units. For example, Exhibit 16.4 summarizes the benefits that are sought by automobile and van buyers representing four different market segments. Exhibit 16.5 summarizes

---

Exhibit 16.4   The Product-Market (SBU) Matrix for Benefits
(For a hypothetical automobile manufacturer)

What is a business? It is a matching of a market and a product or service. What business are we in? What business do we want to be in?

Present Products	Position in Product Life Cycle	SOLD TO THE FOLLOWING MARKET SEGMENTS			
		Consumers	Federal Government	Police	Sales Representatives
		Strategic Business Unit (SBU)			
Automobiles	Mature	Styling Service Price Mileage	Life-cycle costs Price Political	Cost Speed	Comfort Large trunk Value
Vans	Mature	Styling Economy Space	Value	Space	

Cell entries may be for share of our sales, share of our profit, ROI, share of the market, share of the product to a particular market, or growth rates for any of these measures.

The analysis may be repeated using *potential* products to help decide what business we want to be in.

Exhibit 16.5 The Product-Market (SBU) Matrix for Growth Rate
(For a hypothetical automobile manufacturer)

What is a business? It is a matching of a market and a product or service. What business are we in? What business do we want to be in?

GROWTH RATE PERCENTAGES
SOLD TO THE FOLLOWING
MARKET SEGMENTS (CURRENT YEAR)

Present Products	Position in Product Life Cycle	Consumers	Federal Government	Police	Sales Representatives	Product Totals	Product Previous Five-year Growth Rates
		Strategic Business Unit (SBU)					
Automobiles	Mature	0.3%	0.8%	1.0%	1.5%	0.4%	1.0%
Vans	Mature	−1.8	0.8*	1.0	0.1	−1.2	2.5**
SEGMENT PREVIOUS FIVE-YEAR GROWTH RATE		0.05%	0.8%	1.0%	1.2%		

*To be read, "Vans to the federal government grew at the rate of 0.8 percent during the current year."

**To be read, "Vans during the previous five years grew at the rate of 2.5 percent"

Cell entries may be for share of our sales, share of our profit, ROI, share of the market, share of the product to a particular market, or growth rates for any of these measures.

The analysis may be repeated using *potential* products to help decide what business we want to be.

Exhibit 16.6 The Product-Market (SBU) Matrix for Market Share

What is a business? It is a matching of a market and a product or service. What business are we in? What business do we want to be in?

MARKET SHARES
SOLD TO THE FOLLOWING
MARKET SEGMENTS (CURRENT YEAR)

Present Products	Position in Product Life Cycle	Consumers	Federal Government	Police	Sales Representatives	Product Totals
		Strategic Business Unit (SBU)				
Automobiles	Mature	3.0%	20.0%	25.0%	4.0%	3.9%
Vans	Mature	15.0%	25.0%*	30.0%	45.0%	21.0%
SEGMENT PREVIOUS FIVE-YEAR GROWTH RATE		−0.7%	0.0%	−2.0%	−5.0%	

*To be read, "This brand had 25 percent of the van sales to the federal government this year."

Cell entries may be for share of our sales, share of our profit, ROI, share of the market, share of the product to a particular market, or growth rates for any of these measures.

The analysis may be repeated using *potential* products to help decide what business we want to be in.

the growth rates for these strategic business units. Exhibit 16.4 summarizes the market share for each of these units. Similar tables may be made where the cell entries are profit, return-on-investment, or market potential for each of the units.

Once the businesses have been clearly defined, the sales manager may turn to the next critical question: What communication mix is needed to sell to this business and what is the role of personal selling? He or she may want to develop a table like the one that appears as Exhibit 16.3 for each of these strategic business units.

ASKING STRATEGIC QUESTIONS

The development of a strategy requires asking and then answering strategic questions. The following questions are the kind that may be posed by a sales manager.

Goals: What are our financial goals? Our marketing goals?

Marketing Mix Strategy Questions: How is our product positioned? How should it be positioned? How should we use the marketing mix to position or reposition our brand?

Product: What are its benefits? What services are part of the product? Do we use a market segmentation strategy by altering the product for each segment? What are the competitive strengths and weaknesses of our product?

Price: Should we have different prices for different strategies, segments, and channels, or a one-price policy? What are the legal implications of our pricing strategies? Who will determine prices? What factors determine the price level and the timing of price changes in this industry?

Channel of Distribution: Should we use traditional channels or build new ones? Should we use our own sales force or a mixed sales force?

Advertising: What will be the role of advertising? What messages and what media will be used in advertising? How will we measure the effectiveness of advertising?

These questions are simply illustrations of the kinds of critical questions that need to be asked and answered when developing a strategy. Hughes has developed a worksheet approach to help organize the asking of these questions, the collection of facts, the making of assumptions, and the drawing of conclusions in preparation for developing a marketing strategy.[3]

WHAT IS OUR COMPETITIVE POSITION?

When each of the company's businesses has been identified, the next step in developing a marketing strategy is to evaluate the company's competitive position in each of these businesses. This competitive analysis may be done with the aid of a form such as Exhibit 16.7, which continues the example of our hypothetical automobile manufacturer. Each business must be evaluated according to those elements that are necessary for success in this business. Elements would include factors such as product benefits, price, costs, manufacturing, distribution, finance, advertising, sales management, management, and research and development.

Sellers and buyers may have quite different perceptions of product benefits. Exhibit 16.8 illustrates the concept of a communication gap when these differences in perceptions occur. This exhibit illustrates the case of a pharmaceutical company that had developed a new prescription product. The two most important benefits that are considered by physicians when prescribing a drug are maximum effectiveness and minimum side effects. We see in Exhibit 16.8 that the physicians and the company have different perceptions about the effectiveness and side effects of this new drug. The distance between these two perceptions is a communication gap. In this case, clinical research strongly supported the company's position. It then became necessary to close this communication gap with appropriate advertising and sales messages to be delivered by the representatives to the physicians.

Competition may come from present competitors, potential competitors, substitute products, and buyers who decide to make the product themselves. Porter suggests that four forces drive industry competition. On the supply side, there is the threat of new entrants who make a competitive product. On the demand side, there is a threat of substitute products and services. Then there is the bargaining power of suppliers and buyers. Finally, there is competition within the industry among existing firms.[4]

Formal Planning Methods

Since the early 1960s there has been a movement toward more formal planning methods. This movement has been led by consulting firms such as the Boston Consulting Group (BCG), Arthur D. Little (ADL), and McKinsey, as well as by companies that have had extensive experience in planning such as General Electric, Shell International, and

Exhibit 16.7 Analysis of Our Competitive Position in Each Business

OUR RELATIVE POSITION ON
COMPETITIVE SUCCESS FACTORS IN
THIS BUSINESS

	Competitive Disadvantage		Par	Competitive Advantage		Comments
	1	2	3	4	5	
PRODUCT BENEFITS						
Styling	1	2	3	④	5	
Mileage	1	2	③	4	5	
Space	1	2	3	④	5	
Repair Costs	①	2	3	4	5	
Speed	1	②	3	4	5	
Comfort	1	2	3	4	⑤	
Trunk Space	1	2	3	④	5	
PRICE						
Initial Price	1	2	③	4	5	
Life-Cycle Costs	①	2	3	4	5	
COST COMPONENTS						
Experience Curves Position	1	②	3	4	5	
Raw Material Costs	1	2	③	4	5	
Raw Material Availability	1	2	③	4	5	
Superior Purchasing	1	2	③	4	5	
MANUFACTURING						
Production Facilities	1	2	3	④	5	
Engineering Expertise	1	2	3	4	⑤	
Labor Conditions	1	2	③	4	5	
DISTRIBUTION						
Logistics	1	2	③	4	5	
Selling	1	②	3	4	5	
Servicing	1	2	③	4	5	
FINANCE						
Working Capital	1	②	3	4	5	
Credit Position	1	②	3	4	5	
ADVERTISING						
Creativity	1	2	3	4	⑤	
Effectiveness	1	2	3	4	⑤	
SALES MANAGEMENT						
Cost	1	2	③	4	5	
Effectiveness	1	②	3	4	5	
MANAGEMENT						
Capacity for New Ventures	1	②	3	4	5	
Effectiveness	1	②	3	4	5	
RESEARCH & DEVELOPMENT						
Innovative	1	2	③	4	5	
Personnel	1	②	3	4	5	

**Exhibit 16.8   A Brand Map for a New
Prescription Drug**

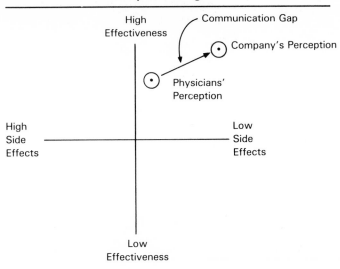

Mead. The sales manager should be aware of the three most popular methods—portfolio analysis, market attractiveness, and PIMS (Profit Impact of Market Strategy).[5]

Portfolio Analysis

Portfolio analysis evaluates each of a company's businesses as though it were a financial investment. Two frequently used variables for this evaluation are the market growth rate (in constant dollars, relative to GNP growth) and market share dominance (the company's market share relative to its largest competitors). Businesses are then classified into one of the four categories that appear in Exhibit 16.9. This strategy matrix, which is used by the Mead Corporation, suggests strategies that are appropriate for businesses that fall in each cell. For example, businesses with a high growth rate and high market share should attempt to achieve cost effectiveness. Businesses in the cell reflecting a high growth rate, but a low market share, should assess chances for leadership and either grow their share aggressively or get out of this business.

Portfolio analysis urges the strategist to develop a balanced portfolio that includes a mix of products with a high growth rate that have a good potential and those with a low growth rate that generate cash because of their low demands for new capital investments. Exhibit 16.10 illustrates how this portfolio matrix aids in the development of business

Exhibit 16.9   Mead Corporation Portfolio Matrix

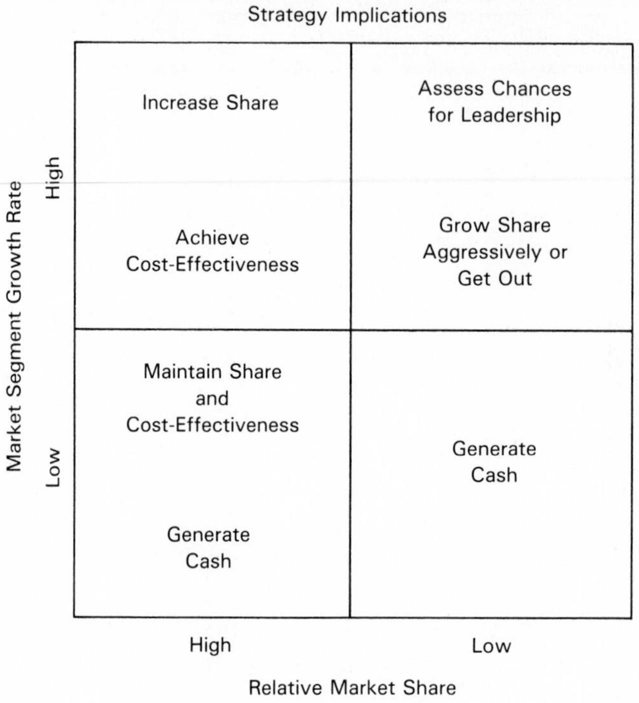

Strategy Implications

	High Relative Market Share	Low Relative Market Share
High Market Segment Growth Rate	Increase Share / Achieve Cost-Effectiveness	Assess Chances for Leadership / Grow Share Aggressively or Get Out
Low Market Segment Growth Rate	Maintain Share and Cost-Effectiveness / Generate Cash	Generate Cash

Relative Market Share

Mead Corporation, Dayton, Ohio.

strategies. For example, business A will be supported aggressively, but the strategist should anticipate a decline in market share as competitors enter the field. The present strategies for products B and C should be to continue to maintain present market shares in these lower growth markets. Business D may require investing in acquisitions to improve its market share dominance. Business E may need a strategy of reducing the number of models and focusing more specifically on a single segment of the market. The company should divest itself of businesses F and G.[6]

Day points out that we are in a period of critical reappraisal of many of the planning approaches because unqualified enthusiasm has been replaced by thoughtful skepticism.[7] (See Exhibit 16.10.) He notes that there is evidence that misuse of these techniques can produce misleading strategic guidance. The methods also seem to be sensitive to improper measurements and violations of underlying assumptions. The desire of consultants to differentiate their services has led to a confusion of terminology.

Exhibit 16.10   Balancing the Portfolios of Business

(Diameter of circle is proportional to product's contribution to total company sales volume)

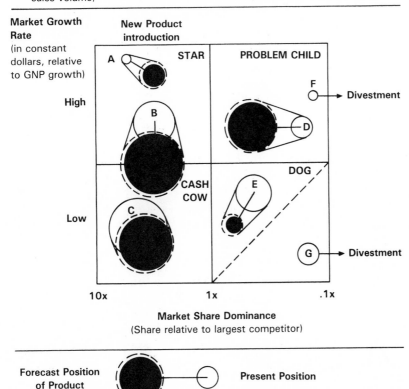

G. S. Day, "Diagnosing the Product Portfolio," *Journal of Marketing* 41, no. 2 (April 1977): 34. (Published by the American Marketing Association.)

Exhibit 16.11 summarizes some of the methods of portfolio assessment. Business portfolios may be established in terms of market structure, risk assessment, operating performance, and financial factors. Each of the resulting portfolios may be divided further into the variables that are used by analysts and the proponents of this method.

Portfolio analysis encourages the effective allocation of resources, but the analysis tends to be static, ignoring the dynamics of the marketplace. It also focuses on current capabilities rather than encouraging a search for new opportunities. The management reward systems that are associated with portfolio analysis tend to emphasize short- or medium-

Exhibit 16.11   A Comparison of Strategic Planning Models

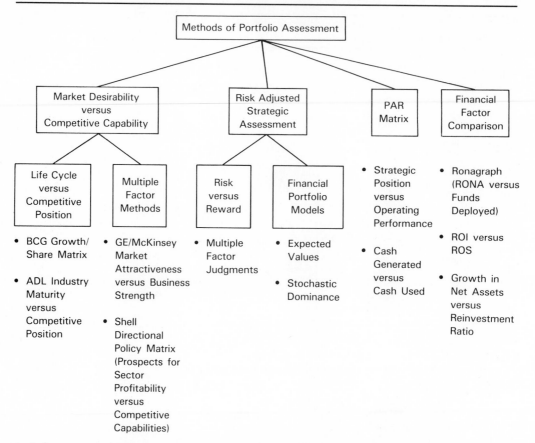

G. S. Day, ''Analytical Approaches to Strategic Market Planning,'' *Review of Marketing, 1981,* ed. Ben M. Enis and Kenneth J. Roering, (Chicago: American Marketing Association, 1981), p. 100.

term operating performance goals rather than long-term goals. Instead, managers should be looking for opportunities to shift the business into a more attractive sector by developing new business strengths or using a market segmentation strategy that fits the company's present strengths.[8]

Market Attractiveness

Criticism of the portfolio approach has led to the development of two-dimensional displays that use axes labeled ''market attractiveness'' and ''business position.'' The market attractiveness of a business will be determined by multiple factors, such as whether it is growing, whether the margins are high, whether it is regulated, and the success factors that are required to take advantage of an opportunity within this market.

The position of the business will be measured by such variables as the business share of the market, its growth rate, the bargaining power of suppliers and customers, its vulnerability to new technology, etc.[9] These multiple dimensions may be reduced by statistical and/or judgmental means into single dimensions to produce an investment opportunity matrix such as Exhibit 16.12. Strategists will want to move a business from the lower right-hand quadrant of this matrix to the upper left-hand quadrant.

PIMS Analysis

PIMS (Profit Impact of Market Strategy) is an empirical model that is based on data supplied by 150 large and small companies who are in over 1,000 businesses. The data include measures such as market share, product quality, vertical integration, growth rate, industry stage of development, capital intensity, profitability, cash flow, and other variables that may reflect the effects of changes in strategies. The PIMS data base provides a means for testing the effect of a change in the strategy of an individual business.

Exhibit 16.12   Investment Opportunity Matrix

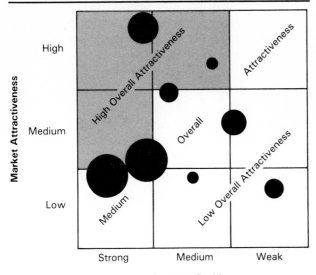

Derek F. Abell and John S. Hammond, *Strategic Market Planning: Problems and Analytical Approaches.* © 1979, p. 213. Reprinted by permission of Prentice-Hall Inc., Englewood Cliffs, N.J.

The PIMS model provides estimates of what effect a given market environment, market position, degree of competitive differentiation, and use of investment will have on return-on-investment and cash flow. A strategist may compare his or her return-on-investment against a par value for a comparable business in the PIMS data base.

CREATING A PERSONAL SELLING MIX

When the communication needs of the marketing strategy have been defined (Exhibit 16.3), the sales manager must turn to creating a personal selling mix. This mix may include the company's own sales force, the use of manufacturers' representatives, trade shows, brokers, direct mail, and telephone selling.

Manufacturers' representatives perform the function of a sales force for a manufacturer who cannot afford his or her own sales force, or who wants to supplement the sales force in areas where it would be too expensive to reach small clients. These representatives generally work on a straight commission. The most recent Census of Wholesale Trade indicates that many companies are reducing their sales branches and increasing their use of manufacturers' representatives in their search for lower-cost alternatives for personal selling.[10]

Trade shows are used extensively by industrial marketers, jewelry manufacturers, housewares and hardware distributors, business machine companies, furniture industries, and fashion clothing industries. The trade show can reduce travel costs because the prospects come to the seller. Techniques must be developed, however, for evaluating the quality of the prospects, because many persons who attend a trade show are not prospects.

The use of direct selling approaches, such as mail and telephone, have been accelerated by many new developments. Mailing and telephone lists that are classified by zip code, occupation, and income provide means for screening prospects. The computer makes these data available on a low-cost basis. The high mobility among the population reduces the loyalty to retail stores, making mail and telephone buying more acceptable. The wide use of credit cards facilitates this form of selling. The large proportion of women in the work force reduces the time available for shopping, making telephone and mail shopping more attractive. Computer technology can facilitate writing personalized letters and automatically dialing a prospect's telephone, thereby reducing the costs of these methods.

Travel costs are greatly increasing the cost of a personal selling call, making mail and telephone sales more attractive. Some companies are using telephone selling to cover country territories that are too sparse to send a salesperson, to cover territories left vacant by a promotion or termination of a representative, and to provide coverage in a territory when a representative is out of the territory for additional training. Telephone selling is also being used in industrial marketing. One well-known manufacturer of office typewriters is testing telephone selling as an alternative to personal selling because the margins in these units no longer justify a personal call.

There is a growing list of examples of successful telephone sales strategies. Uniroyal generated $2 million in tire sales to automobile dealers using telephone sales. It also used telephone strategies to sell small recappers, with the dramatic results of shifting two recapping plants from a position of excess capacity to a twenty-four-hour-a-day operation. Telephone selling has been used successfully to introduce new products. A new antibacterial drug was introduced to the veterinary market. A medical nutritional product sold to hospitals was introduced to nursing homes. A new reflective highway warning device that was required by a new federal regulation was introduced directly to truck fleets, bypassing traditional channels and gaining a 20-percent market share before competitors could react.[11] These examples illustrate some of the advantages of telephone sales, which include speed, flexibility, control over the selling effort, and lower costs that can make marginal accounts profitable.

RECENT SALES MANAGEMENT STRATEGIES

To illustrate how some of these concepts are used in developing a strategy and to see the role of sales management in this development, we will examine recent marketing strategies for several well-known companies.

American Telephone and Telegraph Company (AT&T)

AT&T developed a market-oriented strategy in the early 1970s when deregulation permitted competitors into the communication industry and when rapid technological development made many of its products and services obsolete. The company aligned its organization according to market segments and proceeded to analyze the total communication needs of customers. It took a systems selling approach toward the development of a communication system that meets the individual needs of each customer.[12] An aggressive recruiting and training program was developed to create a sales force of communication consultants.

Goulds Pumps

Goulds Pumps has stuck to a product strategy of selling only industrial and consumer pumps. Rather than add new products, it chose to find new markets for existing products. Many of its recent organizational changes supported this product strategy by putting it in closer touch with the marketplace. It changed from a centralized corporate structure to divisional profit centers. It shifted from using independent sales representatives to selling mainly through its two separate company sales forces—industrial and consumer pumps. It hired marketing managers for each division to work on product strategies.[13]

Pepsi-Cola

In its race to overtake Coca-Cola, Pepsi-Cola faced a comparative disadvantage in the soda fountain market. While Coke and Pepsi sell through franchise bottlers, the Coke franchise enables the company to deal directly with large accounts, while Pepsi must rely on the selling effort of bottlers, who have generally regarded the soda fountain market as unimportant. Pepsi initiated a training program to stimulate bottlers' sales forces in this market.[14]

R. J. Reynolds Tobacco

The three success factors in the cigarette business, according to R. J. Reynolds, are quality products, media advertising, and sales representatives who know their business. Reynolds put more decision-making authority in the field by creating five area sales managers who have the responsibility for budgeting, merchandising, and vending sales. Moving these decisions closer to the marketplace gives Reynolds a competitive edge on monitoring trends and consumer-buying preferences. The Reynolds sales force consists of these five area sales managers, 30 regional managers, 180 division managers, and 2,000 representatives. These representatives call on 360,000 retail outlets with call frequencies ranging from once a year to several times per week. Representatives meet quarterly with their division managers to evaluate their progress and set their objectives for the following quarter, which include call scheduling, unit sales, and display placements. Assistant division managers spend most of their time training new representatives. Representatives are trained in merchandising techniques to help retailers improve their profits. This effort has paid off for Reynolds by giving it the fastest coverage for its new brands and the largest market share.[15]

Strategies for Low Market-Share Businesses

Maximizing market share does not always result in maximizing profits because of increased competition and diminishing returns in advertising, sales promotion, and personal selling efforts. Some companies, such as Burroughs Corporation, Crown Cork and Seal Company, Incorporated, and the Union Camp Corporation, produced strong sales, healthy margins, and a good return-on-investment with small market shares. Their success was based on the strategy of competing only in market segments where they had particular strengths that were highly valued by the buyers, by making efficient use of limited research and development budgets, by avoiding growth for growth's sake, and by having leaders who were willing to question conventional wisdom.[16]

Seiko Watches

Seiko, which emphasized the quartz watch rather than more conventional ones, had certain price advantages through automation of its production facilities. It kept its personal selling costs low by using existing jewelry distributors rather than building its own sales force. It gained national distribution quickly through this strategy because it avoided the discount houses, thereby getting extensive support from jewelry retailers.[17]

WHY PLANNING FAILS

The current popularity of strategic planning has left some managers disillusioned with the process. There is a tendency to focus on the broad, general strategic dimensions of management with insufficient effort spent on programs that will implement these strategies. Koontz has observed that planning may fail for one or more of the following reasons: (1) a lack of commitment to planning by operating personnel; (2) a lack of clear, actionable, attainable, and verifiable objectives; (3) a failure to weight properly assumptions regarding economic, market, technological, political, social, and ethical environments; (4) a failure to place strategies within the total planning process; (5) a failure to develop policies that give discretion and direction to decision making; (6) time spans are not clearly defined; and (7) a failure to identify and weight the importance of critical or limiting factors in the plan.[18]

RECENT RESEARCH IN SALES MANAGEMENT

During the last decade there has been renewed interest among academic researchers in the topic of sales management. Some of this research has already been noted in the discussion of the selling process (Chapter 4) and motivation (Chapter 11). The discussion in this chapter will be limited to that research that has focused on sales management. At the risk of overgeneralization, the discussion will be divided into cognitive models and behavioral models.

COGNITIVE MODELS

Churchill, Ford, and Walker are proponents of the cognitive approach. Their research focuses on variables such as the representative's role perception, motivation, and job performance.[19] These authors view sales management as consisting of six components. The *environment* includes external environments (potential customers, competition, legal restrictions, technology, resources, and social), as well as the organizational environment (objectives, human resources, and nonmarketing capacities). The marketing *strategy* considers the positioning of personal selling in the marketing mix for a target market. *Sales management activities* include activities such as sales force organization, planning, territory design, selection, training, motivating, and compensating personnel. *Determinants of a salesperson's performance* deal with the salesperson's perception of the job, aptitude, skills, and motivations. *Outcomes* include sales volume, profitability, service, and reports. *Control* includes evaluation of performance, sales analysis, and cost analysis.[20]

Ryans and Weinberg criticize this approach because it focuses on the operations, not the tactics and strategy, of sales management.[21] The latter authors suggest a three-level model of personal selling and sales management. The three levels examine the strategy, tactics, and implementation phases of sales management.

Ryans and Weinberg argue that this three-level model is more desirable than a single-integrated sales management model for two pragmatic reasons. First, strategic, tactical, and implementation decisions tend to occur at three different levels within the organization. Second, they argue that three models make it easier to conduct research if each decision level is examined separately. The Ryans-Weinberg models appear in Exhibits 16.13, 16.14, and 16.15.

BEHAVIORAL MODELS

Behavioral models focus on observable behavior, such as sales, rather than psychological variables, such as job satisfaction or attitudes.

Ryans and Weinberg have examined the determinants of sales force performance by measuring territory characteristics and an organizational variable—span of control. Four territory characteristics were considered: sales potential, the concentration of potential in a few large accounts, geographic dispersion, and work load, which was measured by the number of accounts per representative. Potential and concentration were found to be positively related to sales, geographic dispersion was negatively related to sales in most situations, and territory work load was not found to be an important determinant of sales in a terri-

Exhibit 16.13   The Strategy Level

Exhibit 16.14   The Tactical Level

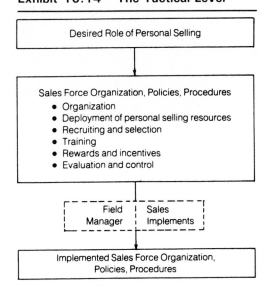

Exhibit 16.15   The Implementation or Operational Level

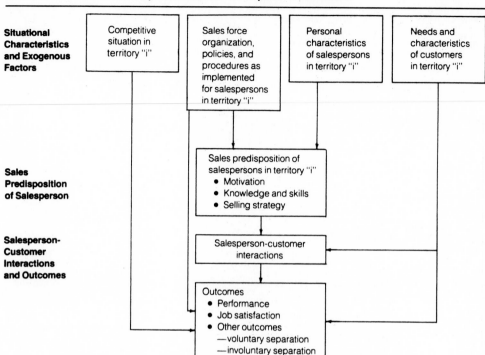

A. B. Ryans and C. B. Weinberg, "Sales Force Management: Integrating Research Advances," © 1981 by the Regents of the University of California. Reprinted from *California Management Review*, volume XXIV, no. 1, p. 79 by permission of the Regents.

tory. They found also that increasing the number of representatives under a first-line supervisor lowered territory sales. The authors illustrated how their models may be used for organizing the sales force and establishing sales territories.[22]

Beswick and Cravens developed a multistage decision model for sales force management that reflects the complex interactions when a manager decides the role of personal selling in the organization; allocates the selling effort to customers, geographic areas, or products; sets sales force size; designs sales territories; and manages the sales force. The authors emphasized that considering these decision areas separately results in suboptimization of the marketing system. Their model examines these decisions in interrelated stages. This multistage decision model, which appears in Exhibit 16.16, is based on managerial judgment

Exhibit 16.16   A Multistage Division Model for Sales Force Management

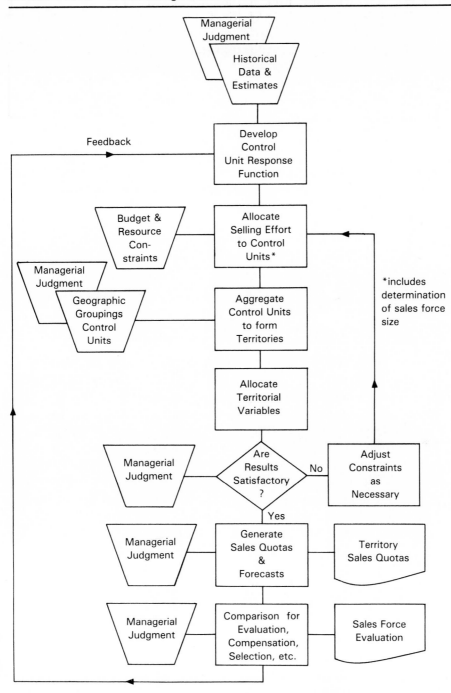

Charles A. Beswick and David W. Cravens, "A Multistage Decision Model for Sales Force Management," *Journal of Marketing Research* 14 (May 1977): 135–144. (Published by the American Marketing Association.)

and historical response data. Managerial judgment is introduced at several points in the model to determine if results are satisfactory. Hence, the manager does not lose control of the process.[23]

SUMMARY

The major difference in the management functions that are performed by general sales managers and field sales managers is that the general manager is more involved in planning and organizing than are the field sales managers. Furthermore, the nature of general sales managers' involvement in staffing, directing, and controlling is different from that of field managers in that it tends to be limited to a review of the field managers' performance of these functions and the overall productivity of the unit.

The general sales manager may play an important role in developing corporate strategy by identifying market segments with opportunities and problems, evaluating and selecting market segments, participating in the development of strategies for these segments, and then developing a personal selling mix strategy. To develop the selling mix strategy, the general sales manager must first understand the communication tasks that are necessary for selling this product. Next, he or she must allocate these tasks among the communication functions of advertising, personal selling, market research, and channels of distribution.

The general sales manager will be part of a marketing team that develops the corporate marketing strategy. He or she will participate in asking and answering strategic questions such as, "What business are we in? What is our competitive position?" Formal planning methods, such as portfolio analysis, market attractiveness analysis, and the PIMS data base, may be used to help answer these and other critical questions.

The sales manager will be assigned the primary responsibility for developing the personal selling mix that may include the company's own sales force, manufacturers' representatives, trade shows, and mail and telephone selling.

Behavioral and operations researchers have developed models that promise to make useful contributions to general sales management by aiding in the identification of cognitive problems in motivation and role clarity, the territorial and organizational determinants of sales force performance, and such decisions as determining the role of personal selling in the organization, allocating selling effort, designing territories, and setting the sales force size. These models will receive wider attention as they are tested in a variety of selling organizations.

ASSIGNMENTS/DISCUSSION QUESTIONS

1. Analyze the problems and opportunities for the company in Exhibits 16.4 through 16.6.

2. Do a literature search of publications such as *Business Week, Sales & Marketing Management, Forbes, Harvard Business Review,* and *Industrial Marketing* for current examples of sales management strategies.

3. Invite the manager of the campus store to class to aid in the completion of a business matrix for a college store, as illustrated in Exhibit 16.17. How could this matrix help a college store plan for the future? How could it help companies that sell to college stores? What is the outlook for those businesses that are in cells 1 through 8?

4. Form class teams and develop business matrices, such as Exhibits 16.4 through 16.6, for local companies of various sizes and industries. Complete also a communication mix matrix such as Exhibit 16.1.

5. Compare each of the management activities of the general sales manager (GSM) and the field sales manager (FSM) in fulfilling their directing responsibilities.

6. Compare each of the management activities of the general sales manager (GSM) and the field sales manager (FSM) in fulfilling their controlling responsibilities.

7. What should the field sales manager do in the case of a sales rep with a complaint who wants to take the complaint to the general sales manager?

8. What should a general sales manager do in the case of a rep who brings a complaint to him or her? Why?

9. Who should announce to a sales rep his or her promotion? Who should announce the promotion to the entire field sales staff? Why?

10. How should a general sales manager reply to a sales rep with whom he or she has worked in the field for a day and who inquires at the end of the day, "Tell me, what do you think of my performance?" Why?

11. Using the arguments of Ryans and Weinburg, "Determinants of Sales Force Performance," discuss the total effect on sales of increasing the number of potential clients contacted within the same suburban territory by lengthening the promotional cycle from ten to twelve weeks.

Exhibit 16.17   A Business Matrix for a College Store

What business are we in? (A business is a matching of a product or service to a market.) (It is not necessary to complete each cell. Row and column totals may be sufficient for planning.)

MARKET SEGMENTS
CELL ENTRIES: % BUSINESS/% GROWTH RATE

Products or Services	Degree Students	Faculty	Adm.	Staff	Alumni	Cont. Educ.	Update Courses	Loyal Friends	Vendors	Five-Year Trend
Books	30%/9%	2%/3%			19%/3%	7%/15%				100%/11%
Supplies	1									
Food										
Health Care	2									
Clothing										
Jewelry										
Recreation (sports, records, etc.)		5			3			4		
Services										
Money	6									
Information	7									
Other									8	
Segment Five-year Trend	45%/6%					12%/20%				

CASE 16.1:
Datec,* Inc.

Martin Johnson, the newly hired sales manager for Datec, Inc., arrived April 23, 1981, at his new job and was concerned about the challenge facing him. Bill Jefferson, Datec's founder and president, gave Martin his first assignment—the expansion of sales in California and other western states.

Located in Carrboro and Durham, North Carolina, Datec manufactured four types of acoustic couplers for the computer industry, ranging in price from $75 to $350. Its nonacoustical coupler, the Datec 212, sold for about $750 and could communicate at four times the speed of an acoustical coupler.

These couplers, known as modems, allow computers to communicate with each other by converting computer signals into audio frequencies suitable for transmission over telephone lines. Jefferson was proud of Datec's distinctive competence in making superior products. They had less than a 1-percent failure in the field during their first year, versus competitive failure rates up to 40 percent. Datec used higher quality components and tested extensively before shipment. Its prices were equal to or lower than competition and it could deliver most orders within four weeks.

Datec sells its product line primarily through fifteen distributors of computer peripheral equipment located through the eastern half of the United States. Distributors receive a 40-percent discount off the suggested retail price. Datec's discount is comparable to its competitors. About 90 percent of Datec's field sales are through distributors. The Datec salesperson keeps distributors technically up-to-date by stressing the competitive advantages of Datec equipment. These salespersons, known as sales coordinators, encourage distributors to sell Datec units. Coordinators work with end users on specific applications and with original equipment manufacturers (OEM), who integrate Datec products into their own equipment.

The company had three independent manufacturer's representatives in Washington, Texas, and Chicago, who developed strong dealer relations by "hand holding," communicating the advantages of Datec products, and entertaining distributor salespeople. These manufacturing reps received a 5-percent commission on sales to distributors. Recently, Datec hired its first company salesperson and assigned him to the Southeastern market, an area of its present strength.

*Datec is the registered trademark of Datec Incorporated.

The case is based on an actual business situation, with some names and figures disguised. The case was prepared by Bryan Joyner and Edward Martin, second-year MBA students, University of North Carolina, under the direction of Professor G. David Hughes.

Exhibit 16.18   Trade Journal Advertising

The people who know more about acoustic couplers know why you should buy Datec.

The heavy-duty coupler   ...Datec did it.

There is a reason so many Datec customers are communication line technicians, computer engineers and data processing experts. They recommend Datec for the simple, solid state, rugged design that has proven to be more reliable than bigger name couplers.

Acoustic couplers are the work horses of a data communications system. They should work every time, every day, so that you can install them and then forget them.

No wonder communication line technicians have nicknamed the Datec 32 the "heavy duty" acoustic coupler.

CRYSTAL CONTROL

Crystal controlled transmitter and receiver insures long-term stability and reliability, even in the most unfriendly operating environment.

BIG EARS

Rugged, tight-fitting rubber cups effectively seal out vibration and room noise. They aren't beautiful, but they work.

BURNED-IN

Datec may be the only company that torture-tests every PC board by burning-in each one for 168 hours at elevated temperatures.

This process reduces the probability of field failure below 2% for the first 1000 hours of operation. We find the faulty one before we ship it.

TALKS WHEN IT RAINS

Datec couplers are highly sensitive, operating at received levels of -55dBm or lower. Our sensitive receiver can pull weak signals out of the "mud" of leaky, rain-soaked telephone cables.

GUARANTEED

Remove a few screws and the PC board pops out. It couldn't be simpler. Any problems incurred through normal use, and it's replaced or repaired free with no questions asked during the first year.

READILY AVAILABLE

Datec 300 bps acoustic couplers are readily available in both originate and originate/answer models. All Datec equipment including the new Datec 212 is Bell compatible. OEM inquiries are welcome.

DATEC INCORPORATED
200 EASTOWNE DRIVE, SUITE 114
CHAPEL HILL, N.C. 27514 919/929-7135

Reprinted with permission of Datec Incorporated.

Exhibit 16.19

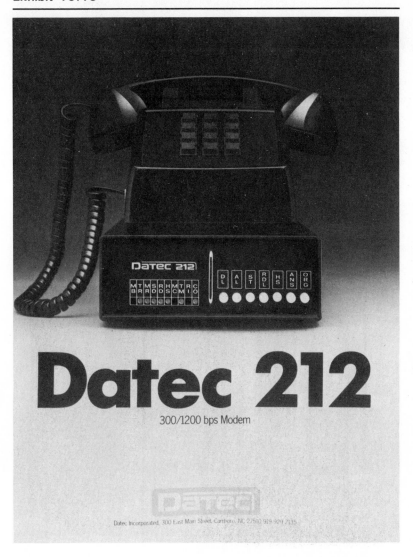

(continued)

Exhibit 16.19   Continued

Keep It Simple, Keep It Datec.

Datec – Simply Innovative

Datec's 300/1200 bps modem is the simple answer to your data movement needs – whether you're installing a new system or upgrading an existing one. The Datec 212 is a versatile modem with an exclusive combination of features: an easily accessible voice/data switch, full- or half-duplex operation over both dial and leased lines with **any** type phone, and AA1 lead control.

Simple Installation
The Datec 212 connects to both dial network and 2-wire leased line systems by simply plugging it in to the desired connection. There's no need to spend money changing your existing phone system.

Simple Operation
Saves time, reduces line charges. In the answer mode, the Datec 212 automatically sets its speed to match that of the originating modem. When originating a call, you select the transmitting speed of your choice with either the front panel pushbutton or automatically through the RS-232-C interface.

Simple Testing
Easy to use front panel buttons control seven simple diagnostic tests which let the user isolate any problem in seconds instead of hours.

Efficient Operation
You can customize your Datec 212 with a wide variety of user-selectable options. Select speed options, clock options, synchronous or asynchronous options and many more through the three DIP switches mounted on the printed circuit board. Programmed or permissive transmission, full- or half-duplex operation at all speeds – just two more Datec innovations!

Reliable Communications
Datec has Carrier-On and Ring Indicator LED's. The modem operator can confirm connection **before** starting data transmission, saving valuable time and money. Datec's exclusive built-in "A" control helps prevent interruptions on key telephone systems by lighting the line button. The built-in telephone line equalizer gives the Datec 212 one of the best receiver sensitivities in the industry.

Burned-In Reliability
Datec torture-tests every modem printed circuit board for one full week (168 hours) at elevated temperatures. This process reduces the probability of field failure below one percent for the first 1,000 hours of operation. We find the faulty ones before they leave the factory.

Datec 212 – Guaranteed
Datec, Inc. warrants its equipment to be free from defects in materials and workmanship for a period of one year from the date of shipment. Datec, Inc. will replace or repair, at its option, any defective equipment, FOB our factory.

Easy to Read Indicator Lights

MB/Make Busy
Indicates that local modem is busy and will not answer incoming calls.

TR/Terminal Ready
Lights when your terminal is ready to transmit and receive data. Must be on for modem to operate.

MR/Modem Ready
Lights when the modem seizes the line.

SD/Send Data
Lights for space, out for mark sent from local modem.

RD/Receive Data
Lights for space, out for mark received by local modem.

HS/High Speed
Lights when modem is in the high speed mode (1200 bps).

MC/Modem Check
Lights in the idle mode. Off with established link or in the test mode. Blinks to indicate errors in the self test mode.

TM/Test Mode
Lights for all test modes.

RI/Ring Indicator
Blinks when your modem receives a call. Stays on to indicate answer mode for the duration of link. (Switch Selectable Option)

CO/Carrier On
Lights when local modem detects a carrier tone from a remote modem.

(*continued*)

Exhibit 16.19 Continued

Simple Voice/Data Control

The Datec 212 lets you switch from voice to data communication and back again without having to hang up and redial. So you save time and money. You can also place the modem in the originate mode without an exclusion key. This enables you to use the Datec 212 with any phone system. Voice/data control—another Datec innovation!

Allows you to manually place the modem in the answer mode.

Simple Testing— Minimum Downtime

The Datec 212 has seven built-in diagnostic tests. Most problems can be isolated quickly by using only one or two of these tests.

Check local modem's transmission and reception. The Analog Loop Self-Test generates an internally looped pseudo-random pattern so you can test the modem circuitry without using a terminal or telephone line. Can be used in high or low speed mode.

Test local modem/terminal interface. The Analog Loop Test is initiated by the local terminal, looped through the modem and returned to the terminal for interface verification.

Test telephone line, local and remote modems. In the End-to-End Self-Test, each modem generates a pseudo-random test pattern which checks the telephone line and the other modem's transmission and reception.

Test local modem, remote terminal/modem and telephone line. The Digital Loopback Test routes data from the remote terminal/modem to the local modem and back to test the local modem's reception and transmission.

Test remote modem, telephone line and local modem. In the Digital Loopback Self-Test one modem tests the other's ability to receive a remotely generated pseudo-random test pattern. Use primarily with low speed operation.

Test local modem, telephone line, and remote modem/terminal. The Remote Digital Loopback test routes data at high speed operation from the local site to the remote modem/terminal, which loops it back for verification by the local terminal.

Test local modem, telephone line, and remote modem. In the Remote Digital Loopback Self-Test the local modem sends a pseudo-random test pattern to the remote modem. The remote unit loops the pattern back to the local modem for automatic verification.

(continued)

Exhibit 16.19 Continued

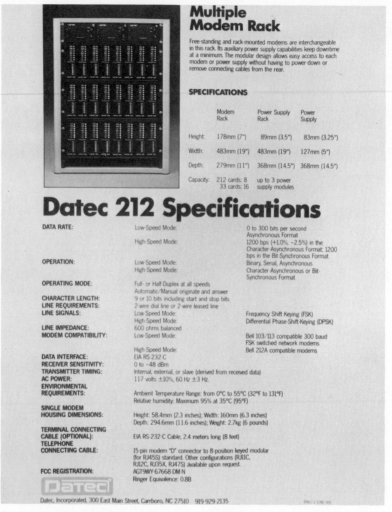

Multiple Modem Rack

Free-standing and rack-mounted modems are interchangeable in this rack. Its auxiliary power supply capabilities keep downtime at a minimum. The modular design allows easy access to each modem or power supply without having to power-down or remove connecting cables from the rear.

SPECIFICATIONS

	Modem Rack	Power Supply Rack	Power Supply
Height:	178mm (7")	89mm (3.5")	83mm (3.25")
Width:	483mm (19")	483mm (19")	127mm (5")
Depth:	279mm (11")	368mm (14.5")	368mm (14.5")
Capacity:	212 cards: 8 33 cards: 16	up to 3 power supply modules	

Datec 212 Specifications

DATA RATE:	Low-Speed Mode:	0 to 300 bits per second Asynchronous Format
	High-Speed Mode:	1200 bps (+1.0%, -2.5%) in the Character-Asynchronous Format; 1200 bps in the Bit-Synchronous Format
OPERATION:	Low-Speed Mode:	Binary, Serial, Asynchronous
	High-Speed Mode:	Character-Asynchronous or Bit-Synchronous Format
OPERATING MODE:	Full- or Half-Duplex at all speeds Automatic/Manual originate and answer	
CHARACTER LENGTH:	9 or 10 bits including start and stop bits	
LINE REQUIREMENTS:	2-wire dial line or 2-wire leased line	
LINE SIGNALS:	Low-Speed Mode:	Frequency Shift Keying (FSK)
	High-Speed Mode:	Differential Phase-Shift-Keying (DPSK)
LINE IMPEDANCE:	600 ohms balanced	
MODEM COMPATIBILITY:	Low-Speed Mode:	Bell 103/113 compatible 300 baud FSK switched network modems
	High-Speed Mode:	Bell 212A compatible modems
DATA INTERFACE:	EIA RS-232-C	
RECEIVER SENSITIVITY:	0 to -48 dBm	
TRANSMITTER TIMING:	Internal, external, or slave (derived from received data)	
AC POWER:	117 volts ±10%, 60 Hz ±3 Hz	
ENVIRONMENTAL REQUIREMENTS:	Ambient Temperature Range: from 0°C to 55°C (32°F to 131°F) Relative humidity: Maximum 95% at 35°C (95°F)	
SINGLE MODEM HOUSING DIMENSIONS:	Height: 58.4mm (2.3 inches); Width: 160mm (6.3 inches) Depth: 294.6mm (11.6 inches); Weight: 2.7kg (6 pounds)	
TERMINAL CONNECTING CABLE (OPTIONAL):	EIA RS-232-C Cable, 2.4 meters long (8 feet)	
TELEPHONE CONNECTING CABLE:	15-pin modem "D" connector to 8-position keyed modular (for RJ45S) standard. Other configurations (RJ11C, RJ12C, RJ35X, RJ47S) available upon request.	
FCC REGISTRATION:	AGT9WY-67668-DM-N Ringer Equivalence: 0.8B	

Datec, Incorporated, 300 East Main Street, Carrboro, NC 27510   919-929-2135

Reprinted with permission of Datec Incorporated.

For 1981, the company had budgeted $50,000 for trade journal advertising. (See Exhibit 16.18.) They had also developed sales brochures. (See Exhibit 16.19.)

Since Bill Jefferson founded the company in 1976, Datec has experienced phenomenal growth. (See Exhibit 16.20.) He is planning for sales of $1.1 million in 1981, and $1.8 million in 1982. While such growth puts a strain on cash flow, Jefferson believes that bank and private financing will be available to support this growth rate.

Exhibit 16.20 Datec Sales ($,000)

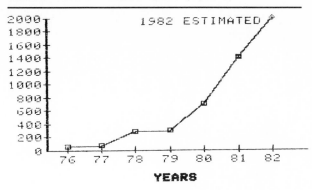

Datec's modem market is dominated by several small companies located in California and New England that sell through their own sales forces. (See Exhibit 16.21.) In 1981, the American Telephone and Telegraph Company had the largest share of the modem market, but they were not direct competitors of Datec. AT&T could only lease its equipment, but a pending divestiture case by the U.S. Justice Department may remove this restriction. If the lease market is included, then AT&T has 50 percent of the market.

The number of modems used depends on the application. A modem will generally be required for each station that is more than 1,000 feet from the computer. Each distant remote station will require a modem and the computer will require at least one modem. One modem at the computer may be able to service several remote modems. Modems would be located throughout a manufacturing plant at production and inventory points. Modems may be needed at

Exhibit 16.21 Datec Major Competition for Modems

COMPANY	SALES (MILLIONS)	EMPLOYEES	MAJOR LINES
Racal-Vadic Cali.	$25	250	Modems complete line
Prentice Corporation	10	100	Modems 25% of business
Rixon, Inc.	20	250	Modems 50% of business
General DataComm	54	1000	Modems 5% of business
UDS	30	350	Modems complete line

Reprinted with permission of Datec Incorporated.

remote locations for some word-processing systems. Research laboratories may need terminals at each laboratory that wanted to communicate with a mainframe computer. Modems are needed for sales force applications, where the home office wants to communicate with the field offices and representatives. Microcomputer hobbyists need modems to communicate with each other, with larger computers, to subscribe to data bases, and to send and receive "electronic mail." Hobbyists tend to buy on price.

Because modems have a derived demand, which is tied to the demand for mainframe computers, Jefferson claims they are purchased almost as an afterthought. Their low unit price, compared to other peripheral equipment, also contributes to this lack of customer awareness. Almost all purchases are initiated by an end-user calling a distributor to inquire about his or her modems. Purchase decisions are based more on brand name awareness, quality, and distributor recommendation than on price. The distributor frequently will sell modems as a small part of a large computer system package.

When Martin Johnson was hired, Bill Jefferson stated that Johnson's first priority was to penetrate the western U.S. market. This area had minimal Datec sales at present, as may be seen in Exhibit 16.22. It was a stronghold of Datec's major competitors. Jefferson believed that despite certain regional loyalties, the end-users would desire Datec products because of their high quality and reliability. Because of the size of computer activities in the far West, Jefferson also believed that this untapped market had a huge sales potential. Johnson believed that he had three alternatives in penetrating the western market:

1. Find and convince western distributors to carry Datec's line.
2. Commission independent manufacturer reps to sell in this market.
3. Hire an in-house salesperson to promote sales in this market.

Exhibit 16.22   Datec Sales Breakdown by Region and User

Region		Origination		Final User	
Southeast	55%	Distributors	75%	Colleges, univ,	50%
Northeast	14%	OEM accounts	10%	gov't agencies	
Midwest	25%	Phone orders	15%		
West	6%			Industry: Fortune 500	30%
				Smaller	20%
Totals	100%		100%		100%

Note: Repeat orders are 90% of present business.

Reprinted with permission of Datec Incorporated.

In-House Sales Rep Strategy

Johnson believed that a dedicated, full-time Datec salesperson located out West offered an excellent opportunity to expand sales in a short period of time. He also was attracted to this alternative because Datec would have greater control on the selling activities of the rep, and could obtain accurate market information from him or her. Johnson was concerned, however, by the substantial investment cost this would require. Recruiting costs, training costs, rep compensation, and initial sales development expenses would be substantial before the rep generated any revenue. The company's strained cash position made "investments" of this nature difficult to justify, compared to capital equipment needs of Datec. Jefferson, an electrical engineer, commented that the company could afford to allocate 5 percent of sales to the selling effort. Since he estimated that a first-year sales rep's salary and expenses would be about $50,000, a rep must generate $1 million to break even. Jefferson was also concerned that it would take six months to determine whether the hired rep was worth anything. Johnson wondered too about the difficulty of managing a rep 3,000 miles away, and what this position's job description should include, if this alternative were chosen. Hiring and training strategies would also have to be devised.

Distributor Strategy

A less risky option would be to locate distributors in the West who were willing to carry and push Datec's modems. Because the majority of modem sales are through distributors, Johnson believed this strategy would still give it high sales potential, high availability, and high market penetration at a much lower investment. Datec's margin per sale would be higher due to the elimination of sales rep expenses or manufacturer's rep commissions. Distributors, according to Jefferson, would be easier to locate than manufacturer's reps. Johnson was concerned that this alternative would be costly in the short run. High expenses and large amounts of his time would be needed in traveling, trying to "sell" distributors on Datec's products. In addition, the lack of continual personal selling to distributors might make it difficult to convince these distributors to actively push Datec's line. Finally, Johnson knew that direct sales to original equipment manufacturers would be difficult without field personnel. He felt that this would be a large future market segment for Datec. If he chose this option, Johnson knew he must come up with a detailed plan to best solicit distributors in the most cost-effective manner.

Outside Manufacturer's Reps

Johnson reasoned that he could limit the cash investment and provide a high degree of personal selling by commissioning independent reps who would obtain distributor sales outlets on their own. Original equipment manufacturer sales would also be possible with these manufacturer's reps. Like the distributor option, this alternative precluded having an in-house sales force. Based on Datec's East Coast experiences, Johnson was concerned about the difficulty of locating dedicated reps who would aggressively push the Datec product line above the established "brand name" competition. In addition, this option ensured that sales in the West would require a 5-percent commission. Finally, manufacturer's reps would reduce the control that Datec could have over the selection of West coast distributors, and also isolate Datec from the marketplace. This was considered a serious problem because Datec expected only about a five-year product life on its present line. Datec needs market input in designing the new generation of modems for the future computer/phone network interface market. Like the distributor option, Johnson knew he would need to decide how to best locate and "sell" manufacturer's reps on accepting Datec's products.

CASE QUESTIONS

1. What are Datec's businesses?
2. List five strategic questions that Johnson should ask.
3. What are the Datec benefits that should be stressed to the end-user? To the distributor?
4. What alternative methods of selling should Johnson consider? In the short run? In the long run?
5. What are some of the key elements that should be in Johnson's recommendation?
6. Recommend a communication matrix (like Exhibit 16.3) for Datec and discuss your recommendations.
7. Analyze the competitive position of Datec.
8. What incentives can Johnson recommend to stimulate distributors? Should these incentives be decided before making the decision on how to penetrate the West coast market?
9. What do you recommend regarding entering the West Coast market?

REFERENCES

1. F. W. Gluck, S. P. Kaufman, and A. S. Walleck, "Strategic Management for Competitive Advantage," *Harvard Business Review* (July–August 1980): 158.
2. Ibid., p. 159.

3. G. David Hughes, *Marketing Management: A Planning Approach* (Reading, Mass.: Addison-Wesley Publishing Company, 1978).

4. M. E. Porter, *Competitive Strategy* (New York: The Free Press, 1980), p. 4.

5. This discussion is based on D. F. Abell and J. S. Hammond, *Strategic Market Planning* (Englewood Cliffs, N.J.: Prentice-Hall, Inc., 1979), pp. 11–12 and Chapters 4, 5, and 6.

6. G. S. Day, "Diagnosing the Product Portfolio," *Journal of Marketing* 41, no. 2 (April 1977): 31–34.

7. G. S. Day, "Analytical Approaches to Strategic Market Planning," In *Review of Marketing 1981,* ed. B. M. Enis and K. J. Roering (Chicago: American Marketing Association), pp. 89–105.

8. Gluck, Kaufman, and Walleck, "Strategic Management," p. 156.

9. For a detailed list of variables to measure market attractiveness and business position, see Abell and Hammond, *Strategic Market Planning,* p. 214.

10 T. C. Taylor, "A Raging 'Rep'idemic," *Sales & Marketing Management* (June 8, 1981): 33–35.

11. For additional discussions of mail and telephone sales see J. C. Pope, "Telephone Selling," in *The Sales Manager as a Trainer,* ed. J. F. Harrison (Reading, Mass.: Addison-Wesley Publishing, 1977), pp. 177–182; Murray Roman, *Telephone Marketing* (New York: McGraw-Hill, 1976); John D. Yeck, "Reducing the Cost of Sales Through Marketing Support Mail," *Industrial Marketing Management* 6, no. 2 (1977): 95–97; J. M. McAllister, "Marketing by Telephone to the Industrial/Wholesale Account," an Address at the Conference Board's 1978 Marketing Conference, October 18, 1978.

12. "Behind AT&T's Change at the Top," *Business Week* (November 6, 1978): 114–139.

13. C. Ungaro and D. Korn, "Goulds Keeps on Pumping," *Sales & Marketing Management* (December 1978): 27–29.

14. "Pepsi Takes on the Champ," *Business Week* (June 12, 1978): 88–97.

15. Sally Scanlon, "Richard Joshua Reynolds Would be Proud," *Sales & Marketing Management* (November 8, 1976): 43–46.

16. R. G. Hamermesh, M. J. Anderson, and J. E. Harris, "Strategies for Low Market-Share Business," *Harvard Business Review* (May–June 1978): 95–102.

17. "Seiko's Smash," *Business Week* (June 5, 1978): 86–97.

18. Harold Koontz, "Making Strategic Planning Work," *Business Horizons* 19, no. 2 (April 1976): 27–34.

19. O. C. Walker, Jr., G. A. Churchill, Jr., and N. M. Ford, "Motivation and Performance in Industrial Selling: Present Knowledge and Needed Research," *Journal of Marketing Research* 14 (May 1977): 156–168.

20. G. A. Churchill, Jr., N. M. Ford, and O. C. Walker, Jr., *Sales Force Management: Planning, Implementation, and Control* (Homewood, Ill.: Richard D. Irwin, 1981).

21. A. B. Ryans and C. B. Weinberg, "A Sales Force Management Model: Integrating Managerial and Research Perspectives," Research Paper No. 485, Graduate School of Business, Stanford University, March, 1979.

22. A. B. Ryans and C. B. Weinberg, "Determinants of Salesforce Performance," Marketing Science Institute Research Program Project Description, Report 79-113 (Cambridge, Mass.: Marketing Science Institute, December, 1979); A. B. Ryans and C. B. Weinberg, "Territory Sales Response," *Journal of Marketing Research* 26 (November 1979): 453–465.

23. Charles A. Beswick and David W. Cravens, "A Multistage Decision Model for Sales Force Management," *Journal of Marketing Research* 14 (May 1977): 135–144.

SUGGESTED READINGS

Abell, D. F., "Strategic Windows," *Journal of Marketing* (July 1978): 21–26.

Abell, D. F., and Hammond, J. S., *Strategic Market Planning* (Englewood Cliffs, N. J.: Prentice-Hall, 1979).

Corbin, A., "Using a Team Approach to Market-Oriented Planning," *Management Review* 66, no. 6 (June 1977): 9–15.

Crissey, W. J. E., and Mossman, F. H., "Matrix Models for Market Planning: An Update and Expansion," *MSU Business Topics* 25, no. 4 (Autumn 1977): 17–26.

Jauch, L. R., "Toward an Integrated Theory of Strategy," *Academy of Management Review* 6, no. 3 (1981): 491–498.

Kerin, R. A., and Peterson, R. A., *Perspectives on Strategic Marketing Management* (Boston: Allyn and Bacon, Inc., 1980).

Kimberly, J. R., and Evanisko, M. J., "Organizational Innovation: The Influence of Individual, Organizational, and Contextual Factors on Hospital Adoption of Technological and Administrative Innovations," *Academy of Management Journal* 24, no. 4 (1981): 689–713.

King, W. R., and Cleland, D. J., *Strategic Planning and Policy* (New York: Van Nostrand Reinhold Co., 1978).

Shapiro, B. P., "Industrial Product Policy: Managing the Existing Product Line," Cambridge, MA.: Marketing Science Institute, Report #77-110, September, 1977.

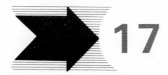

17

MEASURING MARKET POTENTIAL AND FORECASTING*

Strategic sales management begins with a measure of market potentials and a forecast of these potentials into future planning horizons. Sales forecasts reduce some of the uncertainty of planning by predicting *what* will be sold to *whom* and *when*.

Market measures and forecasts require answers to the following questions: Who needs market measures and forecasts? At what levels should we measure? What variables should we measure? Should we segment the market? In which direction should we measure? How can we forecast market measures? Where do we find the information for these measures and forecasts? Who participates in the forecasting? How are forecasts evaluated? This chapter will attempt to answer each of these questions.

WHO NEEDS MARKET MEASURES AND FORECASTS?

The sales forecast plays important roles in the total corporate strategic planning effort. The long-run and short-run needs will be examined briefly.

*The authors acknowledge with gratitude the helpful comments of Professor S. C. Wheelwright. Parts of this chapter will appear as Chapter 2, "Sales Forecasting Requirements," in S. Makridakis and S. C. Wheelwright, eds., *Handbook of Business Forecasting Techniques* (New York: John Wiley, 1982).

LONG-RUN NEEDS

Exhibit 17.1 shows graphically where the long-run sales forecast fits into the corporate strategic planning process. This forecast is needed for organizational changes, such as divisional decentralization, changing the sales force organization, opening new territories, acquiring new companies, developing new channels, and changing advertising agencies. Adding new products, extending the product line, and dropping old products require long-run sales forecasts. The capital budgeting process and changes in the production facilities will require a long-run sales forecast.

SHORT-RUN NEEDS

The left-hand side of Exhibit 17.1 shows how the annual sales forecast is used in the short-run planning process. First, a forecast for next year may help to evaluate the current strategy. The success or failure of the present strategy may be explained as the forecaster examines the trends in the determinants of sales. What looked like an outstanding strategy may have been simply that we underestimated the growth of the market last year. Conversely, a great strategy may have been buried in a declining market.

The short-run forecast is needed for each of the elements in the marketing mix. *Product planning* requires a forecast for estimating inventories that will be required at various times throughout the year and at various geographic locations. Timing *price* changes, channel discounts, and promotional deals requires good sales forecasts. Estimates of sales potential for market segments are a prerequisite for the *advertising* decisions that include copy themes and media strategies. A sales forecast may reveal the need for expanding the *sales force,* which will require plans for recruiting, hiring, training, and deployment. A change in the location of potential sales may require altering the *channel* strategy. All of these marketing strategies will appear in the cash budget as marketing expense items.

The sales forecast is needed for planning the production of a product. Scheduling, purchasing raw materials, inventory planning, hiring and training personnel, and estimating overhead charges require estimates of the timing and magnitude of company sales.

In summary, virtually all departments have some need for the annual sales forecast. Production, finance, personnel, accounting, and all of the marketing functions use the sales forecast in their planning activities.

Exhibit 17.1 The Role of the Sales Forecast in Corporate Strategic Planning

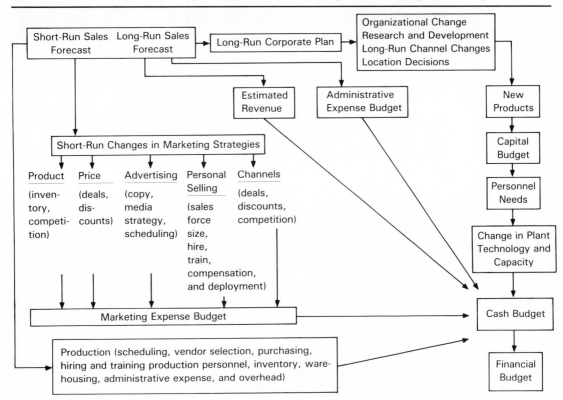

AT WHAT LEVELS SHOULD WE MEASURE?

Markets may be measured at various levels of aggregation, ranging from the highest level of aggregation, known as "market capacity," to the smallest unit of measurement, the "territory sales quota." To eliminate confusion, it is necessary to define these terms.

MARKET CAPACITY

Market *capacity* is the number of *units* of a product or service that could be absorbed by a market at a given time, irrespective of product prices or the marketing strategies of sellers. Market capacity includes unmet needs for which a product or service does not exist. Thus an analysis of market capacity could be the first step in developing a new product.

Market capacities could be expressed in terms of the total market or in terms of disaggregated, homogeneous subsegments of the market that have similar needs or similar buying styles. For example, we may forecast the total market for automobiles, or we may forecast the economy segment, the sporty segment, the luxury segment, and the fleet segment. Each segment would have different demographic, economic, educational, and social-psychological profiles. Buyers' needs would be similar to others within the segment, but quite different from those persons in other segments. The capacity of each of these segments is the *market segment capacity*. The total market capacity (*C*) is simply the sum of all of these market segment (*k*) capacities, thus

$$C = \sum_{k=1}^{n} C_k, \tag{1}$$

where there are *n* segments.

To measure this capacity, we must measure the number of persons with a need and the proportion of these persons who will meet their need with our type of product. Hence, market capacity (*C*) may be defined as the number (*N*) of persons who have a given need multiplied by the proportion (*Pr*) who use the product in question to meet the need and the rate (*R*) at which they use the product. This relationship may be expressed algebraically as follows:

$$C = (N)(Pr)(R) \tag{2}$$

For example, if there are 50,000 fans at a football game, *N* equals 50,000. If the product category is soft drinks, we need an estimate of the proportion (*Pr*) of fans who will drink at least one cup of a soft drink during the game. Let's assume that this proportion is 0.20. Finally, we need to know the number of cups of soda that will be consumed during an average game, given an expected temperature. If we assume that the average number of cups per consumer is 2.25, we may calculate the market capacity for all soft drinks during the game as follows:

$$C = 50,000 \times 0.20 \times 2.25 \tag{3}$$
$$= 22,500 \text{ cups of soft drinks}$$

MARKET POTENTIAL

The market potential, which is also known as the industry potential, will be less than the market capacity because the concept of a market potential introduces economic and distribution constraints. Economic constraints include the product's price, the consumers' income, and the availability of credit. Thus a family may have a need for a house, but be unable to purchase it because of the high selling price, their low income, and the unavailability of mortgage credit.

The market potential may also be considerably less than the market capacity due to inadequate product distribution throughout the industry. For instance, continuing our example of soft drinks at football games, the vendors working the aisles of the stadium may be more interested in the game than in selling soft drinks. Our market potential will therefore fall short of the capacity of the crowd to consume soft drinks.

The market potential will also be determined by industry promotional efforts. The potential will expand as the product category receives more advertising and personal selling effort.

The market potential (P) for a product category, given the market capacity (C); economic variables (E) such as price, income, and credit; distribution (D); and promotional effort (PE), may be expressed as follows:

$$P = f(C, E, D, PE) \tag{4}$$

If our soft drink vendors covered only 75 percent of the stadium, restricting themselves to that part of the stadium where they could see the game, the distribution rate would be 0.75, and the market potential would be 16,875 cups, which is the market capacity of 22,500 cups times 0.75.

The market potential differs from the market capacity in that potential is measured in terms of products, while capacity is measured in terms of needs. Potential introduces the concept of the ability to buy a product, as determined by economic variables, distribution, and the awareness that the product exists, which is determined by promotional effort.

COMPANY POTENTIALS

Company potentials are a set of maximum sales that a company could realize with various product, pricing, marketing, and production strategies. The company will test a number of these strategies to determine which combination will enable it to meet its objective best. After examining these potentials, the company may decide to increase its production and marketing capacities, subcontract to others for these capacities, or let some of the potential go to competitors.

The concepts of a company's marketing effort and competitors' efforts are summarized in the concept of market share, which is simply the share of industry sales that goes to a specific company. A company that sells $20 million in an industry that sells $100 million has a 20-percent share. The company potential for company "j" (CP_j) may be computed by multiplying the market potential (P) times its market share (M_j), thus

$$CP_j = M_j P \qquad (5)$$

The market share is the result of the effectiveness of marketing effort, relative to competitive effort, thus

$$M_j = f(Pd_j, Pr_j, D_j, A_j, PS_j) \qquad (6)$$

where Pd_j, Pr_j, D_j, A_j, PS_j are measures of the relative effectiveness of company j's product, price, distribution, advertising, and personal selling effort, respectively. In some cases it may be possible to include a variable that will reflect the cumulative effect of previous marketing effort.

What will be the market share for our brand of soft drink at the football game? That will depend on consumers' past buying patterns (which reflect the cumulative effect of our past strategies) and our current marketing strategies. Perhaps we generally get a share of 0.15, but we sold the vendor on using our cups, which show our brand name on one side of the cup and the name of the home team on the other side. From previous experience, we have found that this promotion increases our share to 0.20. Thus in this case we may expect a company potential of 4,500 cups (0.20 × 22,500) if the distribution rate is 100 percent, or 3,375 (0.20 × 16,875) cups if the distribution rate is 0.75.

SALES GOALS

Sales goals are a hoped-for sales level for a company. They are generally *higher* than the company potential to provide motivation, especially for the sales force. Goals must be within reach, however, or they will be discouraging and therefore demotivating.

SALES QUOTAS

A *sales quota* is a goal that has been broken down into smaller units, such as a region, a district, or a specific representative's territory, to provide a management objective. The quota is generally part of a motivation plan that is linked to compensation plans for sales managers and representatives.

WHAT VARIABLES SHOULD WE MEASURE?

After the two previous questions have been answered, the market analyst must identify those variables that determine the market capacity and potential.

VARIABLES TO MEASURE MARKET CAPACITY

Market capacity represents the total number of units that could be absorbed, regardless of persons' ability to pay. For many products and services, there are limitations. There is a limit to how much one can eat. One haircut per person per week may be the upper limit for that service. One automobile per person may be the market capacity for that industry.

Identifying this capacity is necessary before making a commitment to a product. But there have been some classic cases in underestimating the market. When the first adding machine was developed, the market capacity was estimated to be 9,000 units—one for each bank branch in the United States and Canada. Fifty years later, the computer industry made a similar underestimate when it estimated that the capacity for computers was one for each major university and governmental agency.

Marketing capacities are based on the needs of individual consumers and firms. The needs of individuals may be defined in broad terms, such as the need for food, shelter, safety, clothing, socialization, self-esteem, and self-actualization. A company has needs associated with its basic mission. For example, a manufacturing company will need machinery, materials, capital, trained labor, and management.

The magnitude of a need is measured by variables that are known as *market factors*, which are variables that either cause or are associated with the magnitude of the need. For example, a consumer's age will be related to food, clothing, and social needs. By knowing the number of persons in different age groups, we can estimate the market capacity for baby food, soft drinks, and geriatric foods. Additional market factors for individual consumers include birth rates, marriage rates, education, geographic location, and the ages of children in the family. Sources of data for these market factors include the U.S. Census of Population and the "Survey of Buying Power," published annually by *Sales & Marketing Management*. Data sources will be discussed further at the end of this chapter.

In industrial marketing, market factors for a prospect that is a manufacturer may be the number of units sold, the dollars of value added, or the number of employees in a company. The U.S. Census of

Manufacturing, Transportation, Retailing, and Wholesaling and the "Survey of Industrial Buying Power," published annually by *Sales & Marketing Management* provide measures of such factors that may be used for estimating industrial market capacity.

VARIABLES TO MEASURE MARKET POTENTIAL

The market potential forecast is a refinement of the market capacity forecast because it includes the additional variables of price, economic capacity to buy, and the effect of the marketing strategies within the industry. Here we are trying to answer questions such as, "How much would sales increase if we lowered price 1 percent?" or "How much will sales drop if disposable personal income drops 1 percent?" These are the concepts of price and income elasticity, as developed by economists.

Market factors for the ability to buy include not only income levels, but employment rates, the availability of credit, inflation rates, and economic expectations for the future. Market factors for a firm's ability to buy include the gross national product, inflation, the availability of capital, government policies, and executives' expectations for the future.

Additional variables will be needed to forecast potentials for specific market segments. Market factor variables that are used to identify market segments include variables such as beliefs, attitudes toward the product, heavy user-light user, and life style variables, such as stylish, worrisome, economical, and sporty. These variables generally require primary research by the marketer.

SHOULD WE SEGMENT THE MARKET?

WHAT IS SEGMENTATION?

A market is a time and place where product or service utilities are exchanged. Markets may be defined further in terms of their geographic location, the type of products exchanged (consumer or industrial), the characteristics of the materials in the product (durables such as cars and appliances, or nondurables such as food and clothing), the shopping habits of buyers (convenience, shopping, and specialty goods), the end use of industrial goods (major equipment, accessory equipment, supplies, parts, and semifinished ingredients), and the personal characteristics of the buyers (age, income, education, life style, and personality). Market segmentation consists of dividing a large market into these smaller markets according to market factors that will cause the purchase of a product or service. These more homogeneous market segments make it easier to focus a marketing strategy.

Exhibit 17.2 Market Segments for the Automobile Industry

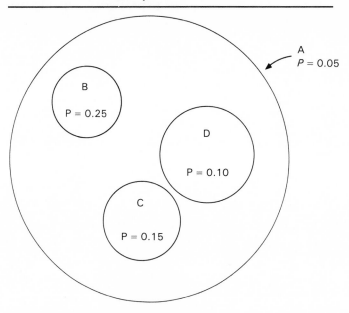

Note: The size of the circle reflects the number of persons in the segment. *P* is the probability of buying a car in a given year.

Exhibit 17.2 illustrates graphically the concept of market segmentation. The large circle, A, represents the population of the United States. The smaller circles, B, C, and D, represent the number of people having different probabilities of buying a new automobile. Commonly used research techniques will help a market analyst to identify the demographic, economic, and psychographic profiles of each of these segments. For example, segment B, with a probability of 0.25, may be professional persons, twenty-five to forty years old, living in a suburban area, and earning $25,000 to $35,000 per year. This segment may be divided into smaller segments according to marital status and life style. This additional segmentation may reveal that persons in segment B who are single and have a sporty life style tend to buy sports cars, while a married person with young children has a higher probability of buying a station wagon. Additional segmentation will identify the profiles of buyers of sedans, vans, and pickup trucks. This information will help the automobile manufacturer to estimate the market potential for these body styles and to develop copy themes and media strategies that will reach these segments effectively. Similarly, a soft-drink bottler will want to measure the profiles of light, medium, heavy, and nonusers of colas, lemon flavors, and diet drinks to estimate product potentials and to develop marketing strategies.

Industrial marketers segment markets by end uses of their products and services. For example, an aluminum smelter may divide its market into beverage containers, packaging, and building and construction segments. Building and construction segments may be divided into finer segments, such as residential doors and windows, screen frames and screening, awnings, mobile homes, ducts, store fronts, bridge rails, street signs, gutters and downspouts, venetian blinds, and weather stripping. Each of these market segments would have a unique set of market factors that would be used to measure potential demand and develop marketing strategies.

The geographic location of the buyer is frequently used as a basis for market segmentation because of the influences of weather, culture, and life style factors that will influence sales. For instance, clothing sales in New England and southern California will be different because of weather and life style differences.

Segments may be defined by supplier characteristics as well as buyer characteristics. For example, we may need to forecast sales through various types of retailers. We may also want to forecast the sales of competitors.

SEGMENTATION EXAMPLES

Exhibit 17.3 illustrates how the profiles differ for four selected brands of hair shampoos, which have similar market shares of primary users. Breck appeals to the older homemaker age group who lives in a city in the mid-Atlantic or southeastern states. Johnson's Baby Shampoo, for obvious reasons, appeals to the younger homemaker with young children. This homemaker tends to be located in the suburbs. Head & Shoulders shampoo provides an interesting contrast to the previous two brands because of its ability to appeal to a broad age group, a national market, and to all income groups. Prell appeals to suburbanities living in the west-central and mid-Atlantic states, and a larger proportion of persons who did not graduate from high school. Prell seems to appeal to a larger proportion of persons representing minority races.

Reading across the psychographics row, we see that shampoo users have the common personalities of being planners and trustworthy. Users of Johnson's Baby Shampoo regard themselves as kind and tense, traits that are common to parents of young children.

Exhibit 17.3 Market Segments for Selected Shampoos

SEGMENT PROFILE VARIABLE	BRECK	JOHNSON'S BABY SHAMPOO	HEAD & SHOULDERS	PRELL
Homemaker's Age	35–49	25–34	25–49	25–49
Geographic Location	City, Mid-Atlantic, and Southeast	Southeast and Mid-Atlantic, Suburban	National, except low in New England	Suburban, West Central, Mid-Atlantic,
Education	Graduated High School	Graduated High School	Graduated High School	Non-High School Graduate
Household Income	$10,000 to $15,000	$10,000 to $15,000	Fairly even income distribution	$10,000 to 15,000
Race	White 94% Black 5% Other 1%	White 91% Black 6% Other 3%	White 92% Black 4% Other 3%	White 89% Black 7% Other 4%
Years Married	20 or more	10 or more	20 or more	20 or more
Age of Children	12–17	2–5	2–17	6–17
Psychographics (Personality, self reported)	Planner, Cautious, Trustworthy	Trustworthy, Kind, Planner, Tense	Trustworthy, Kind, Planner	Trustworthy, Kind, Planner
Number of Primary Users (Millions)	6.3	7.3	8.2	6.0
Market Share of Primary Users	11%	12%	14%	10%

1976 Target Group Index, published by Simmons Market Research Bureau, Inc.

These profile variables help sales managers to develop strategies regarding the distribution of their products, in-store promotional displays, and sales force training.

Markets are frequently segmented according to the benefits that are sought by the user. Consumer preferences may be plotted in two-dimensional brand maps. Exhibit 17.4 is a hypothetical brand map for soft drinks, where the two primary product benefits are the flavor and degree of carbonation. The size of the circle reflects the number of persons who share a common preference for flavor and carbonation levels. The small letters represent the consumers' perception of the positioning of available brands in this two-dimensional space. For example, brands d and e are positioned well inside the largest segment, B. Segment C represents a demand for a low-carbonated, tart soft drink, but no existing brand seems to be meeting this need. Brand c seems to be missing this market and segment A, which demands a high-carbonated, tart beverage. Brand maps can be extremely useful in developing product and promotional strategies.

Exhibit 17.4   A Brand Map of Soft Drinks

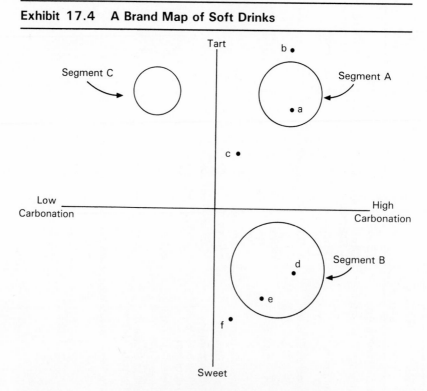

Note: The size of the circle reflects the number of persons in the segment. The small letters represent consumers' perception of the available brands.

Industrial markets may be segmented according to specific clients or similar clients, where the segmentation is according to portfolio criteria, such as return-on-investment, growth rate, or market share. (See Chapter 5.) The long-term growth rate for a client or an industry is a critical variable for long-range planning.

Marketing segmentation is an important concept for the development of marketing strategies, but it has some serious limitations that are frequently overlooked. Segmentation, like any classification procedure, attempts to form groups of people who are very similar to others within the group, but are very different from individuals in other groups. In marketing terms, this means that a product that appeals to individuals in one market segment will not appeal to individuals in another segment. Thus a marketer who uses this strategy must be certain that the present potential and the future potential of a segment are sufficient to be able to absorb present and future production capacities. The breaking of markets into finer and finer segments sharpens the focus of product and promotional strategies, but it can have the effect of turning long production runs into job-shop operations and specifying promotional strategies for segments that do not have unique media.

Should we segment the market? There is no absolute answer to this question. Marketing strategists must balance the efficiencies of more sharply focused product strategies against the inefficiencies in production. A long production run may be possible by selling an undifferentiated product to different segments by segmenting the *promotional* strategy, using different messages and media.

IN WHICH DIRECTION SHOULD WE MEASURE?

The two basic approaches for measuring market potential are the breakdown method and the buildup method. The breakdown approach, as we have seen, begins with an estimate of the market potential and breaks it first into a company potential that may be divided further into district, region, and territory quotas.

THE BREAKDOWN METHOD

RCA uses the breakdown approach to measure color television markets (Exhibit 17.5). It begins with an econometric model that forecasts gross national product (GNP) in constant dollars by using variables to reflect the current supply of money, government expenditures during periods of full employment, a price deflator, and dummy variables to reflect

Exhibit 17.5   Flowchart of Economic and Color TV Forecasting Model, RCA Corporation

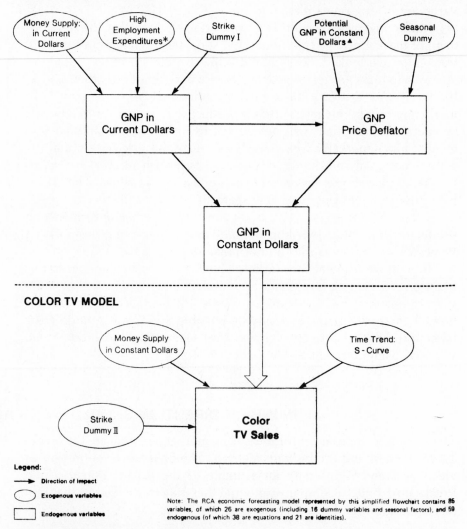

Gross National Product Model

COLOR TV MODEL

Legend:

→ Direction of impact

⬭ Exogenous variables

▢ Endogenous variables

Note: The RCA economic forecasting model represented by this simplified flowchart contains 85 variables, of which 26 are exogenous (including 16 dummy variables and seasonal factors), and 59 endogenous (of which 38 are equations and 21 are identities).

✻ High employment expenditures: level of government expenditures under conditions of full employment.

▲ Potential GNP: level of GNP under conditions of full employment.

David L. Hurwood, E. S. Grossman, and Earl L. Bailey, *Sales Forecasting*, Report No. 730 (New York: The Conference Board, 1978), pp. 110–112.

seasonality and periods when strikes occurred. The color television model uses this forecasted estimate of GNP in constant dollars as one input along with estimates of the money supply in constant dollars (which would reflect the availability of consumer credit), a dummy variable for strike conditions (segments that would be temporarily off the market for major purchases), and the position of color television in its product life cycle, expressed as an S-Curve. The total model includes eighty-five variables.

The Timken Company makes bearings for railroad freight cars. It forecasts its sales using the breakdown method (Exhibit 17.6). Timken uses two equations to derive the demand for new and rebuilt freight cars. The first equation derives the demand for railroad ton-miles per day by first estimating the total intercity ton-miles for the next year. This estimate is multiplied by railroads' estimated share of the market to produce the railroad ton-miles for the coming year. This yearly estimate is divided by 365 to produce a daily demand.

The second Timken Company equation estimates the supply of freight service that is available, expressed in terms of ton-miles per serviceable freight car. The size of the fleet that will be required during the coming year is derived by dividing the projected railroad ton-miles per day by the ton-miles per serviceable freight car. Because only 85 percent of the cars are available for service at one time, this estimated fleet size must be divided by .85 to yield the total fleet that is required for the forecasted year. To this figure, the Timken Company adds the number of cars that will be retired next year and subtracts the size of the fleet at the end of the previous year. The net result of this computation is the market capacity for new and rebuilt freight cars.

COMBINING THE BREAKDOWN AND BUILDUP METHODS

The Cummins Engine Company uses a breakdown and a buildup approach to forecast the sales of its diesel truck engines (Exhibit 17.7). The breakdown approach uses an econometric model and an estimate of Cummins's market share to derive a company forecast. The buildup forecast is based on a detailed study of the needs of each Cummins account. This analysis includes market factors, such as the account's present engine inventory and back orders, as well as the account's marketing program that may increase its truck sales. The resulting forecast is reported by account, model, and month. These individual account forecasts are added to produce a company forecast, which is then reconciled with the company forecast that is derived by the breakdown method.

Exhibit 17.6 Flowchart of Long-Range Freight Car Requirements, The Timken Company

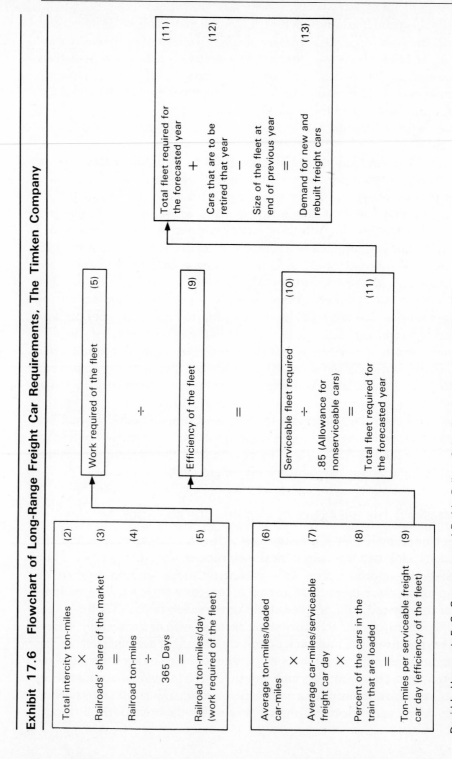

David L. Hurwood, E. S. Grossman, and Earl L. Bailey, *Sales Forecasting*, Report No. 730 (New York: The Conference Board, 1978), pp. 110–112.

**Exhibit 17.7   Two Approaches to Sales Forecast,
Cummins Engine Company**

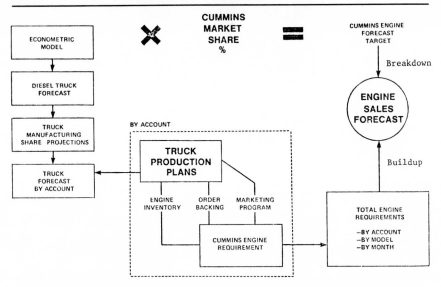

David L. Hurwood, E. S. Grossman, and Earl L. Bailey, *Sales Forecasting*, Report No. 730 (New York: The Conference Board, 1978), pp. 110–112.

Which is better, the breakdown or the buildup method? There are no positive answers to this question. The breakdown method tends to be less expensive when it can use aggregate forecasts that have been made by others, such as the government, universities, or consulting firms. Errors tend to be offsetting in highly aggregated forecasts, but the aggregate forecasts may be too general for strategic planning. The buildup method generally requires the forecaster to collect more data. With regard to reliability, Cummins reports that the breakdown method is more reliable for six months and beyond, while the buildup method tends to be more reliable for shorter periods.[1] Thus the planning horizon seems to determine the appropriateness of the sales forecasting method. This point will be discussed further later in this chapter.

The introduction of the planning horizon requires that we ask, "How far into the future are we forecasting?" If we are making a one-year forecast, variables such as birth rates and geographic shifts in population are not important because there would be only slight changes. If, however, we are making a ten-year forecast, these demographic variables become extremely important.

HOW CAN WE FORECAST MARKET MEASURES?

The measures of market potential took place at one point in time, but to develop strategies for the future we must forecast these potentials to the future. Forecasting techniques range from very simple case history approaches to very complicated mathematical techniques. This section will be limited to a description of those techniques that are appropriate to strategic sales management with emphasis on the accuracy, cost of development, development time, data required, and illustrative applications. More extensive discussions of forecasting techniques may be found in the suggested readings at the end of this chapter. The techniques may be classified as judgmental, time series analysis, and causal.[2]

The judgmental and time series techniques move sales into the future in one of two ways. The judgmental techniques gather information from persons who would be knowledgeable about a market and therefore able to make an estimate of future market potentials. Time series techniques assume that previous patterns such as trends or seasons will repeat themselves in the future so that forecasting will be possible. Both of these techniques may be illustrated algebraically as follows:

$$\text{Sales}_t \rightarrow \text{Sales}_{t + n} \tag{7}$$

Causal models will contain one or more variables, known also as market factors, that explain sales. The forecasting task becomes more complex because each of these variables must be forecasted in order to forecast sales. For example, our model of industry potential for forecasting to time period n would appear as follows:

$$\text{Industry Potential}_{t + n} = N_{t + n} \cdot Pr_{t + n} \cdot R_{t + n} \tag{8}$$

Where N equals number of persons, Pr equals the proportion of this group using the product, and R equals their usage rate. Each of these variables may change over time. For example, a manufacturer of replacement batteries for automobiles may find that the proportion of persons buying replacement batteries increases during a recession when consumers are less likely to buy a new automobile.

One problem in forecasting is the meaning of terms such as *short-run* and *long-run forecasts*. These terms cannot be defined according to a specific number of years because the terms have different meanings in different industries. For example, a long-run forecast for an electrical utility will be ten to fifteen years because of the long lead time in developing new generating capacity. In a highly competitive grocery products market, however, long-run forecasts may be two or three years.

JUDGMENTAL TECHNIQUES

The most frequently used judgmental techniques include case histories, expert opinion, the Delphi method, consensus opinion, survey of users, and buyer intentions. Each of these techniques is compared in Exhibit 17.8 according to accuracy, costs, development time, data required, and applications.

Case Histories and Analogies

Case histories and analogies simply compare new products with the growth experiences of existing products. The resulting forecasts are fair to good, after the initial three months. The cost and developmental time depend on the availability of historical data for similar products.

Expert Opinion

Fair short-term forecasts can be made by using knowledgeable individuals who have good records for judgment and insight. The costs and developmental time can be low if the company can use its own staff.

Delphi

The Delphi method uses a panel of experts who are surveyed anonymously to avoid the effects of the power structure of an organization. Results are summarized by an independent secretary and fed back to the experts so that they may revise their judgment. This technique develops fair to good forecasts. This technique is frequently used for long-range product development. The cost and developmental time depend on the availability of experts and their level of cooperation.

Exhibit 17.9 illustrates a Delphi approach that was used by a company for market forecasting. The example appears here in disguised form. In this example the demand for Pesticide #3 is being forecasted for two market segments—the corn earworm and cabbage inchworm segments. The experts in this case were research and development personnel, the product managers, and the sales managers. They were asked to estimate index numbers that would reflect changes in the number of users, the rate of use, the effect of competition, and the effect of federal regulation. Furthermore, they were asked to state the assumptions that were behind their estimates. The lower part of this table shows how these index estimates are turned into a percent estimate of the sales of

Exhibit 17.8   A Comparison of Forecasting Techniques

TECHNIQUE	ACCURACY	COSTS	DEVELOPMENT TIME	DATA REQUIRED	ILLUSTRATIVE APPLICATIONS
JUDGMENTAL					
Case History/ Analogy: Compare new product with growth of similar existing products.	Fair to good after initial three months.	Variable, depends on data availability.	At least one month.	Several years of history for similar products.	New products and profit forecast.
Expert Opinion: Estimates by knowledgeable persons who have good records for judgment and insight.	Fair for short term.	Minimal, if current staff is used.	Several weeks.	Experts give several future scenarios.	New product and margin forecast.
Delphi: Panel of experts are surveyed anonymously and results are fed back so experts may revise opinions in the light of new information.	Fair to good in medium and long term; fair to good in identifying turning points.	Panel members' time is the major cost. Cooperation is required.	Two months.	Coordinator develops, edits, and reissues questionnaires.	Long-range product development.
Consensus Opinion: Panel of key executives or the sales force makes estimates.	Good for short-range planning. Subject to organizational biases and quota effects; poor to fair in identifying turning points.	Major cost is time of executives and sales force.	One month or less.	Two sets of reports over time.	New product sales and margin forecasts.
Survey of Users: Users' estimates of needs, especially in industrial marketing.	Good for periods less than one year.	Varies according to complexity and size of the market. Using the sales force may not be the least expensive.	Three months.	Two sets of reports over time.	New product sales and margin forecasts.

Technique	Accuracy	Cost	Time Required	Data Required	Applications
Consumer Intentions and Confidence Surveys: Measure intentions regarding durable purchases and the public's opinion about economic conditions.	Better for aggregate events, such as GNP, than disaggregates such as product purchases.	Low if secondary sources are used.	At least several weeks if surveys are conducted.	Primary or secondary opinion data. Surveys are conducted by U. of Mich., Survey Res. Center, Sindlinger Corp. and the Conference Board.	Sales forecasts of product classes.
TIME SERIES					
Trend Fitting: Trend line is fitted to historical data for projection to the future.	Very good for periods less than one year. Good for longer periods; poor in identifying turning points.	Costs depend on data availability.	One day if data available.	Five years if annual data.	New product forecasts.
Moving Average: Data are averaged for a fixed number of months, dropping the oldest month as the new month is added to smooth the series and identify seasons.	Good for one year forecasts; poor in identifying turning points.	Inexpensive if computer program available.	One day.	At least two years of monthly data.	Inventory control for standard items and financial projections.
Exponential Smoothing: A smoothing procedure where more recent data points are given more weight. Adaptive control techniques use iterative procedures to determine weights.	Very good in the short term, poor for longer projections; poor in identifying turning points.	Inexpensive if computer available.	One day.	At least two years of monthly data.	Inventory control for standard products and financial projections.
Box-Jenkins: a mathematical technique that enables the computer to select the model that best fits the time series data.	Excellent for three months, poor to good for longer periods; fair in identifying turning points.	Low, if computer is available. High expertise required.	One day.	At least fifty historical data points.	Production and inventory control, financial projections.

(continued)

Exhibit 17.8 Continued

TECHNIQUE	ACCURACY	COSTS	DEVELOPMENT TIME	DATA REQUIRED	ILLUSTRATIVE APPLICATIONS
Learning Curves: Developed in the aircraft industry to forecast technological development and estimate future production costs. The learning curve is a logarithmic function that reflects the fact that when the cumulative number of units produced doubles, the cumulative average costs and the unit costs are reduced by a constant learning percentage. The learning rate may change over the life cycle of the product.	Very good for forecasting short-, intermediate-, and long-term production costs.	Inexpensive, using manual techniques or log-log graph paper.	One day.	Production costs for two points in time and cumulative units produced.	Forecasting new product production costs; competitive pricing decisions.
CAUSAL					
Regression: An equation that relates sales to independent predictor variables such as advertising effort, number of sales calls, product quality, etc. Leading indicators may be used in regression equations.	Good to very good for periods up to two years; very good in identifying turning points.	Less than $100 if data is available and relationships known.	Depends on knowledge of relationships.	At least two years of monthly data.	Forecasts of sales by product class, forecast margin.

Technique	Accuracy	Cost	Time required	Data required	Applications
Econometric: A system of interdependent regression equations that describe some sales or profit activity.	Good to excellent for short-, medium-, and long-term forecasts; excellent for identifying turning points.	Expensive. High expertise required.	At least two months.	At least two years of monthly data.	Prediction of market potential, company or division.
Input-Output Models: A matrix of industries or departments showing the flow of inputs required for certain outputs.	Good intermediate- and long-range forecasts for aggregated data, especially commodities. Fair in identifying turning points.	Very expensive, $100,000 or more. High expertise required.	At least six months.	Fifteen years of data in considerable detail.	Forecast sales for division or company.
Brand Switching Models: These models use patterns of past brand switching and brand shares at equilibrium.	Users report highly accurate. These models predict but do not explain brand behavior.	The costs and developmental time are not available because the most widely used model, the Hendry model, is proprietary.		Consumer panel purchase data.	Market share, competitive analysis, and optimal marketing expenditures for frequently purchased consumer brands.
Attribute Models: Various models are used to relate buyers' perceptions of product attributes to brand choice.	Limited accuracy in predicting brand behavior. These models help to explain brand behavior better than switching models.	Moderately expensive and time consuming because survey or laboratory methods are needed.			Product developments; promotional strategy.

Sources: John C. Chambers, Satinder K. Mullick, and Donald D. Smith, *An Executive's Guide to Forecasting* (New York: Wiley Interscience, 1974); George C. Michael, *Sales Forecasting* (Chicago: American Marketing Association, Monograph Series #10, 1979); Vithala R. Rao and James E. Cox, Jr., *Sales Forecasting Methods: Recent Developments* (Cambridge, Mass.: Marketing Science Institute, Report No. 78-119, 1978).

Exhibit 17.9 A Delphi Approach to Market Forecasting for 1985

PRODUCT: PESTICIDE #3	USE: CONTROL CROP PESTS	MARKET SEGMENT:	#1 CORN EARWORM #2 INCHWORM, CABBAGE
Estimate % change in N, number of potential users by 1985	Estimated % change in R, rate of usage of pesticide	Effect of Competition, C, on the usage rate for 1985	Estimated Effect of Public Policy, P, for 1985.

(An index number of 1.00 = no change; 1.10 = 10-percent increase; 0.90 = 10-percent decrease.)

$N_1 = 1.15$ $N_2 = 1.00$	$R_1 = 1.05$ $R_2 = 0.95$	$C_1 = 1.00$ $C_2 = 0.80$	$P_1 = 1.30$ $P_2 = 1.00$

Under the following assumptions: (Spelled out briefly)

N_1 Corn crop increase because of exports, new technology

N_2 No change in cabbage plantings.

R_1 Higher pest pressure due to closer planting of rows

R_2 Lower usage for economic and environmental reasons.

C_1 No known competitive developments.

C_2 Competitor will introduce a new product in 1984.

P_1 Environmental Protection Agency will ban a competitive product in 1985

P_2 No known action pending.

Estimated Percent Changes in Market Segment:

#1 Market Segment Index = $1.15 \times 1.05 \times 1.00 \times 1.30 = 1.57$
Percent Change = (Index − 1.0) × 100
= (1.57 − 1.0) × 100
= +57%

#2 Market Segment = $1.00 \times 0.95 \times 0.80 \times 1.00 = 0.76$
Percent Change = (Index − 1.0) × 100
= (0.76 − 1.0) × 100
= −24%

this product in 1985. In this case the corn earworm segment is forecast at a 57-percent increase, while the cabbage inchworm market will decline 24 percent. These results were cycled through the experts again so that they could revise their estimates after seeing the estimates of other experts. Ideally the process is continued until a consensus is reached, but executives tire of the process so the forecaster must be content with a range of estimates.

Consensus Opinion

The consensus opinion approach is simply a panel of informed executives or salespersons who have a knowledge of the marketplace. They are convened as a panel and submit their opinions subject to all of the biases of the power structure of the organization. This approach is generally used in cases where expediency is most important. The quality of the forecasts is doubtful.

Survey of Users

Industrial manufacturers frequently use a survey of end users to determine how much of their products will be used. For example, a paint manufacturer may survey furniture manufacturers and automobile manufacturers to determine their paint needs for the next year. The Cummins Engine Company used this approach in the buildup forecast, Exhibit 17.7.

Consumer Intentions and Confidence Surveys

Consumer expenditures account for 60 percent of the gross national product (GNP); therefore, forecasters use measures of consumer buying intentions and confidence in the economy to forecast GNP and to attempt to forecast the sales of products such as automobiles and houses. A long history of these measures has shown that they are better for measuring aggregate economic events, such as changes in GNP, than for measuring the disaggregates, such as product purchases. The Survey Research Center of the University of Michigan was the first organization to make these measures on a continuing basis with a standard questionnaire. It began in 1946. The Conference Board began its survey about 1967. Although these organizations are interested in the same problems, they use different methods regarding sample size, data collection, questions asked, and data analysis techniques (especially the treatment of neutral answers). The Conference Board seasonally adjusts its data, while the Survey Research Center does not. A comparison of the forecasting ability of these two indices for recent years suggests that the Conference Board is better in predicting quarterly economic changes, while the Center index is better for long-term trends in the economic events.[3]

Components of the Conference Board index have predicted short-term changes in the economy, but they have been unable to predict the magnitude of these changes. Its utility as a leading indicator has suffered because its lead time has varied between three and six months. "The Board's buying plans survey series has failed to demonstrate a convincing capacity to forecast consumer demand for the specific products included with a consistency sufficiently reliable to allow for marketing decision-making."[4]

Staelin and Turner[5] note that errors in judgmental sales forecasts come from two sources. If a total sales forecast is obtained by summing the forecasts of district sales managers, the total error component will be the sum of the variance for each forecaster plus the covariances between these forecasters. This covariance term will be larger if these forecasters tend to estimate in the same direction because they share a common set of misinformation regarding the environment or the company. Staelin and Turner call this second error effect the *contagion effect.* Its relative influence on a forecast may be examined by studying the positive correlation between forecasters' judgments. The authors suggest that these sources of errors be examined statistically and steps be taken to reduce them. These steps would include providing the judgmental forecasters with better information about the environment and the company. A second means for reducing these errors is to give careful consideration to the location of the forecasters within the firm, perhaps minimizing the number of aggregations that are necessary.

TIME SERIES ANALYSIS

Time series techniques search for patterns in the data that may be repeated in the future, thereby permitting a forecast. Frequently used techniques include trend fitting, moving averages, exponential smoothing, Box-Jenkins, and learning curves.

Trend Fitting

Trend fitting consists of fitting a line to a series of historical data, generally using a least-squares approach. Forecasts can be very good for short periods of time and the cost and development time can be low if the data and a computer are available. Short-term forecasts will probably use a linear trend line, but longer forecasts for ten or twenty years will require nonlinear curves that reflect market saturation and varying adoption rates by different market segments. Exhibit 17.10, TV-set sales by year, illustrates the need for nonlinear trend fitting. Retail sales of televisions reached their peak and started to decline slightly in 1972, but this total was composed of two elements—a rapidly declining trend in new-owner sales and a rapidly increasing trend in replacement sales.

Exhibit 17.11, yearly color penetration versus income, shows the penetration percent of the color TV market by segments that are defined in terms of yearly income. We note that the trend is turning toward the horizontal, the saturation level, at the highest income bracket, while the trend in the lowest income brackets is beginning to rise sharply. All of these curves combined to form the total penetration S-shaped curve that appears as a solid line in the middle of this exhibit. The S-shaped penetration curve is explained by the sociological phenomenon known as the *diffusion of innovation.* Exhibit 17.12, the sales curves for different adoption types, illustrates that the total sales for a new product is the sum of sales to segments of society who are innovators, early adopters, early majority, late majority, and laggards.[6]

Exhibit 17.10   TV-Set Sales by Year

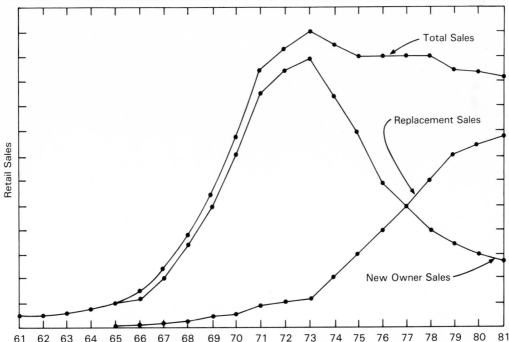

J. C. Chambers, S. K. Mullick, and D. D. Smith, *An Executive's Guide to Forecasting* (New York: John Wiley, 1974), p. 155.

Exhibit 17.11 Yearly Penetration of Color TV Sales by Income Segments

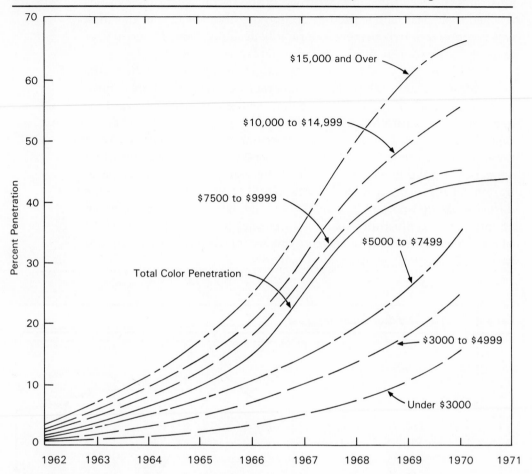

J. C. Chambers, S. K. Mullick, and D. D. Smith, *An Executive's Guide to Forecasting* (New York: John Wiley, 1974), p. 153.

Moving Averages

The moving average technique smooths a time series by averaging the data for a fixed number of months, dropping the oldest month as the new month is added. The method is used frequently in time series decomposition to identify seasonal patterns. The technique is good for short-term forecasts. It is inexpensive, and it is quick if the data and a computer are available. It is used frequently for inventory control and financial projections.

Exhibit 17.12   Sales Curves for Different Adoption Types

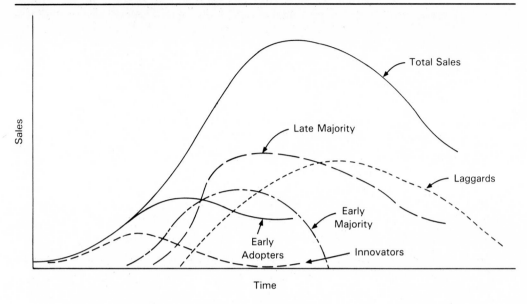

J. C. Chambers, S. K. Mullick, and D. D. Smith, *An Executive's Guide to Forecasting* (New York: John Wiley, 1974), p. 154.

Exponential Smoothing

Exponential smoothing techniques weight the most recent data more heavily, thereby reflecting recent trends that may predict the future. Adaptive control techniques use iterative procedures to determine the most appropriate smoothing weight. These techniques give good short-term projections, so long as turning points are not involved. Turning points are sharp increases or decreases in the series. Exponential smoothing can be low cost and produced rapidly when data and computers are available.

Box-Jenkins

The Box-Jenkins approach uses a mathematical technique that enables the computer to select the model that best fits the time series data. While some forecasters found the short-term projections to be good and the system fair in identifying turning points, Wheelwright concluded that it is not very stable in model identification and does not perform uniformly better than other short-term methods.[7] It may be a high-cost procedure because of the high level of expertise that is required for implementation.

Learning Curves

Learning curves were developed in the aircraft industry to forecast technological development and estimate future production costs. This is a logarithmic curve that reflects the fact that when the cumulative number of units produced doubles, the cumulative average cost and the unit costs are reduced by a constant learning percentage. This learning rate may change over the life cycle of the product. This technique must be used with care so that scale effects, which reflect the cost advantages of larger plants, are distinguished from experience effects, which are the result of practice, repetition, and learning.[8] The technique gives good production cost forecasts over all ranges, is inexpensive if the data are available, and can be produced in one day. It is particularly useful for forecasting new product production costs and for competitive pricing decisions.

CAUSAL MODELS

The philosophy of causal models differs from that of judgmental or time series models. Judgmental and time series models try to predict *what* will happen. Causal models attempt to explain *what* and *why* an event will occur. Causal models frequently contain variables that reflect buyers' needs, their ability to buy, and promotional efforts by the company and competitors. These models can become quite technical, but the discussion that follows will be limited to nontechnical discussions of applications.

Regression

Regression equations relate changes in sales to one or more independent predictor variables, such as income, price, product quality, advertising, and selling effort. Regression techniques are used widely because they give good forecasts and they can be developed quickly and cheaply. Regression is possible on many small, low-cost hand-held calculators. The ease with which regressions may be computed leads to the danger of misapplication, especially spurious relationships between independent variables and sales.

Six examples of regression forecasting models using a single predictor variable appear in Exhibit 17.13. The first two models represent market potential models that attempt to predict and explain *industry* sales. The last four models are *company* potential models.

Figure (a) in Exhibit 17.13 illustrates the income effect of disposable personal income on industry sales. The line slopes upward to the right, indicating that sales will increase as disposable personal income increases. The line starts at zero, indicating that there will be no sales if there is no disposable personal income. The dashed line is the forecasted sales for the higher levels of personal income. The closeness of the dots to the line indicates that this equation would be a good fit, thereby yielding a high correlation.

Figure (b) illustrates the price effects on sales. This is the familiar downward-sloping demand curve from economics. It reflects the fact that sales will decline as prices move toward $7.50, and will increase as the price approaches zero. The market saturation at price $0 is 14.

Figure (c) shows how regression may be used to identify trend and seasonal effects in data. In this figure, the month number is the predictor variable. The time pattern shown here could be for a suntan lotion. We see a slightly high season in January and February, skiing months, and a very high-seasonal effect during the summer months. This seasonal effect may be identified by adding a dummy variable that is equal to one during the summer months and is equal to zero for the nonseasonal months. Dummy variables may be better measures of seasonal effects when the timing of the season is constant over many years, but the amplitude of the effect varies over years.

A company may attempt to estimate the effect of competitive strategies on its sales. Figure (d) illustrates this point. Here we see that there is a slightly downward-sloping line that reflects the fact that competitive advertising expenditures will have a slight negative effect on our sales. We see also that the dots (the observations) are spread widely about this line, reflecting the fact that this is not a good fit. Such a poor fit is to be expected because our sales should be more influenced by our marketing efforts than by our competitors' advertising. It will be noted in Figures (b) and (d) that the dashed lines go to the right and left of the observation. These dashed lines are the forecasts of what would happen if price or competitive advertising were increased or decreased.

Figure (e) shows a nonlinear curve that reflects diminishing returns. In the case of this company, the representative must make at least two calls to make any sales at all, but calls become ineffective after eight calls per year.

Exhibit 17.13 Regression Forecasting Models (Dashed Lines are Forecasts)

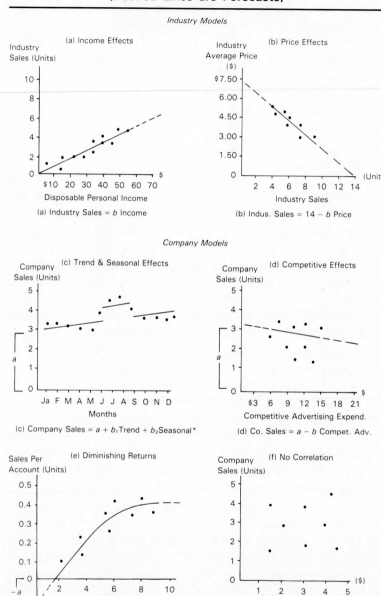

Industry Models

(a) Income Effects

Industry Sales (Units)

(a) Industry Sales = b Income

(b) Price Effects

Industry Average Price ($)

(b) Indus. Sales = 14 − b Price

Company Models

(c) Trend & Seasonal Effects

Company Sales (Units)

(c) Company Sales = $a + b_1$Trend + b_2Seasonal*

(d) Competitive Effects

Company Sales (Units)

(d) Co. Sales = $a − b$ Compet. Adv.

(e) Diminishing Returns

Sales Per Account (Units)

(e) Sales = $−a + b$(No. Calls)$^{1/2}$

(f) No Correlation

Company Sales (Units)

Dealer Training Expenditures

*Trend is month number and Seasonal is 1 during June, July, August; otherwise, 0.

Figure (f) shows a plot for which there is no correlation between sales and the predictor variable, dealer training expenditures, so it is not possible to fit a regression line. A finding such as this suggests that the sales manager will want to evaluate the dealer training program.

The equations for Figures (a) through (e) appear below each figure. These equations are of the following basic form:

$$\text{Sales} = a + bX \tag{9}$$

An equation that used multiple-market factors would appear as follows:

$$\text{Sales} = a + b_1X_1 + b_2X_2 + b_3X_3 \tag{10}$$

Sales & Marketing Management magazine uses a multiple factor equation to compute a Buying Power Index for all counties, cities, and Standard Metropolitan Statistical Areas in the United States and Canada. This index uses three predictor variables as follows:

$$\begin{aligned}\text{Buying Power Index} = {} & .5 \text{ (percent U.S. effective buying income)} \\ & + .3 \text{ (percent of total U.S. retail sales)} \\ & + .2 \text{ (percent of total U.S. population)} \tag{11}\end{aligned}$$

The weights of .5, .3, and .2 reflect this magazine's opinion of these market factors in explaining the sales of consumer products. A market analyst could use the raw data published by this magazine and multiple regression techniques to identify the specific weights for his or her consumer product. In this index, buying income reflects the consumers' ability to buy, percent retail sales reflect the distribution of the consumer product in question, and the percent of the total population is a rough measure of market capacity.

Econometric Models

Econometric models are a system of interdependent regression equations that describe sales or profit activities. The RCA Corporation econometric model in Exhibit 17.5 contained thirty-eight equations. Exhibit 17.14 shows a flow diagram for the forecasting model for the American Telephone & Telegraph Company. This model is composed of three submodels that examine the effect of the environment, corporate policy, and management decisions. The environmental model reflects the effects of the national economy, regulatory agencies, and wages. The corporate model reflects prices, demand schedules, capital market, production, and financial relationships. The management model reflects the inputs and outputs of the management decision process.

Exhibit 17.14 AT&T Forecasting Model for Corporate Policy Analysis

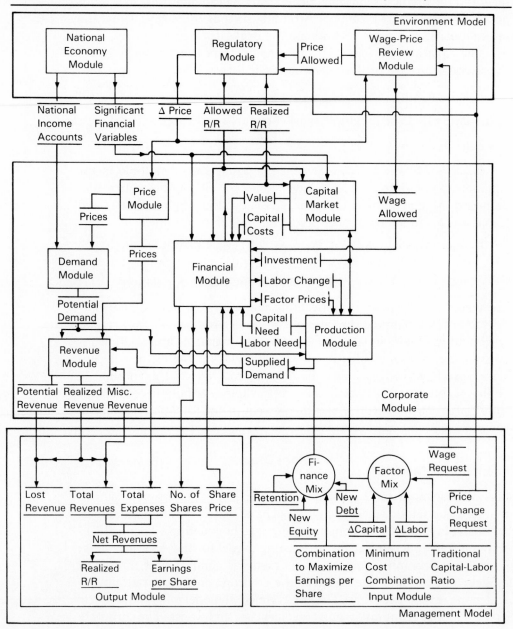

B. E. Davis, G. J. Caccappolo, and M. A. Chaudry, "An Econometric Planning Model for American Telephone and Telegraph Company. Copyright 1973, The American Telephone and Telegraph Company. Reprinted with permission from *The Bell Journal of Economics* (Spring 1973).

Econometrics are expensive to develop in terms of the expertise that is required, the data that must be gathered, and computer time. Econometricians generally credit econometric models with excellent forecasts and an excellent ability to identify turning points. Armstrong concluded that the evidence did not support such generalizations, and that they were due to the selective perception of the econometricians, an opinion that was not supported by econometricians who responded to Armstrong's article.[9]

Input-Output Models

Input-output models are matrices that show the amount of input that is required from each industry for a one-dollar output of the industry whose demand is being studied. These models give good intermediate- and long-range forecasts for major industries, such as automobiles, metals, power utilities, and commodities. They are very expensive to develop in terms of expertise, data requirements, and time. They would be more appropriate in industrial marketing situations than in consumer industries.

Brand Switching Models

Brand switching models use estimates of the probability of a consumer switching from a present brand to another brand. Data are gathered by having consumers report in a diary their weekly brand purchases, which permits analysis of brand switching. Past patterns of switching are analyzed to forecast brand market shares. Brand switching models are good predictors of brand behavior, but they do not provide insight into why people switch brands. Attitudinal research may be required to provide insight for strategy reformulation.

The Hendry Corporation developed a system of models for describing consumer purchase patterns that can be used to predict sales of new brands in specific product categories under specified marketing-mix scenarios.[10] The switching relationships are also used to examine the competitive market structure that occurs as a result of brands competing according to clusters of attributes.

Because the Hendry system is proprietary, it is not possible to compare its accuracy and cost with other methods. Users do report privately that it forecasts market shares well. Because it forecasts only market shares, it is necessary to use other techniques, such as time-series or regression models, to forecast the industry sales.

Attribute Models

Attribute models are based on the fact that buyers do not purchase a product; they buy a bundle of attributes that will meet their needs. Some needs are more important than others, which may be reflected in the model by weighting procedures. Buyers perceive brands as possessing different amounts of these attributes, which are measured in terms of attitudes towards the brands. Various metric and nonmetric methods have been devised for measuring these attitudes. These measures are used for consumer profiles, brand maps, and buying models. The strength of attribute and attitudinal models is in diagnosing why consumers buy one brand rather than another brand. Attitudinal models tend to be poor predictors of brand share.

Conjoint analysis is a set of techniques that enables the market analyst to decompose consumers' overall evaluation of a product into separate utility functions for individual attributes. These utilities are then mapped into probabilities of choice, thereby enabling the researcher to predict the future demand for a new product.[11]

INDUSTRY PREFERENCES FOR METHODS

The preceding brief discussion of forecasting techniques leads us to the conclusion that there is no one technique for all occasions. The appropriate choice of techniques will depend on the characteristics of the product, the product life cycle, the planning horizon, the developmental costs, the speed with which the technique can be developed, the desired accuracy of the forecasts, and the costs of forecasting. Buying intentions may be appropriate for industrial products, but inappropriate for consumer goods. Judgmental techniques may be necessary during the early stages of a product's life cycle because no other data are available, but more quantitative approaches may be used later in the cycle as time-series patterns stabilize. The competitive dynamics of the marketplace may not allow time for extensive econometric models in consumer goods marketing, but such models may be appropriate in a mature industry such as an electric utility.

The forecasting costs include the development of the model, data gathering, data storage, program storage, and the operation of the methods. In many instances, the cost is probably the overriding criterion for selection.

Surveys of forecasters have revealed that the techniques used most frequently are the judgmental techniques of executive opinion and sales force composites, followed by the simpler time-series analysis methods, including trend projections and moving averages.[12] Many firms use several forecasting methods and then reconcile the differences. The multiple-methods approach is similar to a navigator who takes bearings on three objects along the shore and assumes that the ship is at the center of the small triangle formed by these bearings. While many firms use multiple methods, there is no theory of triangulation in sales forecasting.

The ideal forecast will predict the event that will occur, the time when it will occur, and the magnitude of the event. The sales forecast must go one step further and explain why the event will occur at the specified time and in the predicted magnitude. An accurate forecast will require reliable and valid predictions for each of these four steps. Reliability means simply that the method will give similar results over time. Validity means how close the prediction was to the outcome. In the case of the weather forecaster, a prediction is valid if we observe rain after rain was predicted.

To understand these special problems of validating a sales forecast, we must consider the concepts of self-fulfilling forecasts and self-defeating forecasts. A self-fulfilling forecast would occur if a competitor started a rumor that a bank was about to fail and all depositors withdrew their funds, thereby causing the failure. A self-defeating forecast would occur when a sales forecast for a bad year provided the motivation for creating better marketing strategies and stimulating higher sales force productivity, thereby invalidating the forecast. While this is a happy ending for the company, it ruins the forecaster's record. Thus *the ultimate test of a sales forecast is whether it made the marketing strategy a better strategy.*

WHO MAKES THE FORECAST?

The person or department that is responsible for making a forecast will vary among firms and will frequently occur in many different departments, with little coordination of forecasts. The marketing department will make a sales forecast that is part of the decision process for recruiting and training sales representatives. The production department will create a forecast to develop optimal production runs. The finance department will forecast to determine capital needs. Company-wide forecasts are frequently made the responsibility of the chief executive officer and may be performed by a corporate planning department that is directly under this officer.

The staff support for designing the forecasting model, collecting the data, storing the data, and running the model may be supplied by the operations research department, the marketing research department, outside suppliers who specialize in forecasting, or outside consultants.

SALES MANAGEMENT INFORMATION SYSTEMS

Measures and forecasts of market potential require data. The data may be classified as internal or external. Internal data include sales data that are collected as a byproduct of the normal accounting procedures. External data are data that are collected especially for measuring and forecasting market potentials. These external data may be divided into two broad categories—secondary and primary sources. Secondary sources are those information sources that have been collected for purposes other than to meet the needs of the marketer, but may be adapted to the marketer's needs at a very low cost. Primary sources are those marketing research studies that have been undertaken to meet a specific marketing need.

SECONDARY SOURCES

The most familiar of secondary sources are the censuses that are collected by the federal government. The most familiar censuses are those of population characteristics and household characteristics. Less familiar are the censuses of manufacturers, wholesalers, retailers, and selected service industries. The most frequently used federal censuses are summarized in the appendix to this chapter.

The census data becomes out-of-date quickly because it is collected only every ten years. *Sales & Marketing Management* magazine provides an annual estimate of the population and its income for national, regional, state, city, county, and Standard Metropolitan Statistical Areas. This magazine also makes an annual estimate of industrial purchasing power by manufacturing plants, thereby supplementing the federal census of manufacturers that is conducted every five years. Further details of these surveys may be seen in the appendix to this chapter. The surveys conducted by *Sales & Marketing Management* magazine have compared favorably with federal censuses. For example, the 1977 Census of Retail Trade was only 0.1 percent higher than the Survey.[13] The "Survey of Buying Power" reports the number of households, their income, and retail sales. These data have been published by *Sales & Marketing Management* magazine for over fifty years and have been shown to have good accuracy.[14]

A good business library can be very helpful in supplying data for measuring market potentials and for measuring competition. Financial services such as *Value Line, Investment Survey, Standard & Poor's Industries Surveys,* and *Moody's Manuals* can provide useful information for consultative selling, as well as insights into competitive behavior and possible acquisitions. *Predicasts* provides one-line abstracts on growth expectations of industries as arranged by Standard Industrial Classification. Periodical indices such as those for the *Wall Street Journal* and the *New York Times* can be useful in identifying current articles about companies. The *Business Periodicals Index* classifies periodical articles according to the major business functional areas. The *Funk and Scott Index of Corporations and Industries* provides a weekly abstracting service of over 750 U.S. business and trade publications arranged by Standard Industrial Classification number. These are just a sample of the indices and directories that may be found in a good business library.[15]

SYNDICATED SOURCES

Some research firms collect information and make it available to marketing organizations for a fee. For example, Dun's Marketing Services transforms the data that are collected by Dun & Bradstreet for financial reasons into a form that can be useful for marketers. Other research companies provide syndicated data on brand usage by restaurants, retail sales in drug stores and supermarkets, and the reading, listening, and viewing habits regarding the major media. Other companies provide detailed statistics on the movement of products to food stores and drug stores using the computer tapes of food wholesalers and drug wholesalers. Extensive syndicated sources are available in the pharmaceutical industry to provide marketing strategists with information about physicians' product uses and the marketing expenditures of competitors. Some of these information systems are now available in computer time-sharing systems so the strategists may work directly with the data.

PRIMARY SOURCES

A primary source of data is one in which the data were gathered by the analyst to solve a specific problem. These data are proprietary, so they are not available to competitors. A marketing research survey of buyers' needs or brand preferences is an example of a primary data source.

Sales representatives are used frequently to provide market information regarding the growth or decline in market segments and competitive activities. We have seen already that the Cummins Engine Company requires the representatives to report the truck production plans of accounts (Exhibit 17.7). Using sales representatives as market researchers has several limitations. They may choose to underestimate the market to keep their quota low. A representative who is compensated by a straight commission has no incentive to perform any activity that is not a selling activity.

For a feedback system to be effective, the representative must be convinced that the data supplied are actually being used and that they will help him or her in future selling efforts. Some companies make this marketing research activity part of the job description and training given to their representatives.[16]

SUMMARY

This chapter deals with the dual problems of measuring the size or potential of a market and then forecasting this potential into the future. A sales forecast is necessary in sales management in order to forecast labor force needs and selling costs, but also for all other departments in the company. In order to conduct a sales forecast, a series of decisions must be made regarding the level of market aggregation to forecast, the variables that will best predict and explain changes in the market, whether the market should be divided into homogeneous market segments, whether the forecast should be derived by breaking an aggregate forecast down into small units such as territories, or building up the total forecast by measuring customers' needs, and, finally, which of the many forecasting techniques will be used. Once these decisions have been made, the next problem is gathering data to implement the forecasting procedure. All of these topics have been discussed in this chapter.

ASSIGNMENTS/DISCUSSION QUESTIONS

1. If you were the sales manager for a manufacturer of corrugated and solid fibre boxes, how would you determine the market potential and pentration rates by Standard Industrial Classification numbers for Fresno County, California? The company sold $1.5 million in the county in 1976, 85 percent of which went to the food and kindred products industry, and 15 percent to firms manufacturing stone, clay, and glass products.

  a. Describe the model that you would use to measure potential. To measure penetration.
  b. What would be your assumptions and procedures?
  c. What information sources would you use?
  d. What quotas would you establish?

2. A manufacturer of automobile tires has asked you to develop national, state, and county sales quotas and potentials for tire replacements.
  a. Describe the model that you would use. What assumptions does it make?
  b. What would be your procedure and sources of data?

3. In the fall of 1982, after a successful tour of field selling, you have been rotated through the home office of your company, a paper products manufacturer. You have been assigned to the product strategy team for a brand of facial tissues that were introduced ten years ago. You have been asked to develop a forecasting method that will search for the position of the product on its life cycle and identify seasonal patterns.

The data are as follows:

DATE		TISSUE SALES (,000 CASES)	DATE		TISSUE SALES (,000 CASES)
1979	3	52.070	**1981**	1	147.320
	4	71.120		2	187.960
	5	71.120		3	168.910
	6	62.230		4	140.970
	7	44.450		5	128.270
	8	58.420		6	125.730
	9	43.180		7	72.390
	10	71.120		8	77.470
	11	116.840		9	85.090
	12	91.440		10	110.490
1980	1	99.060		11	146.050
	2	172.720		12	166.370
	3	186.690	**1982**	1	175.260
	4	147.320		2	187.960
	5	123.190		3	190.500
	6	101.600		4	191.770
	7	69.850		5	154.940
	8	77.470		6	125.730
	9	58.420			
	10	99.060			
	11	116.840			
	12	123.190			

   a. Search for the position of the product on life cycle under the following assumptions:
   1) the trend is linear,
   2) during this period the trend has been one of growth, but is starting to turn down,
   3) during the period the trend has been one of slow growth, but it has started to reach the point of rapid growth,
   4) the product has grown and reached a saturation point during this period.
   b. Using the trend for the linear assumption and the data for March 1979 through February 1982, compute a seasonal index.
   c. Using the linear trend and the seasonal index, forecast the sales for March 1982 to February 1983. Compare your forecast with the observed months of March to June of 1982.

REFERENCES

1. D. L. Hurwood, E. S. Grossman, and E. L. Bailey, *Sales Forecasting* (New York: The Conference Board, 1978, Report #730), p. 118, fn 5.
2. J. C. Chambers, S. K. Mullick, and D. D. Smith, *An Executive's Guide to Forecasting* (New York: John Wiley and Sons, 1974). For other taxonomies, see S. Makridakis and S. C. Wheelwright, "Forecasting: Issues & Challenges for Marketing Management," *Journal of Management* 41 (October 1977): 24–38; V. R. Rao and J. E. Cox, Jr., *Sales Forecasting Methods: A Survey of Recent Developments* (Cambridge, Mass.: Marketing Science Institute, 1978, Report No. 78-119), Chapter 3.
3. Fabian Linden, "The Measure of Consumer Confidence," *Across the Board* (April 1979): 74–79.
4. Ibid., pp. 77–78.
5. Richard Staelin and Ronald E. Turner, "Error in Judgmental Sales Forecasts: Theory and Results," *Journal of Marketing Research* (February 1973): 10–16.
6. For a discussion of this relationship, see F. M. Bass, "A New Product Growth Model for Consumer Durables," *Management Science* 15, no. 5 (January 1969, Series A): 215–227. For a discussion of other penetration models, see V. R. Rao and J. E. Cox, Jr., *Sales Forecasting Methods: A Survey of Recent Developments* (Cambridge, Mass.: Marketing Science Institute, 1978, Report No. 78-119), pp. 59–66.
7. S. C. Wheelwright, Private communication, July 22, 1981.
8. George S. Day, "Analytical Approaches to Strategic Marketing Planning," *Review of Marketing 1981,* ed. Ben M. Enis and K. J. Roering (Chicago: American Marketing Association, 1981), pp. 89–105.
9. J. Scott Armstrong, "Forecasting with Econometric Methods: Folklore versus Fact," *Journal of Business,* 51, no. 4 (1978): 549–564. For comments by econometricians, see Ibid., pp. 565–600.
10. V. R. Rao and J. E. Cox, Jr., *Sales Forecasting Methods: Recent Developments* (Cambridge, Mass.: Marketing Science Institute, Report No. 78-119, 1978), pp. 51–58.

11. Ibid., pp. 66–72.
12. Ibid., pp. 25–32; D. J. Dalrymple, "Sales Forecasting Methods and Accuracy," *Business Horizons* 18 (December 1975): 69–73; Steven C. Wheelwright and D. G. Clarke, "Corporate Forecasting: Promise and Reality," *Harvard Business Review* (November–December 1976): 40–65ff; R. M. Hogarth and S. Makridakis, "Forecasting and Planning: An Evaluation," *Management Science* 27, no. 2 (February 1981): 115–138.
13. "Comparing S&MM's Survey with the Census," *Sales & Marketing Management* (February 4, 1980): 16–17.
14. Charles Waldo and Dennis Fuller, "Just How Good is the 'Survey of Buying Power'?" *Journal of Marketing* (October 1977): 64.
15. For an extensive annotated bibliography of information sources, see G. David Hughes, *Demand Analysis for Marketing Decisions* (Homewood, Ill.: Richard D. Irwin, Inc., 1973), Appendix A.
16. T. R. Wotruba and Michael L. Thurlow, "Sales Force Participation in Quota Setting and Sales Forecasting," *Journal of Marketing* 40 (April 1976): 11–16.

SUGGESTED READINGS

Bolt, Gordon J., *Market and Sales Forecasting—A Total Approach* (New York: Halsted Press Division, John Wiley and Sons, Inc., 1972).

Makridakis, S., and Wheelwright, S. C., eds., *Handbook of Business Forecasting Techniques* (New York: John Wiley & Sons, 1982).

Makridakis, S., and Wheelwright, S. C., *Forecasting: Methods and Applications* (New York: John Wiley & Sons, 1978).

Measuring Markets: A Guide to the Use of Federal and State Statistical Data (Washington, D.C.: U.S. Department of Commerce, Industry and Trade Administration, August 1979).

Montgomery, D. B., and Wittink, D. R., eds., *Market Measurement and Analysis* (Cambridge, Mass.: The Marketing Science Institute, 1980, Report No. 80-103).

Stephens, K. T., and Wilde, R. W., "On-Target Sales Forecasting: Basis for Better Planning," *Product Marketing* 6 (March 1977): 21–25.

Thomopoulos, Nick T., *Applied Forecasting Methods* (Englewood Cliffs, N.J.: Prentice-Hall, Inc., 1980).

Wheelwright, S. C., and Makridakis, S., *Forecasting Methods for Management,* 3rd. ed. (New York: John Wiley & Sons, 1980).

Appendix: Selected Secondary Data Sources for Demand Analyses

VARIABLES MEASURED	GEOGRAPHIC COVERAGE	FREQUENCY OF MEASURE	PUBLICATION TITLE	ISSUING ORGANIZATION
CONSUMER GOODS				
Population Characteristics				
Number of persons classified by sex, race, birth date, citizenship, household relationship	National, regions, divisions, states, urban, rural, farm, SMSAs, census tracts	Decennial for years ending in "O"	U.S. Census of Population	Bureau of the Census, U.S. Department of Commerce
Number of houses occupied, tenure, ethnic groups, persons per room	Similar to above coverage	Decennial	U.S. Census of Housing	Same as above
Estimates of population by age, school enrollment	National, regional, and state	Annual	Population Estimates (P-25 Series), Social and Economic Characteristics	Same as above
Number of households, families, group quarters, unrelated individuals by type, age, and family characteristics, mobility	National	Annual	Current Population Report, Population Characteristics (P-20 Series) Household and Family Characteristics	Same as above
Number of persons, percent of U.S. population, age distribution	National, regional, state, city, county, SMSA	Annual	"Survey of Buying Power," July issue	*Sales & Marketing Management* magazine
Number of persons and some population characteristics	County, city, and some regional	Annual		Individual state governments

Income Statistics

Data	Geographic Area	Frequency	Publication	Source
Total money and median income of families and unrelated individuals, family composition, educational attainment, major sources, marital status, characteristics of head of household such as age, sex, color, occupation and industry	National, regions, divisions, states, urban farm and nonfarm, urban SMSAs	Decennial, year preceding census of population	U.S. Census of Population	Bureau of the Census, U.S. Department of Commerce
Proportion of families and persons at various income levels by age, sex, color, family size, education, occupation, work experience	National, region, metropolitan, nonmetro., farm, and nonfarm	Current and selected prior years	Current Population Reports (P-60 Consumer Income)	Same as above
Number of tax returns, adjusted gross income, sources of income, exemption types, taxable income and tax items	National, state, counties, some SMSAs	Annual	Statistics of Income, Individual Income Tax Returns, Small Area Data	Internal Revenue Services, U.S. Treasury Department
Aggregate personal income by source	National	Monthly	Survey of Current Business	Bureau of Economic Analysis
Disposable personal income	National	Quarterly	Same as above	Same as above
Per capita personal income	National, regions, states	Quarterly	Same as above	Same as above
Effective Buying Income, totals, median per household, and percent distribution by four income classifications	National, regional, state, city, county, SMSAs	Annual	"Survey of Buying Power," July issue	Sales & Marketing Management magazine
Personal income, wages, salaries	State, county, some SMSAs	Annual, some quarterly or monthly		Individual state governments

(continued)

Appendix: Continued

INDUSTRIAL GOODS

Employment Statistics

VARIABLES MEASURED	GEOGRAPHIC COVERAGE	FREQUENCY OF MEASURE	SIC DIGIT DETAIL	PUBLICATION TITLE	ISSUING ORGANIZATION
Employment, aggregate payroll	National, states, SMSAs, counties, cities	Decennial	2–3	Census of Population	Bureau of the Census, U.S. Department of Commerce
Annual average quarterly employment, annual payroll for manufacturers	National, divisions, SMSAs	Every 5 years, years ending in 2 and 7		Census of Manufacturers	Same as above
Employment level for week including March 12, annual payroll for retail establishments	National, state, SMSAs, counties, cities	Same as above	2–3–4	Census of Retail Trade	Same as above
Same as above, for wholesale trade	Same as above	Same as above	2–3–4	Census of Wholesale Trade	Same as above
Same as above, for selected services	Same as above	Same as above	2–3–4	Census of Selected Services	Same as above
Same as above, for government	Same as above	Same as above	Not applicable	Census of Government	Same as above
Employment level in mid-March; aggregate annual and first quarter payroll.	National, states, counties	Annual	2–3–4	County Business Patterns	Same as above
Annual employment and aggregate payroll	National	Annual	2–3–4	Annual Survey of Manufacturers	Same as above
Employment and earnings	National	Monthly	1–2–3	Employment and earnings	Bureau of Labor Statistics, U.S. Dept. of Labor

Information	Coverage	Frequency		Publication	Source
Employment and earnings statistics	States, SMSAs	Annually	2–3	Employment and Earnings Statistics for States and Areas	Same as above
Employment and earnings	National	Monthly	1–2–3–4	Monthly Labor Review	Same as above
Quarterly and annual employment, weekly and hourly earnings	National	Monthly	1–2	Survey of Current Business	Bureau of Economic Analysis, U.S. Department of Commerce
Employment and earnings	State, counties, some smaller units	Monthly	1–2		State governments
Sales Statistics Value of shipments Retail sales Wholesale sales Receipts of selected services	See Census of Manufacturers, above See Census of Retail Trade, above See Census of Wholesale Trade, above See Census of Selected Services, above				
Value by shipment by product class	See Annual Survey of Manufacturers, above				
Receipts, deductions by type, profits	National	Annual	2–3–4	Statistics of Income—Business Income Tax Returns	Internal Revenue Service, U.S. Treasury Dept.
Value of shipments and selected receipts	National and some states	Annual	3–4	U.S. Industrial Outlook	Bureau of Domestic Business Development, U.S. Dept. of Commerce
State sales taxes	State and counties	Annual	Varies		State governments
Number of manufacturing plants; total shipments and percent of U.S. shipments.	State and counties	Annual	4	"Survey of Industrial Purchasing Power," April issue	*Sales & Marketing Management* magazine

18

DEVELOPING SALES ORGANIZATIONS

DESIGNING A SALES ORGANIZATION

Few general sales managers will have an opportunity to develop a new sales organization for a company or a product, but many managers will find it necessary to reorganize a sales organization as a result of new products, changing strategies, or market potentials. This chapter discusses current thinking in designing sales organizations and developing territories for representatives.

WHAT IS AN ORGANIZATION?

An organization is a cluster of activities that are connected by communication links in order to achieve an objective. A change in the objective or the strategy for achieving the objective will alter the importance of specific activities. Thus a change in a company's objectives or strategies might require that it change its organizational design. The clusters of activities are known as *roles*. An individual may perform one or more roles in an organization.

Objectives determine strategies, and strategies determine activities. These activities determine the roles that one must play. The roles that these activities create determine the type of person who should be in the organization and the relationships that this individual has with other members of the organization. Hence, when a new organization is created, its objectives and strategies determine the organizational structure.[1] The redesigning of an organization, however, will be influenced by the power structure (i.e., who controls the rewards) within the organization, because this structure determines the objectives, the strategies, and the reward systems.

Differences in role expectations will cause organizational conflicts. These differences can frequently be traced to inadequate job descriptions and job performance standards.

Role specialization leads to horizontal organizations. For example, marketing departments divide activities into advertising, sales promotion, personal selling, logistics, and market research, as is illustrated in Exhibit 18.1. This horizontal organization requires provision for coordination of these activities. The coordination of activities among the marketing departments is generally provided by the marketing plan, the final responsibility of which rests with the marketing manager, who is over these functional areas.

When the workload for a cluster of specialized activities, such as personal selling, exceeds the capacity of one individual, then authority for some of these activities is transferred to subordinates. This delegation of authority to increase capacity gives the organization its vertical structure. The process of delegation requires performance standards and measures of performance to assure that the delegated activities are being done. The final accountability for these delegated activities rests with the delegator.

Exhibit 18.1   Various Sales Force Designs

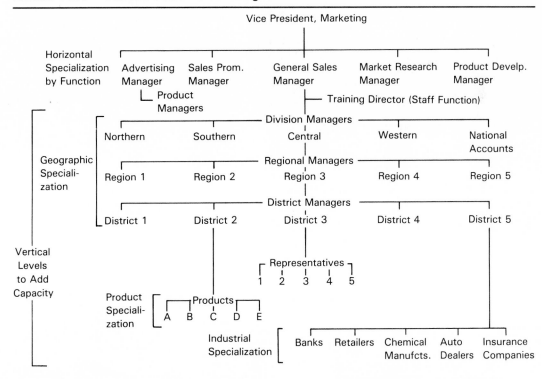

Many sales organizations will use additional role specializations that are defined in terms of geographic location, products, industries, or applications. Such specialization introduces a horizontal dimension to the sales force structure. Diagrams of these organizational designs appear in Exhibit 18.1.

WHY ORGANIZE?

The basic reason for an organization is that it makes people more productive than they would be as a group of individuals. As noted previously, horizontal organizational designs permit specialization, and vertical designs increase capacities for performing an activity. Furthermore, formalized communication links and control mechanisms, such as policies and procedures, expand the capacities of managers to manage. Clear definitions of authority and responsibility for activities assure that all activities will be performed. These definitions also reduce organizational conflict, thereby reducing unproductive activities.

An organization provides continuity, but this continuity can be the major weakness in an organization if it leads to inflexibility and a resistance to the changes that are dictated by the uncertainties of its environments. Lawrence and Lorsch found that decentralized organizational designs were better for firms in an uncertain environment, while the more successful firms in a predictable environment used centralized organizational designs.[2] Many companies in the consumer goods field have decentralized the decision-making process of sales management to the regional level in order to move it closer to the marketplace, thereby permitting a more rapid response to changes in market conditions.

COMMON ORGANIZATIONAL DESIGNS

Exhibit 18.1 illustrates how organizational concepts are translated into an organizational structure. The horizontal positions represent role specialization and the vertical positions represent the need to increase the capacity of the organization. This exhibit illustrates functional, line, and staff designs with specialization at several levels within the organization. Exhibit 18.4 illustrates the matrix design.

Functional Design

The first line on Exhibit 18.1 illustrates the specialization of marketing activities into the functional roles of advertising manager, sales promotion manager, general sales manager, market research manager, and product development manager. Specialization increases the quantity and quality of output of the organization, but it has its costs. It requires systems for communication and coordination. Communication links may be formal or informal. The coordination is usually accomplished in marketing organizations through the annual marketing plan.

At some point, the costs of functional specialization may more than offset the productivity gains. The organizational designer must be careful to stop specialization short of this point, but identifying this point is difficult.

Line Design

The vertical section of Exhibit 18.1 illustrates how a vertical organization increases the capacity of the organization to perform specific activities (in this case, selling activities). The selling capacity will be determined by the span of control of each manager and the number of levels of management.

Exhibit 18.2 illustrates the relationship between span of control and levels of management. Ideally, the organizational designer will want to keep the span of control low so that a manager can give maximum attention to each representative. The designer will also want to use the minimum number of levels in the organization, thereby reducing communication problems and administrative costs. Exhibit 18.2 illustrates how the designer may choose between span of control and organizational levels.

A sales manager will determine first the size of the sales force that is needed after considering factors such as market potential, desired market penetration, product complexity, product life cycles, the fre-

Exhibit 18.2 Tradeoffs Between Span on Control and Organizational Levels for Sales Forces of Various Sizes

	TOTAL NUMBER OF REPRESENTATIVES AT EACH ORGANIZATIONAL LEVEL				
Span of Control	One Level	Two Levels	Three Levels	Four Levels	Five Levels
4	4	16	64	256	1,024
5	5	25	125	625	3,125
6	6	36	216	1,296	7,776
7	7	49	343	2,401	16,807
8	8	64	512	4,096	32,768
9	9	81	729	6,561	59,049
10	10	100	1,000	10,000	100,000

quency, scheduling, and length of the sales calls, and company resources.

To illustrate how Exhibit 18.2 is used, assume that five years ago the sales manager concluded that the sales force should be approximately 200 representatives. The manager selected an organizational design with a span of control of six and three levels of management—a general sales manager, regional sales managers, and district sales managers. Exhibit 18.2 shows that this design will provide appropriate management for 216 representatives (6^3). Assume further that during the five years since this organization was designed the company added new products and competition increased so that the sales force grew to 500 representatives. The general sales manager may decide to redesign the organization, increasing the span of control to eight. Recruiting, training, directing, and controlling eight representatives could exceed the capacity of the typical manager. The general sales manager may decide to solve this problem by performing some of these activities with a centralized staff for activities such as recruiting and training. By centralizing these staff functions, field sales managers' capacities are expanded for activities that cannot be centralized, such as counseling and measuring performance.

If we assume that our hypothetical company continues to grow through new products and markets until a sales force of 700 is needed, we see in Exhibit 18.2 that the general sales manager faces two alternative designs. He or she could increase the span of control to nine and add additional staff functions, or he or she could use a fourth level of management and reduce the span of control to five. The latter case would increase the capacity of field sales managers and permit such activities as recruiting and training to be returned to the field level.

One of the dangers of adding additional levels of management is the misperception of roles. Exhibit 18.3 reports a survey of sales managers at various levels in twenty-five companies. (For details of this survey, see Chapter 2.) Analysis of variance across the first-line, second-line, and general sales management levels revealed no significant differences in the perceptions of the first-line sales manager's job as defined by the twenty-two management activities. Analysis of individual activities revealed that only three were significantly different at the .05 level of probability. Hence, generally these companies do not have a role perception problem. The only one that seems to warrant management attention is "take corrective action." First-line sales managers attach lower importance to this activity. The lack of misperception in roles across these three levels of management suggests that these companies have good communications and probably have adequate job descriptions and performance appraisals.

Exhibit 18.3 Misperceptions in Roles
The Percent Importance of Management Functions and Activities of the First-Line Sales Manager as Perceived by the First-Line, Second-Line, and General/Marketing Managers. Respondents allocated one hundred points among twenty-two activities.

	IMPORTANCE TO FIRST-LINE MANAGER AS PERCEIVED BY:			Probability of Nonsignificant Differences Across Management Levels
	First-Line Manager	Second-Line Manager	General/Marketing Manager	
FUNCTIONS/Activities	%	%	%	
PLAN	17.6	18.0	17.8	
Forecast	2.2	2.2	2.0	.88**
Set Objectives	3.8	4.3	4.1	.43
Develop Strategies	3.4	3.6	3.6	.82
Develop Policies	1.6	1.2	1.5	.24
Develop Programs	3.5	3.9	3.8	.52
Set Procedures	1.8	1.6	1.7	.68
Budget	1.3	1.3	1.1	.79
ORGANIZE	4.2	3.5	5.4	
Estab. Organ. Structure	1.9	1.9	2.3	.74
Create Posit. Descrip.	1.1	0.7	1.6	.03
Estab. Posit. Qualif.	1.2	0.9	1.5	.15
STAFF	34.7	33.5	27.6	
Recruit/Select	8.7	9.4	8.0	.65
Orient/Train	9.2	8.7	9.6	.79
Develop Personnel	16.8	15.4	10.1	.04
DIRECT	21.1	22.6	23.6	
Delegate	4.3	4.5	4.6	.77
Motivate	9.6	10.4	10.3	.58
Coordinate	3.3	3.7	4.2	.21
Manage Change	3.8	3.9	4.6	.51
CONTROL	22.4	22.5	25.6	
Estab. Rept. Systems	2.5	2.4	2.6	.90
Develop Standards	3.3	3.0	2.8	.47
Measure Perform.	5.8	6.1	6.6	.53
Take Corrective Action	5.5	6.1	7.8	.01
Reward	5.4	5.0	5.9	.44
Totals (Subject to rounding error)	100.0%	100.0%	10.0%	
Total Number of Managers	600	69*	25	

*Some second-line managers did not answer this question.

**To be read as follows: There is a 0.88 probability that there is no difference among the perceptions of the forecasting activities of first-line managers. Thus, in nineteen of twenty-two activities, managers at all levels share the same perception of the first-line manager's activities. An analysis of variance across all twenty-two variables showed no significant difference across management levels.

Staff Designs

Staff positions may be added to an organization for reasons of specialization or to increase the capacities of line persons. Staff persons have no authority to issue orders. Exhibit 18.1 has two staff positions—product managers and director of training. Product managers may come under the advertising manager in companies where advertising is the dominant medium in the communication mix. Procter & Gamble has its product managers under the advertising manager. Such a design permits the product manager to concentrate on the advertising strategies for his or her product. The director of sales training would permit the company to specialize in training methods and follow new developments in methods and equipment. Legal and other requirements may dictate a need for centralized training. For example, the pharmaceutical industry must train its representatives carefully regarding the benefits and side effects of its products. The company may be held legally responsible for inaccurate statements made by its representatives.

Specialized Designs

Various forms of horizontal specialization may be used in the sales force design. Geographic specialization is the most common, but the utility of geographic designs is breaking down for a variety of reasons. Doody and Nickels point out that changes in buying habits and more complex products make geographic specialization inappropriate for some sales organizations.[3] Decisions are being centralized at the home office and companies are buying systems, such as computer systems, for the entire company, which prevents decisions from being made in local geographic territories. Many companies want to establish long-term relationships with sellers so that the seller may anticipate the customer's future needs, develop delivery schedules to reduce inventory requirements, and reduce capital investments.

While some companies are moving away from geographic designs, others are moving toward them to gain better control of their operations. The United Services Automobile Association (USAA) moved from a functional to a regional design because of the increased complexity in insurance laws. The company had four functional departments that handled automobile insurance servicing, automobile claims, property insurance servicing, and property claims. Within each of these areas, employees were required to know the laws and regulations of fifty states and many foreign countries. This design was adequate when there was uniformity among the states, but the passage of a wide variety of no-fault automobile insurance laws made it impossible for one employee to cope with the wide variety of coverages and options. To cope with the changing environment, in 1978 USAA shifted to a design of six geographic regions so that personnel could be expert in the insurance laws.[4]

A sales force may be specialized also according to products and industry. Technical or complex products may require two or more sales forces because no one representative can fully understand the products and their applications and because these products tend to be purchased by different individuals within the company. For example, Caterpillar distributers have two separate sales forces—one for the earth-moving equipment and one for materials handling equipment. The volume of sales in the grocery products industry will require a multilevel sales organization.

Industry specialization comes in many forms. Computer manufacturers may specialize their sales forces according to applications, such as banks, retailers, chemical manufacturers, auto dealers, and insurance companies. In 1981, International Business Machines Corp. (IBM) shifted from an industry-specialized sales force to two general sales forces, both selling IBM's full product line to their assigned customers. The National Marketing Division, headquartered in Atlanta, will sell to large, medium, and small customers throughout the United States. The National Accounts Division, with headquarters in White Plains, N.Y., will be primarily responsible for selected large customers with complex information processing needs. This design was to take greater advantage of rapid technological change and to provide better service for customers as they grow.[5]

An industry may divide its customers according to how and why they buy. For example, a tire manufacturer may have a sales force to sell to automobile manufacturers, a separate sales force will handle the replacement market, and a third sales force will sell tires to large fleet buyers. The sales force could be divided also according to the buying needs of different channels of distribution, such as wholesalers, retailers, export channels, and government channels. Many companies are adding a new form of sales force specialization, that of national account selling.

National Account Designs

Mergers, acquisitions, and growth are creating larger companies that seek economies of scale in purchasing. Purchasing is becoming centralized at a home office. Purchasing managers are sophisticated and trained in negotiation skills. Domestic and foreign competition is increasing. Because traditional sales force structures will frequently not cope with these changes, many companies are turning to a national accounts program. A national accounts program assigns an account manager to these large accounts. This manager is responsible for the profitable development of the account. These programs have many benefits for the vendor, such as better sales forecasting and planning, more efficient production runs, better service and communications with customers, and an opportunity to establish customer loyalty through consultative selling techniques.

The development of a national accounts program requires answers to many difficult questions. What criteria should be used to classify a key account for the national accounts program? How does the servicing of these accounts differ from other accounts? How should national accounts managers and representatives be recruited, trained, supervised, compensated, and promoted? What are the possible organizational structures for implementing a national accounts program?[6] There are at least four possible organizational designs for these programs: training present representatives, using senior sales management personnel, developing a national accounts sales force, and setting up a separate division for national accounts. The latter designs represent greater commitments to national accounts programs.

Train Representatives to Call on Key Accounts.   Rather than have separate sales forces or use managers in selling roles, some companies are developing key account programs around the present representatives by providing them with additional training. This training, which would be done by staff trainers from the home office, would include topics such as needs analysis, negotiation, and the legal aspects of large sales. Cargill, Inc., a grain processor and exporter, created the following eight-step program for developing key accounts:

1. Analyze the products and services sold by this account during the past year and the potential for next year.

2. Identify the names and titles of people involved in the buying decision.

3. Classify each buying influential according to whether it makes the economic decisions, personally uses or sells the product in question, makes judgments regarding the technical worth, quality, price, or logistics of the product, and which influentials may coach the representative through the buying organization.

4. Evaluate the current business conditions of the account, searching to determine if it is in a growth, stable, or declining stage in its life cycle, or if it is overconfident about its business and that of competition.

5. Identify the specific *business* needs of each buying influential. The economic buyer will have a need for the right price delivered at the right time. The technical buyer will have technical specifications that are required.

6. The personal or motivational needs of each buyer must be understood. (See Chapters 4 and 11 for extensive discussions of these needs.)

7. The relative strengths and weaknesses of competitors are evaluated relative to the company.

8. The last step in the Cargill program is an evaluation of the current relationships with the key account.[7]

Training representatives is generally less costly than using account managers because travel costs are reduced. It also eliminates the conflict between account managers and the territory representative.

Sales Managers. Some companies use their senior sales or marketing management personnel to call on key accounts. This practice tends to be more prevalent among smaller firms that cannot afford a separate national accounts sales force. While this approach has the advantage of lower costs, it has the disadvantage of taking these managers away from their principal activities. It gives top management a distorted view of the marketplace. A variation of this approach uses field sales managers to call on key accounts.

Separate Sales Force. A separate national accounts sales force that is staffed with experienced representatives works well if the key accounts have relatively little effect on manufacturing operations so that representatives do not have to be concerned with details, such as production schedules. In this case, the national accounts sales force will not need special training in such topics as production schedules.

Separate Division. A separate division may need to be established to coordinate sales, marketing, and manufacturing decisions that must be integrated to meet the needs of large accounts. Companies that supply components in subassemblies to original equipment manufacturers or sell under chain brand names, such as Sears, Wards, or Penneys, may find that the integrated division approach is best for implementing a national accounts program.[8]

Matrix Design

Hierarchical organizational designs are frequently inadequate when a business diversifies, when products become more complex, and when the marketplace becomes more competitive. Many companies are using a matrix-form design that pushes decision making to the lower levels of an organization where there is expertise for making the decision. General Electric, Equitable Life Insurance Company, TRW Systems, Citicorp, Dow Corning, and Shell Oil all use matrix designs in parts of their organizations.

A matrix-form design recognizes that two or more lines of authority may exercise equal influence over the allocation of resources and decision making. A typical matrix design has functional specialization, such as manufacturing and marketing, forming vertical chains of command, while product line divisions form horizontal chains. The result is management by compromise. This design may take four or five years to be operational because of the problems and conflicts that it can produce.[9]

An example of a matrix design organization appears in Exhibit 18.4. This figure describes a product-strategist matrix organizational design as developed by Burroughs Wellcome Company, a pharmaceutical firm. Marketing functions appear in the vertical columns and product planning activities appear in the horizontal rows. Thus the product strategist who heads the planning team for a product may come from any of the functional areas. Each planning team consists of a representative from sales management, marketing research, and the advertising agency. This design helps to overcome some of the limitations of the traditional product management system, such as insufficient experience of product managers, poor communications within the organization, lack of continuity of planning due to the short tenure of product managers, too many functions performed by a product manager, and misapplications of the product management system.[10]

HOW TO ORGANIZE

The development of an organizational design begins with a definition of the objectives for that organization. In general terms, the objectives may be growth, survival, or power. In more specific terms, the objectives will be defined in terms of profit, market share, and sales levels. When the objectives have been defined clearly, in terms of magnitude and time for completion, the next step that determines the organizational struc-

Exhibit 18.4   A Product Strategist Matrix Organizational Design

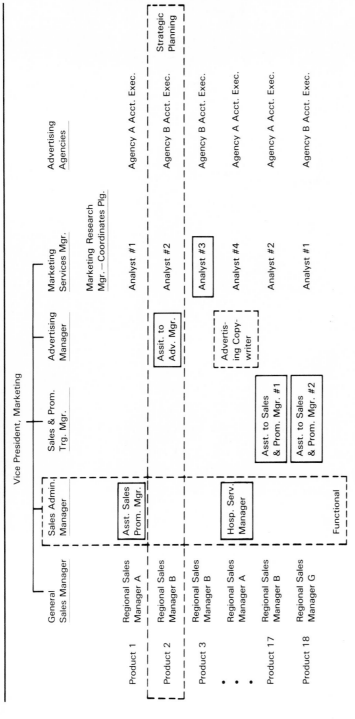

The person in the box is the Product Strategist and team chairperson. This person presents the plan to the Marketing Policy Committee that is composed of the Vice President for Marketing (Chairman), General Sales Manager, Sales Administration Manager, Advertising Manager, Marketing Services Manager, the Marketing Research Manager, and the Sales Promotion and Training Manager.

The person in the dotted box is an assistant strategist.

ture is the development of strategies. These strategies must consider the market segments, the benefits that each segment seeks in a product, and their buying habits. The third step is to select activities that will implement the strategies. It will be recalled from Chapter 2 that sales managers at all levels perform a common set of management activities, but that managers at the lower level are more concerned with operational activities, while those at the higher levels focus on planning activities.

When the activities have been clearly defined, the fourth task is to cluster related activities to form a role or roles to which it is feasible to assign people. Kilmann has used multivariate statistics and computer routines to generate alternative organizational designs. The data for these designs were generated by persons within organizations completing a questionnaire on the activities that they would like to perform and other persons with whom they would like to work.[11] This approach recognizes the fact that roles may have changed, but the organizations did not.

These role clusters form the boxes on organizational charts. At this point, responsibility, authority, and accountability must be defined clearly for each role. Responsibility may be defined as the obligation to perform an activity; authority is the right to perform the activity without seeking permission; and accountability is the obligation to see that the activity was performed and to report the activity performance level to a superior. Communication links and control mechanisms must be established to accomplish effective delegation of authority.

It should be noted that in the grouping of roles into horizontal boxes of specialization and vertical boxes to increase capacity, each decision represents a tradeoff between costs and benefits in the organizational design. The productivity gains in specialization must be weighed against the increased costs of coordination, communication, and inflexibility. The increased capacity gained by additional layers of an organization must be weighed against the cost of communication and administration. Communication costs must include the increased error rate that occurs from additional administrative levels.

The next step in the process is to write job descriptions and performance standards that describe the activities and roles for each position in the organization, the reporting and communication links, as well as responsibility, authority, and accountability obligations.

When the job descriptions are complete, it is possible to assign or reassign people to these positions. Some of these assignments may be on a temporary basis, contingent on the environmental conditions in which the organization operates. For example, a person may be assigned temporarily to a team that will introduce a new product.

The final step in organizational design is a continuous one. The appropriateness of the design must be continually monitored so that it may be changed as the company's environment and strategies change.

THE JOB DESCRIPTION

The present discussion should reinforce a point made in Chapter 2, which was that the job description and accompanying performance standards are the basic tools of sales management. In earlier chapters, we saw that these tools were the basis for recruiting, hiring, motivating, evaluating, counseling, coaching, rewarding, and promoting or terminating. The job description translates the objectives of the organization into strategic and tactical objectives that are then assigned to persons within the organization. These persons are then assigned activities, responsibility, and accountability in ways that will allow them to achieve these objectives as optimally as possible. Communication and reporting links are then established among the various positions. The job description codifies all of these assignments. The performance standards translate these assignments into statements of magnitude and times for completion, thereby adding motivational and control dimensions to the job descriptions.

Exhibit 18.5 illustrates how the sales management organization is translated into a position description for a general sales manager. The corporate objective is translated into the sales staff objective and the appropriate management skills are identified. Activities for achieving the objectives are assigned under the general functions of planning, organizing, staffing, directing, and controlling.

Job descriptions for representatives and sales managers are generally created by a job analyst from the personnel office or an outside consulting firm. The methods that are used generally include group interviews, individual interviews, analyses of existing records, survey questionnaires of operating personnel, and personal observations.

The initial task of the analyst is to identify and confirm the activities that a successful representative performs. The analyst will begin with a group interview that includes the general sales manager and field sales managers to get their perceptions of the major success factors. The analyst will then test these activities against existing records to see if these activities do distinguish between successful and unsuccessful representatives. Records may include call reports, itineraries, field managers' evaluations, and sales statistics for the territories. It may be appropriate at this point for the analyst to interview marketing managers to make certain that the role of the sales representatives in the marketing mix has been defined correctly.

Exhibit 18.5 A Position Description for a General Sales Manager of a Pharmaceutical Company

---

POSITION TITLE: General Sales Manager of the Pharmaceutical Division

OBJECTIVE: To plan, organize, lead, and control all activities and personnel within the pharmaceutical field sales staff in order to achieve the planned level of sales within the approved levels of expense.

MANAGEMENT SKILLS

ANALYZING: Analyze patterns in existing market and sales force data for opportunities and problems. Evaluate new data sources.

DECISION MAKING: Recognize decision-making responsibilities. Exercise judgment in problem-solving situations. Resolve problems or communicate needs, concerns, grievances, and achievements of the sales force to the Vice President of Marketing and appropriate departments.

COMMUNICATING: Keep the sales force informed of all company objectives and programs. Keep the Vice President of Marketing informed of important changes in the market, and sales force performance.

FUNCTIONS AND ACTIVITIES

Plan
- Prepare projections for expenditures, space, equipment, services, and personnel requirements for the field sales staff.
- Achieve national sales objectives by setting sales force objectives that are behavioral, individual, specific, achievable, measurable, and time and budget oriented.
- Develop programs, policies, and procedures to achieve sales objectives within the approved levels of expense. Challenge existing programs, policies, procedures, and budgets.
- Recommend to the Vice President for Marketing programs, policies and procedures that will improve the performance of the sales force. Inform the Vice President when present plans will not achieve their objectives.
- Manage assigned assets, the time of others, and own time in the most productive manner.

Organize
- Develop organizational structure and personnel requirements for all activities within the sales force.

Staff
- Develop and maintain a recruiting program to ensure the continuing availability of personnel within the sales force.
- Develop and train the representatives and field sales managers to ensure capable management succession.

Direct
- Motivate the sales force to work efficiently and independently to achieve the sales objectives and minimum expense.

Control
- Maintain performance criteria and evaluate all personnel in the sales force according to these criteria in order to recognize and reward achievements and to detect unsatisfactory performance at an early stage to assure that prompt and appropriate corrective action is taken when necessary.
- Apply to the sales force all standard Company programs, procedures, and policies, including those pertaining to relevant statutory regulations governing labor relations, equal employment opportunities, fair employment practices, and safety.
- Provide adequate compensation for the sales force by monitoring industry starting salary, minimums and maximums, bonuses, and expenses. Eliminate biases. Recommend changes.

The analyst will then gather information from the representatives themselves. Survey questionnaires and personal observations are frequently used at this point in the process. The analyst will then want to review the list of activities with a sample of the representatives.

The analyst is now ready to complete a job analysis form that lists a brief description of the skills and behavioral traits that are necessary to perform successfully the identified activities. For example, what mental skills are necessary for analyzing customers' needs? Which product attributes will meet these needs? What interpersonal skills are necessary to establish empathy and understanding with the buyer? What level of written and oral communication skills is necessary? What self-disciplinary behavior is required? Successful behavioral patterns include the ability to work independently, sales ability, motivation for sales, resilience, persistence, energy, adaptability, decisiveness, integrity, planning and organizing ability, initiative, judgment, and oral fact-finding ability. The analyst must develop working definitions for these job-related behavioral characteristics.

The analyst is now ready to return to the general sales manager and field sales managers for their review of this list of activities and behavioral skills and their definitions. After receiving the managers' refinements, the analyst is ready to write a job description.

Care must be taken when writing this description to be certain that it does not discriminate against minority and protected groups. The job description is now ready for the approval of the sales managers and, ultimately, the representatives. This management approval should include an agreed upon date for the review and revision of the job description as the environment and strategy change.[12]

RESEARCH IN THE DESIGN OF SALES ORGANIZATIONS

Behavioral scientists have applied their theories and techniques to the selling process (Chapter 4) and motivation (Chapter 11). Research on sales force organizations has tended to focus on role perceptions. Role conflicts and misperceptions are highly likely in a sales organization because these roles are based on strategies and objectives that are determined by the dynamics of the marketplace, which is in a constant state of change. Research on role conflict in sales management emphasizes the need for frequent updates of job descriptions and improved communications in sales organizations.

Churchill, Ford, and Walker, after reviewing the literature and from their own research, concluded that three forms of role misperception could reduce a salesperson's performance and mental well-being.[13] These misperceptions include perceived role ambiguity, perceived role conflict, and perceived role inaccuracy. Ambiguity occurs when the representative does not know what activities to perform, how to perform them, or how this performance is evaluated. Role conflicts may occur within the company when activities are perceived as being unassigned or as having been assigned to more than one person. Role conflicts for representatives also occur at the boundary between the company and the customers. A customer may want a special price or delivery date that is not consistent with company policies. Trying to reconcile role conflicts can be a very uncomfortable experience for boundary-role persons.[14] These persons are the links between organizations. Role inaccuracies occur when the salesperson's perception of a role partner, such as a field sales manager, is inaccurate. When the representative says, "I didn't know I was supposed to do that," we have a role ambiguity.

Donnelly and Ivancevich found that ". . . the greater the role clarity present, the greater the job interest, the opportunity for innovation and job satisfaction, and the less job tension and propensity to leave."[15] Teas, Wacker, and Hughes have shown that performance feedback and participation in decision making are positively related to role clarity.[16] In a study of sales managers' bases of social power, Busch concluded that "Sales management may want to emphasize the expert power base when trying to improve role clarity or reduce turnover among male sales personnel."[17]

Several researchers have examined the effect of organization structure on job satisfaction. Churchill, Ford, and Walker concluded that 40 percent of the variance in job satisfaction was explained by seven job environment variables—closeness of supervision, influence over performance standards, amount of communication, number of departments in the organization, innovativeness, ambiguity, and time in the position.[18] Closer supervision was positively related to job satisfaction. The variable that had the most impact on job satisfaction was the representatives' perception that they had influence in determining their performance standards. Frequency of communication was only slightly related to satisfaction, and the number of departments influencing the representatives did not significantly affect satisfaction. When representatives are required to innovate, there is less satisfaction with supervision, company policies and support, and promotions and advancement, all of which reflect a feeling on the part of representatives that they lack adequate training. Role ambiguity led to dissatisfaction with the job, fellow workers, company policies and support, pay, and customers. The most satisfied representatives were on the job less than two years, and the least satisfied had their jobs from five to fifteen years. It comes as no surprise that the least satisfied group had negative attitudes toward the job, pay, promotion, and advancement.

Ivancevich and Donnelly studied the effect of organizational structure on the satisfaction, anxiety, and performance of trade sales persons.[19] They examined three organizations with structures that were tall, medium, or flat. They found that representatives in flat organizations (i.e., few levels) perceived more satisfaction with respect to self-actualization and autonomy. These representatives sensed lower amounts of anxiety and stress. Furthermore, their performance was more efficient than that of representatives in medium and tall organizations. The representatives in the flat organizations probably felt a sense of being closer to those persons who established performance standards. General sales managers will want to consider these findings when making decisions regarding span of control.

This brief review of research into the design of sales organizations emphasizes two points that have been made throughout this book. First, position descriptions and performance standards are basic tools of sales management. They are a prerequisite for effective recruiting, selecting, training, motivating, coaching and counseling, and rewarding. Second, research and successful management practice clearly indicate that performance standards need to be negotiated with each individual, thereby meeting his or her unique set of needs.

DEVELOPING TERRITORIES

A *territory* is a part of a company's sales potential from present accounts and prospective ones that has been assigned to a salesperson. These accounts and prospects may be grouped to form territories according to their geographic location, industry, product use, method of buying, or channel of distribution.

WHY HAVE TERRITORIES?

When designing a sales organization, the general manager will want to consider the reasons for and against having territories. Sales territories result in better coverage of the market because they permit better planning, more even coverage, efficient call patterns, better customer service, clearer statements of responsibility, and the opportunity to match representatives to accounts. Territories permit the coordination of selling efforts with other marketing efforts, such as sales promotion and advertising. Territories also permit the control of expenses and better evaluations of representatives' performance because performance may be measured against territory potential.

While these advantages are substantial, there are cases where territories are not appropriate. A small company may find that the benefits of territories are less than the cost of administering them. A company that is expanding rapidly, so that coverage is below potential, may not have sufficient representatives to cover the company's market potential with the penetration that it would like. Therefore it permits representatives to "skim the cream" until it gets broad distribution. When distribution is achieved, it will then turn to penetration and form territories. Some services, such as insurance, stocks, and mutual funds, are sold on the basis of social and personal contacts. Companies selling these services tend not to have territories.

TERRITORY DECISIONS

The general sales manager must answer many questions regarding territory designs. Should we have territories? How many? Should they be defined geographically, according to industry, or some other classification? How should representatives be assigned to the territory? Should representatives be scheduled and routed or should they do it themselves?

Once the decision to have territories has been made, the next question to be answered is, "How should the company's market potential be divided among territories?"

ESTABLISHING TERRITORIES

There is a wide variety of models for developing sales territories, but most of them reduce to one of three forms: the breakdown method, the buildup method, or the incremental method. These techniques could be used for building new territories or revising existing ones.

Breakdown Method

The breakdown method begins with an estimate of the company's market potential. This potential is divided by the average productivity per representative, which yields an estimate of the total number of representatives needed. This method may be described by the following equation:

$$N = cp/r \qquad (1)$$

where

N = the number of representatives needed,

cp = the company market potential (contribution or profit could also be used), and

r = the average productivity per representative.

While most people use estimates of market potential when using this method, contribution may be used to reflect differences in the profit contributions for various product mixes and to reflect marketing and selling costs (Chapter 5).

The advantage of this method is its simplicity. Its disadvantage is the use of an average productivity estimate. These averages can vary widely due to the abilities of representatives and different workload factors. Workload includes factors such as differences in travel time, different buying methods, and differences in response rates of customers to sales effort. Managers who use the breakdown method must further refine it according to these workload factors. Like the breakdown and buildup methods in forecasting, this method may be used as a first estimate of the number of territories needed, and then reconciled with the estimate created by the buildup method.

Buildup Method

The buildup method for creating territories may be described in the following six steps:

1. Select the smallest control unit for which market potential data are available. This unit could be a state, a trading area, counties, cities, Standard Metropolitan Statistical Areas, zip codes, or Standard Industrial Classification (SIC) numbers. SIC numbers are frequently used when industrial sales forces are organized according to industrial applications.

2. Estimate the market potential for each unit, using methods and sources of data that are described in Chapter 17.

3. Estimate the workload for each unit. The amount of work required to tap the potential of a unit will vary according to many factors. There will be different response rates to promotional effort. In some cases, a minimum number of calls is necessary to make any sale. In other cases, there is a maximum number of calls per account beyond

which calls are wasted because they produce no additional sales (Exhibit 5.2, Chapter 5).

The workload will also vary according to the desired service levels for each account or account classification and the desired penetration rates. A company entering a new territory may decide to seek broad distribution first and penetration later. Companies selling to closely organized markets, such as the medical market, may choose a lower penetration at first and depend on word-of-mouth diffusion from early adopters of a product.

The territory workload may also vary according to account concentration, distribution rates, warehouse locations, and media support. Territory designs must adapt to uncontrollable events, such as local political and regulatory environments. Finally, there are geographical differences, such as mountains and lakes, that greatly alter the travel time between accounts.

Workloads in a territory could also vary according to the number and skills of competitive representatives in a control unit. If control units are defined in terms of specific accounts or industry classifications, then the mix of products that this account or industry buys will alter a representative's workload. For example, a new product or a complex product will require more selling effort than one that is simply a staple.

4. Estimate the length of call and call frequency required per account or per prospect. Translate these call patterns into the number of hours that a representative must spend with each account or prospect. Sum the hours for all accounts and prospects to produce the total number of selling hours needed for a sales force. Dividing this total by the average hours available per representative provides an estimate of the number of representatives needed in the sales force. This procedure may be illustrated in the following equation:

$$N = H/h \qquad (2)$$

where

$N =$ the number of representatives needed,
$H =$ the total number of selling hours needed for the company, and
$h =$ the average number of selling hours available to a representative.

The sales manager may also use this equation to determine the effect of programs to increase representatives' selling hours on the size of the total sales force.

5. Combine the control units to create the number of territories computed in equation (2). Because a sales manager will be realigning territories more frequently than building them from scratch, he or she will keep a representative's strengths in mind when combining control units to build a territory. These control units are generally combined around a trading area.

6. The general sales manager will want to review the territory designs with the field sales managers and representatives. After refinements, the designs must be tested. This test must include estimates of the compensations that will be generated by each territory because territory design is closely linked to the compensation scheme. After approvals, the new territory designs must be implemented, which will call on the communication and counseling skills of sales managers at all levels.

Data gathering for the buildup method may be extensive and expensive. Some expense will be the time spent by representatives in making subjective estimates, such as the number of sales calls needed for specific accounts. A new company may not have sufficient experience or data to use this approach.

Incremental Method

The incremental method, which in economics terms is the marginal approach, can be described in terms of gold mining. A gold miner with three mines, each with three different assay levels, does not assign miners according to the assay level of each mine. Instead, all of the miners are put into the mine with the highest assay rate and then moved to the next lower assay mine as the vein of the first mine is depleted. Similarly, sales managers should allocate representatives according to the highest profit contribution per hour invested. The manager should stop allocating hours when the cost of the hour equals the profit contribution that it generates. This incremental approach is identical to the economic concept of operating at that point where marginal revenue equals marginal cost. In practical terms, sales managers apply this concept by using the ratio of return per dollar of sales expense. A manager may find it necessary to stop short of this ideal point because there are insufficient representatives' selling hours available. At this point, the manager must explore ways for making representatives more efficient, increasing their available selling hours, or adding to the sales force.

The incremental method may sound theoretical and complex, but it can be implemented rather easily by the representative if adequate territory management techniques are used. Exhibit 5.4 (Chapter 5) illustrates account records that can be translated easily into market potential per call or market potential per hour. These individual account cards can then be sorted in descending order according to those with the highest market potential per call or hour. The representative then proceeds to call on those accounts with the highest potential until available selling time is exhausted.

Some companies have built the incremental concept into a computer model for allocating sales calls. Xerox developed a sales allocation model by laying a grid over a map to create cells of customers. Each cell contains the expected number of customers, the expected revenue from each customer, and the expected number of calls per day per representative. The computer model allocates calls sequentially to the customer with the highest revenue per call value until all accounts are called on and all potential is realized. Cells are combined until the representative's maximum time limit is reached. The resulting set of cells constitutes a territory.[20] Similarly, Xerox will shift salespersons within a branch and region to equalize the productivity of those units.

The incremental method shares some of the problems of the breakdown method. Both methods assume representatives have similar abilities and that the only difference among accounts is their potential.

Scheduling and Routing

There are two extremes in scheduling and routing representatives. Some call patterns are regular and predictable, such as milk or bread representatives who call regularly on supermarkets. In this case, the company could schedule and route the representatives to assure adequate coverage and to minimize driving time. At the other extreme, a representative selling technical equipment, such as a computer or an oil drilling rig, engages in consultative selling activities that are not predictable. In such cases, the routing and scheduling of calls is determined by the representative. Between these two extremes are companies that provide some guidance but leave the final routing decision to the representative.

RECENT RESEARCH IN TERRITORY FORMATION

Zoltners states, "In terms of normative modeling and computer software, sales force planning is one of the most developed decision areas in marketing."[21] There are large incentives for developing these models. The sales force can be a large share of the marketing budget in many companies. Sales calls for industrial products are frequently estimated to cost more than $100. The dynamics of the marketplace require continuous reevaluation and redesigning of sales territories. The shift in population from the snow belt to the sun belt has caused many companies to reduce the number of territories in the northeast and increase the number in the south and west. Computerized data bases have become more sophisticated and more available in control units as small as zip codes. Algorithms that search for the best territory configuration and then graphically plot maps are now available.

Models tend to focus on two types of sales management decisions: organizing the sales force and allocating selling effort to geographical territories, products, customers, or some combination of methods for classifying market potentials. The decade of the 1970s saw the development of many models, which are too numerous to summarize here.[22] The present discussion will be limited to a description of the concepts behind two classes of models: territory design and the allocation of sales effort.

Territory Design

In the early 1970s, GEOLINE, which was derived from a legislative districting model, was used to design sales territories of approximately equal potential and workload. Applications were reported by CIBA Pharmaceutical Company and the IBM World Trade Corporation.[23]

One of the earliest studies on sales force size was reported by Semlow.[24] While this model is widely quoted, Lucas, Weinberg, and Clowes note that the relationships are spurious. These authors note that the independent variable "territory potential" appears as the denominator in the dependent variable.[25]

Lodish developed a mathematical programming model and heuristic solution procedure for the realignment of sales territories.[26] The model uses an objective function that is the anticipated profit generated by the sales force. It also considers the problems of account call frequency, travel time, and combining calls on accounts into trips.

Glaze and Weinberg developed a sales territory alignment program and account planning system (TAPS) that seeks to maximize company sales for a given sales force size. TAPS is a heuristic procedure that uses geographic information and account-specific sales response functions to locate salespersons in the territory, assign them to accounts, and allocate their time to these accounts. The procedure attempts to equalize the workload among salespersons where the workload is defined to include travel and selling time. It is also designed to minimize total travel time. By running the model iteratively for different sizes of the sales force, a sales force response function may be developed.[27]

Toward the end of the 1970s, there was a synthesis of techniques for territory alignment. Zoltners built upon existing procedures to develop a unified approach to sales territory alignment and then used graphic routines to create territory maps that this method formed. The technique was then tested with several firms. Zoltners reported that management was pleased with his system and implemented the final territory configuration.[28]

Effective sales territory development is dependent on a market information base. Heschel reports a procedure that was used by FMC Corporation's Machinery Group to develop a territory information system. The information base was built upon plant and industry file data based on government surveys, census information, trade publications, customer feedback, and limited sampling.[29]

Allocation of Sales Effort

Lodish developed CALL PLAN, an interactive call planning system that is one of the earliest and most frequently cited models of this type.[30] CALL PLAN produces an account call frequency schedule to maximize anticipated profit, given limited time to make calls. The input to the model is the representatives' estimate of the sales responses that would follow from various call frequencies, travel time, time per call, and account profitability. Adjustment factors are available to alter the emphasis on product mixes or account types. In 1980, Lodish introduced the effect of the product mix more directly by examining the sales response that a call about a product would have on a typical member of a market segment. This model could also be used to estimate the optimal size of the sales force.[31]

Zoltners, Sinha, and Chong criticize CALL PLAN because the incremental analysis algorithm can significantly over-allocate sales representatives' time and because such incremental techniques can also be expensive in terms of computer time. They suggest an integer programming approach that uses concave piece-wise linear functions.[32] Zoltners and Sinha suggest a general integer programming model that incorporates multiple sales resources, multiple time periods and carry over effects, nonseparability, and risks.[33]

Many of the models for allocating sales effort focus on a particular problem or technique. Armstrong used an interactive model that requires inputs from representatives on each account's potential, call lengths, profit contribution percent, and estimated penetration.[34] He introduced concepts of uncertainty and he used mathematical programming to solve the concave functions. Parasuraman and Day focused on the problem of the allocation of resources of a sales force over customer units. These researchers heavily weighted judgmental inputs and they modeled the representative-customer interaction and carry-over effects from previous sales efforts.[35] Moriarty and Adams explored special issues in sales territory modeling using Box-Jenkins forecasting techniques.[36]

Some of the more recent models examine territory design and selling effort allocation in a single model. Beswick and Cravens present such a model.[37] These researchers present a seven-stage decision model that combines managerial judgment and historical data to estimate response functions, and uses dynamic programming to allocate selling time to control units. The model output is optimum sales force size and a plan for territory design. The flow chart for this model appeared as Exhibit 16.16 in Chapter 16.

Companies that use allocation models report a variety of benefits. Some companies think that the rigor of gathering the data and inputting judgments provide insights into territory design and sales management problems. Some companies are reporting that they revised their territories using these models. Other companies report that they use the models to check their intuitive thinking in territory designing. While the models are becoming more sophisticated and are getting closer to reality, some companies report that the models fail to consider human factors adequately. The fatigue of travel and staying away from home at night can be important dimensions in accepting a new territory design. The quantity and quality of competitive representatives are not explicitly considered in these models. The uneven distribution of other marketing variables, such as warehouse location and advertising support, can affect the productivity of a territory, but have not been reflected in allocation models. Summary articles, such as the one by Cravens,[38] will help researchers to understand where we have been and where we should be heading in the development of sales force decision models.

Comer notes that each model tends to assume away many sales force complexities in order to be operable. As a result, we have a series of models examining separate sales management problems with no basis for linking them together. He provides some links by developing theoretical constructs for sales effort allocation.[39]

SUMMARY

The development of sales force organizations may be divided into the related activities of designing a sales organization and developing territories. An organization is a means for grouping activities that are necessary to achieve an objective into roles that can be further grouped into positions that will be assigned to individuals. Organizations increase productivity by specialization and increase the capacities to produce through additional administrative levels. These gains, however, are offset by the costs of administrative networks for communication and the coordination of activities. The sales manager must carefully weigh the gains and losses when developing a sales force organization. The job description and performance standards are logical extensions of the sales force organizational design. Recent research in sales management design has confirmed indirectly that these two documents are critical for good sales force management. The dynamics of the marketplace and changes in basic marketing strategies will require the sales manager to evaluate the design of his or her sales organization continuously.

After the organization has been designed, the next step is to decide how to allocate the responsibility and authority for developing market potential to representatives. Three commonly used methods to establish territories are the breakdown method, the buildup method, and the incremental method. Operations researchers have made extensive contributions to the problems of territory design and the allocation of sales effort.

ASSIGNMENTS/DISCUSSION QUESTIONS

1. Evaluate the job description for the general sales manager in Exhibit 18.5. Compare it with the job description for the district sales manager in Exhibit 7.4, Chapter 7. What are the similarities and differences?

2. Create job descriptions for the general sales manager and representatives of Westmont Business Forms, Chapter 23.

3. Get the cooperation of a local company and develop a job description for its representatives.

4. Give at least six reasons and examples when a company would reorganize a sales organization.

5. In addition to changing the size of the field sales force, what other changes in the sales operation could result from new products, changing strategies, or changing market potential?

6. Compare the control advantages and disadvantages of organizational structures A and B.

TITLE	NUMBER OF PERSONS IN:	
	STRUCTURE A	STRUCTURE B
General Sales Manager	1	1
Area Sales Manager	0	2
Regional Sales Manager	8	14
District Sales Manager	56	84
Sales Representatives	675	675

7. Discuss the possible reasons a company would have its product managers organized under the advertising manager instead of under the marketing manager.

8. In a company whose products are purchased centrally for multiple locations, what type of organization would be most suitable for the field staff, and what purpose would local reps assigned geographically have?

9. What are the advantages of training present reps to call on key accounts, instead of using senior sales management or setting up a separate sales force?

10. What are the advantages and disadvantages of the matrix-form design for the marketing planning function as identified with the Burroughs Wellcome Company?

11. Discuss the roles that formal and informal leadership may have in a sales organization.

12. Compare the communication problems inherent in sales organizations A and B.

| | NUMBER OF PERSONS IN: | |
TITLE	STRUCTURE A	STRUCTURE B
General Sales Manager	1	1
Regional Sales Manager	0	2
District Sales Manager	12	16
Sales Representatives	144	144

13. In addition to the use of a good analyst from the personnel office or an outside consultant, how else might job descriptions for sales reps and sales managers be prepared?

14. After a job description has been designed and approved by all interested parties, what must be done to make the job description a useful working document?

15. What are the advantages to the sales rep of having a well-defined territory?

16. Discuss the advantages and disadvantages of two alternative methods of working territory where the rep is unable to spend sufficient time to achieve an optimum number of calls on all potential customers in an area, and (1) concentrates on the customers in the metropolitan area, or (2) includes customers in the suburban and rural areas as well as the metropolitan areas.

17. Discuss the advantages and disadvantages of creating a territory that matches the rep's skills, experience, and individual needs for growth.

CASE 18.1:
The Southern Pharmaceutical Company

For the past several years, Joe Martinez, General Sales Manager for the Southern Pharmaceutical Co., had been very much aware of the need to supplement his field sales force, particularly in the southeast. Information from the company's Marketing Services Department had documented the gradual increase in the field staffs by Southern's major competitors and new competitors in the marketplace. The company's share of all representatives in the field was declining measurably. In addition to these data, he had been subjected to a steady stream of concerned messages from his Regional and District Sales Managers about inroads in sales that were being made in certain parts of the country by a number of competitors primarily as a result of their staff increases. Since Southern relied primarily on the promotional efforts of their representatives, as contrasted with journal advertising and direct mail, this information was critical to the long-term planning of the company. Until last year, there was no easy solution in the face of the company's flat sales curve and increasing expenses as a result of inflation. Fortunately, last year was a good sales and profit year and the Executive Committee approved Mr. Martinez's budget recommendations for adding a total of eight new territories in Texas, Oklahoma, the Carolinas, and Virginia. These territories would be a significant step forward toward restoring the company's competitive field staff balance.

Mr. Martinez has agreed in general with the recommendations made by Jim Smithison, the District Sales Manager for North Carolina and Virginia, and approved by the Regional Manager, Harry Camp, for two new territories in Jim's district. The growth in terms of total population, additional physicians and hospitals, along with the increase in sales in the area for the whole pharmaceutical industry, supported Jim's arguments. But, before Mr. Martinez would give a final green light, he wanted to see formal proposals, including the make-up of the territories, physician counts, and Working Orders for the new territories, as well as for those affected by the changes.

Ordinarily, Mr. Martinez would not have become involved with this degree of detail. Instead, he would have relied solely on Harry Camp's approval. In this case, he wanted to use the opportunity to check the quality of Jim Smithison's business and planning judgment, and because he saw the mid-Atlantic area as an increasingly important market.

With three existing territories in Virginia and the direction in which the health care population had grown, planning a new territory in the Richmond area had been a relatively easy task for Jim Smithison. In addition, starting in Virginia and working south had enabled him to develop the new data with which to prepare a preliminary design for the second new territory on the border of Virginia and North Carolina. This was conveniently adjacent to Territory 26 in Raleigh and Territory 20 in Greensboro, both of which had heavy MD populations, market potential, and the dollar sales to support the expense of a new representative. His next task was to juggle the data from Territories 26 and 20 with the new Territory 29 to come up with the best fit from the standpoint of market potential, doctor counts, and ease of working to take advantage of the sales opportunities and representative overloads that existed there. (See map, Exhibit 18.6.)

The Market Analysis Reports for Territory 20 (Greensboro), Territory 26 (Raleigh), and the preliminary Territory 29 appear as Exhibit 18.7. In writing the formal proposal for the territory design for each of the three territories and the revised Working Order for Territory 26 (Raleigh), the following criteria and definitions apply:

1. The selling plan used by Southern Pharmaceutical is based on a two-month cycle.

2. A representative covers the complete territory in an eight- or nine-week working order (Exhibit 18.8), and will see as many physicians, hospitals, and drug stores as practical in that period. *Note:* a working order is an approved sequence of calls in cities within the boundaries of the territory for which the representative is responsible. The representative is expected to maintain the rotation in the working order.

3. A representative will make approximately forty physician calls per week.

4. As classified in the Market Analysis Report,

   "A" physicians are those with large practices and are to be called on once each month

   "Other" physicians are to be called on once every two months

   "U" physicians are unclassified and not called on. Usually they are new physicians or those who have moved into the area.

   Market Potential is a factor that reflects a composite of data, including the weighted prescribing value of physicians by specialty, the current dollar sales for all major companies for selected classes of pharmaceutical products, and the dollar sales for Southern Pharmaceutical Co.

   Dollar Sales is the current dollar sales for the Southern Pharmaceutical Co. in each of the cities listed. Cities with less than two MDs have not been included.

Exhibit 18.6   Territory Map, Southern Pharmaceutical Co., North Carolina District

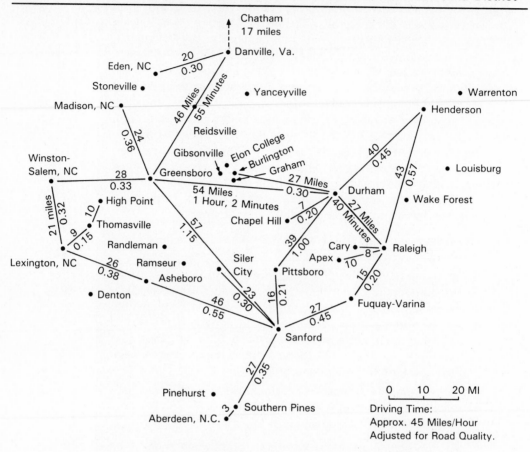

Exhibit 18.7   Southern Pharmaceutical: Market Analysis

TERRITORY 20 (GREENSBORO)

CITY	NUMBER MDs*			MARKET** POTENTIAL	DOLLAR*** SALES
	"A"	"OTHER"	"U"		
Madison	3	—	—	360	$13,500
Stoneville	2	—	1	151	1,700
Asheboro	15	14	1	1,594	33,700
Gibonsville	2	—	1	125	4,800
High Point	20	40	5	3,272	90,100
Eden	3	9	1	812	28,200
Ramseur	1	—	1	63	1,200
Randleman	1	1	1	146	3,600
Reidsville	14	8	3	1,200	31,600
Siler City	7	2	3	554	16,000
Greensboro	84	116	23	9,438	223,900
	161	190	40	17,715	448,300

(continued)

Exhibit 18.7 Continued

TERRITORY 29 (NEW PRELIMINARY)

CITY	"A"	NUMBER MDs "OTHER"	"U"	MARKET POTENTIAL	DOLLAR SALES
Chatham, Va.	4	—	—	191	$ 5,800
Danville, Va.	23	30	5	2,879	82,900
Winston-Salem	11	3	—	2,948	67,300
Burlington	18	30	—	2,502	66,100
Denton	—	2	—	118	3,400
Elon College	—	2	—	116	2,900
Graham	3	—	—	315	9,800
Lexington	9	14	—	1,261	67,600
Thomasville	8	12	—	1,239	29,200
Yanceyville	1	2	—	238	7,000
	77	95	5	11,807	$342,000

TERRITORY 26 (RALEIGH)

CITY	"A"	NUMBER MDs "OTHER"	"U"	MARKET POTENTIAL	DOLLAR SALES
Pittsboro	1	1	2	254	$ 3,700
Sanford	10	18	2	1,448	43,600
Apex	3	—	—	258	9,600
Cary	12	16	—	835	25,800
Fuquay-Varina	3	1	—	358	11,300
Henderson	10	10	—	1,025	38,000
Louisburg	4	2	—	440	19,200
Wake Forest	1	1	—	161	6,400
Warrenton	4	—	—	196	8,900
Raleigh	28	86	22	5,187	127,800
Durham	25	40	27	5,453	190,200
Aberdeen	2	3	—	330	12,000
Pinehurst	10	7	1	975	37,000
Southern Pines	4	4	—	312	15,000
	117	189	54	17,232	$548,500

Definitions
*"A" MDs to be called on each month.
"Other" MDs to be called on every two months.
"U" MDs are not to be called on at all.

**Market Potential is a factor that reflects a composite of data including the weighted prescribing value of physicians by specialty, the current dollar sales for all major companies for selected classes of pharmaceutical products, and the dollar sales for the Southern Pharmaceutical Co.

***Dollar Sales is the current dollar sales for the Southern Pharmaceutical Co. in each of the cities listed. Cities with fewer than 2 MDs have not been included.

Exhibit 18.8   Working Order Territory 26 (Raleigh)

WEEK 1
  Raleigh—3 days
  Henderson—1 day
  Wake Forest—1/2 day
  Warrenton & Louisburg—1/2 day

WEEK 5
  Raleigh—3 days
  Henderson—1 1/2 days
  Warrenton & Louisburg—1/2 day

WEEK 2
  Durham—3 days
  Southern Pines—1/4 day
  Pinehurst—1 1/4 days
  Aberdeen—1/2 day

WEEK 6
  Durham—3 days
  Pinehurst—1 1/2 days
  Southern Pines—1/2 day

WEEK 3
  Raleigh—3 days
  Cary—2 days

WEEK 7
  Raleigh—3 days
  Cary—2 days

WEEK 4
  Durham—3 days
  Sanford—1 1/2 days
  Pittsboro—1/2 day

WEEK 8
  Durham—3 days
  Sanford—1 1/2 days
  Apex & Fuquay-Varina—1/2 day

WEEK 9

CASE QUESTIONS

1. What factors should influence a territory design?

2. Which is the most important factor?

3. What is the approximate average Market Potential, the average Number of Physician Calls, and the average current Dollar Sales for the three territories?

4. Which cities in the three territories are producing dollar sales currently that are in excess of 20 percent *below* the average for their Market Potential?

5. Which cities in the three territories are producing dollar sales currently that are in excess of 20 percent *above* the average for their Market Potential?

6. From the working order for Territory 26 (Raleigh), Exhibit 18.8, calculate the percentage of time the representative spends in each city, the percentage of Market Potential each city has, and identify the cities with major variations.

7. Should your recommended territory design for the three territories be eight or nine weeks in length? Why?

8. Prepare a recommended Market Analysis Report for each of the three redesigned territories.

9. Add a column headed "Number Days Allocated" to your Resources Report for each of the three territories, and calculate the number of days that should be allocated to each city based on an eight- or nine-week working order (whichever you choose).

10. Prepare a recommended working order for revised Territory 26 (Raleigh).

11. In which cities should efforts be made to add Unclassified Physicians to the active call list?

REFERENCES

1. A. Chandler, *Strategy and Structure: Chapters in the History of Industrial Enterprise* (Cambridge, Mass.: The MIT Press, 1962); J. R. Galbraith and D. A. Nathanson, *Strategy Implementation: The Role of Structure and Process* (New York: West Publishing Co., 1978).

2. P. E. Lawrence and J. W. Lorsch, *Organization and Environment: Managing Differentiation and Integration* (Boston: Division of Research, Graduate School of Business Administration, Harvard University, 1967).

3. A. F. Doody and W. G. Nickels, "Structuring Organizations for Strategic Selling," *MSU Business Topics* (Autumn 1972): 27–35.

4. *United Services Automobile Association (USAA) Annual Report, 1978*, p. 2.

5. International Business Machines press releases, Oct. 1 and Dec. 3, 1981.

6. B. P. Shapiro and R. T. Moriarty, "National Account Managment," *Project Description* (Cambridge, Mass.: Marketing Science Institute, Report No. 80-104, July 1980).

7. Gene Sprinkel, "Developing Key Accounts," NSSTE Editorial Contribution, September 15, 1980.

8. Alternatives 2 through 4 are based on Shapiro and Moriarty, "National Account Management," pp. 1–2.

9. "How to Stop the Buck Short of the Top," *Business Week* (January 16, 1978): 82–83.

10. P. S. Howsam and G. D. Hughes, "Problems with Brand Management? Consider Product Strategist System," *Marketing News* (June 26, 1981): section 2, pp. 1, 8.

11. R. H. Kilmann, *An Organic-Adaptive Organization: The MAPS Method* (New York: American Management Association, 1974); R. H. Kilmann, M. A. Lyles, and I. I. Mitroff, "Designing an Effective Problem Solving Organization with the MAPS Design Technology," *Journal of Management* 2, no. 2 (1977): 1–10; I. I. Mitroff, V. P. Barabba, and R. H. Kilmann, "The Application of Behavioral and Philosophical Technologies to Strategic Planning: A Case Study of a Large Federal Agency," *Management Science* 24, no. 1 (September 1977): 44–58; R. H. Kilmann, "On Integrating Knowledge Utilization with Knowledge Development: The Philosophy Behind the MAPS Design Technology," *Academy of Management Review* 4, no. 3 (1979): 417–426.

12. For a detailed discussion of job analysis techniques, see C. Lambert, *Field Sales Management Performance Appraisal* (New York: Ronald Press, 1979); E. J. McCormick, *Job Analysis: Methods and Applications* (New York: American Management Association, 1979).

13. G. A. Churchill, Jr., N. M. Ford, and O. C. Walker, Jr., *Sales Force Management* (Homewood, Ill.: Richard D. Irwin, Inc., 1981), Chapter 10.

14. J. S. Adams, "Interorganizational Processes and Organization Boundary Activities," *Research in Organizational Behavior* 2 (1980): 321–355; H. O. Pruden, "The Outside Salesman: Interorganizational Link," *California Management Review* 21 (Winter 1969): 57–65.

15. J. H. Donnelly, Jr., and J. M. Ivancevich, "Role Clarity and the Salesman," *Journal of Marketing* 39 (January 1975): 71–74.

16. R. K. Teas, J. G. Wacker, and R. E. Hughes, "A Path Analysis of Causes and Consequences of Salespeople's Perceptions of Role Clarity," *Journal of Marketing Research* 16 (August 1979): 335–369.

17. Paul Busch, "The Sales Manager's Bases of Social Power and Influence upon the Sales Force," *Journal of Marketing* 44 (Summer 1980): 91–101.

18. G. A. Churchill, Jr., N. M. Ford, and O. C. Walker, Jr., "Organizational Climate and Job Satisfaction in the Salesforce," *Journal of Marketing Research* 13 (November 1976): 323–332.

19. J. M. Ivancevich and J. H. Donnelly, Jr., "Relation of Organizational Structure to Job Satisfaction, Anxiety-Stress, and Performance," *Administrative Science Quarterly* 20 (June 1975): 272–280.

20. Peter J. Gray, "Computers and Models in the Marketing Decision Process," in *Computer Innovations in Marketing,* ed. Evelyn Konrad (New York: American Management Association, 1970), pp. 158–167.

21. A. A. Zoltners, "Models & Computer Software Can Help Make Sales Force Decisions," *Marketing News* (November 16, 1979): 6.

22. For a summary of these models, see D. W. Cravens, "Sales Force Decision Models: Research Progress and Needs," in *Critical Issues in Sales Management: State-of-the-Art and Future Research Needs,* ed. G. Albaum and G. A. Churchill, Jr. (Eugene, Oregon: Division of Research, College of Business Administration, University of Oregon, June 1979), pp. 127–151; and A. A. Zoltners and P. Sinha, "Integer Programming Models for Sales Resource Allocation," *Management Science* 26 (March 1980): 242–260.

23. S. W. Hess and S. A. Samuels, "Experiences with a Sales Districting Model: Criteria and Implementation," *Management Science* 18 (December 1971): 41–54.

24. W. J. Semlow, "How Many Salesmen Do You Need?" *Harvard Business Review* 37 (May–June 1959): 129–132.

25. H. C. Lucas, Jr., C. B. Weinberg, and K. W. Clowes, "Sales Response as a Function of Territorial Potential and Sales Representative Workload," *Journal of Marketing Research* 12 (August 1975): 298–305.

26. L. M. Lodish, "Sales Territory Alignment to Maximize Profit," *Journal of Marketing Research* 12 (February 1975): 30–36.

27. T. A. Glaze and C. B. Weinberg, "A Sales Territory Alignment Program and Account Planning System," in *Sales Management: New Developments from Behavioral and Decision Model Research,* ed. R. Bagozzi (Cambridge, Mass.: Marketing Science Institute, 1979), pp. 325–343.

28. A. A. Zoltners, "A Unified Approach to Sales Territory Alignment," in *Sales Management: New Developments from Behavioral and Decision Model Research,* ed. R. Bagozzi (Cambridge, Mass.: Marketing Science Institute, 1979), pp. 360–372.

29. M. S. Heschel, "Effective Sales Territory Development," *Journal of Marketing* 41 (April 1977): 39–43.

30. L. M. Lodish, ''CALLPLAN: An Interactive Salesman's Call Planning System,'' *Management Science* 18, no. 4, II (December 1971): P25–P40; Leonard M. Lodish, ''Vaguely Right Approach to Sales Force Allocations,'' *Harvard Business Review* 51 (January– February 1974): 119–124.

31. L. M. Lodish, ''A User-Oriented Model for Sales Force Size, Product, and Market Allocation Decisions,'' *Journal of Marketing* 44 (Summer 1980): 70–78.

32. A. A. Zoltners, P. Sinha, and P. S. C. Chong, ''An Optimal Algorithm for Sales Representative Time Management,'' *Management Science* 25, no. 12 (December 1979): 1197–1207.

33. Zoltners and Sinha, ''Integer Programming Models.''

34. Gary M. Armstrong, ''The SCHEDULE Model and the Salesman's Effort Allocation,'' *California Management Review* (Summer 1976): 43–51.

35. A. Parasuraman and R. L. Day, ''A Management-Oriented Model for Allocating Sales Effort,'' *Journal of Marketing Research* 14 (February 1977): 22–23.

36. Mark Moriarty and Arthur Adams, ''Issues in Sales Territory Modeling and Forecasting Using Box-Jenkins Analysis,'' *Journal of Marketing Research* 16 (May 1979): 221–232.

37. C. A. Beswick and D. Cravens, ''A Multistage Decision Model for Salesforce Management,'' *Journal of Marketing Research* 14 (May 1977): 135–144.

38. D. W. Cravens, ''Salesforce Decision Models: A Comparative Assessment,'' in *Sales Management: New Developments from Behavioral and Decision Model Research,* ed. R. Bagozzi (Cambridge, Mass.: Marketing Science Institute, 1979), pp. 310–324.

39. J. M. Comer, ''Toward a Theoretical Construct: Salesforce Effort Allocation,'' in *Sales Management: New Developments from Behavioral and Decision Model Research,* ed. R. Bagozzi (Cambridge, Mass.: Marketing Science Institute, 1979), pp. 344–359.

SUGGESTED READINGS

Cravens, D; Woodruff, R.; and Stamper, J., ''An Analytic Approach for Evaluating Sales Territory Performance,'' *Journal of Marketing* 36 (January 1972): 31–37.

Daniels, T. D., ''Investing Sales Time for Maximum Return: Developing Key Account Sales Strategies,'' *AMA Forum* (October 1977): 39–41.

Futrell, C. M.; Lamb, C. W.; and Swan, J. E., ''Benefits and Problems in a Salesforce MBO System,'' *Industrial Marketing Management* 6, no. 4 (1977): 265–272.

Gestetner, David, ''Strategies in Managing International Sales,'' *Harvard Business Review* 52 (September–October 1974): 103–108.

Hanan, Mack, ''Reorganize Your Company Around Its Markets,'' *Harvard Business Review* (November–December 1974): 63–74.

Pruden, Henry O., and Reese, R. M., ''Interorganizational Role-Set Relations and the Performance and Satisfaction of Industrial Salesmen,'' *Administrative Science Quarterly* 17 (December 1972): 601–609.

''The New Lean, Mean Xerox,'' *Business Week* (October 12, 1981): 126–132.

19

TRAINING AND DEVELOPING FIELD SALES MANAGERS

NEGLECTED ACTIVITIES

The training and development of sales managers are neglected activities in most companies. A survey by the American Management Association revealed that half of the sales managers surveyed had never seen a job description; 78 percent reported that they had no training or were dissatisfied with their training to prepare them to be a sales manager; and less than 3 percent of the companies surveyed had any kind of a company-sponsored sales management training program.[1] Furthermore, an examination of sales management textbooks will reveal that the topics of training and developing sales managers are not mentioned.

THE NEED FOR TRAINING AND DEVELOPMENT

The terms *training* and *development* carry different meanings. Training means preparing an individual for his or her present job. Development means preparing an individual for a future job. Few companies have training programs for sales managers, but even fewer have programs for developing managers for future management positions.

The increased dynamics of the marketplace create an ever-increasing need for training field sales managers. These managers must have a knowledge of market research techniques and the applications of computers to field management. They need to know many laws and regulations that relate to sales management. In the early 1970s, a sales manager needed to know only some of the antitrust laws. By 1980, he or she needed to have a working knowledge of laws and regulations regarding deception, equal employment opportunities, product safety and liability, warranties, and a deeper knowledge of antitrust as it relates to price fixing, tying contracts, and other topics that are covered in Chapter 6. Competitive new products, foreign competitors, energy crises, the high cost of capital, and government regulations regarding the environment all add to the uncertainty and stress in which a contemporary sales manager must work. Thus there is a need for continuous training and development of these managers, but few companies undertake these activities. Why?

WHY THESE ACTIVITIES ARE NEGLECTED

In many companies the problem can be traced to the fact that no one has taken responsibility for training sales managers. The general sales manager is not an expert in training. Furthermore, the general sales manager is frequently dealing with the pressures of short-term problems and never gets around to the task of training managers for their present jobs and developing them to meet the future needs of the company. Training programs by the personnel or organizational development department tend to be directed toward persons who are managing within the company, such as the management of production workers or secretaries. This type of training is not specific enough to the problems of the sales manager who is managing individuals who must operate in a very unpredictable environment. A production supervisor may be dealing with varying levels of technology, while a field sales manager is managing people almost exclusively.

Using the sales trainer to train sales managers introduces other problems. This trainer tends to focus on training representatives and may not have materials or experience in training field sales managers. Second, in many companies the sales trainer does not report to the general sales manager, but instead may be under sales promotion, the personnel department, or organizational development. This organizational design can create problems because the trainer and the general sales manager may have quite different views on the content of the course. Lacking control over the content of the course, the general sales manager fails to give adequate support to the trainer and reinforcement to the managers who have returned from such programs. Finally, while the sales trainer probably was promoted to that position from the field staff as a representative, few have had field management experience. In fact, the job of sales trainer is frequently an interim position before promotion to field sales manager. Hence, while the sales trainer had experience in selling, he or she may not have had management experience.

Two reasons for not training managers are the infrequency of a need for such training and the need to fill a suddenly vacated management position. If a company has a few managers and turnover is low, there is little incentive for developing a sales management training program. It is also difficult to sell top management on the need to budget for these managers to attend outside training courses. A representative may be promoted to field sales manager on very short notice because the position became vacant due to a sudden promotion, resignation, or death. In such instances, there is little opportunity to train the representative before he or she assumes the new role. In too many instances, the new manager is too busy coping with crises to have time for adequate training.

In earlier chapters, we saw that good sales management does make a difference in the productivity of the sales force. Many companies are beginning to realize that sales management training and development have not kept pace with the training and development of representatives. These companies are meeting these needs in a variety of ways. Some companies cycle promotable representatives through the home office for management experience. After this experience, they may be promoted or placed in a pool until a field management position opens.

TRAINING AND DEVELOPMENT METHODS

Training and developing field sales managers require answers to the same questions that were posed in Chapter 10 on the training and development of representatives. The present discussion will focus on five questions. What should the content of this training be? Who will train? When will the training be given? How will it be done? And where will it take place? The question, "Who should receive training?" can be answered simply—all managers, because it is a continuing process.

DETERMINING "WHAT" THROUGH A NEEDS ASSESSMENT

The needs assessment must identify the individual's needs and the company's needs.

Corporate Needs

Management training programs begin with the assessment of the company's needs for managers in the future. A company that anticipates a rapid growth in the sales force or has high management turnover will have a greater need for this type of training than a company with no growth and little turnover. Is sales management a training ground for marketing managers and higher levels of corporate managers? In some companies, sales management may be a temporary stepping stone to a higher level of management. In such cases, developing sales managers may be part of an overall program for developing corporate managers.

Corporate policies regarding promotion from within will also determine the need for training. Promoting from within provides high motivation for representatives, but it may induce inbreeding and the lack of new ideas. On the other hand, recruiting managers from outside the company may introduce fresh ideas, but there is no assurance that these are good managers; they may be just the highly mobile ones who will move on to other opportunities, taking our ideas with them. The survey that was reported in Chapter 2 revealed that the perception of the importance of activities for first-line field sales managers varies across companies and industries. Thus hiring from outside may create initial conflict until these perceptions are corrected.

Individual Needs

The needs assessment must determine whether the newly appointed or the present sales manager needs training in management knowledge, attitudes, skills, or habits (KASH). A performance evaluation that is based on a recent job description is the first step in a manager's needs assessment. For the new representative, this evaluation can only suggest potential for management, but it will reflect management deficiencies for present sales managers. This performance evaluation will reveal common deficiencies, such as the inability to get things done through others, a need for status that interferes with the development of others, or a fear of failure that may make a manager an uncompromising disciplinarian. The training program must help such a manager to understand how these needs are interfering with his or her management style. The counseling session that follows such a performance evaluation may actually reveal that the fear of failure is based on a lack of training and development.

A needs assessment for a new manager could include written tests, in-basket tasks, and cases that would identify areas where training is necessary. The sales management trainer would then negotiate with the manager on the topics and methods for training. During the negotiation, the trainer should emphasize the point that the new manager need not be defensive about deficiencies because training for management is a continuous process. It may be likened to an engineer who is said to have a knowledge whose half-life is seven years. This means that one-half of an engineer's knowledge is obsolete seven years after graduation. Similarly, a sales manager must be open to learning and view it as a continuous process.

General sales managers should encourage field sales managers to engage in personal career planning, as discussed in Chapter 10. Career counseling sessions include the identification of personal objectives, a realistic evaluation of these objectives, an evaluation of personal strengths and weaknesses, identification of areas where training and development are needed, and a program and schedule for acquiring this training and development. The identification of strengths and weaknesses is a natural extension of the performance evaluation (e.g., Exhibit 7.4, Chapter 7).

Some companies use *needs assessment center* approaches to identify training needs. These are multipersonnel appraisal groups that evaluate individuals' potential for promotion. While these centers are generally under the jurisdiction of the personnel department, the assessment group includes regional and general sales managers. In addition to evaluating the promotability of a representative to first-line sales management or a first-line sales manager to a higher level of management, these assessment centers evaluate candidates' interest in promotion, attitudes toward their job and the company, and their willingness to relocate. Needs assessment centers are not without controversy. Their advantages include multiple inputs and less bias because some of the analysis is by persons outside the sales management function. On the other hand, general sales managers view these centers as usurping the authority of sales management.

A review of outlines for courses that are available to new sales managers revealed the following topics: motivation, interpersonal relationships, communicating, appraising performance, problem solving and decision making, planning and organizing, managing time, delegating work, recruiting, selecting and training, appraising and counseling, and controlling, which are topics that were discussed in Chapters 7 through 15.

WHO WILL TRAIN?

As noted, there is frequently a conflict among general sales managers, trainers, and organizational developers on who will be responsible for training field sales managers. This conflict provides an opportunity to practice the negotiation phase of decision making that was discussed in Chapter 14. Clearly, the cooperation of these three groups could result in an outstanding program with each area contributing its expertise. Failure to negotiate on the goals and methods will assure, at best, an inferior program or, at worst, no program at all.

WHEN TO TRAIN?

Companies that have a continuous need for a flow of management recognize the long developmental time that is required to train a sales manager. These companies will make provision in the organization chart for such training. For example, Procter & Gamble has a position on its organization chart between a representative and the first-line field sales manager. This position, titled "District Field Representative," includes such activities as training new representatives and assisting with some field management activities. Successful performance in this position leads to a promotion to unit sales manager.

While organization charts provide in-training positions for first-line sales managers, they rarely make provisions for such training positions prior to promotion to regional or general sales management. Some companies send promotable candidates to university executive development programs. Other companies are considering sabbaticals for this purpose. The smaller companies are generally faced with crisis management and cannot afford the luxury of such sabbaticals.

HOW SHOULD MANAGERS BE TRAINED?

There is general agreement that the case method is probably the best method for training sales managers. It provides experience in all of the appropriate activities and especially in the skills of analysis, decision making, and communicating. Young managers attending training programs with persons from other industries have been surprised to learn the similarity of sales management problems across industries and how much can be learned from other participants during case discussions.

WHERE SHOULD THE TRAINING BE CONDUCTED?

A frequent training pattern is to use on-the-job training and short courses that are given outside the company. These courses are offered by the National Society of Sales Training Executives, the American Management Association, the Sales & Marketing Executives Clubs, some universities, and consultants. These courses generally last from two or three days to ten days.

Some companies have a formal program for developing sales managers that combines on-the-job training and courses. For example, the Carnation Company annually selects ten new college graduates for its sales management development program. These individuals are selected on the following criteria: intelligence, competitive spirit, maturity, leadership, industry and drive, sales and marketing interest, positive and cooperative attitude, and geographic flexibility. Trainees must qualify for promotion to a management assignment within two years. Those not qualifying will be reviewed for additional help or termination.

The Carnation program includes training in selling methods that are appropriate for all classes of customers, merchandising skills, market research, new product tests, competitive evaluation, territory management, recruiting, selection, training, skills in conducting meetings, motivation, goal setting, and controlling. Advanced management development programs that are available to newly appointed group managers, field managers at all levels, and general managers illustrate the point that in some companies sales management training is a continuous process.[2]

THE GENERAL MANAGER'S ROLE IN TRAINING AND DEVELOPMENT

The general sales manager has the final responsibility for providing a continuous flow of sales management talent. General sales managers may need training in the training and development of field managers. The general sales manager may also need assistance in how to build on the training that is done by corporate and outside training programs. Without such line-management reinforcement, a newly trained field manager becomes frustrated and could actually be a poorer manager after the training. Most general managers would quickly identify this problem if a first-line field manager failed to reinforce the training of a new representative, but it is difficult for them to see that the problem exists for them.

Another important role for the general sales manager is maintaining the continuous stream of management talent. This role includes motivating and rewarding promotables so that they will not be pirated by other companies or management recruiting firms. There is also the need to keep promotables in a learning mode.

Top management must be committed to training the sales managers. This commitment is reflected in their support of training programs, their performance appraisals after training, and their follow through on developmental needs, both in the long run and short run. Too frequently, the pressure of short-run problems dominates and long-run development suffers.

A general sales manager must provide emotional support for sales managers. This support may be simply to be a good listener during periods of change, such as the initial stages of becoming a field sales manager. Managers will also need support during periods of training, and stress from mid-life crisis, illness, financial problems, and family problems. Support will also be needed if demotion is the best course of action and at retirement. These activities on the part of the general manager build team efforts and loyalty.

CREATING SALES MANAGEMENT TRAINING PROGRAMS

INITIAL TRAINING PROGRAMS

Some companies have well-organized training programs for new sales managers. One such company is N. L. McCullough. This company, which is a division of N. L. Petroleum Services Company, is a leader in cased hole logging in the oil drilling industry. N. L. McCullough has a ten-day course, complete with its own manual. The contents of this course are summarized in Exhibit 19.1. It covers topics such as marketing fundamentals, market information systems, market analysis, the marketing mix and product mix, and managing and directing representatives.

ADVANCED TRAINING PROGRAMS

Some companies, such as American Greetings Corporation, a manufacturer of greeting cards, have advanced training programs for managers that feature "people problem" inputs from the manager-participants. Approximately forty-five days prior to the seminar, each participant is requested to describe three "people problems" that presently exist in his or her district. These case histories are the basis for 60 percent of the seminar. In this way, the participants are assured that the training program will be relevant to their needs and not on theoretical subjects. Each participant develops management knowledge and skills, and learns alternative solutions to daily people problems. Managers are very enthusiastic about such training programs.[3] Sales management training programs run by the National Society of Sales Training Executives also use this approach of having participants submit difficult management problems.

BENEFITS OF TRAINING MANAGERS

The benefits of training managers are similar to the benefits derived from training at any level within an organization. The training helps the new sales manager to exploit existing talents and develop those talents that are weak. Training develops confidence so that they are not defensive and they are more willing to delegate authority and responsibility.

Exhibit 19.1   Area Sales Manager's (ASM) Program, For N. L. McCullough, A Division of N. L. Petroleum Services

UNIT I CONTENT, 2 DAYS	Content
Marketing Fundamentals	Discussion Questions
	Answers Reviews
	Historical Development of Marketing
	Film
	Job Description
	Seminar Discussion
	Market Concept Case
	A.S.M.'s Role in the Management Information System (MIS)
Market Information System	Overview of the MIS
	Market Research
	Market Research Case
UNIT II CONTENTS, 2 DAYS	*Content*
	Market Behavior and Characteristics
Market Analysis	Market Segmentation and Targeting
	Market Share
	Current Program and Activity
	Market Forecasting
UNIT III CONTENT, 2 DAYS	*Content*
	Overview of the Marketing and Product Mix
	Present Mix and Resources
Marketing Mix and Product Mix	Needed Market and Product Mix
	Strategy Determination
	Market Plus Fit
	Market Mix Case
UNIT IV CONTENTS, 4 days	*Content*
	Recruiting and Directing Sales Effort
Managing and Directing Sales	Training New and Existing Salesmen
	Counseling and Appraising Salesmen
	Identifying and Utilizing Resources
	Presentation Skills

N. L. McCullough Area Sales Manager's Program. Courtesy of Mr. Keith Fitzgerald, Director of Marketing.

This delegation helps to train subordinates to become managers, thereby increasing the pool of trained managers in case of expansion, promotion, death, or resignation of present managers. By training the field managers, the company also expands the pool of management talent for higher levels of management. Trained managers are better able to motivate their subordinates and create a team spirit.

The dangers of not training are the obverse of the benefits, but some additional dangers need to be noted. The failure to train is a demotivator that will cause high producers to leave the company quickly. There will be the loss of the immediate production and the longer range effects of a weak management pool. Managers who are not trained are forced to "rediscover the wheel" and they become very defensive about their methods. As a result, they do not delegate; subsequently, they become overloaded and discouraged.

BEHAVIORAL SCIENCE CONTRIBUTIONS TO TRAINING MANAGERS

Industrial organizational theorists have developed a theory of social learning that has been very effective in training first-line supervisors in production to interact more effectively with subordinates. This theory would seem to have direct application to the training of first-line sales managers, especially in developing their skills in coaching. The theory is based on the concept of *behavior modeling.*

BEHAVIORAL MODELING

Social learning theory is based on the fact that most human learning is the result of observing and modeling (that is, imitating) the behavior of others. Social learning theorists conclude that to model the behavior of others we must process the information by coding it for future use when the prescribed behavior is appropriate. This is the cognitive component of the theory. There are also behavioral and environmental components. It is the *interaction* of these three components that makes behavioral modeling a powerful learning method.

Bandura summarizes the theory when he states that, "In the social learning view, people are neither driven by inner forces nor buffeted by environmental stimuli. Rather, psychological functioning is explained in terms of a continuous reciprocal interaction of personal and environmental determinants."[4] Latham and Saari introduce the concept of self-selection of stimuli when they note, "Moreover, the theory states that people do not merely react to external influences but actually select, organize, and transform stimuli that impinge on them."[5] Which stimuli will be perceived, retained, and acted upon will be determined to a large degree by the individual's perception of the rewards that are associated with the prescribed behavior.

THE MODELING PROCESSES

Bandura has found that when an individual models the behavior of another person, he or she engages in four distinct processes.[6] These processes include attention, retention, motor reproduction, and motivation.

Attention

In order to imitate behavior an individual must attend to and perceive accurately the critical features of the behavior that is to be modeled. The level of attention given to learning this behavior will depend on many factors, such as the expected rewards, or avoidance of punishment, that are associated with engaging in the prescribed behavior. Attention will also be determined by the complexity of the behavior and uniqueness of its features. Individual differences in the observer, such as his or her sensory capacities, arousal levels, perceptual set, cognitive style, and past reinforcements for learning new behavior, will also determine the level of attention that is given to modeling observed behavior.

Retention

To retain information about the modeled behavior, the observer must code information about the behavior by using symbols that can be stored and recalled for future reference. These symbols will be familiar images and words. The coding process will be greatly enhanced if the modeling process is expressed in verbal and image symbols that are familiar to the observer. Repetition of these symbols increases retention. The ability of the observer to organize new information cognitively improves retention. This ability may be enhanced by previous training and experience. Practice of the modeled behavior not only increases retention of the cognitive codes, it also develops the motor skills that are necessary to translate the cognitions into actions.

Motor Reproduction

The conversion of cognitive symbols into appropriate actions is known as the *motor reproduction process*. Impediments to perfect reproduction occur when there is faulty coding of information, poor retention of coded information, inadequate feedback after performance (such as the inability to observe one's own behavior in tennis or golf), and physical limitations (including being out-of-shape).

The coach plays an important feedback role in the motor reproduction process. He or she serves as a model of behavior, checks on the knowledge that has been retained, and provides feedback regarding motor reproduction skills. The person who is self-taught misses the fine tuning in these skills that transforms a good performance into a superior one.

Motivation

Social learning theory distinguishes between the acquisition of information about the prescribed behavior and the actual performance of this behavior.[7] The adoption and replication of behavior is more likely to occur if the behavior is rewarded in ways that are valued highly by the trainee. Rewards are highly valued when they meet an individual's most important needs, as was seen during the discussion of motivation in Chapter 11. A trainee may successfully complete the first three processes of modeling, including motor reproduction in training sessions, but not replicate the behavior on the job because the perceived rewards associated with the behavior do not seem to meet the individual's needs on the job. Hence, motivation for modeling the behavior must be provided on the job.

TRANSLATING THEORY INTO TRAINING

Latham and Saari described an experiment in which they applied behavioral modeling in training programs for first-line supervisors.[8] The training groups focused on management activities such as orienting a new employee, giving recognition to an average employee, motivating a poor performer, correcting poor work habits, discussing potential disciplinary action, reducing absenteeism, handling a complaining employee, reducing turnover, and overcoming resistance to change.

Each of the training sessions used the following format:

ACTIVITY	PROCESS
1. Topic Introduction	Attention
2. Film modeling good supervision	Retention
3. Group discussion	Retention
4. Practice	Retention, Motor Reproduction
5. Class feedback	Motivation

The film depicted a supervisor model effectively handling one of the management activities. The supervisor was effective because he or she applied three to six learning points that were shown immediately before and after the film. For example, the learning points for overcoming resistance to change were as follows: (1) describe the details of the change clearly, (2) explain the reasons for the change, (3) discuss how the change will affect the employee, (4) stress the positive aspects of the change, (5) listen carefully to the employee's concern about the change, and, (6) seek the employee's help in implementing change, and, if necessary, schedule a follow-up meeting.

During the practice sessions, the trainees assumed the roles of the supervisor and the employee. There was no script. They were asked to re-create a problem that was relevant to the film and that had happened to them within the previous six months. The trainers supervised the sessions and coached the trainees on how to make constructive comments.

At the conclusion of each session, the trainees were given copies of the learning points and instructed to apply their new supervisory skills on the job. They were asked to report their successes and failures during the next session. They explained their difficulties to the class and were given the opportunity to reenact the event with another trainee playing the role of the hourly employee.

To assure that there would be additional support on the job, the superintendents of the trainees were given an accelerated two-session training program in behavioral modeling. These sessions role played the superintendent-supervisor relationships. Superintendents were trained in providing proper praise for their supervisors.

The results of these training sessions by Latham and Saari are impressive.[9] Participants' initial hostility for being required to take the training turned to positive support after they found that the learning points really worked on the job. Some participants even returned from vacation to complete the sessions.

Comparisons between the test and control groups showed statistically that behavioral modeling was a more effective training technique than other training methods. Participants in the test group did significantly better than those in the control group in a test of their learning that used eighty-five situational questions. Superintendents of the test-group trainees evaluated the test group higher in management skills.

Latham and Saari concluded that "the integration of both cognitive and behavioralistic principles within the context of social-learning theory brings about a relatively permanent change in supervisory behavior in what to supervisors is the most difficult part of their job, managing people."[10] Some sales organizations are just beginning to apply behavioral modeling to the training of field sales managers. This technique could be an important means for increasing the productivity of the sales force.

SUMMARY

The need for a continuous flow of trained sales managers will vary among industries and companies, but few companies provide adequate training and development to meet this need. Failure to provide this training may be traced to several reasons, including (1) no one takes the primary responsibility for the training, (2) top management thinks on-the-job training is sufficient, and (3) instant promotions become necessary when sudden openings occur, thereby leaving no time for training.

Training and development methods begin with a needs assessment. This assessment includes an analysis of the corporate needs for future management and the individual needs of promotable representatives and inexperienced managers. To develop a training and development program for managers, one must answer the same types of questions that needed to be answered for training programs for representatives. Who will do the training? When will it occur? How will the training be done? And where will the training take place?

The general sales manager may have neither the time nor the proper training for conducting these programs. He or she will, however, have the important role of supporting the programs and reinforcing the training that was given to field managers.

A company may have a mixture of sales management programs, some for new managers and some advanced studies for experienced managers. The programs may be conducted by in-house staff, or managers may be sent to programs that are run at management development programs, universities, and by consultants.

ASSIGNMENTS/DISCUSSION QUESTIONS

1. What reasons would explain why the training and development of sales managers have been neglected?
2. Discuss the relative importance of the need for sales management training and sales management development.
3. How might a company with a policy of promotion from within avoid the problem of inbreeding?
4. Discuss the value of experience as a first-line field sales manager to a sales training manager.
5. Discuss the value of experience as a first-line field sales manager to a marketing services manager.
6. Discuss the value of a rotational assignment within the marketing services department to a sales representative ultimately promoted to first-line field sales manager.

7. If a sales rep who was recently promoted to first-line field sales management was successful as a sales representative primarily because of his or her drive and ability to get results, identify at least two sales management activities in which the individual will probably need training.

8. If a sales representative who was recently promoted to first-line field sales management was successful as a sales representative primarily because he or she saw the best in everyone, was well liked by the customers, and generated their trust, identify at least two sales management activities in which the individual will probably need training.

9. Discuss the reasons for the importance of a field sales manager coaching a sales representative following the latter's successful completion of a sales training program.

10. With whom should the final responsibility rest for the content and effectiveness of a sales management training program? Why?

11. Why could a newly trained field sales manager become frustrated and actually be a poorer manager because of management training?

12. What are the benefits of training to the field sales manager?

13. Design a five-day program for new sales managers in a company that averages five new first-line field sales managers per year. Select an industry that interests you.

CASE 19.1:
Sandy Cooper

After trying a variety of jobs over a three-year period after graduation from the University of Washington, Sandy Cooper felt that he was finally doing what he enjoyed—selling for Northwest Industries, Inc. The opportunity to interact with people, the challenge and sense of achievement in persuading others to his point of view, the freedom to work independent of close supervision, all appealed to him. These personal appeals, plus his robust good nature, quick wit, and ability to get along with others and to have them like him quickly, combined with his initiative and imagination to make Sandy an excellent candidate for a career in sales.

Sandy had previously worked as a technical assistant in a food-processing plant, an inventory processor, and later as an inspector for the county welfare department, before learning of the opening in sales with Northwest Industries, Inc. Concerned about his previously unsatisfactory attempts to start a career, Sandy talked with as many people as he knew in sales, and eagerly took advantage of the offered opportunity to ride with one of Northwest's salesmen during the interviewing process. Following a series of interviews with Alex Peterson, the local district manager, and a final interview with Bob Heinman, the regional manager, Sandy was pleased when Mr. Heinman phoned him to offer him a sales territory in Spokane, Washington.

Full of ambition and the belief that at last he had found the field that best suited his talents, Sandy applied himself full throttle and the results of his efforts soon appeared. While he had inherited a territory in which sales had been above the regional average, both in dollars and in sales versus forecast for each of the past five years, Sandy's efforts widened the gap. In his first year, he was selected as Salesman of the Year for his region and was second runner-up for national honors. In each of the next four years, he finished among the top three in the region, winning the award again in his third and fourth years on the job, and qualifying for the President's Board of Advisors after five years with the company, which was his first year of eligibility.

No one is perfect and Sandy didn't pretend to be. On more than one occasion, his district manager, Alex Peterson, had to remind him about overdue reports and other support activities, such as recruiting follow-up, relaying marketing information, etc., that weren't high on his list of favored activities. When this occurred, Sandy usually brought his administrative activities up to date and maintained them satisfactorily—at least for a while. Another annoying practice of Sandy's that Alex was less successful in correcting was an outgrowth of Sandy's imagination and creativity (which, in part, contributed to his success). It was his good-humored put-down of company strategies and tactics in favor of his own methods. Alex was less concerned when this happened in private than in front of the other reps at district sales meetings. Considering Sandy's success, Alex Peterson wasn't certain he really wanted Sandy's compliance; nevertheless both were aware of the subtle test of strength that occurred on these occasions.

Further indication of Sandy's success was the high esteem in which he was held by his customers and competitors. He was invited by a group of customers to travel with them to their annual convention in San Francisco, and later was appointed chairman of their industrial relations committee. He was also elected president of the local professional sales representatives club. Although his early and continued successes initially sparked some antagonism among the more senior sales reps with the company, Sandy's easy manner and robust good humor soon won over the remaining holdouts, and with increasing experience he took over the role of unofficial leader in the district.

Alex Peterson was pleased with Sandy's productivity and development. He had recruited Sandy, guided his early training, and wished there were more in the district who were equally productive. In his appraisal and counseling sessions, Alex encouraged Sandy to think ahead and prepare himself for additional responsibility. Sandy's response was always positive. In conversations with Bob Heinman, the regional sales manager, and Bill Eastland, the general sales manager, during a recent visit to the company headquarters in Chicago, Alex had recommended Sandy as his most qualified candidate for promotion to district manager. Two months later, Sandy's chance came. He was offered a promotion to district manager in Denver. With a sense of pride in his achievement, Sandy quickly accepted.

Sandy breezed through the three-week management training program. His experience and intelligence gave him insights into the discussions about the reasons for the supervisory policies, procedures, and management responsibilities. His natural "people skills" enabled him to do well during the case studies about people problems. He was somewhat surprised at the number of controls in the form of reports and various forms of documentation required, as well as the amount of marketing and performance data available to him about his representatives. He was aware that several years prior to his promotion, Northwest Industries had rewritten the reporting procedures, created new job descriptions and performance appraisals, and generally was operating a more highly structured management system. While this was never Sandy's area of strength, he felt that since it was part of the job, he'd learn how to do what was required. He spent a week with Bob Heinman getting a rundown on the reps in his district, reviewing the personnel records, and gaining an understanding of Mr. Heinman's management philosophies. He also spent some time picking up the district sales records and reviewing the district market potential with his predecessor, who was being shifted to the metropolitan San Francisco district.

Sandy's performance as a district sales manager reflected his enthusiastic personal style of interacting with people. He had no difficulty winning the confidence of his reps, and he enjoyed the opportunity to interact with new customers. He quickly took over the role of trouble shooter in resolving difficult selling situations or customers who were hard to deal with, and he responded eagerly to emergency calls from his reps to "fight fires" that occurred in the field. He relished the opportunity to display and maintain his selling skills. His district sales meetings were usually highly participative with considerable enthusiasm displayed by the reps. When disagreement arose about the suitability of various selling plan strategies, Sandy was highly supportive of the reps' point of view. The overall district sales figures continued to be moderately above average, even though two territories that had been producing significantly below average on his arrival were still only slightly improved after almost four years. Sandy's explanation to Bob Heinman was that both territories were in economically depressed areas, and "anyway, the reps were only marginally satisfactory performers at best."

Beginning about two years ago, the activities and outputs in Sandy's district attracted Bob Heinman's attention. Bob continued to monitor the performance of the individual territories and studied the action plans Sandy and the two reps had devised for the two below-average territories. Bob also studied the field reports Sandy submitted after working with these reps. Recently, Bob remembered that he still had not received any recommendations for promotions from Sandy since he had been in management, even though he had discussed this with Sandy at last year's performance review. Although these recommendations were voluntary, they were supposed to be considered annually. While Bob had not expected any recommendations during Sandy's first year, it was usual that second-year managers were championing at least one of their reps for promotion. Sandy's lack of recommendations after nearly four years was unusual, particularly in the light of the overall better-than-average productivity of his district. Over the past year, the sales administration department had alerted Bob to a continuing delinquency or failure on Sandy's part to submit the selling plan evaluation reports that were required following the preceding promotional period.

As troublesome as these deficiencies were, the aspect of Sandy's performance that was of most concern to Bob Heinman was the trip reports and semi-annual performance appraisals Sandy was required to submit after each bimonthly field trip with his eleven reps and semi-annually after their performance reviews. During his first two years in supervision, Sandy submitted the reports more or less on time, but their content was far too brief to be useful. Although examples of model reports were given to all new district managers during their training, Bob Heinman resupplied Sandy and tried to make sure that he fully understood how they were to be prepared and their importance. In talking about the performance of his reps, Sandy described their activities in detail. Bob pointed out that it was this type of detailed information that should be included in the trip reports and evaluated in the semi-annual performance appraisals. Improvement was temporary, and, at Sandy's counseling session last year, Bob discussed his dissatisfaction with Sandy's continuing reporting problems and included a lengthy analysis in his performance appraisal report, a copy of which he gave Sandy. Sandy didn't dispute the facts or provide any explanation. Instead, he repeatedly referred to the sales data and the fact that his district was performing above the regional average and it was the sales output that was more important. When the reasons for the importance of the reporting and other administrative responsibilities were reviewed, Sandy said he would try to do better.

For a while, the quality and timeliness of Sandy's performance improved, but during the past six months he reverted to his previous habits. By the year end, he had failed to submit eighteen of the required field trip reports, and half of the semi-annual appraisals were significantly late and their content was short of what Bob considered a fair review of the reps' performance. Determined to resolve this problem, Bob Heinman discussed Sandy's performance at length with John England, the general sales manager, and suggested that they have a three-way conference with Sandy. Depending on the outcome of that conference, Bob further recommended that he put Sandy on probation for the next year, during which time he would have to submit the delinquent reports, have all future reports in on time, and improve their quality to meet Bob's approval.

John England agreed with Bob's recommendation and the three-way conference was held. It proved to be an awkward experience for everyone, particularly Sandy. Bob Heinman commended Sandy for his overall effort and for the sales productivity of his district, but stated that Sandy's performance of his administrative responsibilities was totally incomprehensable and unacceptable. He reviewed the various occasions on which they had discussed the same problem, Sandy had agreed with the discussions and agreed to improve, only to lapse into his previous deficiency. When pressed by Mr. England for an explanation, Sandy first contested the importance of reporting, noting that he knew his people well and could supply any information anyone wanted. Then he tried to make a case of his record of working regularly with his reps in the field, getting the desired sales reports and that multiple trip reports were unnecessary, and "anyway, there was too much paperwork overall." Bob reminded him this was not a negotiable requirement, and that none of the other district managers had any difficulty complying with the reporting requirements. At the end of the interview, when Bob Heinman told Sandy that he was so concerned about the duration and recurrence of Sandy's problem in the face of repeated warnings that he was putting him on a year's probation, the fight went out of Sandy and he promised to mend his ways. Bob then outlined the conditions of probation on which he and Mr. England had agreed, and told Sandy he would have to show a good faith effort if he were to retain his job. He offered to give Sandy any help he felt he needed to change his habits, and the meeting ended with Sandy voicing his appreciation for the frankness of the exchange and the opportunity to resolve his problem.

Although Sandy submitted all of the delinquent reports, after five months he unfortunately once again began to fall behind, and the content of his reports no longer did justice to the performance of the representatives with whom he worked.

CASE QUESTIONS

1. What is the problem and its cause(s)?

2. How would you explain the statement that "usually second-year managers were championing at least one of their reps for promotion"?

3. Why are field trip reports and semi-annual performance appraisals important?

4. What potential harm could Sandy Cooper's reps suffer from his reporting deficiencies?

5. What potential harm could Sandy's reporting deficiencies have caused Northwest Industries?

6. What evidence is there of the effect of Sandy's reporting deficiencies on his reps?

7. Discuss the advisability of Bob Heinman's recommendation to Mr. England to put Sandy on probation, in the face of Sandy's sales record.

8. Why would Bob Heinman, a regional manager, discuss Sandy's performance problem with Mr. England, the general sales manager, rather than take action on Sandy independently?

9. What would be the advantages of a three-way conference on performance deficiency between a district manager, a regional manager, and a general sales manager?

10. What alternate courses of action can Bob Heinman take? Which do you recommend and why?

11. What problems, if any, do you foresee resulting from the answer to question #10?

REFERENCES

1. C. G. Stevens and D. P. Keane, "How to Become a Better Sales Manager: Give Sales People How To, Not Rah Rah," *Marketing News* (May 30, 1980): 1ff.
2. Carnation Company recruiting brochure, August 1977.

3. R. W. Davenport, "Managers: Design Your Own Seminar," Editorial for the National Society of Sales Training Executives, March 21, 1974.
4. Albert Bandura, *Social Learning Theory* (Englewood Cliffs, N.J.: Prentice-Hall, 1977), p. 11.
5. G. P. Latham and L. M. Saari, "Application of Social-Learning Theory to Training Supervisors Through Behavioral Modeling," *Journal of Applied Psychology* 64, no. 3 (1979): 239–246.
6. Bandura, *Social Learning Theory,* pp. 22–29.
7. Ibid., p. 28.
8. Latham and Saari, "Application of Social-Learning Theory," pp. 240–246.
9. Ibid., pp. 242–245.
10. Ibid., p. 245.

SUGGESTED READING

Koontz, H., *Appraising Managers as Managers* (New York: McGraw-Hill, 1971).

20

CONTROLLING THE SALES FORCE WITH PLANS, PRODUCTIVITY AND BEHAVIORAL ANALYSIS, POLICIES, AND PROCEDURES

The general sales manager has many tools available for controlling the sales force, most of which have been discussed in earlier chapters. The activities of developing policies and procedures were introduced in Chapter 2. The use of personal objectives for achieving selling goals appeared in many chapters. In Chapter 5, we saw how the representative manages his or her territory by setting personal objectives. In Chapter 13, we saw how a field sales manager and a representative will negotiate objectives during the appraising process. In Chapter 17, we saw how forecasting techniques are used to develop quotas, which are quantified objectives for each representative. In this discussion of the controlling systems for the general sales manager we will examine how the general sales manager uses these systems to control the entire sales force. This chapter will introduce two topics that have not been discussed in previous chapters—the selling plan and productivity analysis. The next chapter will discuss the roles of financial rewards and compensation schemes as controlling devices.

THE SELLING PLAN

The selling plan is the means by which a marketing strategy is implemented through the sales force. It translates marketing objectives and strategies into action plans for the sales representatives. For example, the strategy of a manufacturer of garden supplies would be to promote hoes and rakes for the spring season and snow shovels and ice scrapers for the fall season. Magazine and television advertising would be timed to coincide with these seasons. The personal selling plan would require the representatives to sell specific seasonal products. The plan would identify frequent objections and means for overcoming them. It would identify competitors and compare the company's products with those of competitors, stressing the comparative advantages of the company's products.

A detailed selling plan will include specific short-term objectives for products and accounts. Specific market segments will be targeted for promotional effort and a brief summary of the state of this market given. The competitive position of each targeted product in each targeted market will be identified. A competitive analysis will help the representative to anticipate and overcome competition. Some selling plans provide representatives with benefit and proof statements to overcome competition. The plan will anticipate buyers' objections and supply representatives with benefit statements and proofs to help them overcome these objections (Chapter 4). The plan will also include promotional materials and equipment that are available to the representative with instructions on how to use them. These promotional materials may be carried by the representative or mailed to the buying influence as part of a direct mail campaign. Some selling plans even provide the representative with suggested closes. In short, the selling plan summarizes where we are, where we would like to be, and then provides specific tactics for getting there.

Some companies conduct market tests of their selling plans prior to implementing them. Others rely on feedback from representatives and field sales managers. The final plan should represent the best thinking within the company for achieving the sales objectives. To accomplish this end, sales plans must be adjusted for local conditions, such as differences in weather, growth patterns, competition, and economic environments. The first-line field sales manager will work with the representative to customize a plan for each territory. By involving the representative in this customization, the manager gets his or her commitment to implementing the plan.

The selling plan would probably be introduced to the sales force in a district sales meeting in order to answer broad questions or concerns and generate enthusiasm. If the introduction is important, the selling plan may be introduced at a regional or national sales meeting with the company's top officials as part of the introductory team. The district sales manager would then work with each representative to customize the plan to each territory. After the representative and the manager agree on a plan, they may turn to implementation and compliance details. Productivity analysis and behavioral analysis provide means for measuring compliance with the plan.

Who writes the selling plan? The plan will be written by internal staff, but external consultants may be used to develop the strategy and to implement it. The sales promotion department writes the selling plan based on the marketing plan that has been written by the product manager and approved by higher management. In writing the selling plan the sales promotion department will seek input from the field sales staff regarding competition and the success of previous plans. Input for the plan would be sought from internal staff persons including internal sales managers, the marketing research department, the advertising department, and the legal department.

Outside consultants are used to provide the additional capacity and special knowledge that may be necessary for a new product launch or for major products. These external firms assume the responsibility for coordinating the production of selling aids, special equipment, display material, launch programs, display booths for conventions, training materials, video programs, films, and contracting with actors and other outside professionals.

PRODUCTIVITY ANALYSIS

Productivity analysis consists of performance standards and measures that are used to evaluate a sales strategy and to determine if the sales force is complying with the selling plan and if the objectives are being achieved. This analysis consists of three elements—a clear statement of selling objectives, analysis of historical data, and experiments to confirm or reject hypotheses regarding why the selling effort did or did not reach its objectives.

OBJECTIVES

Without a clear definition of objectives, it is impossible to measure the productivity of the sales force. It will be recalled from Chapter 2 that an objective must be defined in measurable terms that state the *magnitude* of the result that is to be achieved and the *time period* for its achievement. A sales objective may be defined in terms of unit or dollar sales, numbers of orders, calls per day, presentations per month, new accounts per year, expenses, and contribution to profit. A sales quota is a representative's part of the total selling objective for the sales force. This quota will be derived from the sales forecasting process (Chapter 17). Field sales managers will be assigned or negotiate quotas for the districts and regions for which they will be held responsible. Quotas may be assigned various names by companies, such as expected sales, sales forecasts, or sales goals, but, regardless of the terms used, they are objectives and part of the management control system.

Budgets are a different kind of objective. Budgets establish limits on the allocation of resources to programs that have been designed to achieve the objectives of the organization (Chapter 2). These resources include people, working capital, and information. Field sales managers will be assigned budgets for their respective districts and regions. A representative who manages his or her territory as a profit center will also think in terms of territory budget limitations. Representatives must budget their time, expenses, and promotional materials. Exhibit 17.1 (Chapter 17) illustrated how sales forecasts provide inputs for marketing expense budgets and the total corporate budgets, including cash budgets and financial budgets. While the budgeting process is usually unique to each company, a few generalizations are possible. A budget forces specificity in planning and provides a basis for accountability. A budget must retain some flexibility so that the selling effort may be adjusted to the dynamics of the marketplace. The budget is an important element in the coordination and communication that is necessary between line and staff functions and between horizontal and vertical positions in an organizational design (Chapter 18). Negotiated quotas and budgets provide the basis for motivating and evaluating the performance of representatives.

HISTORICAL ANALYSIS

A comparison of historical sales and expense data with objectives and budgets provides the basis for much of the control of the sales force by the general sales manager. If the accomplishments exceed the goal—a happy situation—the manager may want to consider reallocating resources to sections of the program that did not achieve their objectives. Another approach is to add more resources to this successful program. When programs, representatives, or managers fall short of their objectives, an analysis of historical data is necessary to identify why these shortfalls occurred.

Historical analysis is part of the scientific process that attempts to explain the behavior of any system, including sales management systems. This analysis leads to hypotheses, which may be defined briefly as "a shrewd guess at why something happened." These hypotheses are then tested with either the analysis of additional data or through experimentation.

Sales Analysis

Data for sales analysis come from many different sources, such as territory records (Chapter 5), order forms, invoices, call reports, expense accounts, customer and prospect records, financial records, warranty cards, reports from distributors and dealers, store audit reports, and survey research. The wide availability of computers and multivariate statistical techniques makes it possible to analyze sales data according to categories that are almost limitless. In fact, one of the problems of the first-line field sales manager is the proliferation of reports that must be absorbed. When deciding what reports to provide sales managers, a good rule is to provide only those reports and details that are necessary. Providing information that "may be interesting" contributes to the information inundation of management and reduces the probability of any report being read. Thus when developing sales analysis for field managers, one should find out how they make their present decisions and the types and forms of data that they need to improve these decisions.

Common classifications for analyzing sales data include absolute and relative changes in sales volume expressed in dollars or units, by product, customer, industry, class of trade, geographical area, channel of distribution, and product application. Statistics may be created on the number and the size of orders, the number of new accounts added, the number of planned versus unplanned sales calls, the number of presentations made, the number of letters written to prospects, the number of calls required to produce an order, the number of dealer meetings held, costs per sales call, the value of orders booked per call, selling expenses and expense ratios, and gross profit margins.[1] Each of these indices may then be compared with stated objectives and budget figures, as were discussed in Chapter 5.

Activities Analysis

Sales may be a poor measure of a representative's efforts because of differences in market potential, market shares, advertising support, and competition.[2] In Exhibits 5.5 and 5.9 (Chapter 5), we saw that some companies use measures of activities to evaluate representatives' productivity. Frequently used activities include selling days, calls per day, new accounts, accounts lost, number of approaches, number of needs surveys, number of demonstrations, number of presentations, number of closes, and number of sales. Analytical ratios are frequently computed from these measures to diagnose representatives' weaknesses. For example, a low hit ratio (number of sales divided by number of sales calls) may reveal that the representative is having trouble overcoming objections or is afraid to close the sale. Additional important ratios are the sales productivity (dollar sales divided by number of calls), travel costs per call, average order size, the asset turnover rate, and the territory return-on-assets managed. Return-on-assets managed puts the general sales manager's request for additional working capital or sales personnel in the financial terms that are accepted by corporate management. Inflation accounting methods may be applied to these return-on-assets analyses to make them realistic to current inventory and asset replacement costs.[3]

Product Mix Analysis

Two accounts that generate identical sales volume may not make identical contributions to profits if they buy different mixes of products. One account may buy items with a low margin, while the other account buys high-margin products (Exhibit 5.10, Chapter 5). A product mix analysis may identify weaknesses in the compensation scheme or the selling plan that need adjustments. This analysis may suggest switching the compensation scheme from a commission on gross sales to a commission on profit contribution. The latter compensation encourages the representative to put his or her efforts on the high-margin products, assuming that the representative wants to maximize personal income.

Basing a compensation scheme on gross margins should not be confused with delegating the pricing authority to the sales force. A survey of wholesale distributors of medical supplies that was conducted by Stephenson, Cron, and Frazier, suggested that sales forces with the highest degree of pricing authority generated the lowest sales and profit.[4] Basing the compensation scheme on gross margin does not require management to relinquish pricing authority. In fact, it is not necessary to reveal margins for specific products. Commissions may be varied across classes of products to encourage sales representatives to sell certain classes of products, without revealing the margins for the products or the classes.

Expense Analysis

An annual survey of selling costs, conducted by *Sales & Marketing Management* magazine, indicates that selling costs climb at a rate equal to or greater than the consumer price index.[5] Many general sales managers are evaluating these cost trends and developing alternate strategies for sales calls. Some of these strategies include more extensive use of distributors for small accounts, and the use of telephone sales to supplement or take the place of representatives' calls. Some companies are using telephone sales for small or distant accounts, and to cover open territories.

In Exhibit 5.11 (Chapter 5), it was seen that the allocation of marketing and selling expenses to specific accounts helped to identify those accounts that made the greatest net contribution to profits. Unfortunately, very few companies attempt to allocate marketing costs to specific accounts, channels of distribution, or products. When they do, they are surprised to learn the profitability gains from either eliminating small accounts, unprofitable channels, and products, or developing more economical strategies for selling them. The techniques for allocating marketing costs to customer classes and products are generally known as "Distribution Cost Analysis." These techniques and examples are described extensively by Sevin.[6] Distribution cost analysis was used extensively during the 1940s and 1950s as a defense against charges under the Robinson-Patman Act (1936). This act provides for a defense against price discrimination when it can be demonstrated that the difference in price was justified by a difference in the marketing costs associated with sales to a particular customer. The technique became less popular as the courts looked with less favor on this defense. The disuse of this technique is unfortunate because it can be an important analytical tool for increasing the profitability of the sales effort. Perhaps the increasing availability of computers will encourage some sales managers to explore its potential.

EXPERIMENTATION TO TEST HYPOTHESES

Historical analysis provides hypotheses regarding explanations for deviations from sales objectives. Controlled experiments are the most scientific means for testing these hypotheses. These experiments provide the basis for better sales and marketing strategies. Sevin has used the term "marketing productivity analysis" to describe the combination of the historical analysis of marketing costs data and marketing experimentation to test proposed marketing strategies.[7] Sevin notes that the following kinds of marketing errors occur because of insufficient information regarding productivity: the marketing budget for a given product is too large, the budget for a given product is too small, the marketing mix is inefficient (too much is probably being spent on advertising), and marketing efforts are grossly misallocated among products, customers, and territories.[8]

Sevin provides several examples of how controlled market experiments in a few territories were used to test hypotheses that have been developed with cost analysis. In one case, a manufacturer with twelve products found that 81 percent of the total profit was contributed by three products and that two unprofitable products lost 15 percent of the company's total net profit contribution.[9] A controlled market experiment was conducted in which personal selling effort was shifted from the unprofitable product to the profitable one. Despite the drastic reduction in sales effort from the unprofitable product, its sales remained relatively stable and it became profitable because of the reduction of personal selling costs. The contribution from the profitable product increased from 16 percent to 31 percent. Sevin provides other examples of productivity analyses that resulted in the dropping of products and the changing of channels of distribution, all with a substantial increase in contributions to profits. Sevin describes in considerable detail techniques for allocating functional costs, such as selling, advertising, promotion, storage and shipping, and order processing, to product groups, accounts, and sales territories. These allocations produce profit and loss statements for products, customers, and territories. The bases for allocating these costs are summarized in Exhibit 20.1.

BEHAVIORAL EVALUATIONS

Evaluations of subordinates' behavior meet the organization's need for maintaining control, for measuring the efficiency of human resources, and for relating the productivity analysis to the behavior. These appraisals also establish a formal communication link between a subordinate and a superior. These communication links, it will be recalled from Chapter 18, are central to the existence of any organization. Performance appraisals also meet several needs of the subordinate, such as structure and feedback. This structured work environment reduces ambiguity, stress, and internal tension for the subordinates. It lets the individual know how he or she stands in the eyes of the organization and how others will react to what is said and done. Thus performance appraisals meet the needs of subordinates, as well as meet the organization's needs for staffing, management development, promotion, and succession.[10]

The general sales manager's involvement in behavioral evaluations occurs at three levels. First, he or she will monitor the evaluations that district sales managers have made of representatives and that the regional sales managers have made of the district sales managers. Second, the general manager will continuously evaluate the evaluation system. Third, the general sales manager needs to evaluate and counsel field sales managers.

MONITOR FIELD MANAGERS' EVALUATIONS OF SUBORDINATES

A general sales manager with a field force of hundreds of representatives must delegate the authority for evaluating the performance of these representatives, but must retain the responsibility for their evaluations. The

Exhibit 20.1 The Bases for Allocating Functional Costs to Products, Customers, and Territories

BASES OF ALLOCATION

Functional-cost Groups	To Product Groups	To Account-size Classes	To Sales Territories
1. Selling—direct costs:	Selling time devoted to each product, as shown by special sales-call reports or other special studies	Number of sales calls times average time per call, as shown by special sales-call reports or other special studies	Direct
2. Selling—indirect costs:	In proportion to direct selling time, or time records by projects	In proportion to direct selling time, or time records by projects	Equal charge for each sales-man
3. Advertising:	Direct; or analysis of space and time by media; other costs in proportion to media costs	Equal charge to each ac-count; or number of ulti-mate consumers and prospects in each ac-count's trading area	Direct; or analysis of media cir-culation records
4. Sales promotion:	Direct; or analysis of source records	Direct; or analysis of source records	Direct; or analysis of source records
5. Transportation:	Applicable rates times ton-nages	Analysis of sampling of bills of lading	Applicable rates times ton-nages
6. Storage and shipping:	Warehouse space occupied by average inventory. Num-ber of shipping units	Number of shipping units	Number of shipping units
7. Order processing:	Number of order lines	Number of order lines	Number of order lines

C. H. Sevin, "Marketing Profits From Financial Analysis," *Financial Executive* (May 1966): 28; C. H. Sevin, *Marketing Productivity Analysis* (New York: McGraw-Hill, 1965), pp. 13–15; C. H. Sevin, *Distribution Cost Analysis* (Washington, D.C.: U.S. Department of Com-merce, 1946).

general manager must establish a monitoring system that assures that these evaluations are done according to schedule and according to uniform standards across territories and districts. The manager must make certain that these appraisals meet the corporate policies and the requirements of legislation regarding equal employment opportunities.

EVALUATE THE EVALUATION SYSTEM

In addition to complying with existing policies, the manager has an obligation to recommend changes in the evaluation system so that it may better meet the needs of the company and the individuals who are evaluated. This evaluation of the system requires answers to many questions. Does the system need updating? Are appraisals being conducted on schedule, accurately, and fairly? What are the overall effects of appraisal on motivation at all levels within the organization? What are the relationships between appraisals and salary administration? What are the equal employment opportunity implications resulting from appraisals on women, minorities, protected age groups, or from actions resulting from appraisals relative to promotions, demotions, separations, probation, and salary changes?

EVALUATE AND COUNSEL THE FIELD SALES MANAGERS

The general sales manager must apply the same concepts when appraising, coaching, counseling, and correcting field managers as the field managers used with representatives (Chapter 13). The goals of management evaluation systems are even the same—knowledge, attitudes, skills, and habits—but the content is different.

The general sales manager must train managers in problem solving, decision making, and communication skills (Chapters 14 and 15). The field sales managers will need to gain knowledge in planning and organizing, staffing, directing, and controlling the field salespersons. Some field sales managers will have difficulty in developing proper habits for managing their time as they first make the transition between selling and management. New managers may also need assistance in redirecting their thinking so that they develop the attitudes of a manager. And finally, managers, like representatives, need to be motivated. Thus the evaluation and counseling of field sales managers is an opportunity to identify their needs and to develop means for meeting the needs (Chapter 11).

Research on the control systems for sales representatives has shown that the success of the system depends on the clarity of the goals, the linking of rewards to performance, and the degree of influence that the representative has in establishing the work environment and performance standards.[11] No research has been conducted on the evaluation systems for field sales managers, but it seems reasonable that these three conditions for the success of a control system for representatives would also apply to a control system for field sales managers. Similarly, measures of role perceptions, attitudes, skill levels, and motivation levels that have been the basis for research on sales representatives' performance[12] may also be a fruitful area for researching the performance of field sales managers.

AUTOMATIC CONTROLLING THROUGH POLICIES AND PROCEDURES

Policies are standing decisions regarding recurring strategic matters, while procedures are standardized programs of actions regarding recurring tactical matters (Chapter 2). Policies and procedures are automatic decision makers for managers, and free them from the need to rethink routine matters. They provide uniformity, fairness, and efficiency, and they simplify communication. Many companies have detailed policy and procedure manuals. A pharmaceutical company has a procedures manual that covers the following topics:

1. Advertising—product request forms, literature and stationery order form, and professional services mailing list.

2. Automobile—operating instructions, reporting expenses, insurance and accident reports.

3. Conventions—convention reporting, hospitality suites, shipping, setting up, and dismantling exhibits.

4. Correspondence and filing—standard field file, mail, and field information system.

5. Expenses—general information, instructions for completing reports, and audit adjustments.

6. Government—selling to the federal government, government terminology, and government distribution systems.

7. Insurance and Pensions—benefits, medical insurance, sickness and accident plan, retirement plan, and investment savings plan.

8. Legal—tax deductions for office in home, taxation and moving expenses, handling of samples, and illegal substitution and misbranding.

9. Marketing—product complaints, shipping and receiving specimens, and working with product planners.

10. Personnel—equal employment opportunity policy, patents and confidentiality, performance and pay, health and safety, separations, scheduled absences, educational opportunities, and relocation program.

11. Recruiting—recruiting policies and guidelines.

12. Territory management—call-reporting forms, due dates, supervisor's activity reporting procedure, and consignment of equipment.

13. Training—catalog of courses, continuing education programs, and product proficiency examination program.

14. Wholesale—wholesale distribution policies, shipping procedures, and return goods policies.

While policies and procedures manuals are automatic decision makers, the general sales manager must monitor compliance with them. It is this monitoring that provides the control, not the manuals themselves. The amount of control applied generally increases as one moves down the organizational hierarchy. In working with these manuals, general sales managers should remember the old dictum, "People do what you inspect, not what you expect."

THE ROLE OF THE COMPUTER IN CONTROL SYSTEMS

Computers are playing important roles at all levels of sales management. Earlier discussions included the use of microcomputers in managing a territory as a profit center (Chapter 5), controlling districts (Chapter 13), and the measurement of market potential and forecasting (Chapter 17). Some companies are developing elaborate computer-based reporting systems at the company level. For example, Burroughs Wellcome Company, a pharmaceutical company, has a computer-based reporting system that requires representatives to complete a computer card. Pillsbury Company uses mathematical models for allocating sales effort and has made continual improvements in its call reporting system. After Pillsbury decided to reallocate the effort of the representatives, the next question was, "Are representatives making the calls as directed?" To answer this question, Pillsbury used preprinted and precoded forms that were processed by an optical scanner.[13] A good computer-based sales management control system can give a company a competitive advantage, which explains why so few of these systems are published in the marketing literature.[14] The Computer Instrumentation Division of

Westinghouse Corporation installed an electronic sales-information system that frees salespeople from paperwork and gives management current information on the status of marketing plans. This division credits the system with the following productivity gains: a 27-percent increase in sales contacts, new customer contracts per salesperson up 300 percent, and cost per sales call decreased 25 percent.[15] These results should encourage other companies to explore the benefits of electronic reporting systems.

SUMMARY

The general sales manager has the final responsibility for controlling the sales force to assure that it meets the objectives that have been assigned to it by the marketing plan. This control is accomplished through the selling plan, productivity analysis, behavioral evaluations, and policies and procedures.

The selling plan represents the best thinking in the sales force for the development of tactics that will implement the selling strategy specified in the marketing plan. Productivity analysis, which includes historical analysis and experimentation, helps to explain why sales objectives were not met and to develop new strategies and tactics for meeting them. The general sales manager's role in behavioral evaluations includes monitoring field managers' evaluations, evaluating the total evaluation system, and, finally, evaluating the field sales managers themselves. Policies and procedures provide automatic decision making for the sales manager, thereby freeing him or her to focus on decisions that do not occur regularly. Policies and procedures must be monitored continuously if they are to be effective. The computer is playing an increasingly larger role in the controlling systems at all levels of sales management.

ASSIGNMENTS/DISCUSSION QUESTIONS

1. How does the selling plan relate to the job description of a sales representative?

2. If the sales representative and field sales manager set a dollar sales objective on product A because of lagging sales in the representative's territory on that product, what will the representative do about the promotion of that product during the time product A is not listed in the selling plan?

3. Why would a sales representative promote a product not listed in the selling plan?

4. What factors could adversely affect the average number of calls per day of a sales representative? What can the representative do to minimize that adverse effect?

5. Discuss the pros and cons of using a sales representative's behavioral activities as an index of compliance with the selling plan.

6. What conclusions would you reach about the performance of a sales representative whose call average and record of products promoted per call are satisfactory but whose dollar sales are unsatisfactory?

7. If a sales representative's performance is evaluated on the basis of dollar sales achieved against a quota as a result of knowledge regularly and skillfully communicated to an assigned group of customers, how would you evaluate the performance of the field sales manager?

8. What factors would influence the selection of sales figures versus behavioral activities to measure the effectiveness of the selling plan in achieving its objectives for a specific period of time?

9. How can a general sales manager be reasonably sure that the field sales manager's appraisal of the sales representative is accurate?

CASE 20.1:
The Inflated Appraisal

After an indepth analysis of the productivity of the sales representatives in the six districts in his region, Jack Hunter was convinced that the relative productivity in terms of dollar sales versus potential in two of his districts did not match the individual performance appraisals submitted by the district sales managers. This seems particularly true in the case of Carol Thompson's district. Judging by the annual performance appraisals submitted by Carol, the overall performances of her ten representatives ranged from a "high satisfactory" to "outstanding" rating. By contrast, the total sales productivity of Carol's district was significantly below the regional average, and three of her representatives were at the bottom of the regional list and none was in the top quartile when compared on sales versus potential.

At the last district sales managers' quarterly conference, Jack conducted a workshop with a series of case studies on the importance of realistic performance appraisal reports, and stressed the fact that he had contributed to this problem in the region by accepting annual appraisals, which his better judgment had told him were inflated. At the same time, he served notice that he planned to tighten up this procedure on the appraisals that were due during the next quarter.

As a result, he was annoyed a month later to receive an envelope from Carol Thompson containing five annual appraisals, all of which, in Jack's opinion, were inconsistent with the comparative sales data. In checking further into his files, Jack dug out copies of correspondence from Carol to her representatives, and a series of trip reports that Carol completed following each working visit with her representatives, all of which provided documentation to support Jack's conclusion that the appraisals were inflated.

After agonizing over the situation for a day, and feeling that the problem had existed far too long and had to be solved, Jack telephoned Carol and told her that three of the five reports were unacceptable and would have to be resubmitted. As expected, Carol protested, contending that the appraisals reflected her best judgment of the activities ratings of these representatives. Jack's rejoinder was that if the sales results were inconsistent with the ratings of the activities that produced these results, then the ratings were inflated. He added that if Carol could not provide evidence to justify the higher ratings, then she'd have to reduce them before Jack would accept them. While Carol conceded the logic of Jack's position, she argued that she couldn't recall and change the appraisals because she had already held the performance appraisal and counseling sessions with these representatives, had them sign the appraisals, and had given them their copies. At this point, Jack insisted, saying that he had made his position clear at the last managers' conference and that the problem was Carol's to resolve but that Jack would not accept these reports as originally submitted.

CASE QUESTIONS

1. What is Jack Hunter's problem?
2. What is Carol Thompson's problem?
3. What are the possible reasons for Carol's inconsistency in appraising her sales representatives?
4. What options are available to Carol?
5. If Jack will not yield, how could Carol conduct the reappraisals in an effort to minimize the trauma?
6. What harm is done by inflated appraisals?

REFERENCES

1. *Measuring Salesmen's Performance* (New York: National Industrial Conference Board, Business Policy Study, No. 114, 1965), pp. 14–15.
2. D. W. Cravens, R. B. Woodruff, and J. C. Stamper, "An Analytical Approach for Evaluating Sales Territory Performance," *Journal of Marketing* 36 (January 1972): 31–37.
3. F. E. Webster, Jr., J. A. Largay, III, and C. P. Stickney, "The Impact of Inflation Accounting on Marketing Decisions," *Journal of Marketing* 44 (Fall 1980): 9–17.
4. P. R. Stephenson, W. L. Cron, and G. L. Frazier, "Delegating Pricing Authority to the Sales Force: The Effects of Sales and Profit Performance," *Journal of Marketing* 43 (Spring 1979): 21–28.
5. This study appears in *Sales & Marketing Management* during the third week in February.
6. C. H. Sevin, *Marketing Productivity Analysis* (New York: McGraw-Hill, 1965); C. H. Sevin, "Marketing Profits from Financial Analyses," *Financial Executive* (May 1966): 22–25; D. R. Longman and M. Schiff, *Practical Distribution Cost Analysis* (Homewood, Ill.: Richard D. Irwin, Inc., 1955).
7. Sevin, *Marketing Productivity Analysis*.
8. Sevin, "Marketing Profits," pp. 23–24.
9. Ibid., p. 24.
10. This paragraph is based on W. E. Hill, "The R. T. French Company, Management Performance Appraisal and Development," Editorial for the National Society of Sales Training Executives, September 30, 1980.
11. C. M. Futrell, J. E. Swan, and J. T. Todd, "Job Performance Related to Management Control Systems for Pharmaceutical Salesmen," *Journal of Marketing Research* 13 (February 1976): 25–33.
12. O. C. Walker, G. A. Churchill, Jr., and N. M. Ford, "Where Do We Go From Here?" In *Critical Issues in Sales Management: State-of-the Art and Future Research Needs*, ed. G. Albaum and G. A. Churchill, Jr. (Eugene, Oregon: College of Business Administration, University of Oregon, 1979), pp. 10–75; O. C. Walker, G. A. Churchill, Jr., and N. M. Ford, "Organizational Determinants of the Industrial Salesman's Role Conflict and Ambiguity," *Journal of Marketing* 39 (January 1975): 32–39.
13. L. M. Deboer and W. H. Ward, "Integration of the Computer into Salesman Reporting," *Journal of Marketing* 35 (January 1971): 41–47.
14. For example, Cravens, Woodruff, and Stamper, "An Analytical Approach for Evaluating Sales Territory Performance."
15. T. C. Taylor, "Talk about Sales Productivity!" *Sales & Marketing Management* (July 6, 1981): 38–39.

SUGGESTED READINGS

Bailey, R. E.; McDermott, Dennis R.; and Wilson, John, "Time Allocation of a Pooled Industrial Sales Force," *Industrial Marketing Management* 5 (1976): 343–350.

Dunne, P. M., and Wolk, H. I., "Marketing Cost Analysis: A Modularized Contribution Approach," *Journal of Marketing* 41 (July 1977): 83–94.

Hughes, G. D., "A New Tool for Sales Managers," *Journal of Marketing Research* 1 (May 1964): 32–38.

Small, R. J., and Rosenberg, L. J., "Determining Job Performance in the Industrial Sales Force," *Industrial Marketing Management* 6 (1977): 99–102.

21

CONTROLLING
THROUGH FINANCIAL
REWARDS

It may seem strange that a topic as important as financial compensation appears near the end of a textbook on sales management. This is not because it is an unimportant topic, but rather this positioning represents the natural flow of management activities. An effective compensation plan must be built on effective plans for hiring, training, motivating, and evaluating. Too frequently, compensation plans are viewed as the only means for directing and motivating the sales force. In such cases, these monetary motivators are short term in their effects because the weaknesses in the preliminary steps of management will ultimately surface. No compensation plan can overcome basic weaknesses in sales management. "One of the most common errors in designing a compensation plan is to overburden the plan with objectives more appropriately assigned to other areas in sales management."[1]

A representative receives directly only about 75 percent of a company's cost for maintaining that representative. The remainder is divided about equally between fringe benefits and expenses. The compensation that is received by the representative will consist of various components, such as salaries, commissions, drawing accounts, bonuses, contest awards, and profit sharing.

A compensation plan should be based on four principles:

1. Pay a meaningful incentive in a timely fashion.
2. Base the incentive payment on performance.
3. Be certain that the performance is based on activities that can be controlled by the representative.
4. Use performance criteria that are observable and measurable.[2]

594

THE ROLE OF COMPENSATION PROGRAMS

Compensation programs must simultaneously meet the needs of the company and those of the representatives. The fact that these needs are quite different makes it easy to understand that there is no perfect compensation plan because compromises must be made between the needs of the company and those of the representative.

CORPORATE NEEDS

The corporation's needs may be described simply as the optimal deployment of sales effort across customers, territories, product lines, and such activities as prospecting, setting up displays, training customers' employees, and account collection. To accomplish these broad objectives, the company needs a compensation scheme that will attract and retain desirable salespersons, provide control over specific selling activities, reward outstanding performance, develop long-term relationships with customers, and accomplish all of these without excessive sales administration.

The compensation plan must establish some stability and security within the sales force, but, on the other hand, it must be flexible so that it can respond to changes in the company's product or marketing mix and the dynamics of the marketplace. The compensation plan cannot be decided upon until basic decisions have been made regarding the role of sales management in the marketing mix and the role of compensation plans in motivation, territory designs, quota systems, programs for career planning, and the availability of marketing information systems that will make it possible to develop and implement a compensation plan.

A well-designed incentive system can provide a general sales manager with an automatic control device over representatives. The system also provides representatives with an opportunity to evaluate their own performances and take appropriate actions. A good compensation scheme will be fair to the company, its customers, and the sales force.

REPRESENTATIVES' NEEDS

In Chapter 11, we saw that the individual needs of a representative included the physiological, security, social, esteem, and self-actualization needs. Many of these needs are met by nonfinancial incentives, such as opportunities for advancement and responsibility. A stimulating work environment may help to meet the need for self-actualization. But financial compensation is necessary to meet the physiological needs, security needs, and to buy those social, esteem, and self-actualization needs that cannot be met on the job.

In designing the compensation plan, the general sales manager must consider the needs of the typical representative. A young representative who is meeting his or her basic physiological needs may not be concerned with security needs, but instead is concerned with social recognition. This representative needs a compensation plan that gives opportunities for this recognition through visible rewards, such as bonuses and contests. An older representative with family obligations may be concerned with security needs so that his or her ideal compensation plan may include such features as a stable income, stock option plans, health insurance, and a retirement plan. Thus the compensation plan cannot be developed until there is a clear understanding of what needs patterns motivate the representatives.

From the representative's point of view, the compensation plan must provide incentive for superior performance of activities that are within his or her control. To be fair and equitable, compensation must be competitive within the industry. The plan must also be understandable by the representative. *Understandable* does not mean that the compensation scheme must be simplistic. It does mean, however, that when complex compensation plans are necessary, they must be explained carefully to representatives.

STEPS IN DEVELOPING A COMPENSATION PLAN

DEFINE THE OBJECTIVES

A representative's compensation scheme must be linked to the role of personal selling in the marketing mix. Does it perform the entire communications task? Or does it perform a minor role with advertising and the channels of distribution providing the major communications effort? What are the short-term and long-term selling objectives? Are the short-term objectives sales, developing accounts, or getting product distribution? Each of these objectives requires a different compensation plan. For example, an objective of a short-run increase of market share suggests a compensation scheme that has a large incentive factor, such as a commission. An objective of developing long-term relationships with an account would require a scheme that was largely salary.

RELATE COMPENSATION TO THE JOB DESCRIPTION AND PERFORMANCE APPRAISALS

The job description and performance appraisal system are prerequisites to a well-designed compensation plan. The job description will identify the activities that are required of the representative, and the performance appraisal system will provide a means for measuring the quality of performing these activities. Once again, we see that the representative's job description is the basic tool for sales management. The rewards should also reflect the accomplishment of personal objectives that a representative negotiates with his or her manager.

ESTABLISH COMPENSATION LEVELS

Within the basic job description for a sales representative, there may be several levels of compensation, such as trainee, junior representative, representative, and senior representative. There may also be salary grades for special representatives who call on a particular class of customers, such as hospitals, insurance companies, etc. National accounts representatives may also have a separate salary grade. It is necessary to establish total compensation packages for each of these levels. It may also be necessary to distinguish between field salespersons and internal sales support services, such as telephone and counter sales personnel, systems design engineers, and installation persons. Within each grade a company may establish upper and lower salary limits.

When developing a compensation plan for representatives, the general manager must also consider the compensation plans for first-line field sales managers. Should there be an upper limit on representatives' total compensation so that they do not earn more than their superiors? Some companies have a philosophy that a representative can make more than anyone in the company, including the president. Other companies maintain a differential between the representative and his or her manager. Some companies allow a limited overlap between representatives and managers. By making this differential a matter of policy, the company reduces the chances of a star salesperson consistently outearning his or her manager, thereby raising questions of the value of managerial abilities. This guaranteed differential encourages the manager to motivate the representatives to maximize their income, without concentrating on his or her own incentive earnings.

A wide differential has several advantages. It helps the new manager to think like a manager rather than a super salesperson. It encourages the development of star salespersons into sales managers. This wide differential gives room for adapting representatives' income for areas with high cost-of-living without upsetting the salary chain throughout management. A wide pay differential may eliminate the need for a maximum compensation statement for sales representatives, thereby giving the impression that unlimited earning potential is available to all persons. Companies that maintain a differential pay the manager, on the average, 30 percent more than the representatives.[3]

Most field sales managers are compensated with a salary and a bonus. In most cases, the bonus is calculated in the same way as the bonus that is given to salespersons. In some cases, however, there is also an executive bonus that is calculated on the same basis as the bonuses that are given to executives above the manager.[4]

DETERMINE THE INCENTIVE PROPORTION

When the total compensation has been determined for representatives' salary grades, the next step is to determine what proportion of this income should be related to an incentive program. A common point of departure is a 75–25 split, where 25 percent of the compensation plan is based on an incentive system.[5]

The incentive portion may be increased to 40 percent, but it should be recognized that as the incentive portion increases, the need for closer supervision of nonselling activities (e.g., collections, reports, etc.) increases. Similarly, reducing the incentive portion to 10 percent will reduce the administrative load of the nonselling activities, but the incentive may be too small to be effective.

When the proportion of incentive income has been decided, the next decisions are the forms that these incentives will take and the frequency of payment. The typical forms include commissions, bonuses, and contests. Contests generally serve more as a short-term motivator than as a form of compensation, but they are discussed in this chapter because of their financial component. (Nonfinancial motivators were discussed in Chapter 16.) Commissions tend to be paid more frequently than bonuses and contests. Bonuses are scheduled at irregular intervals to meet special incentive needs. Commissions and bonuses tend to have longer range effects than contests.

PRETEST THE PLAN

The compensation plan should be pretested in a variety of ways. One of the early pretests should be a simulation of several alternative plans with different incentive proportions. This "desk-top" pretest would use historical data and subjective estimates to estimate the effect of different compensation schemes on specific representatives' income. A field test of the plan may occur at several levels. First, there would be feedback from managers regarding their perception of how the plan would stimulate representatives to achieve the prescribed goals. At the next level, the pretest would solicit similar inputs from the representatives. The final pretest would be a limited installation of the compensation plan in the field. If this limited field test proved successful, the plan would be rolled out to the entire sales force.

IMPLEMENT THE PLAN

The implementation plan must make provisions for developing sales volume goals and creating monthly or quarterly compensation statements for the representatives and all levels of sales management. A program for introducing the compensation to the representatives must be developed. This plan should give a statement of the reasons for changing from the old plan to the new plan, the objectives of the new plan, the benefits to the representatives, the representatives' role in developing the plan, and the time schedule for its introduction.

EVALUATE THE PLAN

The dynamics of the marketplace require that the compensation plan, like all major sales management decisions, must be evaluated on a continuous basis. It is extremely important during the installation of a new compensation plan to monitor the effect of the plan on the objectives, such as an increase in sales, profits, or new accounts. There must be an immediate followup on any problems that develop. Later, the review may be shifted to quarterly and subsequently to annual reviews to determine if fine tuning or major overhauls are necessary.

CHOOSING COMPENSATION METHODS

The most common compensation methods are straight salary, commission only, and salary plus some form of incentive. Each of these methods is appropriate for different situations and industries, and each method has its own advantages and disadvantages. The situations, industries, advantages, and disadvantages are summarized in Exhibit 21.1, and will be discussed briefly.

STRAIGHT SALARY

Straight salaries are commonly used when selling is a group effort, when many nonselling tasks are required (e.g., taking inventory, setting up displays, and collecting accounts), and when the selling process is a long one so that the commission method would result in violent swings of income. Companies in the steel, cement, airframe, defense, and service industries frequently use a straight salary plan.

Straight salaries have the advantages of avoiding disputes among a selling team. The income is level for the representative and predictable for the company. A salary plan is easy to administer and it provides greater control over the activities of the representative.

Exhibit 21.1   A Comparison of Sales Compensation Methods

	STRAIGHT SALARY	COMMISSION ONLY	SALARY PLUS COMMISSION	SALARY PLUS BONUS
SITUATIONS:	1. When a sales team is used, including technical persons, inside personnel, and representatives in other territories. 2. When sales are cyclical or take a long period. 3. To achieve nonselling objectives. 4. When sales impact is difficult to measure.	1. A company or product is in early stage of life cycle and it is difficult to establish territories. 2. When a company has limited working capital. 3. When few nonselling activities are needed. 4. When representatives are part time.	1. When security, incentive, and control are needed.	1. When long-term incentives are needed. 2. When it is difficult to measure individual performance.
INDUSTRIES:	Steel, Cement, Airframe, Defense-Oriented Industries and Service Industries.	Wholesaling	A wide variety of industries including consumer goods, services, and wholesaling.	A wide variety of industries use bonuses for about 15 percent of total compensation.
ADVANTAGES:	1. Avoids disputes. 2. Evens income level. 3. Easy to administer and budget. 4. Control over representatives is increased for nonselling tasks and servicing. 5. Increases company loyalty. 6. Makes total sales compensation predictable. 7. Easier recruiting.	1. Conserves capital by avoiding fixed cost and spreading risk between the company and the sales person. 2. Maximizes sales force incentive to develop the market. 3. Sales costs per sales dollar are predictable and generally lower. 4. System is easy to understand and compute. 5. Attracts high achievers.	1. Great flexibility with many incentive options. 2. Improves performance over straight salary. 3. More control than straight commission over nonselling activities.	1. Bonuses cannot become excessive because they are based on percent of goals. 2. Forces establishment of annual sales or profit contribution quotas for each territory. 3. Provides flexibility for rewarding extra effort.

DISADVANTAGES:

1. Discourages achievement oriented representatives.
2. High fixed costs if sales decline.
3. Little relationship between sales and sales compensation.
4. Inflexible.
5. Concentrates effort on products that are easiest to sell.
6. Tends to reward length of employment rather than performance.

1. Little control over activities.
2. Highly cyclical income in cyclical industries.
3. May create dissatisfaction among nonsales peers if salespersons have very high salaries.
4. May require representative to take a reduction in income if promoted.
5. Wide variances in income between representatives.
6. Administrative problems when cutting territories.
7. Tendency of representatives to skim the cream.
8. Tendency to ignore nonsales work such as attending trade shows and collecting accounts.
9. Difficult to start a new representative.

1. Complex, requiring more administrative work.
2. Danger of individual adjustments eliminating uniformity and fairness.
3. Incentive may not be high enough for all representatives.
4. Unduly rewards territories with high potential.

1. More complex to establish and administer.
2. The typical quarterly or annual payment reduces the incentive effect.
3. Sometimes the bonus is based on the subjective judgment of management.

The major limitation of the salary plan is that it provides no direct incentive that links sales effort to sales results. It may result in representatives concentrating their efforts on products that are easiest to sell. which may be the low-price and low-margin products.

COMMISSION ONLY

Fewer than 15 percent of manufacturers, service companies, wholesalers and distributors use a commission only plan.[6] Such a plan pays a representative a percentage of the sales or gross margin on a product. The payment is made after the sale. A commission with a drawing account differs from the commission-only plan by allowing the representative to draw income against future commissions. Thus a commission with a draw retains all of the incentive of a commission plan, but some of the wild fluctuations are reduced. While few manufacturers use a commission with a draw method, 10 percent of the service companies and 26 percent of wholesalers and distributors used this method.[7] A general sales manager who uses a commission with a draw plan must decide the appropriate level of draw for each representative. A representative who continues to "owe the company" may become extremely demotivated and quit, never having covered the amount of the draw.

A commission-only compensation plan may be appropriate during the early stages of a company's or product's life cycle, when it is difficult to establish territories. The method is used also by companies with limited working capital, thereby shifting much of the risk for sales to the representative. The method may be appropriate in situations where the need for incentive is high and the availability of sales supervision is low.

A commission-only approach avoids fixed costs and makes the costs per sales dollar predictable and generally lower. The system is generally easy to understand and compute, thereby maximizing its effect as an incentive.

While the commission-only system provides maximum incentive, it has many disadvantages. It results in highly cyclical incomes, which may discourage new representatives. The sales manager has little control over representatives' nonselling activities with this plan. The method may prove to be inflexible regarding administrative problems, such as cutting territories.

A critical decision when designing a commission plan is the base that will be used for computing the commission to be paid. Should the commission be applied to total sales or gross margin?

Research Findings

The problem of designing a commission rate structure for a multiproduct sales force has been examined by many researchers. In summarizing the research in this field, Srinivasan notes that most of the research has been concentrated on how commission rates and their basis for computation affect how representatives allocate their time among several products.[8] Some of the earliest research on this topic was done by Farley in 1964, in which he noted that when production costs and prices are constant over a relevant range of output, basing the commission system on the gross margin for each product provides optimal results for the company and the representative.[9] Farley and Weinberg note that the task becomes more complicated when variable costs are rising or falling. These authors suggest an algorithm that is based on experimental data of representatives' assessment of the relationship between their efforts and sales. These time-effectiveness functions may be used to develop commission rates and control models for allocating selling efforts.[10]

Srinivasan addresses the problem of a compensation scheme that is not limited to allocating a fixed number of hours for representatives. Instead, he considers the effect of a compensation plan on the total time that a salesperson will spend on selling tasks. Some salespersons will respond by increasing the total number of hours, while others may choose to have more leisure. Srinivasan suggests that commission rates be set higher for products with greater elasticities relative to the selling time spent on the product. Representatives would then call on accounts that are highly responsive to personal selling, thereby generating the greatest productivity from a limited resource—salespersons' time.

A study of highly motivated and experienced representatives would probably reveal that many of them adjust the time spent to certain product-account mixes in ways that suggest they intuitively are aware of the product-account response function relative to the amount of time spent, and that they attempt to optimize their time accordingly. Unfortunately, such empirical studies have not been conducted.

Weinberg states, "An equal gross margin commission system is jointly optimal when the sales person is an income maximizer; when he or she seeks to minimize work subject to an income constraint; or when he or she explicitly trades off time against money."[11] We must conclude, therefore, that while not all researchers agree, there is strong evidence that a commission based on gross margin will lead toward optimality for the company and the representative.

Practical Considerations

Some companies prefer the commission based on gross margin when the representative has the authority to vary the price. A survey of wholesale distributors of medical supplies revealed that this practice will not necessarily maximize profits or sales.[12] A representative may have a different utility function for income than the company, thereby not choosing to maximize personal income.

One manufacturer of business forms had an interesting variation on the policy of allowing salespersons to set prices. It paid representatives a fixed commission on sales when the price generated a gross margin between 20 and 25 percent. If the price quoted by the representative was high or low, the company split with the representative any gains or losses above or below this margin range. The system has worked successfully for twenty-five years.

The commission system requires corporate policies on special problems, such as phone and mail orders. Should the representative get a full commission when the sale was made by an internal representative? How should house accounts and team sales be handled? What commission should a field representative receive for servicing an account that was sold by the national accounts representative at the customer's headquarters? How should returned products, allowances for product damage, and bad debts be reflected in a representative's commission? These commission complexities have convinced some companies to use a straight salary.

SALARY PLUS INCENTIVE

A compensation plan that is based on a salary plus an incentive is clearly the most popular. This type of plan is being used by 66 percent of manufacturers, 52 percent of service companies, and 43 percent of wholesalers and distributors.[13] The most common incentives that are used with salaries are commissions and bonuses. A salary plus commission compensation plan can have the security and control advantages of a salary and the incentive component of the commission. On the other hand, if the plan is not well designed, such a combination plan can have the worst features of a salary plan and of a commission plan, with the additional disadvantage of greater administrative complexity. Hence, the general sales manager must design combination plans with great care.

Exhibit 21.2 provides a graphic example of a combination plan that is based on a salary, a commission, and a bonus. It also illustrates an upper limit that is designed to preserve a 30-percent differential between the representative and the field sales manager. This illustrative plan

Exhibit 21.2   A Graphic Example of a Salary, Commission, and Bonus Plan, with an Upper Limit for Representatives

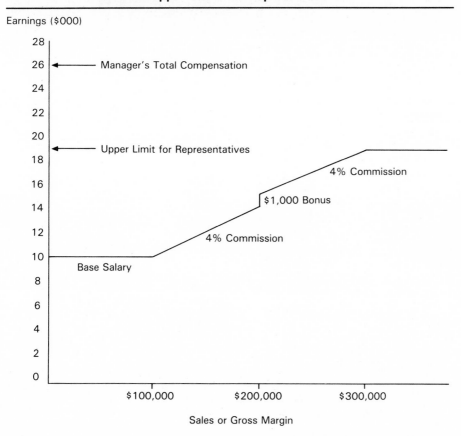

Earnings ($000)

Sales or Gross Margin

pays a base salary of $10,000 and a 4-percent commission rate. At a sales or gross margin level of $200,000, a bonus of $1,000 is paid. The 4-percent commission continues until a level of $300,000 in sales or gross margin is reached. At this point, the representative reaches the upper limit that has been established to preserve an income differential between a representative's compensation and his or her manager's compensation. If a higher incentive is required after the bonus is paid, the general sales manager may want to consider using a commission rate higher than 4 percent on sales beyond the $200,000 level.

When a strong incentive program is necessary but it is difficult to relate activities to results, some managers use a point system. This system awards points to representatives for performing activities such as soliciting new accounts, doing needs assessments, setting up displays, or, perhaps, gathering marketing data. Bonus points may be given for exceeding quotas for each of these activities. Points may then be translated into dollars or, in some cases, trading stamps. Many companies have found that trading stamps will involve a representative's spouse in the incentive program. Trading stamps simplify the implementation of incentive programs because the trading stamp company administers the details, such as shipping products.

BONUSES

Bonuses are lump sum payments for achieving a specific objective, such as meeting quota. They are frequently used with a straight salary plan to provide some incentive in those situations where a compensation plan requires incentives but a commission plan is inappropriate. As noted, the bonus plan may also be used when a salary plus commission plan is used. Exhibit 21.2 illustrates that a commission plan gives immediate and continuous stimulation. A bonus, in contrast, provides longer-term incentives. In Exhibit 21.2, only one bonus is available to the representative. Bonuses may be spaced throughout the year for achieving various levels of performance.

Bonuses tend to be about 5 to 15 percent of the total compensation package for several reasons. A large incentive that is placed out of reach of most representatives is no incentive at all. Furthermore, if the incentive is large, and therefore represents a major source of income to the representative, a downturn in the industry or economy may put the bonus out of reach. In this case, the net effect would be a cut in income—a substantial demotivator.

Many bonus plans are based on a bonus pool that is determined by the total sales force performance in a district or a region. The pool is then allocated to representatives according to a point system that reflects each individual's contribution to the pool. The total pool may be determined by the combined sales force achieving various levels of the total sales force quota. Individual points will be assigned according to many different achievements. For example, one company bases the points on the percent increase over the sales for the previous year. An increase of 18 percent was required for special bonus points. However, if the representative received bonus points the previous year, then only a 13-percent increase was required to receive bonus points during the current year. First-year representatives received bonus points if they reached a 25-percent increase over their territory for the previous year. By varying the percentages for bonus points, the general sales manager is able to encourage a steady increase in sales rather than widely fluctuating ones.

Another company used a group pool system and bonus points to gain rapid distribution of new products. Persons selling new products got more points than those who sold older products that were easier to sell.

To create competition among territories, one company developed a sales district pool that was based on the performance of that district versus a national average. The pool was allocated among representatives according to performance activities by each representative. Competition among districts can create a high level of cooperation and team spirit within districts.

CONTESTS

Contests are short-term motivators with an economic component. Many sales managers have found that sales contests that give prizes, such as televisions, trips, trading stamps, premium merchandise, and other products for the family, generate more incentives than the dollar value associated with the prize. Such response on the part of a salesperson is easy to understand if he or she has met the physiological and security needs and wants to meet some social needs. A new color television set, a personal computer, or a trip to Hawaii is very visible among the neighbors.

A sales contest, however, must be designed carefully to avoid its becoming a disaster and a demotivator. Objectives, such as new accounts or the sale of off-seasonal products, must be defined clearly. There should be a reasonable probability of rewards for all individuals. Rewards must be attractive to representatives so that they will motivate them. There must be proper follow through after the contest to assure that all winners receive their prizes.

Contests, probably more than any other compensation plan, tend to be abused. They cannot be used too frequently because representatives will regard them as a regular part of their income. Furthermore, they do not solve basic long-term sales management problems, and when used as such become demotivators. Representatives tend to reply with, "Yes, but what have you done for me lately?"

PROBLEMS DURING INFLATION

Inflation can have various impacts on representatives according to the compensation plan under which they operate. If their compensation is based on a percent of total sales, and if the price of the product increases at or above the rate of inflation, there is no problem: the representative receives an automatic increase as prices increase. If, on the other hand, the commission is based on a gross margin and the cost of manufacturing the product increases at a greater rate than its price, then the representative receives a reduction in pay as costs increase. Similarly, salaries and bonuses must be adjusted to keep representatives' salaries competitive so as to maintain their loyalty and services.

Inflation can have a greater impact on the younger representatives who have a smaller income. For this reason, many companies are reexamining their compensation packages and giving a greater percentage increase to the younger staff members and rippling increases of lesser amounts through the rest of the sales force. This solution to the inflation problem is based on the assumption that younger representatives will have greater financial needs than older representatives who have established their homes.

EXPENSE PLANS

The basic philosophy of an expense plan for representatives is that it should not be regarded as a source of income to the representative, but rather as an investment of corporate funds for the mutual benefit of the company and the representative.

An expense plan, like a compensation plan, needs to be fair to all parties. It should not discourage a representative from making a distant call on a potential account or buying a customer's lunch. Conversely, it should not encourage the representative to cheat on the expense account because this may have tax advantages for the representative and the company. (The representative would not pay income taxes and the company would not pay social security taxes.) Fairness also requires prompt payment of expenses when the representative used his or her own funds and did not receive an advance or the use of a company credit card.

Most companies have policies for reimbursing expenses beyond those personal expenses, such as laundry, that were incurred while on company business. The least controversial expenses are transportation (automobile, taxis, and airfare) and communications (telephone, postage, etc.). The controversial expenses include personal ones such as laundry, cleaning, telephone calls home while on the road, entertainment of clients, and gifts.

Methods of paying expenses range from unlimited expense plans to no reimbursement. There might be no reimbursement plans when a representative is paid a commission and required to pay his or her own expenses out of total commissions. In such cases, there is a strong incentive for reducing expenses. Between these two extremes there is a wide variety of expense plans that are based on per diems, quotas, and percentages of sales. These expense plans must be frequently negotiated with representatives to adjust for variations in territories.

Automobile expenses present a particularly complex problem for general sales managers. Should the representatives be reimbursed for using their own automobiles or should the company supply them? If the company supplies them, what should be the arrangement for the representative to use the automobile for private use? If the company supplies an automobile, should this be part of the incentive system? Perhaps senior representatives are given a more prestigious car.

Before a new expense plan is implemented, it should be tested. This test should follow steps similar to those that are used when testing a new compensation plan. At first, the expense plan should be tested on historical data, and then by using feedback from various levels of the field managers, and finally from the representatives themselves. There should also be a program for implementing a change in an expense plan that is similar to the program for introducing a new compensation plan.

THE GENERAL SALES MANAGER'S ROLE IN COMPENSATION

The general sales manager plays a critical role in developing and monitoring compensation plans. He or she must anticipate competitive and market conditions that will necessitate changes in these plans to assure the effectiveness of the present sales force and the continuous flow of new recruits. The general sales manager will want to develop a method for continuously monitoring salary and incentive systems within the industry to avoid any sudden raiding of star representatives. It will be necessary to anticipate the effect of new product introductions, product discontinuances, and major market disruptions on compensation. The general manager will also monitor the field sales managers' equitable implementation of incentive programs and expense plans.

The general manager must also develop and monitor compensation and expense plans for field sales managers. These expense and compensation plans must be translated into a sales budget that becomes an important part of the corporate budget. (See Chapter 17.) The general sales manager must report to higher management any great variations that are anticipated in the selling budget.

The field manager is concerned largely with implementing the compensation plan, but he or she should make recommendations for changes and report special problems, such as competitors' compensation plans or unusual expenses in local living costs.

SUMMARY

Compensation programs begin with an identification of the corporate and representatives' needs. The corporate needs should have been identified in the marketing plan and selling plan. The representatives' needs should have been identified as part of the motivation activities.

There are many prerequisites to the development of a good compensation plan. Selling objectives must be defined clearly. The job description and performance appraisal steps must have been completed. Good management practice in recruiting, selecting, training, motivating, and controlling must be in place because a compensation plan cannot correct long-term weaknesses in any of these areas.

A compensation plan should allow for various grades of representatives, such as trainees, senior representatives, and representatives who have been assigned to special tasks. The next step is to determine that portion of the compensation that should be assigned to an incentive system. The most commonly used incentive systems are commissions, bonuses, and contests. After the plan has been developed, it should be pretested using, first, historical data and then input from field sales managers and representatives. Finally, a program for implementation and evaluation needs to be developed to gain the full support of the sales force.

Expense plans attempt to reimburse representatives for expenses that were incurred for the benefit of the company and the representative. These expense plans include systems in which the company pays all expenses, expenses up to fixed limits, or pays no expenses. In the latter case, the representative is generally on a commission-only plan.

The role of the general sales manager in the development and implementation of compensation and expense plans is a continuous one. It is necessary to make certain that the company plans are on a parity with other companies in the industry to avoid difficulties in recruiting and high turnover. The general sales manager must also develop and monitor compensation and expense plans for field sales managers, and their equitable administration of such plans for their representatives.

ASSIGNMENTS/DISCUSSION QUESTIONS

1. Discuss the seemingly contradictory definitions of "incentives" and "compensation" in the reward systems used for field sales representatives, and indicate why you believe one is more accurate.

2. If a company has 500 field staff members and provides benefits that add an additional 25 percent to the total compensation package, and that company contemplates increasing salaries $100 per month, how much must be added to the budget to cover these costs?

3. Of a compensation plan comprised of salary and incentive bonus, what percentage of the total compensation should the incentive bonus consist of? Why?

4. Discuss the pros and cons of a special cost-of-living allowance for areas with a high cost of living.

5. Should the salary ranges (not the actual salaries of individuals) for all field sales staff positions be published? Why?

6. Why is compensation in its various forms considered to be a short-term motivator?

7. For what reasons would a sales representative consider a compensation plan based on dollar sales as unfair?

8. Why does an increase in the incentive bonus portion of a sales representative's total compensation increase the need for closer supervision of nonselling activities (e.g., collections, reports, etc.)?

9. Design an incentive bonus plan, based on achieving quota, that will reward or penalize all sales representatives.

10. What criteria can be used variably on which to base an incentive bonus?

11. What are the advantages and disadvantages of contests featuring prizes appealing to the family?

12. What is the effect on compensation during periods of inflation of giving greater percentage increases to the younger staff members and rippling increases in lesser amounts through the rest of the staff?

CASE 21.1:
Vanguard Business Systems, Inc.

In May 1981, Vanguard Business Systems, Inc., was enjoying the rapidly expanded international demand for products in its field. Small computers, word-processing equipment, and communications hardware and software orders enabled the company to double its sales of $80 million in less than four years. Along with the increase in sales, its field sales staff and internal support systems just less than doubled. With new entries into the market, competition had intensified, but the sales forecasts for the next several years looked particularly strong—primarily because of Vanguard's commitment to research and development and the new products that were on stream.

That was the bright side of the responsibilities of Stan Lewis, Vanguard's Vice President and General Sales Manager. The most troublesome flaw at this time was the availability of good field sales representatives and sales engineers. The company's compensation plan and benefits package were at a generally above-average level, and the company's growth rate and policy of promotion from within offered predictable rewards to career-oriented employees. The problem was self-generated in that the company's success created a continuing need for qualified personnel. Since Vanguard's major competitors were also expanding, recruiting was an industry-wide problem and pirating of the best producers gradually appeared, along with leap-frog increases of starting salaries for inexperienced trainees and premiums for experience. As the salary increases of the existing field staff did not keep pace with the premiums for experienced new hires, a compression of the top and bottom salaries gradually occurred, compounded by an inflation rate of approximately 11 percent.

More and more correspondence from the field sales managers and more manager's conference time dealt with complaints from experienced Vanguard sales representatives that, in the light of the new starting salaries, their salaries did not reflect their experience. Additionally, there were the complaints that seniority meant little because new representatives with experience were being hired at about the same level as the existing staff with the same length of experience. The most frequent complaint at the time of last year's merit salary review, when the general increase was 12 percent, was that it was only slightly ahead of the inflation rate and, in some cases, they actually lost ground. Because there were no easy answers to these recurring problems, resignations occasionally resulted, thus intensifying the recruiting problem.

Stan Lewis's compensation problems were further complicated by the replies from his field sales managers to a recent industry survey sent out by the Wage & Salary Administrator, Tim Landers, showing that Vanguard's average salary for the field staff was equal to the industry level, but that the starting salary was about $150 per month under the average. The responses from the vast majority of field sales managers agreed with those findings and one-third gave examples of a promising candidate whom they had recently lost to a competitor with a higher starting salary.

As a result of the survey and the comments of the field managers, Mr. Lewis appointed a special committee comprised of the Sales Administration Manager, the Wage & Salary Coordinator, the Personnel Manager, and himself to examine alternative ways to implement an increase in the company's starting salary for the field staff. That an increase had to occur was accepted, but the question was: How much and what adjustment, if any, would be made in the salaries of the existing staff?

As in past years, because of the continuing inflation, an increase of $100 per month in the starting salary had been budgeted, along with a pool equal to $50 per month for the existing staff of 390 sales representatives and sales engineers, 42 district sales managers, and 7 regional sales managers, though this was not always spent. To obtain a larger amount would require approval of the Board of Directors along with a strong set of reasons.

The salary range at Vanguard was currently set at $14,400 to $33,600 for sales representatives and sales engineers; $21,600 to $43,200 for district sales managers, and $26,400 to $54,000 for regional sales managers. Grouped in brackets of 10 percent of the salary range (deciles) from the minimum up, the distribution of field sales staff members was as follows:

SALES REPRESENTATIVES AND SALES ENGINEERS		DISTRICT SALES MANAGERS		REGIONAL SALES MANAGERS	
Actual Salaries	Number Reps	Actual Salaries	Number DSMs	Actual Salaries	Number RSMs
$14,400 to $16,319	75	$21,600 to $23,759	0	$26,400 to $29,159	0
16,320 to 18,239	35	23,760 to 25,919	1	29,160 to 31,919	0
18,240 to 20,159	45	25,920 to 28,079	1	31,920 to 34,679	1
20,160 to 22,079	75	28,080 to 30,239	3	34,680 to 37,439	1
22,080 to 23,999	65	30,240 to 32,399	6	37,440 to 40,199	1
24,000 to 25,919	35	32,400 to 34,559	11	40,200 to 42,959	3
25,920 to 27,839	30	34,560 to 36,719	10	42,960 to 45,719	1
27,840 to 29,759	20	36,720 to 38,879	8	45,720 to 48,479	0
29,760 to 31,679	8	38,880 to 41,039	1	48,480 to 51,239	0
31,680 to 33,600	2	41,040 to 43,200	1	51,240 to 54,000	0
	390		42		7

After considerable deliberation, the special committee considered four alternatives before agreeing unanimously on their decision:

1. Increase the starting salary for sales representatives and sales engineers by $100 per month as budgeted, and increase the salaries of all existing field sales staff by $50 per month;

OR

2. Increase all salaries, including the starting salary for the field sales staff, by $100 per month, across the board, and ask the Board for the extra funds;

OR

3. Increase the starting salary for sales reps and sales engineers by $100 per month, and in some variable amount starting with $100 per month for those sales reps and sales engineers receiving less than 50 percent of the maximum in their pay grade;

OR

4. Increase the salary for sales reps and sales engineers by $150 per month and in some variable amount starting with $150 per month for the entire field sales staff.

CASE QUESTIONS

1. What is the problem and its cause?

2. How do turnover, continuing recruiting, and pirating of higher producers influence the salary level for the Vanguard representatives?

3. If Vanguard had no turnover and hired no new reps, what would the cost of additional salary increases of Alternatives #1, #2, #3, and #4 be for the next fiscal year?

4. If Vanguard added thirty-six new representatives evenly throughout the next fiscal year, had no turnover of their existing staff, and calculated the Vanguard Benefits Package (life insurance, hospitalization, dental plan, education reimbursement plan, etc.) as an additional 37 percent of salaries, what would be the total amount that would have to be budgeted for the additional sales reps, using the existing starting salary plus a $100 per month increase?

5. What are the relative advantages and disadvantages of each alternative in Question #3, and which would you support if you were Stan Lewis?

6. What should Vanguard's wage and salary policy be for field sales reps and sales engineers?

7. How can a District Sales Manager answer an experienced rep who complains that in the light of the new starting salaries, his or her salary does not reflect his or her length of experience?

8. Should sales reps with experience be hired at the same average salary level as existing reps with the same length of experience? Why?

9. How can a District Sales Manager answer a sales rep who states that his or her percentage salary increase was only slightly ahead of (or even with, or behind) the increase in the cost of living?

REFERENCES

1. Frederick E. Webster, Jr., "Rationalizing Salesmen's Compensation Plans," *Journal of Marketing* 30, no. 1 (January 1966): 55–58.
2. Roger M. Peterson, "Sales Compensation Seminar," Seminar Sponsored by Drug Distribution Data, New Orleans, March 1980.
3. This paragraph is based on "Compensating the Field Sales Manager," *Sales & Marketing Management* (February 19, 1973): 21–24.
4. "New Approaches in Compensating the Field Sales Manager," *Sales Management* (March 5, 1973): 35–37.
5. Peterson, "Sales Compensation Seminar," p. 12; J. P. Steinbrink, "How to Pay Your Sales Force," *Harvard Business Review* (July–August 1978): 111–122.
6. "Managers on Compensation Plans," *Sales & Marketing Management* (November 12, 1979): 41–43.

7. Ibid.

8. V. Srinivasan, "An Investigation of the Equal Commission Rate Policy for a Multi-Product Salesforce," *Management Science* 27, no. 7 (July 1981): 731–756.

9. J. U. Farley, "An Optimal Plan for Salesman Compensation," *Journal of Marketing Research* 1 (1964): 39–43.

10. J. U. Farley and C. B. Weinberg, "Inferential Optimization: An Algorithm for Determining Optimal Sales Commissions in Multiproduct Sales Forces," *Operations Research Quarterly,* 26, no. 2 (1975): 413–418.

11. Charles B. Weinberg, "Jointly Optimal Sales Commissions for Nonincome Maximizing Sales Forces," *Management Science* 24, no. 12 (August 1978): 1252–1258.

12. P. R. Stephenson, W. L. Cron, and G. L. Frazier, "Delegating Pricing Authority to the Sales Force: The Effects on Sales and Profit Performance," *Journal of Marketing* 43 (Spring 1979): 21–28.

13. "Managers on Compensation Plans," p. 42.

SUGGESTED READINGS

Barry, John, and Porter, Henry, *Effective Sales Incentive Compensation* (New York, McGraw-Hill, 1980).

Darmon, R. Y., "Setting Sales Quotas with Conjoint Analysis," *Journal of Marketing Research* 16 (Feburary 1979): 133–140.

Darmon, R. Y., "Alternative Models of Salesmen's Response to Financial Incentives," *Operations Research Quarterly* 28 (1977): 37–49.

Darmon, R. Y., "Salesmen's Response to Financial Incentives: An Empirical Study," *Journal of Marketing Research* 11 (November 1974): 418–426.

Futrell, C. M., and Jenkins, O. C., "Pay Secrecy versus Pay Disclosure for Salesmen: A Longitudinal Study," *Journal of Marketing Research* 15 (May 1978): 214–219.

Gonik, Jacob, "Tie Salesmen's Bonuses to Their Forecasts," *Harvard Business Review* (May/June 1978): 116–123.

Greer, W. R., Jr., "Sales Compensation: Conflict and Harmony," *Management Accounting* 55, no. 9 (March 1974): 37–41.

Nagle, Thomas, "Pricing by the Sales Force: Resolving the Discrepancy Between Theory and Data," Working Paper, University of Chicago, April, 1980.

"Sales Force Compensation," *Sales & Marketing Management,* Special Report, August 23, 1976.

Scanlon, Sally, "Incentive Game Plan," *Sales & Marketing Management* (April 7, 1980): 56–76.

Scanlon, Sally, "Who's Keeping Score on Incentive Results?" *Sales & Marketing Management* (September 1978): 63–65.

Winer, Leon, "A Sales Compensation Plan for Maximum Motivation," *Industrial Marketing Management* 5, no. 1 (March 1976): 29–36.

Winer, Leon, "The Effect of Product Sales Ouotas on Sales Force Productivity," *Journal of Marketing Research* 10 (May 1973): 180–183.

Welks, D. A., *Compensating Salesmen and Sales Executives* (New York: Conference Board, 1972, Report 579).

22

THE CHANGING ENVIRONMENT OF SALES MANAGEMENT

OVERVIEW

The decade of the 1980s will see many demographic and economic changes in the population that will have important implications for sales management. There will be greater racial and ethnic pluralism. There will also be rapid growth in two segments of the population: the very young and the elderly. The trends of the 1970s regarding changing social structure, particularly in the family, and personal values will continue through the 1980s. These changes will have predictable effects on the composition of the work force. Changes in the level of family income and the distribution of income will have important marketing and sales management implications.

CHARACTERISTICS OF THE UNITED STATES' POPULATION[1]

RACIAL AND ETHNIC PLURALISM

By 1990, more than one out of every five Americans will be Hispanic, black, or a member of another racial minority. It is quite possible that considerable market potential is not being realized by marketers because they fail to contact these minority market segments in terms of their own culture and language and through their media. These minority markets can be segmented further. For instance, the Hispanic market breaks down into Puerto Rican, Mexican, Cuban, and "other," each with different age and income distributions. The black market seems to be fragmenting into political segments that are liberal or conservative.[2]

AGE DISTRIBUTION

The most startling characteristic of the population for the decade of the eighties is the aging of the population. Senior citizens are on the verge of outnumbering teenagers. While the total population will increase during the next decade at the rate of slightly less than 10 percent, the number of teenagers will decrease 17 percent, persons over 65 will increase 20 percent, young adults (20–34) will increase only 3 percent, while the middle-age group (34–54) will increase 28 percent. The college market age group (18–24) will decline by 3.8 million persons, or 13 percent.

These shifts in the age distribution of the population can have important marketing implications. For example, one textbook publisher is becoming more selective in the books that it publishes. Manufacturers are developing products for the older market. For instance, "Wrinkles Away," a product to remove wrinkles temporarily, was positioned for the older market segment. Wilson Sporting Goods developed new golf clubs for the middle-aged golfer that will help him or her get the ball into the air faster. Recreational travel is a large budget item for the "over-49" segment, a fact well known to recreational vehicle manufacturers. Wild Strawberries, a restaurant chain in California, developed a menu with no salt, heavy sauces, or hard liquor for the market target of middle-aged business executives trying to lose weight. The aging population is having its impact on the demands for housing. The older group wants townhouses with lots of gadgets, formal dining rooms, and large living rooms to facilitate entertaining.

Marketers are discovering that this "graying market" has a green lining and that it is willing to spend for itself, rather than leave it to offspring.

A population with a very large number of elderly and a very large number of young persons can create an intergenerational conflict that has important social and political implications. Such conflicts have been seen in Broward County, Florida, where the old-to-young ratio reflects the 1995 demographic projections for the nation. The elderly demand social services, while the younger demand education, thereby putting strain on public funds.

Because many states have increased or removed entirely the upper mandatory retirement age, sales managers can no longer depend on retirement to solve the problem of an older representative whose performance is deficient. The manager must now choose between retraining and terminating the older representative. Either alternative is difficult. The success rate of retraining is low and termination would be traumatic to the employee, the manager, the company, and society.

The aging of the United States' population can have international implications as it deals with young populations in Latin America, Africa, and Asia. Youthful demands for immediate results can strain diplomatic relations. There may also be pressure toward the United States to increase immigration, thereby affecting the composition of the labor force.

POSTWAR BABY BOOM

The persons born between 1946 and 1964 have been labeled the baby boom. This boom was the result of delayed family formation until the end of World War II and a subsequent birth rate of 3.7 children per woman, unprecedented in western society. This birth rate seemed to be the result of changes in attitudes toward family size and a period of great economic growth. The crest of this boom has moved through the various age groups and placed considerable stress on public institutions as it passed through. We saw the overwhelmed secondary schools in the late 1950s, the unrest on college campuses in the 1960s, the large unemployment rates among young adults in the 1970s. We saw a new youth culture that greatly affected clothing, automobiles, life styles, and sexual values. This group gathered considerable political power because of its large proportion of the population. In the coming decade, as this group moves into the middle-age classification, the phrase "don't trust anyone over 30" may be changed to "don't trust anyone under 40." As this baby boom moves into the family formation stage, the stress periods of life and the demand for housing, social services, and schooling will place considerable demands on federal, state, and local treasuries.

On the positive side, productivity should increase in the 1980s as the baby boom moves solidly into the work force, as may be seen in Exhibit 22.1. As it moves into the family formation stage, it will generate demands for housing, baby cribs, diapers, and piano lessons.

A SECOND BABY BOOM

In 1980, the birth rate had dropped to 1.8 babies per woman, one-half the rate during the previous baby boom, but the decade of the eighties may see another baby boom for two reasons. First, the earlier baby boom is now in the family formation stage. Second, many women who chose a career first are now planning families. By the mid-1980s, we may see as many as four million babies born per year. It is hoped that business and public institutions will be better equipped to handle this boom than they were a generation ago.

Exhibit 22.1 Distribution of the Population, By Age and Sex: July 1, 1979

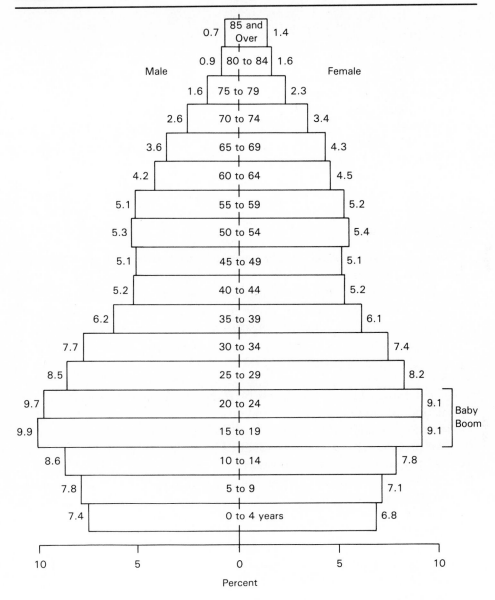

Source: "Social and Economic Characteristics of Americans During Midlife," *Current Population Reports,* Special Studies, Series P-23, No. 11, June 1981, p. 2.

GEOGRAPHIC DISTRIBUTION

The geographic shift in the U.S. population was from the frostbelt to the sunbelt. While the growth rate for the entire population was 11.4 percent between 1970 and 1980, the rates for the colder regions were as follows: New England, 4.2 percent, Mideast, −0.5 percent; Great Lakes, 3.5 percent, and Plains, 5.2 percent. In contrast, the warmer regions were as follows: Southeast, 20.1 percent, Southwest, 28.5 percent, Rocky Mountain, 30.8 percent, and Far West, 20.6 percent. The migration patterns are being determined by where people want to live, rather than where the jobs are.[3] Of course, sales managers will want to examine the growth rates for specific states, counties, and territories before reallocating personal selling resources.

FAMILY COMPOSITION

The composition of the family has gone through many changes during the 1970s and this trend is likely to continue during the 1980s. The important changes that have occurred include the number of households, the average size of the household, the number of single-parent householders, and the number of households that are headed by women.

NUMBER OF FAMILIES

The number of households grew by 25 percent during the 1970s, but the number of persons per household declined sharply. For the first time in the nation's history, over half of all households consist of only one or two persons. This decline is explained by social events, such as children leaving parents earlier, the postponement of marriage and child bearing, divorce, delays in remarriage, cohabitation, sole survivors due to increased life span, and the elderly maintaining their homes after retirement and not moving in with the children, as was the case in previous generations.

COMPOSITION OF FAMILIES

The composition of family units will change dramatically. *Nonfamily* units will expand by 9.8 million, reflecting independence and experimentation with alternative living arrangements. *Family* households will increase by 10.9 million, and will be composed of 4.3 million one-spouse families and 6.5 million two-spouse families. Family and nonfamily household types that are headed by a female will increase by 4.5 million.

CHANGES IN THE LABOR FORCE

The composition of the labor force is going through many changes, including the increase of women in the labor force, changes in the characteristics of the jobs, and the effects of higher levels of education.

WOMEN IN THE LABOR FORCE

The percent of women in the labor force increased from 31 percent in 1950 to 51 percent in 1980. Of the 23 million working women, 16.1 million have children under 18 years of age and 6 million have children under age 6. Many of these women are the sole support of the family. Others are attempting to maintain the family consumption pattern during periods of high inflation and the cost of children in college. These families become candidates for labor-saving and time-saving devices, such as microwave ovens and food processors, as the very busy family members share in the household tasks.

Traditionally, women have assumed the primary caretaking role for children and elderly family members. With this change in the composition of the work force, we must now establish other support systems.

SHIFT FROM BRAWN TO BRAINS

White collar jobs will grow at a rate 14 percent higher than the general rate, according to the Bureau of Labor Statistics. However, the better jobs, such as professional, technical, managerial, and administrative, are likely to increase at a rate 6 percent slower than all other jobs. There may be a surplus of college graduates during the early part of the 1980s. About one of four college graduates entering the labor market settles for a job traditionally filled by someone without a college degree. The growth will be in the service industries, especially information and communication industries, rather than in manufacturing.

To the extent that overtraining occurs for some jobs, employee dissatisfaction and frustration may result, presenting managers with additional challenges for job enrichment and motivation. The filling of jobs with overqualified persons may make it increasingly difficult for disadvantaged groups to climb the economic ladder.

ECONOMIC CHANGES

ATTITUDES TOWARD PRODUCTIVITY

The slower growth rate in Gross National Product in the United States has been explained in part by some observers as Americans' desire for additional leisure, less pressured jobs, and a higher quality of life. They have also sought a cleaner environment where it meant a tradeoff with lower productivity.

CONSUMPTION PATTERNS

The Gross National Product growth rate of the 1960s was not maintained during the 1970s, but the consumption rate per person was almost maintained through a reduction in household savings rates and second incomes provided by working wives. There is some question about how long consumption rates can be maintained through these two mechanisms.

Inflation and anti-inflation policies create considerable economic uncertainties in the marketplace. The cost of inflation falls most heavily on those with fixed incomes, investors, and savers, especially small savers. Anti-inflation policies, however, may place a cost on a quite different group—investors in cyclical industries, the unemployed, and the communities where these groups live.

Many couples are sharing working through dual careers, and even more are sharing the decision process for spending. A survey revealed that 72 percent of the couples reported that they shared the spending decisions. This means that marketers must promote to husbands and wives.[4]

CHANGING PERSONAL VALUES

The decade of the 1970s was a period of changing and fragmenting personal values. There was a decline in the trust of traditional institutions of all types, including government, universities, churches, and business. Some of the college student radicalism of the 1960s turned toward conservative values during the late 1970s with preppie clothing replacing blue jeans, a desire to rise within professions, and goals of earning money. The value structures of teenagers and young adults suggest that they are more experimental and must experience events for themselves.

MULTIPLE GOALS AND FRAGMENTED POLITICAL SYSTEMS

One pattern that is emerging is that sections of society have clear and definite value structures that seek political response. As a result, the political system has become fragmented, responding to single issues and pressure groups. These multiple goals and fragmented political approaches raise questions about the long-term best interests of society. Conger argues that the present social systems are incapable of solving problems like poverty, interracial accord, reducing crime, and overcoming addiction. He concludes that more social inventions are needed to solve these problems. He regards marriage, religion, cities, schools, democracy, trade unions, and "sit-ins" as social inventions.[5]

SALES MANAGEMENT IMPLICATIONS

The changing environment for sales management will greatly alter the way sales management is practiced in the coming decade. Population changes will change the type of goods and services that are demanded. There will be considerable changes in how sales management is practiced.

SHIFTS IN GEOGRAPHIC DISTRIBUTION OF POPULATION

Shifts in the geographic distribution of the population require the continuous evaluation of the degree of coverage of the new market potential and the revision of territory assignments. Many companies are combining territories in the northeast and giving them to a single representative while they are dividing territories in the sunbelt, adding representatives, and creating new districts.

    The cost of living and operating territories is frequently higher in the areas with a high growth rate. Some industries have found it necessary to have cost-of-living salary adjustments for representatives in these high-growth areas.

    These shifts in population have also influenced changes in policies regarding transfers. Representatives are now encouraged to request transfers to new markets. This transfer policy has increased the budgets that are associated with transferring employees. Traditional budget items included visits to the new community, moving expenses, and motel expenses for the first week or so. Lately, many companies have been assisting transferred employees by subsidizing their mortgage payments, because of the greatly increased interest rates.

CHANGES IN FAMILY COMPOSITION

The great increase in the number of smaller households can have a great impact on all industries selling to households. For example, the demand for housing will shift to smaller homes, condominiums, and apartments. The demand for furniture will be to more but smaller units. Kitchen appliances will reflect time-saving devices, such as food processors and microwave ovens. Food manufacturers will see a shift in demand from large family-sized to smaller-sized packages. Automobile manufacturers will experience a demand for fewer station wagons and smaller, more fuel efficient, and more personal automobiles.

THE DYNAMICS OF THE LABOR FORCE

The aging of the labor force and the increasing number of women in the labor force are greatly altering the practice of sales management. Older representatives who "retire on the job" cannot be forced to retire at age sixty-five. They may be less motivated by money than younger representatives. Thus managers must find new ways to retrain and motivate them. Dual-income families may also be less motivated by monetary incentives. Dual-income families also face difficult decisions when one spouse receives a promotion that requires a transfer. Two cases at the end of this chapter deal with the problems of the aging representative and the dual-career couple who must evaluate a transfer.

A large number of women are moving into personal selling because it does not require brawn and it rewards effective communication. Objections such as, "Customers will not accept them," "They will not get along with men in the organization," or "They cannot do the job" have not proven to be valid. In earlier chapters, however, we have noted that women representatives may require different methods for recruiting and selecting (Chapter 9) and for orienting and training (Chapter 10).

The mobility of society may reduce loyalty to a company. More recent trends reveal a reluctance or refusal to relocate when offered a promotion, not only because of the cost of relocation and possible differences in cost of living, but because of current satisfaction with housing, schools, friends, etc. The long-term consequences of a decision to turn down a promotion for reasons such as these have yet to be experienced.

The rapidly changing technology and changes in the make-up of the labor force will require new and continuous training of representatives and managers. This high mobility and technological change will lead to many persons having two or three careers between college and retirement. For some individuals, these career changes can be exciting, while for others they are traumatic. Sales managers will need to develop orientation, training, and development programs for older representatives who bring a variety of experiences to selling. This will be at least different and possibly a more difficult task than training new college graduates.

The growing number of dual-career couples provides sales managers with a growing challenge because mobility has been central to gaining experience and promotion in sales management. Hence, the mobility of the spouse is becoming an important consideration for the representative when career opportunities are evaluated. Divergent careers can strain a relationship. Couples have taken many alternatives, such as accepting the promotion and the spouse quitting his or her job, the promoted spouse moving and returning to the home base on weekends, turning down the promotion, negotiating with the company to find the spouse a job in the new area, negotiating with the spouse's company for a transfer to the same area, and divorce. The presence of children raises questions about schooling and friends.

Regardless of the final decision, there will be strains, gains, and losses for all parties. The decision will signal whose career will dominate. The net financial impact could be negative. There will be social and psychological costs, as well as benefits. The decision may have an effect on the job performance of one or even both spouses.

Some couples are using decision theory (Chapter 14) for such personal decisions. For example, they may identify the attributes of the living and work environments that are important to them. Then they will evaluate each alternative in terms of these attributes. Perhaps they will decide to score them on a scale from -5 to $+5$. The next step would be to estimate the probability of the event occurring. The expected value of each attribute may be computed. Finally, the expected values for each alternative are totaled.[6]

A couple's decision model might appear as Exhibit 22.2. This decision analysis suggests that the choice is not clear. The couple will need to gather additional information on the attributes for the transfer to improve the low probability estimates. Thus the couple is really performing a sensitivity analysis for a personal decision.

Exhibit 22.2 A Couple's Transfer Decision Model

Attribute	REJECT TRANSFER			ACCEPT TRANSFER		
	Value	× Prob.	= Expected Value	Value	× Prob.	= Expected Value
Housing and living environment	3	1.0	3.0	5	0.6	3.0
A better job (now or in future)	4	0.7	2.8	5	1.0	5.0
Spouse job	5	1.0	5.0	3	0.4	1.2
School system	−1	1.0	−1.0	1	0.4	0.4
Total expected values			9.8			9.6

Adapted from Francine S. Hall and Douglas T. Hall, *The Two-Career Couple* (Reading, Mass.: Addison-Wesley, 1979), p. 195.

CHANGING PERSONAL VALUES

Changing personal values can affect the demand for goods and services, and the worklife in which they are created. Youthful values that stress immediate personal experience when translated into retailing may mean that they demand a wide selection of quality merchandise attractively displayed to encourage their experimental and experiential desires. The young seek the promise of personal growth and personal competence, which may increase their demand for travel, sports equipment, books, cooking equipment, wines, and hobby products, such as cameras. They seek immediate gratification for desires, which, in retailing, means items must be in stock, credit must be readily available, travel agents must make arrangements immediately, and this group has an aversion to saving.

The role of an individual in the work force is changing from an extension of a machine to a complement to a machine. Exhibit 22.3 summarizes Trist's observations of organizational profiles when a work force moves from a management style of technological imperatives to joint optimization. The shift is toward recognizing the individual as an individual, collaboration, and innovation—points that have been stressed in this textbook as necessary for successful sales management.

CHANGING MANAGEMENT STYLES

Sales management styles are changing and will continue to change. Some changes are organizational in their origin because of growth, mergers, acquisition, or new designs, such as matrix organizational forms. The computer is making substantial impact on the design of organiza-

---

Exhibit 22.3   Quality of Worklife Shift in Values

FROM: TECHNOLOGICAL IMPERATIVE	TO: JOINT OPTIMIZATION
Man as an extension of the machine	Man as complementary to the machine
An expendable spare part	A resource to be developed
Task breakdown, single, narrow skills	Task grouping, multiple, broad skills
External controls (supervisor, etc.)	Internal controls (self-regulating)
Tall organizational chart: autocratic	Flat organizational chart: participative
Competition, gamesmanship	Collaboration, collegiality
Organization's purposes only	Members' and society's purposes also
Alienation	Commitment
Low risk-taking	Innovation

Reprinted with permission from *Portrait: The Network Builder*, by Warren Bennes, The Wharton Magazine © 1978, by the Wharton School of the University of Pennsylvania, Vol. II, No. 4.

tions, territory design, call allocation, routing, and strategic planning.[7] Some food marketers are equipping their representatives with hand-held computers for taking inventory in stores and sending orders via telephone directly to the computer that will ship and bill the products.[8]

Computer developments are part of the information revolution that is making the information industry the fastest growing sector of the U.S. economy. Not only will this revolution change the way that representatives and sales managers operate, it will also create a need for representatives and sales managers. By the year 2000, only 2 percent of the U.S. work force will work in agriculture, 22 percent will be in manufacturing, and 66 percent will be allied with information.[9] Molitor predicts that computers, like TV and radio, will be subject to abuse, which will lead to a wave of regulation related to computers. We have seen some attempts to prevent insurance company computers sharing information about applicants.[10]

Shifts in personal values are causing some managers to realize that old systems of motivation will not work. This places greater emphasis on a manager treating each representative as an individual and understanding his or her individual needs, as was discussed in Chapter 11. We saw in earlier chapters that representatives are more productive when they participate in developing the standards by which they will be evaluated. This is part of a general movement in the United States in which workers participate more in management. Some authors refer to this new style as "Theory Z," and refer to the successful application by the Japanese.[11] This theory increases involvement, purpose, and a sense of responsibility—all of which tended to be missing in other management styles. This style of management is particularly appropriate in selling, where the representative must frequently operate as a loner.

Educational patterns of sales management are changing. Previous patterns were that promotion was based on experience, not formal education. The complexity of the job is changing this mix, but not without problems. On the one hand, there are sales managers who have been promoted to positions for which they have inadequate training and for which retraining is not readily available (Chapter 19). On the other hand, some college graduates, especially MBAs, are anxious to be managers and do not want to take the time to gain the necessary minimum of experience in selling, account management, territory management, etc. Solutions to these twin problems will require better planning for the human needs of sales management. Alternatively, the value and need for sales management training is being recognized increasingly and implemented to identify and eliminate the unsatisfactory performer, to develop and to reward the above average producer, and to motivate increased productivity.

New matrix organizational designs may alter how some organizations buy. Buying influences may be greatly decentralized, thereby complicating the selling process for representatives.

The increased cost of a sales call has resulted in some companies shifting part of their selling effort to telephone selling. IBM uses a combination of newspaper advertising and telephone selling to sell typewriters because the profit margin can no longer justify repeated personal sales calls. We have shown in many points throughout the text how microcomputers can aid sales managers.

SUMMARY

The changing environment of sales management includes shifts in the age and location of the population, both of which will have profound effects on the demand for goods and services, and therefore on sales management decisions. The aging of the work force, the increasing number of salespeople, and the dual-career families create new challenges for sales managers in the areas of selecting, training, and motivating salespersons.

Technology has increased the complexity of products. Purchasing managers use economic analysis and value analysis when making decisions. Buyers are trained in negotiations skills. All of these trends raise the level of sophistication of selling so that the salesperson is a consultant and must manage his or her territory as a profit center. This new sophistication requires persons with analytical skills, as well as communication skills. Methods for selection and training must reflect these changes in the role of the saleperson.

Organizational changes, centralization of purchasing, and computerized inventory systems are changing the way large national companies are buying. Sales managers are adapting to these changes with new selling organizations, such as the creation of national account managers.

The explosion of knowledge and data, the speed of communications, and the reduced cost of computers will compound and confound the judgmental decision-making process of buyers and clients. This complexity will create opportunities for salespersons to be consultants. It will also require them to use the kinds of analytical methods and tools that are used by buyers.

Some observers predict that the increasing costs of selling, especially travel costs, will result in a relative reduction in the role of personal selling in the communication mix and a relative increase in the role of mass media, such as print, radio, and television. Other observers predict that an avalanche of mass communications will confuse buyers of complex equipment, thereby creating a need for a consulting salesperson who can distill information and make recommendations.

Sales management might be the organizational innovators in many companies with the introduction of open, collaborative organizational designs. These designs are being used increasingly in sales management to define salespersons' objectives and performance standards.

The complexity of the selling process and the new type of person who is needed in selling will require better methods of training, better management training, improved communications schemes, expanded coaching and counseling, and frequent performance appraisals. Appraisals are needed not only to resolve problems of deficient behavior, but also to recognize and reinforce positive behavior, thereby increasing the salesperson's commitment to the sales objectives.

In conclusion, sales management in the coming decade will be different from previous decades. For those persons who like challenges and can handle uncertainty, the changes will be exciting and rewarding.

ASSIGNMENTS/DISCUSSION QUESTIONS

1. What effect will computers have on the people management activities of sales management?

2. Identify and explain the principal management activities in Exhibit 2.1, Chapter 2, applicable to the problem of an older sales representative whose performance is deficient.

3. Specifically, what different "people management" activities listed in Exhibit 2.1, Chapter 2, will be called for in the management of a younger salesperson versus a mature or older salesperson?

4. In what area of the sales representative's job responsibilities could an increase in the number of single-parent households create a problem for a field sales manager?

5. Discuss the potential problems of a dual-career couple where both partners are employed as sales representatives by competing companies.

6. Discuss the potential advantages and disadvantages of a dual-career couple where both partners are employed as sales representatives by the same company.

7. Discuss the advantages and disadvantages to the individual and to the company of transferring the individual to a different territory because of shifting population.

8. What long-term consequences may be experienced by an individual who turns down a promotion that requires relocation?

9. What factors will influence whether the effects of high mobility and technological change, and two or three careers between college and retirement, will be exciting or traumatic?

10. Discuss the impact of joint optimization in Exhibit 22.3 on the motivation of a sales representative.

11. Why is the style of management referred to as Theory Z particularly appropriate to selling?

12. How might one solve the twin problems of (a) sales managers who have been promoted to positions for which they have been inadequately trained and for which training is not readily available, and (b) some college graduates, especially MBAs, who are anxious to be managers and do not want to take the time to gain the necessary minimum experience in selling, territory management, etc.?

CASE 22.1:
"What the Hell Do I Do?"

Pat and Sarah Hopkins first met in Economics 1-A during their sophomore year at Indiana State University. Pat had enrolled at ISU as a second-year student after a year at a junior college in his hometown of Evanston, Illinois. Sarah won a Regents scholarship from high school in Cincinnati. Two years later, they were married during their summer vacation. Neither, however, had much of a vacation at any time during college. Both worked at any type of employment that was available. Pat was a campus guide, a cook, and spent one summer selling Bibles in the South. Although Sarah's tuition was paid by her scholarship, she covered her other expenses by tutoring in math and doing freelance typing, and still found time to work on the college paper, serving as editor in her senior year. They graduated without difficulty four years ago, Pat with a B.S. in Business Administration, and Sarah with a B.A. in Economics.

Upon graduation, Pat joined Continental Electric Company as a sales representative in Atlanta. Sarah wasn't very enthusiastic about moving south, but they had agreed that they would live wherever Pat found a good selling job. Although Continental Electric marketed its products primarily east of the Mississippi at the time Pat joined the company, in the past three years, the company's expansion westward was proceeding on schedule. As a result, Pat's hopes soared when his District Sales Manager, Charlie Johnson, made an appointment for him to come by the office and "discuss his future." Pat's expectations were realized the next day when Mr. Johnson offered him the opportunity to take over the New Orleans district from John Stewart, who was being promoted to head the new regional headquarters in Kansas City. Pat was most enthusiastic in his immediate acceptance of the offer and reassured Mr. Johnson that he had worked hard for this opportunity and would make the most of it. Charlie Johnson was pleased with Pat's response, but suggested that perhaps he should talk it over with Sarah before giving his final answer. Mr. Johnson knew that although Sarah had not been anxious to move to Atlanta initially, she had told Charlie's wife at a recent company party that she really enjoyed living in Atlanta and that she found her job responsibilities very challenging.

During the first year after their move to Atlanta, Sarah had tried an assortment of temporary jobs, none of which utilized her talents, until she was hired by the Atlanta Computer Services Co. During her three years there, Mr. Bach made increasing use of Sarah's educational background and natural talents. As a result, Sarah was promoted twice with increasing administrative responsibilities. It was against this background that Mr. Johnson had quipped to Pat as he was about to leave the office, "Maybe you'll change your mind overnight because Sarah won't want to move—perhaps." Pat reassured him that there would be no problem because Sarah was as interested in his success as he was and they'd been married seven years now and understood one another and what was best for their future. He also related that Sarah had once told him it didn't matter where they lived as long as it was together. And, anyway, she'd now be able to quit working and raise a family. Pat and Mr. Johnson parted with the agreement that Pat would get back to him in the morning with a firm answer.

Pat's analysis of Sarah's reaction was wide of the mark. Although she was pleased for him, she had her own surprise. Her boss had offered her the job of managing the Data Processing Department at Atlanta Computer Services and she was equally as excited about her opportunity as Pat was about his. As she saw it, the extra college courses she took at night during the past several years had finally paid off and she was being given the chance to use her talents to their fullest. A move at this time was out of the question. "Why, I'd have to start all over at the bottom in a new company. Opportunities like this are few and far between." When Pat enumerated all the benefits that would go with his promotion, and the fact that Sarah could now afford to stop working and raise a family, Sarah brushed this aside by saying, "Why does the man's job always have to come first? And, anyway, we can have a family later."

> Their conversation continued without resolution long into the evening until finally, Pat summarized the situation by saying, "We both want our promotions, but there is no way we can have them. Someone is going to have to give in, but no matter who does, there's going to be resentment. I don't want this to drive a wedge between us, but what in the hell am I supposed to do?"

CASE QUESTIONS

1. What options are open to a dual-career couple or family faced with a transfer due to promotion of one of the spouses?

2. If a dual-career family is faced with a transfer due to promotion of one of the spouses, what factors should the couple consider in making their decision?

3. What, if any, responsibilities does a company have for offering financial remuneration for the loss of the spouse's income and career opportunities?

4. What are some of the things companies might offer to compensate for the spouse's loss of income and career opportunities?

5. Is it realistically possible to avoid disappointing one or both of the spouses of a dual-career couple or family faced with a transfer due to promotion of one of the spouses?

CASE 22.2:
MidWestern Appliance Distributors

Although it was a beautiful April day in St. Louis when Doug Santoro walked out of the office of Walter Gates, the general sales manager of Midwestern Appliance Distributors, Doug had some strong misgivings that he couldn't quite put into perspective. He knew that Mr. Gates was not an unreasonable or impulsive person, and he knew that Walter Gates was right in saying it was time to take some kind of action on John Rankin, but his gut reaction was that the situation was more complicated than it seemed. On the other hand, he knew that his six months' experience in management didn't qualify him to second-guess the general sales manager. Even before he was promoted to district sales manager, Doug was aware of John Rankin's problem, but he thought it was of a different nature. Walter Gates's summary of John's productivity caught Doug off guard, and he wasn't prepared to argue.

Doug and John Rankin had adjacent territories when Doug was a rep, and while John had not been involved in Doug's field training when he joined Midwestern Appliance four years ago, Doug later wondered why not, since Ken Chartmen, who trained him, certainly left something to be desired. Doug and John had lunch together now and then, and arranged to meet on more than one occasion when Doug had a sales problem about which he needed some help and didn't want to bother his DSM. John knew the answers. In addition to solving some of Doug's problems during their get-togethers, they discussed company activities in general, and Doug began to realize that for all practical purposes John was on his own. While John was a kindly gentleman who rarely was critical of anyone, it was clear that he was being ignored, and he resented it. As he put it, "After all the years I've put into this company, I think I deserve better treatment than this. When I started, we had only three sales reps and must have done less than 5 percent of what we sell today. I helped build this business!"

John Rankin, aged sixty-three, had been with Midwestern Appliance for twenty-eight years. This was his second job after leaving the Army in 1946, after World War II. He had completed one year of college before being drafted, and another year at night school after being discharged, but he never got a degree. He had married during the war, and had three youngsters, so most of his spare time he spent selling in order to support his young family.

On returning home from his visit with Mr. Gates, Doug reviewed John's evaluation reports for the last five years and found that, for the first three of those five years John generally made quota; but during the last two years things started to deteriorate. He made 80 percent of quota overall, with 95 percent on the older products and 60 percent on the new products. Although the evaluation reports were copied to John, they contained no comment by him. "John is a nice old guy and the customers love him," Walter Gates had said, "but we're losing too much business in his territory. We must do something and do it fast."

With those words ringing in his ears, Doug tried to sort out the alternative courses of action. He tried to recapture the essence of some of the conversations he and John had years back to identify when John's performance began to change and the possible causes, but to no avail. He also tried to recall some of the things he had learned in college some six years ago, but there didn't seem to be any ready answers. Something that kept coming up in his mind was a memorandum from the company president, Mr. Howell, that he'd received shortly after he was promoted. It was a confidential memorandum to all company managers, to which was attached a copy of a newspaper article about one of the appliance manufacturers whose line of products they distributed. The article had described a huge E.E.O.C. settlement that the appliance manufacturer had entered into with one of their employees, as a result of what was judged to have been an unfair practice in terminating the employee who was fifty-eight years of age, and thus in the forty- to, sixty-five-year-old protected age group. Mr. Howell's covering memorandum had reminded them that although Midwestern Appliance was a much smaller organization, the same fair employment practice laws applied to them, and that they should develop a heightened awareness of their responsibilities in this area.

Midwestern Appliance Distributors is a wholesaler for name brand appliances, such as washing machines, dryers, dishwashers, refrigerators, freezers, ranges, microwave ovens, hifi radios, television sets, and videotape recorders. Customers include appliance retailers, furniture dealers, and department stores. Headquartered in St. Louis, Midwestern covers a territory that includes the eastern half of Missouri, and parts of Iowa, Arkansas, Illinois, and Tennessee. The territory is covered by twenty-eight representatives and four district managers. The reps live in their territory, so they are rarely away at night.

Customers frequently regard the Midwestern rep as their consultant in the merchandising of appliances. The rep reports local trends in demand and competitive activities, and advises on products that will sell well at a particular store. The duties include training the customer's sales staff in the best techniques for selling Midwestern's products. The rep advises on advertising campaigns and suggests newspaper layouts featuring the Midwestern line. Midwestern has a cooperative advertising program, which the rep is expected to help the retailers use, to the advantage of both parties. In-store displays and window displays are also part of the rep's activities. Thus the Midwestern representative has many of the activities of a product manager, plus the responsibility for getting and servicing the sale.

Representatives are expected to maintain the productivity of their outlets. They are to evaluate the financial and management strengths and weaknesses of present dealers and potential new dealers. Their recommendations for dropping or adding a dealer are to be supported with a careful evaluation of a retailer. Many relationships have been built up over the years, and Midwestern does not want to treat this goodwill casually.

Representatives are paid a salary and a bonus that is based on quota. The salary is generally 70 percent of a representative's total compensation, except in the case of John Rankin, where it was 100 percent. This system went into effect about four years ago. All reasonable expenses are reimbursed. It is assumed that the compensation is adequate because few representatives have gone to competitors. Turnover is about three reps per year.

When Doug first worked with John, he had mixed reactions. John was well received by everyone in the store—the owner, the buyer, and the floor salespersons. He knew them all by name. To some, he seemed to be almost a father figure. Doug sometimes wondered who John worked for. During several discussions of company policy with regard to the return of unsold merchandise, John sided with the customer against the company. Generally, John's attitude toward Midwestern was positive.

John operates out of his home in Columbia, Missouri. He is very active in community affairs through his service organization and his church, and he recently headed the local United Fund drive. He plays tennis several times a week in the summer and vacations on a lake where he likes to sail. His three children have left the nest, and he would like to travel, but his wife's increasingly chronic and incapacitating illness keeps him near home. On a recent working trip, Doug and John briefly discussed John's wife's illness. John had said that because of the increasing expenses and the fact that it wasn't possible for her to travel, he was glad that Congress had enacted the changes in the retirement laws (Federal Age Discrimination in Employment Act, 1978), which would make it possible for him to continue to work until age seventy. He added that this would help pay the expenses and give him something to do.

CASE QUESTIONS

1. Identify and define the problems.

2. What are the potential causes for John Rankin's deteriorating performance?

3. What could Doug Santoro have done, possibly to have prevented John Rankin's problem from developing into the complex problem it now poses?

4. What are the duties and responsibilities of a Midwestern Appliance sales rep, and how is his or her performance evaluated?

5. What evidence is there to indicate John Rankin's performance potential?

6. What effect could John Rankin's potential have on his actual performance?

7. What were Walter Gates's instructions to Doug Santoro, and how could they be interpreted?

8. Should John Rankin be fired? Explain.

9. What are the chances of meeting Mr. Gates's deadline of "doing something fast"? Why?

10. What plan of action should Doug Santoro recommend to Walter Gates? How should he introduce it to Mr. Gates, and why is it necessary in this case to introduce it carefully?

11. What are the multiple benefits that could result from this action plan?

REFERENCES

1. Much of the discussion is based on articles in the current marketing literature, such as the following: "55+: A Gray Market with a Green Lining," *Sales & Marketing Management* (Feburary 5, 1976): 37; "Generational Justice," *Forbes* (Feburary 18, 1980); "Households: Growing Fast, and Shrinking Fast," *Sales & Marketing Management* (Feburary 5, 1979): 39; Fabian Linden, "Singular Spending Patterns," *Across the Board* (July 1979): 31–34; J. S. Lubin, "Marketers Discover Free-Spending Group: Affluent Middle-Aged," *Wall Street Journal* (April 16, 1979): 1, 22; *Sales & Marketing Management*'s annual "Survey of Buying Power" and its feature articles on population and economic trends can be very helpful in detecting important sales management environmental change. This chapter is also based on the *Current Population Reports* of the U.S. Census. (For details of these reports, see the Appendix of Chapter 17.)

2. "Hispanics: Markets within a Market," and "Blacks: A Market that's Beginning to Fragment," *Sales and Marketing Management* (July 27, 1981): 33–35.

3. T. C. Taylor, "Targeting Sales in a Changing Marketplace," *Sales & Marketing Management* (July 27, 1981): A-6–A-16.

4. Nancy Giges, "Study Follows Baby Boom Spenders," *Advertising Age* (May 11, 1981): 45.

5. D. S. Conger, "Social Inventions," *1999 The World of Tomorrow* (Washington, D.C.: World Future Society, 1978), pp. 139–148.

6. Adapted from Francine S. Hall, and Douglas T. Hall, *The Two-Career Couple* (Reading, Mass.: Addison-Wesley, 1979), p. 195.

7. J. M. Comer, "The Computer, Personal Selling, and Sales Management," *Journal of Marketing* 39 (July 1975): 27–35.

8. M. L. King, "Computer Age Quickens Pace of Salesman," *Wall Street Journal* (March 20, 1981): 27.

9. G. T. T. Molitor, "The Path to Post-Industrial Growth," *The Futurist* (April 1981): 23–30.

10. Ibid.

11. C. G. Burck, "Working Smarter," *Fortune* (June 15, 1981): 68–73; Jeremy Main, "Westinghouse's Cultural Revolution," *Fortune* (June 14, 1981): 74, 84–93.

SUGGESTED READINGS

Johnson, Barbara P., ''Women Marketers: Their Aspirations and Frustrations,'' *Product Marketing* 6 (January 1977): 17–22.

Howard, Niles, ''Sales Jobs Open Up for Women,'' *Dun's Review* (March 1978): 86–88.

Levine, Arthur, *When Dreams and Heroes Died: A Portrait of Today's College Students* (San Francisco: Jossey-Bass, 1980).

Robertson, Dan H., ''Saleswomen: Perceptions, Problems, and Prospects,'' *Journal of Marketing* 41 (July 1977): 66–71.

''Women in Selling: The Problems and the Promise,'' *RIA Marketing Alert* (New York: Research Institute of America, Inc., May 15, 1974).

V.

INTEGRATED
CASE

23

WESTMONT BUSINESS
FORMS, INC.*

At the end of December 1980, Drew Westmont, President of Westmont Business Forms, Inc., was examining the sales data for the year. He was wondering why his sales were flat, while the industry seemed to be growing. (See Exhibits 23.1, 23.2, and 23.3.)

THE BUSINESS FORMS INDUSTRY

The business forms industry supplies business with a variety of standard and custom forms, such as invoices, checks, computer continuous forms, and sales orders. It is characterized by many national and regional firms that sell directly and through independent distributors. Westmont Business Forms, Inc., is an Atlanta-based company that serves the Southeastern United States.

The business forms industry enjoyed a healthy growth during the period of the 1970s, with its highest growth rate between 1978 and 1980, reaching 11.7 percent per year. Due to alternatives such as CRT, computers, and high-speed printers, the rate after 1980 is expected to drop to 8.3 percent per year. The rate of profitability may not follow this growth in sales because a possible recession may increase competition and reduce margins. In the 1975 economic recession, many forms companies had large inventories of standardized forms and paper, which

*Written by Ms. M. V. Terryn Douglas under the direction of Professor G. David Hughes, University of North Carolina. The observations of Mr. Robert Wesley, Chairman, and Mr. Richard Wesley, President of Wesley Business Forms, Inc., are gratefully acknowledged. Cases are for classroom discussion and are not examples of good or poor management techniques.

Exhibit 23.1   Westmont Business Forms Co.
Income Statement 1979

SALES	6,320,000
Materials	2,281,520
Labor	2,009,760
Variable Factory Expenses	214,880
Costs of Goods Sold	4,506,160
GROSS PROFIT	1,813,840
Depreciation	347,600
Selling & Administrative Expenses*	1,068,712
	3,230,152
OPERATING PROFIT BEFORE TAXES AND INTEREST	397,528
Interest	632
NET PROFIT BEFORE TAXES	396,896

*Includes advertising, personal selling, market research, distribution, administrative, and R&D expenses

Exhibit 23.2   Westmont Business Forms Co.
Balance Sheet 1979

ASSETS	
Fixed Assets	$1,500,000
Cash Assets	270,000
Receivables	765,000
Inventory (LIFO)	891,000
Other	36,000
Total Assets	$3,462,000
EQUITY	
Accounts Payable	$ 234,000
Debt Due	72,000
Other	333,000
Current Liabilities	$ 639,000
Owners' Equity	2,823,000
Total Equity	3,462,000

turned out to be an advantage when there was a shortage of paper. They had lower inventories in 1980.

During 1979, the industry passed cost increases, averaging 11.5 percent, along to its customers as price increases. This strategy may not be possible in the future for several reasons. If there is a recession, customers may switch from the showy, customized forms, to stock forms that are very competitive and have a lower margin. Customers who have purchasing agents are tending to ask for bids, thereby reducing price and increasing the cost of getting a job.

Exhibit 23.3 Westmont Sales and Expense Percentages

	1981*	1980	1979	1978	1977	1976	1975	1974	1973	1972
SALES	$6.73	$7.16	$6.32	$6.17	$5.68	$5.62	$4.98	$5.30	$4.47	$3.74
VARIABLE COSTS:										
MATERIAL		36.6%	36.1%	36.4%	36.5%	36.6%	36.2%	35.8%	36.2%	36.6%
LABOR		32.0	31.8	31.9	32.3	32.5	32.1	31.5	32.0	32.5
VARIABLE FACTORY		3.4	3.4	3.4	3.5	3.6	3.5	3.4	3.5	3.7
TOTAL C.G.S.		72.0	71.3	71.7	72.3	72.7	71.8	70.7	71.7	72.8
MARKETING COSTS:										
ADVERTISING		1.5	1.3	1.5	1.6	1.7	1.5	1.4	1.6	1.8
PER. SELLING		5.5	5.5	5.5	5.5	5.5	5.5	5.5	5.5	5.5
MKT. RESEARCH		1.0	1.0	1.0	1.0	1.0	1.0	.9	1.1	1.2
DISTRIBUTION		2.0	2.0	2.0	2.0	2.4	2.0	2.2	2.1	2.2
TOTAL MKTING COSTS		10.0	9.8	10.0	10.1	10.6	10.0	10.0	10.3	10.7
TOTAL VARIABLE COSTS		82.0%	81.1%	81.7%	82.4%	83.3%	81.8%	80.7%	82.0%	83.5%
FIXED COST:										
ADMINISTRATIVE		7.0	7.0	7.0	7.0	7.5	7.5	7.5	7.5	7.5
DEPRECIATION		5.5	5.5	5.5	5.5	5.5	5.5	5.5	5.5	5.5
INTEREST		.01	.01	.01	.01	.01	.01	.01	.01	.01
R&D		.13	.11	.10	.18	.16	.13	.18	.16	.12
TOTAL FIXED COSTS		12.64%	12.62%	12.61%	12.69%	13.17%	13.14%	13.19%	13.17%	13.13%
PROFIT		5.36%	6.28%	5.69%	4.91%	3.53%	5.06%	6.11%	4.83%	3.37%

*estimated

It is not clear whether this trend toward bidding is the result of the recession or a continuing trend toward cost cutting.

Competition in the forms industry is strong and may become more so if bidding becomes an industry trend. There has also been a proliferation of small printers in the industry. Products are diverse, so competition depends more on what product lines are carried than on where one competes. Thus some companies compete on many levels, while others do not compete at all.

WESTMONT BUSINESS FORMS, INC.

Westmont Business Forms is a relatively small company for the forms industry, but competes successfully in the southeast. It is based in Atlanta, but sells from Virginia to Florida and westward to Alabama and Tennessee. At present, it has 144 employees, 7 of whom are sales representatives. Westmont has no plans for expansion that would increase company size. Its production facilities can handle a 30-percent expansion in present markets or the addition of new ones without an increase in labor power or equipment.

Westmont Business Forms was founded nearly a century ago by George S. Westmont. Since that time, it has had a reputation for producing top-quality forms and, thus, a somewhat expensive line. Westmont also tries to offer service of the highest standard. The company works with its customers in such a way that it has many longstanding customers, generally handled by the vice president.

Westmont carries standard forms in inventory and makes custom forms to customer specifications. Standard forms include sales and purchase orders, receiving reports, invoices, credit memos, reply message forms, bills of lading, delivery and packing tickets, repair order forms, requests for quotations, ledger cards, journals, labels, hospital bills, and mortgage loan sheets. Westmont imprints the customer's name on the blank form.

Custom forms may include special customized formats to reflect a customer's artwork and colors. These forms include payroll, accounts payable, dividend checks, magnetic striped ledgers, computer continuous forms for bank trust tax summaries, stock certificates, restaurant customer checks, invoices, and letter sets.

Westmont sells directly to several thousand customers and indirectly through approximately 150 distributors. Standard and customized products are sold through distributors. These distributor accounts are handled by the sales manager and one new representative. Most of the business of Westmont is in the custom line, which is more consistent with its policy of providing service and quality at a fair price. Forms are usually purchases in order sizes of about $400. Delivery time is three to four weeks for all forms.

Since its founding, the company has stayed within the family. At present, Drew Westmont, the great-grandson of the founder, is president and has been for seven years. The Westmont family controls stock ownership with 51 percent, while the remaining stock is held by Carter Price, the vice president. Both men have worked in sales, but Westmont also spent some time in production; thus top management has a complete picture of the workings of the company.

Westmont and Price are joint decision makers, but Westmont oversees production while Price is in charge of Sales with the assistance of the Sales Manager, Cathy Umstead. She and Price are both involved in selling, as well as in managerial activities. Westmont wants to keep the organizational structure informal because he feels it allows for more communication within the company.

Drew Westmont presents the company as one that is: ". . . very close-knit and tightly run, yet informal. Our staff is competent and company-minded. Wages are high with good benefits; thus we have no union to deal with. Carter and I make decisions together. We grew up in the business so we feel that basically two heads are better than one. Even when we disagree, I don't use my position to override him. Eventually, we compromise.

"This may not seem to be a sophisticated management style, but we're small, we don't really need fancy techniques. We're doing fine without them.

"With a recession a possibility, we may have a few tight years coming up, but we can handle it. Lately, our growth has been somewhat slower than the industry's, but that's probably because we're smaller."

Carter Price backs up Westmont's views of the company. He adds: "Company growth has almost come to a halt and I can find no clear-cut reason for it. We're known and have a good reputation—maybe a little expensive, but our customers have always been willing to pay for our quality.

"We need to increase our sales. I guess we could use a larger sales force, but we have no training program, so we have to hire the experienced sales rep who knows accounting and accounting machines. Right now, they aren't easy to find. Cathy, the sales manager, is still selling, but not as much as a full rep.

"One trend that bothers me is the move toward bidding for a job. We are more expensive than some of our competitors, so often our bids are higher and we don't get the job. Maybe two out of five jobs are lost on bids. Our sales reps don't want to cut the price too much, and who blames them?—the company wants a profit and they want their commission. Hopefully, this trend is temporary and will die shortly with the recession. We've a few problems, such as sales and production rarely being balanced. There are frequent bottlenecks in order writing, composition, and shipping. But this type of thing is common in the forms business.

"I'd like to see us add about a million and a half in sales in the next year so that we could absorb some of our unused capacity. I think that we could do it with a little effort on everyone's part."

Management sees the future of Westmont Business Forms as strong. The trend toward competitive bidding is seen as temporary, and as the economy grows stronger, companies will return to the customized form. Once the economy is back on a growth cycle, management feels any problems in the company will correct themselves. No changes are needed from inside; as Westmont puts it, "It's been working like this for almost one hundred years. Why make changes now?"

WESTMONT'S SALES FORCE

Westmont's sales force (Exhibit 23.4) is directed by Carter Price with the assistance of a part-time sales manager, Cathy Umstead. Price continues to handle a few of his old accounts because he feels they're extremely important to the company. As the company has grown, Price feels he has less and less time to spend on these accounts and is considering turning them over to Umstead. He hesitates because he is afraid of the customers' reactions to such a move.

Cathy Umstead, the sales manager for the past year, has been with Westmont for six years. Along with her managerial duties, she is responsible for sixty-five distributor accounts. She took over these when she became manager because she thought that they required less time than her industry customers. At present, Cliff Styres is in charge of Umstead's old accounts.

Umstead tries to work most of the week at the Atlanta office on her managerial activities, but does travel each week in Florida, Georgia, and Alabama. Time away from the office varies between one and three days a week. Her administrative duties include all reports on sales reps, including recruiting, selecting, training, and evaluating them. Her job could easily be full-time without the selling activities. Umstead also tries to be available to the reps for assistance with any special problems they may encounter. With so many duties, Umstead neglects some that she feels are unimportant, such as the weekly call reports of the sales reps. She believes she gets more out of direct contact with the reps.

Exhibit 23.4   The Westmont Sales Force

SALES REP	TERRITORY	YRS WITH CO.	AGE	EXPERIENCE/ EDUCATION
Cathy Umstead (Manager)	distributors in Florida, Alabama, Georgia	6	29	sales, administrative work
Ron Emerson	1/2 North Carolina, South Carolina	15	46	work in production, then sales
Cliff Styres	Tennessee, 1/2 Alabama	4	31	administrative work with some selling
David Whitaker	Atlanta, and Georgia	4	35	sales in another business forms company
Rick Hackney	1/2 Alabama, Florida	3	30	MBA
Margaret Linden	1/2 North Carolina, Virginia	2	26	college graduate, one year selling experience
Jeff Cobb	distributors in North Carolina, South Carolina, Tennessee	1	24	college graduate

Umstead describes her job as being ". . . a sales representative with some administrative duties. I could actually spend all my time on my accounts, but instead divide it up to include my managerial duties.

"Right now I'm most concerned about getting a couple of new reps. Even with the recession, there is a large untapped market in our area that needs reaching. I feel this should be our top priority, but Price thinks with new reps we can go into new territories. Then none of our problems would be solved.

"Getting new reps is going to be hard since we have no training program. We need people who can sell and, at the same time, know the industry. Jeff Cobb, our newest rep, is handling the other distributor accounts because they are the easiest way to learn something about the forms industry. He isn't ready to take on industry customers, so I can't move him out to let a new inexperienced rep take over Cobb's distributors. He has potential, so I don't want to push too hard. I doubt we'll be able to get experienced reps immediately because with the recession people want to stay in the security of their old jobs. As soon as I get new reps though, some changes on the force will be made."

Ron Emerson, Westmont's senior rep, has been with the company for fifteen years. Emerson was considered the top candidate for the sales manager's job, but turned it down. He believes he is better off with his sales commission of 5.5 percent than with the manager's salary. Emerson has been in sales with Westmont for ten years and has a strong group of established customers. He no longer does much prospecting because he is satisfied with the income that his present customers allow him to make. He travels most of the week, but the majority of his work consists of checking on his customers and taking new orders.

Emerson described his selling style as follows: "I check on each account every six weeks and spend three or four nights a week on the road. Occasionally I check in on a potential customer recommended by one of my accounts, but otherwise I really don't look for new accounts. I'm making an adequate salary with my commission—better than if I'd taken the manager's job, so I'm satisfied. Plus, management doesn't push me to do more prospecting so why bother?

"Another reason I didn't take the manager's job is its structure. It should be full-time. Umstead doesn't have time to fulfill all her duties. Knowing this, I don't even turn in all the required reports and sometimes she doesn't even notice. I'm not blaming her though. The top people need to put some structure into the company. The sales force can't do it all."

The five remaining members of the sales force (Exhibit 23.4) have all been with the company for under five years. Umstead believes that Whitaker, Styres, and Linden are doing well with their territories, but could use some help in covering such large areas. Umstead is having problems with Hackney and feels that his work should be better after three years. If she can get new reps, Umstead is considering firing Hackney.

Cobb, the newest rep, has been with Westmont for one year and handles distributorships in North Carolina, South Carolina, and Tennessee. These accounts are the easiest to handle, so Umstead put Cobb on them to aid in his training.

Cobb sees his job as an "order taker. I do very little, if any, real selling. Umstead tells me to look after all the old customers and don't worry about getting new accounts; yet, at the few sales meetings we have, she continually talks about the need to reach more of the market. Half the time, I don't think management knows what they want, and even if they did set goals, they wouldn't have any plans on how to reach them.

"The company pays well and could be great to work for, but I have my complaints. After a year, I still have no real selling experience and I wasn't even trained to start with. Sure, college gave me an idea of what to expect, but it really is a lot different out there. If the job market wasn't so bad right now, I'd probably be out looking for a new job.

Maybe it's me, but I don't know what the company expects of a rep, and as a new member of the force, I feel I need some guidance."

Price and Umstead both see the need for some new reps. Price believes that once the sales force is larger, the problems in this area will work themselves out. Umstead, on the other hand, feels some changes are needed, especially some structure added to the work of the company.

With the expansion of the sales force, Price is considering making the manager's job full-time, but isn't sure the job really requires that much effort. Another area he is considering changing is the size of the territories. He has discussed with Westmont the possibility of going into some new states. Price feels that "we're doing great where we are; why not branch out?"

COMPETITION

The strongest competitors of Westmont sell customized forms. (See Exhibit 23.5.) Cobb Corp., Inc., sells nationally; Johnston Forms Co. sells in the eastern United States; and American Paper Products sells in the South and Gulf regions. American is noted for its excellent quality, service, and delivery commitments, so it is Westmont's closest competitor in the minds of forms buyers. Johnston uses some of the newer high-speed presses, so its prices tend to be lower, in the long run, than Westmont, but its quality is not always good. Because of its size, Cobb offers the largest line of forms. It can be very price competitive and does very good work. Westmont worries that Cobb may expand its sales force in the southeast. The sales for these companies appear in Exhibit 23.6.

Exhibit 23.5   Westmont Business Forms, 1979
Top Competitors* ($ millions)

COMPANY	SALES	REGION	PRODUCTS
Cobb Corp. Inc.	$137.70	national	business forms, custom packaging
Johnston Forms Co.	$ 23.85	eastern U.S.	customized forms, std forms, data systems equipment
American Paper Products	$ 10.30	south and gulf regions	forms for computers and business machines, printing, catalogs, textbooks

*Most competition is in the area of customized forms — these companies are a bit larger than Westmont with a broader range of products.

Exhibit 23.6 Sales for Westmont's Competitors
1972 to 1980 ($ millions)

	1980	1979	1978	1977	1976	1975	1974	1973	1972
Cobb	$153.0	$137.7	$119.1	$106.6	$ 94.8	$ 90.5	$ 92.9	$ 52.8	$ 44.9
Johnston	24.75	23.85	19.49	17.06	15.22	13.84	15.04	11.50	9.71
American	11.7	10.30	8.59	7.40	6.62	5.90	5.01	3.68	3.25
	$189.45	$171.85	$147.18	$131.06	$116.64	$110.24	$112.95	$ 67.98	$ 57.86

ASSIGNMENTS/DISCUSSION QUESTIONS

1. What are the problems Westmont has that are contributing to the reduced growth of sales?

2. What changes in the marketing and sales strategy do you recommend? Relate your recommendations to the anticipated demographic, economic, and technical trends for the next decade.

3. Develop a retraining program for *existing* representatives.

4. Develop a training program for three new representatives who were hired out of college with no industry experience.

5. Assume that Cathy Umstead will be a full-time sales manager. Write a job description for her, noting any organizational changes that you recommend.

6. Develop a control process for the sales representatives. Distinguish between those controls that are automatic and those that are not automatic.

7. What are the problems with the compensation plan? Design a new compensation plan and include the objectives of your recommendation.

8. What are the motivational problems in this case? What do you recommend to motivate the representatives toward greater activity?

AUTHOR INDEX

651

SUBJECT INDEX